T0338235

Manufacturing and Managing Customer-Driven Derivatives

Manufacturing and Managing Customer-Driven Derivatives

DONG QU

WILEY

This edition first published 2016
© 2016 Dong Qu
First edition published 2016

Registered office
John Wiley & Sons Ltd, The Atrium, Southern Gate, Chichester, West Sussex, PO19 8SQ, United Kingdom

For details of our global editorial offices, for customer services and for information about how to apply for permission to reuse the copyright material in this book please see our website at www.wiley.com.

Library of Congress Cataloging-in-Publication Data is Available

ISBN 9781118632628 (hardback)   ISBN 9781118632529 (ePDF)
ISBN 9781118632536 (ePub)

Cover Design: Wiley
Cover Images: Top Image © stocker1970/Shutterstock; Bottom Image © photofriday/Shutterstock

Set in 10/12pt Sabon LT Std by SPi-Global, Chennai, India
Printed in Great Britain by TJ International Ltd, Padstow, Cornwall, UK

To my wife and children: all of them have contributed in their own ways.

Contents

Preface

Derivatives have long diffused into the financial systems as trading, hedging and risk management instruments, on and off balance sheets, embedded in assets and liabilities. In an industry that is increasingly focusing on value-added activities, customer-driven derivatives will continue to play key roles in the retail, private, corporate and institutional derivatives markets.

Managed properly, customer-driven derivatives business can be a rewarding business with high capital efficiency. It offers tailor-made investment and hedging solutions to the customers, and can be a very valuable source of funding for banks, even in a time of crises. The capital efficiency mainly comes from the fact that the bulk of the business is customer-driven. By its nature, this business requires efficiency and flexibility in product offering.

While it is true that the customer-driven derivative products have overall become simpler, manufacturing and managing these products has actually become more complex, due to macro factors such as the multi-curve environments triggered by the recent financial crises, stricter regulatory requirements of consistent modelling and managing frameworks, and the needs to optimize risk/reward profiles.

This book aims to present a holistic view of the customer-driven derivatives business, coupled with forensic quantitative model analyses from a practical perspective:

- It explains the life cycle of the derivative products, the manufacturing process of turning models into products, the key pillars of the business infrastructure and the regulatory framework, including Basel III and beyond.
- It explores quantitative pricing models and their applications, explaining various model paradigms and non-arbitrage models used in real equity and interest rate derivatives business. Smile/skew topics are examined in depth. The multi-curve environment and its practical impact on interest rate derivatives pricing are discussed extensively. Key derivative risks are also highlighted, and the focus is on combining or balancing the model simplicity with the necessity to capture the risks.
- It examines a wide range of customer-driven structured derivative products, their investment or hedging payoff features and associated risk exposures.
- It analyses a number of real-life derivatives embedded in real-life financial products, zooming into their risk characteristics.

Customer-driven derivatives business is a complex business, and it is often surrounded by some mystery. Certain derivatives may look simple, but are actually complex, others may look complex, but are actually simple. Complexity/simplicity does not necessarily equate to or explain the riskiness. This book hopes to demystify some aspects of the customer-driven derivatives and increase the transparency.

The book pays attention to risks and raises risk awareness. The customer-driven derivatives business is always an evolving business. Risks evolve with the business offerings, driven by customers' and banks' risk appetites. Better understanding of derivatives risks and how such risks should be captured and quantified can help managers and practitioners to adopt better organizational setup and control framework.

Acknowledgments

I have been fortunate to have worked with many financial industry professionals, with whom I shared knowledge and insight of the customer-driven derivatives business.

Starting from my early banking career, I was exposed to real-world derivative products and gained first-hand experience of their pricing and hedging. I worked with a number of industry experts including Edmond Levy, Robert Benson, Mario Pytka, Andrew Brogden, William Lyons, Mark Simmons, Tim Mortimer, Peter Glancey, Andrew Law and so on, with whom I had opportunities to deep-dive into pricing and risk managing a wide range of structured derivative products.

I have appreciated the experience of working with some remarkable business executives, including TJ Lim, Guy Laffineur, Tong Lee, Ferdinando Samaria, Terence Tsang, Steven Oon, Richard Williams et al, all of whose business and management wisdom influenced me in many ways. The opportunities to work with Henrik Neuhaus, Peter Jäckel, Russ Bubley, Bruno Dupire, Dariusz Gatarek, Dingqiu Zhu, Frank Mao, Franz Maier et al on derivatives models and techniques have certainly been beneficial and rewarding.

Over the years I have interacted and worked closely with many skilled quants, including Chris Reynolds, Matthew Steiner, Andrew Fenlon, Philip Cowdall, James Roberts, Panta da Silva, Julien Hok, Alexander Giese, Rolando Santambrogio, Simone Costa, Daniel Wilheim, Andreas Geisselmeyer and Bernd Geisselmeyer. Their dedication to the quantitative profession is impressive. I also very much enjoyed my professional interactions with Paul Wilmott, Fabio Mercurio, Han Lee, Lane Hughston, Ken Yan, Marek Lusztyn and Juliusz Jabłecki.

Finally, I'd like to thank my families in UK, China and Poland for their continuous support, which have made my day-to-day professional life and book-writing enjoyable and sustainable.

About the Author

Dong Qu (屈冬宁) obtained a BSc in Physics in China. He came to the UK to pursue a higher degree and completed a PhD in Statistical Laser Optics from Imperial College London. He started working in the City of London in the mid-1990s.

In the late-1990s, working with colleagues, Dong was instrumental in industrializing barrier reverse convertibles, which have since become one of the most popular structured products. The barrier protection mechanism designed to reduce the risk of capital loss is now an industry-standard risk-reduction tool. It has become a stalwart of the structured product markets and is embedded in many products such as autocallables.

Dong is currently the global head of the quantitative product group at UniCredit, having previously worked at banks including HSBC, Nikko and Abbey/Santander. He has in-depth knowledge of customer-driven derivatives across major asset classes, including equity, interest rate, FX, credit and real estate. He has spent many years on derivative pricing and hedging models, associated trading and risk management infrastructures, and has first-hand experience of how the customer-driven derivatives industry is operating in the competitive business and regulatory environments.

Overview of Customer-driven Derivative Business

The derivative business environment has evolved and changed dramatically. Many lessons have been learned, and financial regulations have become more sophisticated and demanding. Product offerings bearing geographic features reflect the importance of the customer-driven derivative business. In order to cope with the evolving business environment and optimize business efficiency and safety, executives need to create an effective organizational structure, streamline the development process for new products and modernize product distribution techniques.

Financial risk management and the banking global rule book Basel III are the generic parts of the business. Executives must manage economic and regulatory capital requirements along with leverage and liquidity, all of which attribute significantly to the business's bottom line.

CHAPTER 1

Evolving Derivative Business Environment

The derivatives business has evolved in terms of customer needs, product ranges and models and infrastructure required for managing the derivatives products. It is a business that requires comprehensive understanding of the quantitative and organizational setup, and one must pay attention to the overall picture, as well as individual components.

CUSTOMER-DRIVEN DERIVATIVE PRODUCT CATEGORIES

Derivative products are explicitly or implicitly embedded in many financial product types:

- retail structured products;
- insurance investment products;
- pension products;
- securitization products;
- real estate (property) products;
- etc.

There are many different ways to categorize customer-driven derivative products: by asset classes, by payoffs, by client sectors, etc. At the high level, they can also be categorized by the intended purposes of the derivative products, as seen in Table 1.1.

Retail structured derivative products are by far the most varied in product types and payoffs innovation across all major asset classes, including equity, commodity, interest rate, FX and credit. Structured derivative products modify the risk/reward profile and hence the risk-adjusted returns. Their returns can therefore be better defined and clarified. One can also incorporate protection barrier features into many types of product to reduce the risk of losing capital.

Structured life insurance products also become popular in the low interest rate environment, whereby insurance companies look into new investment areas and

TABLE 1.1   Customer-driven derivative products

Category	Intended Purpose
Structured Derivative Products	Structured derivative products are primarily intended for investment purposes. They offer investors alternative investment opportunities and access to new asset classes or markets. The buy side includes retail investors, high net worth and private banking customers, and institutional investors.
Derivative Hedging Products	Derivative hedging products are primarily designed for the hedging needs of institutional and corporate clients. They can be and should be used as effective risk management and mitigation tools. Large proportions of such products are interest rate hedging products.

products, in order to fulfil the promised coupons embedded in certain products. As life insurance institutions will be subject to Solvency II capital requirement, the products with low guarantee will attract lower capital requirement.

Structured derivative business has undergone profound changes over the years, in manufacturing processes and distribution mechanisms. The products become more tailor-made, coupled with the fact that distribution channels are moving towards e-platforms, which in turn encourages more individual product features. The manufacturing process encompasses product design, quantitative modelling, trading and risk systems integration, and validation. The overall process has become much more complex and infrastructures must also build in various required regulatory constraints. Therefore an integrated comprehensive manufacturing approach is vital to keep the whole process economically viable. The products' competitions have also been extended towards the longer end, from traditional short-dated (e.g. typically < 5 years) products to long-dated products, including pension products serving the ageing population.

Financial promotions of derivative products not only require the sell sides to get facts right, i.e. what the product does, what the cash and tenure commitment is it is also a compliant requirement to explain clearly to the customers the risks involved. Setting a strict and high standard on products and their risk management ensures a sustainable product design process which is vital for the long-term success of the derivative business.

LESSONS IN DERIVATIVES AND CRISES

Financial derivatives are a double-edged sword. Understanding and using them well, derivatives can be valuable investment tools, and effective risk management and mitigation instruments. Misunderstanding and misusing them can lead to amplified losses. Over the decades, there have been many documented and undocumented derivative losses. Table 1.2 lists some of the well-known and high profile cases dating back to early 1990s. These derivative losses resulted either from outright wrong and misunderstood positions or from unwinding losses because of forced margin calls.

Derivative Losses

As can be seen in Table 1.2, derivative losses have happened frequently in the past. While the frequency of these occurrences may have become less on average, the individual loss amount has actually become larger. This indicates that lessons have not been learned fully. Derivatives are highly leveraged instruments. One must fully understand the risky nature of the derivatives as well as their practical operational details. It is essential to build adequate technical and operational frameworks before embarking on highly leveraged activities. Derivatives business should consist of a comprehensive set of technical, risk management and operational control tools.

Table 1.2 does not include rogue trading that occurred at Barings, Société Générale and UBS. For completeness, they are listed in Table 1.3 and it is striking to see how similar they all look. The last column shows one of the common features of rogue trading; they all involved liquid index futures. Strong internal operational control is the key to prevent such rogue trading activities.

TABLE 1.2 Sample derivative losses

Decade	Organization	LOSSES	Transactions
1990s	Metallgesellschaft	$1.3 billion	Energy futures
1990s	Codelco	$207 million	Copper futures
1990s	Cargill (Minnetonka Fund)	$100 million	Mortgage derivatives
1990s	Kashima Oil	$1.5 billion	Currency derivatives
1990s	Procter & Gamble	$157 million	Leveraged interest rate and currency swaps
1990s	Askin Capital Management	$600 million	Repo and mortgage derivatives
1990s	Air Products and Chemicals	$113 million	Leveraged interest rate and currency swaps
1990s	Piper Jaffray Cos.	$700 million	Mortgage derivatives
1990s	Sears	$237 million	Swaps
1990s	Orange County, Calif.	$1.6 billion	Leveraged repo
1990s	Capital Corporate Federal Credit Union	$126 million	Mortgage derivatives
1990s	Sumitomo Bank	$1.8 billion	Copper futures
1990s	First Capital Strategists	$128 million	Stock index futures
1990s	Postipankki	$110 million	Mortgage derivatives and structured notes
1990s	NatWest	$90 million	Interest rate options
1990s	UBS	$170 million	Equity derivatives

(*continued*)

TABLE 1.2   (*Continued*)

Decade	Organization	LOSSES	Transactions
1990s	UBS	$120 million	Equity derivatives
1990s	UBS	$75 million	Convertible bonds
1990s	LTCM	$500 million	Leveraged spreads
2000s	Allied Irish Banks	$700 million	Currency derivatives
2000s	China Aviation Oil	$550 million	Commodity derivatives
2000s	China State Reserve Co.	$300 million	Copper futures
2000s	Hedge funds	Undisclosed large sum	Credit tranche baskets
2000s	Credit Suisse	$120 million	Equity derivatives (Korea)
2009	A European Bank	€100 million	Bermudan swaptions
2009	Brazilian Corporates	$28 billion	FX Tarfs (Real)
2009	Korean Corporates	$4 billion	FX Tarfs (Won)
2009	Citic Pacific	$2.4 billion	FX Tarfs (Australian Dollar)
2012	JP Morgan	$6 billion	Credit derivatives index
2013	A Portuguese entity	€450 million	Exotic swaps with accumulating coupons
2014	Asian corporates	$3 billion	FX Tarfs (offshore renminbi)

TABLE 1.3   Derivative rogue trading losses

Year	Organization	LOSSES	Transactions
1995	Barings PLC	$900 million	Stock/index futures
2009	Société Générale	$4 billion	Stock/index futures
2011	UBS	$2 billion	Stock/index futures

Credit Crunch and European Debt Crisis

The banking landscape has changed forever following two major financial crises: the sub-prime triggered credit crunch in 2007/08 and European sovereign-debt crisis in 2012/13. Both crises led to the freezing of the global credit market. Derivatives were certainly not the cause of the crises, although in some cases they were misused. Many lessons can be learnt from the analysis of how the crises happened, as can be seen in Table 1.4.

Direct financial losses incurred by the financial institutions were massive during the crises. The losses in many large banks were running into tens of billions each. Ironically, the losses due to traditional banking activities such as (bad or excessive) lending

TABLE 1.4 Financial crises and their causes

Crisis	How Did It Happen?
Credit Crunch 2007/08	▪ Prior to the crisis, desire for home ownership and easy access to loans led to a boom in sub-prime mortgages in the USA. ▪ Those very risky sub-prime mortgages were re-packaged using CDO pricing technologies by the banks, and sold to many other institutional investors worldwide. ▪ The risks in the re-packaged instruments were massively underestimated and mispriced. The ratings were wrong too, as many of those instruments were rated AAA. As a results, investors worldwide held massively inflated and overpriced assets on their balance sheet. ▪ When the US housing bubble burst in 2007, predictably, the values of those sub-prime repackaged instruments plummeted. ▪ The liquidity in those sub-prime repackaged instruments dried up. ▪ This in turn led to a wider liquidity crisis across the board, which eventually triggered a credit crunch in the entire financial market. ▪ The credit crunch of 2007/08 extended its shadow from Wall Street to the High Street.
European Debt Crisis 2010/13	▪ Excessive national debt in the some European countries had long worried investors. The sharply deteriorated debt-to-GDP ratio led to the fear of sovereign default. ▪ When the new Greek government in late 2009 revealed that the previous budget deficit had been under-reported, investors' fear of sovereign default became real. ▪ It eventually triggered a massive sell-off of sovereign debts and caused a sovereign debt crisis. ▪ Contagion: the sovereign default crisis quickly spread from Greece to Ireland and Portugal, and later to the larger economies of Italy and Spain. ▪ The sovereign debt crisis also exposed the fundamental imbalance within the eurozone.

were many magnitudes higher than the derivative losses if compared like-for-like, even though derivatives are perceived as more risky by the general public.

In the aftermath of the financial crises, financial institutions started fundamental changes and repositioning to de-risk and de-leverage. For example, one bank's leverage ratio (total assets exceeding tier 1 capital) was reduced from 68 times in December 2007 to 44 times in December 11. High leverage means high volatility in P&L, resembling derivatives. Leverage itself is a derivative on society, and too much of it will expose the economy.

REGULATIONS AFFECTING DERIVATIVE BUSINESS

The financial regulatory landscapes have evolved dramatically during and after the crises. Banks have been under increasingly tighter regulatory regimes, at various levels, from capital to liquidity to operational details. Financial regulations have become an extremely important part of the derivative business. Both the USA and the EU have been introducing various laws and directives that will affect the business profoundly. All of these have implications on the day-to-day management of the business, and knock-on impact on derivative models and infrastructures.

Dodd–Frank and EMIR

No one can have a sound and prosperous derivatives business without embedding the relevant financial regulations into its operation framework and reporting infrastructures. Regulatory requirements can in fact affect the viability of certain trading and products distribution activities. The recent wide-ranging regulations affecting derivatives include:

- Dodd–Frank (the Dodd–Frank Wall Street Reform and Consumer Protection Act);
- EMIR (European Market Infrastructure Regulation).

Dodd–Frank has been written into law in 2010 in the USA. It covers areas of monitoring systemic risks, limiting/banning banks' proprietary trading (the "Volcker rule") and new regulations on derivatives and consumers protection. All the major aspects of the banking activities, from trading to customer/consumer services, have been under intensive regulatory analysis and scrutiny. The "Volcker rule" effectively bans banks' proprietary trading activities, although trading activities of "market making" are exempt. Clearly, the definition of "market making" is very important in this context. As for customer/consumer services, transparency and accountability together with investor protections are specifically mentioned and emphasized, which have profound implications for how financial institutions should be run and managed.

EMIR was brought into force in 2012 by the European Parliament, putting strict regulations on OTC derivatives, central counterparties (CCPs) and trade repositories (TRs), with a view to controlling systemic risks and reducing counterparty credit risks associated with OTC derivatives. Under EMIR, the relevant financial institutions must observe the following obligations: central clearing for certain categories of OTC derivatives; risk mitigation techniques for non-centrally cleared OTC derivatives, such as using collateral and having adequate capital coverage; trade reporting to TRs; organizational and prudential requirements for CCPs and TRs.

The regulatorily required CCP clearing of certain OTC derivatives (such as IRS, OIS) can also bring about real capital and operational efficiency. Some clearing houses have already introduced trade compression for IRS, OIS, Basis, FRA etc. to reduce the line items and net notional. For example, a trade compression for a portfolio of fixed legs of the same counterparty will net the cash flows of the fixed rates having the same coupon dates. In essence, it generates a synthetic fixed leg with a weighted average blended fixed rate. By replacing those fixed legs with one synthetic fixed leg, compression can greatly reduce the number of line items. As a result, it can achieve much enhanced operational efficiency and reduced capital requirements for all counterparties. It is conceivable that the trade compression technique can be further extended to cover all linear instruments to achieve greater business efficiency.

Both Dodd–Frank and EMIR are designed with a view to preventing another financial crisis and promoting financial stability. Their scopes are wide-ranging, and their effectiveness clearly depends on how effectively they are implemented in the financial systems by the relevant financial institutions.

European Markets and Structured Products Governance

The European Securities and Markets Authority (ESMA) governance paper on structured retail products maps out the expected good practices for issuers and providers when manufacturing and distributing the products. The expected good practices are aimed at improving product providers' ability to protect investors, in particular in relation to the complex structured retail products, the nature and range of investment services and activities undertaken in the course of business, and the type of investors they target. The good practices guidelines cover a wide range of topics, including product design and testing, target market and distributing strategy, value at the date of issuance and transparency of costs, secondary market and redemption, and the review process.

It is conceivable that other types of financial instruments such as asset-backed securities or contingent convertible bonds being sold to professional clients will be under increasingly tighter governance. The regulator insists that sound product governance arrangements are fundamental for investor protection purposes. When properly implemented, it can reduce the need for product intervention actions by competent authorities.

The European Parliament has also approved MiFID II, the full implementation of which ESMA will oversee by 2017. MiFID II will directly impact on the product manufacturing and customer value chain with to the following two aspects:

- Much enhanced market transparency: The scope and scale of the financial instruments covered by MiFID II have been much widened, to include equity and fixed income markets, derivatives, bonds, commodity, etc. It requires transparency and accountability in both manufacturing and distributing process. Trading venues must be transparent and adequately controlled to provide level-playing fields. Institutions must ensure pre- and post-trade transparency, timely reposting etc.
- Much-increased investors' protections: The requirements will govern how financial firms should design, advise on or distribute MiFID instruments. MiFID II makes clear that complex products, including complex structured deposits, cannot be sold to investors on an execution-only basis. The requirements will promote greater price transparency, allowing retail investors to see more clearly the actual prices of various financial instruments, enabling them to compare prices and find the most competitive offer available.

Table 1.5 summarizes some key MiFID II features and coverage, and the relevant regulations derived from it relating to structured products.

EU-11 Financial Transaction Tax

The EU-11 Financial Transaction Tax (FTT) will be introduced in 11 EU countries: Austria, Belgium, Estonia, France, Germany, Greece, Italy, Portugal, Slovakia, Slovenia and Spain. It will levy tax on financial transactions involving EU-11 counterparties. The financial instruments covered by FTT include cash management products, securities, derivatives and repos. FTT will impact the financial markets in a variety of ways and it will also impact derivatives pricing. The affected derivative instruments can impact end products pricing, either directly or via hedging.

TABLE 1.5   Regulations and key features

Regulations	Key Features
MiFID II (Markets in Financial Instruments Directive II)	MiFID rules cover Europe's overall markets and trading infrastructure. They include both conduct of business requirements (for example, gathering sufficient information to ensure the products are suitable or appropriate for the client) and organizational requirements (for instance, identifying and managing any conflicts of interest). One of the key elements for the structured products industry is the introduction of a stronger harmonized investor protection framework, in relation to financial instruments, such as shares, bonds, derivatives and structured products. On the regulation of OTC derivatives, MiFID II can further improve transparency, support orderly pricing and prevent market abuse. It complements EMIR, which mainly deals with central counterparties and trade repositories.
PRIPs (Packaged Retail Investment Products)	PRIPs can be viewed as a subset of MiFID II. It covers structured products and the Insurance Mediation Directive (IMD) rules for insurance-based investment products.
UCITS (Undertakings for Collective Investments in Transferable Securities)	Under MiFID II, shares or units in UCITS will be classified as complex or non-complex instruments. Previously, all UCITS have been classified as non-complex instruments. MiFID II introduces the exception of "structured UCITS", which will now be treated as complex instruments for the purposes of the execution-only regime.
UK's RDR (Retail Distribution Review)	This is UK-specific on investment advice. Independent advisers will need to match the client's profile and interests against a broad array of products available in the market. They will state whether they will provide the client with a periodic assessment of the suitability of advised products.

Corporate and retail customers will be exempted from FTT. Market-making activities will also be excluded from FTT, although the definition of "market-making" involves some details. The FTT will be levied at between 1 and 10 basis points per transaction. The direct and indirect impacts of FTT include:

- Transaction costs: Additional transaction costs due to FTT can be substantially higher than the headline tax rate (1 ~ 10bps). The real cost will be the sum of the entire transaction chain, for example from an asset manager, via a broker, through a clearing member to the clearing house, and round trip. Each one of them has to pay, say 10bps. So a headline tax rate of 10bps for a government bond transaction could on average become 40bps (for the tax collector) after going through the whole chain.
- Indirect costs: If financial institutions cannot or won't absorb the additional transaction costs, they will pass some or all costs to the end users. This will have knock-on effects on bid-offer spreads, liquidity, volume etc., increasing the indirect costs of financial transactions.

The impact of FTT on the derivatives business could be substantial. It will make certain hedging and risk management activities more expensive. EU-11 domiciled banks and counterparties who are subject to FTT can potentially lose their competitiveness in the affected derivatives markets. Specific to the derivatives business:

- Derivatives pricing: Transaction costs due to FTT cannot be ignored any more in some affected derivative products. Pricing in the transaction cost is therefore important, considering increased hedging costs. Intuitively, options with larger Gamma will be affected more by the transaction cost, as one needs to rebalance the delta hedge more often if Gamma is larger. Pricing in transaction costs can be challenging, though, as calculating local Gamma and/or cross Gamma is a computationally heavy task.
- Derivative package/product: A derivative product transacted with an end user often consists of and is hedged by a number of simple instruments. For example, a cross-currency swap can be replicated and hedged by single currency swaps, plus basis and FX swaps. The total cost of FTT on such derivative products can potentially mushroom during the course of risk managing and hedging. It is important for practitioners to understand FTT impacts properly, and make appropriate business adjustments accordingly.

STRUCTURED DERIVATIVE PRODUCTS GEOGRAPHIC FEATURES

Structured derivative products markets are very different in size and product types across geographic boundaries. The dominant business model for structured products has been to develop and distribute country-specific products tailored to specific markets (e.g. country indices or stocks) and appetites. The United States is by far the largest market in terms of issuance and complexity of products. In Europe, Germany and Italy have the largest structured derivative products issuances, followed by the United Kingdom. China's structured derivative products business is sizeable in volume but still in its early development stages. Every country has its own market features and product preferences. In the following, we shall summarize some of the key market and product features in the selected countries, to obtain a holistic snapshot of the geographic characteristics.

United States

The US structured product market has evolved for many decades since the 1980s, and is more mature than the others. The majority of the structured products are now issued in the forms of structured notes, structured funds and structured deposits. These products are typically sold over-the-counter, although some may be listed on the exchanges. The annual sales do vary from year to year, and it is estimated to be in the range of USD\$55 ~ USD\$75 billion.

In terms of product types, US has certainly the most complex structured products in all major underlyings, including equities, interest rates, commodities, credit and currencies. Even in the era of credit crunch and European debt crisis when most of the other countries only having very simple products, one can still find rather complex products in the US across all major asset classes.

The equity-linked products are among the most popular categories, with underlyings in equity indices and single stocks. In the prolonged low volatility environment whereby the structured products pricing is difficult, there are more single stock underlyings as they tend to have larger volatilities than those of equity indices. From time to time, theme-based investment demands also drive the creation of single stock structured products. For example, auto-callable products based on internet single stocks are popular in the aftermath of giant internet company IPOs.

The issuances in currency basket, hybrid basket (e.g. CMS and S&P500), commodity index and long-dated equity for leveraged return products are also frequent. Although the embedded callable or auto-callable features can shorten the durations, in general the products in the US are longer-dated than their European or Asian counterparts.

Compared to other countries, the US market has more retail structured products based on interest rate exotics. For example, products such as callable inverse floater, callable (step-up) fixed-rate note, callable CMS steepener, fixed to floating rate notes are often issued by banks to retail investors. In Europe, these types of interest rate exotic products are deemed as more suitable for professional (institutional or corporate) clients.

European Union

In the European Union, structured product landscapes are very different in different countries. Germany and Italy are the largest in terms of market size and volume, followed by Switzerland, Spain and the UK. In each country, usually only one or two asset classes (e.g. equities and/or interest rate) are the dominant reference underlyings that driving the vast majority of the issuances. In the following, we shall have an overview of Germany, Italy and the UK.

Germany   In Germany, the annual sales of retail structured products are in the order of EUR€40 ~ EUR€50 billion, and the open positions are in the region of EUR€100 billion. Many structured products are listed in exchanges, and the exchange annual turnover is in the order of EUR€45 billion. Public distribution is a very important distribution mechanism in Germany and product demands are often driven by macroeconomics.

The major underlying asset classes are equities and interest rate. Equity-linked products tend to be larger in the number of issuances, although interest rate-linked products can sometimes be larger in volumes. While simple interest rate (EURIBOR or LIBOR)-linked products remain popular, equity-linked structures have been increasing from previous years. The current increase in equity-link products is mainly driven by the capital protection structures that the equity asset class can offer in the low interest rate and low volatility environment. Underlyings that have potentials of delivering higher yield such as blue chip stocks and baskets have been chosen to enable capital protection and attractive pricing.

Sub-dividing the overall structured product volume into investment and leverage product category, interest rate underlying can account for more than 55% of the volume in the investment product category, while equities account for more than 80% of the volume in the leverage product category. The other asset classes such as credit, currencies and commodities tend to be rather small in size.

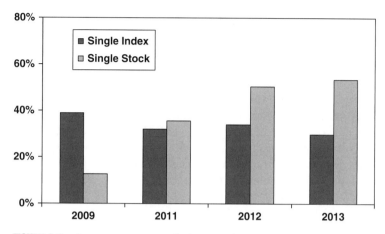

FIGURE 1.1   Germany equity underlying (index, stock)

Among the equity-linked products, single index and single stocks are the largest underlyings. Figure 1.1 illustrates the proportions of the two classes of underlyings over a 4-year period. During this particular sample period, the single stock products were becoming more popular, although there was substantial portion in the single index products. The pattern may change over time, but both single index and single stock are key components in the German market.

Structured notes and certificates are two popular product wrappers in Germany. The product payoffs are wide-ranging, from capital-protected notes to express and bonus certificates. Reverse convertibles, discount and tracker certificates are also very common. More products are being listed and distributed on the exchanges, partly due to the less stringent requirements of form filling compared to issuing products via bank branches for example. Additionally, leverage products are in demand and they are well suited for exchanges. The exchange-traded warrants and structured mini-bonds, partly due to their leverage nature, are gathering popularity.

Italy   Italy's structured products landscape was severely impacted by the collapse of Lehman Brothers in 2008. Lehman had sold many index-linked products to the Italian insurance sector, which were subsequently distributed to retail policy holders. Theoretically, the end users (retail policy holders) would bear the counterparty risk (the collapse of Lehman). However, for a variety of practical reasons, the insurance companies had to compensate retail policy holders, effectively taking up the Lehman counterparty risk even though they were technically intermediaries. Subsequently, Italy's insurance regulator ISVAP decreed that the insurers would carry the counterparty risks of any products they sell. The viability of distributing prepackaged structured products via insurers is now in question.

For the structured products as a whole, Italy's securities market regulator CONSOB stipulates that product distributors have to formally distinguish between "liquid" and "illiquid" products. For "illiquid" products, which include OTC derivative products, strict documentation, pricing and reporting standards are required. If a distributor wishes to sell an "illiquid" product, including a structured product, it has to have an internal independent price evaluation models and provide investors with regular reports on the product's performance. Typically, separate Monte Carlo pricing and statistical analysis is needed for every product issuance, in order to meet CONSOB's prospectus requirements.

CONSOB pays a great deal of attention to the products considered as "complex" and/or "dangerous" in the retail market. To limit retail customers' risks to such products, CONSOB compiled a list of "complex financial products" (including asset-backed securities, convertible, structured and credit-linked products, etc.) and recommended intermediaries not to offer them to retail investors. The intermediaries are expected to maintain the coherence between the products offered and customers' profiles, at the distribution stage as well as the product design stage. CONSOB also requires structured products providers to abstain from offering and placing certain "very highly complex financial instruments" to retail investors.

Annual sales of retail structured products in Italy is in the region of EUR€35 ~ EUR€45bn. Overall the volume of issuance with equities as underlyings is broadly similar to those with interest rates as underlyings. The issuances of certificates linked to equity underlyings are on the rise in the low interest rate and low inflation environment.

For the equity-linked products, single index and single stocks are the two key categories of underlyings. Figure 1.2 illustrates the proportions of the two classes of underlyings over a 4-year period. During this particular sample period, the volumes of single stock products had increased relative to the single index. The rise of single stock products was mainly driven by the demand for higher coupons and more interesting payoffs. The pattern may fluctuate over time, and a substantial portion of the equity-linked products was still referencing a single index.

Structured certificates and fund-linked products have a range of payoffs, including protected tracker, capped or uncapped call, reverse convertibles, digital and callable. As all listed products are automatically classified as "liquid" under CONSOB's rules, there is a strong incentive to get products listed on the Borsa Italiana. Listed products tend to be the simple payoff types. Leverage products are also in demand and they are well suited to listing on the exchange. Certificates designed to suit the specific financial environment can sell well in Italy. For example, in 2014/2015, when the

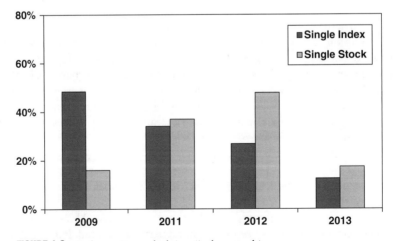

FIGURE 1.2   Italy equity underlying (index, stock)

markets were steadily positive and moving sideways, autocallable (express) certificates and capital-protected certificates were popular with investors. These short-term (e.g. 3-year) certificates have indeed generated good returns for investors.

United Kingdom   In terms of the market size, UK structured products annual sales are in the order of GBP£10 ~ GBP£15 billion. The total outstanding client positions are in the region of GBP£60 billion. The vast majority of the retail structured products are equity-linked, and there is little in the way of FX, commodity or interest rate-linked products in the retail space.

The typical product wrappers are:

- Investment plans: These plans are typically offered via intermediaries, such as Independent Financial Advisers (IFAs). They are administrated either by a third party or the issuer. The plans are often targeted to the NISAs and SIPP investors who have no tax liability on the returns. The plans are also marketed as tax-efficient investments (within the limit) as, for the direct investors who pay UK tax, the returns of the plans will be treated as capital gain instead of income.
- Structured deposits: These are offered by banks and building societies as fixed-term deposit/saving accounts. The returns will be treated as interest income and subject to income tax, unless it is wrapped in a NISA. The deposit/saving with authorized firms is protected by the Financial Services Compensation Scheme (FSCS).
- Exchange-traded structures: These are typically issued as certificates, and are listed on the London Stock Exchange as full tradable securities. The listed securities have the benefit of transparency and liquidity. The exchange-traded structures are quoted throughout the trading day.

For the equity-linked products, single index is very dominant in the UK as shown in Figure 1.3. FTSE-100 is the most popular index followed by EURO STOXX 50 and S&P 500. Basket of indices is often used, but there is very little in single stocks.

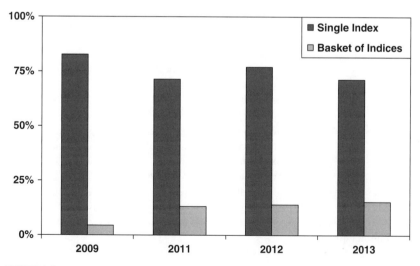

FIGURE 1.3   UK equity underlying (index, basket)

Apart from underlying liquidity and investors' risk appetite and familiarity with the indices, UK's stamp duty on share transactions may have depressed the single stock-based product offering. It is conceivable that financial transaction tax on stocks, which makes hedging single stock-based products very expensive, can skew the markets and product offerings.

Over the years, the mainstream structured product payoffs in the UK have been fluctuating among capped or uncapped call, digital, reverse convertible and kickout (auto-callable). In the low interest rate and low volatility environment, kickout products are very popular and they constitute a very large portion of the business. Basket underlying is sometimes used in the kickout products to enhance the headline rate.

China

China's financial systems are still evolving. Its structured products markets are very different from the western counterparts in both framework and contents. The overall picture therefore seems to be more complex from a western perspective.

Markets and Drivers In China, commercial banks including city commercial banks, rural commercial bank and rural credit cooperatives, can issue structured products to attract short-term deposits. Trust products, private equity limited partnership products and increasingly the internet products are the other main forms of structured (fixed income) products in the market. The so-called "shadow banking" encompasses segments including trust companies, wealth management and private lending among individuals. Structured products are typically categorized as part of wealth management products (WMPs) family, as illustrated in Table 1.6.

TABLE 1.6 WMPs and structured products

WMPs Family	Key Features
Fixed Coupon Products (Non-Structured WMPs)	Paying fixed coupon, typically higher than the bank deposits. They are effectively credit products. Because they are perceived as having an "implicit guarantee" by the distributing banks, they appear to be more attractive than equivalent bank deposits. These WMPs do not involve the use of options or derivatives, and they are equivalent to fixed-term deposits with short maturities (e.g. less than a year). These asset pool products tend to roll over after maturity.
Structured Products	These are genuine structured products with purpose-built risk profiles. Although they contain issuer credit risks, they are principally exposed to the risks in interest rate, equity, FX, gold, etc. Private banking and retail investors are the key customers.

The market size is varying, but the overall trend is growing. An estimated annual issuance of all short-dated (< 1 year) WMPs is in the order of 10 trillion Yuan, equivalent to about USD$1.7 trillion. Among WMPs, the actual structured product issuance is in region of USD$25 ~ USD$35 billion equivalent in 2015.

One of main issuers of WMPs is the trust companies. The investment trust industry is one of the main players in WMPs. The trust companies are usually selling the trust products through the wealth management divisions of commercial banks. The products distributed by banks are perceived as having "implicit guarantees", meaning that the distributing banks may compensate investors if products default. Whether the "implicit guarantee" holds when default happens or it is simply a misunderstanding on the investors' part, can only be decided when a real default case sets a precedent. Nonetheless, when the credit-risky fixed coupon products paying much higher yields are perceived as guaranteed by banks, investors will go for those products rather than banks' deposits of similar maturities.

Another main wrapper for structured products is structured deposits. These are aimed at Chinese domestic savers and investors. Providers can also issue through the QDII (qualified domestic institutional investors) scheme, which allows Chinese institutional investors to invest abroad. Through QDII, these investors can be introduced to some of the best-selling structures abroad.

Both customers' investment needs and banks' desire for alternative funding drive the rise of the issuance of WMPs. It is true that some investors are looking at the return side of the high-yielding WMPs without paying adequate attention to the associated risks. They are drawn by the expected return rate and the implicit capital guarantee, while the risks in products are often overlooked. However, investors' increasing awareness of credit risks in the fixed coupon products will shift their attention to the structured products in the WMPs family.

The liquidity needs can encourage banks to raise cash through the issuance of WMPs targeted at deposit-rich companies and households. China regulatory framework is also evolving, and it can have significant impact on the product issuance. For example, the introduction of the asset management plan pilot scheme by the regulator triggers a volume increase of alternative funding products via the structured product channel.

Overall, the biggest demand for structured products is from the retail investors, accounting for about 70% of the total notional. Institutional investors have a market share of around 20%. The remaining gap is filled by private banking customers etc. Insurance companies have become a potential driving force for structured products, following the introduction of new relaxed rules by the China Insurance Regulatory Commission (CIRC) over the use of derivatives for hedging purposes by insurers. Insurance companies can now use OTC options and swaps to hedge market risks on their equity holdings or lock-in profits from winning open positions.

Regulatory Development   China Securities Regulatory Commission (CSRC) in 2012 gave the green light to banks and securities firm to issue structured products, provided it is risk-neutral, namely they are collateralized and have no risks on issuers' books.

In order to better control the risks associated with alternative funding through WMPs, the regulator recently introduced the use of asset management plans (AMPs) among domestic banks. AMPs will not be able to assign expected returns to their offerings and providers of such products are required to regularly publish net asset values, and disclose the underlying assets backing the products. Specifically, under the AMPs scheme:

■ banks can sell asset management plans directly to customers, instead of via other local banks;
■ an implicit guarantee of principal and yield by WMPs in the form of expected return is removed;
■ banks earn an explicit management fee simply by issuing asset management products to customers, instead of implicit fees from the spread between the actual return and the cap promised to investors;
■ banks no longer have to use third-party intermediaries to structure off-balance products. As publicly-traded instruments, the asset management schemes provide enhanced transparency to investors.

Key Products and Trend   The payoffs of structured products in China are much simpler than their counterparts in the West. Vast majority of the issuances are capital-protected vanilla products, and typical embedded options are call, digital, up-and-out call (shark fin), etc. The popular underlyings are gold, FX, interest rates (Shibor-linked) and some equities. Most of the products are typically very short-dated (3 months or 6 months). Investors had preferred short-dated products because of their higher flexibility and liquidity. However, there are severe limitations on short-dated products in terms of market exposures and potential higher returns. As the structured products market becomes more mature and investors have a better understanding of the products, the dominance of short-dated products is being contested by a gradual trend for longer-dated (more than 1 year) products. Longer-dated products allow investors not only higher expected returns, but also exposures to more underlyings including commodities, domestic and overseas equities.

Chinese investors tend to pay more attention to yield than the underlying. Up to now the global product offerings involve underlyings that are mostly overseas assets. The choice of domestic stocks as suitable underlyings for the structured products is limited but expanding. Since the introduction of future contracts on the SSE (Shanghai Stock Exchange) Composite Index, the stock market underlying has become a reality, again mostly for short-dated products ranging from a few days to two years. In February 2015, China introduced its first exchange-listed option on Exchange Traded Fund (ETF). The option underlying Huaxia SSE 50 ETF tracks the performance of the SSE 50 index, which consists of 50 blue chip stocks. The introduction of ETF listed options is an important step forward in the development of China's listed and OTC derivative markets. It facilitates hedging, price finding and market transparency, allowing practitioners to build more reliable implied volatility surfaces for example. It is expected that after ETF options, stock index options and single stock options will be introduced in due course on SSE and SZSE (Shenzhen Stock Exchange). Structured products based on blue chip stocks will be boosted as a result.

China's OTC Shibor-linked derivatives market is also expanding. Standardized Shibor-linked vanilla derivatives have also been rolling out. Standardized Shibor-linked derivatives can be used as interest rate hedging tools, and will facilitate interest rate liberalization in the country through enhanced market transparency. Some of the latest examples include 1-month OIS based on the overnight Shibor rate, 3-month swap based on the one-week Shibor rate, 3-month swap based on the seven-day repurchase rate and 3-month Shibor FRA. These provide standardized points of reference, catering for the growing demand for more efficient trading and hedging of interest rate risks from practitioners, including structured products issuers.

It is clear that structured products based on local currency and local underlyings will become popular in the future, when domestic market hedging capabilities are built up. As China is also undergoing interest rate liberalization, high-yield fixed income products may gradually lose their attraction. Sensibly designed structured products can be viable replacements in the long term.

China's financial markets are still evolving with its economic development and social needs. One example is how the country should handle its demographic situation and look after older people financially. There have been numerous discussions on the topic and new policies are emerging along the line of "utilizing houses to look after pensioners". It is conceivable that equity release (reversion) products will be manufactured and distributed by the insurance companies. As these types of products often have embedded real estate derivatives, it is vital for the Chinese customers to understand the benefits as well as the risks in those products.

CHAPTER 2

Pillars in Structured Derivative Business

Structured derivative business encompasses exotic derivatives, in addition to vanillas. The key elements to understand in structured derivatives are Models, Risks, Applications and Hedges (MRAH). Given the risky nature of the structured derivatives, failing to understand MRAH, structured derivatives can backlash and HARM you. Grasping MRAH requires an effective and "simpler" business value chain, with an efficient and well-functioning product development and distribution processes.

DERIVATIVE BUSINESS VALUE CHAIN

Structured derivatives business is not a stand-alone trading or stand-alone sales business. It is an integrated risk management business. A coherent and consistent risk management business value chain consists of the key pillars in Figure 2.1.

The pillars consist of:

- Trading: It is much more than just buying and selling. It is about understanding the risk characteristics of derivative products and hedging the risks. Risk management should be part of its DNA. In the process of risk managing the positions, trading is putting fingers onto the market pulses and making appropriate hedging decisions accordingly.
- Hedging derivatives requires deep understanding of potential pitfalls. "Gamma trap" is a classic example. To hedge short gamma and short volatility positions, traders have to buy the underlying when it goes up and sell when it goes down. If volatility suddenly spikes, the underlying will move rapidly against them and the dynamic hedging can exacerbate the underlying movement, in particular during the downward spiral. This type of "chasing own tails" hedging can lead to sharp V-shaped underlying movement known as "Gamma trap", which can amplify losses of the short gamma positions. If large numbers of institutions hold similar short gamma positions and perform similar hedging, the "Gamma trap" can cause wider market distortion and stress, as observed many times in the past.

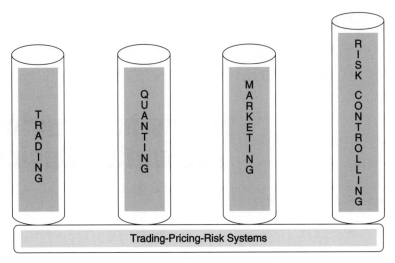

FIGURE 2.1 Key Pillars of Structured Derivatives Business

- Quanting: Quantitative modelling is the core part of derivative products development. In the modern day and age, the models need to be consistent front to back for pricing and risks, to ensure consistency and transparency across the value chain. Quants should play a driving role in the development of trading and risk infrastructures;
- Marketing: This client-facing function includes structuring and sales. Client-driven product design, distribution process and channels are constantly evolving. Clients and market feedbacks play important roles in the new products development and manufacture process.
- Risk controlling: This is a four-eyes principle-based independent risk management function that should work with the front office functions very closely, to identify and control risks including market, credit and operational risks.
- Trading/pricing/risk systems underpin day-to-day derivative activities. It is actually scandalous that the derivative industry has wasted many billions on IT systems spending due to lack of integrated vision and lack of coherent business and technological management.

The pillars illustrated in Figure 2.1 are fundamental to the structured derivatives business. The whole business value chain needs to function efficiently and coherently, to ensure an effective and safe business. The widely acclaimed IPD (Integrated Product Development) management philosophy can and should apply to the derivative products development, taking into account the business as a whole.

MODEL AND PRODUCT DEVELOPMENT PROCESS

Financial derivative products are not tangible, and ultimately they are based on models. Quantitative analysts (quants) must be a risk-conscious business group. Its roles encompass developing derivative pricing and hedging models, providing quantitative supports, formulating and developing derivatives model-related trading and risk systems. Quants should be one of the drivers along the industrialized production line for derivatives.

Derivative pricing models are vital in the structured derivatives and risk management business. Many client-driven derivative products have no direct traded markets for bench-marking, and they will have to be **marked to the models**, although the vanilla markets are used for calibration. In such a (de facto) marking-to-model business environment, the quality of the models is paramount, as it not only impacts P&L, but also the day-to-day hedging and risk managing activities. Banks must establish and standardize a process for developing quality pricing and hedging models, as a key part of the efficient and reliable production line which can also minimize the model risks.

Principles of Model and Product Development

Model specification, its numerical implementation and development testing need to follow a number of critical principles. Independent model validation is also an essential part of the model and product development process.

Model Specification   Speculation is human, hedge is divine. The central part of the non-arbitrage derivative pricing framework rests on the divine principle of hedge. The model specification must comply with this general framework. The model mathematical formulation, scope, applicability range and any limitations should be clearly specified. Any model assumptions deviating from those defined in the model framework should be thoroughly assessed with the business. Assumptions and potential implications of hedging should be explicitly explained. The bank must seek to eliminate or minimize the model mis-specification risks at source.

It is very important that the models are specified and implemented as close as possible to the real world, and they are suitable for day-to-day business usage. Quants should be aware of the common and best market practices, remembering that the models are not only used for pricing, but also for risk analysis and hedging. As a general guideline, good model specifications aim to achieve the following qualities:

- capturing market risks which matter from a hedging perspective;
- calibrating reliably to the markets to enable reliable hedging;
- numerical stability for pricing and computing risk sensitivities (Greeks);
- computationally efficient for front office pricing as well as downstream risk calculations.

Model Implementation Process   Model implementation is an interactive process among quants, traders, IT and risk managers. It entails the following stages:

- Quants develop pricing models including all the necessary calibration routines in a quant library. It is vital that the quant library is structurally well-designed and object-oriented.
- Quants, working with IT, develop system and user interfaces for the trading and risk systems.
- Quants conduct model development testing to examine the validity and implementation of the model. The model test scopes as well as the results should be documented.

- IT develops the downstream applications, including the relevant Risk and Back Office requirements.
- Risk conducts independent model validation.

A typical model/product implementation flow chart is shown in Figure 2.2.

Note that the model trading/risk system integration should be accomplished during the model development stage as a parallel task, rather than after. This is because most of the model integration and interfacing works are not specific to a particular model. In a well-designed object-oriented quant library, the permitted parallel approach can greatly enhance the overall model and product development efficiency.

Model Testing   Quants model testing is to ensure that the model is implemented properly. It is aimed to minimize the implementation risks, which constitute a very large portion of model risks occurred in real life. Model testing should include development testing and system testing.

Development testing checks the fundamental mathematical and numerical implementation. Whenever possible, an alternative model should be developed for comparison purposes. The comparison between the models can reveal differences and deficiencies. Differences should be thoroughly examined and understood; some are due to legitimate differences in numerical methods and some due to implementation bugs.

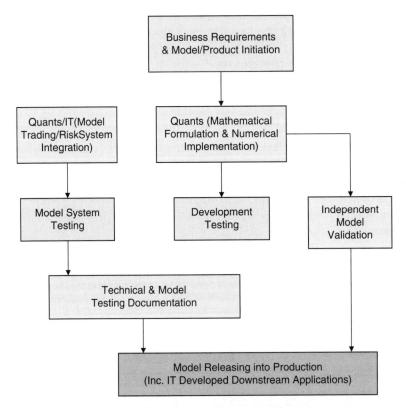

FIGURE 2.2   Typical model/product implementation flow chart

Model system testing is to ensure that the implemented model performs as expected in the production environment. The testing within the trading and risk systems enables an assessment on model's pricing stability and its capability in generating sensible risk sensitivities, for hedging over a wide range of real market data at portfolio level. It is beneficial to run system tests using the live system overnight daily risk report and analysis tools. The impact of the new model on the live portfolio in terms of P&L and risk sensitivities should be assessed and fully understood.

System testing is vital for new model development. It is also essential for model change control. Live models may be changed and updated, and they should be subject to release change control procedure, including thorough system regression tests. All live models should be version-controlled, and this can usually be done easily by the source code's repository. Accompanying each model release, there should be a release note explaining any model changes together with version number and date, etc.

Independent Model Validation Independent Model Validation (IMV) is based on the four-eyes principle to verify the model theory and test the model implementation. In practice, IMV develops its own equivalent models independently to conduct model comparison and testing. The actual model testing tends to be a large part of the work, as many implementation details need to be verified.

Once the models have been tested and approved by IMV, they can be released into production for pricing and hedging. It is the best practice that IT carries out the model release into trading and risk production systems independent of quants and trading. IT should manage and maintain production systems following a standard but independent procedure.

Quants should communicate effectively with the IMV team to facilitate its model validation, and more importantly model testing tasks. Some of the key information is listed in Table 2.1.

IMV is a very important development and control function, and its focus should be on mathematical verification and actual model testing. It should avoid spending time to go through front office quants' source codes for obvious reasons:

- The amount of tiny detail in the source codes is overwhelming. Going through source codes does not help with the independent mathematical or numerical verification.
- It does not help either with the most important part of IMV: the actual thorough model testing.
- It can potentially compromise IMV's "independent" validation.

TABLE 2.1 Key model information

Mathematical and Numerical Techniques	■ Stochastic process and model formulation ■ Numerical and analytical techniques employed ■ Quants development test results ■ etc.
Model Description	■ Products the model is intended and suited for ■ Inputs and outputs of model ■ Risk sensitivities to be generated by model ■ Any known limitations on parameters ■ etc.

- It substantially increases the bank's security risks of model source codes leaking out.
- Overall it consumes valuable resources and prolongs the validation process with little real benefit on control or business.

Object-Oriented Quant Library

A quant library consisting of implemented models is the engine in the modern derivatives business. It should be scalable, simple and transparent, allowing generic, efficient and user-friendly modular interfaces to the pricing tools, trading and risk systems. The quant library requires a well-designed architecture at the outset as well as ongoing enhancement to survive and succeed.

The quant library should be written in an object-oriented framework. Object-oriented programming and design has many advantages. At the programming level, the (C++ or C#) programs are well-structured and modular. At the practical level, it permits orthogonal combinations of objects. For example, by keeping the instrument/product objects distinctively separate from the valuation/model objects, the orthogonal combination allows one to price a particular instrument/product with any suitable model using any suitable numerical approach. This can be done at trade as well as portfolio level, reusing the same objects without coding repetitions.

Key Objects in a Quant Library   Table 2.2 lists some examples of the key objects or components in a quant library.

When all the required objects are coded up properly in the quant library, it will allow efficient and flexible interactions among the objects in the process of developing new models and products. A generic description of a product can be constructed

TABLE 2.2   Key objects in a quant library

Object Categories	Objects
Market Data Objects	- Index (actual or synthetic underlyings) - Yield curve (to include basis) - Volatility surface or cube (to include functional forms)
Calibration Objects	- Yield curve calibration (including bootstrapping) - Volatility term structure calibration - Volatility smile/skew calibration
Advanced Security Objects	- Cash flow - Legs, swaps - CMS (convexity), CMS spreads
Instrument or Product Objects (describing cash flows and payoffs)	- Terminal payoffs (e.g. piece-wise representation) - Path-dependent payoffs - Exercise rights
Basic Numeric Objects	- Numeric recipes, to include for example integration routines; matrix operations; interpolation/extrapolation - etc.
Advanced Numerical Engine Objects	- Monte Carlo engines - Tree or lattice mechanics - PDE solvers (1D, 2D, 3D)

Object Categories	Objects
Model Objects	▪ Vanillas (e.g. Black–Scholes, etc.) ▪ 1-factor models (e.g. LV, LGM, etc.) ▪ Replication models (e.g. CMS) ▪ Stochastic volatility models (e.g. LSV)
Operator Objects (constructing complex payoffs)	▪ Arithmetic operators: +, -, *, / ▪ Boolean operators: <, >, and, or, not ▪ Conditional operators: if ▪ Others: max/min
Utility Objects	▪ Dates ▪ Error handling ▪ etc.
Risk Engine Objects	▪ Delta, Gamma, Vega ▪ Smile/skew risk sensitivities ▪ etc.

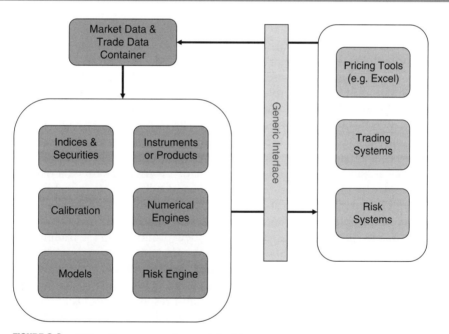

FIGURE 2.3 Object Interconnection and Architecture

naturally by connecting together the relevant objects. For example: a *swap* consists of legs, a *leg* consists of cash flows, and *cash flow* consists of various attributes including currency, notional, pay/receive and auxiliary information. All the required details are wrapped up in an organized way that permits easier understanding and repeated usage without code repetitions.

Objects Interconnection and Architecture   Figure 2.3 illustrates how the objects are interconnected from the architecture perspective.

TABLE 2.3   Example attributes table

Attribute	Value
Barrier Type	DownIn
Barrier Style	Continuous
< Cash Flow >	< Sub-Table >
... ...	... ...

Generic interface should be very thin, and its sole task is to transit and map data, reformatting data as necessary. Interfacing is extremely important, as the quant library must be integrated into trading and risk systems to be of value to the business. A badly designed interface will significantly increase the time and costs of developing new products. In the following, the "attributes table" approach is explained as an example of a generic interface for systems.

In trading and risk systems, common attributes such as spot, notional, currency, yield curve, etc. are readily available and a quant developer can simply pull them out and group them into objects that are fed into the pricing models and/or risk engines. For the exotic (or even common) attributes, an attributes table can be created inside the trading system. An example can be seen in Table 2.3.

Once the attribute table is set up inside the trading system, the quant developer can simply loop through the table, and pass all attributes in the table into the model interface. The model interface should be designed so that it can recognize the attributes and map them into the relevant objects. The beauty of this approach is that the looping codes are simple, and they do not change, no matter what the attributes are. This makes the quant developer's job much easier and more standardized. For some risk engines or back office systems that sit outside the trading system, a risk developer can use similar looping codes to read attributes and call the same model interface. The attribute table approach makes it possible for the same looping codes to be used in the trading and downstream systems, for many different products. It is therefore feasible that once quants have developed and added a new product into the trading system, all downstream systems will automatically work.

Object-oriented quant library architecture is fundamental in meeting the challenges in modern derivatives business. Many banks had to rewrite their quant libraries every a few years, wasting a huge amount of time and resources, because their prevailing libraries were not properly designed and constructed or simply became too complex to handle.

A quant library should be a child born from the marriage of brilliant mathematical modelling and skilful IT programming. A well-designed and constructed, object-oriented quant library can offer:

- Integrated business efficiency and much-enhanced productivity, including streamlined interfacing to systems and infrastructures.
- Standardization of model development and testing process, and minimization of model implementation risks.
- Application of higher-quality operational control procedures, allowing four eyes to watch a centralized piece.

TABLE 2.4   Key quantitative documents

Document	Description
Model Technical Documentation	Should provide a full description of the model, and contain sufficient mathematical and numerical details to allow independent model assessment and validation.
Model Testing Documentation	Should provide a full description of test scope and detailed test results performed on the model. Assessment of model as well as limitations and recommendations will be stated in the document. It should also include a thorough model testing in the trading systems.
Model User Manual	Will allow users to easily understand the intended products and payoffs, inputs and outputs of the model, etc. Restrictions on market or model parameters should be clearly stated where applicable. User manual should cover both desk tools (e.g. Excel) and trading and risk systems. All the necessary market data, parameters and fixings should be clearly specified.

Finally, an object-oriented quant library should be kept simple. Overly complicated object structures are tempting, but they may in fact defeat the purpose of having an efficient quant library. So keep it simple and object-oriented (KISOO).

Quantitative Documentation   Derivative models developed by Quants must be documented comprehensively. The key quantitative documents are listed in Table 2.4.

Table 2.5 and Table 2.6 show examples of the model technical and testing documentation templates respectively. These tables are given to illustrate the scopes and details required for achieving a high documentation standard.

TABLE 2.5   Technical documentation template

Sections	Specifications and Details
Executive Summary	▪ Model and/or product description with payoffs. ▪ Class of products for which model is suited for. ▪ Pricing tools and systems to which the model has been implemented.
Mathematical Framework	▪ Specify whether the model is built within the non-arbitrage framework. If not, specific hedging or/and economic assumptions need to be stated clearly. ▪ Specify the underlying stochastic processes, including stochastic volatility if applicable. ▪ Specify stochastic processes for each underlying as well as the correlation structures in the multi-factor case. ▪ Specify the underlying stochastic evolution process explicitly when appropriate, as in the case of valuing strong path dependency products (e.g. forward volatility and forward skew products, cliquet and vol bond). ▪ Specify other key modelling features, such as smile/skew dynamics.

(continued)

TABLE 2.5   (*Continued*)

Sections	Specifications and Details
Numerical Techniques	■ Specify the numerical techniques used in the model implementation, for example PDE, Monte Carlo, Tree or multi-nodes lattice, etc. ■ Specify in detail the numerical techniques implemented, for example in PDE, which solver scheme (explicit/implicit, Crank–Nicolson, Douglas, ADI) is used. ■ Specify any non-standard numerical routines in the implementation. ■ Specify calibration procedure and subsequent steps in pricing and risk calculations.
Model and Product Analyses	■ Analyse key features of the model, preferably using examples, on both valuations and risk sensitivities. ■ It is important that the model produces expected economic behaviours of intended products. ■ When appropriate, comparison with alternative models should be made.
Conclusions	■ Summarize the overall suitability of the model. ■ Summarize any restrictions to the use of the model. ■ Other key statements.
References	■ Cite key reference papers quoted in the technical document.
Appendix	■ More technical/mathematical details if necessary.

TABLE 2.6   Model testing documentation template

Sections	Specifications and Results
Testing Scope	■ Specify testing scope and coverage (e.g. prices and risks). ■ Specify testing procedure and methodology. ■ Specify the alternative model for comparison when applicable.
Pricing Analysis	■ Analyse numerical convergence of the model, such as price versus time step, grid spacing or Monte Carlo runs. ■ Analyse pricing behaviours using typical market input parameters to demonstrate that the model produces sensible prices. ■ Analyse pricing behaviours when the input parameters converge the model to vanilla. ■ Analyse pricing behaviours using extreme market input parameters to check possible extreme cases and boundaries, whenever possible. ■ Analyse pricing behaviours in special and critical regions (e.g. when spot is around barriers, or "as of" dates are around coupon dates) when applicable. ■ Analyse calibration behaviours in various scenarios. ■ Analyse specific cases (such as spot or coupon fixings) during the life cycle of a trade.

Sections	Specifications and Results
Risk Sensitivity Analysis	▪ Analyse standard risk sensitivities (Greeks), Delta, Gamma, Theta, Vega, etc. Full ladders such as spot ladder and volatility ladder should be analysed as they contain more risk information. ▪ Analyse curve parallel shift and time-bucketed sensitivities, including interest rate and/or CDS curve, volatility term structure. The parallel shift sensitivities should match reasonably well with the sum of time-bucketed sensitivities. ▪ Examine product-specific risk sensitivities when applicable. ▪ Analyse the stability of the model in producing risk sensitivities. ▪ Analyse risk sensitivity behaviours in special and critical regions (e.g., when spot is around barriers, or "as of" dates are around coupon dates) when applicable. ▪ Analyse risks with extreme market input parameters to check possible extreme cases and boundaries, whenever possible.
Trading System Testing	▪ When possible, models integrated into the trading system need to be tested by Quants too. ▪ Describe test cases, market and trade data details used in the tests. ▪ Reconcile prices with those, say, in the Excel environment. ▪ Reconcile risks with those, say, in the Excel environment. ▪ Examine special cases, such as fixings, coupon dates, or in the lookback period. ▪ Examine relevant test portfolios using comprehensive overnight pricing and risk batch whenever possible.
Conclusions	▪ Summarize the overall test results. ▪ Summarize issues and limitations clarified during the testing. ▪ Impose restrictions to the use of the model when appropriate. ▪ Other key statements.

Model technical and testing documents also serve as the audit trail of the quantitative works done during the model/product development. These works are essential to pursue the highest possible quality for the model and the quant library as a whole.

PRODUCT ISSUANCE AND WRAPPERS

This section explains the typical mechanism of product issuance and hedge, and product wrappers with their characteristics.

Issuance and Hedge

When a structured derivative product is issued, it typically involves three parties: investors, an issuer and a derivative desk. The investors buy the product (e.g. a structured note) from the issuer, who subsequently hedges the derivative risks with a derivative desk. The flow is illustrated in Figure 2.4 and described in Table 2.7.

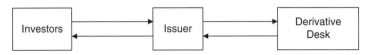

FIGURE 2.4   Flow of product issuance and hedge

TABLE 2.7   Flow description

	On Issue Date	On Coupon Dates	On Maturity Date or Being Called
Investors	Pay initial notional.	Receive structured coupons.	Receive the specified final payoff.
Issuer	▪ Receive initial notional, and invest it with its funding desk at $L_f = L + s_1$; ▪ Transact a swap hedge with a derivative desk: pay floating $L_f - s_2$, receive structured coupons.	▪ Pass through structured coupons from the derivative desk to investors; ▪ Pay floating coupons $(L_f - s_2)$ to the derivative desk. ▪ Net-net, the issuer achieves sub-market funding by spread of s_2.	▪ Pass through the specified final payoff from the derivative desk to investors.
Derivative Desk	▪ Transact a swap hedge: receive floating $L_f - s_2$, pay structured coupons.	▪ Pay structured coupons to the issuer; ▪ Receive floating coupons $(L_f - s_2)$ from the issuer.	▪ Pay the specified final payoff to the issuer.

Notes:
[1] Issuer's position can be booked as a floating rate note (with coupon L_f) plus a swap. Net-net this is equivalent to a zero coupon bond plus an option.
[2] Issuer's total funding level (L_f) includes issuer-specific credit spread (s_1). L_f is an important factor in derivatives pricing given it is included in the swap hedge.
[3] If the structured note is callable or autocallable, the swap and funding leg are also callable or autocallable. One needs to assess or value the associated callable effects.

From investors' perspective, in addition to the market risks, the counterparty (issuer) risks in the structured products must be taken into account when they make investment decisions. The pricing of the products must include the counterparty (issuer) risks and it is typically manifested in issuer's funding spread.

Wrapper Categories

Structured products are distributed to investors via different channels in various wrappers. Different wrappers have different features and benefits. In a nutshell, a wrapper specifies what the product will be issued as (e.g. a security or bank saving account), and their subsequent tax and financial protection treatment. Naturally, different jurisdictions have different preferences in terms of meeting investors' needs.

Table 2.8 lists some of the key structured product wrappers and their features.

TABLE 2.8 Key structured product wrappers

Wrapper	Key Features	Benefits
Deposit	It is a bank deposit, although the interest rate may be linked to stock market, for example. The return is treated as income from tax perspective. Deposit is typically protected by financial authority protection schemes up to certain limit. The offerings must be via deposit-taking institutions in the relevant jurisdictions.	It is the safest wrapper for investors from the counterparty risk point of view. However, structured deposits tend to have worse pricing than the equivalent notes because of better safety.
Note or Certificate	Both Notes and Certificates are debt securities. Investors are exposed to the counterparty risks as well as the market risks embedded in the products. They can be in the form of Medium Term Note (MTN). They are a suitable form of wrapper for the issuers looking for retaining some liquidity for their balance sheets. They can be issued by the agents.	The pricing of notes and certificates tends to be transparent. They are cheaper to trade, facilitating a secondary market and liquidity. The return is typically treated as capital gain from tax perspective.
Exchange-Traded Note or Certificate	An Exchange-Traded Note (ETN) or Certificate (ETC) is essentially a note or certificate. They are synthetic structured products issued and traded via exchanges. An example is a mini-future, which is a type of open-ended certificate linked to single stocks, equity indices, commodities or FX. It provides a return equivalent to a leveraged long or short position in the underlying with a stop loss clause. The stop loss level can be adjusted regularly depending on the underlying spot and implied financing of the leveraged position.	Public distribution to wider range of investors, and allowing e-trading and leveraging. Examples of leveraged certificates include leverage long with stop loss and leverage short with stop loss, in which if the underlying touches a specified stop loss level (aka barrier or knock-out level) the product ends and returns the net position at that time.
Warrant	Warrants are essentially options, guaranteed by the issuers. They tend to be on single stock underlyings and listed in the stock exchanges. The maturity tends to be longer than standard exchange-traded options.	Public distribution to wide range of investors, and allowing e-trading.

(*continued*)

TABLE 2.8   (*Continued*)

Wrapper	Key Features	Benefits
Fund (Mutual fund or UCITS – Undertakings for Collective Investment in Transferable Securities)	In USA, a range of structured products including capital-guaranteed range can use the mutual funds wrapper. In Europe, structured funds can either be in the form of UCITS or Specialized Investment Funds (SIFs) with derivative based payoffs. An investment fund company can be set up to manage the funds.	This form of collective investments is specifically regulated, and it offers transparency and flexibility. In Europe, UCITS-compliant platforms governed by European Commission directive can be an attractive wrapper for retail investors. They can be open-end companies collateralized in line with UCITS IV regulations.
Life Assurance	Life assurance (insurance) bonds are insurance products that pay out upon the death of the insured person. Typically the bonds have life policy elements embedded, and their investment elements can be linked to structured product payoffs. Life assurance bonds are clearly long-term investment products.	The varieties of the bonds and their tax treatments are country-dependent. It is possible to use life assurance bonds for tax planning purpose, for example in terms of tax deferral.
Investment Plan – Tax-Efficient Scheme	The product is sold by intermediaries and then administrated either by a third party or the issuer. The plan administrator will face the investors and handle proceeds and payoffs. It can be a tax-efficient product as the return is typically treated as capital gain, as opposed to income.	The plan is popular in UK. It can be bought as a direct investment, or as a NISA (New Individual Savings Account), or within a personal pension scheme.

SPVs for Collateral

Banks sometimes set up special purpose vehicles (SPVs) to issue structured products. SPVs can be used to hold collateral, among other tax and rating conveniences. After the SPV issuing a note, it will enter a swap transaction to completely hedge the product payoff. The SPV can then use the proceeds of the issuance to purchase collateral as security for the note principal repayment, for example. If dealers use their own bonds as collateral for the structured products they originated, then when they collapse, as in the case of Lehman Brothers, the value of collateral will also collapse. In such cases, the losses on the structured products are due to the significant decline in the collateral value, even if the derivatives embedded in the products may perform well.

A SPV with good collateral management will substantially reduce investors' counterparty risks. It is therefore very important for SPVs to seek high-quality and safer collateral for structured products.

PRODUCT DISTRIBUTION

Derivative product distribution is not simply selling products. There is a comprehensive set of principles and rules one must follow to the word and in spirit, in particular relating to the retail customers.

Organization

In retail structured derivative business, organizationally there is a clear distinction between the manufacturing and distribution functions. The two functions have very different policies, processes as well as regulatory requirements. Product providers (manufacturers) and distribution functions need to agree and have distinct responsibilities towards investors. The product providers should interact with intermediaries who are the direct client-facing functions. In broad terms, intermediaries include private banks, independent financial advisors, and various modern distribution platforms that are subject to very strict regulation and compliance rules as client-facing functions.

As client-facing functions, investors' suitability and products suitability are extremely important topics that need to be included in the distribution process. In the context of product transparency, the marketing materials need to be clearly articulated to enable investors evaluating the products from the perspective of risk/reward and their specific investment objectives. One should make sure the materials are clear and not misleading, and it is also important to make proper risk disclosure, including market risks, credit risks, liquidity/unwinding costs, tax consideration. The fees and costs need to be disclosed clearly. The overall documentation standard must remain very high in stating products accurately, fairly and explaining the risks clearly and accurately.

While managing the relationship between investors and distribution functions is a key task, distribution functions also need to fully understand the new products themselves. Distribution functions should review and understand the products, whether they are developed by themselves or by a third-party provider. There should be an internal review process, taking into account the nature of the products, target investors, their risk appetite and assess the appropriateness for the intended target markets. The overarching rules in the structured products distribution should be KYC (know your customers), KYD (know your distributors) and KYPP (know your product providers).

It is also extremely important for the business and distribution functions to analyse and manage conflicts of interests around retail structured products. For example, some of the investment and debt products are indeed complex and linked to issuer's proprietary index. For firms that issuing structured products linked to their own or their affiliate's indices, addressing embedded conflicts is critical in order to avoid serious problems of favour issuers over investors. Some proprietary indices based on complicated algorithms and strategies may potentially harm investors' economic interests. Selling callable products to investors who adopt a buy-and-hold strategy could have a negative impact on investors. The firms have responsibilities to customers and managing conflicts of interest is a very important aspect of the structured derivatives business.

Due to increasingly strict regulatory rules on distributing "complex" derivative products to retail customers, banks are increasingly exploring the option to outsource certain distribution functions to third-party specialist research/marketing/servicing companies.

Documentation

In Europe, the regulation on Key Information Documents (KIDs) for Packaged Retail and Insurance-based Investment Products (PRIIPs) has been adopted by the European Council (EC). It will be deployed by end of 2016, and it is aimed at increasing market transparency for retail investors. PRIIPs covers investment funds, structured deposits and life insurance policies with investment elements. Retail investors will be provided with compulsory information on all products intended for them, and KIDs will be required to explain clearly all the risks associated with the investment products. KIDs must contain risk and performance scenarios and cost disclosures. The risk matrix and risk scenarios need to be shown and explained very clearly to investors.

The new mandatory KIDs for PRIIPs must comply with a set of uniform rules on the format as well as content, to enable better understanding by retail investors. It will include the features of the product, including whether the capital is at risk, cost and risk profile and relevant performance information. The format, presentation and content of KIDs should be calibrated to maximize retail investors' understanding and to allow them to compare different PRIIPs. As a pre-contractual information document, KIDs will be required before retail investors buy an investment product offered by a bank, an insurance company or an investment fund. KIDs will have to indicate what the product invests in, what its risks and potential rewards are and what total costs will be during the product's life cycle. It will cover a wide range of investment products that retail investors can buy through banks, financial intermediaries and on the internet. KID is designed to offer better disclosures about the features, risks and costs of products. Its more standardized information can facilitate easier comparability among investment products.

EC has made exemptions, and the new regulation on KIDs will not be applicable to the following product categories:

- deposits (only structured deposits and securities will be subject to KIDs);
- non-life insurance products;
- life insurance contracts whose benefits are only payable upon death or in the event of incapacity due to injury, sickness or infirmity;
- pension schemes that are officially recognized;
- pension products whose primary purpose is to provide investors retirement incomes;
- individual pension products whereby an employer contribution is required.

Distribution Channels

Traditional and modern distribution channels include bank branches, financial advisers, money managers, public distribution on exchanges and e-platforms. The often observed trend is that the volume per product becomes lower, but there are many more small tickets. This, together with the fact that we are in the internet age, have made e-platforms an essential part of the modern distribution mechanism. Single issuer e-platforms have automated production and distribution process and substantially reduced costs. Also emerging are the independent multi-issuer platforms, which either supplement or compete with in-house e-platforms, providing investors a single marketplace.

Each distribution channel has its own purposes and features. Through intermediary, it is typically supply-driven, rather than explicit demands from end-consumers. The end-consumers are increasingly bypassing the intermediaries to buy directly from banks and retail distributors. Public distribution for listed products, including covered warrants are mainly for vanilla products. However, the trend is a more homogenous distribution channels with increased share of e-platform. Multi-issuer platforms have become a trendy subject, and both sell-side and buy-side institutions are increasing the infrastructure investment in the field.

In line with the natural evolution of financial e-commerce, practitioners need to position themselves to capitalize on the internet- and technology-driven distribution landscape. Financial e-commerce platforms can enhance transparency, choices and convenience for customers. It will become a core part of the modern integrated wealth management service and distribution model.

CHAPTER 3

Financial Risk Management, Basel III and Beyond

Needless to say, derivatives business is not just about pricing and trading. Financial risk management and the banking global rule book Basel III play essential and overarching roles. Executives must manage the derivatives business in line with the economic and regulatory capital requirements, and seek to optimize risk-adjusted overall business performance.

RISK MEASURES AND FINANCIAL RULE BOOKS

Risk measurement and economic and regulatory capital management are crucial parts of the business. Apart from risk sensitivities for hedging, such as Delta Gamma Vega, a range of other risk measures and quantities are also the essential ingredients of day-to-day risk management activities. Table 3.1 itemizes some of such essential risk measures and quantities:

TABLE 3.1   Essential risk measures and quantities

Risk Measures	Category
Value at Risk (VaR)	Market risks
Stressed VaR (sVaR)	Market risks in financial crisis
Expected Shortfall (ES)	Market risks including tail risks
Incremental Risk Charge (IRC)	Default and credit migration risks
Incremental Default Risk (IDR)	Default risks
Comprehensive Risk Measure (CRM)	Incremental charge for correlation books
Potential Future Exposure (PFE)	Counterparty credit risk
Credit Value Adjustment (CVA)	Counterparty credit risk
Initial Margin	Counterparty credit risk
Funding Valuation Adjustment (FVA)	Collateral and funding

(continued)

TABLE 3.1   (*Continued*)

Risk Measures	Category
Liquidity Ratios	Liquidity risk
Economic Capital	Risk capital best estimated to cover the risks
Regulatory Capital	Ma ndatory capital required by regulators

The activities on these risk measures and quantities are not only driven by best practices, but also financial regulations including tighter capital adequacy rules and stricter collateral requirements for un-cleared derivative trades. Financial rules and regulations have become key elements in the derivatives business, and they are gaining increasing importance. They are among the key drivers for risk management modernization and more efficient and reliable risk infrastructures. It is therefore vital to understand the relevant regulations and their implications on the derivative business, with a view to optimizing capital usage and risk/return.

Basel III

Basel III (Basel 2010, Basel 2013) is a comprehensive set of reform measures that are designed to strengthen the regulation, supervision and risk management of the banking sector. It was developed by the Basel Committee on Banking Supervision as the global banking rule book, and endorsed by G20 countries. While Basel III sets the international standards and rules, they need to be adopted and implemented by individual countries or jurisdictions. In Europe, Basel III is implemented through the legislative package Capital Requirements Directive IV (CRD IV), and the associated Capital Requirements Regulation (CRR).

Basel III has profound business and quantitative impacts on a number of frontiers:

- Capital: Laying down stricter capital rules for the financial firms, with detailed requirements on the quality of capital, capital loss absorption and minimum capital ratios and buffers. The capital ratio is defined as:

$$Capital\ Ratio = \frac{Eligible\ Capital}{Risk\ Weighted\ Assets(RWA)}$$

where *RWA* is a risk-based capital measure and its calculation involves risk models and methodologies designed to capture all key risks. RWAs include credit risk as well as market risk RWAs, linking the capital treatments directly to the financial risks including derivative risks. Operational risks also contribute to RWAs.

- Leverage: Setting prudent leverage ratio limit to avoid excessive leverage in financial institutions and in financial systems. The leverage ratio is defined as:

$$Leverage\ Ratio = \frac{Total\ Assets}{Capital}$$

where *Total Assets* include on- and off-balance sheet assets, and they are not risk-weighted. Setting a floor to the leverage ratio will force financial institutions to optimize assets and capital, in conjunction with RWAs.

- Liquidity: Setting adequate liquidity standards and defining the important liquidity measures, including short-term Liquidity Coverage Ratio (LCR) and long-term Net Stable Funding Ratio (NSFR).
- Systemic risks: Addressing systemic risks within the financial systems and proposing some regulatory incentives to mitigate them. It covers the topics of counterparty credit risk (CCR), provision of capital incentives for using Central Counterparties (CCP), higher capital requirements for systemic derivative instruments, usage of contingent capital, collateral, trading book, securitization, reputation and operational risks, etc.
- Management and supervision: Addressing management principles and policies, firm-wide governance, supervisory policies and practices, market discipline including transparency and disclosure, and remuneration policy.

Solvency II

The much tightened and refined financial regulations on capital and risk management are not only a theme for the banks, they have also become major business topics for the insurance industry. The Solvency II Directive is an EU Directive aiming to unify and harmonize the regulations for the EU insurers, and reduce their risks of insolvency. Solvency II will impose tough requirements on the amount of capital an insurer should hold, governance, quantitative risk measurement, risk management, reporting and disclosure. Indeed, some of the insurance products in real life (e.g. variable annuities) are quite complex and their embedded hybrid derivative risks can be a major source of instability if not measured and managed properly. Hence an appropriate regulation regime for the insurance industry can serve the purpose of raising general risk management standards and optimizing capital and asset allocation. To this end, insurers can learn from banks in terms of implementing internal models under regulatory directives, and balance sheet and business optimization as a result of regulatory compliance.

BASEL III TECHNICAL REQUIREMENTS

The evolution of regulatory regime impacts the banks in such a way that Basel III may determine whether some business is still viable. Banks must pay a great deal of attention to the regulatory changes and requirements of risks and capitals. Compared to the previous Basel accord, Basel III has broadened to a combination of measures including capital, liquidity and funding ratios, in addition to market risks. Banks will have to comply with all the measures and corresponding rules, as opposed to one single narrow measure, hence creating more balanced and stable financial environments and systems. Within this regulatory framework, banks need to optimize the capital usage and efficiency, and carry out appropriate infrastructure projects to comply with the rules.

Capital Structure

A Basel III-compliant capital structure can be shown schematically in Figure 3.1.

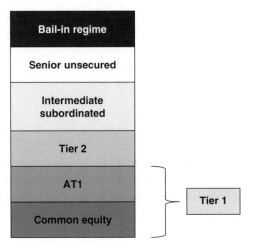

FIGURE 3.1   Basel III-Compliant Capital structure

The key components in the capital structure possess the features in Table 3.2.

TABLE 3.2   Capital components features

Tier 1 Capital	Tier 1 capital includes Common Equity Tier 1 (CET1) and Additional Tier 1 (AT1) capital. Tier 1 capital is the going-concern capital supporting the ongoing business activities and helping to prevent insolvency. ■ CET1: Fully loaded CET1 consists of share capital, plus reserve and minus regulatory reductions. Goodwill is also deducted. ■ AT1 has equity features of no fixed maturity and is subordinate to most other claims. AT1 has a mandatory loss absorption trigger set at 5.125% by Basel III. ■ AT1 has the benefits of being non-dilutive and tax efficiency compared to the equity capital. When AT1 instruments are treated as debt, the interest payments are tax-deductible. ■ AT1 is cheaper than the cost of equity. The main AT1 issuance drivers are to meet the capital as well as leverage requirements.
Tier 2 Capital	Tier 2 capital includes undisclosed reserves and subordinated term debt. Tier2 capital is viewed as the gone-concern capital. If the bank collapses, it will be used to repay depositors and senior creditors. ■ Must be subordinate to bank's depositors and general creditors. ■ Must have an original maturity of at least five years. It does not need to be perpetual. ■ Must be callable by the issuer, after a minimum of five years. 10% bail-in buffer is one of the Tier 2 issuance drivers.
Bail-in regime	Includes secured debt, small deposits, payment/clearing systems, etc.

Basel III and CRD IV set clear capital requirements as detailed in Table 3.3.

TABLE 3.3 Basel III capital requirements

Capital and Buffers	Basel III and CRD IV Requirements
Common Equity Tier 1 (CET1) Capital	Minimum 4.5% of risk-weighted assets (RWA).
Tier 1 Capital (CET1 + AT1)	Minimum 6% of risk-weighted assets (RWA). Additional tier 1 (AT1) capital can consist of hybrid debt. This is considered as a measure of solvency under the current rules.
Total Capital (Tier 1 + Tier 2)	Minimum 8% of risk-weighted assets (RWA).
In addition, the following capital buffers are required to further safeguard the systems:	
Capital Conservation Buffer of 2.5%	Even if CET1 meets the minimum requirement of 4.5%, but if it falls below 7%, i.e. breaching the capital conservation buffer, the (coupon) distributions will be restricted accordingly.
Discretionary Counter-Cyclical Buffer	Between 0% and 2.5% of RWA for CET1. National regulators can adjust the size according to economic cycles.
Buffer For Systematically Important Banks (SIBs)	Still in discussion in Basel Committee, but can be between 0% and 2.5% of RWA for CET1.
AT1 Instruments Trigger	If CET1 falls below 5.125% of RWA, it will trigger principal loss absorption on the AT1 instruments.
Pillar 2 Requirements	Pillar 2 refers to other risks such as concentration and reputation risks, etc. It is conceivable that additional CET1 will be required by the national regulators to cover Pillar 2 risks.

The capital requirements and buffers in Table 3.3 are illustrated in Figure 3.2.

In the worst-case scenario, the minimum CET1 requirement including all buffers could be as high as 12% 4.5% + 2.5% × 3. Usually banks will also have their internal CET1 buffer (e.g. 1.5%) held in equity as an additional protection. Note that the banks must also hold sufficient AT1 (1.5% minimum) to meet the basic requirement, otherwise their internal CET1 buffer will be used to fill the AT1 shortfall. This is one of the drivers/motivations for the banks to issue contingent convertibles (CoCos) to ensure they have sufficient AT1 capital.

Capital Requirements

RWA is the common denominator of capital ratios, and it injects the risk weightings into those ratios. Capital requirements under Basel III, on the other hand, are explicitly linked to the risks. From a risk and capital management perspective, both RWAs and capital requirements should be kept at minimum and optimum. Seeking capital-light business and optimizing RWAs are key business objectives.

Capital requirements must reflect the true risks in the trading and banking books and securitization positions, including both market and credit risks. Contributions from various risk measures to the capital requirement are schematically given by:

$$Capital\_Charges = a \times VaR + b \times sVaR + IRC + CRM + Secu + CCR + CVA\_VaR$$

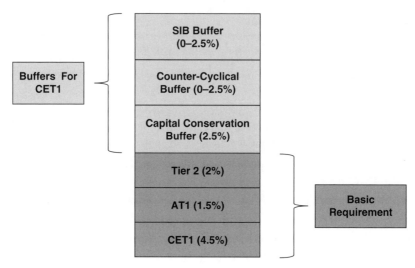

FIGURE 3.2   Basel III capital requirements and buffers

where:

VaR	■ Captures market risk scenarios. ■ a is the multiplier dependent on model and VaR backtesting.
sVaR	■ Captures financial crisis scenarios. ■ b is the multiplier dependent on model and sVaR backtesting.
IRC	■ Captures default and credit migration risks of non-securitized positions. It is measured over a 1-year horizon at 99.9% confidence level, taking into account liquidity horizons of individual positions.
CRM	■ Captures risks in the correlation trading positions (e.g. CDOs).
Secu	■ Captures securitization exposures.
CCR	■ Captures counterparty credit default risks, based on Internal Model Method (IMM). ■ Risks of default are measured by effective expected positive exposure (EEPE).
CVA_VaR	■ Captures marking-to-market losses of expected counterparty risks, due to spread widening, for example. ■ Exemptions: trading with European non-financial corporate is currently exempted from CVA VaR charge. This European CVA exemption is valuable for both banks and corporate. Clearing via central counterparties (CCP) or securities financing transactions (SFT) are also qualified for CVA exemption. ■ For some non-financial end-users, such as qualified energy firms and pension funds, they are granted derivative clearing exemptions by the regulators. Some are also exempted from posting margins on non-centrally cleared swaps.

The Basel Committee, in its fundamental review of the trading book (FRTB) consultative document, has proposed to replace VaR by Expected Shortfall (ES) as the new risk measure for market risk management and trading book capital calculation. By moving the quantitative risk metrics to ES, banks are expected to better capture and manage tail risks. We will discuss FRTB and ES in more details later.

Counterparty Credit Risks   Basel III strengthened the CCR requirements, and introduced CVA capital charges. It requires banks to hold capital both against potential losses due to counterparty default (CCR) and changes in counterparty credit quality (CVA). For derivatives that are centrally cleared, the capital charge is relatively low. CCP clearing houses have become important avenues to mitigate counterparty credit risks, as transactions cleared through CCP benefit from less stringent capital requirements. For those products that cannot be centrally cleared, the CVA capital charge can be large, and the banks are strongly incentivized to find ways to reduce the charges. If the counterparty can and is willing to post collateral, the exposure at default and risk can be reduced.

In counterparty risk modelling, the following key Monte Carlo steps need to be taken:

- scenario generation ➜ instrument valuation ➜ portfolio aggregation;
- current and potential future exposures ➜ exposure profiles;
- calculating effective expected positive exposure (EEPE);
- model validation and back-testing.

The CCR modelling and computation will encompass key market risk factors such as exposure at default (EAD), and key credit risk quantities such probability of default (PD), loss given default (LGD) and internal credit ratings of the counterparties. Netting, correlation of market and credit risk, and wrong way risks are also key factors in the CCR modelling and computation.

Regulations have encouraged financial firms to optimize their OTC derivatives portfolios, including migrating trades to clearing platforms, increasing collateralized transactions and requesting high-quality collaterals. The Basel Committee has introduced the new standardized approach for measuring counterparty credit risk exposure (SA-CCR), which will replace both the Standardized Method (SM) and the Current Exposure Method (CEM) in the capital adequacy framework. The (IMM) shortcut method will also be phased out once SA-CRR has gone live in early 2017.

SA-CCR is a rule-based approach for measuring CCR of OTC and exchange-traded derivatives, and long settlement transactions. It retains two key regulatory components: replacement cost (RC) and potential future exposure (PFE). The sum of the two components adjusted by an alpha factor gives rise to the exposure at default (EAD): $EAD = \alpha \times (RC + PFE)$, where α is the regulator-set multiplier (e.g. $\alpha = 1.4$), RC is the PV of the portfolio netting set and PFE is the add-on accounting for the potential future exposure over a one-year period for uncollateralized netting sets, or over the margin period for collateralized netting sets. As such, SA-CCR has some risk sensitivities, and the netting and over-collateralization effects are included in the multiplier α which only partially recognizes the collateral benefits.

The capital requirement is calculated as the EAD multiplied by the risk weight of the given counterparty. SA-CCR is a risk-sensitive methodology that differentiates between margined and unmargined trades, with a degree of recognition of netting benefits. Its design aims to incentivize centralized clearing of derivative transactions. Comparing to IMM though, SA-CCR can be a lot more conservative for the following reasons:

- In SA-CCR, netting is only allowed among trades belonging to the same hedging set, which is defined as a subset of trades within an asset class that share common attributes. If a hedge is across the SA-CCR predefined hedging sets, the calculation is based on the worst-case correlations and no netting is granted. In most cases this means that the allowed netting is restricted to trades with the same underlying. In contrast, IMM can model and calculate different underlyings netting using correlations among risk factors.
- Because SA-CCR does not fully recognize the netting effects, its estimations of EAD and capital requirements can be substantially more than those of IMM, especially for large portfolios with many different underlyings whereby the benefits of diversification and netting across different underlyings are mostly lost.
- With SA-CCR, the benefit of initial margin or initial negative mark-to-market value of the netting set is only partially accounted for, since it is added on top of the calculated EAD. In most cases this leads to conservative estimates of the exposures.
- SA-CCR is calibrated to historic market stress scenarios. For products with optionalities, the calibrated regulatory implied volatilities based on stressed market scenarios are more conservative. Because of calibrations to the historic market stress periods, it projects a static view of risk that is less sensitive to the current market volatilities and correlations.

Basel III intends to introduce capital floor based on SA-CCR. The capital floor (*Floor*) will be set at a percentage (r) of the capital calculated by the standardized approach (*SA*): $Floor = r * SA$. Assuming $SA = 2 \times IMM$ (*SA* capital is twice that of *IMM*), if r is set by the regulator at 75%, then $Floor = 75\% \times 2 \times IMM = 1.5 \times IMM$, meaning the capital requirement due to the capital floor is 50% more than that of *IMM*.

CCR Hedging Consideration   Banks can theoretically use CDS to hedge EAD, hence reducing the capital charges. However, the CDS hedge positions have to be accounted for at fair value and it will appear in accounting P&L. The problem is that the changes in EAD are not included in the accounting CVA. Therefore there is a mismatch between the regulatory charge under Basel III and the CDS hedge from an International Financial Reporting Standards (IFRS) perspective. While banks can reduce their Basel III CVA capital charge by CDS hedges, simultaneously they suffer from the accounting issue that the CDS hedges have no offsetting and are naked. The net outcome is the additional fair-value volatility in the financial statements. From the accounting perspective, banks are a net protection buyer. A counterintuitive outcome is that widening of credit spreads will generate positive P&L, increasing equity under IFRS and consequently boosting regulatory equity.

While the counterparty exposure exists in both the IFRS and bank capital rules, the Basel methodology is more punitive. When Basel III's CVA charge is added, the counterparty risk recognized by the capital rules can be far higher than under IFRS. The above inconsistencies and conflicts between IFRS and regulatory CVA lead to a situation that it is very difficult to simultaneously mitigate regulatory capital under Basel and P&L volatility under IFRS. In other words, CDS hedges can reduce the regulatory CVA risk charge and achieve capital relief, but at the cost of P&L volatility.

Leverage

Prior and during the financial crises between 2008 and 2012, many banks were very highly leveraged. In parallel to the stricter requirements on regulatory capital, the systemic risks of excessive leverage are also being addressed by Basel III. Basel III reduces the leverage by introducing a limit on the leverage ratio, which is defined as:

$$Leverage\ Ratio = \frac{Tier1\ Capital}{Exposures}$$

The *Exposures* is the sum of all assets and off-balance sheet risk exposures, including derivatives and various required add-ons. The exposures are calculated on a gross basis, and not weighted by asset riskiness.

Basel III requires the minimum leverage ratio of 3%, meaning the risk exposures cannot be more than 33.3 times of Tier1 capital. This is substantially less and safer than some of the risky banks whose risk exposures were hundreds of times Tier1 capital during the crises. Under Basel III, given the leverage ratio limit of 3%, most of the banks limit themselves between 3.5% and 4% to be on the safe side.

The leverage ratio is calculated on Tier 1 capital, as opposed to common equity. This means that the AT1 instruments can fulfil capital shortfalls as well as leverage ratio requirements. Meeting the regulatory required minimum leverage ratio is another incentive for banks to issue AT1 hybrid debt, such as CoCos.

The flip side of reducing leverage is that it can reduce banks' lending to the real economy. However, because the leverage ratio calculations are non-risk-based, it can still incentivize lenders to take on higher risk/reward business.

Liquidity

Lack of liquidity can kill a bank even if it may be solvent. Basel III introduced two liquidity measures to strengthen banks' liquidity risk management, for both short-term liquidity and long-term funding:

- Liquidity Coverage Ratio (LCR):

$$LCR = \frac{High\ Quality\ Liquid\ Assets}{Net\ Liquidity\ Outflows\ Over\ 30\ Days} \geq 100\%$$

The short-term liquidity measure requires financial institutions to hold high-quality liquid assets to cover net liquidity outflows over a stress period of 30 days. In calculating LCR, assets are liquidity-weighted in the context of defining "high-quality". For example, cash and some government bonds have a weighting of 100%, while corporate bonds between 0% and 50%. The 30-day stress scenarios include both systemic and firm-specific factors.

- Net Stable Funding Ratio (NSFR):

$$NSFR = \frac{Available\ Stable\ Funding}{Required\ Stable\ Funding} \geq 100\%$$

NSFR requires financial institutions to manage and maintain stable funding structures over the long term. It has an embedded duration element, reflecting stability. In calculating Available Stable Funding, liabilities with maturities longer than 1 year tend to attract higher weighting to reflect the stability requirement. For the same stability rationale, Tier 1 capital attracts higher weighting than core retail deposits and core retail deposits attract higher weighting than unsecured wholesale funding. In calculating Required Stable Funding, in the same spirit, different weightings are applied to the assets to incentivize banks to achieve higher NSFR.

Under Basel III, financial institutions are required to report LCR at least monthly, and NSFR at least quarterly. These liquidity rules pose challenges to financial institutions on how to calculate and manage LCR and NSFR, and how to effectively design the funding strategy within the liquidity risk management framework.

INTERNAL MODEL METHOD (IMM)

Under the Basel framework, banks that wish to use the IMM to calculate market and credit risk capital requirements must have a rigorous and comprehensive risk infrastructure and engine. It must be capable of conducting reliable scenario runs and stress-testing, and carrying out prudent statistical analyses. The IMM can substantially reduce banks' capital requirements compared to the Standardized Method (SM). This provides a strong incentive for banks to build solid and efficient risk architecture for regulatory purpose, as well as pursuing best risk management practices.

Risk Infrastructure

The IMM is inherently more complex than the SM, as banks need to develop a risk-sensitive approach that is aligned with internal risk management policies as well as their risky positions. All positions in the trading books, including derivative, repo (reverse repo) and securities lending, are subject to both market risk and counterparty credit risk capital requirements.

Up to now, the IMM risk infrastructure has been very heavily dependent on VaR. VaR calculated at a pre-determined time horizon (e.g. 10 trading days) and confidence interval (e.g. 99% one-tailed) is one of the most important market risk measures contributing to capital requirements and trading limits setting. For a given VaR (VaR_{t-1}) and sVaR ($sVaR_{t-1}$) calculated overnight ($t-1$), the VaR contributions to the daily capital requirement are given by:

$$Capital_{VaR} = max\left(VaR_{t-1},\ m_c \cdot VaR_{avg}\right) + max\left(sVaR_{t-1},\ m_s \cdot sVaR_{avg}\right)$$

where VaR_{avg} is the daily average VaR and $sVaR_{avg}$ is the daily average sVaR for the previous 60 business days. The multiplication factors m_c and m_s are decided by regulators on the basis of their assessment of bank's risk management systems, subject to a minimum (for example, 3).

The capital requirements for market risk are calculated on a consolidated basis. This determines that the required risk infrastructure must be designed and implemented enterprise-wide in order to fully capture portfolio aggregating effects. Because the VaR calculations involve all derivative positions across all asset classes for all risk factors, the system or engine design and implementation should leverage the developments in the front office trading systems, to ensure overall consistency as well as future business efficiency.

The schematic diagram in Figure 3.3 illustrates a risk architecture that leverages the front office trading systems and quant pricing model library. When technically possible, the best and simplest implementation is for the risk infrastructure to supply and impose risk scenarios onto the positions already booked in the trading systems, and re-run the entire books. The quant pricing model library already integrated into the trading systems will be used automatically. This setup will ensure consistency and enhance model transparency across the value chain. It will substantially improve the new products development process in the future.

In the second best case, the same quant pricing model library used for trading should be integrated and used in the risk systems. A risk system should not be a stand-alone system, as such a system will run into issues of consistency and costs, and potentially hamper the business.

Risk engines at enterprise-wide level for all asset classes and all risk factors involve a combination of pricing models and huge amount of data. Data analysis, capture, storage, search and transfer matter a great deal and they are the main factors affecting the computational efficiencies. The data topic in this finance context is potentially bordering the pioneer topic of "big data". "Big data" is not just about the size, it is more about how to achieve computational efficiency given the size of data, extract new risk information and provide new management service from the big data.

VaR Engine – A Key Component   A VaR engine allows banks to recognize and measure the risks into the future. There are several key ingredients in VaR calculation, including determination of risk factors, scenarios, ways of daily changes (multiplicative or additive) and VaR methodology. Broadly speaking, there are three VaR methodologies as seen in Table 3.4.

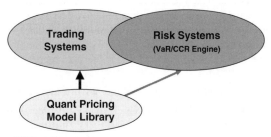

FIGURE 3.3   Risk architecture for consistency and transparency

TABLE 3.4   Major VaR methodologies

Historical Simulation (Non-Parametric)	▪ Historical data is used to derive change distributions. For example, 10-day change distributions of risk factors are calculated from the fixed length historical data. The minimum historical data observation length is 1 year. ▪ The historical change distributions can then be applied to the current market data and positions to compute VaR. ▪ The historical data sampling window is moving every day for daily VaR.
Variance-Covariance Matrix Method (Parametric)	▪ Using historical data, simple risk factors statistics including mean and variance, correlations etc. are estimated. ▪ By making a strong assumption that the change distribution in risk factors is normal, for a given confidence level the expected profit and loss on the portfolio can be calculated. ▪ The normal distribution assumption is reasonable if it is for a very short (e.g. 1 day) holding period. In such cases, one can also adopt the delta approach, using the first derivative of the changes in the VaR calculation. ▪ In a nutshell, this method fits normal distributions to historical data!
Monte Carlo Simulation (Non-Parametric)	▪ This method generates a wide range of future scenarios for all risk factors, and applies them onto the existing positions. ▪ The most sophisticated approach is to generate risk-neutral scenarios and then fully re-value the positions. ▪ Stress scenarios can include, but are not limited to, equities and interest rates market swings, commodity, credit and currency fluctuations. ▪ Backtesting is essential, and it is a key performance test required by the regulators to examine bank's internal models.

The normal distribution assumption in the parametric (variance-covariance) method is too strong to be flexible for banks' wide variety of non-linear derivative instruments. The vast majority of banks opt for non-parametric VaR methodology, either historical simulation or Monte Carlo simulation.

Risk Systems Evolution   Risk systems have evolved with time to become more sophisticated in line with the advance of risk management technology and practice. To a large extent, the evolution is also driven by the regulatory requirements. One of the latest such regulatory impacts could be the outcome of "fundamental review of the trading book". Basel Committee, in its fundamental review of the trading book consultative document, has proposed to revise market risk framework. Among a number of proposals, the following two components can potentially alter the risk systems substantially:

- Proposal to replace VaR by Expected Shortfall (ES) as the new risk measure for market risk management and trading book capital calculation. ES is mathematically/statistically a more plausible risk measure, but it is computationally much more demanding. Back-testing ES is also challenging, and it requires new researches and techniques to meet the VaR back-testing standard.
- Proposal to enhance the roles of revised Standardized Methods:
  - banks must regularly calculate the standardized charge for each trading desk as if it were a stand-alone regulatory portfolio;
  - banks should publicly disclose standardized charges and capital requirements in their regulatory reports, regardless of whether they are using models-based charges;
  - apply a standardized-based floor or surcharge to the model-based capital charges.

By enhancing the roles of revised SM, it can help to create a public benchmark across firms and jurisdictions, and reduce model-based discrepancies seen among the banks. For those who are already using IMM, there will be additional risk systems requirements and evolution. The incentives and benefits of current risk-sensitive IMM will be reduced.

Scenarios Generation

There are three key steps when using the IMM to calculate risk exposures (VaR, ES, CCR) and capital requirements:

- scenarios generation for relevant risk factors into a set of future dates;
- evaluation of all relevant risky positions under the generated scenarios;
- computation and aggregation of risk exposures, taking into account collateral and netting where applicable.

Scenarios generation is a key risk engine component in the IMM. In the process, a scenarios generator is designed to also capture the specific characteristics of certain portfolios for specific risk capital requirements, and stress scenarios for sVaR.

Risk factors' dynamics are specified by SDEs. Risk-neutral scenarios are generated using calibrated market data including yield curves and volatilities. They are of course model-dependent and driven by assumed underlying and yield curve dynamics. The techniques of generating high-quality risk-neutral scenarios are therefore closely related to the Monte Carlo pricing of relevant derivatives. For example, the risk-neutral yield curve scenarios are closely related to the Monte Carlo pricing of interest rate derivatives.

For some risk calculations (e.g. CCR, PFE), some practitioners prefer the real-world measure (*P*-measure), mainly because they prefer to use past history to assess the severity of the tail events and calibrate the scenarios to them. In this context, a real-world measure scenarios generator is used to calculate the effective expected positive exposures (EEPE) for regulatory capital requirements, and PFE for credit lines and limits management.

Let's assume the SDEs for the risk factors (X_i) under the P-measure are given by:

$$dX_i = \mu_i^P dt + \sigma_i dZ_i$$
$$(dZ_i \cdot dZ_j) = \rho_{ij} dt$$

where $\mu_i^P = \mu_i + \lambda_i \sigma_i$, μ_i is the drift under the risk-neutral measure and λ_i is the market price of risk for X_i.

For scenarios generation in the real-world measure, the drift (μ_i^P) or market price of risk (λ_i), volatility (σ_i), variance-covariance matrix etc. can be estimated from historical time series. Table 3.5 lists some example dynamics from which the scenarios for the risk factors can be generated.

TABLE 3.5 Example dynamics for scenario generation

Risk Factor	Example Dynamics
Equity	Log-Normal: $X_i = \ln S_i$; Scenarios can also be generated in the local volatility space.
FX	Log-Normal: $X_i = \ln F_i$; Scenarios can also be generated in the local volatility space.
Interest Rates	Simulate the entire zero curve. Each zero rate (r_i) at a $(i$-th) bucket is assumed to follow a SDE (e.g. Log-Normal or CIR process).
Credit Spreads	Can use the same method as for interest rates, each zero spread is simulated. Additionally, random default events (e.g. jumps) and recovery rate stochastic fluctuation can be included in the simulation.
Commodity	Can be simulated either as indices or a curve;
Inflation	Can be simulated either as indices or a curve;
Implied Volatilities	The volatilities are stochastic and they are risk factors too.

In general, it is more difficult to generate high-quality yield curve scenarios than to generate, for example, equity scenarios. In the following, we shall focus on the discussion of interest rate yield curve scenarios generation.

Yield Curve Scenarios

The reliability of risk calculations (sVaR or PFE or CCR) heavily depend upon the quality of the yield curve scenarios. Below we will use a zero yield curve to illustrate how to enhance the quality of the yield curve (YC) scenarios generation.

YC Scenarios Using Brute Force Monte Carlo
A zero yield curve consists of a vector of zero rates $(r_1, r_2, \cdots, r_n)$. To simulate the whole curve into the future using historical or calibrated parameters (drifts and volatilities), one could use brute force Monte Carlo to simulate a basket of n correlated components. Once the stochastic process of the zero rates are assumed (for example, log-normal), the simulation technique is standard. An example of brute force Monte Carlo scenario simulation is shown in Figure 3.4.

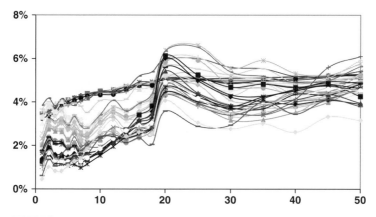

FIGURE 3.4 Brute force Monte Carlo YC scenarios

The simulated yield curves at future times are plotted in the figure. Most of the curves certainly do not look pretty, not only visually but technically. Among the curves generated, a large proportion of them look too "bumpy" to be realistic. The real-life yield curves are usually much smoother. If these types of "bumpy" yield curve scenarios are used in the sVaR or PFE or CCR calculations, a large amount of computational time and resources will be simply wasted on calculating unrealistic scenarios, and the sVaR or PFE or CCR numbers can be unreliable. Moreover, some of the sharp downward slopes in the curves may indicate arbitrage opportunities, hence can crash the pricing models. Clearly, we need a better yield curve scenario generation technique.

YC Scenarios Using Principal Component Analysis   One such technique is based on Principal Component Analysis (PCA). PCA is a well-known technique in the fields of statistical data analysis, signal processing and finance (Jamshidian and Zhu). In essence, it extracts principal components (or factors) which contribute the most to the dynamics of the underlying process. A typical example of PCA is actually on a yield curve, its dynamics can be characterized as parallel shift (as the 1st component), tilting (as the 2nd component) and curvature change (as the 3rd component). The yield curve scenario model taking these principal components as the driving factors will clearly generate much more realistic scenarios.

The yield curve scenarios generated using the PCA technique are plotted in Figure 3.5. The scenarios are generated under the identical conditions as those using brute force Monte Carlo. By comparing Figure 3.4 and 3.5, PCA scenarios look much prettier, visually and technically.

The mathematical details of the PCA technique are outlined below. Given a zero curve $(r_1, \cdots, r_i, \cdots, r_n)$, assuming they are log-normally distributed:

$$\frac{dr_i}{r_i} = \mu_i \cdot dt + \sigma_i \cdot dw_i$$

with correlation $\langle dw_i \cdot dw_j \rangle = \rho_{ij} dt$, the eigenmatrix operation can be conducted on the correlation matrix $R\{\rho_{ij}\}$:

$$R \cdot \beta_j = \lambda_j \cdot \beta_j$$

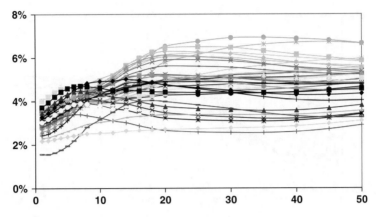

FIGURE 3.5   Principal component analysis YC scenarios

where β_j is the j-th eigenvector of the correlation matrix and λ_j is the j-th eigenvalue.

Given R is a symmetric positive definite matrix, its eigenvectors are orthogonal to each other, and eigenvalues are all positive. The eigenvectors can be normalized such that:

$$|\beta_j|^2 = \sum_{i=1}^{n} \beta_{ij}^2 = \lambda_j$$

in which the eigenvalues have been sorted in the following order:

$$\lambda_1 \geq \lambda_2 \geq \cdots \geq \lambda_n$$

The eigenmatrix operation enables us to identify β_1 as the 1st principal component, β_2 as the 2nd principal component, β_3 as the 3rd principal component, and so on.

The Wiener variable dw_i can then be expressed using the orthogonal principal components:

$$dw_i = \sum_{j=1}^{n} \beta_{ij} \cdot dz_j$$

By taking the first three principal components $\beta_{i1}, \beta_{i2}, \beta_{i3}$, the zero curve dynamics can be rewritten as:

$$\frac{dr_i}{r_i} = \mu_i \cdot dt + \sigma_i \cdot \left(\beta_{i1} \cdot dz_1 + \beta_{i2} \cdot dz_2 + \beta_{i3} \cdot dz_3 \right)$$

where dz_1, dz_2, dz_3 are independent random (Wiener) variables. This is the SDE used in the PCA technique to generate yield curve scenarios. The dimensionality of the simulation has been reduced to three from n (and n is typically more than 10).

The PCA technique is much better than the brute force Monte Carlo in terms of yield curve scenarios generation. Note that the PCA model only works well if the underlying variables are reasonably correlated. This is generally true for the interest rate yield curves, where the rates of different maturities tend to move in a correlated manner.

For sVar or PFE or CCR, one can also use Nelson–Siegel model to generate yield curve term structure scenarios. Instead of generating individual points on the yield curve, the Nelson–Siegel model uses the following functional form for the zero yield curve:

$$r(t) = a_0 + a_1 \left(\frac{1 - e^{-\lambda t}}{\lambda t} \right) + a_2 \left(\frac{1 - e^{-\lambda t}}{\lambda t} - e^{-\lambda t} \right)$$

where a_0, a_1, a_2 and λ are model parameters which can be fitted to or characterized by the relevant market or historic data. These parameters can certainly be made time-dependent to increase the flexibility. Additionally, it is possible to formulate the Nelson–Siegel model in an arbitrage-free manner for generating risk-neutral yield curve scenarios.

BEYOND BASEL III

While Basel III strengthens the requirements/rules for credit counterparty risks (e.g. CCR, CVA), its market risk framework largely remains the same as Basel 2.5. Fundamental Review of the Trading Book (FRTB) (Basel 2013, Basel 2014) proposes the next generation of the market risk framework. Given its significant changes, some practitioners already call FRTB "Basel IV".

Fundamental Review of Trading Book

The FRTB-compliance market risk framework is expected to be implemented by banks from the end of 2018. The significant policy and operational changes proposed by FRTB include:

- Capital requirements and the internal models will be assessed and approved at the trading desk level. This is much more granular than at the enterprise level.
- The boundary between the trading book and banking book will be revised.
- Different liquidity periods (ranging from 10-days to 250-days) will be included in the capital calculations.
- Equity positions will be included in the default risk framework.
- Banks will be required to follow more stringent disclosure rules.

FRTB also proposes fundamental changes in the risk methodology:

- Internal Models Approach (IMA):
  - Expected Shortfall (ES): to replace VaR and sVaR.
  - Incremental Default Risk (IDR): to replace incremental risk charge (IRC).
  - For a trading desk to qualify for IMA, it must meet the criteria of independent model assessment, back testing, P&L attribution, etc.

- Standardised Approach (SA):
  - Standardised approach for market risk will be based on risk sensitivities. It is known as Sensitivity Based Approach (SBA).
  - SA will be used to calculate a floor for the internal model. Hence even if IMA is approved for a trading desk, SA may still have an impact on its capital calculation.
  - All banks will be required to calculate and disclose SA capital charges for all trading book positions, including those under IMA. The disclosure will be on a monthly basis and mandatory.

Practically, for a trading desk using IMA, the capital charge will consist of the following three components:

- **Expected Shortfall (ES):** ES will be used to calculate the market risk for the modellable risk factors. Modellable risk factors are those having sufficiently frequent and high-quality historical observations. Each risk factor is subject to liquidity horizon scaling. The liquidity horizon is deemed to be the time to unwind the position in the market without causing significant market movement. The aggregated ES is the weighted average of expected shortfalls over different liquidation horizons.
- **Incremental Default Risk (IDR):** IDR measures the jump to default risk, and it'll include sovereign and equity trading positions. Securitization products are not allowed for internal model treatment. IDR is similar to IRC under Basel III, except that IDR excludes migration risk as it focuses on the default component.
- **Non-Modellable Risk Factors add-on:** FRTB divides the risk factors into modellable and non-modellable risk factors. The internal models can only be applied to the modellable risk factors. Capital charges from non-modellable risk factors will be via add-ons, which are based on stress testing and scenario analysis. As an example, "correlation" is often considered as a non-modellable risk factor by many practitioners.

It is important to note that the total capital charge calculated using IMA will be subject to a floor calculated using the SA. The regulator will decide a percentage (r) of SA capital as floor, i.e. $floor = r \times SA$.

For a trading desk that has to use the SA, the capital charge will consist of the following components:

- **Sensitivity-based Approach (SBA):** SBA will use risk sensitivities (delta, Vega, curvature) and apply 1bp shift (absolute shift for interest rate and credit, relative shift for equity, commodity and FX) to calculate capital. The outcome of SBA is strongly dependent on the allowable offsetting. For example, if a trading desk hedges a position with an instrument, and if for capital purposes their risks are not allowed to offset, then the exposure from capital perspective will be amplified by the hedge. Hence in practice one needs to consider hedging also taking account of allowable offsetting in capital calculation.
- **Incremental Default Risk (IDR):** This will involve the calculation of jump to default. Under certain conditions offsetting is allowed.
- **Residual risk add-on:** This is for instruments whose payoffs cannot be written as a linear combination of European or American vanilla put and call options on a single underlying of equity price, commodity price, exchange rate, bond price, CDS

price or interest rate swap. Hence any non-vanilla options (including digitals) are within the residual risk add-on scope. The total add-on is calculated by multiplying the total absolute notional by a regulator-determined multiplier. The residual risk add-on is effectively a "non-vanilla option notional add-on".

The Basel Committee on Banking Supervision (BCBS) is still consulting financial institutions and addressing outstanding issues. Certain rules and implementation details are still evolving and subject to changes. The finalized FRTB will set out the new market risk capital rules, which are more streamlined than those in Basel III. It will also incentivise banks to further re-organise and optimise their trading desks.

In addition, it is worth pointing out that some capital rules have not been in line with market hedging practice. BCBS is also trying to align the rules better with the risk management reality. For example, it is examining the derivatives counterparty risk capital framework with a view to better aligning the regulatory requirements with market practice.

Expected Shortfall Versus VaR

By using expected shortfall (ES) as the new risk measure for market risk management and trading book capital calculation, banks are expected to better capture and manage tail risks. ES will run using stress scenarios, hence the risk measure can cover and replace both VaR and sVaR.

For a given time horizon (e.g. 10 days), and probability percentile α (e.g. $\alpha = 3\%$), its VaR is defined as:

$$P\left(\Delta V < -VaR\right) = \alpha$$

where ΔV is the value change of the relevant portfolio. VaR is a single number. It does not contain any information on loss distribution, or on the tail beyond α percentile.

ES is defined as the expectation of losses beyond the α percentile:

$$ES = \frac{1}{\alpha}\int\limits_{0}^{\alpha}VaR(p)\cdot dp$$

ES is actually the average VaR covering the tail area, as illustrated in Figure 3.6. By definition, ES is sub-additive, and VaR is not.

As a risk measure, the tail risk is captured by ES. Let us use an example to further illustrate this. For 99% and 10-day holding period, the VaR can be 10 million, i.e. 1% chance of losing more than 10 million. However, VaR cannot state how much more one can lose beyond 1%. ES is to fill this gap by considering the shape of loss distribution in the tail. ES will be the expected loss beyond 1% and it will be always larger than VaR, depending on the shape of loss distribution.

It is entirely possible to have a portfolio with small VaR, but very large ES, since VaR does not capture the tail risks. For example, it is possible to have a VaR of 10 million, i.e. 1% chance of losing more than 10 million. However, the portfolio can have a 1% of chance of losing 50 million, which can only be captured by ES. The trading risks and limits measured and set by VaR have serious shortcomings.

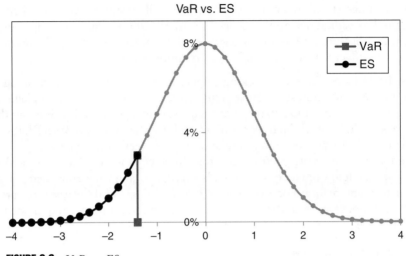

FIGURE 3.6   VaR vs. ES

Regulators have so far proposed to set the ES confidence level at 97.5%, as opposed to 99% for VaR. Although lower ES confidence level will reduce the calculated expected loss, there are good numerical and economic reasons for the lower threshold:

- The tail risk calculation will numerically be more stable and more reliable.
- With a larger tail, people can be more focused on the risks they know better and are sure of, rather than at the mercy of just a few extreme tail events.
- It can also facilitate back testing in terms of statistical reliability.

Comparing VaR and ES from computation perspective:

- ES requires moderately more computational power than VaR, as ES integrates over VaRs at different percentiles.
- The tail distribution required by ES is harder to obtain or estimate in practice, and one will need more data with substantially higher quality to ascertain the tail distribution. Extrapolating distribution to the tail end is also a difficult process.
- It is therefore a challenge to conduct back-testing of ES, although some of the latest researches (e.g. Acerbi and Szekely) are proposing possible ways forward.
- Since ES is sensitive to the extreme events contained in the tail distribution, numerically it can be less stable than VaR.
- Overall, ES possesses many good properties. However, its implementation can pose some numerical, infrastructure and operational challenges to the financial institutions.

The ES engine is a critical component. It must be able to conduct reliable scenario runs and stress-testing, and carry out prudent statistical analyses. Although the IMM (or IMA) risk infrastructure originally developed for VaR can be adapted for ES, banks should also optimise the fundamental architecture of ES engine, including centralising quantitative pricing library across the value chain. In order to benefit fully from IMM, banks must have a reliable and comprehensive risk infrastructure with a very efficient ES engine.

Two

Equity Derivatives

Equity derivatives have specific market, product and model features. Most equity underlyings have discrete dividends which introduce discrete jumps into the continuous stochastic process. The volatility surfaces typically show pronounced smile/skew, and the volatility surfaces typically move with the time and spot. These specific equity market features make equity derivative models unique, and it is a challenge to model and risk manage structured equity products, taking into account the discrete nature of the underlying and volatility dynamics.

In Part II, key equity derivatives market features will be presented. Various quantitative modelling paradigms and practical insights will be examined. Moving from theoretical and academic framework to real-world modelling is a giant step forward. Much attention will be given to the practical aspects, as to how to modify and adapt the theoretical frameworks to work with the real-world market features.

CHAPTER 4

Equity Derivatives
Market Features

The number of equity underlyings (stocks, indices, funds, etc.) across the globe is almost unlimited, which bring about a wide range of settlement rules. This is in contrast to the FX or interest rate derivative business, where a limited number of currency pairs and interest rate yield curves are the underlyings. In this chapter, we shall summarize some of specific equity derivatives market features, including key equity index underlyings, features of discrete dividends, option settlement rules, quanto effect and convexity in the equity futures.

Volatility smile/skew is also a very pronounced feature in the equity markets. Modern equity derivatives models are designed to handle smile/skew. Managing implied volatility surfaces is fundamental in equity derivatives pricing and the topic will be discussed in details in this chapter.

EQUITY INDEX UNDERLYINGS

A large number of structured products are linked to equity index underlyings. These index underlyings can expose investors to a wide range of equity risks. The exposures can be chosen in geographic terms and/or sectors, for example to large-caps (e.g. FTSE-100, S&P 500, EURO STOXX 50) or small-cap segments (e.g. Russell 2000). Table 4.1 summarizes some of the major indices in the global equity markets.

DISCRETE DIVIDENDS

One of the complications in equity derivative modelling is how to treat discrete (cash) dividends. On ex-div dates, the underlying spot drops by the dividend amount, ignoring tax. This introduces discrete deterministic jumps into the geometric Brownian process

TABLE 4.1   Major equity indices

Index Category	Key Features	Examples
Market Cap Weighted Index	The weighting of each constituent stock is proportional to its prevailing market value.	FTSE-100, S&P 500, EURO STOXX 50, NASDAQ Comp, Russell 2000, CAC 40, Hang Seng Index, SENSEX
Equal Weighted Index	Every constituent stock has the same weighting.	S&P 500 EWI, EURO STOXX 50 EWI, NASDAQ100 EWI
Price Weighted Index	The weighting of each constituent stock is proportional to its prevailing market price.	Dow 30, Nikkei 225
Total Return (TR) Index	Includes stock price changes as well as dividend reinvestment.	DAX, S&P 500 TR, FTSE 100 TR
Strategy Index	Typically measures the performance of an investment strategy, including fund strategies, currency beta, inverse and leverage, dividend, etc. The weightings are rules-based.	S&P Chinese Renminbi, S&P 500 2x Leverage Daily
Dividend Index	It tracks the total dividend payments from the constituent stocks. The index resets to zero periodically, for example quarterly or annually.	Dow Jones Dividend Indices, STOXX Select Dividend Indices
Risk Control Index	Tracks the return of a dynamically rebalanced portfolio or index, to control the volatility of the overall investment.	S&P RC indices, STOXX RC indices, MSCI RC indices
Excess Return (ER) Index	Measures the performance of investment on borrowed money. The excess return index is unfunded, equal to the underlying index minus the borrowing costs.	S&P 500 Average Daily Risk Control 5% USD ER, FTSE 100 Risk Target ER
Volatility Index	Tracks implied volatility of a specified underlying and tenor, e.g. S&P 500 9-day or 30-day implied volatility. Relevant quoted option prices are used for its calculation.	VXST, VIX, VSTOXX

assumed in the Black–Scholes framework. Ignoring the equity repo rate, the underlying stochastic process in the presence of discrete dividend can be expressed as:

$$\frac{dS}{S} = rdt + \sigma dz$$

$$S_{t+} = S_{t-} - D_t$$

where r is the risk-free rate and D_t is the discrete dividend on ex-div date, S_{t+} is the spot just after the ex-div date and S_{t-} is the one just before the ex-div date.

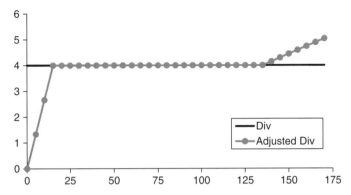

FIGURE 4.1 Schematical diagram of discrete dividend adjustment
Horizontal axis is the spot level.

Handle Discrete Dividends in PDE

In a PDE (Partial Differential Equation) grid (or during Monte Carlo simulation), at the very low spot grid points, a discrete dividend can make the spot after the dividend negative. This is undesirable, and one can make simply dividend adjustment to avoid negative spot. As seen in Figure 4.1, at a given time slice, with the discrete dividend D_t, the adjusted discrete dividend D_{adj} can be made as a function of spot (S_{t-}):

$$D_{adj} = \begin{cases} \dfrac{D_t}{S_L} S_{t-} & S_{t-} \leq S_L \\ D_t & S_L < S_{t-} < S_U \\ \dfrac{D_t}{S_U} S_{t-} & S_{t-} \geq S_U \end{cases}$$

- S_L is a low spot level. From there downwards the adjusted dividend becomes a proportional dividend with a fixed proportion of D/S_L.
- S_U is a upper spot level. From there upwards the adjusted dividend becomes a proportional dividend with a fixed proportion of D/S_U.
- The upper side is used to compensate the downside. S_L and S_U should be chosen such that the probability weighted forward after the dividend date still calibrates to the market.
- The large middle part ($S_L < S < S_U$) is unchanged, and this can minimize the potential side effect of the dividend adjustment.

Discrete Dividends Versus Continuous Dividend Yield

Very often, various dividend assumptions are made to simplify the underlying process. One commonly used is to convert discrete dividends into an equivalent continuous dividend yield q, and the underlying stochastic process then becomes:

$$\frac{dS}{S} = (r - q)dt + \sigma dz$$

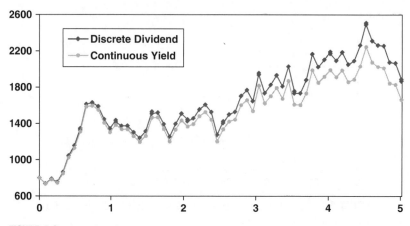

FIGURE 4.2 Simulated spot paths

The continuous dividend yield assumption actually alters the underlying stochastic process. Figure 4.2 compares two simulated spot paths for a single stock. One path is generated using the discrete dividends process (dividend every 6 months, amount of 2.5% spot), and the other path using the equivalent continuous yield process (annualized 5% yield). Both paths are generated using exactly the same random sequence.

The difference shown in Figure 4.2 is due to different dividend assumptions. It is clear that the simplified continuous dividend yield process is close to the discrete process at the short end. The difference between the two processes becomes large at the longer end. The obvious implication is that longer-dated derivative products could be mispriced if the continuous yield process is used improperly. This is true not only for path-dependent options, but also for European options even if the forwards match under the two different dividend assumptions.

In the following, we compare the price differences between the discrete dividend process and the continuous dividend yield process. The comparisons are made when the two corresponding models use the same market data, including risk-free curve and implied volatility surface.

Comparison of European Options

To handle discrete dividends accurately, they are incorporated into a smile/skew Partial Differential Equation (PDE) solver. The discrete dividends on ex-div dates meet the following jump conditions:

$$S_{t+} = S_{t-} - D_t$$
$$V_{t+} = V_{t-}$$

where S_{t+} is the spot just after the ex-div date and S_{t-} is the one just before the ex-div date, and V_{t+} and V_{t-} are the corresponding option prices. The jump conditions can be implemented by interpolating within the PDE mesh on ex-div dates.

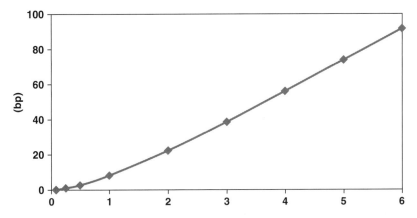

FIGURE 4.3 Price difference (call) vs maturity

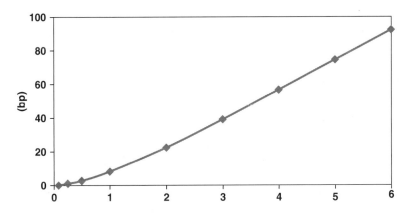

FIGURE 4.4 Price difference (put) vs maturity

In Figure 4.3, the ATM European call price differences between discrete dividend PDE solver and Black–Scholes with equivalent dividend yield are plotted for a range of maturities. The underlying is a typical equity index and the same market data is used in both models. The price differences are expressed in basis point (bp).

The price difference increases dramatically with the maturity. For the same volatility input, European calls using discrete dividend PDE is more expensive that those using continuous dividend yield Black–Scholes. Figure 4.4 shows a similar picture for European puts.

Both calls and puts are more expensive under the discrete dividend process. As the forwards are kept the same this is in line with put-call parity. The price discrepancy is largely due to the fact that in the discrete dividend case, discrete jumps increase the overall variance (volatility) of the process. If both discrete dividend and continuous dividend yield model are calibrated to the same market-quoted option prices, the resulted implied volatility of the discrete dividend model will be lower than that of continuous dividend yield model.

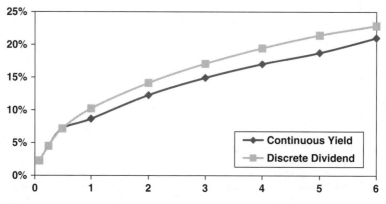

FIGURE 4.5   American calls vs maturity

The examples showed above used an equity index whose dividends are fairly spread out. Yet the longer-dated vanilla prices could still be quite different under different dividend assumptions. For single stocks whereby the discrete dividends are lumpier, the pricing difference can be even larger.

Comparison of Path-dependent Options

For American and barrier options, the dividend processes also affect the optimum exercise boundary and barrier touching probabilities. In the following we use a single stock to illustrate these effects. The example single stock pays the first dividend in 6 months' time and every 6 months thereafter, of the amount of 2.5% of the current spot – the equivalent of an annualized 5% continuous dividend yield.

American Options   Figure 4.5 displays the price versus maturity for ATM American calls under different dividend assumptions. The price difference starts at the maturity of 6 months when the first dividend is due.

The substantial price difference is due to the fact that discrete dividends alter the optimum exercise boundary of the American option. Under the discrete dividend process, on passing the ex-div date the downwards jump of the stock makes the call option less valuable after the dividend than before it. Clearly, if the option is in the money, one might exercise the option before the dividend. Under the continuous yield process, however, since there is no jump on the ex-div date, the early exercise of an American call does not produce extra gain for the option holder. Consequently the American calls under the discrete dividend process are more expensive than their continuous dividend yield counterpart.

Barrier Options   Figure 4.6 compares barrier one-touch probabilities under the two different dividend processes. The barrier is at 80% of the spot. The difference between the two starts at 6 months when the first dividend is due. In this example, under the discrete dividend process, the spot drift ($\mu = r$) at non ex-div dates is higher than that in the continuous yield case ($\mu = r - q$). The spot on average drifts higher and away from the barrier in the discrete case and hence a lower one-touch probability.

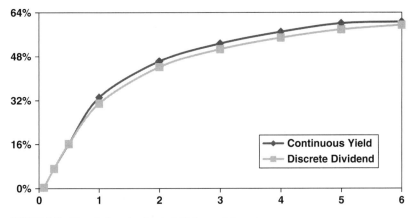

FIGURE 4.6 Touch Barrier Probabilities vs Maturity

Summary

The numerical implementation of discrete dividends is non-trivial. However, the alternative, converting discrete dividends into continuous dividend yield, could produce significant pricing and risk management errors for longer-dated and/or path-dependent option (e.g. American and barrier options).

In theory, it is possible to adjust partially for the discrete dividend effects by recalibrating the implied volatility surface at the long end using appropriate models. In practice, however, given the poorer liquidity of long-dated options, one tends to extrapolate the short-end volatility surface into the long end and partially calibrate some points on the implied volatility surface. When the short-end volatility is extrapolated into the long end, it should be used in conjunction of rigorous option models, which should use the correct discrete dividend process.

Dividend assumptions can affect derivative pricing significantly. In general, equity dividends can be assumed to have both cash and yield element on ex-div dates:

$$D\big(t,\ S_t\big) = a\big(t\big) + b(t)\cdot S_t$$

where $a(t)$ represents the cash dividends, $b(t)$ is the yield element and S_t is the prevailing spot. Note that both elements are discrete, happening on ex-div dates. Typically the cash dividends have heavier weight at short end as they can be reasonably predicted, while the long-end dividends can be better represented by the yield. The advantage of this approach is that by associating longer-term dividends with spot process, one can partially capture and hedge dividend exposures. It is not a good idea to assume cash dividends only when pricing longer-dated equity derivatives. In the aftermath of market crashes, dividends will typically be marked down as the real economies will be affected adversely. The derivative positions modelled using cash dividends only will have P&L jumps. Post the Lehman Brothers collapse in 2008, some financial institutions suffered significant losses due to the fact that the cash dividends had to be marked down.

For some major equity indices and blue chip stocks, exchange-traded dividend futures and options can be used to hedge dividend risks. Dividend has evolved to become a tradable asset in itself.

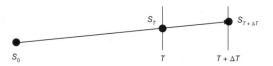

FIGURE 4.7   Option settlement time interval

OPTION SETTLEMENT DELAY

Figure 4.7 illustrates the option settlement time interval.

The option expires at time T, and the delayed settlement either cash or physical happens at $T + \Delta T$.

In the case of cash settlement, the settlement delay is easy to handle. One can usually apply additional discount to the option premium for the delayed period ΔT. Almost all exchange-traded equity options are cash-settled, so are the majority of OTC equity options including options on equity indices, and their settlement delays are handled in this way.

In the case of physical settlement mostly associated with bespoke single stock options, one needs to take into account additional factors. For example, there may be dividends falling between the option maturity date and delivery date. The forward at the settlement date does have an impact. The option payoff or exercise decision can also be affected by the settlement delay, which in turn impacts the value of the option.

Physical Settlement: Automatic Exercise

For a call option, if the exercise is automatically determined at expiry T, with the exercise condition set at $S_T \geq K$, then the price expectation integration of S_T should be from K to ∞. The actual payoff, however, is the physical delivery at $T + \Delta T$, namely the forward at delivery $F_{T+\Delta T} = S_T e^{(r-q)\Delta T}$. Therefore the call option price is given by the following expectation integration:

$$Call = e^{-r(T+\Delta T)} \int_K^\infty \left(F_{T+\Delta T} - K \right) \cdot g\left(S_T \right) dS_T$$

$$= e^{-r(T+\Delta T)} \left[F_{T+\Delta T} \cdot N\left(d_1 \right) - K \cdot N(d_2) \right]$$

where r is risk-free rate, q is dividend yield, σ is the volatility, $N(\cdot)$ is the cumulative normal distribution,

$$d_1 = \frac{\ln\left(\dfrac{F_T}{K} \right) + 0.5\sigma^2 T}{\sigma\sqrt{T}}$$

$$d_2 = d_1 - \sigma\sqrt{T}$$

Note that d_1 contains F_T instead of $F_{T+\Delta T}$. This is because the integration of S_T is from the actual K to ∞.

Similarly, for a put:

$$Put = e^{-r(T+\Delta T)} \int_{-\infty}^{K} \left(K - F_{T+\Delta T} \right) \cdot g\left(S_T \right) dS_T$$

$$= e^{-r(T+\Delta T)} \left[K \cdot N\left(-d_2 \right) - F_{T+\Delta T} \cdot N\left(-d_1 \right) \right]$$

For physical settlement, the automatic exercise type is less common. However, it is sometimes embedded in the client-driven structures, and it should be handled differently from the more common type: optimum exercise.

Physical Settlement: Optimum Exercise

The most common European option type is the optimum exercise, as the holder has the right (but not the obligation) to exercise. For a call option with a delayed physical settlement, if the exercise decision is determined by the condition $F_{T+\Delta T} \geq K$, rather than $S_T \geq K$ as in the previous case, the option exercise is optimum and the pricing formula is yet again different.

$F_{T+\Delta T} \geq K$ can be rewritten as $S_T \geq Ke^{-(r-q)\Delta T}$. This indicates that the expectation integration is from the modified strike $X = Ke^{-(r-q)\Delta T}$ to ∞. Therefore the call pricing formula is given by the following expectation integration:

$$Call = e^{-r(T+\Delta T)} \int_{X}^{\infty} \left(S_T e^{(r-q)\Delta T} - K \right) \cdot g\left(S_T \right) dS_T$$

$$= e^{-r(T+\Delta T)} e^{(r-q)\Delta T} \int_{X}^{\infty} \left(S_T - X \right) \cdot g\left(S_T \right) dS_T$$

$$= e^{-r(T+\Delta T)} e^{(r-q)\Delta T} \left[F_T \cdot N\left(d_1 \right) - X \cdot N(d_2) \right]$$

$$= e^{-r(T+\Delta T)} \left[F_{T+\Delta T} \cdot N\left(d_1 \right) - K \cdot N(d_2) \right]$$

where:

$$d_1 = \frac{\ln\left(\dfrac{F_T}{X} \right) + 0.5\sigma^2 T}{\sigma\sqrt{T}} = \frac{\ln\left(\dfrac{F_{T+\Delta T}}{K} \right) + 0.5\sigma^2 T}{\sigma\sqrt{T}}$$

$$d_2 = d_1 - \sigma\sqrt{T}$$

Note that d_1 contains $F_{T+\Delta T}$ instead of F_T. This is because the integration of S_T is from the modified strike X to ∞.

For a put option, similar principles apply:

$$Put = e^{-r(T+\Delta T)} \int_{-\infty}^{X} \left(K - S_T e^{(r-q)\Delta T} \right) \cdot g\left(S_T \right) dS_T$$

$$= e^{-r(T+\Delta T)} \left[K \cdot N\left(-d_2 \right) - F_{T+\Delta T} \cdot N\left(-d_1 \right) \right]$$

The above physical settlement principles consider the forward at $T + \Delta T$, together with the standard deviation $\sigma\sqrt{T}$ at T. When $\Delta T > 0$, delayed physical settlement can make a material difference in option price.

QUANTO EFFECT

Many equity-linked structured products contain Quanto options. A Quanto option has a payoff linked to underlying(s) of one currency, but the payoff is made in another currency. For example, for an option on FTSE-100 (GBP underlying) Quanto into EUR, if at expiry the option payoff is 100, it will pay out 100 in EUR (as opposed to GBP). In many practical cases, Quanto options allow investors to take on equity exposures in foreign markets, and get paid in their domestic currency. Such Quanto options have foreign underlying(s), and the payoff is made in domestic currency.

From an option holder's perspective, Quanto option enables them to expose to the foreign underlying(s) without taking on any FX risks, as the FX rate is effectively fixed at the outset. In the following, we shall examine how a Quanto option is hedged to gain more insight on its pricing and risks.

Quanto Hedging

Let us use a Quanto product example to illustrate the life cycle of the embedded Quanto option and how it can be hedged. Investors in the eurozone buy a simple growth product with capital protection and an equity exposure to a foreign market (e.g. S&P500). Both notional and payoff are in domestic currency of EUR, while the equity underlying S&P is in USD.

The product issuer must hedge the embedded Quanto option – call on S&P500 Quanto into EUR. Denoting the FX rate X_t, the following steps in Table 4.2 need to be taken to delta hedge the exposures.

Intuitively, FX rate X_t impact on the **EUR amount** is through its correlation with S&P500 spot during the delta hedge rebalancing. The **EUR amount** represents the delta position from EUR perspective, as opposed to from the S&P500 currency (USD)

TABLE 4.2 Quanto delta hedge

Initial hedge	Convert delta amount from EUR into USD using X_0. Put on the delta hedge of S&P500 in USD.
Rebalancing the delta hedge	If S&P500 spot moves, the delta hedge needs to be rebalanced. One would either convert additional amount of EUR into USD to increase the delta hedge, or reduce the delta hedge and repatriate the excess USD back into EUR, using the prevailing FX rate X_t. The correlation of S&P500 spot and FX rate X_t has a direct impact on the **EUR amount** needed or repatriated to rebalance the delta hedge.
Final payoff	At option expiry, the delta hedge position should cancel out the S&P500 call position, in the context of continuous hedge theory. The final option payoff is the accumulated **EUR amount** throughout the rebalancing process.

perspective. This leads to the following mathematical formula for the standard Quanto drift adjustment.

Quanto Adjustment

If an option payoff P is in the underlying currency 1 (Ccy1), under its Martingale measure Q_1 the SDE for the underlying S is given by:

$$\frac{dS}{S} = \mu dt + \sigma dW^{Q_1}$$

If the same payoff P is payable in currency 2 (Ccy2), namely Quanto into Ccy2, the option needs to be valued under the measure Q_2. Using the measure change technique and through Girsanov's theorem, the following relationship between Brownian motions under different measures holds:

$$W^{Q_2} = W^{Q_1} - \rho \sigma_{FX} T$$

where ρ is the correlation between S and X_t. X_t is the FX rate expressed as the units of Ccy1 per unit of Ccy2.

The above formula allows us to derive the underlying SDE under the measure Q_2:

$$\frac{dS}{S} = \mu dt + \sigma dW^{Q_1}$$
$$= \left(\mu + \rho \sigma \sigma_{FX}\right) dt + \sigma dW^{Q_2}$$

Therefore the Quanto options can be valued by making a simple drift adjustment and using the discount factor in the payoff currency:

$$DF_2 \cdot E^{Q_2}[P]$$

The above standard Quanto adjustment can be used for vanilla and exotic options alike. Usually ATM volatility is used to adjust the Quanto forward. In the presence of discrete dividends, one can construct an equity repo curve if there isn't one and make the Quanto adjustment to the equity repo curve alone.

Quanto Risks

In implementing Quanto adjustment, the correlation between S and X_t will change sign if the FX rate X_t is quoted differently (Ccy1Ccy2 versus Ccy2Ccy1) on the market. While this may sound like a trivial detail, it is important to get it right for all the currency pairs needed for Quanto options.

In the presence of volatility smile/skew, Quanto adjustment becomes more complex. Giese [2012] presented a comprehensive paper discussing Quanto adjustment in the presence of stochastic volatility which is used to model the volatility smile/skew. Not surprisingly, in addition to the standard drift adjustment, an additional Quanto adjustment to the volatility is also required in the stochastic volatility modelling setup. This intuitively can be viewed as a smile/skew contribution to the Quanto adjustment.

The constant correlation assumption and FX volatility smile are two more sources of uncertainties in Quanto pricing. During past financial crises, practitioners witnessed correlation moving to extreme values (very high correlation or anti-correlation depending on FX quoting conventions) and much-increased FX volatility smile effect. In such scenarios, the equity Quanto books showed substantial (too much) FX exposures, sometimes with undesirable outcomes due to practical difficulties in the Quanto hedging. Practitioners therefore need to make some allowance for these effects in risk managing Quanto positions.

FUTURE VERSUS FORWARD

The difference between **forward** and **future** arises from the fact that **forward** is settled only once at the end of the contract, while **future** is settled daily until the end of the contract, with a margin account maintained. A margin account either earns interests or incurs funding costs, depending on long or short position as well as equity market performance. Hence **future** is path-dependent due to daily margining. Its fair value is determined by the expectation that makes the continuous rebalancing margin account zero PV. Mathematically, the forward (Fwd) and future (Fut) can be defined by:

$$E_0^Q\left[\frac{S_T - Fwd}{B_T}\right] = 0$$

$$E_{t-1}^Q\left[\frac{Fut_t - Fut_{t-1}}{B_t}\right] = 0$$

where B_t is the cash account numeraire. The solutions for the forward and future can be expressed as:

$$Fwd = \frac{E_0^Q[S_T/B_T]}{E_0^Q[1/B_T]}$$

$$Fut = E_0^Q[S_T] = E^Q[S_T \mid F_0]$$

As can be seen from the above, Forward is driven by the expectation of deflated spot process, which is a martingale. Only the terminal spot values contribute to the expectation and Forward. Future is, however, the conditional expectation on the filtration at time 0 (F_0). Embedded in the conditional expectation, Future is subject to day-to-day stochastic interest rate impact, including the correlation between equity spot and short-term interest rate. If S_t and B_t are independent under the Q-measure, then $Fwd = Fut$.

Convexity Adjustment For Future

The convexity adjustment in Future is model-dependent. In the simplest case, one can assume the equity spot S and short interest rate r follow the following stochastic processes:

$$\frac{dS}{S} = \mu dt + \sigma dw_s$$

$$dr = -\kappa r dt + \alpha dw_r$$

$$\langle dw_s dw_r \rangle = \rho dt$$

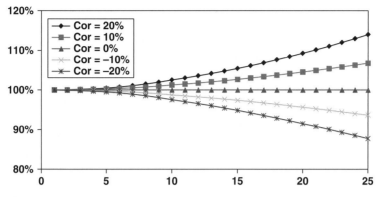

FIGURE 4.8 Future convexity adjustment [$C(T)$]

where κ is the mean reversion and α is the absolute volatility of the short rate, and ρ is the correlation between the equity spot and short rate.

Taking the conditional expectation as defined for the **future**, and after some algebra, the following relationship can be established: $Fut = C(T) \cdot Fwd$, where the convexity adjustment $C(T)$ is given by:

$$C(T) = exp\left(\int_0^T \rho\sigma\sigma_r(t)\,dt \right)$$

$$\sigma_r(t) = \alpha \frac{1 - e^{-\kappa t}}{\kappa}$$

Plugging $\sigma_r(t)$ into $C(T)$, the convexity adjustment is:

$$C(T) = exp\left(\rho\sigma \int_0^T \alpha \frac{1 - e^{-\kappa t}}{\kappa}\,dt \right)$$

$$= exp\left(\rho\sigma\alpha \frac{T}{\kappa}\left(1 - \frac{1 - e^{-\kappa T}}{\kappa T} \right) \right)$$

Figure 4.8 plots the convexity adjustments versus the maturity T, at various correlation levels for an example set of equity index market data. As expected, the longer the maturity T is, the larger the convexity adjustment becomes. The long-dated convexity adjustments can become quite significant depending on market data.

The correlation has significant effect on the convexity adjustment. The effects can be understood as follows:

- If one longs a future, with a positive correlation between the equity forward and interest rate (i.e. on average both go up or both go down together):
  - when market and rate go up, the margin account will be settled with a credit, which in turn earns a higher interest;
  - when market and rate go down, the margin account will be settled with a debit, which in turn incurs a lower funding cost;

■ this constitutes a systematic advantage for the person who longs the future, hence the future price must be higher than the forward;

■ If one longs a future, with a negative correlation between the equity forward and interest rate (i.e. on average they move in opposite ways), the same logic as above indicates that there is a systematic disadvantage for the person who longs the future. Hence the future price must be lower than the forward.

Convexity Effects On Long-dated Hedge

The difference between **forward** and **future** will affect the delta hedging error/cost if the latter is used to hedge the former. In long-dated equity structures, the long-dated equity forward is priced in. The delta hedges for the forward positions often involve trading futures on the relevant equity indices. Forward is not equal to future if the interest rate is stochastic. Hence for long-dated delta hedges, the convexity adjustment for long-dated future, i.e. the difference between the future and forward needs to be taken into account.

Given that $Fut = C(T) \cdot Fwd$, the hedge ratio (delta) has the following relationship:

$$\frac{\partial(Fut)}{\partial S} = C(T)\frac{\partial(Fwd)}{\partial S}$$

Therefore to hedge one forward contract, $1/C(T)$ future is needed. For example, if one is **selling** forward in the structured products **and** using future to hedge, the adjustment of $1/C(T)$ (instead of $C(T)$) should be adopted.

The convexity analysis can be extended to other asset classes, such as the convexity adjustments to interest rate futures. Convexity adjustments on interest rate futures will be significantly higher than those for equity futures. The correlation between the interest rate future underlying (which is an interest rate itself) and interest rate is very high. Hence one observes sizeable market price differences between interest rate futures and FRAs, starting from a fairly short time horizon onwards.

IMPLIED VOLATILITY SURFACE

Prior to the infamous October 1987 stock market crash, equity options were priced using Black–Scholes with flat implied volatility. There was no volatility smile/skew. During the crash, as shown in Figure 4.9, the massive drops happened within a very short period, measured in hours and days. The volatility shot up during the crash in equal measures. The market psychology was shaken permanently by the events. The fear of market crash has since been built into the option pricing, manifested as volatility skew. Volatility skew has since become a permanent feature in almost all equity markets globally.

Figure 4.9 caption: S&P500 and FTSE100 price movement during the October 1987 stock market crash. Both indices are normalized as of 3 July 1987 and labelled by the left axis. The right axis is the label for the S&P500 volatility movement during the crash.

Today, although equity volatility skew can be attributed to a number of other reasons, including supply and demand, the downside crash protection is still a major factor. An essential component in the derivative pricing and hedging is the volatility

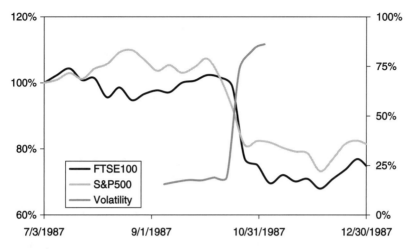

FIGURE 4.9 Oct 1987 market crash

smile smile/skew modelling. Implied volatility surface along maturity and strike is the prime source of market smile/skew information, and its construction is vital in all smile/skew modelling paradigms.

General Non-arbitrage Conditions

The shapes and curvatures of the implied volatility surface cannot be arbitrary, as the option prices calculated using the implied volatility surface must satisfy certain non-arbitrage conditions.

A call option with strike K and maturity T is defined by:

$$C(K,T) = e^{-rT} \int_0^\infty \max(S-K,0) p_T(S) dS$$

where r is the risk-free rate and $p_T(S)$ is the probability density function. Differentiating it against K:

$$\frac{\partial C}{\partial K} = -e^{-rT} \int_K^\infty p_T(S) dS$$

Differentiating it again against K:

$$\frac{\partial^2 C}{\partial K^2} = e^{-rT} p_T(K)$$

From the above, the non-arbitrage conditions along the K-axis can be easily obtained. Together with those along the T-axis, Table 4.3 summarizes the essential non-arbitrage conditions in the construction of an implied volatility surface:

TABLE 4.3   Non-arbitrage conditions of an implied volatility surface

Options	Non-arbitrage Conditions	Economic Rationale
Call Spread	$-e^{-rT} \leq \dfrac{\partial C}{\partial K} \leq 0$	For the same maturity, a call with higher strike must be less valuable than the call with lower strike.
Butterfly	$\dfrac{\partial^2 C}{\partial K^2} \geq 0$	Butterfly at strike K must have a positive value.
Calendar Spread	$\dfrac{\partial C}{\partial T} \geq 0$	For the same strike, a call with longer maturity must be more valuable than the call with shorter maturity.
Variance $(V = \sigma^2 T)$	$\dfrac{\partial V}{\partial T} \geq 0$	Total variance must increase with time.

Finally, if the local volatility bootstrapped from an implied volatility is non-negative everywhere, then the implied volatility surface is arbitrage-free. This is the ultimate non-arbitrage test.

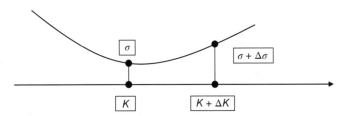

FIGURE 4.10   Call Spread Strikes and Corresponding Volatilities

Non-arbitrage Smile/Skew Boundaries   The volatility smile/skew at the short end is more pronounced than that at the long end, and the long-end smile/skew tends to decay. While this market phenomenon can be explained by some trading intuitions, it is ultimately determined by the non-arbitrage conditions.

Taking the call spread as example, for a given maturity T, the strike (K) and volatility (σ) are marked schematically in Figure 4.10.

The non-arbitrage condition states that the call spread must be less than or equal to zero ($\partial C / \partial K \leq 0$). Hence:

$$\Delta C = C\left(K + \Delta K, \sigma + \Delta \sigma\right) - C\left(K, \sigma\right) \leq 0$$

The value of ΔC comes from two incremental elements, one is due to the strike change (ΔK), and the other from the volatility change ($\Delta \sigma$) due to smile/skew. Therefore:

$$\Delta C \approx \frac{dC\left(K, \sigma\right)}{dK} \Delta K + \frac{dC\left(K, \sigma\right)}{d\sigma} \Delta \sigma \leq 0$$

In the standard Black–Scholes framework with standard B-S notations:

$$\frac{dC(K,\sigma)}{dK} = -e^{-rT} \cdot N(d_2)$$

$$Vega = \frac{dC(K,\sigma)}{d\sigma} = Se^{-qT}\sqrt{T}N'(d_1) = Ke^{-rT}\sqrt{T}N'(d_2)$$

$$d_1 = \frac{\ln(S/K) + (r - q + 0.5\sigma^2)T}{\sigma\sqrt{T}} \qquad d_2 = d_1 - \sigma\sqrt{T}$$

where $N(\cdot)$ is the normal cumulative probability and $N'(x) = \exp(-x^2/2)/\sqrt{2\pi}$. Plugging them into call spread non-arbitrage condition ($\Delta C \le 0$), one can obtain the volatility smile $\Delta\sigma/\Delta K$ boundary:

$$\frac{\Delta\sigma}{\Delta K} \le \frac{e^{-rT} \cdot N(d_2)}{Ke^{-rT}\sqrt{T}N'(d_2)} = \frac{N(d_2)}{KN'(d_2)}\frac{1}{\sqrt{T}}$$

Using the put spread non-arbitrage condition:

$$\Delta P = P(K + \Delta K, \sigma + \Delta\sigma) - P(K,\sigma) \ge 0$$

and following the same logic, the volatility skew $\Delta\sigma/\Delta K$ boundary is given by:

$$\frac{\Delta\sigma}{\Delta K} \ge \frac{-e^{-rT} \cdot N(-d_2)}{Ke^{-rT}\sqrt{T}N'(d_2)} = \frac{[N(d_2) - 1]}{KN'(d_2)}\frac{1}{\sqrt{T}}$$

Denoting the smile/skew boundaries as:

$$b_{smile} = \frac{N(d_2)}{KN'(d_2)} \cdot \frac{1}{\sqrt{T}} \qquad b_{skew} = \frac{[N(d_2) - 1]}{KN'(d_2)} \cdot \frac{1}{\sqrt{T}}$$

we have $b_{skew} \le \dfrac{\Delta\sigma}{\Delta K} \le b_{smile}$ which defines the volatility smile/skew boundaries at a given T. b_{smile} and b_{skew} are simple functions of K given T and σ. One can potentially use this simple relationship to analyse the smile/skew boundaries at extreme strikes.

b_{smile} and b_{skew} are also simple functions of T given K. The ATM case when $K = S$ is of particular interest. Figure 4.11 plots the ATM smile boundary (b_{smile}) versus maturity (T) for three different ATM volatilities (10%, 30%, 60%), with $K = S$, $r = 3\%$ and $q = 1\%$. In these examples, the smile boundaries decay with maturity.

With the same parameters, the ATM skew boundary (b_{skew}) versus maturity (T) for three different ATM volatilities are plotted in Figure 4.12. While they tend to decay with maturity, the long end smile/skew boundary is ultimately determined by non-arbitrage conditions, and it does not always decay as in the case of $\sigma_{atm} = 60\%$.

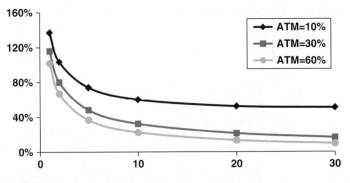

FIGURE 4.11   Smile decay

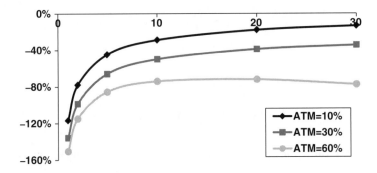

FIGURE 4.12   Skew decay

Extrapolating Smile/Skew to the Long End   In many practical applications, given the lack of market data at the long end, one needs to extrapolate the short-end smile/skew to the long end. The above boundary analysis provides a sound basis for such smile/skew extrapolation. One should not naively flat extrapolate the smile/skew, i.e. using the same smile/skew at the long end, as this can lead to arbitrage.

Assuming the short-end smile/skew is already within the non-arbitrage boundaries, the long-end smile/skew can be extrapolated using the ATM smile/skew boundary formulae (b_{smile} or b_{skew}) to ensure it stays within the non-arbitrage boundaries. The smile/skew boundary formulae (b_{smile} or b_{skew}) are very simple and they can be used directly to extrapolate smile/skew proportionally. For example, if the smile at year 5 is known (δ_{5y}), the smile at year 10 can be extrapolated as $\delta_{10y} = \delta_{5y} \cdot (b_{10y} / b_{5y})$, where b_{10y} and b_{5y} are the ATM smile/skew boundary at year 10 and 5 respectively. Figure 4.13 shows an example of smile extrapolation to the long end using the boundary formula b_{smile}.

Some practitioners use a Sqrt(T) decay scheme to extrapolate smile/skew:

$$\frac{\Delta\sigma}{\Delta K} \propto \frac{1}{\sqrt{T}}$$

Figure 4.14 compares the ATM b_{smile} boundary decay scheme with the Sqrt(T) decay scheme, using $\sigma_{atm} = 50\%$, $r = 3\%$ and $q = 1\%$. The two smile decay schemes can be

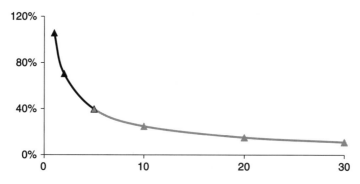

FIGURE 4.13   Boundary decay smile extrapolation

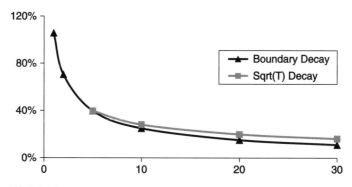

FIGURE 4.14   Smile extrapolation schemes (ATM = 50%)

quite different. As the boundaries do depend on other parameters (not just T), the b_{smile} and b_{skew} boundary smile/skew decay schemes are much more reliable and they are very simple to implement.

Provided the Black–Scholes implied volatility is quoted against the strike, i.e. in the K space, the boundary decay scheme works in other asset classes too. If, however, the implied volatility is quoted against the delta, such as in FX option markets, one needs to make the necessary conversion between the delta and K space for the boundary smile/skew decay scheme. Further details can be found in chapter 15, where the FX volatility smile extrapolation is discussed.

Non-parametric Implied Volatility

Equity implied volatility surfaces are usually referenced to ATM spot. For some equity underlyings, such as major equity indices, there are option price quotes for different strikes and maturities. The implied volatilities at the quoting points can then be interpolated and extrapolated along both K-axis and T-axis, to construct a non-parametric implied volatility surface. Assuming the market data is clean, the implied volatilities directly from the quoted option prices should be arbitrage-free. One therefore needs

TABLE 4.4 Non-parametric interpolation schemes along strike

K-axis Interpolation Schemes	Features
Cubic Spline Volatility Versus Moneyness	It has the advantage of being numerically smooth, and continuous in both first and second derivatives.
Linear Volatility of Moneyness	Suitable for pricing vanilla options only. It has discontinuity in first and second derivatives.
Linear Volatility of Logarithmic Moneyness	Suitable for pricing vanilla options only. It has discontinuity in first and second derivatives.
Linear Variance of Logarithmic Moneyness	Suitable for pricing vanilla options only. It has discontinuity in first and second derivatives.

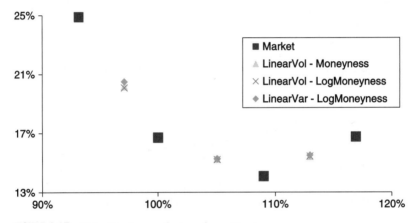

FIGURE 4.15 Volatility interpolation along *K*-axis

to make sure not to introduce arbitrage during the interpolation and extrapolation process. In the following, some practical schemes are explained for interpolation along the strike (*K*) and maturity (*T*) axis.

Along the *K*-axis There are various simple non-parametric interpolation schemes, as listed in Table 4.4.

Figure 4.15 compares the three linear interpolation schemes, and their interpolated volatilities are plotted against the market points. The horizontal axis is strike in moneyness. While it can be a personal choice, linear volatility against logarithmic moneyness is a popular scheme, partly because it is more in line with the log-normal underlying assumption in the equity world.

It is important to note that linear non-parametric interpolation schemes are only suitable for pricing vanilla options. They are not good enough for stripping local volatilities, and will not behave well in a smile-modelling framework where numerical smoothness and continuity in the first and second order derivatives (implied volatility wrt *K*) are required. While the cubic spline scheme can be adopted in such a situation for smile modelling, using functional form implied volatility can be another alternative.

TABLE 4.5 Non-parametric interpolation schemes along maturity

T-axis Interpolation Schemes	Features
Linear Variance	For any given strike K, the total variance $[\sigma(T, K)^2 T]$ is linear along the T-axis.
Linear Skew	For any given strike K, $\sigma(K,T) = \sigma_{ATM}(T) + skew(K,T)$. $\sigma_{ATM}(T)$ is interpolated using linear variance for ATM, and $skew(K,T)$ is interpolated linearly from the skew components.

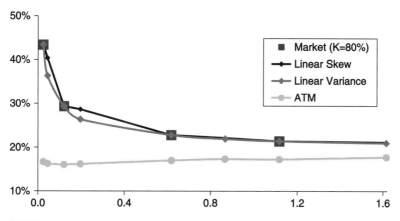

FIGURE 4.16 Volatility interpolation along T-axis

Along the T-axis Typical non-parametric interpolation schemes along the T-axis include linear variance and linear skew, as seen in Table 4.5.

In Figure 4.16, the above two interpolation schemes are compared for the given strike of 80%. The horizontal axis is maturity in years. The linear variance scheme generates smoother curved term structure, and the linear skew scheme generates straighter line between the points. Once again, practitioners may have different preferences. The important thing, though, is to ensure the interpolated volatility term structure is arbitrage-free.

By subtracting the ATM volatility from the implied volatility, the skew term structures are plotted in Figure 4.17 for the two different interpolation schemes. A linear variance scheme creates a curved skew term structure, and a linear skew scheme creates a straight line between the points.

Figure 4.18 shows an example of constructed non-parametric implied volatility surface of EUROSTOXX 50. A cubic spline scheme is used along the K-axis, and linear variance is used along the T-axis.

Non-parametric implied volatility surface can in general fit very well to most of the market quotes. However, some interpolation schemes can only be used for pricing vanilla options, as they cannot ensure continuity in first and second derivatives along the K-axis, which can cause serious problems in the smile modelling.

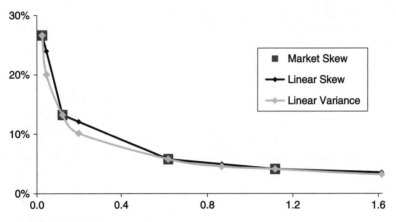

FIGURE 4.17 Interpolated skew along T-axis

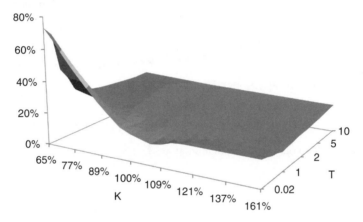

FIGURE 4.18 Non-parametric vol surface (Eurostoxx 50)

Functional Form Implied Volatility

A sensible volatility smile/skew functional form can provide a simple and intuitive way to specify and calibrate smile/skew. Importantly, it can provide numerical smoothness required in the smile/skew modelling. The functional form parameters are obtained by using numerical optimization techniques, fitting to market-quoted implied volatilities. In the case of fitting along the K-axis, it is preferable to fit as exactly as possible to the ATM volatility because they are most liquid and more likely used for hedging. If possible, ATM volatility should replace the relevant parameter in the functional forms as a direct input, and the optimization technique is used to fix the remaining parameters.

Along the K-axis A variety of volatility smile/skew functional forms are used in equity derivatives, including quadratic, SVI (Gatheral 2006) and several others. This is in contrast to the interest rate derivatives, where the consensus is to use SABR as the functional form.

In the following, a Tanh-Cosh volatility functional form is examined. It has the form of:

$$\sigma(X) = \sigma_{ATM} + A \cdot \tanh[B \cdot (X-1)] + C \cdot \left(1 - \frac{1}{\cosh[D \cdot (X-1)]}\right)$$

where $X = K / S$ is the relative strike (moneyness), K is the strike and S is the spot and $\sigma(1) = \sigma_{ATM}$, which is a direct market input. The four parameters (A, B, C, D) in the above functional form can be made time-dependent. At each maturity, A, B, C, D can be calibrated to market-quoted implied volatilities using numerical optimization techniques.

A, B, C, D are also related to the following direct market inputs:

- skew – defined as slope of the implied volatility curve;
- smile – defined as curvature of the implied volatility curve;

Mathematically:

$$Skew = \frac{\partial \sigma(X)}{\partial X}\bigg|_{X=1}$$

$$Smile = \frac{\partial^2 \sigma(X)}{\partial X^2}\bigg|_{X=1}$$

Plugging the functional form into the above equations, the following simple relationships between the parameters and direct market inputs can be established:

$$Skew = A \cdot B$$
$$Smile = C \cdot D^2$$

In the limiting case:

$$\sigma_{X \to \infty} = \sigma_{ATM} + \frac{B}{|B|} \cdot A + C$$

$$\sigma_{X \to -\infty} = \sigma_{ATM} - \frac{B}{|B|} \cdot A + C$$

By specifying the direct market inputs, and converting them to the four parameters, one can construct the volatility surface. This can be useful in interpolating the strike-dependent functional form between time slices. The direct market inputs can be interpolated first in a meaningful way, and the functional form parameters can then be backed out.

Figure 4.19 shows an example of implied volatility surface, generated and calibrated using the Tanh-Cosh functional form. The Tanh-Cosh functional form is flexible and able to fit to a wide range of market-observable smile/skew.

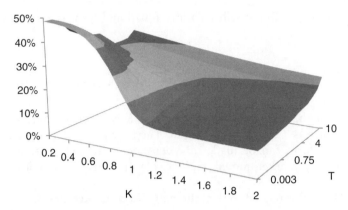

FIGURE 4.19   Parametric vol surface (FTSE 100)

Along the T-axis   An interesting ATM volatility term structure functional form is the following exponential form:

$$\sigma^2(T) = \sigma_\infty^2 + \left(\sigma_0^2 - \sigma_\infty^2\right)\frac{1 - \exp(-\alpha T)}{\alpha T}$$

The parameters $(\sigma_\infty, \sigma_0, \alpha)$ can be obtained numerically by fitting to the quoted ATM volatilities using numerical optimization, such as Levenberg–Marquardt technique. Note that $\sigma(\infty) = \sigma_\infty$ and $\sigma(0) = \sigma_0$, allowing easier first guess in the optimization process. Typically the short end market quotes are used to back out three parameters given the liquidity.

The above exponential functional form is obtained by assuming the instantaneous volatility-squared follows the Ornstein–Uhlenbeck process, from which the expectation of volatility-squared can be derived.

Practical Implementation Choices

Implied volatility surface is used for pricing as well as risk management purposes, each of them has different requirements and constraints. In the following, we shall examine what practical implementation choices work well for pricing and risk managing vanilla options, and what work well for exotic options. The smile/skew volatility surface of illiquid options will also be discussed.

Non-parametric or Functional Form   Along the K-axis, non-parametric interpolation and functional form volatility have pros and cons as listed in Table 4.6.

Given the above pros and cons:

- One can choose to use non-parametric scheme for vanilla options, for faster pricing and easy calculation of strike bucketed Vega sensitivities.
- One can choose to use either functional form or cubic spline for pricing exotic options. For calculating strike bucketed Vega sensitivities, cubic spline works much better than functional form.

TABLE 4.6 Non-parametric vs functional form

Pricing Vanilla	Non-parametric interpolation is ease, quick and accurate enough. Functional form also works, but relatively slow.
Pricing Exotics	Numerical smoothness is essential. Functional form works better. Only some non-parametric schemes, such as cubic spline can achieve numerical smoothness in the smile modelling framework. The other non-parametric schemes, such as the linear schemes, will not work well for exotics;
Vega Sensitivity	Both non-parametric and functional form can work well for parallel shift Vega sensitivity. However, for the strike bucketed Vega: Functional form cannot easily do individual strike volatility bumping. Non-parametric scheme can easily do strike volatility bumping.
Extrapolation	Vegas on the wings are very small. So it will not make much difference which extrapolation scheme to use when pricing vanilla options. However, wings are very important for pricing exotics, so is the extrapolation scheme. Adequately chosen functional form tends to work better in practice.

- A good compromise is to construct original smile/skew (implied volatility surface) using functional form, and then use cubic spline for pricing exotics and calculating risk sensitivities.
- Along the *T*-axis, most practitioners prefer to use non-parametric schemes.

Smile/Skew Volatility Surface of Illiquid Options For illiquid options, such as those of some single stocks or emerging market equity indices, there is little or no reliable market option data to allow a reliable construction of implied volatility surface with smile/skew. In such a circumstance, historic time series can be used to assess the smile/skew information of the underlying (Zou and Derman 1999). The technique uses the historic return distribution to estimate a risk-neutral probability density function (PDF), which can then be used to price options of all strikes. The implied volatilities at those strikes can therefore be derived from the option prices.

The advantage of this technique is that one only needs a reliable set of time series of the underlying to derive a reasonable volatility surface. Typically, such time series is easy to obtain.

The historic time series analysis can provide valuable volatility surface benchmarks, in particular the smile/skew information. As with any historic analysis, it does **not** necessarily indicate for the future. It is possible, however, to blend the current market conditions into the analysis. This can be done by blending simulated data into the historic time series to derive a different volatility surface. For example, it is possible to introduce market crashes into the time series and this will increase the skew into the historic volatility surface.

The technique for illiquid options can also be valuable for those of emergent market underlyings, whereby the smile/skew information is scarce or non-existent. One must remember that even if the volatility smile/skew information is not available in the option market, it does not mean smile/skew risks do not exist. In fact, smile/skew risks exist across equity markets: when markets crash, their volatilities shoot up.

CHAPTER 5

Black–Scholes Paradigm

One of the most fundamental concepts in derivative pricing is hedging. Speculation is human, hedging is divine. A non-arbitrage derivative pricing framework does rest on the divine principle of hedging. The Black–Scholes model paradigm is generally regarded as such a framework, providing simple and practical derivative pricing solutions. Although the original Black–Scholes assumes there is no volatility smile/skew, it has widely been used by practitioners in all asset classes for pricing vanilla as well as certain path-dependent products. The paradox is that even though Black–Scholes formulation is based on continuous hedging, its Greeks for hedging must be adjusted in the presence of volatility smile/skew. It is important to know that Black–Scholes are not necessarily used in its simplest forms by the practitioners, but in a variety of modified ways.

In this chapter, we shall first review some basic modelling framework and formations, followed by discussions on certain vanilla and path-dependent products. The required pricing adjustments for volatility smile/skew will be explained. Finally, the important topic of how to adjust Black–Scholes hedging parameters (e.g. delta) in the presence of volatility smile/skew will be covered.

BASIC MODELLING FRAMEWORK

There are two distinctive modelling methodologies in the Black–Scholes model paradigm. One is to use the probability measure Q ($P \rightarrow Q$) by incorporating risk aversion in the model. The other is to use Ito's differential equation to replicate and hedge the optionalities.

Under Q Probability Measure

The objective probability measure (P) is a real-world measure describing the underlying asset evolution with time. Under P measure, $E^P[S_t] = S_0 exp[(\mu - q)t]$, where μ is the expected rate of return including risk premium, and is larger than the risk-free rate (r). Hence under the real-world (P) measure, investors will be expecting larger returns given the risks taken, namely $E^P[S_t] > S_0 exp[(r-q)t]$. Of course, some securities are riskier than the others, hence it is reasonable to expect higher returns for the riskier securities. This is why P-measure cannot be a martingale even under the numeraire-adjusted price process.

The risk-adjusted probability measure (Q) adjusts the real-world probability such that under Q the numeraire-deflated price process is a martingale. Under Q measure, $E^Q[S_t] = S_0 exp[(r-q)t]$. It is clear that $E^Q[S_t] < E^P[S_t]$, indicating that under Q measure one effectively assigns larger probability weight to the unfavourable events and smaller probability weight to favourable events, to take into account (or counter) the real-world risk-aversion reality. Q measure is therefore equivalent to the risk-neutral concept, and in fact is also known as the risk-neutral measure.

Probability measure change is closely associated with the numeraire change. For a specific chosen numeraire, an equivalent martingale measure or risk-neutral probability measure (Q-measure) is a set of probabilities $Q = (q_1, \cdots q_i, \cdots), q_i > 0$ such that the deflated security value is a martingale:

$$\bar{V}_t = \frac{V_t}{N_t} = E_t^Q\left[\frac{V_T}{N_T}\right] = E_t^Q[\bar{V}_T] \qquad t < T$$

where V is the security, N is the numeraire, V / N is the deflated security and $E_t^Q[\cdot]$ is the expectation under Q-measure. The equivalent martingale measure is always associated with the specific numeraire. Therefore choosing an appropriate numeraire security is crucial in the formulation of martingale pricing.

A very important martingale pricing theorem is that the absence of arbitrage is equivalent to the existence of Q-measure. For a deflated value process, if there exists a Q-measure, then there can be no arbitrage opportunities. Conversely, if there are no arbitrage opportunities, there must exist a Q-measure and the deflated value process of any self-financing trading strategy is a Q-martingale. In a complete market, the Q-measure is unique, which can be used to obtain the value of contingent claims. Accordingly, by taking the Q-expectation of deflated security terminal values, the deflated price at an earlier time, e.g. present value at $t = 0$, can be computed.

Although any positive non-dividend-paying asset can be a numeraire, a properly chosen numeraire can greatly simplify the formulation and pricing of the derivative. Change of numeraire does not alter the self-financing portfolios and their hedges. One such numeraire example is the zero-coupon bond $z(t, T)$, whose maturity (T) coincides with that of the derivative. For a European style payoff, the no-arbitrage derivative pricing formula is reduced to:

$$V_0 = z(0, T) E_0^Q\left[\frac{V_T}{z(T, T)}\right] = z(0, T) E_0^Q[V_T]$$

Because the terminal value of the zero-coupon bond is 1, i.e. $z(T, T) = 1$, the present value of the derivative is simply the discounted expected terminal payoff. This conclusion holds for all major asset classes, including interest rate. The martingale pricing principles are valuable mathematical tools to formulate many types of option payoffs in the Black–Scholes model paradigm.

Partial Differential Equation (PDE)

In B-S framework, the log of the underlying spot is assumed to follow the Brownian motion:

$$\frac{dS}{S} = \mu \cdot dt + \sigma \cdot dz$$

where $\mu = r - q$ is the drift, the difference between risk-free rate (r) and dividend yield (q), and σ is the volatility. Following the practical hedging principle using a continuously rebalanced replication portfolio, and applying Ito's lemma mathematically, one arrives at the B-S PDE for the option value $V(S,t)$:

$$\frac{\partial V(S,t)}{\partial t} + \mu S \frac{\partial V(S,t)}{\partial S} + \frac{1}{2}\sigma^2 S^2 \frac{\partial^2 V(S,t)}{\partial S^2} = rV(S,t)$$

Each term in the above PDE has clear practical meanings. $\frac{\partial V(S,t)}{\partial t}$ is the Theta (Θ) measuring option time decay, $\frac{\partial V(S,t)}{\partial t}$ is Delta and $\frac{\partial^2 V(S,t)}{\partial S^2}$ is the Gamma (Γ_S). In a standard option Delta hedging strategy, one hedges away the first order option value change with respect to the underlying spot change. Mathematically, Delta hedge eliminates all the first order terms in the PDE, and leaves only the Theta and Gamma terms:

$$\Theta + \frac{1}{2}\sigma^2 S^2 \Gamma_S = 0$$

Therefore if an option position is long Gamma, it is in general short Theta, as shown in the B-S PDE. This explains the simple fact that long Gamma position makes money when spot moves, but at the expense of losing time value, and short Gamma position is a nightmare when spot moves, but at some comfort of gaining time value.

Outside B-S paradigm where volatility smile/skew dynamics matters, the option formulation and hedging practices can be a lot more complex. We shall explain some of those aspects in other relevant chapters. As a simple intuitive example, if one assumes the volatility is stochastic, the higher order terms left in the PDE after appropriate Delta hedge can be expressed (Hull and White 1990) as:

$$\Theta + \frac{1}{2}\sigma^2 S^2 \Gamma_S + a \cdot \Gamma_\sigma \sigma^2 + b \cdot \Gamma_{\sigma S}\sigma S = 0$$

where a and b are model-dependent constants, Γ_σ is the Gamma with respect to volatility, and $\Gamma_{\sigma S}$ is the cross Gamma with respect to volatility and spot. It is clear that one needs to consider those additional risk factors in practice as they can alter significantly the B-S hedging parameters (Delta and Gamma). Hedging those additional risk factors is not straightforward. It is, however, possible to include them in the modified Delta hedging strategies, where the first order risk sensitivities and hedging parameters are adjusted, for example to take into account volatility smile/skew.

Stochastic Process and Brownian Bridge

One of the principal assumptions in the B-S model paradigm is that the underlying stochastic process follows a geometric Brownian process. The PDE and Monte Carlo techniques based on the geometric Brownian processes are widely used to formulate and price relevant derivatives. The general stochastic process and its associated mainstream pricing techniques have been discussed extensively in the literatures. In the following, we will only discuss Brownian bridge, a very valuable tool supplementing the mainstream techniques such as Monte Carlo.

Brownian bridge is a stochastic process in which the both ends are tied down. It can be defined as:

$$X(t) = W(t) - \frac{t}{T} W(T), \quad 0 \leq t \leq T$$

where $W(t)$ is a Wiener process ($W(0) = 0$) with a mean 0 and variance $\sigma^2 t$. As can be seen from the above definition, $X(0) = X(T) = 0$, both ends have fixed values. When $0 < t < T$, $X(t)$ is stochastic conditional on the values of both ends. To generalize, assuming the fixed values at time t_a is a, and at time t_b is b, the generalized Brownian bridge can be written as:

$$X_{ab}(t) = a \cdot \left(\frac{t_b - t}{t_b - t_a} \right) + b \cdot \left(\frac{t - t_a}{t_b - t_a} \right) + X(t), \quad t_a \leq t \leq t_b$$

$$= a \cdot \left(\frac{t_b - t}{t_b - t_a} \right) + b \cdot \left(\frac{t - t_a}{t_b - t_a} \right) + \left[W(t - t_a) - \frac{t - t_a}{t_b - t_a} W(t_b - t_a) \right]$$

This is a Gaussian process overlay onto a straight line between (t_a, a) and (t_b, b). Its mean and covariance are given by the following:

$$E[X_{ab}(t)] = a \cdot \left(\frac{t_b - t}{t_b - t_a} \right) + b \cdot \left(\frac{t - t_a}{t_b - t_a} \right)$$

$$Cov(s,t) = \sigma^2 \cdot \left(\min(s - t_a, t - t_a) - \frac{(s - t_a) \cdot (t - t_a)}{(t_b - t_a)} \right)$$

The variance and standard derivation of the Brownian Bridge are:

$$Var = Cov(t,t) = \sigma^2 \cdot \frac{(t - t_a)(t_b - t)}{(t_b - t_a)}$$

$$Std = \sqrt{Var} = \sigma \sqrt{\frac{(t - t_a)(t_b - t)}{(t_b - t_a)}}$$

Note that when $t = \frac{t_b - t_a}{2}, Var = \frac{\sigma^2 \cdot t}{2}$, meaning at the midpoint, the variance of the Brownian Bridge is half of standard Brownian process. This can be illustrated by Figure 5.1, which plots the variance of the Brownian bridge with $\sigma = 1$ and $t_b - t_a = 1$. The mid-point has the largest variance, as both ends are tied down. The overall variance is reduced as a result.

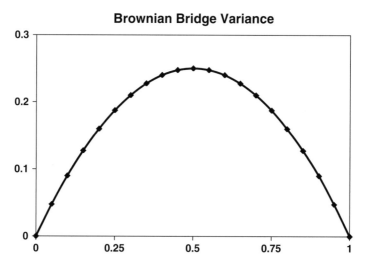

FIGURE 5.1: Brownian bridge variance

For geometric Brownian motion with $X(t) = \ln[S(t)]$, the corresponding Brownian bridge process for $X(t)$ and $S(t)$ is given by:

$$X(t) = a\left(\frac{t_b - t}{t_b - t_a}\right) + b\left(\frac{t - t_a}{t_b - t_a}\right) + \sigma\sqrt{\frac{(t - t_a)(t_b - t)}{t_b - t_a}}\,dZ$$

$$S(t) = S(0)exp\left[\left(\mu - \frac{1}{2}\sigma^2\right)t + X(t)\right]$$

When using low-discrepancy sequences such as Sobol in the Monte Carlo pricing of path-dependent options, e.g. Asian options, it is essential to use Brownian bridge for paths generation. Brownian bridge is used to address the high-dimensionality issues in the Sobol sequences.

In the conventional Monte Carlo path generation approach, the independent increment of Brownian motion (dZ_i) is used in sequence. For example, dividing a time period into many time steps, the following path can be generated sequentially:

$$S(t_i) = S(t_{i-1}) \cdot \exp\left[\left(\mu - \frac{1}{2}\sigma^2\right)\Delta t + \sigma\sqrt{\Delta t} \cdot dZ_i\right] \qquad i = 1, \cdots, n$$

The independent Brownian motion increments (dZ_i) and the path points $(S(t_i))$ are completely in synchronization.

The above standard path simulation scheme will not work properly when Sobol low discrepancy sequences are used in simulation. The variance in Sobol is not even distributed among dimensions, i.e. there is a bias among the dimensions, in particular higher dimensions. Hence if a Sobol sequence is used sequentially in the path generation, it will bring in bias too. The alternative is to use the Brownian Bridge to redistribute the variance as evenly as possible along the simulation path. Instead of generating

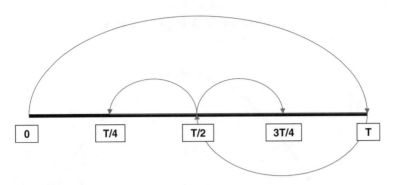

FIGURE 5.2 Recursive bisection

TABLE 5.1 Recursive bisection

Date (t)	$X(t)$
0	$X(0) = 0$
T	$X(T) = \sigma\sqrt{T} \cdot dZ_0$
$\dfrac{T}{2}$	$X(T/2) = \dfrac{X_0 + X_T}{2} + \sigma\sqrt{\dfrac{T}{4}} \cdot dZ_1$
$\dfrac{T}{4}$	$X(T/4) = \dfrac{X_0 + X_{T/2}}{2} + \sigma\sqrt{\dfrac{T}{8}} \cdot dZ_2$
$\dfrac{3T}{4}$	$X(3T/4) = \dfrac{X_{T/2} + X_T}{2} + \sigma\sqrt{\dfrac{T}{8}} \cdot dZ_3$
...	...
$\dfrac{(n-1)T}{n}$	$X((n-1)T/n) = \dfrac{X_{(n-2)T/n} + X_T}{2} + \sigma\sqrt{\dfrac{T}{2n}} \cdot dZ_{n-1}$

the path in sequential order, the end points are generated first, the middle points are then generated iteratively. Figure 5.2 and Table 5.1 show an example of recursive bisection to generate the path of $X(t)$.

Given $X(t)$, $S(t)$ can be obtained by:

$$S(t) = S(0) \cdot \exp\left[\left(\mu - \frac{1}{2}\sigma^2\right)t + X(t)\right]$$

Note that the variance of $X(t)$ is half of that compared with standard Brownian path, this is in line with what one expects in the recursive bisection Brownian bridge scheme. Also the Brownian motion increments (dZ_i) and the path $S(t_i)$ are not in synchronization in the Brownian bridge scheme. This actually helps to redistribute the variance along the path, given much more of the variance in the Brownian bridge scheme is in the first a few steps. The total variance in the Brownian bridge path generation scheme is the same as in the standard path generation scheme. The redistribution of variance reduces the effective dimension of the low discrepancy (Sobol) sequences.

The Brownian bridge scheme can also be a valuable tool in enhancing computational speed of some derivative products. For example, many customer-driven derivative products have Asian tails. Quite often, the pricing model, numerical implementation and computational efficiency of such products are heavily influenced by the tails. This is a good example of the tail wagging the dog! If the tail has many Asian points, it will substantially reduce the computational efficiency, in particular when it comes to computing risk sensitivities of portfolios. One simple yet accurate approximation is to simulate to the beginning and end of the Asian tail, and then use the two end points to simulate and average the middle points. The number of middle points does not need to be as many as the actual Asian points. The two end points have effectively anchored the bridge, and the Asian average can be calculated with high accuracy without too many points.

ASIAN OPTIONS

Asian option is mostly referred to as the arithmetic Asian option. It is meant to be a safer option compared to its European counterpart. Its payoff is designed to be smoother, with reduced overall volatility. An (arithmetic) Asian call has a payoff $C_A = D \cdot E^Q \left[(S_A - K)^+ \right]$, where D is the discount factor, K is the strike and S_A is the weighted arithmetic average of spots S_i:

$$S_A = \frac{1}{W} \sum_{i=1}^{n} W_i \cdot S_i$$

$$W = \sum_{i=1}^{n} W_i \qquad W_i > 0$$

Pricing Models

In the B-S framework where the spot is driven by geometric Brownian motion, the weighted arithmetic sum of the spot does not follow the same stochastic process. Hence an analytical solution for the Asian option is difficult to find. Over the years, one has to either use Monte Carlo or approximate analytical solutions.

When using Monte Carlo to price Asian options, a good combination is to use Sobol together with Brownian bridge. This can achieve much faster convergence and reduce bias. Among various Asian option approximate analytical solutions, the moments matching methods (Turnbull and Wakeman, Levy) are the easiest to implement. But they are less accurate in certain scenarios, e.g. in the case of long-dated and/or out-of-money and/or large volatility. The conditioning geometric mean model (Curran 1994) and Taylor expansion model (Ju 2002) are more robust in practice. In the following, we shall outline the main results of the conditioning geometric mean model, which can also be used for a basket option with Asian tail.

For a series of spots S_i the geometric mean is defined as:

$$G = \left(\prod_{i=1}^{n} S_i^{W_i} \right)^{\frac{1}{W}}$$

The Asian call payoff can be rewritten as the conditional (on G) expectation:

$$C_A = D \cdot E^Q\{E^Q[(S_A - K)^+]|G\}$$

$$= D \cdot \int_0^\infty E^Q[(S_A - K)^+]|G \cdot g(G) \cdot dG$$

$$= D \cdot \left\{ \int_0^K E^Q[(S_A - K)^+]|G \cdot g(G) \cdot dG + \int_K^\infty E^Q[(S_A - K)^+]|G \cdot g(G) \cdot dG \right\}$$

where $g(G)$ is the probability density function of G. By denoting:

$$C_1 = \int_0^K E^Q[(S_A - K)^+]| G \cdot g(G) \cdot dG$$

$$C_2 = \int_K^\infty E^Q[(S_A - K)^+]|G \cdot g(G) \cdot dG$$

we have:

$$C_A = D \cdot (C_1 + C_2)$$

So the Asian call is split into two parts, C_1 and C_2. There is no exact analytical solution for the first part C_1, and it needs to be solved approximately. However, there is an analytical solution to the second part C_2. This certainly enhances the overall accuracy of the conditioning geometric mean model.

The approximation of C_1 depends upon the nature of the correlation structure of the components. Note that the conditioning geometric technique is also applicable to basket options if we take S_A as the sum of basket components. For basket options, the correlation structure of the component underlying can be complicated and the approximation of C_1 shall be done more rigorously (e.g. using a numerical integration of modified Black–Scholes formulae). For Asian options, the correlation structure of Asian fixings is a function of variances of the same underlying. A simpler approximation of C_1 can therefore be used without losing too much accuracy. Using Jensen's inequality, given that $(S_A - K)^+$ is a convex function:

$$C_1 \approx \int_0^K [E^Q(S_A - K)| G]^+ \cdot g(G) \cdot dG$$

$$= \int_0^K [E^Q(S_A | G) - K]^+ \cdot g(G) \cdot dG$$

Assuming $E^Q(S_A \mid G = \tilde{K}) = K$, the above integration can be written as:

$$C_1 \approx \int_{\tilde{K}}^{K} [E^Q(S_A \mid G) - K] \cdot g(G) \cdot dG$$

Namely, if we can find $\tilde{K}$, C_1 can be approximately integrated as above.

For C_2, given that $S_A \geq G$ and the integration is on G from K to ∞ (namely, $G \geq K$), we have $S_A \geq K$ and C_2 can be written as:

$$C_2 = \int_{K}^{\infty} E^Q[(S_A - K)^+] \mid G \cdot g(G) \cdot dG$$

$$= \int_{K}^{\infty} E^Q[(S_A - K)] \mid G \cdot g(G) \cdot dG$$

$$= \int_{K}^{\infty} [E^Q(S_A \mid G) - K] \cdot g(G) \cdot dG$$

Combining C_1 and C_2:

$$C_A = D \cdot \int_{\tilde{K}}^{\infty} [E^Q(S_A \mid G) - K] \cdot g(G) \cdot dG$$

$$= D \cdot \left[\int_{\tilde{K}}^{\infty} E^Q(S_A \mid G) \cdot g(G) \cdot dG - K \cdot \int_{\tilde{K}}^{\infty} g(G) \cdot dG \right]$$

This Asian call integration can be solved analytically. Defining $X_i = \ln(S_i)$ which follows a normal distribution with mean μ_i and variance σ_i^2, the log of G is:

$$X = \ln(G) = \frac{1}{W} \sum_{i=1}^{n} W_i \cdot X_i$$

with a mean of μ and variance σ^2:

$$\mu = \frac{1}{W} \sum_{i=1}^{n} W_i \cdot \mu_i$$

$$\sigma^2 = \frac{1}{W^2} \sum_{i=1}^{n} \sum_{j=1}^{n} W_i W_j \sigma_i \sigma_j \rho_{ij}$$

$$= \frac{1}{W} \sum_{i=1}^{n} W_i \sigma_{X_i}$$

where:

$$\sigma_{X_i} = \frac{\sigma_i}{W} \sum_{j=1}^{n} W_j \sigma_j \rho_{ij}$$

Given that X_i and X follow a bivariate normal distribution, the conditional distribution of X_i is a normal distribution:

$$[X_i \mid X = x] \sim N\left(\mu_i + \frac{\sigma_{X_i}}{\sigma^2}(x - \mu), \ \sigma_i^2 - \frac{\sigma_{X_i}^2}{\sigma^2}\right)$$

The above distribution can be used to obtain the conditional expectation of the average. After some algebra:

$$E^Q[S_A \mid G = e^x] = E^Q[S_A \mid X = x]$$

$$= \frac{1}{W}\sum_{i=1}^{n} W_i \cdot \exp\left\{\mu_i + \frac{\sigma_{X_i}^2}{\sigma^2}(x - \mu) + 0.5 \times \left(\sigma_i^2 - \frac{\sigma_{X_i}^2}{\sigma^2}\right)\right\}$$

By changing variable $X = \ln(G)$ and substituting the above expectation into the Asian call integration:

$$C_A = D \cdot \left[\int_{\ln(\tilde{K})}^{\infty} E^Q(S_A \mid X = x) \cdot f(x) \cdot dx - K \cdot \int_{\ln(\tilde{K})}^{\infty} f(x) \cdot dx\right]$$

$$= D \cdot \left[\frac{1}{W}\sum_{i=1}^{n} W_i \cdot \exp\left(\mu_i + \frac{\sigma_i^2}{2}\right) \cdot N\left(\frac{\mu - \ln(\tilde{K})}{\sigma} + \frac{\sigma_{X_i}}{\sigma}\right) - K \cdot N\left(\frac{\mu - \ln(\tilde{K})}{\sigma}\right)\right]$$

The Asian put (P_A) can be priced using the Asian call-put parity:

$$C_A - P_A = D \cdot \left(\frac{1}{n}\sum_{i=1}^{n} F_i - K\right)$$

where F_i are the forwards on the fixing dates.

Volatility Smile/Skew Adjustment

Geometric conditioning model was originally developed for the term structure volatility only, i.e. no volatility smile/skew. In the presence of volatility smile/skew, the question is how the model should be modified to take volatility smile/skew into account. Similar to a European option, which takes the volatility at strike, at Asian fixing dates it is possible to search for appropriate strikes in order to sample smile/skew volatilities. The sampled volatilities can then be used to price in volatility smile/skew with a fair degree of accuracy.

Given the contractual strike K of an Asian option, let's examine how it can be decomposed into several equivalent Asian strikes K_i on the Asian fixing dates. One such technique is to set Asian strikes as:

$$K_i = \frac{F(t_i)}{S(t_0)} exp\left(\alpha\sqrt{t_i - t_0}\right)$$

Where t_i is the i-th Asian date $(i = 1, \cdots, n)$, $F(t_i)$ is the forward at time t_i and α is a constant. By imposing a constraint:

$$\frac{1}{n} \sum_{i=1}^{n} K_i = K$$

the constant α can be easily solved, e.g. by Newton–Raphson. Once α is obtained, all the Asian strikes K_i can be calculated. The volatilities at (t_i, K_i) can be sampled from the smile/skew volatility surface as follows:

$$\sigma(t_i) = \sigma\left(t_i, \frac{K_i}{S(t_0)}\right)$$

In doing so, the Asian option Vega is spread over the Asian fixing dates along the strikes K_i.

The rationale for the above simple yet effective approach can be seen in the K_i formula, which can be rewritten as:

$$K_i = exp\left(\mu_i(t_i - t_0) + \alpha\sqrt{t_i - t_0}\right)$$

where μ_i is the drift, and α is the standard deviation determined by the K constraint. Hence K_i can be viewed as the most relevant path that is $\alpha\sqrt{t_i - t_0}$ variance away from the forwards at time t_i with a constant volatility gap. Note that when $n = 1$, $K_i = K$, the Asian option converges to a European option. The Asian strikes K_i are calculated on the fly, given their dependence on the forwards. Going through the life cycle of an Asian option, when fixings are in, they will impact averaging so far and remaining K_i.

Figures 5.3 and 5.4 show two examples of Asian strikes, both for a 5-year Asian option with 1-year Asian tail. The Asian fixing dates are monthly for the last year, with 13 averaging points. Assuming the drift is 3%, for a contractual strike $K=120\%$ (flat line), the Asian strikes K_i at the Asian dates are shown in Figure 5.3 with $\alpha = 2.23\%$. The forwards at the relevant Asian fixing dates are also plotted in the graph for reference.

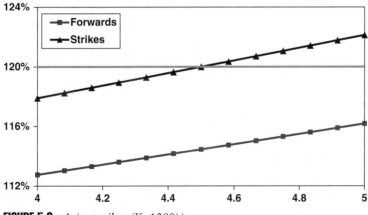

FIGURE 5.3 Asian strikes (K=120%)

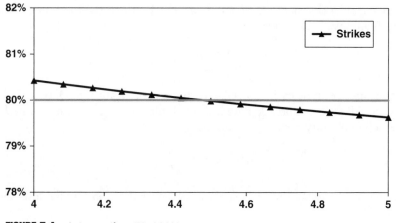

FIGURE 5.4   Asian strikes (K=80%)

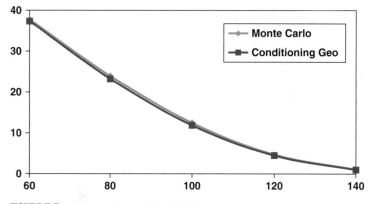

FIGURE 5.5   Asian call vs strike (daily)

For a contractual strike $K=80\%$, the Asian strikes are shown in Figure 5.4 with $\alpha = -16.89\%$.

In Figures 5.5 and 5.6, conditioning geometric Asian call prices are compared with those obtained by Monte Carlo. The prices are plotted versus contractual strikes. The ATM volatility used is quite high at 30%, with a skew of 2.5%. The options all have 3-year maturity. The daily averaging prices are shown in Figure 5.5, and the monthly averaging prices are in Figure 5.6. As can be seen in the figures, conditioning geometric Asian model with the volatility smile/skew adjustment is quite accurate and it compares well with the Monte Carlo pricer. As the model is analytical, it is numerically and computationally very efficient. One should avoid using PDE to price Asian options.

Risk Sensitivities and Hedging

While the Asian model is somewhat challenging, its risks are rather smooth and stable. The hedging becomes easier as the option goes through its life cycle and more fixings are in. In general, you might need a senior quantitative analyst to develop good Asian option models, but a junior option trader should be able to manage Asian option risks.

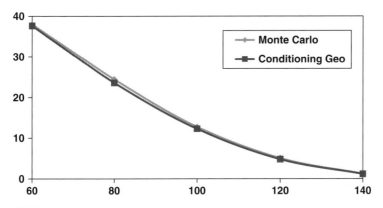

FIGURE 5.6 Asian call vs strike (monthly)

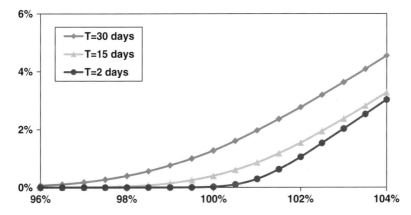

FIGURE 5.7 European price ladder

In Figures 5.7 to 5.9, we compare how the risks evolve as the options going through the life cycle, for a European (Figure 5.7), Asian (Figure 5.8) and digital (Figure 5.9) option. All of them have a maturity of 30 days to start with, and the strike is fixed ATM. The price ladders (price versus spot) are plotted for T=30 days, T=15 days and T=2 days, assuming the market data stay the same. As the options approach expiry, the price ladders at 15 days and 2 days expiry exhibit some of the key risk and hedging characteristics.

Comparing the European and Asian option price ladders in Figures 5.7 and 5.8, as options approach expiry, the ATM curvature of the European option price ladder increases and Gamma becomes larger. For the Asian option, it is the opposite. As more Asian fixings are in, the final average for the payoff becomes more certain, the optionality and hence Gamma becomes smaller and hedging should be easier.

A sharply contrasting case is the digital option as illustrated in Figure 5.9. Closer to the option expiry, the ATM digital has larger risks given increased uncertainty in Gamma as it may change sign. This is the case where a junior quantitative analyst can write a pricing model, but a senior option trader with market experiences should be assigned to manage such risks.

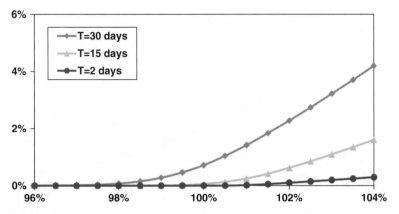

FIGURE 5.8   Asian price ladder

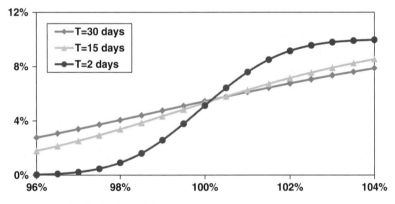

FIGURE 5.9   Digital price ladder

BASKET OPTIONS

For a basket of underlyings (S_i) with the corresponding weightings (w_i), the standard basket option has a payoff:

$$Call = D \cdot E^Q \left[\left(S_B - K \right)^+ \right]$$
$$Put = D \cdot E^Q \left[\left(K - S_B \right)^+ \right]$$

where the basket asset is defined by:

$$S_B = \sum_{i=1}^{n} w_i S_i$$

The basket payoff in fact looks very similar to an Asian option payoff. Instead of a single underlying sampled at different times as in Asian option, the basket option has a number of underlyings sampled at the same time. The fundamental difference between

Asian and Basket option is the correlation structure of the underlying or price samples, namely auto- or temporal-correlation in Asian versus arbitrary correlation in Basket.

Pricing Models

Like Asian option, basket option has long eluded a closed-form analytical solution. There are various analytical approximations. Depending on the nature of the correlation structure, some basket approximations work better than the others. In general the basket correlation structure is more complex and the approximations need to be formulated more rigorously than for the Asian option. In Table 5.2, the major basket option analytical approximations and their key features are summarized.

Given all the above are approximations, they perform differently in different regimes characterized by strike, volatility, correlation and volatility homogeneity. In general the conditioning geometric mean and Taylor expansion models are more accurate and perform better in most of the practical applications. Moment matching is of course the simplest, and very valuable when accuracy is not the priority.

TABLE 5.2   Major basket option analytical approximations

Pricing Model (Approximation)	Key Features
Moment Matching (Levy 1992)	It assumes that the basket as a whole has a log-normal distributed and its first two moments are approximated by those of the sum of basket underlyings. It is a simple and practical method.
Conditioning Geometric Mean (Curran 1994)	It is more complex than moment matching, but a more accurate approximation. It can also be more accurate in dealing with more arbitrary correlations. The Asian tail can also be naturally included.
Geometric Average (Gentle 1993)	It approximates the basket (arithmetic average) with a geometric average. Although it corrects the basket forward in its formulation, the higher order moments can be less accurate.
Edgeworth Expansion (Huynh 1994)	It expands the basket distribution function into a series of log-normal distributions. Series expansion and approximation can be numerically challenging though.
Taylor Expansion (Ju 2002)	It Taylor expands the ratio of the characteristic function of basket (arithmetic) average to that of the log-normal. Intuitively, its first summand must converge to the moment matching approximation. The other terms will give higher order corrections.
Reciprocal Gamma (Milevsky and Posner 1998)	The basket distribution is approximated by the reciprocal Gamma distribution. Although one can subsequently derivate an analytical formula using reciprocal Gamma, it can be a poor approximation for the basket.

When the volatilities of the basket underlyings are inhomogeneous and/or pricing the basket option with Asian tail, one may still rely on the final resort – the Monte Carlo pricing techniques. To achieve acceptable convergence, Sobol together with Brownian bridge is a preferred choice of combination. Using such a Monte Carlo scheme, one must pay attention to numerical efficiency. For example, when dealing with a basket of underlyings (N) together with several Asian tail points (M), one needs to handle a covariance matrix ($N \times M$). Conventionally, Cholesky decomposition can be used to impose the correlation structure onto the entire covariance matrix. However, this may not be optimal. Singular value decomposition (SVD) can be more flexible and allow more effective use of the Brownian bridge. In Cholesky decomposition, a triangular matrix containing correlation structure is created. In SVD, together with the eigenvectors, a diagonal matrix is created with the corresponding eigenvalues in decreasing order. This diagonal feature allows us to deal with the basket underlying dependency and the Asian tail points (time) dependency separately. One can then couple them into a combined matrix, putting all eigenvalues into an order. For example, one can operate SVD on N assets and M Asian dates separately to impose corresponding correlation structures. The resulting eigenvalues can be combined by direct matrix product, which results in a total of $N \times M$ eigenvalues. These eigenvalues can be ordered easily. Note that once the eigenvalues are ordered, one can assign them with appropriate elements in the Sobol low discrepancy sequences. As shown in the Brownian bridge scheme, if one is able to assign appropriate Sobol numbers to the right parts of the path generator (represented by eigenvalues), one can redistribute the variance to make the Monte Carlo pricing much more effective.

Basket Risks

Basket risks can be complex. In addition to the standard option risks, e.g. delta, Gamma, Vega which are related to the individual underlyings in the basket, the other key basket-specific risks are mostly associated with the correlations. A summary of the basket-specific risks is given in Table 5.3.

TABLE 5.3   Basket risks

Basket Risks	Specifics
Cross Gamma Risks (Correlation Risks)	The cross Gamma is defined as $\dfrac{\partial^2 P}{\partial S_i \partial S_j}$, $i \neq j$, where p is the basket option price, S_i and S_j are the underlying spots. The cross Gamma specifies the delta change of the i-th underlying caused by the spot change in the j-th underlying.
Correlation Skew Risks	When large moves occur in the market, the basket correlation tends to spike and this will impact the pricing as well as the risk parameters. These are also referred to as the skewed correlation structure risks.
FX Correlation Risks	In a Quanto or Compo basket, the FX correlation with each individual basket component will impact the price.

Basket Risks	Specifics
Contractual Risks	If merge and acquisition activity happens to the basket member, the basket composition will change and so will its volatility structure. This also applies to the credit default event when the defaulted underlying drops out of the basket.
Jump Risks (Credit Risks)	In a large single stock basket, it is more likely that one or some of the basket underlying default. The corresponding underlying price may jump to zero.
Model Risks	Correlation or co-dependency could be mis-specified.

It is evident that a basket (correlation) book is a complex entity involving significant second order effects that needs to be understood. There are clearly many moving parts glued together by correlation, which is renowned for its misuse and misspecification. In order to manage basket risks sensibly, not only on the risk characteristics of the individual components but also the correlated risk behaviours should be taken into account.

What about volatility smile/skew in and of the basket? With the above-mentioned approximate analytical solutions, the volatilities are typically obtained by using the same basket strike (K) to sample the individual underlying volatility surfaces at (T, K). This is, of course, an assumption on the basket smile/skew. More generally, techniques of pricing and risk managing basket options have very important implications going well beyond standard basket options. Many real-world financial risks that have the portfolio nature (e.g. enterprise-wide CCR and CVA, contagion risks) must be modelled as baskets. We have dedicated a chapter specifically discussing the techniques of managing "Basket Products" later in the book.

DIVIDEND FUTURES AND OPTIONS

Most of the company dividends at the short end are forecasted fairly accurately. In the context of pricing equity derivatives the dividends have long been treated as deterministic, although practitioners do re-mark the dividends from time to time. Dividend swaps in the OTC market and exchange-traded dividend futures provide some market information about the dividend forward price for the given time horizons. Exchange-traded dividend futures are available for some major equity indices and blue chip companies with maturities extending to 5 and 10 years. They are valuable dividend hedging tools and important calibration instruments for dividend options.

A dividend option is a contingent claim on the total dividends paid over a specified time window. The option payoffs are expressed as:

$$DivCall = D_T \cdot max\left(\sum_i d_i - K, 0\right)$$

$$DivPut = D_T \cdot max\left(K - \sum_i d_i, 0\right)$$

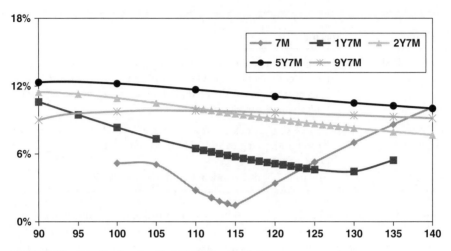

FIGURE 5.10 Div Option Implied Volatility Smile/Skew

A dividend option can be either on an exchange-traded dividend future, or on a bespoke dividend stream. In the former case, the dividend future annual index contract pulls to par towards December and the Black–Scholes formula is typically used for pricing on the underlying future annual index. In the latter case, one can also treat it as an Asian or basket option. A key feature in the dividend option is that the dividends are paid and distributed over time, and the volatility of the dividend underlying decreases as the option approaches maturity. This is actually the typical Asian option feature reflected in the dividend option.

Exchange-Traded Dividend Options

Exchanged traded dividend options include options on EURO STOXX 50 Index Dividend Futures (OEXD) and dividend index options at CBOE (S&P 500 Dividend Index Options). Dividend options also exhibit pronounced volatility smile/skew. Figure 5.10 contains a snapshot of EURO STOXX 50 dividend option implied volatility smile/skew for different maturities. The horizontal axis is strike and the forwards are in the region of 114, albeit the forwards for different maturities vary slightly. As can be seen in the figure, the shortest maturity (7M) has a very low ATM volatility but with a strong smile. This is because of the fact that the short end dividends are either fixed/announced or forecasted with little uncertainty, unless some tail events occur. As the option maturity becomes longer (1Y7M and 2Y7M), the volatility skew is more dominant. The volatility skew flattens for long-dated options (5Y7M and 9Y7M). The general volatility smile/skew features of the dividend options are actually quite in line with those of equity options.

Bespoke Dividend Options

In pricing a bespoke dividend option, the Asian or basket moment matching model can be used. Denoting the dividend basket as:

$$D_{Basket}(T) = \sum_i d_i$$

The expectation of the dividend basket and its second moment are:

$$E\big[D_{Basket}(T)\big] = E\bigg[\sum_i d_i\bigg]$$

$$E\big[D_{Basket}^2(T)\big] = \sum_{i,j} E\big[d_i \cdot d_j\big]$$

Denoting ρ_{ij} as the correlation between d_i and d_j, and assuming dividends follow the log-normal stochastic process, the second moment can be expressed as:

$$E\big[D_{Basket}^2(T)\big] = \sum_{i,j} d_i \cdot d_j \cdot \exp\big(\rho_{ij} \cdot \sigma_i \sqrt{t_i} \cdot \sigma_j \sqrt{t_j}\big)$$

By matching the two moments, we have:

$$D_{Basket}^2(T) \cdot \exp\big(\sigma_D^2 \cdot T\big) = \sum_{i,j} d_i \cdot d_j \cdot \exp\big(\rho_{ij} \cdot \sigma_i \sqrt{t_i} \cdot \sigma_j \sqrt{t_j}\big)$$

The above formula should allow us to calculate the dividend basket volatility σ_D. The Black–Scholes option formula can then be used to price the dividend option. In general:

$$\sigma_D = \sqrt{X^t \cdot \Omega \cdot X}$$

where Ω is the covariance matrix, X^t is the transpose of X, and $X = (d_1, d_2, \cdots, d_n)$.

In Figures 5.11 and 5.12, two examples are shown to illustrate key intuitions in the dividend option. Figure 5.11 shows a 5Y dividend floor (put) price versus the dividend growth. When the dividend growth becomes small, the forward dividends become less and the dividend floor price becomes larger. Importantly, the curve is smooth, which should give rise to stable Greeks.

Figure 5.12 plots the moving dividend floor price and the corresponding dividend basket spot. The option strike and maturity are fixed, while the start date of the dividend basket rolls forward. The horizontal axis labels the start date in days and maturity is fixed at 1280. As the start date rolls forward, the dividend basket spot (left

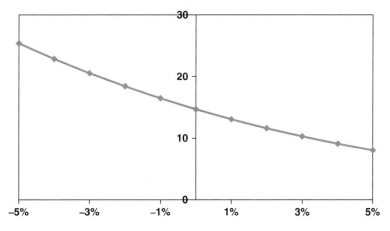

FIGURE 5.11 Div put price vs div growth

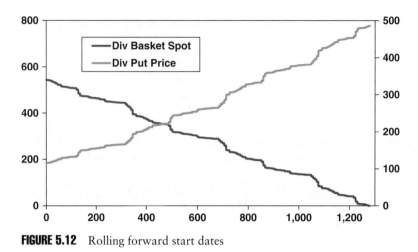

FIGURE 5.12   Rolling forward start dates

vertical axis) becomes smaller and the dividend floor price (right vertical axis) becomes more expensive. The jumps in both curves are in synchronization with each other and coincide with the ex-div dates.

Dividend Risks

Dividend risks can cause significant losses. During the financial crises the forecasted dividends are typically marked down and the resulted losses can be huge if the dividend risks are not hedged or managed. While it is a common practice that dividends are treated as deterministic in pricing equity derivatives, stochastic dividends can have impact in the pricing of the structured products. In fact, dividend options exhibit strong volatility smile/skew. For example, during the financial crises of 2008 and 2010, dividend futures crashed by 50% and this was a classic behaviour of volatility skew.

Structured products issuers use dividend futures to hedge. It is possible that the dividend futures markets can be distorted by supply-demand, as the market can be one-sided. For example, when everybody is selling it'll depress the dividend futures prices. The 3-years to 6-years buckets are typically more vulnerable to this market effect. The short-dated contracts, however, are more driven by fundamentals. In summary, dividend risks in the structured derivative books are real and they should be measured and managed together with other derivative risks.

AMERICAN OPTIONS

Most exchange-traded options on single stocks and some exchange-traded options on equity indices are American options. American options differ from European options in that they can be exercised at any time up to maturity. Consequently, they will always be more valuable than their equivalent European options, and their value must increase with increasing maturity.

A useful concept in American option pricing is the Optimal Exercise Boundary (OEB). For a call (put) option on any given day it is optimal to exercise the option if the stock price is above (below) the OEB. This makes the option path-dependent as the payoff depends on the path the stock price takes, not just its value at maturity. The OEB is not known ex ante, and must be determined as part of the solution during the calculation.

PDE Solution

For a general set of market data, including implied volatility surface with skew, discrete dividends and interest rate term-structure, one has to resort to numerical techniques such as PDE to price American options accurately. The early exercise conditions for the American option can be easily imposed in PDE. The volatility smile/skew effect included in the PDE pricing is consistent with that on the European options.

Discrete dividends can induce early exercises, and their effects can be priced in using PDE. The treatment of discrete dividends can significantly affect the American price. Considering an American call, if there is no dividend it is not optimal to exercise a call option early. If there is a discrete dividend it can be the case that on passing the ex-div date the downward jump of the stock makes the call option less valuable after the dividend than before it. Denoting a discrete dividend D, if the stock price is S just before the dividend, then after the dividend it will be $(S-D)$. Before the dividend the call option is worth $(S-K)^+$, after the dividend it will be worth $(S-D-K)^+$. Therefore the optimal early exercise opportunity of American call would be before the dividend. Applying the same logic, the optimal early exercise opportunity of American put would be after the dividend. The ex-div dates must be treated as important dates in PDE and they must fall onto PDE's time slices. The early exercise condition should be checked before and after every dividend.

Closed-form Solution

Closed-form solutions for American options are approximations. None of the approximations are totally satisfactory even in the case of flat volatility surface. The difficulties arise from the fact that there is no easy way to determine the OEB, given it is path-dependent.

Typically, closed-form solutions use the continuous dividend yield assumption. Dividends before the maturity of the option are present valued and then treated homogeneously as a flat rate. For American options the continuous dividend yield can misrepresent the OEB near the ex-div dates. Consequently the early exercise decisions can be wrong. Therefore under normal market conditions a continuous dividend yield assumption can produce pricing and risk-management errors for American options.

One of the well-known closed-form solutions is the BAW model (Barone-Adesi and Whaley 1987), which uses quadratic approximation to estimate the early exercise premium. Denoting r the risk-free rate, q the dividend yield and σ the volatility, the BAW quadratic equation solutions for $q^2 + bq + c = 0$ are:

$$q_1 = \frac{-b + \sqrt{b^2 + 4c}}{2}, \quad q_2 = \frac{-b - \sqrt{b^2 + 4c}}{2}$$

with $b = \dfrac{2(r-q)}{\sigma^2} - 1$ and $c = \dfrac{2r}{\sigma^2\left(1 - \exp(-rT)\right)}$. The American call and put price can then be approximated as:

$$
AmericanCall(S,T) =
\begin{cases}
EuropeanCall(S,T) + A_1 \cdot \left(\dfrac{S}{S_1^*}\right)^{q_1} & \text{if } S < S_1^* \\[2ex]
S - K & \text{if } S \geq S_1^*
\end{cases}
$$

$$
AmericanPut(S,T) =
\begin{cases}
EuropeanPut(S,T) + A_2 \cdot \left(\dfrac{S}{S_2^*}\right)^{q_2} & \text{if } S > S_2^* \\[2ex]
K - S & \text{if } S \leq S_2^*
\end{cases}
$$

where

$$
A_1 = \frac{S_1^*}{q_1}\left(1 - \exp(-qt)\cdot N(d_1)\right), \ d_1 = \frac{\ln(S_1^* / K) + (r - q + \sigma^2 / 2)\cdot T}{\sigma\sqrt{T}}
$$

$$
A_2 = -\frac{S_2^*}{q_2}\left(1 - \exp(-qt)\cdot N(-d_1)\right), \ d_1 = \frac{\ln(S_2^* / K) + (r - q + \sigma^2 / 2)\cdot T}{\sigma\sqrt{T}}
$$

S_1^* solves for:

$$
S_1^* - K = EuropeanCall(S_1^*,T) + \frac{S_1^*}{q_1}\left(1 - \exp(-qT)\cdot N(d_1)\right)
$$

and S_2^* solves for:

$$
K - S_2^* = EuropeanPut(S_2^*,T) - \frac{S_2^*}{q_2}\left(1 - \exp(-qT)\cdot N(-d_1)\right)
$$

PDE Versus Closed-form

In this section, the American option prices obtained using the PDE are compared with those by the BAW model. All options used in this section have a maturity of 1 year, and the underlying is either an equity index or a single stock with full volatility smile/skew.

In Figures 5.13 and 5.14 respectively, the American call and put (on index) prices are plotted against spot with option strike fixed at 100%. Their price differences are labelled by the right vertical axis. An equity index consists of many individual stocks. The combined index dividends are typically fairly spread out, and the dividend yield assumption works well. The analytical BAW prices match well with those of PDE. In general there is a good agreement between PDE and BAW.

For the American options on single stocks, the BAW analytical solution can mismatch PDE significantly. Single stocks' dividends are much more concentrated and the lumpy dividends can impact early exercise decisions. In the following examples in Figures 5.15 and 5.16, the total dividend yield is the same as in the index option examples, but the dividend is paid every 6 months.

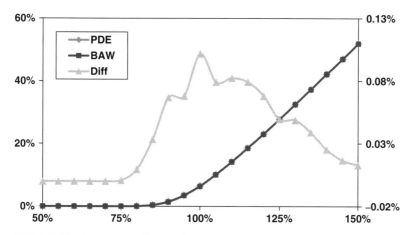

FIGURE 5.13 American call on index

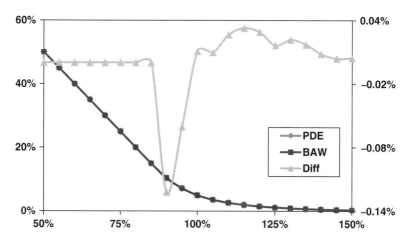

FIGURE 5.14 American put on index

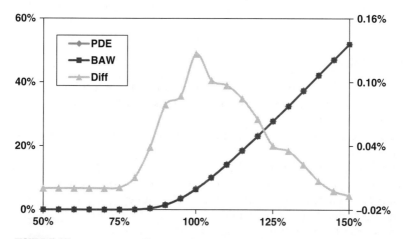

FIGURE 5.15 American call on single stock

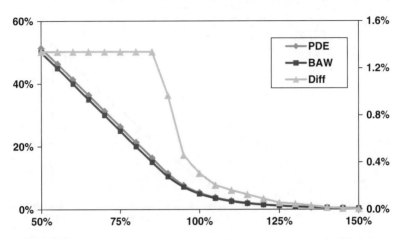

FIGURE 5.16 American put on single stock

The price differences between BAW and PDE become larger, in particular in the American put option case. For American options on single stock, the discrete dividends make the BAW model less accurate. In fact, the timing of the dividends also matters. Not only the dividend amount but also when the dividends occur affects the early exercise pricing.

In general, for American options on an index, conditional on the fact that the index dividends are fairly spread out and the dividend yield is comparably small, the price agreement between the PDE and BAW model for calls and puts in both non-Quanto and Quanto case is good. With due care this offers the attraction of being able to price the whole book very quickly. For American options on underlyings with lumpy dividends, such as single stocks, it is advisable not to use BAW, instead a PDE pricer is necessary.

BARRIER OPTIONS

Barrier options include single barrier and double barrier options, and rainbow barrier options.

Closed-form Solutions

The closed form solutions for all types of barrier options are available in many literatures. For options with a single barrier, barrier types include:

- down-and-out call;
- down-and-in call, in-out parity holds, i.e. $DnOut\ Call + DnIn\ Call = European\ Call$,
- up-and-out put;
- up-and-in put, in-out parity holds;
- down-and-out put, also known as reverse barrier option because of the fact that the barrier is where the option payoff is in-the-money;
- down-and-in put, in-out parity holds;
- up-and-out call, a reverse barrier option;
- up-and-in call, in-out parity holds.

The closed-form solution for double barrier option and partial barrier options (aka window barrier options) are also available in several literatures.

In most of the practical situations whereby the volatility smile/skew is present, the flat volatility analytical solutions will clearly misprice the barrier options. Barrier options are highly path-dependent and volatility smile/skew has direct impact on their pricing and risk sensitivities. To take account of volatility smile/skew, one can resort to the full-blown smile/skew models, including Local Volatility (LV) or Stochastic Local Volatility (SLV) models. Sometimes it is also plausible to formulate approximate solutions within the BS framework to price barrier options under smile/skew. Using a rainbow barrier option is such an example.

Rainbow Barrier Option

In a standard rainbow barrier option, the option payoff is depending on one asset, whose spot and dividend yield are S_1 and q_1, while the barrier (B) is triggered by another asset (S_2, q_2). The closed-form solutions of a rainbow barrier knock-out option are given by:

$$RBO = \omega_1 S_1 e^{-q_1 T}$$

$$\left[M(\omega_1 d_1, \omega_2 e_1; -\omega_1 \omega_2 \rho) - exp\left(\frac{2(r - q_2 - 0.5\sigma_2^2 + \rho\sigma_1\sigma_2)\ln(B/S_2)}{\sigma_2^2} \right) M\left(\omega_1 d_3, \omega_2 e_3; -\omega_1 \omega_2 \rho\right) \right]$$

$$-\omega_1 K e^{-rT}$$

$$\left[M\left(\omega_1 d_2, \omega_2 e_2; -\omega_1 \omega_2 \rho\right) - exp\left(\frac{2\left(r - q_2 - 0.5\sigma_2^2\right)\ln\left(B/S_2\right)}{\sigma_2^2} \right) M\left(\omega_1 d_4, \omega_2 e_4; -\omega_1 \omega_2 \rho\right) \right]$$

where

$$d_1 = \frac{\ln(S_1/K) + (r_1 - q_1 + 0.5\sigma_1^2)T}{\sigma_1\sqrt{T}} \qquad\qquad d_2 = d_1 - \sigma_1\sqrt{T}$$

$$d_3 = d_1 + \frac{2\rho\ln(B/S_2)}{\sigma_2\sqrt{T}} \qquad\qquad d_4 = d_2 + \frac{2\rho\ln(B/S_2)}{\sigma_2\sqrt{T}}$$

$$e_1 = \frac{\ln(B/S_2) - (r_2 - q_2 - 0.5\sigma_2^2 + \rho\sigma_1\sigma_2)T}{\sigma_2\sqrt{T}} \qquad\qquad e_2 = e_1 + \rho\sigma_1\sqrt{T}$$

$$e_3 = e_1 - \frac{2\ln(B/S_2)}{\sigma_2\sqrt{T}} \qquad\qquad e_4 = e_2 - \frac{2\ln(B/S_2)}{\sigma_2\sqrt{T}}$$

$\omega_1 = 1$ and $\omega_2 = -1$ For Down-and-Out Call

$\omega_1 = 1$ and $\omega_2 = 1$ For Up-and-Out Call

$\omega_1 = -1$ and $\omega_2 = -1$ For Down-and-Out Put

$\omega_1 = -1$ and $\omega_2 = 1$ For Up-and-Out Put

and $M(a,b;\rho)$ is the standard bivariate normal cumulative distribution:

$$M(a,b;\gamma) = \frac{1}{2\pi\sqrt{1-\gamma^2}} \int\limits_{-\infty}^{a}\int\limits_{-\infty}^{b} exp\left[-\frac{x^2 - 2\gamma xy + y^2}{2(1-\gamma^2)}\right] dxdy$$

Note that the in-out parity holds for the rainbow barrier options too. Therefore the rainbow knock-in options can be easily derived from the European option and knock-out options.

Volatility Smile/Skew

When searching for an approximation to price a barrier option under volatility smile/skew, one often asks the question of which implied volatility to use or matters most: the one at strike or the one at barrier? It is a difficult question to answer. The rainbow barrier option allows both volatilities to be used in the analytical solution. One can assume two perfectly correlated assets $(S_1 = S_2 = S)$, S_1 is driven by the implied volatility at strike $(\sigma_1 = \sigma_K)$, and S_2 is driven by the implied volatility at barrier (σ_B), then the rainbow barrier option analytical formulae can be used directly to price barrier options with two volatilities.

Note that for two perfectly correlated assets, i.e. when $\rho = 1$, the standard bivariate normal cumulative distribution $M(a,b;\gamma)$ degenerates to standard univariate normal CDF $N(\cdot)$. This will greatly simplify and speed up the numerical calculations of rainbow barrier options.

Specifically, for $\rho = 1$, we have $\gamma = -\omega_1\omega_2\rho = \pm 1$ for various barrier types, the standard bivariate normal cumulative distribution is given by the first principle:

when $\gamma = 1$, $x = y$:

$$M(a,b;1) = \Pr(x \leq a \cap y \leq b)$$
$$= \Pr(x \leq a \cap x \leq b)$$
$$= \Pr(x \leq \min(a,b))$$
$$= N(\min(a,b))$$

when $\gamma = -1$, $x = -y$:

$$M(a,b;-1) = \Pr(x \leq a \cap y \leq b)$$
$$= \Pr(x \leq a \cap -x \leq b)$$
$$= \Pr(x \leq a \cap x \geq -b)$$

If $-b > a$, $M(a,b;-1) = 0$. If $-b \leq a$, then:

$$M(a,b;-1) = \Pr(-b \leq x \leq a)$$
$$= N(a) - N(-b)$$
$$= N(a) + N(b) - 1$$

By replacing the bivariate function $M(\cdot)$ with the relevant univariate CDF $N(\cdot)$ in the rainbow barrier option formulae, barrier options can be priced including some smile/skew effects (using two volatilities) with the same numerical efficiency as the corresponding single volatility barrier option formulae. The two-vol rainbow barrier technique can be valuable in the situations of using cascading barriers to price lookback and hindsight options.

LOOKBACK AND HINDSIGHT OPTIONS

The payoffs for a variety of lookback and hindsight types of options are very much inter-linked. In the following, we shall analyse the linkage and link them eventually to the basic lookback options. The closed-form analytical formulae for the basic lookback options are readily available in public domain literatures. An effective method of incorporating volatility smile/skew effect in the pricing will be discussed.

Payoffs Relationships

All the notations are given in Table 5.4.

- **Lookback Call:** This is the basic lookback call option. Its price is:
$P = e^{-rT} \cdot E\big[\max(S_T - S_{\min}, 0)\big]$
- **Lookback Put:** This is the basic lookback put option. Its price is:
$P = e^{-rT} \cdot E\big[\max(S_{\max} - S_T, 0)\big]$
- **Hindsight Call:** The payoff is $\max(S_{\max} - K, 0)$. Its price is:

$$
\begin{aligned}
P &= e^{-rT} \cdot E\big[\max(S_{\max} - K, 0)\big] \\
&= e^{-rT} \cdot E\big[\max(S_{\max}, K) - K + S_T - S_T\big] \\
&= e^{-rT} \cdot E\big[\max(S_{\max}, K) - S_T\big] + e^{-rT} \cdot (E[S_T] - K) \\
&= LookbackPut\ [with \max(S_{ref}, K)] + e^{-rT} \cdot (E[S_T] - K)
\end{aligned}
$$

TABLE 5.4 Notations

S_0	Spot price
S_T	Terminal spot price.
$S_{\min}$	Minimum spot over the life of the option.
$S_{\max}$	Maximum spot over the life of the option.
S_{ref}	The extreme spot value achieved so far, either minimum or maximum depends on option.
K	Option strike.
T	Option maturity.
r	Risk-free rate.
$E[\bullet]$	Risk-neutral expectation. $E(S_T)$ is the forward.

- **Hindsight Put:** The payoff is $\max(K - S_{\min}, 0)$. Its price is:

$$
\begin{aligned}
P &= e^{-rT} \cdot E\left[\max(K - S_{\min}, 0)\right] \\
&= e^{-rT} \cdot E\left[K - \min(S_{\min}, K) + S_T - S_T\right] \\
&= e^{-rT} \cdot E\left[S_T - \min(S_{\min}, K)\right] - e^{-rT} \cdot (E[S_T] - K) \\
&= LookbackCall\ [with \min(S_{ref}, K)] - e^{-rT} \cdot (E[S_T] - K)
\end{aligned}
$$

- **Minimum Call:** The payoff is $\max(S_{\min} - K, 0)$. Its price can be found using call-put parity:

$$
E\left[\max(S_{\min} - K, 0)\right] - E\left[\max(K - S_{\min}, 0)\right] = E\left[S_{\min}\right] - K
$$

Note that:

$$
E\left[S_{\min}\right] = E\left[S_0 - \max(S_0 - S_{\min}, 0)\right] = S_0 - E[\max(S_0 - S_{\min}, 0)]
$$

Substituting this into the call-put parity and re-arrange the equation:

$$
\begin{aligned}
P &= e^{-rT} \cdot E\left[\max(S_{\min} - K, 0)\right] \\
&= e^{-rT} \cdot E\left[\max(K - S_{\min}, 0)\right] - e^{-rT} \cdot E\left[\max(S_0 - S_{\min}, 0)\right] + e^{-rT} \cdot (S_0 - K) \\
&= HindsightPut[strike = K, with\ existing\ S_{ref}] - \\
&\quad HindsightPut[strike = S_0, with\ existing\ S_{ref}] + e^{-rT} \cdot (S_0 - K)
\end{aligned}
$$

- **Maximum Put:** the payoff is $\max(K - S_{\max}, 0)$. Its price can be obtained by using call-put parity:

$$
E\left[\max(S_{\max} - K, 0)\right] - E\left[\max(K - S_{\max}, 0)\right] = E\left[S_{\max}\right] - K
$$

Note that $e^{-rT} \cdot E[S_{\max}]$ is the HindsightCall with a strike equal to 0.

$$
\begin{aligned}
P &= e^{-rT} \cdot E\left[\max(K - S_{\max}, 0)\right] \\
&= e^{-rT} \cdot E\left[\max(S_{\max} - K, 0)\right] - e^{-rT} \cdot E\left[S_{\max}\right] + e^{-rT} \cdot K \\
&= HindsightCall[strike = K, with\ existing\ S_{ref}] - \\
&\quad HindsightCall[strike = 0, with\ existing\ S_{ref}] + e^{-rT} \cdot K
\end{aligned}
$$

The above relationships allow us to price all other categories using the basic lookback call and put pricer.

Volatility Smile/Skew

Volatility smile/skew has a significant effect on the lookback pricing, given its strong path dependency. Taking the lookback call $\left(S_T - S_{min}\right)^+$ as example, the volatility at the minimum region can be very different from the ATM region. In the equity skew case, the volatility in the minimum region is higher than ATM. With an increased fluctuation in the minimum region, S_{min} will be lower than that in the skewless case. Hence a lookback call will be more expensive when there is a skew. By applying the same rationale, a lookback put $\left(S_{max} - S_T\right)^+$ in the skew case should be cheaper than in the skewless case. So the standard flat volatility analytical lookback pricing formula will misprice in most of the practical cases.

The question is therefore how to take account of volatility smile/skew in the lookback pricing. One could use Monte Carlo in the local volatility pricing framework. However, sometimes it is possible to find a numerically efficient semi-analytical alternative to deal with the smile/skew effect. In the following, we shall examine the cascading barrier technique.

From the first principle, a lookback option can be replicated by a series of cascading barrier options. Using the lookback call $\left(S_T - S_{min}\right)^+$ as example, discretizing the spot space into possible minimum levels starting from $S_{min}^0 = S_0$, we have $S_{min}^0 > S_{min}^1 > \cdots > S_{min}^n$. A lookback call can be replicated by the sum of cascading down-and-in barrier options. The sum includes both long and short positions are shown in Table 5.5.

At each barrier level (S_{min}^i), a short position is knocked-in which cancels the previous long position. The knocked-in long position represents the prevailing lookback payoff with the new minimum as the strike. Cascading barrier method allows one to price a series of barrier options using different implied volatilities at different strikes and barriers, therefore including the smile/skew effects in the lookback pricing semi-analytically. With an adequate spot space discretization scheme it converges fast.

The cascading barrier method is very valuable in the situation where a payoff contains a lookback tail. It is numerically fast and quite accurate. The accuracy is of course also dependent on what model is used to price individual barrier options. The two-volatility rainbow barrier technique discussed in the previous section can further enhance the accuracy.

Risk Analysis

In the following, we shall risk analyse a hindsight put $\left(K - S_{min}\right)^+$ whose payoff was used as a tail in some income products to enhance the yield. It is of course very risky for investors who would be exposed the minimum spot during the lookback period. The hindsight put can be priced using its relationship to the lookback call.

TABLE 5.5 Replicating lookback option by cascading barrier options

Cascading	Long Position	Short Position
At $S_{min}^0 = S_0$	European call $(K = S_{min}^0)$	
Barrier $B = S_{min}^1$	down-and-in call $(K = S_{min}^1)$	down-and-in call $(K = S_{min}^0)$
Barrier $B = S_{min}^2$	down-and-in call $(K = S_{min}^2)$	down-and-in call $(K = S_{min}^1)$
Barrier $B = S_{min}^3$	down-and-in call $(K = S_{min}^3)$	down-and-in call $(K = S_{min}^2)$
and so on	......	......

In Figure 5.17, two spot profiles illustrating the hindsight put delta and gamma features are plotted. One is for a hindsight put with a maturity of 1Y3M and 42 days lookback period. The other is when the option is within the lookback period, with a maturity of 30 days and a recorded minimum spot so far of 90%.

The lookback risk features change when going through its life cycle. Once it is within the lookback period, as can be seen in the figure, the gamma risk becomes larger and it is centred on the recorded minimum region. The gamma is much reduced when spot is at both far ends.

The same comparison is made for the price versus volatility profiles, to examine the Vega features. As shown in Figure 5.18, Vega is actually reduced within the lookback period. This is understandable as when the spot is moving to the far ends the payoff will become more linear.

The spot and volatility risk profiles of lookback/hindsight options can change with time. The higher order risks (e.g. $\partial^2 V / \partial S \partial \sigma = \partial(vega) / \partial S$, $\partial^2 V / \partial S \partial t = \partial(theta) / \partial S$)

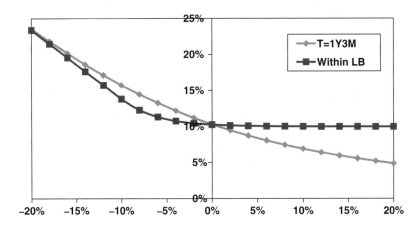

FIGURE 5.17 Price vs spot

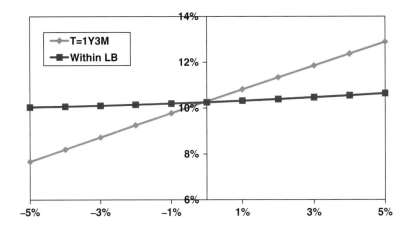

FIGURE 5.18 Price vs volatility

also have impacts on the risk features, which can be complex and sometimes "counter-intuitive". In risk managing such portfolios, one needs to be careful as the net Vega or theta positions can change signs triggered by spot moves.

VOLATILITY SMILE/SKEW DYNAMICS IMPACT ON HEDGING

Derivatives' hedging in the presence of volatility smile/skew is non-trivial in that the delta calculation is subject to assumptions made on volatility surface evolution or volatility dynamics. These assumptions include various volatility regimes, such as "sticky strike", "sticky delta" and "sticky local volatility". The deltas calculated under different dynamics can be substantially different. This raises an important question as to how delta positions should take the volatility dynamics into account.

Volatility Dynamics

For simplicity, denoting the price of an option as a function of spot (S) and implied volatility (σ), $P = f(S, \sigma)$, using the mathematical chain rule the option delta is:

$$\frac{dP}{dS} = \frac{\partial P}{\partial S} + \frac{\partial P}{\partial \sigma}\frac{\partial \sigma}{\partial S}$$

The term $\partial\sigma / \partial S$ specifies the volatility change due to the spot move. It is not a simple term to evaluate. Specifically:

- It specifies the forward volatility dynamics, namely the dynamic (as opposed to static) relationship between spot and implied volatility.
- In most of markets, today's implied volatility surfaces themselves do **not** contain information on the forward dynamic relationship of spot and implied volatility.
- If $\partial\sigma / \partial S$ is calculated somehow from today's implied volatility surface without any adjustments, one has implicitly assumed that the implied forward volatility and forward smile/skew will prevail in the future. In reality, however, this is not the case. As time moves forward the volatility smile/skew tends to persist. The implied forward volatility and forward smile/skew from today's volatility surface is not a good prediction of the future volatility surface evolution.
- Therefore, practitioners must make additional assumptions on volatility dynamics in the calculation of $\partial\sigma / \partial S$ and subsequently the option delta. In the interest rate swaptions whereby SABR model is widely used, the volatility dynamics referred to as backbone is explicitly modelled and widely adopted in the delta hedging. In the equity markets, however, as there is no consensus volatility dynamics model, practitioners need to make specific assumptions on the volatility dynamics based on experience and historic analyses.

Delta Adjustment

Different volatility dynamics will result in different delta hedge positions, and the average hedging P&L over a period of time will be different as a result. In order to include real volatility dynamics in the option delta, at least approximately, one could use today's implied volatility surface to calculate today's "dynamic" term and then make appropriate adjustment to it. Let's assume a simple linear relationship between the real-life volatility dynamics and today's "dynamic" term:

$$\frac{\partial \sigma}{\partial S} = \frac{\partial \sigma_0}{\partial S} L_T$$

where σ_0 denotes today's implied volatility surface, and L_T is a time (option maturity) dependent adjustment factor; the option delta can be rewritten as:

$$\frac{dP}{dS} = \frac{\partial P}{\partial S} + \frac{\partial P}{\partial \sigma}\left(\frac{\partial \sigma_0}{\partial S} \cdot L_T\right) = \Delta_{BS} + Vega\left(\frac{\partial \sigma_0}{\partial S} \cdot L_T\right)$$

Different values of L_T represent different volatility dynamics. The intuitive meanings are shown in the table below for an option with a fixed strike:

$L_T = -1$ Sticky delta: ATM volatility moves with spot.

$L_T = 0$ Sticky strike: Volatility is fixed with strike regardless of spot. The delta is hence the Black–Scholes delta: $dP / dS = \Delta_{BS}$.

$L_T = 1$ Sticky local volatility: Static local volatility delta: $dP / dS = \Delta_{LV}$.

It is interesting to note the following relationship:

$$\frac{dP}{dS} = \Delta_{BS} + \left(\Delta_{LV} - \Delta_{BS}\right) \cdot L_T$$

While the above delta formula provides clear intuitions, the L_T adjustment factors are mostly implemented by directly adjusting the bump-and-run implied volatility surface. For example, for a relative strike volatility surface $\sigma(T, K)$ where strike is expressed as percentage of spot, if the spot S is bumped by ΔS, the new volatility including L_T is:

$$\sigma_{new}(T, K, \Delta S) = \sigma(T, K) - \frac{d\sigma}{dK}\left(\frac{\Delta S}{S}\right) \cdot L_T$$

A similar volatility bump scheme can be formulated for an absolute strike implied volatility surface.

$$\sigma_{new}(T, S, K, \Delta S) = \sigma(T, S, K) - \frac{d\sigma}{dK}\Delta S \cdot L_T$$

Figure 5.19 plots the ATM European call deltas of different maturities for different L adjustment factors. The market data used is a typical FTSE-100 set with pronounced skew.

In Figure 5.19, with $L = -1$ ("sticky delta"), the longer-dated deltas are much larger than those calculated with $L = 0$ (Black–Scholes). As schematically shown in the "sticky delta" diagram in Figure 5.20, when spot shifts up, the ATM strike moves with the spot. Therefore skew will result in an increase in volatility for a given fixed strike and hence a larger option delta. In contrast, with $L = 1$ ("sticky local vol"), when spot shifts up, given a static skewed volatility surface, a smaller volatility is used for calculating the option delta. The longer-dated option deltas are smaller comparing to those calculated when $L = 0$ (Black–Scholes).

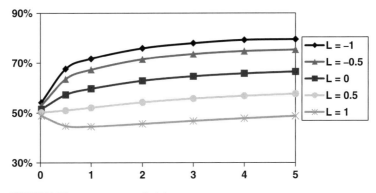

FIGURE 5.19 European call deltas

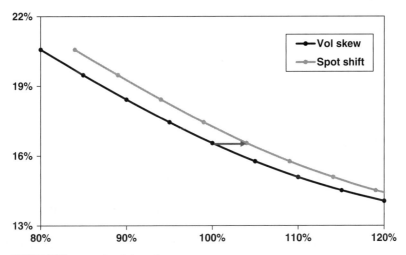

FIGURE 5.20 "Sticky delta" diagram

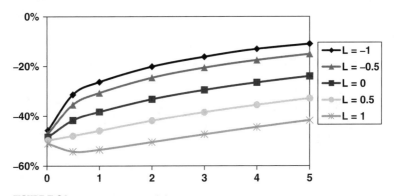

FIGURE 5.21 European put deltas

The deltas of ATM European puts for different L adjustment factors are plotted in Figure 5.21. Similarly, the deltas are very different for different L adjustment factors.

The differences among these curves can be explained similarly as for the European calls.

Adjustment Factor Term Structure

In the equity markets, one often observes that the short end volatility dynamics is different from that of long end. Therefore different L_T adjustment factors may be needed for different option maturities. A term structure of L_T adjustment factors can be used to calculate the overall delta hedging across all option maturities.

The L_T term structure is not something directly observable in the markets. Rather it is derived from market experiences and some historical analysis. An example analysis is qualitatively shown in Figure 5.22, which plots a set of FTSE-100 average ATM implied volatility for various maturities. The daily volatilities (e.g. the 1Y implied volatility) were averaged over one year. The error bars show the magnitudes of the variations of the averaged volatility for different maturities.

As can be seen in Figure 5.22, short-dated volatility exhibits larger variation than the long-dated one. Assuming the implied volatility surface was partially driven by the spot and given the daily spots were different, the short end ATM volatility was seen to be more susceptible to the spot movement, indicating a less "sticky delta" situation. The long-end ATM volatility, however, was relatively more stable with the changing spot, indicating a more "sticky delta" dynamics.

In Figure 5.23, an example equity index L_T term structure inclined towards the "sticky delta" is shown. The value at the 6-month point is about −30% and decays as the maturity gets longer. At short end, the behaviour is closer to "sticky strike". At the longer end, "sticky delta" behaviour becomes more dominant.

For European calls, the absolute cash delta positions calculated using this example L_T term structure are larger than those of Black–Scholes and "static local volatility". For European puts, the absolute cash delta positions calculated off this L_T term structure are less than those of Black–Scholes and "static local vol". A comparison of deltas of European calls of different maturities is plotted in Figure 5.24, whereby the delta curves calculated using B-S, local volatility PDE and L_T adjustment are shown to be quite different.

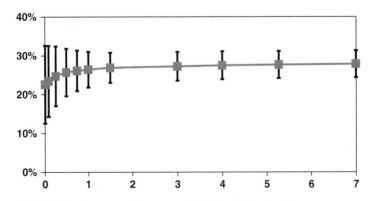

FIGURE 5.22   An example average ATM implied volatility

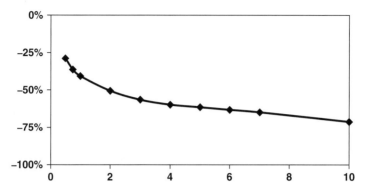

FIGURE 5.23 Adjustment factor term structure

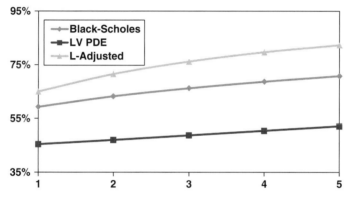

FIGURE 5.24 Comparison of European call deltas

Hedging in Practice

The volatility dynamics is complex but real. It can seriously affect hedging parameters in the B-S framework, in particular deltas. This has implications in the risk management of derivative products and hedging strategies aiming at achieving relatively stable long-term P&L. One needs to analyse and understand the volatility dynamics of individual underlyings in order to formulate realistic tailor-made delta hedge adjustments. Using a L_T term structure one can apply a consistent hedging strategy across all option maturities at portfolio level.

Measuring L_T adjustment factors is not straightforward. One has to use empirical experience together with some specific market information including the implied volatility surface. It is possible to extract some information from historical data, including spots and implied volatility surfaces. Across asset classes, there are several typical volatility dynamics known as "sticky" behaviours:

- Sticky delta: Volatility surface moves with delta, in particular when the underlying is trending.
- Sticky strike: Volatility is fixed with strike, effectively a Black–Scholes model behaviour. This is often observed when the underlying is bounded.
- Sticky local volatility: Volatility surface is static.

In practice, volatility dynamics often exhibits mixed "sticky" behaviours. In fact, the market price/volatility processes do vary between various "sticky" processes when market regime changes. This makes it harder to adjust delta hedges using a particular "stickiness". L_T adjustment technique can be a flexible tool in achieving optimal delta hedging for the relevant derivative positions.

L_T-adjusted delta includes an element of Vega due to spot move. However, one should not confuse this with the traditional Vega which hedges the volatility change due to much broader types of market moves. It is important though to subject the entire portfolio, including exotic or vanilla trades and their hedges, to the same volatility dynamics to ensure overall consistency in delta and Vega hedging.

CHAPTER 6

Local Volatility Framework

In derivative pricing and hedging, one of the most crucial components is the volatility smile/skew modelling. In fact, smile/skew modelling is so fundamental that it can make or break the business. Local volatility model (Dupire, Derman and Kani) is a key category of smile/skew models. The local volatility model is derived within the arbitrage-free framework and can be extended to include extra market features, such as jumps. A number of its variations have been used by market practitioners in pricing and risk managing certain path-dependent derivative products.

LOCAL VOLATILITY STRIPPER

This section summarizes the key local volatility stripping formulation, illustrating the inter-relationships among the call option $[C(K,T)]$, implied volatility $[\sigma_{imp}(K,T)]$ and local volatility $[\sigma_{LV}(S,T)]$.

Log-normal Local Volatility

For a typical equity underlying, it follows the log-normal process:

$$\frac{dS}{S} = (r - q)dt + \sigma(S, t)dW$$

With a given maturity T, a call option with a strike K is by definition related to the probability density function (PDF) $p_T(S)$ via:

$$C(K,T) = e^{-rT} \int_0^\infty \max(S - K, 0) p_T(S) dS$$

Denoting $C = C(K, T)$, and differentiating against strike K:

$$\frac{\partial C}{\partial K} = -e^{-rT} \int_K^\infty p_T(S)\,dS$$

Hence:

$$1 + e^{rT} \frac{\partial C}{\partial K} = 1 - \int_K^\infty p_T(S)\,dS = \int_{-\infty}^K p_T(S)\,dS$$

which is the terminal cumulative probability of spot $S < K$. Differentiating again against strike K:

$$\frac{\partial^2 C}{\partial K^2} = e^{-rT} p_T(K)$$

which is the butterfly at K. Note that although the above relationships are simply different ways of expressing a vanilla call option, they link up the PDF with terminal probability which is by definition associated with a digital option, and local volatility at $S = K$. In fact by applying the Fokker–Planck forward equation to the PDF, one can arrive at the following fundamental local volatility model:

$$\sigma_{LV}^2(K, T) = \frac{2\left(\dfrac{\partial C}{\partial T} + (r - q)K\dfrac{\partial C}{\partial K} + qC\right)}{K^2 \dfrac{\partial^2 C}{\partial K^2}}$$

where r is the risk-free rate, q the dividend yield. The local volatility at $S = K$ can be calculated from the call option with strike K. For a given matrix of vanilla options of different maturities and strikes, a local volatility surface can be constructed in principle.

In practice, the local volatility surface is better stripped out of the implied volatility surface rather than the vanilla option prices directly. This is because either the vanilla option price matrix or the implied volatility surface needs to be made numerically smooth before stripping the local volatility. Interpolating and extrapolating in the implied volatility surface is much easier numerically, and also in the context of ensuring non-arbitrage. Denoting the implied volatility $\sigma_{imp}(K, T)$ as σ_I, the local volatility at $S = K$ and time T has the following relationship with the implied volatility:

$$\sigma_{LV}(K, T) = \sqrt{\frac{2\dfrac{\partial \sigma_I}{\partial T} + \dfrac{\sigma_I}{T} + 2K(r - q)\dfrac{\partial \sigma_I}{\partial K}}{K^2\left[\dfrac{\partial^2 \sigma_I}{\partial K^2} - d\sqrt{T}\left(\dfrac{\partial \sigma_I}{\partial K}\right)^2 + \dfrac{1}{\sigma_I}\left(\dfrac{1}{K\sqrt{T}} + d\dfrac{\partial \sigma_I}{\partial K}\right)^2\right]}}$$

where

$$d = \frac{ln\left(\dfrac{S_0}{K}\right) + \left(r - q + \dfrac{1}{2}\sigma_I^2\right)T}{\sigma_I\sqrt{T}}$$

and S_0 is the spot. Alternatively the above formula can be rewritten as:

$$\sigma_{LV}(K,T) = \sqrt{\frac{2\dfrac{\partial \sigma_I}{\partial T} + \dfrac{\sigma_I}{T} + 2K\mu\dfrac{\partial \sigma_I}{\partial K}}{\dfrac{1}{\sigma_I T}\left(1 + \dfrac{Ky}{\sigma_I}\dfrac{\partial \sigma_I}{\partial K}\right)^2 + K^2\dfrac{\partial^2 \sigma_I}{\partial K^2} - \dfrac{K^2\sigma_I T}{4}\left(\dfrac{\partial \sigma_I}{\partial K}\right)^2 + K\dfrac{\partial \sigma_I}{\partial K}}}$$

where $\mu = r - q$, $y = ln(F_T/K)$ and $F_T = S_0 e^{\mu T}$.

Figures 6.1 and 6.2 show an example of an equity index implied volatility surface, and its stripped local volatility surface. A numerically smoothed implied volatility surface is vital in the local volatility stripping, and it in turn impacts the subsequent derivatives pricing using PDE or Monte Carlo. One can either apply pure numerical optimization schemes or use the best-fit functional form for the implied volatility. Typically, the smoothing starts at each time slice in the K direction, and then globally in the T direction. The functional form of the implied volatility usually refers to the smile/skew in the K direction. In real market situations the local volatilities are typically not smooth, even if the implied volatility surface can be made numerically smooth. This is OK as long as the local volatilities do not go negative. Non-negative local volatilities is a measure of non-arbitrage!

Normal Local Volatility

There are underlyings such as in interest rates whose stochastic process is normal:

$$dS = \mu dt + \sigma_N(S, t)dW$$

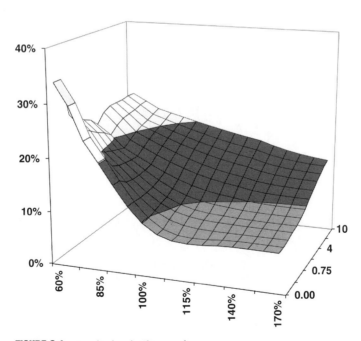

FIGURE 6.1 Implied volatility surface

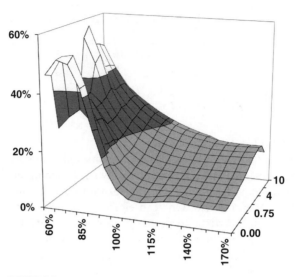

FIGURE 6.2 Local volatility surface

Following the same logic as in the log-normal case, the normal local volatility equation related to the undiscounted Bachelier call $\left(C = E^{Q}\left[(S - K)^{+}\right]\right)$ payoff is:

$$\sigma_{LV}^{2}\left(K,T\right) = \frac{2\left(\dfrac{\partial C}{\partial T} + \mu\dfrac{\partial C}{\partial K}\right)}{\dfrac{\partial^{2}C}{\partial K^{2}}}$$

The undiscounted call is used for the convenience of interest rate swaption underlyings, whereby the discount factor is usually included in the annuity.

The normal local volatility can be stripped from the implied normal volatility (σ_{N}) directly. Given the undiscounted Bachelier call payoff is:

$$\begin{cases} C = \left(F_{T} - K\right)N\left(x\right) + \phi(x)\sigma_{N}\sqrt{T} \\ \qquad x = \dfrac{F_{T} - K}{\sigma_{N}\sqrt{T}} \end{cases}$$

where $N(\cdot)$ is the cumulative normal distribution and $\phi(\cdot)$ is the normal probability density function, the partial derivatives of C are:

$$\frac{\partial C}{\partial T} = \mu N\left(x\right) + \phi\left(x\right)\sqrt{T}\frac{\partial\sigma_{N}}{\partial T} + \frac{\phi\left(x\right)\sigma_{N}}{2\sqrt{T}}$$

$$\frac{\partial C}{\partial K} = -N\left(x\right) + \phi(x)\sqrt{T}\frac{\partial\sigma_{N}}{\partial K}$$

$$\frac{\partial^{2}C}{\partial K^{2}} = -\phi\left(x\right)\frac{\partial x}{\partial K} - \phi\left(x\right)x\sqrt{T}\frac{\partial\sigma_{N}}{\partial K}\frac{\partial x}{\partial K} + \phi\left(x\right)\sqrt{T}\frac{\partial^{2}\sigma_{N}}{\partial K^{2}}$$

$$= \frac{\phi\left(x\right)}{\sigma_{N}\sqrt{T}}\left[\left(1 + \frac{S - K}{\sigma_{N}}\frac{\partial\sigma_{N}}{\partial K}\right)^{2} + \sigma_{N}T\frac{\partial^{2}\sigma_{N}}{\partial K^{2}}\right]$$

Plugging the partial derivatives into the local volatility equation, we can derive the following normal local volatility stripping formula:

$$\sigma_{LV}(K,T) = \sqrt{\frac{2\dfrac{\partial \sigma_N}{\partial T} + \dfrac{\sigma_N}{T} + 2\mu\dfrac{\partial \sigma_N}{\partial K}}{\dfrac{1}{\sigma_N T}\left(1 + \dfrac{(F_T - K)}{\sigma_N}\dfrac{\partial \sigma_N}{\partial K}\right)^2 + \dfrac{\partial^2 \sigma_N}{\partial K^2}}}$$

In summary, local volatility stripping is the core part of the local volatility model in equity. It is also a crucial part of the interest rate local volatility model described in §12.5.

LOCAL VOLATILITY PDE SOLVER

One of the common problems encountered in the implementation of these smile/skew models is the difficulty in achieving numerical stability and convergence. With (binomial or trinomial) trees, it is in general very difficult to achieve numerical stability and convergence. The Partial Differential Equation (PDE) approach is much more robust and stable (Andersen and Brotherton-Ratcliffe) and is a preferred technique to implement the local volatility model. In the following, we shall describe how to implement the smile/skew with PDE incorporating the local volatilities, and how to deal with discrete dividends.

PDE Formulation

A local volatility stripper is an integral part of the smile/skew PDE solver. The smile/skew PDE requires a local volatility surface as input. In a complete market, assuming the underlying is driven by a geometric Brownian process and volatility is a deterministic function of spot and time, Ito's lemma enables us to reach a localized Black–Scholes PDE for the contingent claim V:

$$\frac{\partial V}{\partial t} + (r(t) - q(t)) \cdot S \frac{\partial V}{\partial S} + \frac{1}{2}\sigma^2(S, t) \cdot S^2 \frac{\partial^2 V}{\partial S^2} = r(t) \cdot V$$

where $\sigma(S,t)$ is the stripped local volatility, $r(t)$ is the risk-free rate and $q(t)$ is the continuous dividend yield. In the log space $Z = \ln(S)$, after some algebra, the above PDE can be transformed into:

$$\frac{\partial V}{\partial t} + \left(r(t) - q(t) - \frac{\sigma^2(Z,t)}{2}\right)\frac{\partial V}{\partial Z} + \frac{1}{2}\sigma^2(Z,t)\frac{\partial^2 V}{\partial Z^2} = r(t) \cdot V$$

In the presence of smile/skew, the solution of the above PDE is only applicable within a small localized region in which the volatility is assumed to be constant. It is therefore obvious that in order to solve for the whole surface with smile/skew, a map of PDE solutions of tiny regions and a combination of these solutions are required. The above log space PDE must be discretized to derive numerical equations. Let's denote all parameters as local and we omit typing Z and t, namely r for $r(t)$, q for $q(t)$ and σ for $\sigma(Z,t)$.

Non-uniform Grid

It is important that the discretization scheme allows for non-uniform grid in the log-space Z. In practice, some path-dependent options (e.g. barrier options) will require non-uniform grid to achieve numerical stability and convergence. The following derivation is done within a general non-uniform grid framework for the time and space partial differentiations.

The diagram in Figure 6.3 illustrates a non-uniform grid layout. Along the space direction Z, we need to calculate the first and second order differentiations $\left(\dfrac{\partial V}{\partial Z}, \dfrac{\partial^2 V}{\partial Z^2}\right)$.

To ensure the numerical stability and remove bias, a quadratic fitting scheme going through three points needs to be used as shown in Figure 6.4. Assuming $V(z) = aZ^2 + bZ + C$, the first order differentiation, the pink tangential line, is given by $\dfrac{\partial V}{\partial Z} = 2aZ + b$.

The quadratic fitting is actually equivalent to the distance-weighted differentiation scheme. The generalized full set of differentiations along both t-axis and Z-axis are:

$$\frac{\partial V}{\partial t} = \frac{V_{i+1,j} - V_{i,j}}{dt}$$

$$\frac{\partial V}{\partial Z} = \frac{1-\theta}{dZ}\left(\frac{V_{i,j} - V_{i,j-1}}{dZ_1}dZ_2 + \frac{V_{i,j+1} - V_{i,j}}{dZ_2}dZ_1\right) + \frac{\theta}{dZ}\left(\frac{V_{i+1,j} - V_{i+1,j-1}}{dZ_1}dZ_2 + \frac{V_{i+1,j+1} - V_{i+1,j}}{dZ_2}dZ_1\right)$$

$$\frac{\partial^2 V}{\partial Z^2} = \frac{2\cdot(1-\theta)}{dZ}\left(\frac{V_{i,j+1} - V_{i,j}}{dZ_2} - \frac{V_{i,j} - V_{i,j-1}}{dZ_1}\right) + \frac{2\cdot\theta}{dZ}\left(\frac{V_{i+1,j+1} - V_{i+1,j}}{dZ_2} - \frac{V_{i+1,j} - V_{i+1,j-1}}{dZ_1}\right)$$

$$dZ = dZ_1 + dZ_2$$

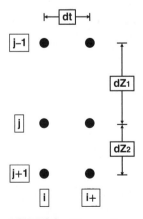

FIGURE 6.3 Non-uniform grid layout

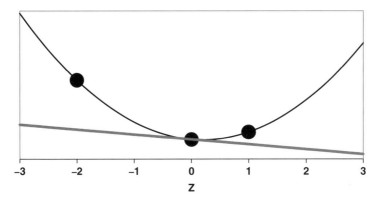

FIGURE 6.4 Quadratic fitting

where i denotes the i-th time space discretization and j denotes the j-th log space discretization, dZ_1 and dZ_2 are steps in log space, θ is the differentiation weighing from the current and forward time step allowing for implicit or explicit scheme. Note that due to the fact that dZ_1 and dZ_2 are not necessarily equal (non-uniform grid), the first and second order differentiations $\left(\dfrac{\partial V}{\partial Z}, \dfrac{\partial^2 V}{\partial Z^2}\right)$ are weighted appropriately as shown in the formulae above.

Substituting the above numerical differentiations into log-space PDE, and after some tedious algebra, one can reach the following discretized PDE:

$$\alpha_j V_{i,j-1} + \beta_j V_{i,j} + \gamma_j V_{i,j+1} = \alpha_j^* V_{i+1,j-1} + \beta_j^* V_{i+1,j} + \gamma_j^* V_{i+1,j+1}$$

where:

$$\alpha_j = \frac{-(1-\theta)}{dZ \cdot dZ_1}\left(\sigma^2 dt\left(1 + \frac{dZ_2}{2}\right) - (r-q)\cdot dt \cdot dZ_2\right)$$

$$\beta_j = 1 + r \cdot dt + \frac{(1-\theta)}{dZ_1 \cdot dZ_2}\left(\sigma^2 dt - \left(r - q - \frac{\sigma^2}{2}\right)\cdot dt \cdot (dZ_2 - dZ_1)\right)$$

$$\gamma_j = \frac{-(1-\theta)}{dZ \cdot dZ_2}\left(\sigma^2 dt\left(1 - \frac{dZ_1}{2}\right) + (r-q)\cdot dt \cdot dZ_1\right)$$

and

$$\alpha_j^* = \frac{\theta}{dZ \cdot dZ_1}\left(\sigma^2 dt\left(1 + \frac{dZ_2}{2}\right) - (r-q)\cdot dt \cdot dZ_2\right)$$

$$\beta_j^* = 1 + \frac{\theta}{dZ_1 \cdot dZ_2}\left(\sigma^2 dt - \left(r - q - \frac{\sigma^2}{2}\right)\cdot dt \cdot (dZ_2 - dZ_1)\right)$$

$$\gamma_j^* = \frac{\theta}{dZ \cdot dZ_2}\left(\sigma^2 dt\left(1 - \frac{dZ_1}{2}\right) + (r-q)\cdot dt \cdot dZ_1\right)$$

In a matrix form, it can be re-arranged into:

$$
\begin{pmatrix}
\beta_1 & \gamma_1 & 0 & 0 & 0 & \text{............................} & 0 \\
\alpha_2 & \beta_2 & \gamma_2 & 0 & 0 & \text{............................} & 0 \\
0 & \alpha_3 & \beta_3 & \gamma_3 & 0 & \text{............................} & 0 \\
 & & & \text{............................} & & & \\
 & & & \text{............................} & & & \\
0 & \text{.......} & & & \alpha_{n-2} & \beta_{n-2} & \gamma_{n-2} \\
0 & \text{.......} & & & & \alpha_{n-1} & \beta_{n-1}
\end{pmatrix}
\bullet
\begin{pmatrix}
V_{i,1} \\
V_{i,2} \\
V_{i,3} \\
... \\
... \\
V_{i,n-2} \\
V_{i,n-1}
\end{pmatrix}
=
\begin{pmatrix}
G_1 - \alpha_1 \cdot V_{i,0} \\
G_2 \\
G_3 \\
... \\
... \\
G_{n-2} \\
G_{n-1} - \gamma_{n-1} \cdot V_{i,n}
\end{pmatrix}
$$

where $G_j = \alpha_j^* V_{i+1,j-1} + \beta_j^* V_{i+1,j} + \gamma_j^* V_{i+1,j+1}$.

This matrix is the core equation that needs to be solved. By applying the boundary conditions according to the option payoffs, one can roll back the PDE grid to obtain the present value of the option. Since it has incorporated the non-uniform grid weighting scheme at the outset, this PDE solver can naturally deal with the pricing of a variety of path-dependent options, including barrier options where non-uniform grids are required. The built-in non-uniform grid capability is crucial in achieving numerical stability when pricing exotics in the local volatility framework.

To price Bermudan or American options, one can impose early exercise condition at all relevant PDE time slices and grid points; the option value is given by:

$$
V = max\left(V_{rollback}, V_{intrinsic}\right)
$$

where $V_{rollback}$ is the roll back option value and $V_{intrinsic}$ is the intrinsic option value.

Discrete Dividends

Discrete dividends introduce jumps into the geometric Brownian process. Jumps themselves do not satisfy the diffusion PDE. The discrete jumps can be viewed as if the PDE grid jumps downwards on the ex-div dates. In reality, during the PDE roll back pricing, linking up misaligned PDE grids is difficult and it will introduce severe numerical instabilities. Instead it is better to keep the same grid and interpolate the option values on the ex-div dates. Of course, one needs to make sure that all ex-div dates are built into the grid.

Typically, jump boundary conditions on an ex-div date are expressed as:

$$
S_- - D = S_+
$$
$$
V_-(S_-) = V_+(S_+)
$$

where $D = D(t, S)$ is the discrete dividend, including both cash and yield element, S_- is the spot just before the ex-div date, S_+ is the one just after the ex-div date, $V_-(S_-)$ and $V_+(S_+)$ are the corresponding option values. As shown schematically in Figure 6.5, the discrete dividend drops the spot by D to the red point. One can first roll back as usual to obtain the option values at time t_+ on the grid points marked black. The option value at the red point $[V_+(S_+)]$ can be interpolated from the black grid points at time t_+. Usually linear interpolation *wrt* to S is sufficiently good. The option value at time t_- on the corresponding black grid point $[V_-(S_-)]$ is therefore obtained as $V_-(S_-) = V_+(S_+)$.

Barrier Options

In the presence of smile/skew and discrete dividends, Smile/Skew PDE is one of the most stable and accurate numerical solvers for some path-dependent options such as barrier options. The formulation in the above section is generic, it is derived allowing arbitrary non-uniform grid spacing. In the case of barrier options, one can use the same PDE formulation to adjust grid spacing to increase the density of the grid in more important regions near the barrier. Figure 6.6 shows the critical region of a Down&Out put; the grid is denser nearer to the barrier and closer to maturity.

Figure 6.7 plots the price versus spot for a 1-month Down&Out put, with strike fixed at 100% and barrier at 80%. The plot exhibits the stable and smooth feature in the pricing, and this make the Greeks calculation stable too. The large curvature near the barrier indicates a very large gamma in that region. As discussed elsewhere in the

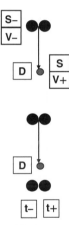

FIGURE 6.5 Handling discrete dividend on PDE grids

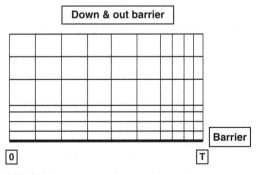

FIGURE 6.6 PDE grid of a Down&Out put

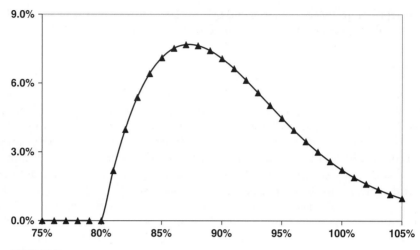

FIGURE 6.7   Down&Out put price vs spot

book, in practice one often needs to deploy the soft barrier technique to mitigate the risks of massive jump in Greeks.

Although LV PDE solver has existed for a long time, and various boundary conditions including discrete dividend jumps look simple, an efficient and stable numerical implementation in the presence of pronounced volatility smile/skew remains challenging, in particular when it is used to run sizeable derivatives positions. One needs to pay attention to a number of critical details, such as discretization weighting scheme, dividend jumps, aligning time slices with all important dates (e.g. ex-div dates, option call dates), aligning space grid with all barriers or option call levels.

LOCAL VOLATILITY MONTE CARLO

Monte Carlo (MC) simulation and pricing in the local volatility framework requires the small step approach. As the term "local" indicates that the local volatilities are for small local regions, and MC must sample many local points along the simulation path to ensure the compliance of the stochastic process, numerical accuracy and stability. The makes the MC simulation and pricing in LV very slow and computationally expensive. There is currently no general or universal solution to this problem. There are, however, faster simulation techniques that bypass the small steps in LV. These simulation techniques use the large step approach and are only suitable for certain types of path-dependent products, such as auto-callables whose payoffs are functions of specified time slices.

Large Step Monte Carlo

For an underlying with its full market implied volatility surface, the terminal distributions incorporating term volatility smile/skew at any chosen time slices can be calculated by using European digitals. The European digitals are of course valued using call spreads to capture smile/skew. In the following we shall assume all the terminal probability distributions (CDFs, PDFs) are known at given time slices. For certain path-dependent products, such as auto-callables, their payoffs are determined by the underlying spots on the call dates. The idea is to simulate the spot paths in large steps, jumping directly from spot to call dates sequentially. For such products, the local stochastic processes between the call dates are less important. What is important is that the temporal correlations and transition probabilities along the simulation paths in the large step approach must be aligned with those of the LV process, approximately but as much as possible. Figure 6.8 illustrates a desired large step simulation path, starting from time 0, one step to time slices T_1 and another step to T_2.

Markov Terminal Mapping Methodology

Assuming there is no volatility smile/skew, the geometric Brownian motion can be simulated using a standard Monte Carlo with large steps without losing accuracy. Once the smile/skew is present, the LV process effectively invalidates the large step approach. Markov terminal mapping (MTM) uses the volatility term structure (without smile/skew) as the driving Markov process, to simulate large step paths, for example going through T_1 and T_2. The obtained terminal distributions at T_1 and T_2 using the driving Markov process are then mapped to the smile/skew terminal distributions at T_1 and T_2, calculated directly from the full implied volatility surface.

Specifically, for a LV process:

$$\frac{dS}{S} = \mu dt + \sigma_{LV}(S,t)dz$$

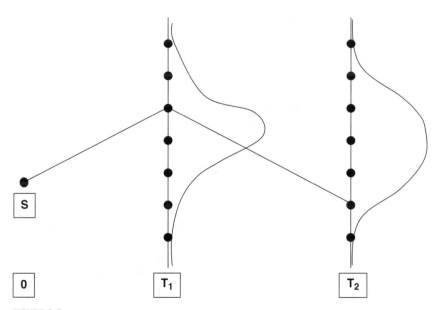

FIGURE 6.8 Large step simulation path

A geometric Brownian motion Y, which has the same ATM volatility term structure as S can be used in the Markov driving process to generate paths at large steps:

$$\frac{dY}{Y} = \mu dt + \sigma_{ATM}(t)dz$$

Clearly the terminal distributions of Y and S will be different. Figures 6.9 and 6.10 show such differences at a given time slice, where the Y distributions are simulated by large step MC, and S distributions are calculated directly from the implied volatility surface using digitals.

Nevertheless, Y and S should have similar temporal correlation structure, namely the incremental cascading correlation between the time steps in Y is a good approximation for that in S. This can be intuitively understood by the fact that they share the same ATM volatility term structure, and a process including smile/skew (S) can be approximated by Taylor expansion as a linear function of Y. Since temporal correlation will not change by a linear transformation, Y and S will have similar correlation structure.

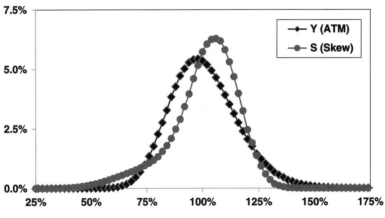

FIGURE 6.9   Terminal PDF (Y vs S)

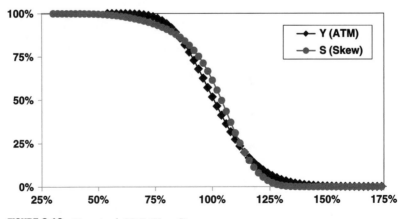

FIGURE 6.10   Terminal CDF (Y vs S)

The correlation perspective is the fundamental reason why a Markov driving factor is chosen to generate the initial paths.

Now, at given time slices, we need to map the Markov terminal distributions CDFs to the market implied terminal distributions containing smile/skew, i.e. mapping Y to S. This can be achieved by matching the relevant Y CDF values which are simulated, to the S CDF values which are simply un-discounted European digital prices. Mathematically, for simulated $Y_i, CDF(Y_i)$, one searches for a S_i on the S CDF such that:

$$CDF(Y_i) = CDF(S_i)$$

As can be seen in Figure 6.11, by drawing a horizontal line across the two CDF curves, for the same CDF value, one can find the corresponding pair Y_i and S_i, hence mapping Y_i to S_i. Because CDFs are monotonic, the mapping from Y to S is monotonic. For every point on Y, there must be a corresponding point on S which has the equal CDF value.

Following the above methodology, at any given time slice, all the simulated Y values $\{Y_1, Y_2, \cdots, Y_i, \cdots\}$ can be mapped and paired up to the corresponding S values $\{S_1, S_2, \cdots, S_i, \cdots\}$.

In summary, the MTM methodology:

- Uses a Markov driving process Y to simulate paths in large steps between the chosen time slices sequentially. This preserves the temporal correlation structure.
- Maps all the Y values at a time slice to the S values using the terminal CFDs: $CDF(Y_i) = CDF(S_i)$. This ensures the terminal distribution is fully calibrated.
- Continues the mapping one-by-one for all chosen time slices. The mapped S values at the time slices can be used to calculate option payoffs in the large step MC;

Copula Terminal Mapping Methodology

Another technique of utilizing large step Monte Carlo is to use the copula technique. Details of the copula technique will be discussed in chapter 9. For a single underlying,

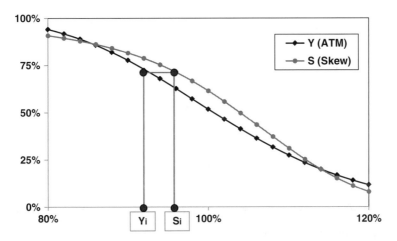

FIGURE 6.11 Terminal CDF (Y vs S)

spot at each time slice can be viewed as a component in a basket that consists of spots at many time slices. Provided we can obtain the correlation (or co-dependence) among the spots at those time slices, the copula technique can be readily used to sample the corresponding terminal CDFs directly.

Once again, the Markov driving process Y can be used to obtain and approximate the temporal correlation structure. Since Y uses the ATM volatility term structure without smile/skew, its temporal correlation matrix is determined by the ratios of relevant variances, i.e. $\left(\sigma_i \sqrt{t_i}\right) / \left(\sigma_j \sqrt{t_j}\right)$. Assuming there are n time slices, their marginal distributions (CDFs) can be calculated. The following steps are taken to simulate a spot path with the Copula Terminal Mapping (CTM) methodology:

- Build CDFs for at all time slices. An example CDF is shown in Figure 6.12, which can be used to sample the spot (S) given a uniformly distributed random number between 0 and 1;
- Generate n independent random Gaussian numbers (g_i) and impose the temporal correlation structure of the Y process. If Cholesky decomposition technique is used, given the decomposed correlation matrix C_{ij}, the correlated Gaussian number is given by $G_i = \Sigma_j C_{ij} \cdot g_j$.
- Convert the correlated Gaussian numbers back to uniformly distributed numbers by reversing the Wiener process $U_i = W^{-1}(G_i)$.
- Use the correlated uniform numbers (U_i) to sample the corresponding CDFs to obtain the underlying spots (S_i). The obtained spots form the spot path going through all the required time splices.

Figure 6.13 plots the 5-year callable note price versus the call trigger level using CTM (copula) and local volatility Monte Carlo. The call dates are annual, and the underlying is a liquid equity index with strong skew. The price difference is labelled by the right axis.

The price difference in this example mainly comes from the fact that the correlation structure in copula is an approximation of realized correlation in the local volatility model. For a single underlying where the computational speed in local volatility Monte

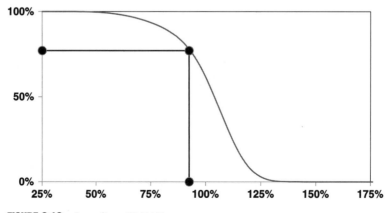

FIGURE 6.12   Sampling CDF (S)

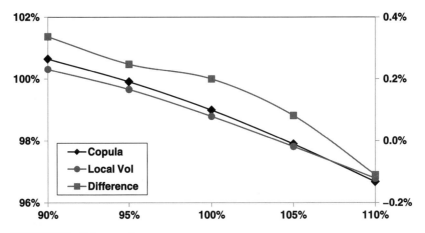

FIGURE 6.13 Price vs trigger

Carlo is not too slow, CTM may not offer too much advantage due to the speed/accuracy balance. For multi-underlying auto-callable products, however, the multi-step copula model can be of good value in terms of speed/accuracy balance. More details on the analysis can be found in chapter 9.

Note that in both MTM and CTM methodology, the mapped S values at the time slices can be used to calculate transition probabilities between the time slices. The terminal distributions at time t_{i-1} and t_i are specified by:

$$\begin{pmatrix} P_i^0 \\ P_i^1 \\ \cdots \\ P_i^n \end{pmatrix} = \begin{pmatrix} p_0^0 & p_1^0 & \cdots & p_n^0 \\ p_0^1 & p_1^1 & \cdots & p_n^1 \\ & \cdots & \cdots & \\ p_0^n & p_1^n & \cdots & p_n^n \end{pmatrix} \cdot \begin{pmatrix} P_{i-1}^0 \\ P_{i-1}^1 \\ \cdots \\ P_{i-1}^n \end{pmatrix}$$

where the terminal probabilities are denoted by capital Ps, and the transition probability matrix is:

$$\begin{pmatrix} p_0^0 & p_1^0 & \cdots & p_n^0 \\ p_0^1 & p_1^1 & \cdots & p_n^1 \\ & \cdots & \cdots & \\ p_0^n & p_1^n & \cdots & p_n^n \end{pmatrix}$$

and:

$$p_0^0 + p_1^0 + \cdots + p_n^0 = 1$$
$$p_0^1 + p_1^1 + \cdots + p_n^1 = 1$$
$$\cdots$$
$$p_0^n + p_1^n + \cdots + p_n^n = 1$$

For the transition matrix, there are $n \times n$ unknowns, with only $2 \times n$ equations. Unless $n \leq 2$, there is no unique solution to the $n \times n$ unknowns in the transition matrix without additional assumptions. In general, the transition stochastic processes and transition probabilities cannot be fully specified by the terminal distributions. Nevertheless, the simulated spot paths across the time slices in both MTM and CTM methodology allow us to calculate transition probabilities between the time slices by fast Monte Carlo. The speed advantage will be more significant for multi-underlying basket products.

In summary, both Markov Terminal Mapping and Copula Terminal Mapping methodology use large step Monte Carlo to avoid the needs of small steps typically required in the LV framework. In doing so, they are only suitable for certain products whose payoffs can be specified by finite number of time slices. Another important application is when one needs to value a portfolio of options with the same underlying at finite time slices. For example, for a portfolio of call/put options (or caps/floors) of different strikes and maturities but with the same underlying, if there is a need to value the portfolio at given forward time slices (e.g. for CVA purpose), the MTM or CTM methodology will be an extremely valuable tool to price in the volatility smile/skew without having to go through many small time steps in the LV Monte Carlo.

LOCAL VOLATILITY TO IMPLIED VOLATILITY

Given an implied volatility surface, a local volatility surface can be easily calculated by using the local volatility stripper. However, the inverse problem is not straightforward. In the presence of volatility smile/skew, it is in general rather difficult to calculate implied volatility from local volatility by inverting analytically. Only when there is no volatility smile or skew, i.e. no K dependency, the local volatility stripping formula collapses into a term structure relationship:

$$\sigma_{LV}^2(t) = 2\sigma_I(t) \cdot t \frac{\partial \sigma_I(t)}{\partial t} + \sigma_I^2(t) = \frac{d\left(\sigma_I^2(t) \cdot t\right)}{dt}$$

and the implied volatility squared can be inversed out of the term structure formula as follows:

$$\sigma_I^2(T) = \frac{1}{T} \int_0^T \sigma_{LV}^2(t) dt$$

Most Likely Path

The MLP concept is useful in the context of obtaining implied volatility from local volatility in the presence of volatility smile/skew. The idea is to have a simple volatility "term structure formula" that is similar, as in the no smile/skew case. Starting from a standard diffusion equation where local volatility is spot- and time-dependent:

$$\frac{dS}{S} = \mu dt + \sigma_{LV}(S, t) dz$$

If at time T, $S_T = K$, the equivalent diffusion equation conditional on $S_T = K$ is given by:

$$\frac{dS}{S} = \mu dt + \sigma_{x|K}(t) dz$$

where $\sigma_{x|K}(t)$ is the local volatility along the MLP, which is implicitly defined in the above diffusion equation as the path x along which the implied volatility for strike K can be calculated by numerical integration (Figure 6.14). For the given local volatility along the MLP, the implied variance can then be expressed as an integral over the MLP, labelled x:

$$\sigma_I(K,T)^2 \approx \frac{1}{T} \int_0^T \sigma_{x|K}(t)^2 dt$$

The question is how to find MLP and compute the implied volatility. Note that the MLP is not really uniquely defined, and it is ultimately an approximation. It can be defined either as the path calculated as the conditional (on $S_T = K$) expectation of x_t with respect to an appropriate density, or the path where the appropriate density is maximized. The techniques of searching for a MLP and calculating the resulted implied volatility range from simple (e.g. small time approximations) to complex (e.g. head kernel expansion) (ref. Gatheral, Guyon et al). The question here is that in practice how far we should go in terms of looking for an ideal solution. In general, we should of course use simple techniques while tolerating approximations. If by seeking the ideal solution the MLP technique becomes too complex, we might as well simply get the implied volatility numerically by computing European prices using local volatility.

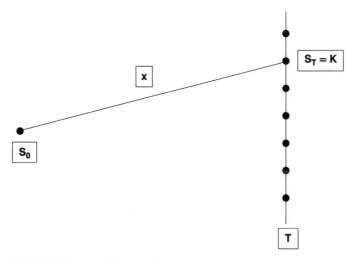

FIGURE 6.14 Most likely path

BBF Formula

An elegant and simple approximation for the implied volatility is given by the BBF (Berestycki, Busca and Florent) formula. For the log-normal process ($dS/S = \mu dt + \sigma_{LV}(S,t)dz$), denoting $x = \ln(S_0/K) + r(T - t_0)$, in the limit of small time approximation $\Delta t = (T - t_0) \to 0$, the implied volatility can be approximated by the following formula:

$$\sigma_I(x,0) \approx x \cdot \left(\int_0^x \frac{ds}{\sigma_{LV}(s,0)} \right)^{-1}$$

Here the implied volatility is the one in the Black–Scholes formula that reproduces the market option prices. By substituting x and $s = \ln(S_0/S)$ into the above equation:

$$\sigma_I(K,T) \approx \ln(S_0 / K) \cdot \left(\int_{S_0}^K -\frac{d\ln(S)}{\sigma_{LV}(k,0)} \right)^{-1}$$

$$= \ln(K / S_0) \cdot \left(\int_{S_0}^K \frac{dS}{S \cdot \sigma_{LV}(S,0)} \right)^{-1}$$

Note that although in the formula the local volatility $\sigma_{LV}(S,0)$ is meant at $t = 0$, i.e. the integration should be along the path from $(S_0,0)$ to $(K,0)$, in practice one can take the local volatility along the path between $(S_0,0)$ and (K,T). Here we effectively treat this particular path as MLP.

Figure 6.15 shows the calculated implied volatility curve from a given local volatility curve using the BBF formula. The spot and ATM strike is 4%. The curvature of the implied volatility curve is less than that of local volatility as expected.

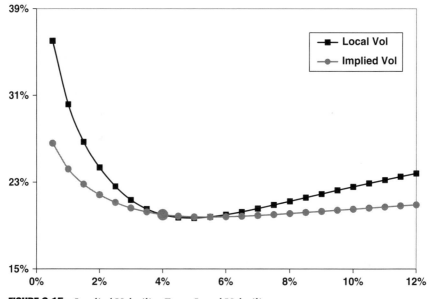

FIGURE 6.15 Implied Volatility From Local Volatility

As mentioned earlier, the local volatility curve can be a slice at $t = 0$ along the K-axis, or a slice along the line of $(S_0, 0)$ to (K, T).

One can make further correction to the above approximation. The correction can be done by using Taylor expansion. Denoting the above BBF formula as the zeroth order $\sigma_{I\_0}(x)$, the implied volatility can be expanded in the power of Δt:

$$\sigma_I(x) = \sigma_{I\_0}(x) + \sigma_{I\_1}(x) \cdot \Delta t + O(\Delta t^2)$$

where the first order correction term $\sigma_{I\_1}(x)$ can be expressed as:

$$\sigma_{I\_1}(x) = \frac{x}{d(x)^3} \ln\left(\frac{d(x)}{x} \cdot \sqrt{\sigma_{LV}(0) \cdot \sigma_{LV}(x)} \right)$$

$$d(x) = \int_0^x \frac{ds}{\sigma_{LV}(s)}$$

Given that $\sigma_{I\_0}(x) = \dfrac{x}{d(x)}$, the alternative formula is given by:

$$\sigma_{I\_1}(x) = \frac{\sigma_{I\_0}(x)^3}{x^2} \ln\left(\frac{\sqrt{\sigma_{LV}(0) \cdot \sigma_{LV}(x)}}{\sigma_{I\_0}(x)} \right)$$

This correction term is actually very sensitive to the integration in $d(x)$, where the curvature of the local volatility needs proper numerical attention.

The above implied volatility approximation is rather simple and useful in practice. The Black–Scholes implied volatility is approximated by an integral of local variances along the most-likely-path. For an option with strike K, the MLP is a line (straight or curvy) from spot at time t to K at time T. This implied volatility proxy can be a valuable numerical tool in some option pricing implementations where the local volatility space is not efficient. It is also interesting to note that the same Taylor expansion method can be used to derive SABR volatility smile/skew widely used in interest rate derivatives (Obloj 2008).

For the normal process $(dS = \mu dt + \sigma_{LV}(S, t) dz)$, the normal implied volatility is defined as the implied volatility used in the Bachelier formula that reproduces the market option prices. There is simple relationship between the (normal) implied volatility and local volatility:

$$\sigma_I^N (K, T) = (K - S_0) \left(\int_{S_0}^{K} \frac{dS}{\sigma_{LV}(S, 0)} \right)^{-1}$$

Comparing to the Black–Scholes implied volatility, there is a beautiful relationship between the log-normal and normal implied volatility, accurate to the zeroth order in the right context:

$$\frac{\sigma_I(K)}{\ln(K) - \ln(S_0)} = \frac{\sigma_I^N(K)}{K - S_0}$$

One of the possible applications of MLP is to calibrate the local volatility surface to the given implied volatility surface by iteration. Although the MLP approach offers natural intuition and can be useful for local volatility stripping in the higher dimension case, its implementation accuracy is subject to a degree of bias. Standard local volatility stripper remains the preferred technique in practice.

The theoretical significance of the BBF formulation is that it provides a methodology and insight for deriving implied volatility from a given dynamics specified in the local volatility space. For example, the spirit of BBF is clearly visible in the SABR volatility model widely used in the interest rate derivatives. Another example is that one can specify basket underlying dynamics and a correlation skew relationship in the local volatility space, and the basket implied volatility smile/skew can be derived incorporating correlation skew.

PRACTICAL ISSUES WITH LOCAL VOLATILITY

Both B-S and local volatility model are calibrated to the vanilla option market. Vanilla option prices contain the static market information only. If they are used to price options that are sensitive to the volatility and smile/skew dynamics, it can lead to serious mispricing. Let us examine a "simple" example of forward start call or put option, where the option strike is set at $x\%$ of the forward. Table 6.1 lists the implied forward volatilities between 1-year and 2-years using linear variance interpolation, given the term volatilities at the two points.

As can be seen clearly, the implied forward volatility is driven by the volatility term structure. When it is downwards sloping, will you sell a corresponding forward start option (1-year into 2-years) priced using the implied forward volatility (7.1%)? When it is upwards sloping, will you buy a corresponding forward start option priced using the implied forward volatility (29.2%)? The answers to both questions are obviously "no", as the "wrong" forward volatilities are used in the "wrong" model. Note that in a forward start option, the strike is actually floating with the forward. One cannot lock into the forward volatility associated with a floating strike by using two term volatilities in the presence of volatility smile/skew. So in this context the forward volatility cannot be properly hedged in practice.

What about implied forward smile/skew? Figure 6.16 compares the 3-month skew calculated using LV at $t = 0$ and the 1-year forward point $(t = 1Y)$. The implied volatilities are normalized by subtracting the corresponding ATM volatility. The skew at the forward point (the forward skew) is clearly flattening. The implied forward smile/skew in LV is not compatible with the persistent smile/skew dynamics observed in the markets.

TABLE 6.1   Implied forward volatility

Term Volatility at 1 year	Term Volatility at 2 years	Implied Forward Volatility between 1 and 2 years
20%	15%	7.1%
20%	25%	29.2%

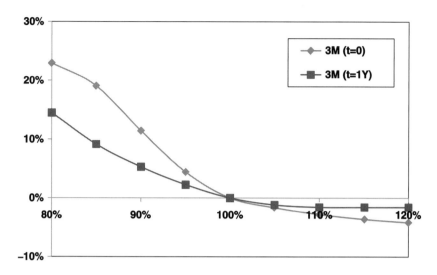

FIGURE 6.16 Forward skew flattening

To counter for this shortfall embedded in the LV model, practitioners often impose their own forward skew by using the spot skew of the same maturity to price forward skew-sensitive products:

$$\sigma_{fwd}\left(t_1,t_2,K\right) = \sigma_{fwd}\left(t_1,t_2,ATM\right)+\left[\sigma_o\left(t_2-t_1,K\right)-\sigma_o(t_2-t_1,ATM)\right]$$

Given that the implied forward volatility/smile/skew in the deterministic volatility models (B-S and Local Volatility) are not really hedgeable, one needs to make other appropriate model assumptions to price in forward dynamics in line with the market observations. Such dynamics include forward volatility variations and persistent volatility smile/skew. Mis-specified volatility smile/skew dynamics can lead to wrong Greeks within the PDE, and LV. To overcome these issues in the LV model, and in fact in the wider deterministic volatility models, suitable stochastic volatility models are called for.

CHAPTER 7

Stochastic Local Volatility Framework

This is the latest class of models capable of handling volatility smile and skew in a consistent way. The local volatility paradigm has some serious issues, its embedded forward volatility does not have market-observable features such as persistent skew. LSV model paradigm addresses this problem by introducing stochastic process in the local volatility space. It is effectively a mixture of local volatility model and stochastic volatility model. This chapter will go through the essential mathematical framework, and examine the practical numerical techniques in stochastic local volatility (LSV) implementation. The chapter will use LSV to examine a number of forward skew-sensitive products, such as cliquet, to compare prices, Greeks and dynamic hedging strategies.

Within the LSV framework, one can also incorporate stochastic interest rates in a similar fashion. A properly implemented LSV infrastructure is very valuable and in fact essential in modern equity and FX derivatives business.

STOCHASTIC VOLATILITY MODELS

In both Black–Scholes and local volatility model paradigm, the volatilities are deterministic and they are (or meant to be) fully calibrated to the markets. The reality is that both realized and implied volatilities do have significant variability in practice, and stochastic volatility is readily observable. Ignoring stochastic volatility should not affect the pricing of vanillas and certain payoffs, because the calibrated implied volatilities (and their equivalent local volatilities) are in fact aggregated and averaged parameters containing those risk factors unaccounted for including stochastic volatility. While this is true for vanillas and some payoffs, stochastic volatility at a granular level can have specific and significant impact on the pricing and hedging of many path-dependent products. Those products include barriers, lookbacks, forward start options, cliquets, volatility swap and option, where one must take into account the forward volatility/ smile/skew evolutions. Stochastic volatility is one of the most important contributing factors in the modelling of smile/skew dynamics.

There have been many attempts to model stochastic volatility in the past, most notably the Heston, Stein & Stein and Hull & White model. Table 7.1 summarizes their stochastic processes which underpin the respective dynamics.

In all of the above stochastic volatility models, the implied volatility is made stochastic, where ξ is the vol of vol. When $\xi = 0$, all models converge to the same deterministic volatility model framework. Making implied volatility stochastic tends to give rise to several practical and numerical issues:

- Full market calibration is difficult. For example, one may be able to calibrate to the long-end smile/skew, but not the short-end smile/skew. A full calibration to the entire volatility surface is rarely possible in practice with the limited number of stochastic volatility model parameters.
- The calibrated model parameters can be unrealistic, i.e. too large or too small to make practical sense. For example, the calibrated vol of vol (ξ) can be as high as 200%, while the historic average is at only 20%.
- Numerical optimization/minimization can be unstable. The semi-analytical solutions of the vanilla options used in the calibrations are associated with Fourier inversions. Mixing them with numerical optimization can have some inherent numerical errors leading to unstable dynamics.

The above practical problems of the stochastic (implied) volatility models can be addressed and largely overcome by the application of Stochastic Local Volatility (SLV) model.

TABLE 7.1   Stochastic volatility processes

Stochastic Volatility Model	Stochastic Processes (SDEs)	Description
Heston	$\dfrac{dS_t}{S_t} = \mu dt + \sigma dz_1$ $d\sigma^2 = \kappa(\theta_t - \sigma^2)dt + \xi \sigma dz_2$ $< dz_1 dz_2 > = \rho dt$	S_t is locally log-normal. σ^2 follows a Cox–Ingersoll–Ross (CIR) process with a long-term average value θ_t.
Stein and Stein	$\dfrac{dS_t}{S_t} = \mu dt + \sigma dz_1$ $d\sigma = \kappa(\theta_t - \sigma)dt + \xi dz_2$ $< dz_2 dz_2 > = \rho dt$	S_t is locally log-normal. σ follows a mean-reverting Ornstein–Uhlenbeck (OU) process, with a long-term average value θ_t.
Hull and White	$\dfrac{dS_t}{S_t} = \mu dt + \sigma dz_1$ $\dfrac{d\sigma^2}{\sigma^2} = \kappa dt + \xi dz_2$ $< dz_1 dz_2 > = \rho dt$	S_t is locally log-normal, and σ^2 also follows a log-normal process.

SLV MODEL FORMULATION

There are several versions of SLV models, each deploying different stochastic local volatility processes. Clearly the choice of the stochastic process can make a substantial difference in practice, in particular from numerical implementation and calibration perspective. For example, with the CIR process, it is much harder to use PDE for a stable and faster outcome, and one may have to resort to Monte Carlo. With the OU process, it is easier to use PDE in pricing and calibration. Table 7.2 lists some of key SLV model variations used by practitioners.

So what are the fundamental differences between the standard stochastic volatility model and SLV model? First of all, we see from the table above that a deterministic term $\sigma(S_t, t)$ is introduced. This spot- and time-dependent term can greatly help make the calibration, as it provides a counterpart to the local volatility term in the local volatility model. The second major difference is that the stochastic term L_t (hence $\sigma(S_t, t)L_t$) can be linked directed to the local volatility in the local volatility model. This direct link and the counterpart term in the SLV model make it possible to map to the local volatility surface. As the local volatility surface is fully calibrated to the market from a theoretical point of view, the full SLV model market calibration is practically possible! In the following, let's examine the link between a SLV and LV model.

TABLE 7.2 Stochastic local volatility models

Stochastic Local Volatility Model	Stochastic Processes (SDEs)	Description
Jex, Henderson and Wang	$\dfrac{dS_t}{S_t} = \mu dt + \sigma(S_t, t)L_t dz_1$ $dL_t^2 = \kappa(\theta_t - L_t^2)dt + \xi L_t dz_2$ $< dz_1 dz_2 > = \rho dt$	S_t is locally log-normal. L_t^2 follows a Cox–Ingersoll–Ross (CIR) process with a long-term average value θ_t.
Ren, Madan and Qian	$\dfrac{dS_t}{S_t} = \mu dt + \sigma(S_t, t)L_t dz_1$ $d\ln L_t = \kappa\big(\theta_t - \ln(L_t)\big)dt + \xi dz_2$ $< dz_1 dz_2 > = \rho dt$	S_t is locally log-normal. $\ln L_t$ follows a mean-reverting Ornstein–Uhlenbeck (OU) process, with a long-term average value θ_t.
Tataru and Fisher	$\dfrac{dS_t}{S_t} = \mu dt + \sigma(S_t, t)L_t dz_1$ $dL_t = \kappa(\theta_t - L_t)dt + \xi L_t dz_2$ $< dz_1 dz_2 > = \rho dt$	S_t is locally log-normal. L_t follows a mean-reverting process.

Gyöngy's Theorem and Markovian Projection

Gyöngy's theorem states that the marginal distributions of Ito processes can be mimicked by a Markovian process. For an Ito process X_t, its dynamics is given by:

$$dX_t = \alpha_t dt + \delta_t dZ_t$$

where dZ_t is the Wiener process. Both α_t and δ_t can be stochastic, hence dX_t is a general form of SDE for a multi-factor model. Gyöngy's theorem states that there exists a lower dimension Markovian process (Y_t):

$$dY_t = b_t(Y_t)dt + v_t(Y_t)dZ_t$$

Its marginal distributions are the same as X_t for every $t > 0$. Both $b_t(Y_t)$ and $v_t(Y_t)$ are deterministic, and they are determined and related to X_t by:

$$b_t(x) = E[\alpha_t \mid X_t = x]$$
$$v_t^2(x) = E[\delta_t^2 \mid X_t = x]$$

Y_t is also called the Markovian projection of X_t. Markovian projection is in general a very valuable tool in financial mathematics. In cases where one has to handle path-dependent (non-Markovian) processes, and one is only interested in the marginal distributions, Markovian projection can be used to convert the process into a Markov and reduce the dimensionality of the problem. In the context of SLV modelling, it provides a method to link up the multi-factor stochastic processes (SLV SDEs) to a one-factor process (LV SDE) via the marginal distributions.

Applying Gyöngy's theorem to the 2-factor SLV SDE:

$$\frac{dS_t}{S_t} = \mu dt + \sigma(S_t,t)L_t dz_1$$

its Markovian projection 1-factor SDE with the deterministic local volatility is given by:

$$\frac{dS_t}{S_t} = \mu dt + \sigma_{LV}(S_t,t)d\tilde{z}$$

and

$$\sigma_{LV}^2(S,t) = \sigma^2(S,t)E[L_t^2 \mid S_t = S]$$

This states that the conditional expectation of the stochastic instantaneous variance in SLV is equal to the local variance in LV. This vital linkage between the 2-factor SLV processes and the 1-factor local volatility process underpins the implementation and calibration of SLV models. In essence, an SLV model is a mixture of stochastic and local volatility model. When $\xi = 0$, it converges to a pure local volatility model. When $\sigma(S_t,t) \equiv 1$, it degenerates to a pure stochastic volatility model.

Fokker–Planck (Kolmogorov Forward) Equation

For a N-dimensional stochastic process vector $\mathbf{X}$:

$$d\mathbf{X} = \mu(\mathbf{X})dt + \sigma(\mathbf{X})d\mathbf{Z}$$

with the drift vector $\mu = (\mu_1, \mu_2, \cdots, \mu_N)$ and the $N \times N$ covariance matrix $D(x) = \sigma(x)\sigma(x)'$, the joint probability density function $p(x)$ satisfies the Fokker–Planck (Kolmogorov forward) equation:

$$\frac{\partial p(x)}{\partial t} = -\sum_{i=1}^{N} \frac{\partial}{\partial x_i}[\mu_i(x)p(x)] + \frac{1}{2}\sum_{i=1}^{N}\sum_{j=1}^{N} \frac{\partial^2}{\partial x_i \partial x_j}[D_{ij}(x)p(x)]$$

SLV example 1: Setting up the Kolmogorov forward equation (forward PDE) for the SLV model with the processes of:

$$\frac{dS_t}{S_t} = \mu dt + \sigma(S_t, t)L_t dz_1$$

$$d\ln L_t = \kappa(\theta_t - \ln(L_t))dt + \xi dz_2$$

$$< dz_1 dz_2 > = \rho dt$$

let $x = \ln S_t$ and $y = \ln L_t$ and the above SDEs can be rewritten as:

$$dx = \left(\mu - \frac{\sigma^2(e^x, t)e^{2y}}{2}\right)dt + \sigma(e^x, t)e^y dz_1$$

$$dy = \kappa(\theta_t - y)dt + \xi dz_2$$

$$< dz_1 dz_2 > = \rho dt$$

Applying the Kolmogorov forward equation and the corresponding forward PDE for the probability density $p = p(x, y, t)$ is given by:

$$\frac{\partial p}{\partial t} = -\frac{\partial}{\partial x}\left[\left(\mu - \frac{\sigma^2(e^x, t)e^{2y}}{2}\right)p\right] - \frac{\partial}{\partial y}\left[\kappa(\theta_t - y)p\right]$$

$$+ \frac{1}{2}\frac{\partial^2}{\partial x^2}\left[\sigma^2(e^x, t)e^{2y}p\right] + \frac{\xi^2}{2}\frac{\partial^2 p}{\partial y^2} + \rho\xi\frac{\partial^2}{\partial x \partial y}\left[\sigma^2(e^x, t)e^y p\right]$$

with the initial boundary conditions of $x_0 = \ln(S_0)$ and $y_0 = \ln(1) = 0$.

SLV example 2: Setting up the Kolmogorov forward equation (forward PDE) for the SLV model with the processes of:

$$\frac{dS_t}{S_t} = \mu dt + \sigma(S_t, t)L_t dz_1$$

$$dL_t = \kappa(\theta_t - L_t)dt + \xi L_t dz_2$$

$$< dz_1 dz_2 > = \rho dt$$

Denoting $x = lnS_t$ and $y = L_t$ the above SDEs can be rewritten as:

$$dx = \left(\mu - \frac{\sigma^2(e^x,t)y^2}{2}\right)dt + \sigma(e^x,t)ydz_1$$

$$dy = \kappa(\theta_t - y)dt + \xi ydz_2$$

$$< dz_1dz_2 > = \rho dt$$

Applying the Kolmogorov forward equation and the corresponding forward PDE for the probability density $p = p(x,y,t)$ is given by:

$$\frac{\partial p}{\partial t} = -\frac{\partial}{\partial x}\left[\left(\mu - \frac{\sigma^2(e^x,t)y^2}{2}\right)p\right] - \frac{\partial}{\partial y}\left[\kappa(\theta_t - y)p\right]$$

$$+ \frac{1}{2}\frac{\partial^2}{\partial x^2}\left[\sigma^2(e^x,t)y^2p\right] + \frac{\xi^2}{2}\frac{\partial^2}{\partial y^2}\left[y^2p\right] + \rho\xi\frac{\partial^2}{\partial x\partial y}\left[\sigma(e^x,t)y^2p\right]$$

with the initial boundary conditions of $x_0 = \ln(S_0)$ and $y_0 = 1$.

SLV NUMERICAL IMPLEMENTATION

The key in the SLV numerical implementation is its calibration to the markets.

SLV Calibration

The deterministic unknown parameters in SLV that need to be calibrated are $\sigma(S_t, t)$, (κ, θ_t, ξ) and ρ. In a sense, the SLV model has "excessive" degrees of freedom, its stochastic volatility parameters (κ, θ_t, ξ) can have different sets of values and all allow the full calibration to the vanilla options (implied volatility surface). Precisely because of these "excessive" degrees of freedom, SLV has the flexibility of benchmarking or specifying forward dynamics for both forward volatility and forward smile/skew, at the same time calibrating to the vanilla options. By "benchmarking", the market exotic instruments such as cliquets, barriers and VIX options are used to calculate (κ, θ_t, ξ). By "specifying", historical time series or trading intuition are used to set and adjust the values of (κ, θ_t, ξ). So in general, the overall SLV calibration consists of two distinctive steps. The first step is to benchmark or specify the forward dynamics, including forward volatility and forward smile/skew, by deciding value of (κ, θ_t, ξ). The second step is to calibrate to the vanilla markets by calculating $\sigma(S_t, t)$. In practice, one can of course use the first step to assist the calibration of the vanilla markets, namely the first step can help the second step, but not vice versa.

Let's analyse the calibration example of a SLV model whose stochastic processes are defined by the following SDEs:

$$\frac{dS_t}{S_t} = \mu dt + \sigma(S_t,t)L_tdz_1$$

$$dlnL_t = \kappa\left(\theta_t - \ln(L_t)\right)dt + \xi dz_2$$

$$< dz_1dz_2 > = \rho dt$$

Step 1 calibration: For (κ, θ_t, ξ), it is possible and convenient to make θ_t a function of (κ, ξ), hence reducing the degree of freedom. One way to do so is to set the unconditional expectation of L_t^2 to 1. Let $X_t = \ln L_t$ and the SDE $d\ln L_t = \kappa(\theta_t - \ln(L_t))dt + \xi dz_2$ can be rewritten as $dX_t = \kappa(\theta_t - X_t)dt + \xi dz_2$, the solution for X_t is given by:

$$X_T = e^{-\kappa T} X_0 + \kappa e^{-\kappa T} \int_0^T \theta_t e^{\kappa t} dt + \xi e^{-\kappa T} \int_0^T e^{\kappa t} dz_2$$

Hence:

$$L_t^2 = \exp(2X_T) = \exp\left[2e^{-\kappa T} X_0 + 2\kappa e^{-\kappa T} \int_0^T \theta_t e^{\kappa t} dt + 2\xi e^{-\kappa T} \int_0^T e^{\kappa t} dz_2 \right]$$

Setting $L_0 = 1$, $X_0 = 0$:

$$E\left(L_t^2\right) = \exp\left(2\kappa e^{-\kappa T} \int_0^T \theta_t e^{\kappa t} dt \right) \cdot E\left[\exp\left(2\xi e^{-\kappa T} \int_0^T e^{\kappa t} dz_2 \right) \right]$$

$$= \exp\left(2\kappa e^{-\kappa T} \int_0^T \theta_t e^{\kappa t} dt \right) \exp\left(2\xi^2 e^{-2\kappa T} \int_0^T e^{2\kappa t} dt \right)$$

$$= \exp\left[2\kappa e^{-\kappa T} \int_0^T \theta_t e^{\kappa t} dt + \frac{\xi^2}{\kappa}\left(1 - e^{-2\kappa T}\right) \right]$$

If we set the unconditional expectation of L_t^2 to 1, i.e. $E\left(L_t^2\right) = 1$, then:

$$\int_0^T \theta_t e^{\kappa t} dt = -\frac{\xi^2}{2\kappa^2}\left(e^{\kappa T} - e^{-\kappa T}\right)$$

differentiating the above wrt T:

$$\theta_T = -\frac{\xi^2}{2\kappa}\left(1 + e^{-2\kappa T}\right)$$

Note that by imposing $E\left(L_t^2\right) = 1$, $\sigma^2(S_t, t)$ is effectively interpreted as the average local variance. The step 1 calibration can therefore be reduced to the calibration of (κ, ξ) if practitioners choose to. These parameters are either benchmarked to certain observable exotics (e.g. barriers, cliquets, etc.) or specified by the practitioners for example using historic time series statistics. The benchmarking for the correlation ρ can follow the same historic analysis. Since correlation ρ mainly controls the skew and vol of vol ξ mainly affects the smile, their distinctive roles are quite separate and their benchmarked/fitted values tend to be stable in practice.

It is very important to note that even if these parameters are benchmarked or specified, they are not calibrated in the context of hedging. Markets do evolve and these parameters do shift in practice, and they surely can produce better risk sensitivities for hedging because of the more sensible forward volatility and smile/skew dynamics (e.g. persistent smile/skew). However, it does not mean the positions exposed to the forward dynamics are completely hedged, because at present, there are no realistically tradable instruments to hedge forward volatility or forward smile/skew, never mind hedging correlation. So the benchmarked or specified parameters (κ, ξ) and ρ represent the best possible educated estimates as far as hedging volatility forward dynamics is concerned.

Step 2 calibration: For $\sigma(S_t, t)$, the key is to utilize the Markovian projection property in the SLV formulation:

$$\sigma_{LV}^2\left(S_t, t\right) = \sigma^2\left(S_t, t\right) \cdot E\left[L_t^2 \mid S = S_t\right]$$

where $\sigma_{LV}(S_t, t)$ is the Dupire local volatility calculated directly from the implied volatility surface. Therefore in order to obtain $\sigma(S_t, t)$, we need to find the conditional expectation of L_t^2 which is defined as:

$$E\left[L_t^2 \mid S = S_t\right] = \frac{\displaystyle\int_0^\infty L_t^2 \cdot p\left(S_t, L_t, t\right) dL_t}{\displaystyle\int_0^\infty p\left(S_t, L_t, t\right) dL_t}$$

Setting $x = lnS_t$ and $y = lnL_t$ the above can be rewritten as:

$$E\left[L_t^2 \mid x = x_t\right] = \frac{\displaystyle\int_0^\infty e^{2y} \cdot p\left(x_t, y, t\right) dy}{\displaystyle\int_0^\infty p\left(x_t, y, t\right) dy}$$

So knowing the transition probability density $p(x,y,t)$ the conditional expectation of L_t^2 can be numerically calculated. As derived earlier, $p(x,y,t)$ satisfies the Kolmogorov forward equation, which is a 2-dimensional PDE in this particular example. Solving a 2-dimensional PDE is a rather standard numerical process where typically the alternating direction implicit (ADI) scheme is used for discretization. Note that in this specific Kolmogorov PDE, there are two unknowns: $\sigma(x, t)$ and $p(x,y,t)$. One cannot solve for them simultaneously, but can solve the PDE iteratively. With the initial boundary condition $x_0 = \ln(S_0)$ and $y_0 = \ln(1) = 0$, Table 7.3 illustrates the time steps and how the corresponding solutions of the two unknowns are obtained iteratively:

Once the model parameters $\left(\kappa, \theta_t, \xi\right)$, ρ and $\sigma(S_t, t)$ are calibrated, either PDE or Monte Carlo can be used to price appropriate derivative instruments. Note that in the SLV formulation, the volatility mapping term $\sigma(S_t, t)$ already contains the spot dependence. Hence in practice, sometimes one assumes the explicit correlation ρ between dz_1 and dz_2 (spot and volatility) is zero, to substantially simplify the numerical implementation. This may make sense in some asset classes (e.g. certain FX currency pairs) where the spot and volatility correlation assumption is not economically apparent. In other asset classes (e.g. equity), the spot and volatility correlation is economically apparent and observable. It is therefore essential to include the explicit correlation between spot and volatility in the SLV formulation and implementation.

TABLE 7.3 Iterative solutions

Time Step	Calculating $\sigma(x,t)$	Solving PDE for $p(x,y,t)$
$t = 0$	Applying boundary conditions, one obtains: $\sigma(x,0) = \sigma_{LV}(x,0)$;	Knowing $\sigma(x,0)$, solve PDE for $p(x,y,\Delta t)$ at the time step Δt;
$t = \Delta t$	Knowing $p(x,y,\Delta t)$: calculate $E\left[L_t^2 \mid x = x_t\right]$ at Δt; calculate $\sigma^2\left(x_t,\Delta t\right) = \dfrac{\sigma_{LV}^2\left(x_t,\Delta t\right)}{E\left[L_t^2 \mid x = x_t\right]}$;	Knowing $\sigma(x,\Delta t)$, solve PDE for $p(x,y,2\Delta t)$ at the time step $2\Delta t$;
$t = 2\Delta t$	Knowing $p(x,y,2\Delta t)$: calculate $E\left[L_t^2 \mid x = x_t\right]$ at $2\Delta t$; calculate $\sigma^2\left(x_t,2\Delta t\right) = \dfrac{\sigma_{LV}^2\left(x_t,2\Delta t\right)}{E\left[L_t^2 \mid x = x_t\right]}$;	Knowing $\sigma(x,2\Delta t)$, solve PDE for $p(x,y,3\Delta t)$ at the time step $3\Delta t$;
...	and so on	and so on

Alternative Calibration Technique

The above "traditional" calibration technique of solving forward PDE is fast and accurate in most of the practical applications where L_t is driven by one stochastic factor. The localized model parameters $\sigma(S_t,t)$ can then be obtained in one-sweep through the low-dimension (2-D) forward PDE. There is, however, another approximate calibration technique (Henry-Labordere 2009) that is particularly suited if L_t is driven by multi-factor and solving higher dimensional PDEs is numerically difficult and computationally expensive. With this approximate technique, one can solve for $\sigma(S_t,t)$ using Monte Carlo simulation during the calibration process, which makes the implementation easier and more straightforward. In the following, we shall explain how the approximate technique works using the same SLV example above.

Let us recall a key component, Markovian projection, in the SLV model that links Dupire local volatility $\sigma_{LV}(S,t)$ with the local and stochastic parameters:

$$\sigma_{LV}^2(S,t) = \sigma^2(S,t)E\left[L_t^2 \mid S_t = S\right]$$

The Markovian projection can also be used to define an term called "effective local volatility" that is only associated with the pure stochastic volatility model. Basically, if one sets $\sigma(S,t) \equiv 1$, the SLV model degenerates to a pure stochastic volatility (SV) model. The "effective local volatility" associated with the SV is then given by:

$$\sigma_{ELV}^{SV}(X,t)^2 = E\left[L_t^2 \mid X_t = X\right]$$

where X is the stochastic process of pure SV, defined as:

$$\frac{dX_t}{X_t} = \mu dt + L_t dz_1$$

Via Markovian projection, Dupire local volatility is linked to SLV model, and "effective local volatility" is linked to SV model. The relationship between the two setups is given by the following:

$$\frac{\sigma_{LV}(S,t)^2}{\sigma_{ELV}^{sv}(X,t)^2} = \sigma^2(S,t)\frac{E\left[L_t^2 \mid S_t = S\right]}{E\left[L_t^2 \mid X_t = X\right]}$$

As shown by Henry-Labordere (2009), if the assumption of a smooth monotone mapping between S and X holds and denoting $X = H_t(S)$, the above relationship can be rewritten as:

$$\sigma_{LV}(S,t) = \sigma(S,t) \cdot \sigma_{ELV}^{sv}\left[H_t(S),t\right]$$

This is an important equation in the context of calibrating $\sigma(S,t)$. The Dupire local volatility is already known. To back out $\sigma(S,t)$, all one needs to do is to simulate the pure SV process to obtain the "effective local volatility" for SV. As shown in the quoted literatures, the Monte Carlo simulation for pure SV process is numerically effective with good convergence. Although finding the mapping function $H_t(S)$ between S and X requires some work and approximation, the overall convergence is rather good. Note that this calibration approach does not need to involve numerical optimization routines.

Once the SLV model is calibrated, one can of course use either PDE or Monte Carlo to price various derivative instruments. The implementation of the SLV model in practice is non-trivial. In fact it is vital to adopt an appropriate numerical scheme balancing the smile/skew dynamics and computational efficiency. One also needs to pay attention to the overall consistency between the calibration and subsequent pricing with PDE or Monte Carlo. To this end, Andreasen and Huge (2011) proposed a scheme in which the calibration, finite difference solution and Monte Carlo simulation can all be based on the same discretization, to ensure the same model prices.

In practice, a consistent model such as SLV may be used to value and run a large portfolio of trades. Hence the calibration view may be global, i.e. not specific to certain products such as barrier or cliquet. In such cases, all the stochastic volatility parameters can be used to fit the market implied volatility surface as much as possible in the step 1 calibration. The remaining calibration errors will be corrected by the step 2 calibration, in which the localized model parameters $\sigma(S_t,t)$ serves to fine tune the iteration process.

SLV NUMERICAL RESULTS

The dynamic features in the SLV models enable them to handle the derivative products that are sensitive to the term volatility and smile/skew, and/or to the forward volatility and smile/skew! In the following, we shall analyse a few such products by comparing the prices of SLV to those of LV, to see how the forward dynamics affecting the pricing. In fact, the features shown below form a fundamental part of the model testing during the SLV model implementation.

The examples that follow use the volatility surfaces of major equity indices. Equity historical implied volatilities exhibit strong mean reversion. The historical vol of vol parameters are quite variable on a short timescale but more stable over longer periods (e.g. 1 year or more), and they are in the order of 120%. Equity spot and volatility is strongly correlated and in the order of –70%. The characters described are used in the results of the examples that follow in the context of stochastic volatility parameters calibration.

Implied Forward Volatility Smile/Skew

As discussed earlier, a feature of the LV model is that it exhibits a rapid decay of the implied forward smile/skew. Figure 7.1 illustrates such an example in which the 1-year into 1-year forward implied volatility against different strikes are plotted. LV skew is clearly flattening compared to today's spot skew (1-year skew). The calibrated SLV skew is much closer to the spot skew, in line with the market expectation.

Figure 7.2 plots the LV forward skews calculated from an equity implied volatility surface where the volatility skew is pronounced. The implied forward ATM skew using the LV model is plotted at various forward points in time, labelled by the horizontal axis in years. At time $t = 0$ the skew is simply the spot skew. The vertical axis is the value of skew calculated by local tangential in strike $\frac{\partial \sigma}{\partial K}\Big|_{K=1}$.

For all the option maturities (1 month, 6 months and 12 months), the corresponding implied forward skew is significantly lower than spot skew, and declining rapidly as we move forward in time. The equivalent results from the SLV model after calibrating to the relevant historical time series ($\xi = 122\%$, $\rho = -85\%$) are shown in Figure 7.3.

As can be seen in the figure, SLV clearly exhibits the feature of persistent skew, whereby the implied forward skew for a given maturity remains at a similar level to spot ($t = 0$) skew of the same maturity. This is what practitioners have been observing in the real world, and it makes the SLV model a superior candidate for pricing forward start options.

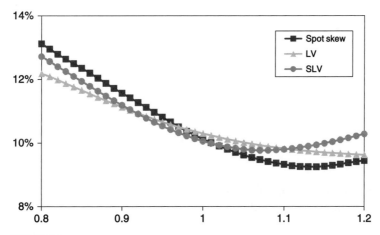

FIGURE 7.1 Forward skew calibration

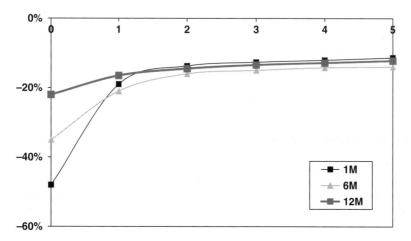

FIGURE 7.2 LV – ATM forward skew

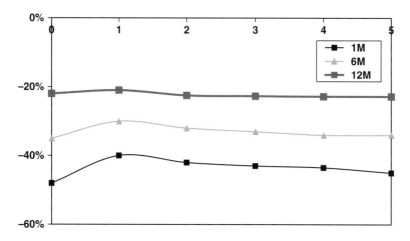

FIGURE 7.3 SLV – ATM forward skew

Digital Option

Digital option is very sensitive to the term volatility smile/skew-sensitive. Taking a digital put as an example, its payoff is defined as:

$$DP_T(K) = D \cdot \int_{-\infty}^{K} p_T(S)\,dS$$

where D is the discount factor and K is the strike. Recall that the PDF has the following relationships with the call spread options in its limit:

$$\frac{\partial C}{\partial K} = -\int_K^\infty p_T(S)\,dS$$

$$1 + \frac{\partial C}{\partial K} = 1 - \int_K^\infty p_T(S)\,dS = \int_{-\infty}^K p_T(S)\,dS$$

So the digital put can be calculated using the spread option $(\partial C / \partial K)$:

$$DP_T(K) = D \cdot \left(1 + \frac{\partial C}{\partial K}\right) = D \cdot \left(1 + \frac{C(K + \Delta K, \sigma_{K+\Delta K}) - C(K, \sigma_K)}{\Delta K}\right)$$

Figure 7.4 compares the digital put prices against the strike using three different approaches, setting $D = 1$ for simplicity. The first is the call spread defined above, and using relevant implied volatility points to capture smile/skew. The second is SLV model pricing digital payoff directly, i.e. not using spread options. The third is Black–Scholes digital simply using the implied volatility at K to calculate the normal cumulative probability. The horizontal axis labels strike K as the distance away from ATM. As can be seen in the graph, SLV is very close to the call spread approach and both have clearly captured the term volatility smile/skew features embedded in the digital options.

As for the BS digital, because it only uses a single implied volatility point in the calculation of CDF, it does not capture the smile/skew information. The price differences are bigger around the ATM region due to the fact that this is a region of more pronounced smile/skew. In fact, for the ATM digital the price difference between SLV and BS can be explained by ATM skew times the BS Vega. So the conclusion here is simple: in the presence of volatility smile/skew, don't use BS to value digital or CDF. Always use spread options or SLV directly for digital options and/or CDF calculations!

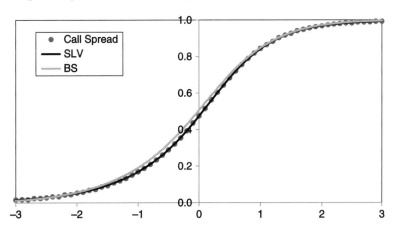

FIGURE 7.4 Digital PV

Barrier Option

Barrier hitting probability in the presence of volatility smile/skew is a complex function of time, spot, drift and barrier level. There is no easy and direct intuition to compare the general barrier case using different models. Figure 7.5 plots the 3-month double-no-touch (DNT) barrier prices against the (equal) distance of two barriers from the spot. The barrier and spot distances are in the unit of standard deviation using ATM volatility at expiry. In this particular example, SLV prices are significantly higher than those of LV when the barriers are close to the spot, and slightly higher when the barriers are far away from the spot. This indicates that SLV has much lower barrier hitting probabilities when the barriers are close. It is important to emphasize that this example cannot be easily generalized to other barrier option cases. The only sure way is to have a proper smile/skew model.

With regard to the BS prices in the above graph, which are calculated using the DNT analytical solution with the ATM volatility, they are much lower than those of SLV when the barriers are close to the spot, and significantly higher when the barriers are far away. This is once again showing the complex relationships between barrier hitting probabilities and volatility smile/skew.

The barrier hitting probability differences mainly come from different smile/skew features in different models. The persistent forward smile/skew in the SLV model versus the flattening smile/skew in the LV model, and versus no smile/skew at all in the BS model, all contribute to the observed DNT price differences. Additionally, for general barrier options pricing, the persistent forward skew also affects the payoff after the barriers are hit. For example, an undiscounted down-and-in digital put (D_T) can be expressed as:

$$D_T = \int_0^T D_t \cdot p_t dt$$

where $p_t dt$ is the probability that the barrier is first hit at time t, D_t is the probability that $S_T < B$ conditional on $S_t = B$, where S_t is the spot, and B is the barrier. Note that D_t is the ATM digital put at time t maturing at time T, conditional on the barrier being hit. As we see earlier, digital options are strongly dependent on the smile/skew at the

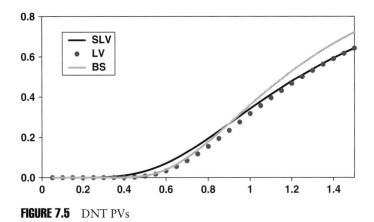

FIGURE 7.5 DNT PVs

time of pricing. So in this example, both barrier hitting probabilities and forward digital pricing are affected by the forward smile/skew in a very convoluted way. This is typical with strong path-dependent options.

Cliquet Option

A standard cliquet option consists of a sequence of forward start options, each may has its own (local) cap and floor. The final payoff is the sum of the forward start options, subject to a global floor. Structured bonds with cliquet payoffs are also known as cannon bonds, due to its cascading and bounded shape. Mathematically, the standard cliquet payoff is expressed as:

$$Cliquet = \max\left\{ \sum_i \min\left[\max\left(\frac{S_i}{S_{i-1}} - 1, LocalFloor \right), LocalCap \right], GlobalFloor \right\}$$

Although the global floor makes the pricing model more complex, it actually trims off some risky optionality and serves to limit the product risks.

As an example, for a 5-year cliquet with 6 month reset period, $GloalFloor = 0\%$, $LocalFloor = -5\%$ and $LocalCap = 5\%$, there will be 10 reset periods, and 9 of them involving forward start options. In all 10 reset periods the local payoffs are capped at 5% and floored at –5%. The sum of 10 local payoffs, including negative values if they turn out to be, is the final payoff subject to the global floor at 0. Clearly this cliquet is exposed to the 6-month forward volatility and forward skew.

With cliquet options, one needs to pay particular attention to the fact that discontinuities in Greeks may occur in transition from one period to the next. Figure 7.6 illustrates this cliquet feature by comparing the spot ladder profiles for one day **before** (labelled **T-1**) and one day **after** (labelled **T+1**) the period boundary. In Figure 7.6, the spot ladder profile changes dramatically across the period boundary, indicating jumps in delta and gamma.

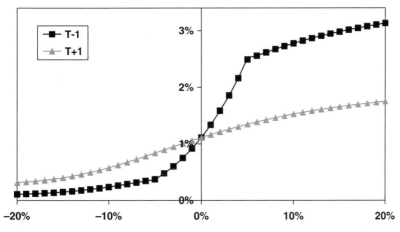

FIGURE 7.6 Price vs spot

How to price a cliquet has long been a subject of discussion and debate. The truth of matter is that there is no good hedge to the forward skew. Of course, cliquet products (e.g. cannon bonds) were manufactured and distributed well before any SLV or SV models were invented. So market practitioners have in the past used various techniques in which the forward volatility and skew for each reset period is specified. Typically this is done by extracting the short end skew from the implied volatility surface and imposing it periodically as the forward (persistent) skew. Although this approach is adequate for pricing standard cliquet, it may misprice other cliquet (e.g. reverse cliquet) when higher order Vega (volgamma and vanna) risks exist. Besides, its lack of internal (skew) consistency makes it difficult to mix the risk sensitivities, in particular the skew sensitivities with those of other derivative products at the portfolio level. The skew sensitivities of cliquets can be artificially too concentrated at certain time buckets, for example at the short end.

In the following, we shall illustrate how forward skew impacts the pricing of a 5-year cliquet with annual reset. The implied volatility surface used has a pronounced skew, but with flat term structure. There are no local floors in the example in order to highlight the skew effects. Figure 7.7 shows the price versus the local cap without a global floor for both SLV and LV model.

Starting with the local cap equal to 0%, which is effectively a forward ATM put, the models have similar prices given that the volatility term structure is quite flat and both are calibrated to the implied volatility surface. As the local cap level increases, the price difference between the SLV and LV increases, as the strike of the put moves away from ATM and forward skew starts to impact the price. In the LV the forward skew flattens at the longer end, while in the SLV, the forward skew has persistent features. This gives rise to a more expensive SLV price in this particular cap structure example. Note that in practice, both forward ATM volatility and skew impact the pricing. For the longer-end cliquet reset periods, the forward ATM volatilities from the models can vary significantly depending volatility term structure and how the SLV is calibrated. The pricing intuition is therefore complex when comparing the SLV to the LV model.

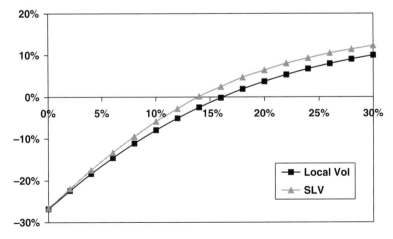

FIGURE 7.7   Price vs local cap (No Local and Global Floor)

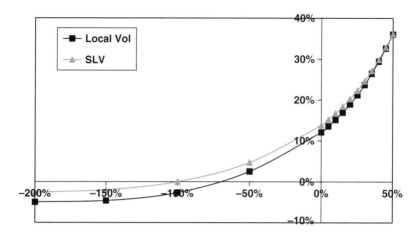

FIGURE 7.8 Price vs global floor

Let's now examine how the global floor can affect the cliquet pricing. Using the same example, and fixing the local cap at 12%, Figure 7.8 plots the price versus global floor. When the global floor is raised, the model differences become smaller, as a globally floored cliquet to some extent resembles a spread and a higher floor level can eliminate contributions from certain skewed down paths. Ironically, although the existence of the global floor makes the cliquet pricing much more complex than a strip of forward start options, it actually reduces the model price differences and associated model risks. In most of the practical cases where the global floor is typically set at zero, the model differences are still sizeable though, comparable to bid-offer spread during cliquet's heydays.

SLV IN PRACTICE

Comparing the SLV model to the LV model, SLV contains the forward volatility and smile/skew dynamics that LV lacks. Comparing the SLV to the SV, SLV's calibration to the vanilla option markets is far better. The SLV model takes the best from both worlds, the superior calibration feature of LV and forward dynamics of SV. In essence, the SLV model is a mixture of the LV and SV model. Due to these desirable features, the SLV model has become a very popular model widely used in pricing equity and FX derivative products. To use the SLV model to run derivatives positions, it is important for the practitioners to understand how the relevant historical implied volatilities have been behaving. The historical analyses of the stochastic volatility parameters are vital, even if they may be calibrated to certain exotic instruments. The stochastic volatility parameters in the SLV and the generated implied forward skews should be broadly consistent with historical statistics! It is possible in practice to use parameters that yield stronger skews that might be considered conservative, analogous to the fact that implied volatilities are usually higher than their historical counterparts.

Although the SLV model can generate more sensible and stable risk sensitivities for hedging, it does not necessarily mean the relevant derivatives positions are completely hedged. This is because the stochastic volatility parameters in the SLV model are benchmarked or specified, they are not strictly calibrated to the tradable instruments. One can run and hedge the relevant derivatives positions with those benchmarked stochastic volatility parameters and hope they are stable over time. If markets have evolved substantially and a regime change has happened, the parameters can shift substantially. This can result in un-desirable P&L jumps and hedging rebalancing. Yes, the SLV model can produce realistic risk sensitivities for hedging because of its more realistic forward volatility and smile/skew dynamics, but practitioners still need to guard against the prospect of mis-hedging risks in the real world. As a general rule of thumb, for exotic models with model parameters, even if they are "calibrated", it does not mean the relevant derivatives positions can be completely hedged. Ultimately, the real and complete hedge is the hedge to the tradable instruments. As far as hedging forward volatility and forward smile/skew is concerned, the SLV model offers a much better chance in practice, but not without possible gaps.

The SLV model can also be formulated and implemented as the discrete version. The computational speed and efficiency of the SLV continuous version is quite adequate in many practical applications. Although one needs to solve for 2-factor spot and local volatility processes, the advanced numerical techniques do exist, making the computations very efficient. However, in certain derivative business areas (e.g. FX options) a desk may have to manage large numbers (many thousands) of smile/skew-sensitive exotic trades. Practitioners hence seek to further reduce the number of dimensionalities in order to achieve a computational speed that is a magnitude faster. For example, one can reduce the 2-factor SLV implementation to effectively a 1-factor numerical implementation by using the discrete version with finite volatility states and assuming no spot and volatility correlation. Although the discrete version may lose some degree of dynamics or accuracy, its analytical tractability and superior computational efficiency can tick the balance towards speed, allowing much more efficient daily valuation of P&Ls and risk sensitivities.

In the discrete version, the stochastic volatility factor L_t is not continuously distributed, but only has a finite number of states. For example, one can assume there are only three pre-determined volatility states: low, medium and high. This particular discretization scheme is similar in spirit to the trinomial tree approach in the volatility space. By assigning transition probabilities (a 3×3 matrix) between the volatility states from time t to time $t + \Delta t$, also assuming the correlation between spot and L_t is zero, the 2-factor PDE in the SLV model can be reduced to three sets of 1-D PDEs. The transition probability matrix can be made time-dependent, which makes flexible calibration. Solving a 1-D PDE is a magnitude more efficient than solving a 2-D PDE, and this makes the discrete version attractive in certain applications. The discrete version can also be viewed as a volatility uncertainty model which has been studied by some practitioners in the past.

CHAPTER **8**

Equity-Linked Structured Products

In this chapter, key equity-linked structured product categories will be analysed in the context of shared common fundamental features. For some popular products, their specific product features, investment rationales and risk characteristics will be discussed. A systematic understanding of the risk profiles of major equity-linked structured products can facilitate practitioners and investors to assess the risk/rewards balance and manage market exposures appropriately.

GENERAL PAYOFF CATEGORY

Structured products have long been regarded as complex products, due to the fact they can be based on different underlyings, and there are vast variety of "fancy" payoff variations, often labelled by jargons. For example, there are products with jargons like Altiplano, Beethoven, Everest, Phoenix, Gladiator, Snowball, Snowblade, Airbag, Turbo, and so on. In reality, however, most of structured products can be simplified into certain categories sharing certain common fundamentals. The fundamental categorization will be analysed below from market risk perspective. The credit aspect manifested in the funding cost will also be briefly discussed.

Fundamental Categorization

Let us first of all take a look at a standard risk-free saving account. As shown in Figure 8.1, at the outset (time 0), the initial capital of 100 is deposited into a risk-free saving account.

At the end of the deposit term (time T), the total return is the full capital (100) plus interest. If we discount both parts back to time 0, the initial capital clearly consists

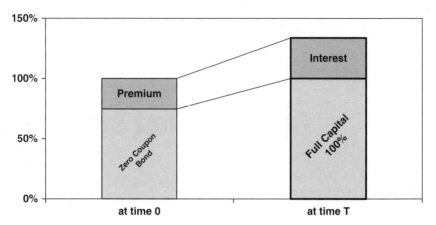

FIGURE 8.1   Risk-free saving A/C

of a zero coupon bond plus a portion labelled premium. This simple graph is actually fundamental to the structured products pricing:

- If one wants full capital protection (in capital-protection products), then one will only use the premium part to buy derivative payoffs in order to participate in the underlying market performance. The zero coupon bond part will not be touched in any way, and this provides full capital protection at maturity.
- If one wants more exposures than the premium can buy, then one needs to take risks on the capital (in capital-at-risk products). The zero coupon bond part will then be exposed to the markets one way or another.
- The premium part is clearly a function of interest rate (and funding rate of the issuer). The higher the prevailing rates are, the larger the premium part is, which naturally leads to a wider range of derivative payoffs one can buy using the premium.
- No matter what the structured derivative products are, and how they are structured, their fair value (sum of all components) at time 0 should be the same as a simple saving account. It is a zero sum game!

Let us illustrate the key categories of structured products: capital-protected growth product, capital at risk growth product and capital at risk income product.

In Figure 8.2, a typical capital-protected growth product is illustrated. The zero coupon bond at the outset will grow to full capital (100%) at maturity, labelled with a solid line box, representing certainty. The premium is used to purchase a call option. The market performance box at time T, in dotted-line representing uncertainty, is the terminal return dependent on the underlying market performance, floor at zero. It is clear that in a low rate environment, due to the fact that premium part is small, offering full capital protection products is challenging as the pricing may not work in customers' favour.

If an investor wants more growth prospect than the limit premium can purchase, then he/she must be prepared to exposure some or all of the capital, i.e. put capital at risk. There are a variety of ways of doing that, and the easiest way is to sell a put as shown in the red part of Figure 8.3. The red part is effectively used to enhance the

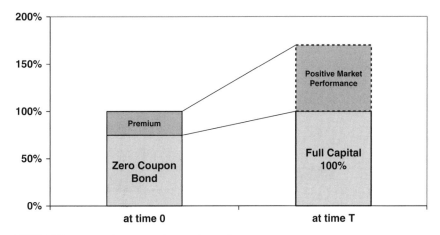

FIGURE 8.2 Capital-protected growth product

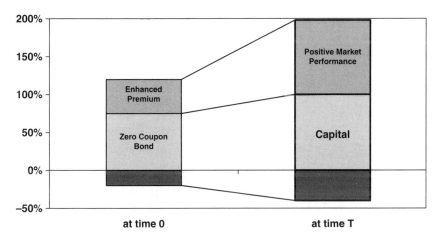

FIGURE 8.3 Capital-at-risk growth product

premium part, and the enhanced premium is used to gear up the upside. As labelled in the graph below, all terminal payoff boxes at time T are dotted lines and they are all uncertain. Given this is a zero sum game, the enhanced upside is accompanied by the fact that the capital is at risk.

Another typical way of using the enhanced premium is to gain above-market fixed income. As shown in Figure 8.4, this type of income products allow investors to obtain fixed higher yield. The yield enhancement is of course at the expense of capital at risk, as governed by the zero sum game rule.

In a nutshell, the pricing of structured products, no matter how simple or complex they are, is governed by the zero sum game rule. The two core components, zero coupon bond and premium, can be modified by using additional components, effectively tailoring the risk profiles or appetite, but the total sum at time 0 must remain the same if the products are priced at fair value.

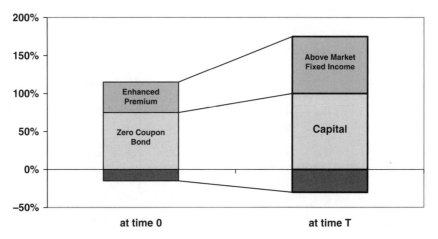

FIGURE 8.4   Capital-at-risk income product

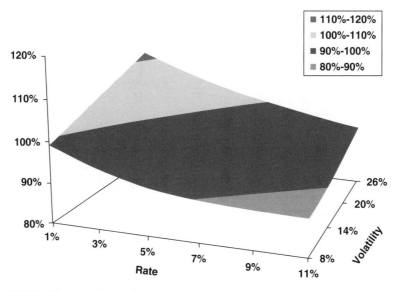

FIGURE 8.5   Growth product price

Growth/Income Products "Eisenhower Matrix"

Eisenhower matrix is an extremely simple tool for time management. By asking two simple questions, "Is it urgent?" and "Is it important?", one can categorize tasks into four quadrants. Using the same simple principle, one can ask two simple questions to judge whether the general market conditions are suitable for capital-secure growth products or capital-at-risk income products. These two questions are "What is the current interest rate?" and "What is the current volatility?" These two questions are related to the macroeconomic environment.

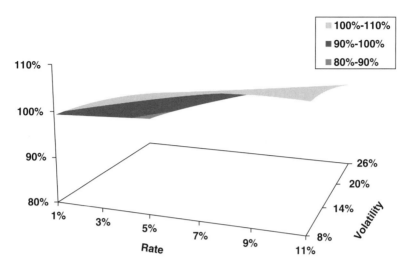

FIGURE 8.6 Income product price

In Figure 8.5, the capital secure growth product note prices versus interest rate and volatility are shown. Given it consists of a zero coupon bond and a call option, high interest rate and low volatility make the price more attractive, as labelled pale grey where the prices are less than 100%. Low interest rate and high volatility hike the note prices, and such products won't work anymore when the prices are higher than 100%, as labelled dark grey and black in the figure. Issuers need to choose low volatility underlyings for the capital secure growth products in the low interest rate environment. An example of low volatility underlying is the S&P 500 Low Volatility Enhanced Index.

For a standard capital-at-risk income product, the note prices versus interest rate and volatility are shown in Figure 8.6. As it consists of an enhanced fixed-rate bond and a short put position, the low interest rate and high volatility make price more attractive, as labelled pale grey in the figure. In the high interest and low volatility part that labelled dark grey, the prices are prohibitively expensive.

The growth/income products linkage to the macroeconomic environment is shown in the matrix diagram in Figure 8.7. Similar to Eisenhower matrix, it consists of 4 quadrants. Two of them have clear tendency. A high interest rate and low volatility economic environment make the capital protection growth product more feasible price-wise. In contrast, in low interest and high volatility economic environment it is challenging to provide capital protection. In such a situation, the market will shift towards capital-at-risk income products. The macroeconomic environment is one of the important driving factors in the product offerings.

In the low interest rate and low volatility region, most product types become difficult as prices are all near the borderline of par. This is actually the least favourable region in terms of product offerings. The high interest rate and high volatility region, on the other hand, offers a great deal of product opportunities. One tends to see many varieties of mixed products meeting investors' risk appetites at the right price level. In all cases, the zero sum rule holds for all products offered at fair values.

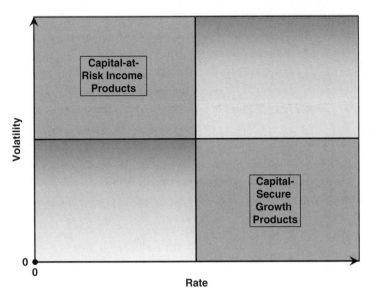

FIGURE 8.7　Product vs macroeconomic matrix

Credit and Funding Spread Effects

In addition to product (market) risks outlined above, investors are increasingly aware of the credit risk of the issuers. Investors' counterparty risks do have prices and they can make a difference in sales. In general, the issuers' credit risks can be priced into the zero coupon bond part by adding, for example, their funding spreads. Clearly including larger funding spreads into discounting will make the structured products cheaper. Theoretically a less creditworthy issuer will have to offer investors better terms for like-for-like products. Ironically, the less creditworthy issuers who have larger funding spreads can be perceived as offering more attractive products if investors only pay attention to the products' headline features without due attention to the credit risks. This interesting phenomenon can affect banks' business decisions. For example, during the credit crisis when the credit quality of the issuers diverge, those with poorer credit quality may opt for issuing more structured products (debts), and those with good credit quality may opt for being OTC hedging providers.

Structured notes are typically issued as senior unsecured debt obligation, as far as credit risk is concerned. Sometimes an issuer can also put forward collaterals (such as bonds) representing credit risks of other institutions that have better credit. Effectively investors' counterparty risks are transferred from the issuer to those institutions related to the collateral bonds. This methodology can also be useful for a less well-known issuer, who can transfer the effective counterparty risks to institutions that are better known to the local investors. It can potentially enhance sales for less known or less creditworthy issuers.

FEATURES OF IMPORTANT STRUCTURED PRODUCT CATEGORIES

In this section we will analyse a number of typical products to understand their key features and market risk profiles. For most structured products, investors don't receive underlying dividends. One needs to bear this in mind in assessing products' overall risk/reward profiles.

Plain Vanilla

Vanilla options are the building blocks for many structured products on the market. Vanilla call, put and digital payoffs are frequently used to create various risk/return profiles, taking into account market conditions and investors' appetites. The simplest capital-protected growth product consists of a zero coupon and vanilla call option. Clearly the capital is protected, and the gearing of the call or participation of the upside is a key parameter from investors' perspective. If a capital-protected growth product has a cap on its final payoff, there is a call spread embedded in the product. The simplest income product is the older version of reverse convertible, where investors are selling vanilla put to gain the yield enhancement, but taking risks of losing capital if markets fall. There are many variations of vanilla products on the markets, created by having a combination of vanilla call and put options. Leveraged return products are created using vanillas. For example, a Buffered Return Enhanced Note (BREN) is leveraged payoff, whose upside is leveraged or accelerated, typically more than 1, e.g. 1.5. The extra leverage must come from somewhere under the zero sum rule, e.g. customer shorting put at a chosen strike. So overall the customer long call and short put, such that their upside has a leverage factor larger than 1 at the expense of putting some capital at risk. An example BREN payoff is shown in Figure 8.8. The buffer amount offers partial capital protection (central, paler part). The investor will lose capital beyond the buffer amount. In return, the investor can have an accelerated upside participation of 1.5.

Hedging and risk managing vanilla products follow relatively "standard" industry practices, although any types of digital risk still deserve attention. The technique of using a spread to represent digital is a common practice in smoothing out jumps in Greeks. Very often, Asian options in the form of Asian tails are used to reduce the

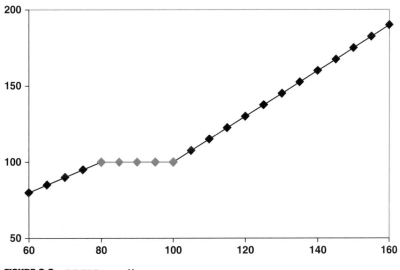

FIGURE 8.8   BREN payoff

risks in the vanilla products, as well as the more exotic types. Note that some of the leveraged products may look vanilla. If the leverage is too large (say 5 or 10 times), one is exposed to gap risks. This is obvious, as any small jumpy movement in the underlying will be magnified by the leverage multiplier. Hedging gap risks is not as straightforward as hedging vanilla options.

Barrier Reserve Convertible

A reverse convertible is a classic income product, in which investors receive enhanced coupons but take risks of losing capital. It is typically linked to equity underlyings, including a stock, an index or a basket of stocks or indices. In a low interest rate and high market volatility environment, reverse convertibles are popular as they provide much enhanced yield for the investors. Prior to the turn of the millennium (2000), reverse convertibles mostly consisted of investors shorting vanilla ATM put options. Investors would lose capital if at maturity the underlying fell below the initial level. To increase the protection for investors, barrier reverse convertibles were invented, whereby investors were instead shorting ATM down-and-in put options. The additional barrier event increased the protection for the investors, as the put option would not come into effect unless the (down) barrier was hit. The barrier protection feature triggered much increased reverse convertible issuances in UK in the early 2000s as well as in the European retail markets. By the early 2010s, the barrier reverse convertibles were also among the most popular structured products in USA.

The older vanilla version of reverse convertible contains a vanilla put, and the newer barrier version contains a down-and-in put option which gives investors more capital protection. The capital repayment at maturity is either full principal, or less if the underlying index falls conditional on the barrier are hit during the lifetime of the product. Figure 8.9 illustrates an example with a barrier set at 60. As investors sell a down-and-in put, they may lose capital once the barrier is hit as shown by the red line

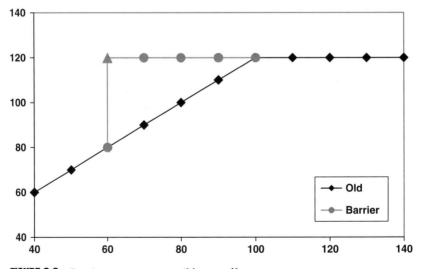

FIGURE 8.9   Barrier reverse convertible payoff

in the graph. At the barrier point, the capital protection is knocked out, and this red cliff point explains why the barrier reverse convertibles are also nicknamed "precipice bonds". It is important to assess the risks of "precipice bonds" in the right context. It is true that the cliff point can knock out a large portion of capital. However, barrier reverse convertibles are much less risky than their old counterparts. In the old version of reverse convertibles where there is no barrier, the downside risk is larger and capital is at risk at a much earlier stage, as shown in the graph. The old version is equivalent to holding underlying equity shares, while the barrier version offers additional protection, making the barrier version less risky than the underlying itself. The introduction of the barrier protection is clearly plausible despite the "precipice" feature. This is why the barrier reverse convertibles are so popular nowadays, and the old version does not really exist anymore as a product.

While the barrier protection feature was beneficial for investors, for the issuers, hedging and risk managing relatively long-dated (e.g. 3~5 years) equity barrier risks can be a challenge. The hedging parameters (Greeks) near the barrier could be unstable, and they might suddenly change which would lead to a massive increase in trading volume. In contrast to FX underlyings, equity underlyings for the reverse convertibles tend to have much less liquidity. The problems would become more severe when the products were issued to the mass retail market. To solve these practical problems in order to manage barrier risks more effectively, financial institutions (issuers) adopted various soft barrier technologies in pricing and risk managing barrier reverse convertibles. While the barrier protection feature has helped reverse convertibles to take a larger share of the structured products for retail and private investors, it is also spreading into many other products including autocallable (kickout) products. Those products, while offering their specific features, often use the barrier protection feature to provide a degree of capital protection. The barrier has become an essential part of capital protection mechanism in the ever evolving market conditions.

Autocallable (Kickout)

The autocallable products are yield enhancement products whose durations can be shortened. When the interest rates are low the autocallable products can be very popular. The market conditions that trigger the autocall (or kickout) are transparent to customers, and the payoffs are very simple for customers to understand. In general, the headline rate at kickout is higher than the fixed rate of a comparable (barrier) reverse convertible at the expense of shorter duration once kicked out.

In a basic autocallable product, there are typically a series of observation dates. At an observation date, if the underlying spot is at and above the specified level, the product will be kicked out (or autocalled) and the investor will be paid a specified enhanced return. If it is not kicked out, the product will continue to the next observation date until maturity. Table 8.1 lists a 5-year autocallable example. At the first observation date (year 1), if the spot is at or above the initial spot level (100%), the investor will be paid 10% plus full capital, and the product will be called off. Otherwise the product will continue to year 2. If the spot is at and above 100% of the initial spot level, the product will be kicked out and the investor will gain 20% plus full capital. The same observation and kickout principle applies to the rest of the observation dates until maturity.

TABLE 8.1   Autocallable coupon return example

Kickout Date	Kickout Level	Kickout Return
1	100%	10%
2	100%	20%
3	100%	30%
4	100%	40%
5	100%	50%

Note that by maturity if the product is still not kicked out, the investor will receive no coupon return at all. Typically the autocallable product contains a capital at risk feature to be able to satisfy the zero sum game rule. With an enhanced return on kickout, the investor will have to make a sacrifice somewhere else. It is possible for the investor to short a vanilla put which exposes the capital. However, the barrier protection feature identical to that in the reverse convertible can be added to lessen the possibility of capital loss. So in typical at-risk autocallable product, the kickout feature for the return and barrier feature for the capital are combined to tailor the risk/return profile. Figure 8.10 illustrates such an example, where the American barrier for the capital protection is set at 60%, and a kickout payout at year 1 is 10%, and year 2 is 20%.

An autocallable can be linked to a single underlying, or a basket of underlyings. The purpose of linking to a basket is to enhance the headline return rate. This has been typically done by using the worst performing underlying in the basket to trigger the kickout as well as barrier protection on capital. Clearly the worst performing underlying can substantially reduce the upside trigger potential as well as increase the chance of capital loss, so the kickout headline rate can look very high. For example, in a

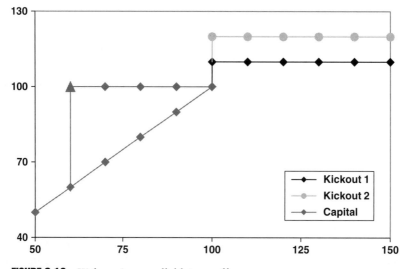

FIGURE 8.10   Kickout (auto-callable) payoff

like-for-like autocallable setup, a single underlying can have an annual kickout rate of 8%, the equivalent worst of three underlyings can have a kickout rate as high as 13%, depending on the correlation of the underlyings. Naturally, the basket version is a lot more risky than the single underlying version.

Specific Autocallable Risks In hedging and risk managing autocallable products, practitioners need to pay attention to two specific features over and above the usual derivative delta/Vega hedging. The first is the digital risks at the call dates, and the second is the interest risks associated with the callability.

In Figure 8.11, the digital feature is displayed by comparing the spot ladders of 1-day before, on and 1-day after the call date. As expected, 1-day before the call date delta and Gamma change sharply when spot is around the trigger level centred in the figure. On the call date, delta and Gamma have discontinuities. 1-day after the call date, delta and Gamma become smooth and continuous again. Standard digital pricing techniques, such as using spreads, should be adopted in pricing to generate smoother risk sensitivities across call dates.

Digital risks in an autocallable also affect its time-bucketed risk sensitivities and hedges. Figure 8.12 shows the time-bucketed Vegas when spot are at 100%, 110% and 90% of the initial fixing from issuer's perspective, with the first call date 1 year away. As expected, the issuer of the autocallable is short Vega around call dates, and long Vega around maturity.

Time-bucketed Vegas can change significantly with the spot due to digital risks. Figure 8.13 shows the time-bucketed Vegas for spot at 100%, 110% and 90% of the initial fixing, when the first call date is 2 weeks away. They are significantly different from each other, due to the fact that the probabilities of kickout at the first call date are very different in the three cases. When the kickout probability is high (S=110% case), the Vegas at the first and subsequent call dates vanish. When the kickout probability is low (S=90% case), the Vega at first call date is very small, and sizeable at subsequent call dates. This changing Vega pattern poses hedging challenges when the autocallable positions are moving across the call dates.

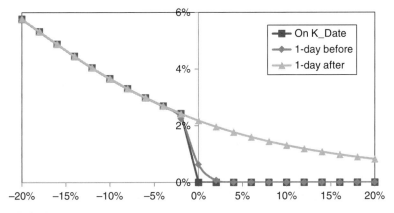

FIGURE 8.11 Price vs spot

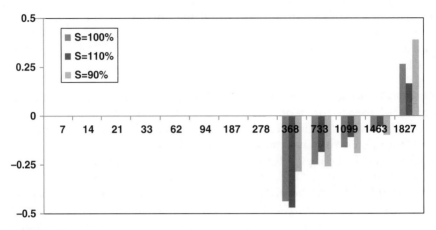

FIGURE 8.12   Bucketed Vega (1Y before 1st Call Date)
5-year autocallable, annual call, call level is 100% of the fixing. First call date is 1-year away. Horizontal axis is in days.

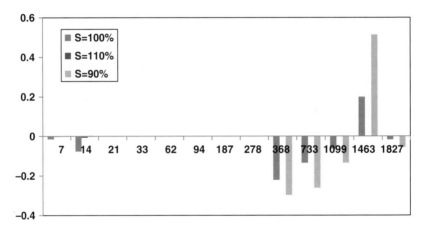

FIGURE 8.13   Bucketed Vega (2W before 1st call date)
Same autocallable with annual call, call level is 100% of the fixing. First call date is 2-weeks away. Horizontal axis is in days.

The second specific feature is the embedded autocallable interest rate risks. In the example of a 5-year autocallable product, the capital is protected at all call dates when a kickout event happens. So do you hedge the interest rate risks (on the capital) to maturity (5 years) or one of the call dates (1, 2, 3, 4 years)? If you hedge to the maturity, you'll have to unwind the hedge when a kickout event happens early. Clearly one is exposed to the rate movement in this scenario. Similarly if you hedge to a call date, you will have to roll up the hedge if no kickout event happens, hence exposing you to rate movement. So autocallable products do have a degree of hybrid risks that are a function of equity and interest rate correlation. In practice, for shorter-dated autocallable products, one can apply equity autocallable probabilities to the funding leg (i.e. the funding leg has the same autocallability as the structured coupon leg), and then manage the residual autocallable interest rate risk with an additional reserve. For long-dated autocallable products, autocallable interest rate risk feature should be modelled rigorously and priced into hedges for the stochastic interest rate.

Autocallable Variations   An interesting variation of the standard autocallable is the shorted-dated airbag autocallable products, which are popular in the USA. For example, for a 1-year airbag autocallable note, the enhanced coupon is payable monthly, and the note will be called at par if the underlying price is at or above the initial price on the quarterly call dates. At maturity, if the note is not called in the previous call dates, the notional payout depends on the underlying price at maturity. If it is at or above the pre-determined conversion price (e.g. 75% of the initial price), notional payout will be at par. Otherwise investors will receive the underlying shares equal to the notional divided by the conversion price, effectively losing capital. Because of the monthly coupons, the digital risks in this type of airbag autocallable products have nearly vanished. The interest risk is also much reduced due to the short maturity.

Another variation of standard autocallable is the Phoenix autocallable. In a Phoenix autocallable certificate:

- On the observation dates, if the underlying is at or above the call level (e.g. 100%), the product will mature early, and the capital together with a due coupon will be paid to investors.
- If the underlying is below the call level (e.g. 100%) but at or above a lower trigger level (e.g. 70%), the certificate will pay a pre-specified coupon and roll on to the next observation.
- If the underlying is below the lower trigger level (e.g. 70%), no coupon is paid and the certificate continues.
- If it reaches the maturity, and if the underlying is at or above the lower trigger level (e.g. 70%), the capital plus the last due coupon will be paid to investors. Otherwise, investors will take a 1:1 participation in the negative performance of the underlying.

A standard autocallable has the coupon memory effect, namely if it is not kicked out on an observation date, the missed coupon rolls on and is added to the next available coupon. Because a Phoenix certificate has the possibility of making coupon payments even if it is not kicked out, it does not have the coupon memory effect as otherwise it will be too expensive.

Basket

Products with a basket as an underlying are typically designed to take advantage of correlation. Depending on how the correlation is structured, it can have either an averaging effect hence lowering the underlying volatility, or amplifying effect with a magnifying underlying volatility. The averaging feature can be found in a standard basket option where the payoff is the average return of the components in the basket. The amplifying feature can be found in best-of or worst-of basket where the best or worst performing component determines the product payoffs. Basket underlying can be used in both growth and income products, and basket components can contain both indices and single stocks. In the example in Table 8.2, we shall discuss a dual-index autocallable example to analyse how the basket underlying modifies the kickout features.

Figure 8.14 shows an example pair of paths of the two indices, where the worst performing index points on the kickout dates including maturity are marked red. Those red points determine the coupon payout as well as capital return. In this particular example, investors will not get any coupon payment, and will lose some capital as the worst performing index points (red) are all below 100%. Although the basket (dual-index) seems to offer higher headline coupons, it has altered the risk profile in such a fundamental way that the product payoffs are significantly affected. We shall analyse more later about basket option in general, but for now it is important to remember that basket and correlation may not as simple as it looks from product perspective. It may have some hidden features that can substantially change the risk characteristics. Hedging and risk managing basket and correlation are always a mixture of science and art.

TABLE 8.2   Dual-index autocallable example

Underlying	Basket of 2 equity indices
Maturity	5 years
Coupons	Every year including maturity, if both indices on any of the kickout dates are at or above their initial levels, the product terminates early and capital is returned in full, plus 13% pa multiplied by the number of years elapsed.
Capital at maturity	100% if both indices are at or above 75% on the maturity date; If either index falls by more than 75% on the maturity date, capital is decreased by 1% for every 1% fall in the worst performing index.

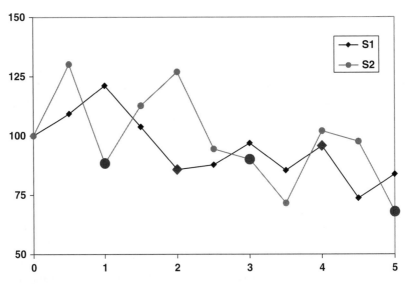

FIGURE 8.14   Dual-index kickout

There are some multi-underlying products whereby the correlation does not play a role in pricing and hedging. Such products do not really belong to the basket category, as underlyings are used individually in the pricing models. For example, the split underlying products, where an underlying is used to generate upside, and a different underlying is used to define downside risks. Such products can simply be assembled using the single underlying products, whether vanilla or exotic.

Target Volatility

Target volatility products are those whose underlying is dynamically rebalanced accordingly to certain volatility rules. Typically, a target volatility is established at a moderate level, say 10%. The underlying, which consists of risky (e.g. stocks) and riskless (e.g. cash) component is then risk controlled to achieve the target volatility. This is done by rebalancing the risky and riskless component. When the market is stable and less volatile, one participates more with bigger portion of risky asset. When market is not favourable and volatile, one reduces risky exposures and shifts to cash. The risky participation is dynamically control using the average realized volatility relative to the pre-determined target volatility as the gauge. The target volatility products are also known as the risk control products. In essence, a target volatility product has an embedded option on a dynamic participation underlying with a stable volatility. Because target volatility products can offer investors greater stability and control of the underlying risk level, a number of Risk Control Indices have been created to tailor the market's needs. For example, the S&P Europe 350 daily Risk Control (RC) index offers several target volatilities, 5%, 10% and 15%. The index utilizes the existing S&P Europe 350 methodology, plus an overlying mathematical algorithm designed to control the index's risk level by dynamically adjusting the exposure to the S&P Europe 350 based on its observed historic volatility. Using a set of historic paths, Figure 8.15 compares the returns of standard S&P Europe 350 index with its daily RC version of 5% and 10% target volatility. It is clear that 5% target volatility index has much less upside and downside than the 10% version and standard index.

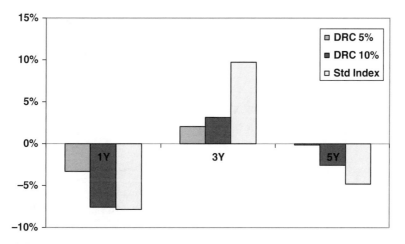

FIGURE 8.15 Annualized indices returns

Target volatility products can be based on risk control indices, as well as bespoke target volatility underlyings. Let's use a bespoke example to see how the target volatility mechanism works. An option on a target volatility underlying is effectively as an option on a "synthetic underlying". The synthetic underlying invests in the actual underlying with varying participation (risky exposure) which is a function of target and realized volatility. The daily value of the synthetic underlying V_t at time t is given by:

$$V_t = V_{t-1}\left[1 + RE_{t-1}\left(\frac{S_t - S_{t-1}}{S_{t-1}}\right)\right]$$

where S_t is the price of actual underlying, RE_{t-1} is the risky exposure, $V_0 = 100$. The risky exposure is determined by specified leverage ratio (L) and target volatility (TV), and running realized volatility (RV_{t-1}):

$$RE_{t-1} = min\left(L, \frac{TV}{RV_{t-1}}\right)$$

The running realized volatility is measured over a specified rolling window, for example 30-day realized volatility. Figure 8.16 plots the risky exposures versus the realized volatility for target volatilities of 5% and 10%, both with a leverage ratio of 120%. As the realized volatility increases, the risky exposures are reduced accordingly. Clearly lower target volatility makes sharper reductions of risky exposures.

Note that the running realized volatility does not have to be the standard annualized version in which every day is equally weighted:

$$RV_t = \sqrt{\frac{252}{n}\sum_{i=1}^{n}\ln\left(\frac{S_{t-i+1}}{S_{t-i}}\right)^2}$$

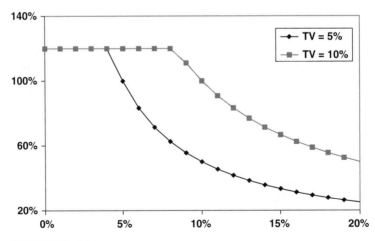

FIGURE 8.16 Risky exposure

In fact, it is better to formulate and measure it in such a way that the more recent price variations have larger weightings and impacts to the overall realized volatility. For example, the following formula can be used to measure the running realized volatility:

$$
RV_t = \sqrt{\frac{252 \cdot \sum_{i=1}^{n}\left(1-\frac{2}{n}\right)^i \cdot \ln\left(\frac{S_{t-i+1}}{S_{t-i}}\right)^2}{\sum_{i=1}^{n}\left(1-\frac{2}{n}\right)^i}}
$$

where n is the number of days in the rolling window, e.g. $n=30$. $\left(1-2/n\right)^i$ is a decay weighting curve when i increases, meaning the more recent days (smaller i) have bigger weights.

Hedging and risk managing options written on target volatility assets (synthetic underlying outlined above + cash portion) require a good understanding of their Vega behaviours. It turns out that in general, the Vega of such options is quite small when the realized volatility is high and risky exposures are dynamically adjusted. Due to the fact that the overall asset volatility is "artificially" maintained to be stable, while an increasing volatility has a positive impact on the value of the option, the decrease in risky participation offsets that impact to keep the overall Vega small. It is conceivable that some target volatility products may have a near-zero Vega in certain volatility range. On the other hand, when the realized volatility goes below the target level, the Vega should be that calculated without subject to "artificial" adjustment.

There is also volatility skew sensitivity embedded in the risky exposures. When the actual underlying S_t increases with decreasing volatility, or decreases with increasing volatility, the risky exposures will vary hence the option price carries an added skew sensitivity. In practice, dynamic rebalancing also carries a degree of gap risk. Despite the specific risks, target volatility products are overall safer products. In low interest rate environments coupled with high market volatilities, target volatility products can appear to be more attractive than the products linked to conventional equity underlyings. Price-wise, target volatility products are more likely to work, serving as cost-efficient alternatives to the conventional underlyings.

Products With Tax Liabilities

In some specific circumstances, structured products issued by life assurance companies need to price in tax liabilities at the outset, such that the investors receive the quoted products net of tax at maturity without further basic rate tax liability. The question is therefore what the gross price of the structured products is when the tax liability is included.

Zero Coupon Bond With Tax Liability   Question: For a zero coupon bond, after paying tax at maturity if the investor must have a net asset worth 100%, what is the gross price of the zero coupon bond with tax liability at time 0?

Answer: Assuming the risk-free discount factor is Z, the gross price including tax at time 0 is X and the tax rate is R, over one tax period at maturity T:

Gross (T)	Tax Payable (T)	Net (T)
$\dfrac{X}{Z}$	$\left(\dfrac{X}{Z} - X\right) \cdot R$	$\dfrac{X}{Z} - \left(\dfrac{X}{Z} - X\right) \cdot R$

Setting net equal to 100%:

$$\frac{X}{Z} - \left(\frac{X}{Z} - X\right)R = 1$$

We have:

$$X \cdot \left[\frac{1}{Z} - \left(\frac{1}{Z} - 1\right) \cdot R\right] = 1$$

If there are multiple tax dates during T, the above one tax period formulation can be generalized into:

$$X_1\left[\frac{1}{Z_1} - \left(\frac{1}{Z_1} - 1\right)R\right] = X_2$$

$$X_2\left[\frac{1}{Z_2} - \left(\frac{1}{Z_2} - 1\right)R\right] = X_3$$

$$\cdots\cdots$$

$$X_{n-1}\left[\frac{1}{Z_{n-1}} - \left(\frac{1}{Z_{n-1}} - 1\right)R\right] = X_n$$

When $X_n = 1$, i.e. the investor's final value is required at par, the above equations can be solved iteratively backwards to obtain the initial gross price X_1 which includes tax liabilities.

Growth Products With Tax Liability   A typical growth structured product consists of a zero coupon bond and a call option:

$$M_0 = g_0 \cdot Z + g_1 \cdot C(K)$$

where g_0 and g_1 are the gearings for the zero coupon bond and call option respectively. At maturity T, the payoff is:

$$M_T = g_0 + g_1 \cdot \max(S - K, 0)$$

If M_T is the required net value at maturity T, we need to solve for the gross price including tax liability.

For a single tax period, at time 0, let's assume we hold A (constant) units of M_0, plus a cash position C_0 to construct the gross structure (X_0) including tax liability:

$$X_0 = A \cdot M_0 + C_0$$

At maturity T, it becomes:

$$X_T = A \cdot M_T + \frac{C_0}{D_T}$$

Denoting R as the tax rate, at time T the following tax equation holds if the required net position is M_T:

$$X_T - (X_T - X_0)R = M_T$$

Substituting X_T into the above equation, we have:

$$\left[A \cdot (1 - R) - 1\right] \cdot M_T + \left[\frac{C_0}{D_T}(1 - R) + X_0 \cdot R\right] = 0$$

This allows two equations to be set up:

$$A \cdot (1 - R) - 1 = 0$$

$$\frac{C_0}{D_T}(1 - R) + X_0 \cdot R = 0$$

Together with $C_0 = X_0 - A \cdot M_0$, the following solutions can be obtained:

$$A = \frac{1}{1 - R}$$

$$P = \frac{X_0}{M_0} = \frac{1}{1 - R(1 - D_T)}$$

$$C_R = \frac{C_0}{M_0} = P - A$$

The gross structure price (X_0) can be calculated once the net value M_0 is known, along with the parameters A and C_0.

The above solutions are valid when the initial gross price X_0 is **not** yet fixed. Once X_0 is fixed, the parameters A and C_t can be calculated directly using:

$$A = \frac{1}{1 - R}$$

$$C_t = -\frac{X_0 \cdot R \cdot D_T}{1 - R}$$

At any time t given the net MTM M_t, the prevailing gross structure $X_t = A \cdot M_t + C_t$ can be obtained.

Let us extend the single tax period to a two tax period case. The second tax period calculations can be done in the same way as above:

$$A_2 = \frac{1}{1-R}$$

$$P_2 = \frac{X_1}{M_1} = \frac{1}{1 - R \cdot (1 - D_{T2})}$$

$$C_{R2} = \frac{C_1}{M_1} = P_2 - A_2$$

To calculate the first tax period, we can use the tax equation for this period:

$$X_{12} - \left(X_{12} - X_0 \right) \cdot R = X_1$$

This leads us to:

$$\left[A_1 \cdot (1 - R) \cdot M_1 - X_1 \right] + \left[\frac{C_0}{D_{T1}} (1 - R) + X_0 \cdot R \right] = 0$$

So the following two equations can be set up:

$$A_1 \cdot (1 - R) \cdot M_1 - X_1 = 0$$

$$\frac{C_0}{D_{T1}} (1 - R) + X_0 \cdot R = 0$$

Note that $C_0 = X_0 - A \cdot M_0$, the solutions from the above equations are given:

$$A_1 = \frac{1}{1-R} \cdot \frac{X_1}{M_1} = \frac{1}{1-R} \cdot P_2$$

$$P_1 = \frac{X_0}{M_0} = \frac{1}{1 - R \cdot (1 - D_{T1})} \cdot P_2$$

$$C_{R1} = \frac{C_0}{M_0} = P_1 - A_1$$

If for the first period X_0 is already fixed, we shall use these solutions:

$$A_1 = \frac{1}{1-R} \cdot P_2$$

$$C_t = -\frac{X_0 \cdot R \cdot D_{T1}}{1-R}$$

At any time t, given the net MTM M_t, the prevailing gross structure price $X_t = A_1 \cdot M_t + C_t$ can be obtained.

In summary, to price in tax liabilities and hedge them correctly, one needs to hold (A) units of net structures **plus** an appropriate (long or short) cash position (C). Both of these parameters are important, and they impact the price of the gross structure (X) as well as its risks.

For multiple tax periods, the parameters (A) and (P) can be calculated by backwards iteration. The cash position (C) can be derived from A and P using a simple equation.

BARRIER REVERSE CONVERTIBLES

The barrier feature was introduced into the reverse convertibles to increase the safety of investors' capital. As a result, the product providers have to manage barrier risks.

Barrier Risks In Barrier Reverse Convertibles

Barrier option books can potentially have unstable Greeks (delta, gamma) when the spot is near the barrier and/or the option near expiry. Figures 8.17 and 8.18 illustrate such an example using a DownOut Put. The option has a maturity of one month, strike of 100% and barrier of 80%. Figure 8.17 plots the option price versus spot and the large curvature near the barrier indicates a discontinuous delta and a large gamma. This is clearly seen in Figure 8.18 where the gamma swings and changes sign.

If one is long gamma, the position may be subject to severe time decay as it shorts theta. If one is short gamma, the delta hedge can be very inefficient and often costly. This is one of the main barrier risks that are very difficult to hedge.

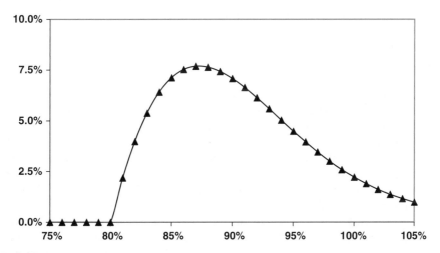

FIGURE 8.17 DownOut put price vs spot

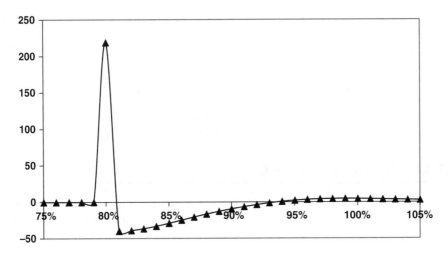

FIGURE 8.18　DownOut put gamma vs spot

Managing Barrier Risks Using Soft Barriers

The soft barrier approach serves to "soften" the barrier risks by splitting the hard contractual barrier into soft barriers. There are a number of soft barrier schemes one can use in practice. For example, in an exponential soft barrier scheme the barrier decays exponentially. Alternatively, one can simply split the contractual barrier into different levels. The barrier option can then be booked as weighted average of soft barrier options and be managed and hedged using the soft barriers. In doing so, one would ensure that the chosen soft barriers make the booking more conservative. Thus, the soft barrier approach includes some reserve for the barrier risks. Let us examine two barrier option examples, both have a maturity of 1 month, spot=100% and strike=100%. A representative set of FTSE-100 market data including a skew implied volatility surface is used in the examples.

Example 1: DownOut Put　Suppose we short a DownOut Put with a hard contractual barrier at 80%. We can split the hard barrier trade into several soft barriers, the first soft barrier is at 80% and the others ranging from 80% to 70%. The weighted average of the soft barriers forms the soft barrier booking. With soft barriers below 80%, the option is less likely to be knocked out than with the hard barrier at 80%. Hence the soft barrier price is more expensive. As we are short the position, the soft barrier booking is more conservative. Figure 8.19 illustrates the above fact for the DownOut Put. Comparing the overall price profiles, the soft barrier profiles are broadened. If the soft barrier profiles are used to hedge, once the hard barrier (at 80%) is touched, the real barrier position jumps down from the soft barrier curve to the hard barrier curve. This jump theoretically represents a hedging windfall, which is the implicit reserve in the soft barrier booking.

Figure 8.20 shows the comparison of gamma profiles of the hard and soft barrier for the DownIn Put. When the spot is near the barrier, the hard barrier gamma shows an unstable nature characterized by a large jump, while the soft barrier gamma is more stable and manageable.

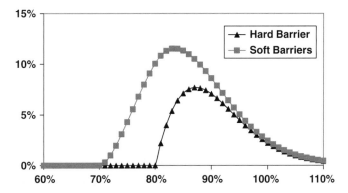

FIGURE 8.19 DownOut put price vs spot

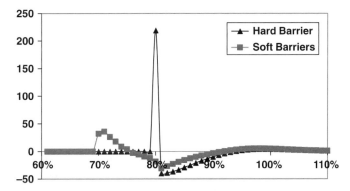

FIGURE 8.20 DownOut put gamma vs spot

Example 2: DownIn Put Suppose we long a DownIn Put with a hard contractual barrier at 80%. We could choose one soft barrier at 80% and decay the rest to 70%. The soft barrier booking is the weighted average of these soft barrier options. With the soft barriers below 80% the DownIn Put is less likely to be knocked in than with the hard barrier at 80%. Given that we long the option, the soft barrier booking is more conservative. Figure 8.21 shows the DownIn Put price versus spot for both hard and soft barriers. Comparing the overall price profiles, the soft barrier profiles are smoothed around the real barrier (at 80%) region. This represents a less sudden price change, and hence a smoother Delta, more stable gamma and reduced barrier risks. If traders follow the soft barrier profile to hedge, once the real barrier (at 80%) is hit, their position jumps up from the soft barrier curve to the real barrier curve. This jump theoretically represents a hedging windfall, which is the implicit reserve in the soft barrier booking.

Figure 8.22 compares the gamma profiles of the hard and soft barrier for the DownIn Put. As can be seen in the figure, when the spot is near the barrier, the hard barrier gamma profile has a large jump and is unstable, while the soft barrier gamma profile is much more stable and manageable.

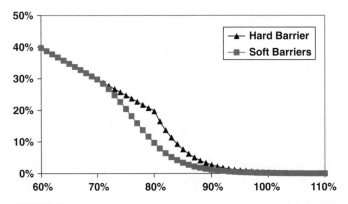

FIGURE 8.21   DownIn put price vs spot

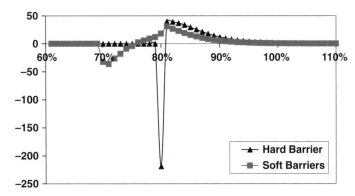

FIGURE 8.22   DownIn put gamma vs spot

Conclusion

The soft barrier methodology is an effective way to manage equity barrier option books. The methodology can be refined to ensure a very smooth gamma profile. In a soft barrier scheme, one can not only move the barrier level, but also alter the barrier duration along the time axis. All these approaches serve the same purpose of softening and reducing the barrier risks. The extra premium required for adopting the soft barrier approaches at the outset tends to be moderate for typical barrier reserve convertibles. Yet it can make the hedging so much better, and the extra premium included in the initial price is effectively the reserved hedging cost.

Soft barrier methodology only softens the impact of the barrier risks; it does not eliminate barrier risks altogether. In practice, the size of the trade, the volatility of the underlying and liquidity of the hedging instruments all contribute towards the how soft barriers are determined and how barrier risks are managed. For example, if equity index futures are used to delta hedge the barrier risks, the daily volume of traded futures shall be a factor to consider in the soft barrier scheme.

CONSTANT PROPORTION PORTFOLIO INSURANCE (CPPI)

Although CPPI is relatively new in the context of structured derivative products, its origin goes back to the late 1980s when it is used as a strategy to dynamically allocate assets over time. It is essentially a fund management (trading) strategy in which the risky investment (stock market) and "risk-free" investment (government bonds or cash) are dynamically rebalanced frequently.

Comparing to standard Option-Based Portfolio Insurance (OBPI), which buys a put to limit the downside risks, CPPI offers the same downside protection without paying upfront cost to buy the put. Extensive comparison within an appropriate stochastic setup of the two portfolio insurance techniques reveals a number of interesting hedging insights. This section, however, will focus mainly on the key features of the CPPI.

CPPI Features

A CPPI is typically referenced to a fund (either real or synthetic), e.g. a FTSE tracker. The CPPI manager guarantees the investors a minimum capital return, say 100%. Investors potentially have full participation in the reference fund appreciation, depending on the fund paths. Dividends paid out by the underlying reference fund will be credited to the investors. Hence typically CPPI is regarded as a total return structure.

In order to achieve the promised guarantee, a disciplined rebalancing scheme needs to be followed. The rebalancing scheme depends on the type of the CPPI setup. Typically, there are two types of CPPI setups:

Open Ended Investment Company (OEIC)   The OEIC CPPI has the gap condition (aka the risk factor) defined as:

$$GC = 1 - \frac{G_t}{V_t}$$

where G_t is the guaranteed fund value at time t (it can be time-varying to include lookback features), V_t is the total fund value at time t, including stocks (risky asset) and cash (riskless asset).

Fixed Maturity   The fixed maturity CPPI has the gap condition (aka the risk factor) defined as:

$$GC = \frac{V_t}{G_t} - DF_{tT} - g \cdot t$$

where DF_{tT} is the discount factor from time t to the maturity T (which can be subject to stochastic interest rate effects), g is the gap provision which is time-weighted in the GC calculation, and it provides a safety buffer in switching from stocks (risky asset) to cash (riskless asset).

Gap condition measures the distance between the prevailing fund value and discounted guarantee. Figure 8.23 shows an example fund value path and the discounted guarantee path assuming the terminal guarantee is 100%.

The gap between the fund value path and guarantee path is plotted in Figure 8.24.

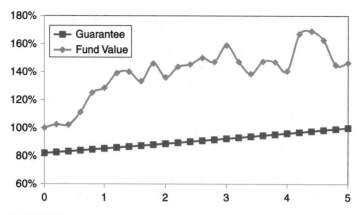

FIGURE 8.23   Fund value path vs guarantee path

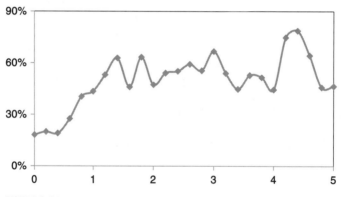

FIGURE 8.24   Gap condition path

Rebalancing Scheme   The gap condition is used to determine the rebalancing scheme. The gap condition is typically calculated daily, and compared to a pre-determined gap condition table to decide the weighting of stock market investment and cash. The gap condition table essentially determines a rebalancing strategy. An example of the gap condition table is shown in Table 8.3.

The gap condition determines the investment weighting (Target Weighting) in the stocks (risky asset). For example:

- If the gap condition is larger than or equal to 2.5%, but less than 5%, the stock investment will be 10%, and the remaining 90% will be in cash.
- If the gap condition is less than 2.5%, all stock market investment will be switched to cash thereafter and forever.
- If the gap condition is larger than or equal to 25%, the stock investment will be 100%.

A gap condition table can be interpolated either linearly (recommended for OEIC CPPI) or in step functions (recommended for fixed maturity CPPI), as illustrated in Figure 8.25.

TABLE 8.3 Gap condition table

Gap Condition	Target Weighting
2.5%	10%
5%	20%
7.5%	30%
10%	40%
12.5%	50%
15%	60%
17.5%	70%
20%	80%
22.5%	90%
25%	100%

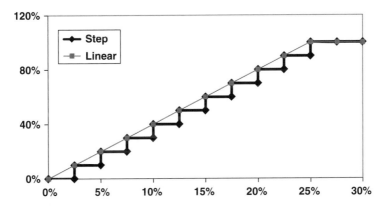

FIGURE 8.25 Risky Investment Proportion vs Gap Condition

The standard CPPI can be extended to include:

- Leverage feature: the maximum risky investment can be set at more than 100%, to allow leverage, namely borrowing cash to invest in risky asset.
- Lookback feature: its return depends on the underlying fund performance as well as the minimum or maximum value ever achieved.
- Non-linear gap condition: to tailor specific investment rebalancing schemes.

CPPI Path Dependence

In Figures 8.26 to 8.30, we use a number of illustrative scenarios to explain CPPI's path-dependency behaviours. The underlying reference is labelled as equity.

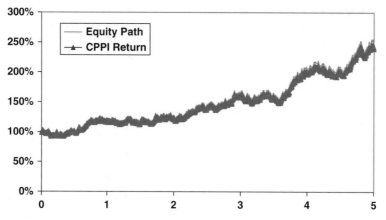

FIGURE 8.26   CPPI return vs equity path

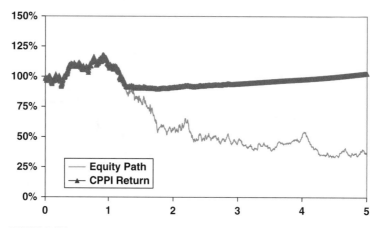

FIGURE 8.27   CPPI return vs equity path

Scenario 1 (Figure 8.26): Equity goes up almost all the way, so does CPPI. They have equal performance.

Scenario 2 (Figure 8.27): Equity goes up, then down. CPPI's floor kicks in, and CPPI's guarantee is honoured. CPPI outperforms the equity underlying:

Scenario 3 (Figure 8.28): Equity goes down almost all the way, CPPI's floor kicks in, and its guarantee is honoured. CPPI outperforms the equity underlying:

Scenario 4 (Figure 8.29): Equity is drifting first, CPPI invests too much in cash. Even if the CPPI picks up at later stage, it underperforms the equity underlying:

Scenario 5 (Figure 8.30): Another case of CPPI's floor kicking in early:

CPPI Gap Option and Hedging

Although CPPI rebalancing scheme is designed to protect the downside risks, it still has gap risks. CPPI providers implicitly protect investors from gap risks. As shown schematically in Figure 8.31, if the risky asset crashes through the guarantee floor, the CPPI fund manager will have to pay the difference. The investors are protected by the embedded CPPI gap option.

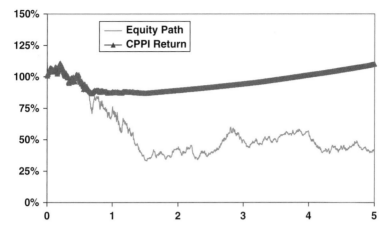

FIGURE 8.28   CPPI return vs equity path

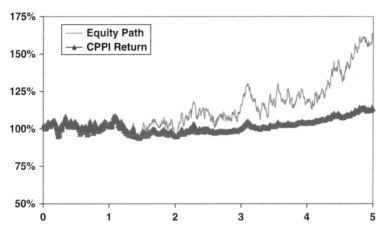

FIGURE 8.29   CPPI return vs equity path

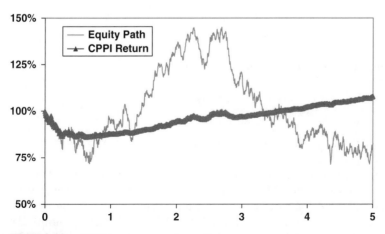

FIGURE 8.30   CPPI return vs equity path

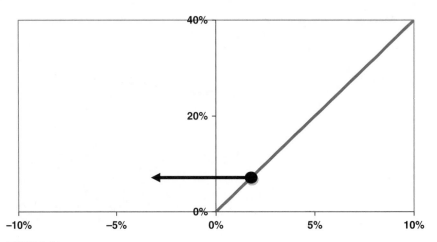

FIGURE 8.31   Risky Investment Proportion vs Gap Condition

Clearly, the gap options need to be priced and risk managed by the CPPI trading desk. On any given day along the spot path, the gap option notional and strike are all path-dependent, driven by the rebalancing scheme according to the gap conditions. One can use Monte Carlo to simulate the CPPI path, and price the gap option at each relevant point along the path.

A single intraday gap option can be modelled using the jump diffusion model with Poisson jumps. The pricing formulae are summarized below:

Given three rather intuitive jump parameters:

J_1 : jump frequency, e.g. 10 jumps per years;

J_2 : average jump size, e.g. -5% (downward jump);

J_3 : standard deviation of the jump size, e.g. 5%;

by defining the following parameters:

$$\lambda = J_1 \cdot (1 + J_2)$$

$$r_n = r - \lambda \cdot J_2 + \frac{n \cdot \ln(1 + J_2)}{T}$$

$$\sigma_n = \sqrt{\sigma^2 + \frac{n \cdot J_3^2}{T}}$$

the European option price with jumps can be written as:

$$P_{Jump} = \sum_{n=0}^{\infty} \frac{\exp(\lambda \cdot T) \cdot (\lambda \cdot T)^n}{n!} P_{BS}\left(S, K, T, r_n, \sigma_n\right)$$

Note that when the jump parameters go to zero, the formula converges to Black–Scholes.

It is not easy to hedge the real gap risks in CPPI, given the notional and strike of the gap option vary along the CPPI performance path. There are, however, some brokers' quotes on standardized gap option on some major equity indices. For example, one can obtain broker's quotes (e.g. 5bp) on EUROSTOXX 50 (SX5E) 3-month daily cliquet put spread with strikes of 80% and 70%. During the 3-month period, if EUROSTOXX

TABLE 8.4 Pros and cons of CPPI

Pros	Cons
▪ Downside protection. ▪ No upfront cost for the downside protection. ▪ Prospect of full participation of the upside of the market. ▪ CPPI funds are total return funds.	▪ Requires fund management approaches, including frequent rebalancing. ▪ If the fund ever touches a pre-determined floor (which is time-varying), the guarantee is payable. It can potentially lose the market upside completely.

50 ever falls below 80% of the previous day's closing price, the option seller pays out subject to a maximum of 10% (80% − 70%). The payout can only happen once to mimic the gap option. Such standardized gap options can only be used as macro hedging tools for the gap risks if the CPPI positions have different underlying funds. In general, the real gap risks can only be partially hedged, and the CPPI gap risks must be monitored and limited by banks' internal procedures.

Summary

CPPI is a relatively low-risk structured product from investors' perspective, and it can be in the forms of investment bonds as well as an OEIC. Its investment return is path-dependent. Table 8.4 summarizes the pros and cons of the CPPI from an investor's perspective:

The fund guarantee element plays a key role in the CPPI's path dependence nature. Different guarantee levels may alter the trading strategies significantly. The gap condition table specifies the rebalancing strategy, which determines the total expected return for the CPPI investors. CPPI managers must manage and hedge the embedded gap options.

Solvency II has been a big driver for the issuance of individualized CPPI (iCPPI) products. Solvency II requires insurers to hedge their financial risk or pay heavy capital charges. Insurers and other retirement solution providers can offer CPPI as long-term investment and saving products, without having to pay for expensive derivatives hedges or taking the market risks on the balance sheets.

iCPPI can meet the demands for more choices and it allows the creation of sets of products based on variations of the CPPI formula. The parameters of an iCPPI product are identical to those of a standard CPPI, although iCPPI is tailored to individual groups of investors' or policyholders' requirements, such as duration, the level of protection and the schedule of contributions. Additionally, iCPPI can cover many different underlying managed funds, to further enhance its investment capabilities and flexibilities.

RISKS DURING RETAIL ISSUANCE PERIOD

In issuing retail structured products, the product providers need to commit to a fixed price for a product that is forward starting and has an uncertain notional, because of the selling and application period required for retail investors. During the selling and application period, the product provider must manage the risks of a forward starting option with uncertain notional. Using a vanilla call as an example, the actual product the issuer has committed to potential investors at time 0 is:

$$N_t \cdot \left(S_T - K \cdot S_t\right)^+ \qquad 0 < t < T$$

where K is the fixed percentage strike, t is the forward start date when the spot fixing (S_t) and hence strike fixing is taken, T is the maturity date. N_t is the unknown notional until t, by then the issuer will know for sure the total notional sold to the retail investors.

Even though the selling and application period is not too long, typically 6 to 8 weeks, the risks in the above payoff can be markedly different from those of a spot start payoff: $N_0 \cdot (S_T - K \cdot S_0)^+$, in which N_0 and S_0 are known and fixed. Managing such retail issuance risks during the selling and application period requires science as well as art.

Forward Start Option Risks

The main risk in a forward start is the forward volatility and forward smile/skew. The product providers tend to make a best estimate of the notional and conduct Vega hedge accordingly. The best estimate of notional is typically based on past and present experiences of the market and investors. The notional estimate is improved over time given the daily feedbacks of the sales figures. While the Vega is calculated by the appropriate forward start option pricing model (science), the rest is indeed art:

- Vega hedge is based on the estimated notional.
- Vega hedge at time 0 is based on a fixed absolute strike.
- However, the actual absolute strike of the product is only fixed at time t.
- The potential mismatch of strikes in the Vega hedge may introduce some smile/skew risks. This can be managed at the portfolio level.
- Delta hedge normally starts at time t, as delta before the spot fixing at time t tends to be rather small.

Leaving the entire retail issuance position unhedged during the selling and application period is a very risky practice, as one is exposed to the forward volatility and forward smile/skew on the entire notional. Simply because the notional is unknown at time 0, it does not mean the forward starting risks do not exist at time t!

Uncertain Notional Risks

To conduct any meaningful Vega hedge started above, one must make a best estimate of the notional. Ultimately, one needs to reply on the analyses from the sales and market experiences. However, it is possible to use simple option models to understand and quantify the risks and set limits if necessary.

Using the same vanilla call example, denoting the best estimate of the notional at time 0 as N_0 and a Vega hedge is put on, the residual unhedged exposure can be expressed as:

$$\left(N_t - N_0\right) \cdot \left(S_T - K \cdot S_t\right)^+$$

One can assume N_t is stochastic, and the following steps can be taken to quantify the residual risks:

- Define a simple stochastic process for N_t, for example log-normal distribution with a mean of N_0 and volatility of σ_N.
- Define the correlation between N_t and S_t. This is of course dependent on the underlying as well as products. For example, when an equity underlying goes up, certain growth products can sell more. There are cases where N_t and S_t are positively correlated.
- In the vanilla call example above, the residual exposure payoff has a compound option element. Either Monte Carlo or a closed-form solution can be used to quantify the residual exposures.
- Once the residual exposures are defined and measurable, risk control measures can be applied, including setting risk limits against them.

CHAPTER 9

Basket Option Analysis

Basket products are correlation products. Basket options have long been important tools in structuring financial products. They are widely used in portfolio management and as retail products as they are typically more cost-effective than multiple single underlying options. The components in a basket can be single stocks, equity indices or funds, or interest rate swap indices. Historically, managing basket option (correlation) books has been problematic and difficult for many financial institutions. Quite often, when the markets move, the basket options and their hedges, which are supposed to offset the basket positions, do not move in the directions as they are supposed to. In these circumstances the basket pricing models used are partially responsible as they fail to capture a certain type of fundamental basket risks. Among them, the **correlation skew** and its structural change triggered by a sudden market move are the key contributors.

In the presence of a volatility smile/skew, pricing basket options becomes much more complicated. It becomes important to understand how the basket skew behaves and how the skewed correlation structure is related to it. In this chapter, we will review some of the key basket option risks, and analyse some basket pricing models, in particular the copula model. The techniques to extract historic basket volatility surface and to construct implied basket volatility surfaces will be presented. We will develop further the copula technique and examine the relationship between the basket skew and correlation skew. The effect of the correlation skew and its structural change on the basket skew will also be examined.

BASKET OPTION RISKS

A typical basket consists of several underlyings with associated weightings. The basket asset return can be expressed in the general form of:

$$S_B(t) = \sum_{i=1}^{n} w_i \frac{S_i(t)}{S_i(0)}$$

where w_i is the weightings, $S_i(t)$ the individual underlying spot at time t and $S_i(0)$ is the individual underlying spot at time $0(t>0)$.

The above general definition covers several practical cases. For example, for a basket with natural weighting, its definition can be generalized into:

$$S_B(t) = \frac{\sum_{i=1}^{n} S_i(t)}{\sum_{i=1}^{n} S_i(0)} = \sum_{i=1}^{n} \frac{S_i(0)}{\sum_{i=1}^{n} S_i(0)} \frac{S_i(t)}{S_i(0)} = \sum_{i=1}^{n} w_i \frac{S_i(t)}{S_i(0)}$$

where: $w_i = \dfrac{S_i(0)}{\sum_{i=1}^{n} S_i(0)}$

The values of standard European call and put options on the basket are calculated from:

$$Call = D \cdot E^Q\left[\left(S_B - K\right)^+\right]$$

$$Put = D \cdot E^Q\left[\left(K - S_B\right)^+\right]$$

The above standard European payoff definition can be extended with an Asian tail. Assuming there are m Asian dates attached to the payoff, then the Asian basket asset can be written as:

$$S_B(t) = \sum_{i=1}^{n} w_i \left(\frac{1}{m} \sum_{j=1}^{m} \frac{S_i(t_j)}{S_i(0)}\right)$$

Where t_j are the Asian dates and $S_i(t_j)$ is the spot of the i-th underlying at time t_j. So the European payoffs can be conveniently used for basket option with Asian tails provided the basket asset $S_B(t)$ is defined adequately.

A basket option book will generally consist of many basket calls and puts, as defined above. In addition to hedging the first order risks (e.g. delta, Gamma, Vega) associated with individual basket underlyings, the correlation-specific basket risk exposures need to be hedged. This type of correlation risks, including cross Gamma, correlation skew risks and FX correlation risks need to be understood. Correlation is renowned for its misbehaviours. The characteristics of the basket volatility surface depend not only on the volatility characteristics of the individual components, but also heavily on the correlation and its skew feature. One should be able to handle basket risks better by understanding the basket co-dependency better, understanding skew risks and the associated correlation issues better.

COPULA PRICING MODELS

In the absence of a volatility smile/skew, a European option on a basket can be priced using various techniques, including moment matching or geometric conditioning. In the presence of a volatility smile/skew, pricing basket options becomes much more complicated. It becomes important to understand how the basket skew behaves and how correlation skew is related to it. Although the **correlation skew** has long been a topic of study in the context of equity derivatives basket, and the **copula** technique was one of the proposed methods to deal with it, it is in the credit derivatives business that the **copula** technique becomes an industry standard to deal with basket of names in the context of defaults. We will here focus on diffusion basket, namely where there are no jumps in the stochastic processes.

Copula Model Framework

For standard European and Asian payoffs, the analytical basket option models can be useful. For example, the conditioning geometric mean approach is effective when it is used appropriately, taking the right volatilities at the basket option strikes, and incorporating adequate correlation skew adjustment. However, the analytical models do suffer from the fact that they cannot price path-dependent basket options, in particular when there is pronounced volatility smile/skew. In contract to the analytical models, the local volatility model is very versatile. It can be used to price standard as well as path-dependent basket options. In the local volatility model, the underlying local volatility surfaces are stripped, and the correlated small step random walks can be performed within those local volatility spaces. Although it is flexible, the numerical and computational costs are substantial, and the risk sensitivities are exposed to Monte Carlo noises.

Copula techniques are valuable tools in dealing with multivariate distribution. For a set of random variables, if the joint probability distribution is specified, then the marginal distributions can be calculated, and the expectation of a given set of states can be computed. In the case that the joint probability distribution is unknown, and instead one only knows the marginal distributions, copula techniques allow us to bind the marginal distributions to specify a joint distribution. This is somehow analogous to the mathematical "inverse problem", but copula can make "inverse problem" simpler. For example, in actuaries' annuity pricing, one can use copula to conveniently specify the relationship of individual incidence and disease, to specify the joint survival probability of husband and wife. In micro-econometrics, the economic and social factors can be bound using copula, as the related variables are each coming from different statistical distribution families. The application of copula in pricing basket derivatives is the main topic of this section.

For a set of random variables $(X_1, X_2, \cdots, X_n)$, denoting their marginal uniform distributions as $F(X_1), F(X_2), \cdots, F(X_n)$, Sklar's theorem (1959) states that there exists a copula that binds the marginal uniforms to give the joint distribution of the multivariates:

$$F(X_1, X_2, \cdots, X_n) = C(F(X_1), F(X_2), \cdots, F(X_n))$$

This joint distribution specified by a copula is bounded by Frechet's Bounds (1951), of the following formulae:

$$F_L(X_1, X_2, \cdots, X_n) \leq F(X_1, X_2, \cdots, X_n) \leq F_U(X_1, X_2, \cdots, X_n)$$

where the lower bound is

$$F_L(X_1, X_2, \cdots, X_n) = \min \left[G(X_1), G(X_2), \cdots, G(X_n) \right]$$

and upper bound is

$$F_U(X_1, X_2, \cdots, X_n) = \max \left[\sum_{i=1}^{n} G(X_i) - n + 1, 0 \right]$$

Knowledge of bounds is of course useful in selecting and assessing an appropriate copula in practice.

By definition the joint probability density function (PDF) is given by:

$$f(X_1, X_2, \cdots, X_n) = \frac{\partial^2 C(F(X_1), F(X_2), \cdots, F(X_n))}{\partial X_1 \partial X_2 \cdots \partial X_n}$$

$$= \frac{\partial^2 C(u_1, u_2, \cdots u_n)}{\partial u_1 \partial u_2 \cdots \partial u_n} \prod_{i=1}^{n} f(X_i)$$

denoting:

$$c(u_1, u_2, \cdots, u_n) = \frac{\partial^2 C(u_1, u_2, \cdots, u_n)}{\partial u_1 \partial u_2 \cdots \partial u_n}$$

$c(u_1, u_2, \cdots, u_n)$ is known as the copula density. The joint PDF is fully specified if the copula density is specified. The basket option can be priced as follows:

$$P = \int payoff \cdot c(u_1, u_2, \cdots, u_n) \cdot \prod_{i=1}^{n} f(X_i) \cdot dX_1 dX_2 \cdots dX_n$$

For a basket consisting of a lesser number of underlyings (say, two underlyings), it is in general more efficient to numerically integrate over the specified basket payoff. For example, the spread option can be calculated using the following integration:

$$\max(S_1 - S_2 - K, 0)$$

$$= \int_{-\infty}^{\infty} \int_{-\infty}^{\infty} (S_1 - S_2 - K) \cdot 1_{S_1 - S_2 - K > 0} \cdot f(S_1, S_2) \cdot dS_1 dS_2$$

$$= \int_{-\infty}^{\infty} \int_{-\infty}^{\infty} (S_1 - S_2 - K) \cdot 1_{S_1 - S_2 - K > 0} \cdot c(u, \upsilon) \cdot f(S_1) \cdot f(S_2) \cdot dS_1 dS_2$$

Numerical integration in general works well for baskets with up to three underlyings. For baskets with more than three underlyings, large step Monte Carlo technique may be more efficient.

Copula has some a number of interesting properties. First, because copula specifies the dependency of the marginal distributions, rather than correlation between random state variables, one can use copula to specify the dependency strength for a particular part of the distribution. For example, if one believes that the tail parts of the distributions have stronger dependency, then one can specify a copula which prescribes a stronger tail dependency. This useful mathematical feature can conveniently be used to model the market crash scenario (tail event) in which the correlations shot up. Secondly, the dependency structure specified by copula is invariant or change in a predictable way when a monotonic transformation is applied to the random state variables. This is understandable, as the copula dependency is on the marginal distributions rather than the state variables. Hence, provided the transformation applied to the state variables does not alter the marginal distributions, the copula dependency will not vary. An example of the invariant property is that the copula dependency on a set of state variables $(X_1, X_2, \cdots, X_n)$ is the same as their logarithmic counterparts $(\log(X_1), \log(X_2), \cdots, \log(X_n))$.

There are a variety of parametric forms for the copula family. They include Gaussian, Student-*t* and Archimedean (e.g. Clayton, Frank and Gumbel) copula. One of the fundamental differences among various copulas is the fact that they represent different dependency strengths for certain parts of the marginal distributions. For example, Student-*t* copula can assign much stronger tails dependency than the Gaussian copula. In the following, we shall examine some copula examples using two random variables.

Gaussian Copula

For a Gaussian copula with two random variables, it is defined as:

$$C_G(u, \upsilon) = \Phi_2\left(\Phi^{-1}(u), \Phi^{-1}(\upsilon)\right)$$

$$= \int_{-\infty}^{\Phi^{-1}(u)} \int_{-\infty}^{\Phi^{-1}(\upsilon)} \frac{1}{2\pi\sqrt{1-\rho^2}} \exp\left(-\frac{x^2 + y^2 - 2\rho xy}{2(1-\rho^2)}\right) dx\, dy$$

where $u, \upsilon \in [0, 1]$, $\Phi(\cdot)$ is the standard cumulative normal distribution and $\Phi_2(\cdot)$ is the bi-variate cumulative distribution. The copula density $c(u, \upsilon)$ is:

$$c(u, \upsilon) = \frac{\partial^2 C_G(u, v)}{\partial u\, \partial v} = \frac{\psi_2\left(\Phi^{-1}(u),\, \Phi^{-1}(v)\right)}{\psi\left(\Phi^{-1}(u)\right) \cdot \psi\left(\Phi^{-1}(v)\right)}$$

where:

$$\psi(x) = \frac{1}{\sqrt{2\pi}} \exp\left(-\frac{x^2}{2}\right)$$

$$\psi_2(x, y) = \frac{1}{2\pi\sqrt{1-\rho^2}} \exp\left(-\frac{x^2 + y^2 - 2\rho xy}{2(1-\rho^2)}\right)$$

Note that in this Gaussian copula example, the correlation coefficient is the only parameter (degree of freedom) in the copula calibration, i.e. calibrating copula to a set of relevant market basket option prices.

t-copula

The Student's t-copula with two random variables is defined as:

$$C_t(u, \upsilon) = t_{2,d}\left(t_d^{-1}(u), t_d^{-1}(\upsilon)\right)$$

$$= \int_{-\infty}^{t_d^{-1}(u)} \int_{-\infty}^{t_d^{-1}(\upsilon)} \frac{1}{2\pi\sqrt{1-\rho^2}} \left(1 + \frac{x^2 + y^2 - 2\rho xy}{d(1-\rho^2)}\right)^{-\frac{d+2}{2}} dx dy$$

where $t_d(\cdot)$ is the Student's t distribution with d degree of freedom and $t_{2,d}(\cdot)$ is the bi-variate version. The copula density for t-copula can be calculated:

$$c(u, \upsilon) = \frac{\partial^2 C_t(u, v)}{\partial u \, \partial v} = \frac{f_2(t_d^{-1}(u), t_d^{-1}(v))}{f(t_d^{-1}(u)) \cdot f(t_d^{-1}(v))}$$

where

$$f(x) = \frac{\Gamma\left(\dfrac{d+1}{2}\right)}{\sqrt{d\pi} \cdot \Gamma\left(\dfrac{d}{2}\right)} \cdot \left(1 + \frac{x^2}{d}\right)^{-\frac{d+1}{2}}$$

$$f_2(x, y) = \frac{1}{2\pi\sqrt{1-\rho^2}} \exp\left(1 + \frac{x^2 + y^2 - 2\rho xy}{d(1-\rho^2)}\right)^{-\frac{d+2}{2}}$$

With t-copula, both correlation coefficient (ρ) and the degree of freedom (d) can be used in the copula calibration. It is of course more flexible than the Gaussian copula calibration.

Power Copula

Both Gaussian and t-copula can be powered up as:

$$C_p\left(u, \upsilon, \rho, \theta_1, \theta_2\right) = u^{1-\theta_1} \upsilon^{1-\theta_2} C\left(u^{\theta_1}, \upsilon^{\theta_2}, \rho\right)$$

where θ_1 and θ_2 are constant. When $\theta_1 = \theta_2 = 1$, the power copula converges to the standard copula:

$$C_p\left(u, \upsilon, \rho, 1, 1\right) = C\left(u, \upsilon, \rho\right)$$

The power copula has two more degrees of freedom (θ_1, θ_2), which will provide more flexibility in the copula calibration process. For example, in the power t-copula there are four parameters ($\rho, d, \theta_1, \theta_2$) which can be used for calibration, while in standard t-copula one can only use (ρ, d). The flexibility of the power t-copula comes at a cost; its partial derivatives require the calculation of bi-variate CDF. The standard t-copula counterparts do not require that, hence it is much more computationally efficient.

Basket Pricing Models Comparison

In this section, we will compare three models for pricing standard basket options in the presence of volatility smile/skew. The standard basket option payoffs are:

$$Call = E^Q < (S_B - K)^+ >$$

$$Put = E^Q < (K - S_B)^+ >$$

where:

$$S_B = \frac{1}{\text{n}} \sum_{i=1}^{n} \frac{S_i(T)}{S_i(0)}$$

where T is the maturity and $S_i(T)$ is the spot of i-th underlying at maturity.

In this section, we shall compare three basket pricing models. The first model is the local volatility model, in which a local volatility surface is stripped for each basket component. One can then use Monte Carlo to generate correlated random paths in the local volatility spaces, and price the basket payoff. The second model is the copula technique explained in the section earlier. It uses big step Monte Carlo to generated correlated random paths without the need of local volatility. Hence it can price basket options more efficiently. The third model is the conditioning geometric mean (CGM) analytical model with a few twists, in order to take account of the volatility smile/skew more effectively.

Note that the correlation coefficient used in the copula model does not have exactly the same mathematical meanings as in the local volatility model or the geometric conditioning model. If the same correlation coefficient is plugged into the copula, local volatility and geometric conditioning models, the basket option prices of the three models may differ. However, if all models are calibrated to the same basket option quotes (if they exist in the market), their prices should be consistent with each other, even while the implied correlation coefficients may be different, as implied correlation is obviously model-dependent.

The volatility smile/skew effects are taken into account by all three models, but in three very different ways. For an European basket payoff:

- Local volatility model: By construction of local volatility surface, the full smile/skew of all basket underlyings are built into the subsequent small step Monte Carlo random walks.
- Copula technique: By construction of the marginal distributions, the full smile/skew of all basket underlyings are built into the big step Monte Carlo samples. It is important to note that the correlation does have a different meaning as in the local volatility model.
- CGM: This analytical model was originally developed for the term structure volatility. If the payoff is European only, then the volatility value at strike K is taken.

Let's compare the prices of European basket options using the three models. The basket consists of three real-life equity indices (FTSE, S&P500, ESTX) with full dividend streams and volatility surfaces. The option has a maturity of 5 years. As shown in Figures 9.1 and 9.2, for both basket calls and puts, local volatility, copula and geometric conditioning model give very close prices across a range of strikes.

For an Asian basket, in which there are n underlyings, and each has m Asian dates, the basket asset is defined as follows:

$$S_B = \frac{1}{n} \sum_{i=1}^{n} \left(\frac{1}{m} \sum_{j=1}^{m} \frac{S_i(t_j)}{S_i(0)} \right)$$

where t_j are the Asian dates and $S_i(t_j)$ is the spot of i-th underlying at time t_j.

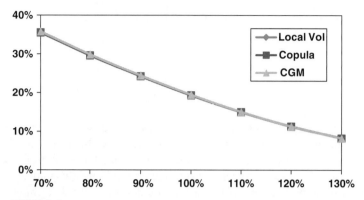

FIGURE 9.1   Basket call

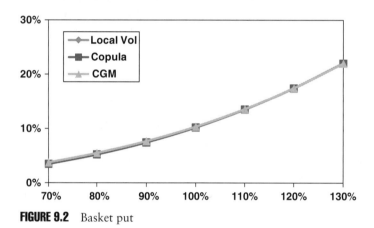

FIGURE 9.2   Basket put

When a basket options has an Asian tail, the volatility smile/skew effects are taken into account by all three models, again in three very different ways:

- Local volatility model: By construction of local volatility surface, the full smile/skew of all basket underlyings are built into the subsequent small step Monte Carlo random walks. This applies to the Asian tail as well.
- Copula technique: By construction of the marginal distributions, the full smile/skew of all basket underlyings are built into the big step Monte Carlo samples. The stock prices at the first and last Asian dates are simulated directly. An additional Monte Carlo Brownian bridge point (or more points) between them can be used to determine the average. Conditional averages can be assumed to be lognormal, and correlation between conditional averages is assumed to be the same as between stocks.
- CGM: This analytical model was originally developed for the flat volatility. If the payoff is European only, i.e. there is no Asian tail, then the volatility value at strike K is taken. If there is an Asian tail, the question is how to modify the model such that the volatility values at appropriate strikes for each Asian dates can price

consistently under smile/skew. Given the contractual strike K, one can decompose it into equivalent strikes (K_j) for each Asian dates, by setting Asian strikes as:

$$K_j = \frac{F(t_j)}{S(t_0)} exp\left(\alpha\sqrt{t_j - t_0}\right)$$

where t_j is the j-th Asian date $(j = 1 \dots m)$, $F(t_j)$ is the forward at time t_j. α is a constant. By imposing a constraint:

$$\frac{1}{n}\sum_{j=1}^{n} K_j = K$$

The constant α can be easily found, e.g. by Newton–Raphson. Clearly once α is obtained, all strikes (K_j) can be calculated and the volatility values can be sampled from the corresponding volatility surfaces as follows:

$$\sigma(t_j) = \sigma\left(t_j, \frac{K_j}{S(t_0)}\right)$$

In doing so, note that the Vega is spread over the Asian tail along the "line" of K_j.

Figures 9.3 and 9.4 plot the basket Asian calls and puts for a range of strikes, using the three models. It is the same basket, and consists of three real-life equity indices (FTSE, S&P500, ESTX) with full dividend streams and volatility surfaces. The correlation used is 70%. The options have a maturity of 5 years, including 6 months' Asian tail, with monthly average. All prices obtained by the local volatility, copula and geometric conditioning models with their corresponding Asian tail methodologies are remarkably close.

Correlation Skew Methodology

Correlation itself is hard to model, never mind correlation skew. However, correlation skew is very much apparent; as markets crash, correlation shoots up. In practice, certain pragmatic schemes can be deployed in the basket pricing models to take account

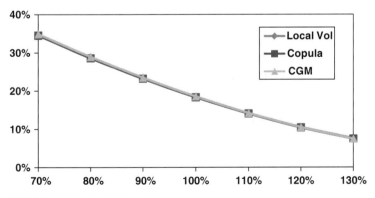

FIGURE 9.3 Basket Asian call

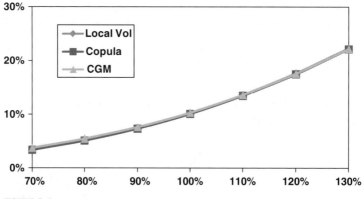

FIGURE 9.4　Basket Asian put

of the correlation skew effect. In the following, we describe two schemes that have a good intuition and are easy to implement.

For an original correlation matrix:

$$\begin{pmatrix} 1 & \rho_{12} & \rho_{ij} \\ \vdots & 1 & \vdots \\ \vdots & \vdots & 1 \end{pmatrix}$$

The correlation between i-th and j-th underlying ρ_{ij} can be adjusted as follows:

$$\rho_{ij}^{adj} = \rho_{ij} + \left(1 - \rho_{ij}\right) \cdot A_{ij}$$

where ρ_{ij}^{adj} is the adjusted correlation and A_{ij} is the adjustment factor, which can either be of the functional form or empirical data.

In the following, we discuss two functional forms for A_{ij}, one is labelled "Tanh1":

$$A_{ij} = 1 - \frac{\tanh\left(a_{ij}\right)}{\tanh\left(1\right)}$$

and the other is labelled as "Tanh2":

$$A_{ij} = \tanh\left(1\right) - \tanh\left(a_{ij}\right)$$

where $a_{ij} = \frac{1}{2}\left(\frac{S_i^t}{S_i^0} + \frac{S_j^t}{S_j^0}\right)$, representing the average movement of the i-th and j-th underlying from over time step t. When $a_{ij} < 1$, it indicates markets are falling on average, and when $a_{ij} > 1$, it indicates markets are rallying up on average. Figure 9.5 compares these two Tanh functional forms of the adjustment factor A_{ij}, plotted against a_{ij}.

As can be seen in the figure, in the first form (labelled Tanh1), when $a_{ij} = 0$, A_{ij} becomes 100% and the adjusted correlation $\rho_{ij}^{adj} = 1$. In the second form (labelled Tanh2), when $a_{ij} = 0$, A_{ij} reaches a maximum of 76.2%, hence the adjusted correlation will be closer to 1 but won't reach maximum of 1. Both adjustment factor forms show that when

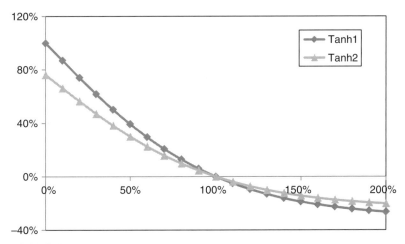

FIGURE 9.5 Adjustment factor

markets crash, the correlation shots up, although Tanh1 form adjusts the correlation to 1, and Tanh2 takes it to less than 1. Both assumptions can be reasonable, depending on underlying markets. When $a_{ij} = 1$, i.e. when markets have not moved, the adjustment factor of both forms is zero, i.e. no adjustment is made to the original correlation. When $a_{ij} > 1$, i.e. markets are rallying, the adjustment factor in both forms level off at a negative value, which adjusts the correlation down, but to a much lesser degree than when markets are crashing. This correlation skew phenomenon can be captured by both Tanh1 and Tanh2 forms. It is also possible to only take the market crashing scenario into consideration during the pricing, by limiting $a_{ij} = min\left[1, \frac{1}{2}\left(\frac{S_i^t}{S_i^0} + \frac{S_j^t}{S_j^0}\right)\right]$,

which only represents the fall in the average of the i-th and j-th underlyings.

As copula model takes large step, in order to incorporate correlation skew in copula, the average basket movement a_{ij} can be determined either the points at the end of the large step or half way. For example, it we decide to use halfway points, one can first use the copula to obtain the spots at the end of large step using the original correlation. The average of the end point spots and the initial spots will be used to calculate a_{ij}, which can then be used to determine the adjusted correlation matrix. The adjusted correlation matrix will be used to re-calculate the spots at the end point using the same numerical parameters, e.g. same Sobol point. The halfway point represents average correlation over the whole path. Note that the correlation skew scheme will make Gaussian copula non-Gaussian because the adjusted correlation is not constant any more.

To incorporate correlation skew into the analytical CGM model for basket option, one can utilize the fact that the basket local variance is a function of the local co-variance and correlation. By assigning a function form to the correlation (or average correlation for simplicity), the basket local variance is then directly linked to the correlation skew functional form. One can subsequently derive, from the spot space to strike space ($S{\rightarrow}K$), the implied basket volatility smile/skew that includes the correlation skew (Lee, Wang and Karim).

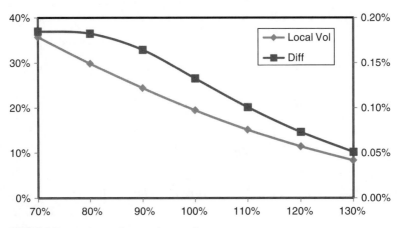

FIGURE 9.6 Basket call (correlation skew)

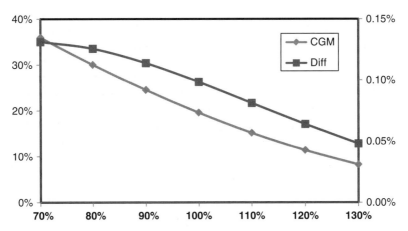

FIGURE 9.7 Basket call (correlation skew)

In the following, we examine a few pricing examples by comparing prices with and without correlation skew. It is the same basket used in earlier example, which consists of three real-life equity indices (FTSE, S&P500, ESTX) with full dividend streams and volatility surfaces. The original correlation input is 70%. Figure 9.6 shows the 5-year basket European call prices at various strikes for the local volatility model without correlation skew. The differences in price after imposing Tanh1 correlation skew is plotted in the same figure and labelled "Diff". As can be seen, correlation skew increases the price, as basket option is long correlation. The price difference is larger for lower strike.

Figure 9.7 shows the correlation skew effect on basket European call prices, for the CGM model.

Figures 9.8 and 9.9 shows Basket European Put with correlation skew.

Note that in the these examples, the original correlation is already 70%. The correlation skew effect may appear to be not too big; this is because the correlation

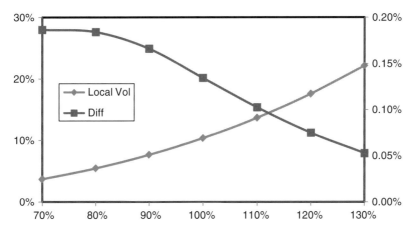

FIGURE 9.8 Basket put (correlation skew)

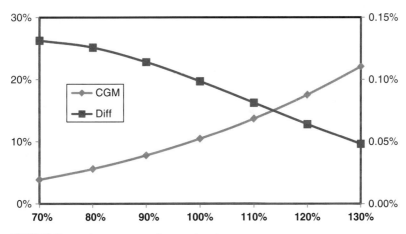

FIGURE 9.9 Basket put (correlation skew)

skew-induced increase is limited to 1. If, however, the original correlation input is low, then correlation skew will have larger effects on prices. In Figures 9.10 and 9.11, we compare the price increases at various strikes due to correlation skew effect for two different original correlation inputs, 70% versus 50%. The model used in the figures is the local volatility model. The basket call price increases for 50% original correlation are much larger than those for 70%, given there is more room for the 50% original correlation to increase when markets crash. The same correlation skew conclusion holds for the basket put price increases.

Figures 9.12 and 9.13 compare the basket deltas for calls and puts at different strikes. As can be seen in both figures, the correlation skew does not appear to affect deltas much. This is because the deltas are usually calculated by shifting the spots by a small amount (say 1%). In a primarily diffusion setup, correlation skew won't affect the small movement much, it'll affect large simultaneous movements that traditional deltas

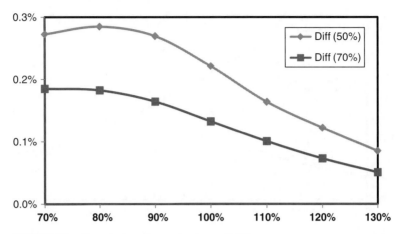

FIGURE 9.10   Correlation skew – basket call LV

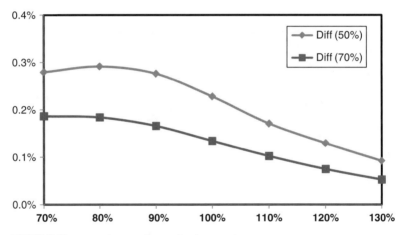

FIGURE 9.11   Correlation skew – basket put LV

won't be able to handle. The practical implication is that although correlation skew schemes may have priced in the possibility of some market crash scenarios, hedging it is still a challenging task which cannot be easily accomplished by continuous delta hedge.

Multi-step Copula for Auto-callable Baskets

The Copula Terminal Mapping (CTM) methodology discussed in Chapter 6 is an efficient numerical technique using large-step Monte Carlo, as opposed to small-step local volatility Monte Carlo, to random walk an underlying through multiple dates. CTM methodology can also be used to price basket auto-callable products. For each underlying, assuming there are M call dates including maturity, an M-dimensional Brownian motion can be used to simulate the spot prices at the call dates. At each call date, each dimension is mapped to the implied distribution, which by construction fully calibrates to the underlying European options.

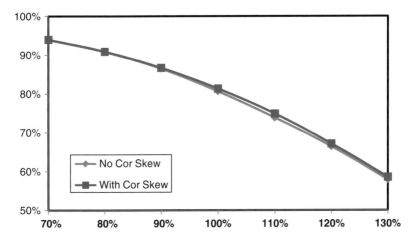

FIGURE 9.12 Basket option delta (call)

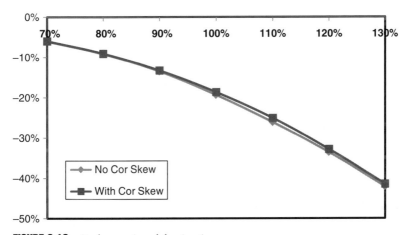

FIGURE 9.13 Basket option delta (put)

For a basket of N underlyings together with M call dates, the covariance matrix has the dimension of $(N \times M)$. In theory, Cholesky decomposition can impose the correlation structure onto the entire covariance matrix. However, singular value decomposition (SVD) is more flexible and effective. In SVD, together with the eigenvectors, a diagonal matrix is created with the corresponding eigenvalues in decreasing order. This diagonal feature allows us to deal with the basket underlying dependency and the call dates (temporal) dependency separately. One can then couple them into a combined matrix, putting all eigenvalues into an order. For example, one can operate SVD on N assets and M call dates separately to impose corresponding correlation structures. The resulting eigenvalues can be combined by direct matrix product, which results in a total of $N \times M$ eigenvalues.

To achieve optimal convergence, Sobol together with Brownian bridge can be used. The SVD eigenvalues can be ordered easily, and one can assign them with appropriate elements in the Sobol low discrepancy sequences. By assigning appropriate Sobol numbers to the right parts of the path generator (represented by eigenvalues), one can redistribute the variance to make the Monte Carlo pricing much more effective.

Once the basket values at the call dates are efficiently calculated from the underlying components, the auto-call decisions can be made. Soft-call features can easily be imposed accordingly to soften the digital risks and Greeks. Figures 9.14 and 9.15 compare the basket auto-callable prices of CTM and LV. The basket has three equity underlyings. Maturity is 5 years with annual call dates. The call trigger is set at 90% of the basket value, and payout upon is 7% for every year passed plus the original capital.

In Figures 9.14 and 9.15, the left vertical axis labels the price, and the right vertical axis labels the price difference between CTM and LV Monte Carlo. The same correlation coefficients are used in both CTM and LV. As stated earlier, the correlation

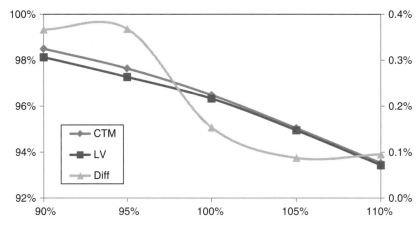

FIGURE 9.14   Price vs trigger (no soft call)

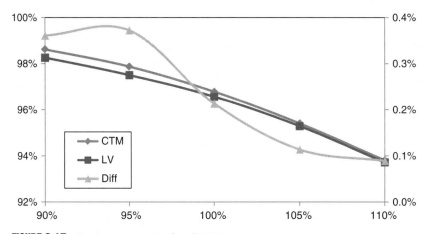

FIGURE 9.15   Price vs trigger (soft call=2%)

coefficient used in copula does not have the same mathematical meanings as in the local volatility. Therefore when the same correlation coefficients are plugged into CTM and LV, the basket option prices of the two models will differ. However, if the correlation coefficients in all models were calibrated to the same basket option quotes (if they exist in the market), their prices could be made more consistent with each other. Importantly, CTM methodology takes large time steps directly to call dates and expiry, resulting in much faster and more stable prices and Greeks than using small-step LV Monte Carlo.

HISTORIC BASKET VOLATILITY SURFACES

It is possible to construct a historic basket volatility surface from the historic time series of the individual basket components. One such approach is to minimize the relative entropy in which a risk-neutral drift-adjusted probability density function (PDF) for the basket can be built. Subject to constraints of the forward and ATM implied volatility, the risk-neutral PDF is used to construct a historic volatility surface for the basket. Specifically, given the historic time series of the basket spot S_i the following steps are taken to build a historic basket volatility surface:

Step 1: Recover the historic PDF for the basket at time interval T by calculating the log-return at appropriate time interval:

$$R_T = ln\left(\frac{S_{t+N}}{S_t}\right)$$

where N defines the time interval. The bucketed log-returns R_T create the historic PDF denoted as P. An example of a historic PDF is shown Figure 9.16.

Step 2: Recover the risk-neutral drift-adjusted PDF (Q) from the historic PDF (P). This is a key step and a numerical optimization technique is used for this. The penalty function for optimization is based on a relative entropy, which is a mathematical measure of the uncertainty of a distribution. The relative entropy of Q to P is defined as follows:

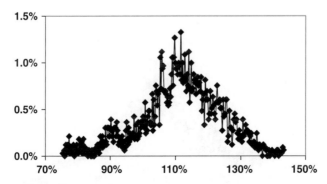

FIGURE 9.16 Historic PDF (mean drift = 9%)

$$S(P,Q) = E^Q \big[\ln(Q) - \ln(P) \big]$$

By minimizing relative entropy $S(P,Q)$, one can solve for Q, subject to the following constraints:

$$\int Q(S_T) \cdot S_T \cdot dS_T = Forward$$

$$\int Q(S_T) \cdot dS_T = 1$$

Additional optimization constraint can also be applied, such as imposing the ATM volatility. The optimization solution for the problem posed above is:

$$Q(S_T) = \frac{P(S_T)}{\int P(S) \cdot \exp(-\lambda S) \cdot dS} \exp(-\lambda S_T)$$

Where λ is a constant that can be obtained by iterating constraints during the numerical optimization. Note that given $P(S_T)$ is always positive, $Q(S_T)$ is guaranteed to be positive. In Figure 9.17, an example of risk-neutral PDF is shown and it is derived from the historic PDF shown previously. The mean drift is the expected drift of the forward given the historic yield curve and dividends.

Step 3: Use the risk-neutral drift-adjusted PDF Q to obtain option prices with different strikes K_i:

$$Call(K_i, T) = DF \cdot \int_K^\infty (S_T - K_i) \cdot Q(S_T) \cdot dS_T$$

$$Put(K_i, T) = DF \cdot \int_0^K (K_i - S_T) \cdot Q(S_T) \cdot dS_T$$

where DF is the discount factor. The option prices can then be used to recover the implied volatility points at K_i. By repeating the above steps at a different time interval T, one can build a historic volatility surface for the basket. Such a historic risk-neutral drift-adjusted volatility surface example is shown in Figure 9.18.

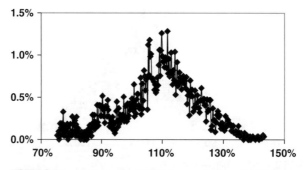

FIGURE 9.17 Risk-neutral PDF (mean drift = 6.75%)

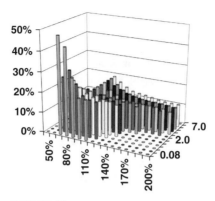

FIGURE 9.18 A historic vol surface

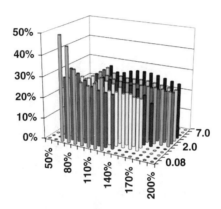

FIGURE 9.19 FT-banks historic vol surface

Let us examine a few more examples of the historic volatility surfaces. The historic volatility surface shown in Figure 9.19 is that of the FTSE-100 banking sector basket. Clearly there is a smile at the short end and skew at the longer end.

The historic volatility surface for an equally weighted index basket of FTSE-100, S&P and EUROSTOCK 50 is shown in Figure 9.20. Again the smile/skew is apparent in the figure.

In fact, the above method for building the historic volatility surface is so general, that it can be used practically for any underlying, whether it is a basket or not. One of the applications is to analyse the historic skew features in the emerging markets where the options quotes are scarce. Figures 9.21 and 9.22 show two examples of the historic volatility surfaces. They are the Bombay SENSEX and the Shanghai Composite respectively. Both were from pre-2008 financial crisis data. SENSEX shows a clear skew pattern, as expected in most equity markets.

However, SHCOMP at that time showed a volatility smile pattern with a very strong upside at the short end. This was due to the fact that the market was expecting

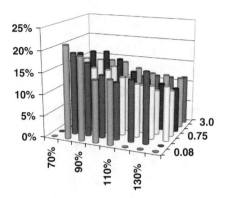

FIGURE 9.20   Index basket historic vol surface

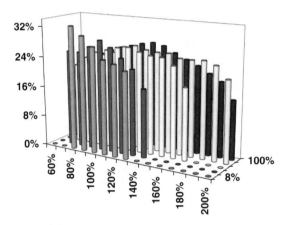

FIGURE 9.21   SENSEX historical vol surface

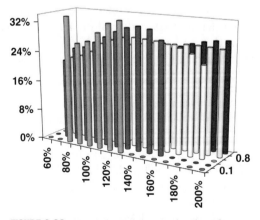

FIGURE 9.22   SHCOMP historical vol surface

strong Chinese stock market performance at the time. It did not materialize as we know, and the stock market (SHCOMP) has since turned back into the typical skew pattern.

IMPLIED BASKET VOLATILITY SURFACES

While the historic basket volatility surfaces provide valuable smile/skew information about the basket, it is relatively static. It is a useful tool for a snapshot and regime change analysis. When the market moves, historical information changes little given that the recent contribution constitutes a relatively small proportion of the time series. For day-to-day trading and hedging purposes, one requires different approaches to cater for rapidly changing market conditions and the basket volatility surfaces should incorporate the latest market information.

It is possible to construct an implied basket volatility surface from the implied volatility surfaces of individual basket components in a variety of ways. One possible approach is to use the local volatility surfaces, in which the stripped local volatility surfaces of the basket components can be integrated with appropriate correlation structures to build an implied basket volatility surface. The local volatility approach is a small step operation and can be computationally expensive. A more efficient technique of constructing an implied basket volatility surface is to use a copula technique, in large steps dealing with the terminal distributions.

Copula Technique to Construct Implied Basket Volatility Surface

In order to build an implied basket volatility surface, one needs to obtain the joint distribution of the basket components. In general, however, knowing the marginal distributions of the individual component and the correlation structure does not guarantee a unique joint distribution. The copula technique allows us to specify a joint distribution function for known marginal distributions with a dependence (correlation) structure. Specifically, for given univariate marginal distributions $F_i(S_i)$, the copula links the univariate marginal distributions to their multivariate joint distribution $F(S_1, S_2, \cdots, S_n)$:

$$F(S_1, S_2, \cdots, S_n) = C(F_1(S_1), F_2(S_2), \cdots, F_n(S_n))$$

Given the implied volatility surfaces of each basket component, the Cumulative Distribution Functions (CDF) at a chosen time slice for the individual component can be built and these CDFs are the univariate marginal distributions. If we impose correlation structures onto these CDFs and link them up using a Gaussian copula, the joint (basket) distribution can be created as follows:

$$F(S_1, S_2, \cdots, S_n) = C(CDF_1(S_1), CDF_2(S_2), \cdots, CDF_n(S_n))$$

The joint distribution given above allows us to simulate the basket spot path by sampling the correlated CDFs. Assuming there are n individual components in the

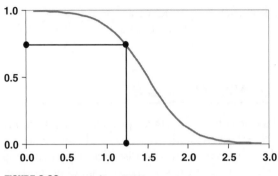

FIGURE 9.23   Sampling CDF

basket, at a given time slice T, the following steps can be taken to construct an implied basket volatility surface:

- Build CDFs for all basket components at a chosen time slice T. This can be achieved by calculating digital calls or puts at the appropriate strikes since a undiscounted digital option specifies the terminal probability for the underlying spot to be above (call) or under (put) the strike. The CDFs are obviously distributed between 0 and 1 and a typical CDF is shown in Figure 9.23. The CDFs can be used later on to sample the individual component spot path given a uniformly distributed random number.
- Generate n independent random Gaussian numbers (g_i) and impose a correlation structure among them. This is a key step in which one can either use a simple correlation number or skewed correlation structure. If Cholesky decomposition technique is used, given the decomposed correlation matrix C_{ij}, the correlated Gaussian number is given by $G_i = \sum_j C_{ij} \cdot g_j$.
- Convert the correlated Gaussian numbers back to uniformly distributed numbers by reversing the Wiener process $U_i = W^{-1}(G_i)$.
- Use the correlated uniform numbers (U_i) to sample individual CDFs to obtain underlying spots (S_i), and in turn calculate the basket spot $S_B = \sum_{i=1}^{n} w_i S_i$.
- Calculate either a call or put on the basket for a given strike K:

$$Call = E < \max(S_B - K, 0) >$$

$$Put = E < \max(K - S_B, 0) >$$

- Calculate the basket implied volatility from either the call or put by reversing the Black–Scholes formula $(\sigma_B(K,T) = BS^{-1}(K,T))$.

The above steps can be repeated for different strikes (K) and maturities (T) to build an entire basket implied volatility surface. It is important to note that in order to obtain a high-quality basket implied volatility surface using this technique, some numerical smoothing techniques are needed in the process. For example, during the Monte Carlo runs, the basket forward should be corrected using the following scheme. Denoting basket underlyings as S_i which are simulated to calculate the basket forward S_B, after M Monte Carlo runs, the average basket forward (prior to any correction) is given by:

$$S_B^M = \frac{\sum_{m=1}^{M} S_B}{M}$$

Since we know exactly what the basket forward S_F is, we can calculate a correction factor f, which can then be used to modify all simulated S_i:

$$f = \frac{S_F}{S_B^M} \qquad S_i' = f \cdot S_i$$

The corrected underlying spots can then be used to calculate basket option payoffs. This simple yet effective correction scheme can make a difference in terms of numerical convergence.

The constructed basket implied volatility surface could be used in a variety of ways. First, it allows one to quantify the basket skew and hence analyse the skew exposures. Secondly, the basket can be treated as a new single underlying and other basket payoffs may be priced and risk managed efficiently in a consistent manner using the same basket implied volatility surface.

Correlation Influence on Basket Skew

In the following, we examine a basket of three underlyings. Their volatility surfaces are shown in the figures below. The volatility surface for the underlying 1 (Figure 9.24) has a relatively low ATM volatility but strong skew. The volatility surface for the underlying 2 (Figure 9.25) has a medium ATM volatility with a medium skew. The volatility surface for the underlying 3 (Figure 9.26) has a high ATM volatility with medium skew.

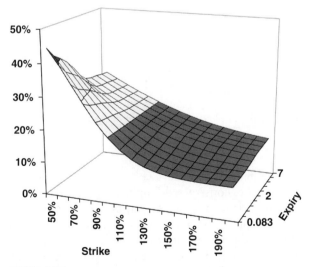

FIGURE 9.24 Implied vol surface (underlying 1)

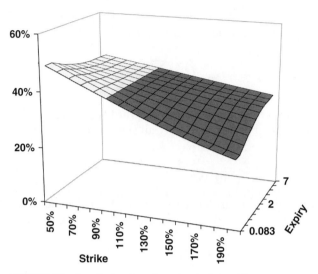

FIGURE 9.25   Implied vol surface (underlying 2)

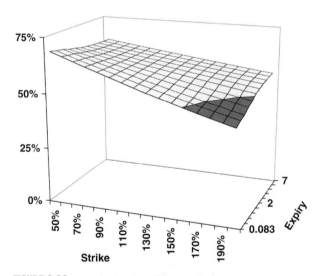

FIGURE 9.26   Implied vol surface (underlying 3)]

The underlying volatility surfaces are chosen to be representative to cover a wide range of possible market μ implied volatility surfaces.

Figure 9.27 shows the constructed implied basket volatility surface using a constant correlation coefficient of 40%. As can be seen in figure, the basket skew is quite pronounced. The implied volatility points in the near right corner of the basket volatility surface for the short maturities and high strikes are not fully recovered. In practice, this is not a problem given that the missing points are in the very low probability region and extrapolation into this region is relatively straightforward.

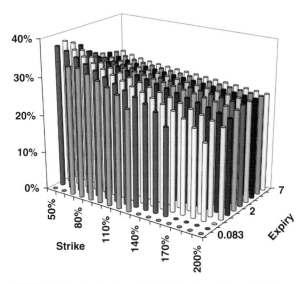

FIGURE 9.27   Basket Implied Vol Surface (Cor=40%)

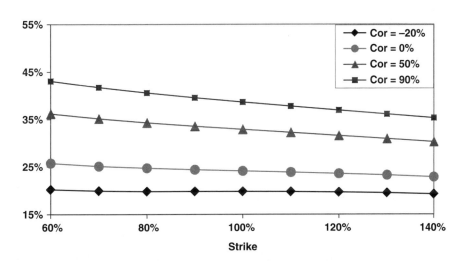

FIGURE 9.28   Basket implied volatility (1Y)

The correlation effect on the basket volatility is shown in Figure 9.28. The implied basket volatility curves (volatility versus strike) at the time slice year 1 for different correlation coefficients (−20%, 0%, 50% and 90%) are plotted in the figure. It is apparent that the higher the correlation, the higher the basket volatility level. This is a well understood fact, as the higher correlations indicate that the basket components move more coherently, resulting in the higher basket volatility.

As can be seen in Figure 9.28, the slope of the volatility curve changes with the correlation. This indicates that the basket skew is also a function of the correlation.

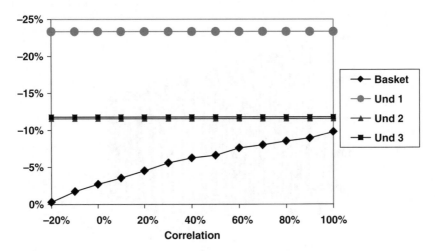

FIGURE 9.29 Skew (1Y) vs correlation

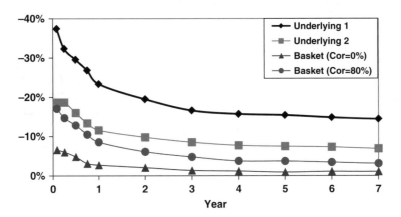

FIGURE 9.30 Skew term structure

In Figure 9.29, we plot the basket skew versus correlation at the time slice year 1. The basket skew is defined as the volatility slope at the strike of 100%. As can be seen in the figure, the basket skew increases (slope becomes more negative) as the correlation increases. This is because the larger correlation makes the constituents of the basket move together more often and increases the probability of the basket spot reaching large extreme values. The resulting probability density function can only be matched by that from an implied volatility curve with a larger skew. When correlation approaches 100%, the basket skew reaches maximum of –9.8%. This is substantially less skewed than the most skewed underlying in the basket, which has a skew of –23.4%. Actually the basket skew is even less than the least skewed underlying, which has a skew of –11.6%.

Let us now examine the skew term structures. Figure 9.30 plots the skew term structures of two basket underlyings and those of basket for different correlation coefficients (0% and 80%). Overall the basket skew tends to be reduced compared with those of the basket underlyings. This can be qualitatively understood from the central limit theorem. Given the skew indicates a non-log-normality, and when there are more basket underlyings contributing towards the joint distribution, the log-normality tends to be preserved and this reduces the skew.

Correlation Skew Influence on Basket Skew

In contrast to a constant correlation, correlation skew illustrates a more complex but realistic relationship among the basket components. In Figure 9.31, we plot a time

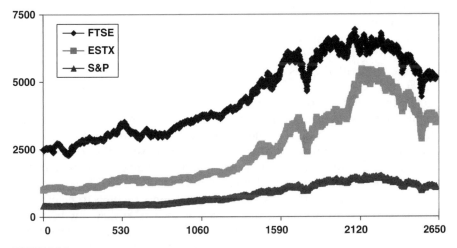

FIGURE 9.31   Historic spot (FTSE, ESTX, S&P)

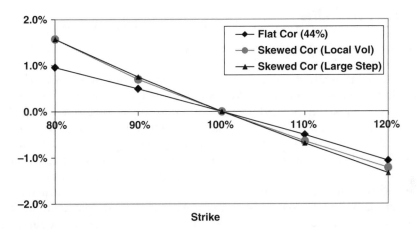

FIGURE 9.32   Basket implied volatility (1Y)

window of 10 years' worth of historic spot time series for FTSE-100, ESTX (EUROS-TOCK 50) and S&P. As can be seen, typically when markets fall dramatically they tend to fall together, indicating a much more correlated market move. A correlation skew structure incorporates the fact that the correlation becomes larger when basket component spots are falling.

The correlation skew structures can be built into the basket implied volatility surface during the construction process outlined in the earlier section. One such approach is to impose a functional form (e.g. linear) correlation structure depending on where the average basket underlying spot is in a simulated path. In Figure 9.32, we plot three basket volatility curves versus strike for a basket of three underlyings. All curves are subtracted by the ATM volatility to highlight the basket skew. The first curve is generated using a flat correlation coefficient of 44%, which is chosen such that the basket ATM volatility equals to that in the second and third curve illustrated below. The second curve is constructed with a skewed linear correlation structure in the local volatility space in small steps. For each small step, the initial correlation of 40% is scaled up linearly to a maximum of 95% when the average of the basket underlying spots falls below the prevailing average at the start of that small time step. It is apparent from the figure that the skewed correlation structure increases the slope of the basket volatility curve and the basket skew. The third curve is created also with a skewed linear correlation structure but using one big step, in which the linear correlation coefficient (between 40% and 95%) is dependent on half of the average of the terminal basket spot drop. The large step approach is effectively an approximation to the small step local volatility approach. This can be clearly seen in the figure as the third curve is very close to the second curve.

In practice, different practitioners may prefer to impose different correlation structures depending on different market views and hedging needs. The copula large step approach is flexible enough to allow various correlation structures to be incorporated into the basket. The correlation structure impact on the basket skew and basket pricing and risk exposures could be significant. Both copula and correlation skew subjects will be dealt with more details in the section below, as they are important.

COPULA APPLICATIONS

The copula pricing model is versatile and efficient, and it can be an efficient tool for pricing relevant basket products. The copula basket volatility surface construction technique is computationally efficient as it is in large steps at finite time slices. Once the basket volatility surface is built, the basket can be treated as a new single underlying and the surfaces could be interpolated or extrapolated for pricing and risk managing basket products in a consistent manner. The risk parameters relevant to individual volatility skew as well as the correlation effects can be generated within the same framework.

For the basket as a whole, its volatility and skew are positive functions of the correlation. Correlation skew structures can be imposed onto the basket during the pricing and volatility surface construction process. The correlation structure impacts the basket skew and basket option prices. A realistic and consistent basket skew framework built by incorporating a skewed correlation structure should be able to capture some risk exposures of dramatic market falls.

It is possible to extend the copula model to price other multi-asset basket payoffs and construct their volatility surface construction. For example, in a worst-of or best-of structure, the basket asset is defined as:

$$S_{min} = min\left(\frac{S_1(T)}{S_1(0)}, \frac{S_2(T)}{S_2(0)}, \cdots, \frac{S_n(T)}{S_n(0)}\right)$$

$$S_{max} = max\left(\frac{S_1(T)}{S_1(0)}, \frac{S_2(T)}{S_2(0)}, \cdots, \frac{S_n(T)}{S_n(0)}\right)$$

The worst-of or best-of basket asset can be treated as the new single underlying, similar to a standard basket underlying S_B. The new single underlying's terminal spots can be simulated using the copula technique which links the individual CDFs with an appropriate dependence (correlation) structure. The simulated spots can then be used to calculate the option prices at different strikes. The implied volatility surfaces for the new single underlying can be backed out from option prices, and the skew risk measurements of these multi-asset option structures can be conducted similarly.

Copula can also be used to price FX basket options. One needs to pay attention to the possible FX crosses ($S_{cross} = S_1 / S_2$) derived from the basket components (S_1 and S_2). For example, if a FX basket consists of GBPUSD and GBPEUR, the derived FX cross is USDEUR. The implied volatilities of GBPUSD and GBPEUR, and FX cross USDEUR contain pair-wise correlation information due to the triangle rule. If the implied volatility surface of the FX cross is available on the market, it should be used to extract valuable implied correlation information of the relevant FX pairs. Calibrating the copula model to the FX cross at a given maturity, the pair correlation can be made strike dependent in order to reprice the FX cross smile (European options at different strikes $[S_1 / S_2 - K]^+$).

In interest rate derivatives, CMS (Constant Maturity Swap) spread option is widely used by practitioners. Copula is capable of pricing CMS spread options in a consistent manner, in the presence of volatility smile/skew, which not only affects the correlated underlying components, but also drives underlying replications. We shall deal with CMS replication and its spread options pricing in a separate chapter.

Correlation and co-dependence is one of the difficult structural risks financial institutions have to manage. Basket option pricing models and techniques in basket volatility surface construction have wider applications than just derivatives pricing. The **copula** model and **correlation skew** are important in the context of basket option; the techniques and the thought process can also be used to simulate and measure contagion risks, either in the context of VaR or explicitly capturing correlation skew risks.

Finally, although this chapter has focused on the Gaussian copula, Student t copula is also a good candidate if one needs more flexibility and degrees of freedom to capture specific basket features, such as those in a CMS spread basket.

PART

Three

Interest Rate
Derivatives

During the recent financial crises, the tenor basis became prominent due to credit, which in turn triggered a multi-curve environment. The multi-curve environment will stay with us, and the interest rate derivatives have gone through a fundamental paradigm shift. In Part III, some of the important aspects of how to handle basis and price in the multi-curve environment will be explained.

In contrast to the equity underlyings, which are "tangible" as single stocks, indices or basket, interest rate derivatives deal with the term structure of yield curves. It is apparent that the underlying stochastic processes are more complex and abstract as a result. Given the underlying complexity, the interest rate derivatives models are less developed in handling volatility smile and skew. Part III will illustrate some of the practical interest rate derivative models, both vanilla and exotic, that are capable of capturing yield curve dynamics and key risk factors. Models that are able to price in the negative interest rates will be discussed. We will also explain the SABR volatility surface construction as well as the volatility wings problems in the context of calibrating both vanilla option and CMS markets.

On the exotic models, from a practical applications perspective, we will examine some short rate models with a focus on Linear Gauss–Markov, and higher-dimension models including LIBOR Market Model and extended Cheyette model. We will also explore the local volatility model framework. The pricing and hedging of the models will be discussed. CMS replication, convexity adjustment, CMS spread option products and their pricing will be examined in depth.

Part III will also discuss some of the important interest rate derivative products, either used as investment products by retail and private investors, or derivatives hedging or funding instruments by institutional and corporate customers. The product payoffs, key risk characteristics and product-specific pricing and/or calibration features will be explained.

CHAPTER 10

Multi-Curve Environment and Yield Curve Stripping

Recent financial crises have triggered a major model paradigm shift towards the multi-curve environment. The credit and liquidity elements have become integral parts of the modern yield curve stripping framework. In the multi-curve environment, the questions of which discounting curve and what collateral are important factors to consider during derivative models and infrastructure development. Collateralized derivative transactions have different economic values compared to uncollateralized ones. The interest rate derivatives modelling framework has certainly become much more complex. Credit and liquidity elements have linked up the themes of discounting, funding, derivative pricing, collateral and CVA in modern finance.

MULTI-CURVE ENVIRONMENT

Before the 2008 credit crisis, little credit element was considered in the yield curve stripping, as people either chose to ignore the small credit element or simply did not know it ever existed. For a given major currency one could strip an arbitrage-free zero curve, and this single curve could be used for both discounting and forecasting cash flows. All derivative instruments, such as swaps, vanilla and exotic options, were discounted using this single curve. The tenors of the rates instruments were practically irrelevant as far as discounting and forecasting were concerned.

The 2007 sub-prime crisis, 2008 credit crisis and subsequent eurozone debt crisis have changed yield curve modelling paradigm. Practitioners were forced to go back to the first principles, starting from yield curve stripping, to take into account the credit and liquidity elements embedded in the market rates, such as LIBOR and EURIBOR. Both credit and liquidity risk elements are functions of tenors (3-month, 6-month, etc.). This has resulted in a tenor-dependent multi-curve environment, i.e. each tenor or index requires its own curve. Yield curve stripping is no longer a simple and straight-forward topic.

OIS and LOIS

An Overnight Indexed Swap (OIS) is a fixed and floating interest rate swap. The floating rate is tied to a daily overnight index rate, often set by the central banks. Some major OIS indices are listed in Table 10.1.

The floating payment in an OIS at the specified payment date is calculated using interest accrued through geometric averaging of the overnight rate, daily over the accrual period. The fixed rate is set such that the sum of the PVs of the two OIS legs is zero at the outset.

It is important to understand the difference between an OIS rate and LIBOR. OIS is a swap, whereas LIBOR (or EURIBOR) is the financing (lending/borrowing) rate. The counterparty exposures in OIS (as a swap) is much less than that embedded in a cash (loan) transaction. Hence the difference between LIBOR and the OIS rate contains important market information of primarily credit, and liquidity. Figure 10.1 plots a snapshot of 3-month EURIBOR curve and EONIA curve. Their spread curve is also shown and labelled by the right vertical axis. It is interesting to see a hump shape of the spread curve, indicating the prevailing market expectation of the credit risk time horizon. The graph is merely a snapshot, and the spread curve does change shape over time.

The spread between LIBOR (or EURIBOR) and OIS is termed LOIS. The fact that LOIS becomes a known market acronym indicates its importance. In Figure 10.2,

TABLE 10.1 Major OIS indices

USD	The Fed Funds Effective Rate, calculated by New York Fed.
EUR	EONIA (Euro Overnight Index Average), calculated by the ECB.
GBP	SONIA (Sterling Overnight Index Average), calculated by the BBA.
CHF	TOIS, a T/N interbank fixing.
JPY	The Mutan (uncollateralized) overnight average call rate, published by BoJ.
CAD	CORRA (Canadian Overnight Repo Rate Average), published by BoC.
AUD	Interbank Overnight Cash Rate, published by RBA.

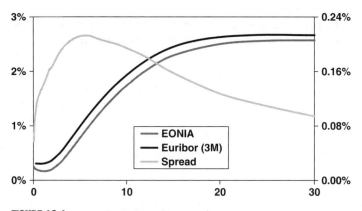

FIGURE 10.1 EURIBOR/EONIA spread

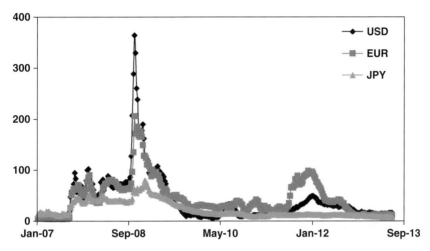

FIGURE 10.2   3M LOIS (LIBOR and OIS spread)

historic LOIS (3-month LIBOR (or EURIBOR) minus the corresponding 3-month OIS rate) values over nearly 7 years are plotted for USD, EUR and JPY. During the 2007 sub-prime crisis, LOIS curves shot up for all major currencies. The spikes during the 2008 credit crisis were huge and they shocked the financial systems. The 2012 euro-zone debt crisis triggered another prolonged jump in LOIS, in particular in EURO.

Credit and Liquidity Elements in LOIS

LOIS will be an important barometer to watch from now on, as it contains market information on credit, liquidity, and in extreme cases stress and the health of the banking system. The size of LOIS may also impact the validity of various derivative pricing models and degree of infrastructure complexities. Intuitively, for a given tenor (T), the credit and liquidity information contained in LOIS can be qualitatively represented by the following components (Crepey and Douady):

$$LOIS \approx \lambda + \sigma\sqrt{T/2}$$

where λ is the credit skew, defined as the difference between CDS spread and short-term funding spread, σ is the normal volatility of the funding spread representing liquidity. Note that it is the credit skew, as opposed to just credit, that represents the credit element in LOIS. Credit skew is the excess part of the credit over and above the funding spread which also has credit element. In general, CDS does not equal to funding spread. The gap between them varies with the market conditions, and is smaller in the normal and calmer markets. During crisis scenarios both credit skew and funding volatility are driven by elements such as panic supply/demand, and LOIS becomes significant.

Note that the liquidity spread term $(\sigma\sqrt{T/2})$ can contribute significantly to LOIS. Figure 10.3 plots the liquidity spread term (in basis point) against the spread volatility

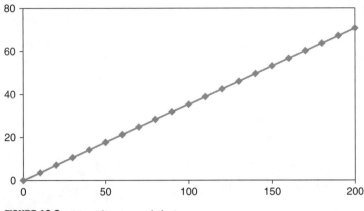

FIGURE 10.3 Liquidity spread (bp)

(in basis point) for a 3-month fixed tenor. For a volatility of 100bp, the liquidity spread is in the order of 35bp. During the past financial crises, such levels were observed and documented.

The above intuitive formulation can be used to estimate the funding spread given LOIS, CDS and funding spread volatility:

$$Funding\_Spread \approx CDS + \sigma\sqrt{T/2} - LOIS$$

A bank's funding spread is not a tradable asset, so it may not be readily observable in the market. If an external analyst wishes to work out a bank's funding spread, for example for discounting its issued structured products, the above estimation method can be useful.

Tenor Basis

Tenor basis is also known as money market basis. In a typical tenor basis swap, both legs are floating and in the same currency. One leg pays a floating rate based on one index, the other leg pays a floating rate based on another index. For example, Fed funds versus 3-month LIBOR, 3-month LIBOR versus 6-month LIBOR, 3-month EURIBOR versus 6-month EURIBOR are common tenor basis swaps. In the past, when the credit and liquidity optionality elements are ignored, both floating legs would pay flat. When the credit and liquidity optionality elements are taken into account, one leg should pay a spread over and above the index. The credit and liquidity optionality elements in the tenor basis come from the same source as LOIS. Figure 10.4 shows a historic graph of the spread for the 1-year 3M versus 6M EURIBOR tenor basis swap.

Let us examine in more detail the credit and liquidity optionality elements embedded in the tenor basis swaps. Starting from cash side, comparing two simple loans of exactly the same maturity, say 6 months, one loan has a single fixed term of 6 months, the other has two consecutive periods of 3 months. It is clear that the single fixed period loan has more credit and liquidity risk than the two consecutive periods loan. The advantage of two consecutive periods is that it offers better liquidity, and there is

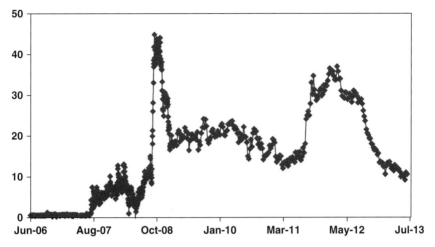

FIGURE 10.4 Euro 1Y basis swap (3M v 6M)

a chance or an option to cancel the loan if the counterparty's credit seriously deteriorates. In the case of LIBOR setting panel for interbank lending, if a panel bank's credit has severely deteriorated, it will be replaced by better one hence an option to achieve better credit quality. Therefore by lending for shorter period, e.g. 3 months, then rolling it up to 6 months, the lender effectively has a 3-month European option on better credit/liquidity. The rolled up rate therefore should be less than the straight 6-month LIBOR, due to the credit and liquidity advantage to the lender.

In the above example, the loan rates, 3-month LIBOR and 6-month LIBOR, have embedded credit and liquidity optionality risks of the cash market. Mirroring these rates in the derivatives market, say in a 3-month vs 6-month tenor basis swap, the credit and liquidity element need to be compensated. This is because such a swap is collateralized and there is no notional exchange, so there is very little credit and liquidity optionality risk in the swap, compared to the cash loan. The swap party receiving the 3-month LIBOR should get an extra positive spread to make it fair against paying 6-month LIBOR.

In Figure 10.5, four market examples of tenor basis swap curves are plotted. It is intuitively understandable that 1M vs 6M has higher spread than that of 3M vs 6M, given the former has higher rolling frequency hence higher credit optionality. Likewise, the same explanation applies as to why 3M vs 12M has larger spread than 6M vs 12M.

Note that the shape of the tenor basis swap curve can change over time. It can be monotonically decreasing or with a hump. Figure 10.6 illustrates how a EURO 3M vs 6M tenor basis swap curve changed levels and shapes over a period of time. In the middle of severe financial crisis (e.g. March 2012), the overall level is higher and the front end is significantly higher than the longer end. For the calmer period (e.g. Nov. 2010, Jun. 2013, Jan. 2015), both monotonic and hump shape can occur. These are simply the reflections of the market's views on credit and liquidity risk time horizon, which fundamentally drive the tenor basis term structure. The dynamics in relation to front and back end movement are interesting and contain certain market expectations.

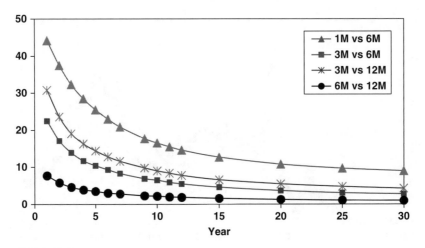

FIGURE 10.5   Tenor basis swaps

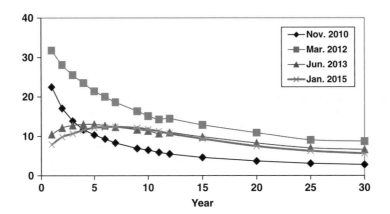

FIGURE 10.6   3M vs 6M basis swap curves

It is important to note that static credit curve CDS itself does not necessarily cause the tenor basis. In fact, the static first order credit risks have already been included in LIBOR or funding spread. It is the rolling credit optionality that is the key contributor to the tenor basis. To some extent, one can call this the second order credit effect, which cannot be ignored any more. Given the fact that tenor basis is driven by rolling credit optionality, it is conceivable that they can be linked up to the credit derivatives market, in particular in the context of credit options.

Cross-Currency Basis

A conventional cross-currency swap (CCS) involves the exchange of coupon cash flows in two different currencies, as well as initial and final notional exchange. For the initial notional exchange, once the notional amount in one currency is chosen, the amount in the other currency is determined by spot FX. The final notional exchange simply reverses the initial notional exchange between the two swap parties. The quoting convention is USD LIBOR flat versus local currency plus/minus a spread (basis) for all currencies, with two exceptions, Mexico and Chile. For Mexico and Chile, their CCS with USD are quoted local currency flat versus USD LIBOR plus/minus a spread (basis). CCS have a number of variations. Table 10.2 lists the key ones.

Conventional CCS is usually transacted with corporate clients. The counterparty risks in a conventional CCS can be substantial, principally due to the notional exchange. Mark-to-market CCS is popular in the broker OTC market due to its much reduced counterparty risk.

Cross-Currency Basis (CCB) in the cross-currency basis swap contains important market credit and liquidity risk information, similar to the tenor basis case. The credit and liquidity risk information in the CCB is of course relative, comparing one currency to the other. Figure 10.7 shows the historical EUR/USD CCB. The negative value added to the EURIBOR leg indicates the higher credit and liquidity risks in EURO relative to USD. The 1-year EUR/USD CCB had widened to −20bp in June 2008 from −2bp, and

TABLE 10.2 Key CCS variations

CCS Variations	Key Features and Comments
Floating/Floating (Conventional CCS)	▪ This is also known as cross-currency basis swap. The spread is the **cross-currency basis** between the two currencies. ▪ Standard initial and final notional exchange with constant notional amounts for both legs.
Floating/Fixed (Conventional CCS)	▪ Standard initial and final notional exchange with constant notional amounts for both legs. ▪ PV is more volatile than the above cross-currency basis swap, due to the fixed leg.
Fixed/Fixed (Conventional CCS)	▪ Standard initial and final notional exchange with constant notional amounts for both legs. ▪ PV tends to be more volatile than the two variations above.
Mark-to-market CCS (Resetting CCS)	▪ Initial notional exchange is determined in the same way as conventional CCS using spot FX. ▪ The notional on the currency paying LIBOR flat (usually USD) is adjusted or reset at the start of next coupon period using the prevailing FX rate. The notional for the other currency is kept constant throughout. ▪ The next coupon is calculated using the reset notional, and the notional excess, i.e. the difference between the reset and previous notional will be exchanged at the reset date. ▪ The counterparty risks in a resetting CCS can be dramatically reduced due to the notional reset feature.
Non-deliverable CCS	▪ Structurally it is similar to a conventional CCS, except the payments in one of the currencies are settled in another currency using the prevailing FX rate. ▪ It is usually associated with the emerging market, where one currency has little liquidity or not even convertible.

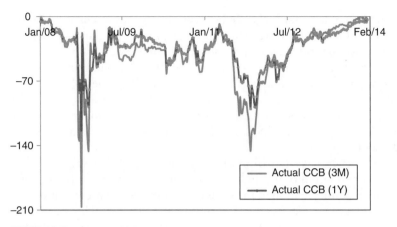

FIGURE 10.7 EURUSD cross ccy basis

peaked at –133bp in October 2008. It has remained between –20 and –60bp until late 2011, and spiking up again during the eurozone debt crisis when the USD funding dried up for European banks.

To illustrate qualitatively where the CCB comes from, imagine a CCS of 3-month USD versus 6-month EUR. It can be viewed as a collection of three swaps: the first is a CCS based on default-free OIS curves, the second is the tenor basis swap in USD 3-month LIBOR versus Fed Funds (USD LOIS), the third is the tenor basis swap in EUR 6-month EURIBOR versus EONIA (EUR LOIS). Hence overall the CCB contains the difference between the two LOISs, plus other cross terms associated the two currencies. Recall that LOIS represents the credit and liquidity quality of the relevant currency, the difference between USD and EUR LOIS will give some indication of CCB in normal and calmer markets. The relationship tends to break down as the cross terms are driven by several practical factors, including supply/demand.

Figure 10.8 compares the actual quoted USD/EUR CCB to the difference between USD/EUR LOISs. Although the difference between LOISs can give some intuition

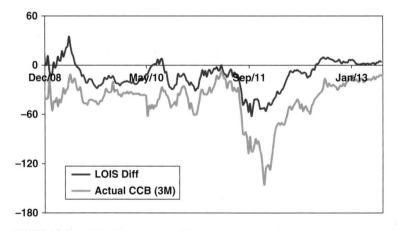

FIGURE 10.8 LOIS difference vs CCS basis

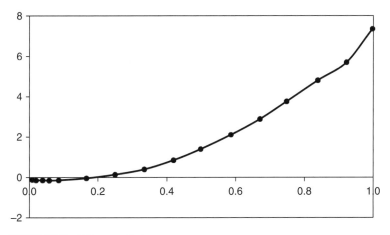

FIGURE 10.9　FX swap (bp)

in the CCB, it is not a good measure of the market-quoted CCB considering the cross terms. In more stressed markets, cross terms can be severely affected by panic supply/demand.

FX Forward/Swap

A FX swap consists of simultaneous transactions of a FX spot and a FX forward that offsets the FX risks. A FX swap is quoted as the difference between a FX forward and spot. Naturally, from the market quotes of a FX swap, one can obtain the market quotes of a FX forward. Figure 10.9 plots a snapshot of market quotes on EURUSD FX swaps. The horizontal axis is in years and the vertical axis is in basis points.

FX forward is clearly related to the cross-currency basis. Because FX forwards above 3 months are collateralized in the same way as IRS and CCS, the credit risk is mitigated and cross-currency basis is closely linked to FX forward. FX forward can be funded in the FX forward market, the shorter-end cross-currency basis swaps must converge to the relevant FX forward. In general for major currencies, the short-term FX forward market is much larger and more liquid. It is dominated by cash management and funding of FX spot positions. The short end spread can therefore be quite volatile, and the basis swap is a reflection of short-term liquidity in the cash market. FX forwards therefore contain important short end market information with regard to cross-currency basis, and they can play a valuable role in the short end yield curve stripping.

YIELD CURVE STRIPPING

In the above sections, we have mentioned "discount curve" in various places. In the old single yield curve environment, there was only one discount curve, so there was no ambiguity. However, in the current multi-curve environment, the question is which curve should be the discount curve.

Cash-collateralized trades should be discounted using OIS rate, as that is the rate collateral earns and accrues interest. In general, the discounting should be linked to the Credit Support Annex (CSA) that governs collateral posting between two counterparties. Trades with CSA counterparties should be discounted using OIS, and trades with non-CSA counterparties should use non-CSA discounting (e.g. LIBOR/ EURIBOR). In the context of yield curve stripping, OIS should be used for discounting, as all the major instruments used for stripping, such as IRS and CCS, are fully collateralized.

Single Currency Bootstrap Framework

Yield curve stripping involves setting up par bootstrap equations and solving for the unknown curves by stepping through time. Let's use a standard swap to illustrate how a yield curve stripper can be formulated. Denoting the notional N and fixed-rate k, the fixed leg PV is:

$$PV_1 = kN \sum_i^n \tau_i D_i$$

where τ_i is the accrual fraction and D_i is the discount factor. The floating leg PV is:

$$PV_2 = N \sum_j^m \tau_j \left(I_j + s\right) D_j$$

where s is spread and I_j is the index rate used for calculating floating cash flows. For example, it can be a 3-month or 6-month LIBOR. Setting $PV_1 = PV_2$, we obtain the **par bootstrap equation**:

$$k \sum_i^n \tau_i D_i = \sum_j^m \tau_j \left(I_j + s\right) D_j$$

The discount factors D_i and D_j are from the discount curve D, and the index rate I_j is from index curve I (also known as projection curve). For a given series of market swap quotes, the par fixed rates k are known. The unknowns in the bootstrap equation are the discount curve (D) and index curve (I). It is important to note that the discount curve and index curve do not need to be the same. Some people may have got used to the single curve environment where the discount curve and index curve were the same. The fact that the discount curve and index curve are not the same leads to the multi-curve environment.

In a similar way, one can set up the par bootstrap equations for OIS and tenor basis swap. These equations together with that of standard swap are summarized in Table 10.3.

TABLE 10.3 Par bootstrap equations

Instrument	Par Bootstrap Equation	Unknown Curves to Solve
Standard Swap	$$k\sum_{i}^{n}\tau_{i}D_{i} = \sum_{j}^{m}\tau_{j}\left(I_{j}+s\right)D_{j}$$	Discount curve (D) and index curve (I). As an example, D can be the OIS curve, and I a LIBOR curve.
Tenor Basis Swap	$$\sum_{i}^{n}\tau_{i}I_{i}^{x}D_{i} = \sum_{j}^{m}\tau_{j}\left(I_{j}^{y}+s\right)D_{j}$$	Discount curve (D) and two index curves. As an example, I_{i}^{x} can be the 6-month LIBOR and I_{i}^{y} the 3-month LIBOR curve.
OIS	$$k\sum_{i}^{n}\tau_{i}D_{i} = \sum_{j}^{m}\tau_{j}R_{j}D_{j}$$ $$R_{j} = \frac{\prod_{d}\left(1+\tau_{d}r_{d}\right)-1}{\sum_{d}\tau_{d}}$$	Discount curve (D) is the only unknown, as the daily overnight rate (r_d) is assumed linked to D: $$r_{d} = \frac{1}{\tau_{d}}\left(\frac{D_{1}}{D_{2}}-1\right)$$ R_{j} is the compound rate of r_{d}.

Armed with the above par bootstrap equations, one can conduct yield curve stripping in various scenarios. Tables 10.4 and 10.5 compare and highlight some key features of single curve and multi-curve environment in the context of yield curve stripping.

TABLE 10.4 Single-curve yield curve stripping

Single-Curve Environment	Key Features	Index Rate I_t	YC Stripping
Standard	$I \equiv D$, index curve is set to be the same as discount curve.	$$I_{t} = \frac{1}{\tau}\left(\frac{D_{1}}{D_{2}}-1\right)$$	1 unknown curve (D) to be bootstrapped using 1 bootstrap equation.
Including funding spread (S_t)	$I \equiv D$, index curve is set to be the same as discount curve.	$$I_{t} = \frac{1}{\tau}\left(\frac{D_{1}}{D_{2}}-1\right)+S_{t}$$	

TABLE 10.5 Multi-curve yield curve stripping

Multi-Curve Environment	Features	Index Rate I_t	YC Stripping
OIS Discounting	$I \neq D$, index curve is **not** the same as discount curve.	$$I_{t} = \frac{1}{\tau}\left(\frac{I_{1}}{I_{2}}-1\right)$$	Several unknown curves to be bootstrapped (OIS, LIBOR curves).
Including funding spread (S_t)	$I \neq D$, index curve is **not** the same as discount curve.	$$I_{t} = \frac{1}{\tau}\left(\frac{I_{1}}{I_{2}}-1\right)+S_{t}$$	

As summarized above, in the single curve environment, there is only one unknown curve (D) in the bootstrap equation. It can be bootstrapped using standard numerical techniques. In the multi-curve environment, however, there are several unknown curves. They should be all bootstrapped in such a way that they can reprice the relevant market instruments, including standard swaps, tenor basis swaps and OIS. Table 10.6 illustrates key steps of yield curve stripping in the multi-curve environment for a single currency.

In the Step 2, although tenor basis swaps are not explicitly used, by construction all the stripped LIBOR curves (e.g. 3-month, 6-month) should be able to reprice relevant tenor basis swaps (e.g. 3M v 6M) with OIS discounting. The choice of Step2 and/ or Step 3 depends on the available market quotes.

Although OIS, standard swap and tenor basis swap are the key instruments for the single currency yield curve stripping, other instruments including deposit, FRA and future also play important roles, in particular at the short end. These instruments are also tenor-dependent, and it is important to use them with the same credit/liquid class of swaps. Some specifics are summarized in Table 10.7.

Yield curve stripping does involve many other details, including interpolation conventions (e.g. log-linear MM convention), fixing and payment conventions (e.g. LIBOR/ EURIBOR are observed two business days in advance and paid at a business day nearest to the end of the interest rate period), LIBOR in arrears features in certain swaps, etc. Sometimes one needs to build/extrapolate a "synthetic" index curve based on a spread over OIS at the very short end (< 3 months). In the context of yield curve stripping, the

TABLE 10.6   Key steps of yield curve stripping

Key Steps	Bootstrap Equation	YC Stripping
Step 1: OIS curve stripping	$I \equiv D$. OIS index curve is set to be the same as the discount curve.	One needs to solve for one unknown curve (D) in the bootstrap equation. As in the single curve environment, OIS discount curve can be bootstrapped using the OIS quotes.
Step 2: LIBOR curve stripping (using LIBOR par rate quotes)	$I \neq D$. LIBOR index curve is **not** the same as the discount curve. However, the (OIS) discount curve is already obtained in Step 1.	One only needs to solve for one unknown curve (I) in the bootstrap equation. This step can be repeated to strip all LIBOR curves (e.g. 3-month, 6-month) one-by-one.
Step 3: LIBOR curve stripping (using tenor basis quotes)	$I \neq D$. LIBOR index curve is **not** the same as the discount curve. OIS discount curve and certain LIBOR are already obtained in Step 1 and 2.	As an example, if OIS and 3-month LIBOR curve are stripped already, with the 3M v 6M tenor basis swap quotes, using the bootstrap equation for tenor basis swap, the 6-month LIBOR curve can be bootstrapped.

TABLE 10.7 The role of deposit, FRA and future

Instrument	Reference Rate	Comments
Deposit	Bank's deposit rate	Bank's credit risk is embedded in deposit. Deposit is not collateralized.
FRA	LIBOR or EURIBOR	Use the right tenor for the corresponding LIBOR curve, e.g. 3-month FRA for 3-month LIBOR.
Future (STIRS)	LIBOR or EURIBOR	Convexity adjustment required. Use the right tenor for the corresponding LIBOR curve, e.g. 6-month future for 6-month LIBOR.

timing convexity due to slight payment mismatch (earlier or later) is usually ignored. One also needs to be mindful that the basis swap convention can be different from that of corresponding swaps. Ways of how to handle such details can be found in the public domain. Figure 10.10 exhibits an example set of EURO zero yield curves bootstrapped from the market quotes. As can be seen in the graph, in the multi-curve environment, the OIS curve, 3-month and 6-month` EURIBOR curve all have different values.

Multi-currency Bootstrap Framework

Let's first examine the cross-currency case in detail, and it can be easily extended to the multi-currency case. In the cross-currency case, one needs to take into account relevant single currency instruments in the two currencies, and cross-currency basis swaps, at the same time. The fact that the collateral is in one currency (usually in USD) makes the matter more complex for the other currency, even from discounting perspective. In the following, we examine how to set up the bootstrap equations for both conventional and resetting cross-currency basis swap.

Conventional CCS   In the conventional version, the notional exchanges only happen twice, one is at the beginning and the other is at the maturity of the swap. The notional amount is determined and fixed at the outset. Using standard FX convention, denoting

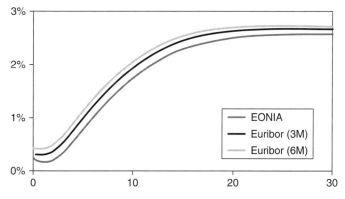

FIGURE 10.10   EONIA and EURIBOR curves

X_0 as the spot FX rate in the units of domestic currency per foreign currency unit, N_0 as the notional in foreign currency, I^d as the floating rate coupons in domestic currency, s as the basis spread and I^f as floating rate coupons in foreign currency, the cash flows for such a CCS are schematically illustrated in Figure 10.11.

In the above, we have denoted the leg receiving domestic currency coupons as the domestic currency leg, and the leg receiving foreign currency coupons as the foreign currency leg. The net position combining the two legs expressed in foreign currency is given by:

$$PV = N_0 \left[\left(D_n^f - D_m^d \right) + \sum_i^n \tau_i^f I_i^f D_i^f - \sum_j^m \tau_j^d \left(I_j^d + s \right) D_j^d \right]$$

The market quoting convention for a CCS is based on notional of 1 unit of foreign currency, i.e. $N_0 = 1$, the above PV can then be simplified to:

$$PV = \left(D_n^f - D_m^d \right) + \sum_i^n \tau_i^f I_i^f D_i^f - \sum_j^m \tau_j^d \left(I_j^d + s \right) D_j^d$$

Resetting CCS   In a resetting CCS, the notional on the currency paying LIBOR flat (usually USD) is adjusted using the prevailing FX rate such that the notional for the other currency is kept constant. Assuming the foreign currency leg paying LIBOR flat and the domestic currency leg paying spread (s), the PV for the domestic currency leg whose notional is kept constant is given by:

$$PV^d = N_0 \left[\left(D_m^d - 1 \right) + \sum_j^m \tau_j^d \left(I_j^d + s \right) D_j^d \right]$$

PV^d is expressed in foreign currency, with N_0 the initial notional in foreign currency.

For the foreign currency leg, the notional changes on the reset dates. Denoting the forward FX rates on reset dates as $X_1, X_2, \dots, X_n$, all expressed in the units of domestic currency per foreign currency unit, in order to keep the notional in the domestic currency leg constant, the adjusted notional in the foreign currency leg on the reset dates must be $N_i = \dfrac{N_0 X_0}{X_i}$, as shown in Figure 10.12.

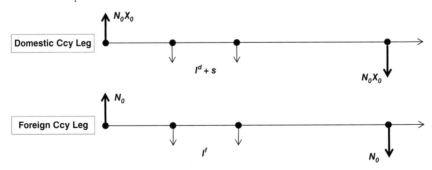

FIGURE 10.11   Conventional CCS cash flows

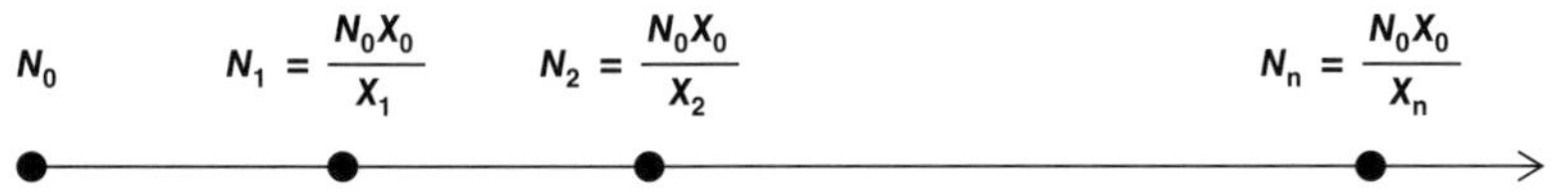

$$N_0 \qquad N_1 = \frac{N_0 X_0}{X_1} \qquad N_2 = \frac{N_0 X_0}{X_2} \qquad\qquad\qquad N_n = \frac{N_0 X_0}{X_n}$$

FIGURE 10.12 Resetting CCS adjusted foreign currency leg notional on reset dates

The sequential notional differences between the reset dates are therefore:

$$\Delta N_1 = N_1 - N_0 = N_0 X_0 \left(\frac{1}{X_1} - \frac{1}{X_0} \right)$$

$$\ldots\ldots$$

$$\Delta N_i = N_i - N_{i-1} = N_0 X_0 \left(\frac{1}{X_i} - \frac{1}{X_{i-1}} \right)$$

These notional differences are used as adjustors on the reset dates. The notional adjustors can be positive or negative (paying or receiving) depending on the prevailing FX rates. If it is positive, one needs to pay extra to make up the shortfall, and if it is negative one needs to receive the shortfall.

The combined cash flows for the foreign currency leg are shown in Figure 10.13. Its PV consists of the following expectations:

$$PV^f = E^Q \left(initial \, and \, final \, notional \right) + E^Q \left(coupons \right) - E^Q \left(notional \, adjustors \right)$$

Substituting the individual terms into above equation, the following is obtained:

$$PV^f = N_0 \left[\left(\frac{X_0}{X_n} D_n^f - 1 \right) + X_0 \sum_i^n E_i^Q \left[\frac{\tau_i^f I_i^f D_i^f}{X_{i-1}} \right] - X_0 \sum_i^n \left(\frac{1}{X_i} - \frac{1}{X_{i-1}} \right) D_i^f \right]$$

As can be seen above, the expectations on the coupons involve the ratios of LIBOR index (I_i^f) to FX rate (X_{i-1}). In such a situation when both variables are stochastic, the expectation will yield convexity adjustment in which covariance and volatility will be involved.

The par bootstrap equation for the resetting CCS can be obtained by setting the net PV to zero:

$$PV = PV^d - PV^f = 0$$

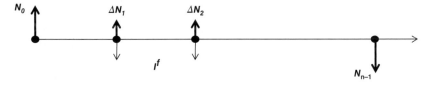

FIGURE 10.13 Resetting CCS combined foreign currency leg cash flows

A resetting CCS can also be viewed as a portfolio of one-period conventional CCS. Because the notional on the currency paying LIBOR flat is adjusted, all the one-period CCS have a common fixed notional for the currency paying the basis spread. One can derive the PV equations using the portfolio of one-period conventional CCS.

In summary, the par bootstrap equations for CCS are in Table 10.8.

Together with the par bootstrap equations for the two single currencies, the CCS par bootstrap equation should be solved to reprice all relevant instruments including IRS and CCS simultaneously. Before starting cross-currency yield curve stripping, an institution must decide which currency is its home currency. For example European banks will treat EUR as their home currency and US banks will take USD as their home currency, and the terms of "home curve" and "foreign curve" referred below are in this context. The key steps of yield curve stripping involving conventional CCS are explained in Table 10.9.

As for the resetting CCS, there is a model-dependent expectation term $[E_i^Q(\cdot)]$ in its par bootstrap equation. In the simplest case, this will give rise to a combo-like adjustment, assuming one can get the relevant volatility and correlation parameters. The FX forwards in the bootstrap equation can be either read directly from the market, or implied from the stripped home and foreign curve of up to one period earlier. Stripping yield curves involving resetting CCS can follow the same key steps as for the conventional CCS.

FX Forward   FX forward is closely linked to the cross-currency yield curve stripping. By interest rate parity, the following relationship holds between FX forward (F_t) and discount curves:

$$F_t = S_0 \frac{D_t^f}{D_t^d}$$

where S_0 is the spot, D_t^d is the domestic discount curve, and D_t^f is the foreign discount curve. The foreign discount curve (D_t^f) is the cross-currency basis adjusted curve

TABLE 10.8   Par bootstrap equations for CCS

Instrument	Par Bootstrap Equation	Unknown Curves to Solve
Conventional CCS	$D_n^f + \sum_i^n \tau_i^f I_i^f D_i^f = D_m^d + \sum_j^m \tau_j^d \left(I_j^d + s\right) D_j^d$	Domestic and foreign discount curves (D^d, D^f), domestic and foreign index curves (I^d, I^f).
Resetting CCS	$X_0 \left[\dfrac{D_n^f}{X_n} + \sum_i^n E_i^Q \left[\dfrac{(1 + \tau_i^f I_i^f) D_i^f}{X_{i-1}} \right] - \sum_i^n \dfrac{D_i^f}{X_i} \right]$ $= D_m^d + \sum_j^m \tau_j^d \left(I_j^d + s\right) D_j^d$	Domestic and foreign discount curves (D^d, D^f), domestic and foreign index curves (I^d, I^f), model-dependent expectations.

TABLE 10.9 Key steps of yield curve stripping involving CCS

Key Steps	Solve For?	YC Stripping Involving Conventional CCS
Step 1: Stripping home OIS and LIBOR curve	D^d and I^d	Same as in the single currency case, both home discount and index curve can be bootstrapped.
Step 2: Setting up foreign currency par bootstrap equations	Foreign currency instruments (e.g. IRS) Plus CCS	Foreign curves cannot be stripped in the single currency manner and then add basis spread, as they would not reprice relevant instruments.
Step 3: Stripping foreign discount and index curve simultaneously	D^f and I^f	Foreign curves have to be constructed differently. The index forwards are still the same, but the discount curve will be different if the CCS spreads are non-zero. One therefore needs to solve two simultaneous par bootstrap equations: one for the foreign currency instruments (e.g. IRS), and the other for CCS.

that can reprice market CCS correctly. Figure 10.14 plots the two error curves on the FX swap. The error curves show the difference between formulae-calculated and market-quoted FX swaps, with horizontal axis in years. The error curve using CCB adjusted foreign discount curve showing much smaller error. The error curve using the unadjusted foreign discount curve gives huge errors. Using unadjusted foreign discount curve for FX forward, or in fact for discounting foreign cash flows of other instruments is simply wrong.

Once the yield curves are stripping taking into account CCS, FX forward can be priced off these curves including the points where interpolation is needed. In practice, one needs to pay attention to certain short-end specifics in the context of pricing FX forwards correctly.

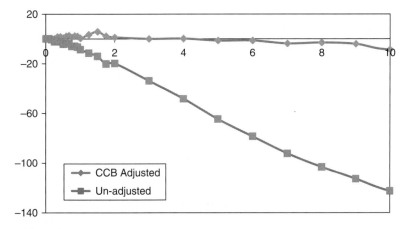

FIGURE 10.14 Error curves (against market quotes)

- In general, one should not use deposits for pricing FX Forwards, as the credit risk in deposits is far higher than that of an FX Forward (loss of principal versus FX move on the forward cash flows of the FX swap). Deposit only works for very short-dated FX forward (< 1 month) when the credit risk is small.
- The short-end curve (e.g. < 3 months) could be constructed by building the front curve as a spread to the OIS curve. This gives a 1-day resolution to the curve and thus better for pricing FX forwards and FRAs. The LIBOR FRAs can be used to calibrate front end tenor basis swap spread, e.g. taking 3-month FRAs (1x4, 2x5 etc.) and adjusting the basis spreads until the spread curve reprices these FRAs. After accounting for the cross-currency basis, the short-end curves can price dated FRAs, FX forwards and CCS. Along with futures, IRS and CCS, they can all feed into the main yield curve stripper for the longer end, being consistent with the rest of the curve.

Numerical Procedures

As discussed in the previous sections, par bootstrap equations for the relevant instruments are used to solve for the unknown curves, being domestic discount and index curve, or foreign discount and index curve. The number of instruments much be equal to or more than the numbers of unknown curves. In the simpler case that the number of instruments is the same as the number of unknown curves, the formation is a well-posed root-finding system. Otherwise one needs to solve the optimization problem.

In many practical situations, one can solve for unknown curves one by one, known as sequential bootstrapping. For example, one can strip a domestic OIS discount curve first, then a LIBOR index curve using the OIS discount curve already stripped. In some other situations, when two curves have a dependency between them, they need to be bootstrapped simultaneously and this is known as double bootstrapping. For example, when stripping foreign discount and index curve, if both of them need to be adjusted by cross-currency basis spread, they are dependent to each other and will be double bootstrapped. In practice, however, one may opt for a sequential approach in which the foreign index curve is assumed to be independent and not adjusted by cross-currency basis spread. Under this assumption, the cross-currency basis adjusted foreign discount curve can be solved, after all other curves have been bootstrapped.

In a sequential bootstrapping, one can either group instruments into maturity buckets in ascending order to solve for curve point bucket-by-bucket, or use optimization to solve for the entire curve points. Multi-dimensional optimization routines such as Levenberg–Marquardt work well as a global optimization routine. The bucket-by-bucket method is capable of fitting every point better, but at the expense of having less smooth forward curve. The global optimization method, on the other hand, can generate a smoother curve, facilitating smoother interpolations, but at the expense of having bigger errors at some points.

It is important to note that yield curve interpolation scheme can also have significant impact on time-bucketed risk sensitivities, such as deltas. For example, global cubic spline interpolation can spread the delta at one time bucket into other buckets far away from the bumping point. This is not desirable and should be avoided. In practice, localized bucket-by-bucket interpolation method is preferred. One such scheme is the piece-wise monotone interpolation in which the monotonicity of the original data is preserved. It can be either monotone quadratic or monotone cubic spline, and the interpolation is on the forward rates. For example, each bucket of three forward rates can be fitted to a local monotone quadratic function form. These local quadratic function forms can then be stitched together with continuous value. Piece-wise monotone interpolation scheme can generate a smooth forward rate curve, and at the same time allows the sensible and stable time-bucketed risk sensitivities.

In the following, we examine two examples of bootstrapped foreign discount curves that are adjusted by cross-currency basis spread. These CCS adjusted discount curves are compared with the corresponding raw OIS discount curves. The currency pair used in the example is EURUSD. In the figure below, assuming USD is the domestic currency, for example for a US bank, the stripped foreign (EUR) discount cure expressed in zero rate is compared with the EONIA discount curve. In Figure 10.15, the CCS adjusted foreign discount curve has **lower** zero rate than that of EONIA. This is in line with the fact that a USD-based bank should see a lower rate EUR discount curve, given that the current market quote of EUR/USD CCS has a positive spread on the EUR leg.

Figure 10.16 examines the flip case in which the foreign (USD) discount curve is bootstrapped from an European bank point of view. The domestic currency is EUR and the CCS adjusted foreign (USD) discount curve is compared with the raw Fed Funds

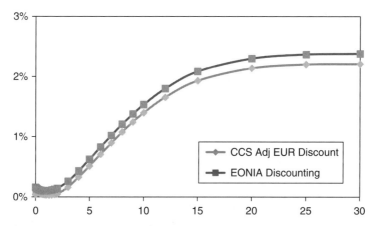

FIGURE 10.15   USD-based: EUR discount curve

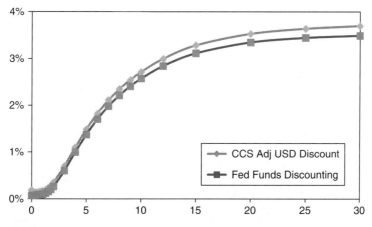

FIGURE 10.16   EUR-based – USD discount curve

discount curve. The CCS adjusted zero rate is **higher** than that of raw Fed Funds. Again this is in line with the market quotes of EUR/USD CCS.

In the above examples, an implicit assumption is that the CCS is collateralized in domestic currency. In reality, most CCS trades are collateralized in USD. This can affect the non-USD based foreign curve stripping if CCS spread is large. When the CCS spread is much less than LIBOR, this collateral effect on the foreign curve stripping can be negligible for the resetting CCS, but not necessarily for the conventional CCS given non-negligible FX exposures. In stressed market conditions when the CCS spread become large or very large, the collateral currency can have sizeable effect on the foreign curve stripping. More details are discussed in the next section, which examines the collateral impacts.

Finally, to extend the cross-currency bootstrapping method to the multi-currency case, one can in principle bootstrap the currency pairs one-by-one, after deciding which currency is the domestic currency and pairing all other currencies with the same domestic currency.

COLLATERAL IMPACTS

Collateral has become an important factor in discounting and derivatives pricing. It serves to reduce and mitigate counterparty credit risks, which in turn impacts the discounting in the multi-curve environment. It is important to handle collateral properly in the context of discounting and yield curve stripping to ensure correct pricing and avoid arbitrage.

CSA and Non-CSA Discounting

Derivative transactions with CSA counterparties should be using OIS discounting, as the trades are collateralized. This is also known as CSA-discounting. For transactions with non-CSA counterparties (e.g. some corporate customers), the discount curve should be LIBOR/EURIBOR of an appropriate tenor. Although this seems just a change of discount curve, it is actually impacting on the methodology of yield curve stripping. The distinction between CSA and non-CSA discounting also impacts derivative pricing in general. Table 10.10 lists some of the key features in the application of CSA and non-CSA discounting.

TABLE 10.10   CSA vs non-CSA discounting

	CSA Discounting	Non-CSA Discounting
Discount Curve	OIS	LIBOR/EURIBOR
Applicable Counterparties	Exchange-traded and majority OTC counterparties.	Mostly corporate counterparties, and some institutional counterparties.
CSA Infrastructure Practicalities	Each counterparty has a different CSA, or no CSA. The CSA details need to be analysed and built into an infrastructure that can accommodate individual curves for all CSA cases. The counterparties can then be tagged in order to determine which discount curve to use.	

A properly designed CSA infrastructure should include the capabilities of attaching individual discount curves to individual counterparties. Some real-life transactions and workflows do require relevant CSA features being represented in the system and priced in properly. Table 10.11 lists three such examples, showing some of the complex features in handling collateral discounting.

TABLE 10.11 Complexity examples of collateral discounting

Workflows ➜		
	Trading with a corporate customer, no CSA.	Hedging with a bank on the OTC market, with CSA.
Example 1: General trading and hedging	If in home currency, use LIBOR for discounting. If in foreign currency, use foreign CCS adjusted curve for discounting. The CCS adjusted curve can either be obtained by stripping in which LIBOR is used for discounting, or approximately incurring the LIBOR CCS adjusted curve $DF^L(CCS)$ from the OIS CCS adjusted curve $DF^{OIS}(CCS)$: $$\frac{DF^L(CCS)}{DF^{LIBOR}_{HomeCcy}} = \frac{DF^{OIS}(CCS)}{DF^{OIS}_{HomeCcy}}$$	If in home currency, use OIS for discounting. If in foreign currency, use foreign CCS adjusted curve for discounting. In the CCS stripping, OIS is the discount curve.
	Different discount curves need to be applied to the client and hedging counterparty.	
Example 2: CCS (e.g. EUR/USD)	CCS is usually collateralized in USD. For an institution that USD is the domestic currency, Fed Funds will be the discount curve, as the relevant IRS (e.g. LCH requires USD as collateral currency) as well as CCS are all collateralized in USD.	For an institution where EUR is the domestic currency, while it uses EONIA to discount EUR IRS, theoretically it cannot use EONIA to discount CCS, as CCS collateral is in USD. To be able to use EONIA consistently, one would need CCS quoted with EUR collateral, although there is no liquidity in such quotes. Therefore in this particular case, a CCS-basis-adjusted-EONIA curve $$\left(E_{adj} = EONIA * \frac{FedFunds}{FedFunds + b}\right)$$ needs to be created specifically for discounting CCS EUR cash flows.
	The choice of discount curve depends on collateral. In some cases, it is rather awkward if the collateral is not the institution's domestic currency. One will have to find practical solutions to deal with the problem. In more complicated cases where the collateral can be in either currencies, the cheapest-to-deliver collateral needs to be taken into account for the CSA-based discounting.	

(continued)

Workflows ➜

Example 3: Swaption (European or Bermudan)	Both option and its underlying swaps require discount curves. If a swaption is traded with a CSA counterparty, OIS discounting for option as well as underlying swaps will be consistent.	If, however, the swaption is traded with a non-CSA counterparty, the option will be discounted using a LIBOR curve. How about the underlying swaps which may be quoted using OIS discounting? An adjustment to the swap is needed in this case.

This nested case where the underlying may use different discount curve as the option can make life complicated. One needs to identify the correct underlying first from discounting perspective, and to ensure the underlying swaps match the market forward rates while applying the non-CSA discounting to the option element of the swaption.

Collateral Arbitrage

Mispricing collateral can lead to arbitrage. During the credit and eurozone debt crisis, a number of high-profile arbitrage "trades" were aimed at collateral mispricing. The simplest case was the pricing of cash collateralized swaps; instead of OIS, LIBOR/EURIBOR curves were used for discounting. This led to pricing errors which were taken advantage of by the arbitragers. An example trade package involves two CCSs in the same currency pair, one is out of the money for the counterparty and the other is flat. If the counterparty were using LIBOR discounting, the arbitrager could offer to pay for the package, which would be cheaper than its fair value. The money paid would immediately be posted back as collateral, which would only earn at OIS rates. The arbitrager would have made profit on the difference for free.

Other forms of collateral arbitrage involve collateral currency switching. The currency of collateral can make a difference. Each currency has its own OIS discount curve, and cross-currency basis spread is the key measure of the relative cheapness between a pair of currencies. If the collateral currency is not specified, one should theoretically post whichever currency is cheapest and switch the currency whenever feasible. There is an embedded switch option which could be very valuable. For example, during the eurozone debt crisis many European banks turned to CCS to raise dollar funding as other avenues dried up, and it was hugely advantageous to receive USD and post EUR in CSAs. EUR was clearly the cheapest-to-deliver collateral in this scenario, and the collateral posting could be optimized if the switch option existed. Although a long switch option position is difficult to monetize in practice, the embedded cross-currency forward option can be of good value in distressed scenarios. Naturally, one should avoid shorting the switch option by giving the CSA counterparty the choice of collateral currency for free.

One arbitrage mechanism carried out during the financial crisis was by back-loading IRS trades into SwapClear, the IRS clearing service at LCH.Clearnet. The clearing house only accepts cash collateral in the currency of the underlying trade, i.e. USD for USD IRS and EUR for EUR IRS. Some unsuspecting counterparties who held in-the-money USD swaps under EUR CSAs were persuaded to backload the trades into SwapClear. Effectively a collateral switch from EUR to USD happened in the back-loading process which must have benefited someone for free.

CME-LCH Basis

The two major clearing houses for interest rate swaps, CME Group and LCH.Clearnet, also allow client clearing. They serve as two CCPs and have different margin/collateral requirements. For example, CME accepts a wider range of assets, such as corporate bonds, as collateral and will offset client's cleared swaps against futures positions. The CCP-specific margin/collateral requirements can lead to differences in funding, liquidity and capital costs, which in turn result in price differences between two CCPs, i.e. two swaps with exactly the same terms but clearing through different CCPs have different prices. The difference in mid swap rates between CME and LCH is known as CME-LCH basis.

In general the CME-LCH basis is expected to be small, in the order of a fraction of one basis point (e.g. 0.15bps). However, certain market conditions can trigger price dislocation, leading to a much larger basis. For example, CME-LCH basis for the 20-year USD swap surged up to 2bps in May 2015. Because of the favourable margin/collateral requirements at CME, more buy-side clients use CME. Buy-side's positions tend to be one-way, e.g. transacting paying-fixed swaps at CME while the rates are deemed low. Interdealers as market makers, however, use LCH for the majority of their business including the hedge trades. Hence interdealers' positions at CME are also largely one-way. With little risk offsetting at both clearing houses, the resulting margin and funding costs become higher, which in turn impacts the swap prices. The build-up of the directional portfolios and exposures at CME in May 2015 therefore drove up the CME-LCH basis significantly.

The CME-LCH basis is tradable and it also has a term structure as shown in the Figure 10.17. The basis can be monetized with a CME-LCH Switch trade (basis swap).

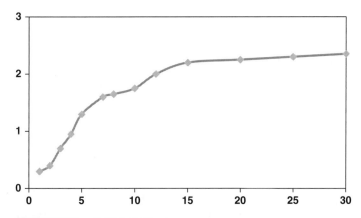

FIGURE 10.17 CME-LCH basis term structure
A snapshot of market-quoted USD CME-LCH basis swaps. The horizontal axis is in years and vertical axis in bps.

Interdealers often use CME-LCH Switch trades to reduce their overall margin/collateral requirements without changing the overall interest rate risks. Increased CME-LCH basis may induce more trading volumes of CME-LCH Switch trades, as interdealers try to optimize the overall profitability and risk profile, taking into account the margin/collateral costs and benefits.

To a large extent, the CME-LCH basis (CCP basis) can be viewed as the market price of the differential fair value adjustments. Because the basis is tradable, it becomes a risk factor in its own right. Not surprisingly, in May 2015 when the CCP basis shot up, some interdealers suffered losses due to increased hedging mismatch between CME and LCH swaps. The CCP basis is unfortunately adding one more dimension to the already complicated multi-curve environments which are characterized by the tenor basis and cross-currency basis. In other words, in addition to tenor basis and cross-currency basis, the trading and risk management systems need to include CCP basis.

CME-LCH basis also affects the futures. For a given time bucket, using CME traded interest rate futures one may not be able to replicate exactly the interest rate swap traded in LCH. During the yield curve stripping, if both CME futures and LCH swaps are used, one would expect a step/spike at the future/swap junction or overlap time bucket. This discontinuity in the stripped yield curve can cause problems in subsequent pricing and risk sensitivity calculations. Technically, one should use LCH futures with LCH swaps to strip a yield curve. Because CME futures and LCH swaps are much more liquid, one may have to mix them in practice. In this case, a basis correction factor to the CME futures can be applied to make them consistent with LCH swaps. The basis correction factors can be obtained by comparing futures to swaps over their overlap time buckets.

MULTI-CURVE MULTI-FACET REALITY

The first order credit risk has long been included in interest rate fixings, e.g. LIBOR/EURIBOR, reflecting the credit quality of the participating institutions. The second order credit and liquidity optionalities, however, are the main sources of tenor basis that lead us to a curve paradigm shift, from the single curve environment to a much more complex multi-curve environment. Cross-currency basis is principally the difference of credit/liquidity spreads in the two currencies in question. As a result of curve paradigm shift, avalanches of complex effects are triggered:

- Index curve used for forecasting the cash flows of a specific tenor is no longer the same as the discount curve. The index curve is independent from the discount curve and they are solved separately from numerical perspective.
- Cash-collateralized OIS curve is regarded as the default free curve, and used as the discount curve.
- Cross-currency basis exists for all currency pairs, as opposed to limited number of currency pairs in the past.
- Each tenor index curve can be intuitively viewed as an individual underlying, for example with its own volatility surface.
- Collateral has direct and substantial impacts in discounting and risk management in general.

- Different collateral and margining methodologies can result in material price differences for the identical instruments cleared by different CCPs.
- And so on...

The multi-curve multi-facet reality is here to stay. Multi-curve environment features must be taken into account in order to formulate a self-consistent yield curve stripping framework. This will in turn affect derivatives pricing and risk management across asset classes. Related to that, collateral discounting, management and optimization should be an important part in banks' risk management systems.

Fundamentally, the credit and liquidity risky elements embedded in the daily financial transactions need to be priced in and managed properly and consistently. In this context, there must be strong links between collateral discounting and other explicit forms of credit risk pricing, such as CVA, FVA, initial/variation margin, as all of them are underpinned by the common credit and liquidity risk factors. Collateral discounting "implicitly" incorporates counterparty credit/default risks, and CVA explicitly measures and calculates the exposures. As for CCPs, their portfolio margining methodologies, either based on VaR or expected shortfall, can have direct impacts on derivatives business.

CHAPTER 11

Vanilla Interest Rate Options

In contrast to equity underlyings, most of which are "tangible" single stocks, indices or a basket of single underlyings, interest rate derivatives deal with term structures, including yield curve and volatility term structures. Many interest rate underlings such as LIBOR, swap and bond are strongly interrelated. The underlying stochastic processes driving the term structures tend to be more complex. Given the underlying complexity, from a practical application perspective, interest rate derivative models are less developed in handling volatility smile and skew. In the following, we shall discuss vanilla interest rate option models and related practical topics, including SABR volatility surface and risk sensitivities.

Vanilla interest rate option trades account for very large portions of banks' derivatives business. The trade has undergone major changes during the financial crises. Those changes have permanently shifted certain market practices, models and system infrastructures in the light of multi-curve environment and very low interest rate regime. Interest rates during the recent financial crises stayed very low and close to zero, which triggered non-negligible probabilities of negative interest rates. In the euro zone, the subsequent quantitative easing coupled with its economic situations have firmly driven interest rates into the negative territory, as shown in the EONIA curves graph in Figure 11.1. As a result, cap/floor and European swaption features have evolved to take into account of these market realities.

MARTINGALE PRICING PRINCIPLE

Martingale pricing theorem states that if there are no arbitrage opportunities, there must exist an equivalent Q-measure and the deflated value process is a Q-martingale. In a complete market, the Q-measure is unique, which can be used to obtain the value of contingent claims.

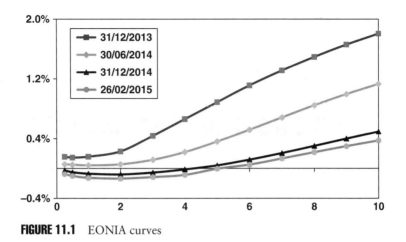

FIGURE 11.1 EONIA curves

Basic Pricing Formula

Using the zero-coupon bond $P(t,T)$ as numeraire, whose maturity (T) coincides with that of the derivative, the non-arbitrage pricing formula for a European style payoff is:

$$V_0 = P(0,T)E_0^Q \left[\frac{V_T}{P(T,T)} \right] = P(0,T)E_0^Q[V_T]$$

Because the terminal value of the zero-coupon bond is 1, i.e. $P(T, T) = 1$, the present value of the derivative is simply the discounted expected terminal payoff. This conclusion holds for all tradable underlyings, including interest rate itself (LIBOR or swap rate). There is no approximation and no contradiction in the above pricing formula. In the context of pricing interest rate options, a deterministic discount factor (zero coupon bond) should be used for discounting even if the interest rate is stochastic.

The martingale pricing principle can be readily applied to cap/floor and European swaption. With the same Log-Normal underlying stochastic process assumption, it yields exactly the same pricing formulae as the original Black formulae. It can, of course, be used to derive pricing formulae for different underlying stochastic processes, for example Normal or shifted Log-Normal process.

In the multi-curve environment whereby the discount curve is different from the index curve (which forecasts the forward coupon cash flows), the expectation of a forward rate $L(t_1, t_2)$ under the discount measure Q_d is no longer a martingale, namely:

$$E_0^{Q_d} \left[L(t_1,t_2) \right] \neq F_0(t_1,t_2)$$

where $F_0(t_1, t_2)$ is the forward rate derived from the curves at $t = 0$. Therefore mathematically a Quanto-like adjustment is necessary (Bianchetti 2010) to make the derivative pricing framework strictly arbitrage-free. Intuitively the two curves are analogous to two currencies, and a FX Quanto-like adjustment can be applied to the forward rate:

$$E_0^{Q_d}\left[L(t_1,t_2)\right] = F_0\left(t_1,t_2\right)\cdot\exp\left(\int_0^{t_1}\mu(t)dt\right)$$

$$\mu(t) = -\sigma_L(t)\sigma_X(t)\rho_{LX}(t)$$

where $\sigma_L(t)$ is the volatility of forward rate and $\sigma_X(t)$ is the volatility of $X(t)$, defined as the ratio of zero coupon bonds $X(t) = P_L(t,t_2) / P_d(t,t_2)$. Note that $X(t)$ behaves like a FX rate that "transfers" the cash flow in one currency (index curve) to another currency (discount curve). $\rho_{LX}(t)$ is the correlation between the forward rate and $X(t)$. The Quanto-like adjustment for the swap rate can be obtain in a similar fashion.

In theory, one can obtain the arbitrage-free pricing formulae by plugging the Quanto-adjusted forward rates or swap rates into the relevant martingale pricing formulae used in the single curve environment. However, the volatility of $X(t)$ and the correlation are not market observable parameters. There is no realistic chance in practice that one can arbitrage those non-tradable parameters. Therefore in practice, instead of making assumptions about the un-observable parameters, it is sometimes better to assume $E_0^{Q_d}\left[L(t_1,t_2)\right] \approx F_0(t_1,t_2)$, in which case the relevant single curve vanilla pricing formulae can still be used. For given market-quoted vanilla prices that all pricing formulae must calibrate to, the approximation errors are absorbed into implied volatilities. Implied volatility is like a sponge, it can absorb various market effects and approximations, including stochastic volatility effects.

Probability Measure Change

Probability measure change can be a very efficient technique in deriving interest rate derivative pricing models. Conceptually, measure change is associated with the change of probability density function (pdf). Denoting $u(x)$ as the pdf of a random variable x, the expectation of $f(x)$ under measure u is given by:

$$E^u\left[f(x)\right] = \int f(x)u(x)dx = \int f(x)\frac{u(x)}{v(x)}v(x)dx$$

Denoting $F(x) = f(x)\dfrac{u(x)}{v(x)}$, one obtains:

$$E^u\left[f(x)\right] = \int F(x)v(x)dx = E^v[F(x)]$$

$v(x)$ is another pdf associated with $F(x)$. The expectation of $f(x)$ under u measure is equal to the expectation of $F(x)$ under v measure.

The measure change formula is formally given as follows. With probability measure Q_A and Q_B corresponding numeraire A and B, for a random variable X_t, its expectation under Q_A can be linked to the expectation under Q_B via the Radon-Nikodym theorem:

$$E^{Q_A}\left[X_T\right] = E^{Q_B}\left[X_T\frac{dQ_A}{dQ_B}\right]$$

where:

$$\frac{dQ_A}{dQ_B} = \frac{A_T}{A_0} \frac{B_0}{B_T}$$

Hence:

$$E^{Q_A}[X_T] = \frac{B_0}{A_0} \cdot E^{Q_B}\left[X_T \frac{A_T}{B_T}\right]$$

This formula provides a convenient way to obtain expectation under different measure, which is often required in the CMS formulation and advanced interest rate derivative models.

CAP/FLOOR

The cap or floor consists of a sequence of caplets or floorlets:

$$Cap = Notional \cdot \sum_{i=1}^{n} Caplet_i$$

$$Caplet_i = \alpha_i D_i \max(F_i - K,\ 0) = Caplet_i(F_i, \alpha_i, D_i, \sigma_i, K)$$

$$Floor = Notional \cdot \sum_{i=1}^{n} Floorlet_i$$

$$Floorlet_i = \alpha_i D_i \max(K - F_i,\ 0) = Floorlet_i(F_i, \alpha_i, D_i, \sigma_i, K)$$

where F_i is the forward LIBOR, α_i is the year-fraction, D_i is the discount factor, σ_i is the caplet or floorlet volatility and K is the contractual strike. As the underlying is LIBOR, one should use appropriate tenor index curve to project cash flows. The discounting curve is the OIS curve if the trade is collateralized. If not, a non-CSA curve needs to be used for discounting depending on the counterparty.

Log-normal, Shifted Log-normal, Normal

Traditionally, the Black model with log-normal underlying had been used for quoting caps and floors. In a very low interest rate environment, given non-negligible probabilities of zero and negative rates, the Black model fails in those regions. Hence the market quotes using the shifted log-normal and normal model had emerged. Table 11.1 summarizes three different cap/floor pricing models.

In Table 11.1, $N(\cdot)$ is the Gaussian cumulative distribution function, and $n(\cdot)$ is the Gaussian probability density function $n(x) = \frac{1}{\sqrt{2\pi}} exp(-x^2 / 2)$.

TABLE 11.1 Cap/floor pricing models

Models	Caplet Formula	Floorlet Formula
	$\alpha_i D_i \left[F_i N(d_1) - K N(d_2) \right]$	$\alpha_i D_i \left[K N(-d_2) - F_i N(-d_1) \right]$
Black Model	$d_1 = \dfrac{\ln\left(\dfrac{F_i}{K}\right) + 0.5\sigma_i^2 T}{\sigma_i \sqrt{T}}, d_2 = d_1 - \sigma_i \sqrt{T}, \sigma_i = \sigma_i(T, K)$ is the Black volatility.	
	$\alpha_i D_i \left[F_i^s N(d_1) - K^s N(d_2) \right]$	$\alpha_i D_i \left[K^s N(-d_2) - F_i^s N(-d_1) \right]$
Shifted Log-Normal (LN) Model	$F_i^s = F_i + s, K^s = K + s, s$ is the rate shift, $d_1 = \dfrac{\ln\left(\dfrac{F_i^s}{K^s}\right) + 0.5(\sigma_i^s)^2 T}{\sigma_i^s \sqrt{T}},$ $d_2 = d_1 - \sigma_i \sqrt{T}, \sigma_i^s = \sigma_i^s(T, K)$ is the shifted Log-Normal volatility.	
Normal (Bachelier) Modela	$\alpha_i D_i \left[(F_i - K)N(d) + \sigma_i^N \sqrt{T}\, n(d) \right]$	$\alpha_i D_i \left[(K - F_i)N(-d) + \sigma_i^N \sqrt{T}\, n(d) \right]$
	$d = \dfrac{F_i - K}{\sigma_i^N \sqrt{T}}, \sigma_i^N = \sigma_i^N(T, K)$ is the Normal volatility.	

The shifted Log-Normal model has the following important features:

- Whilst the interest rate can indeed go to zero or negative, it is inconceivable that it can be arbitrarily negative. Therefore a moderate shift in the shifted Log-Normal model, say 1%, is in general sufficient to cover most of the eventualities.
- The shifted Log-Normal model can still utilize SABR model where a displaced SABR volatility surface is used.
- When $s \neq 0$ the implied volatility smile/skew in the shifted Log-Normal model changes compared to that of the Black model. The shift has a direct impact on the implied volatility smile/skew. Although here the shift is discussed in the context of handling zero or negative interest rate, it (aka displaced diffusion) can be a very useful tool in the modelling and calibration of interest rate volatility smile/skew.
- Many past and recent empirical studies (from the years of high inflation to the years of very low rates) have shown that the interest rate behaviours vary between Log-Normal and Normal, and best fit to Log-Normal process. Shifted Log-Normal model exhibits the flexibility to cater for the dynamics of both Log-Normal and Normal process.
- Overall, shifted Log-Normal is a simple and flexible model to handle very low or negative interest rates. It can conveniently converge to the Black model by setting shift to zero if and when the rates become high.

Comparing Black with Normal (Bachelier) model, the following key points are worth noting:

- Normal (Bachelier) model implies arbitrarily negative interest rate, which is not realistic in practice.
- Both Black and Bachelier price are a monotonic function of the volatility, although Black price is bounded and Bachelier price is unbounded as volatility becomes very large.
- For every Black volatility, there is a corresponding Bachelier volatility giving the same price.
- For every Bachelier volatility, however, there is no guarantee one can find a corresponding Black volatility. This is because numerically the problem is ill-posed in some cases. Translating a Bachelier normal volatility into a Black volatility depends on the underlying rate. A moderate Bachelier normal volatility could be corresponding to a very large Black volatility, and a small perturbation in Bachelier normal volatility could lead to arbitrarily large perturbation in Black volatility. This could make the numerical solution (Bachelier volatility → Black volatility) complicated and unstable.

The cap/floor volatility smile/skew is quite pronounced. A EUR example of market-quoted cap Black volatility surface is shown in Figure 11.2. It is plotted against maturity in years and strike in actual rates.

Calibrated to exactly the same market-quoted cap/floor prices, the shifted Log-Normal with 1% shift, and Normal volatility surfaces are plotted in Figures 11.3 and 11.4 respectively.

Comparing the Black, shifted Log-Normal and Normal volatility surfaces calibrated to the same prices, the surface "smile" shapes along the strike axis vary dramatically. The term structures along the maturity direction have similar shapes.

Volatility Term Structure

For major currencies, cap/floor implied volatility surface together with volatility term structure have liquid quotes and contain important market information. The volatility

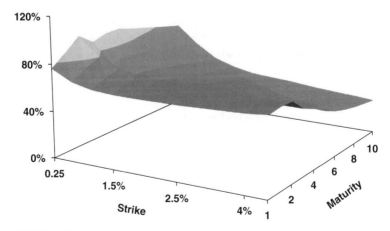

FIGURE 11.2 Cap volatility surface (Black)

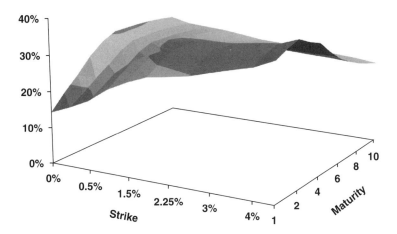

FIGURE 11.3 Cap volatility surface (shifted LN)

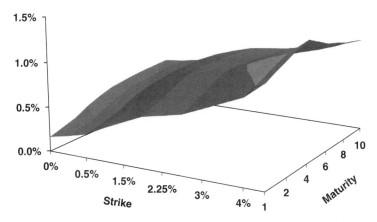

FIGURE 11.4 Cap volatility surface (Normal)

term structure is the at-the-money-forward (ATMF) volatility, and the strike is the corresponding forward swap rate with appropriate compounding frequency. The ATMF for the cap is not necessarily the ATMF for the caplets. This is an important factor to consider when stripping the flat cap volatility into caplet volatilities.

Figure 11.5 displays an example EUR cap volatility term structure using Black model. The quoting convention for EUR is that with a maturity up to 2 years, the cap underlyings are the 3-month EURIBOR caplets. For a maturity equal to or longer than 3 years, the cap underlyings are 6-month EURIBOR caplets. In the multi-curve environment where underlying tenor and tenor basis do matter, mixing 3-month EURIBOR and 6-month EURIBOR can cause complications which must be dealt with. For the Yen caps and floors, the reset frequency is 3-month LIBOR for 1-year, and 6-month LIBOR from 2-years onwards. Fortunately for the USD caps and floors, all caplets are based on 3-month LIBOR.

As can be seen in the graph, the cap volatility term structures typically exhibit humps at about the 2-year point. The volatility hump is actually an important market

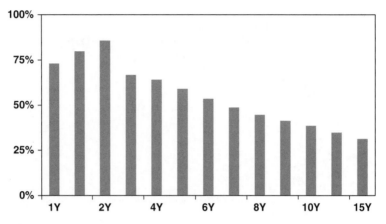

FIGURE 11.5   Cap ATMF volatility (Black)

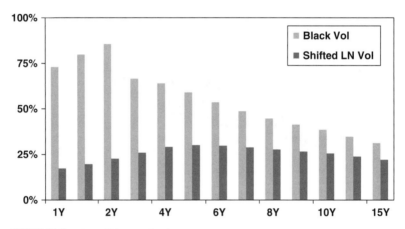

FIGURE 11.6   Cap ATMF volatility

feature which needs to be captured in interest rate derivative models. One plausible macroeconomic explanation of the hump is that it is mainly caused by central bank's intervention. Central banks, including the US Federal Reserve, have the tools and means to control short end interest rates to execute their monetary policies. They have less control over the long end interest rates, which are mostly driven by the market. Given their desires to maintain a stable interest rate environment, sometimes in the name of forward guidance, and the fact that they have means to do so, the short end volatility is driven down as a result.

The interest rate can indeed go negative, as the short end CHF interest rates went in 2013! In a very low interest rate environment, given the measurable probabilities of zero and negative interest rate, practitioners also use shifted log-normal model and normal model to price cap/floor. Figure 11.6 compares the ATMF-implied volatility term structures of (1%) shifted log-normal model with the Black model, implied out from the same market prices. The hump in the shifted log-normal volatility term

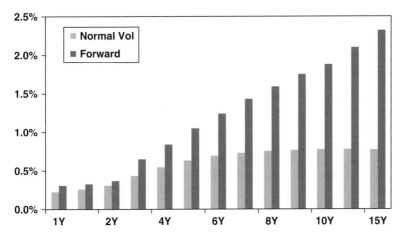

FIGURE 11.7 Cap ATMF volatility (Normal)

structure is still visible and it is pushed back towards the long end by the artificial rate shift. Given the volatility in the shifted log-normal is on $(r + 1\%)$ as opposed to (r) in the Black model, for the same cap or floor prices the implied volatilities (parameters) in the shifted log-normal model are different from those of the Black model. This is true in general when the shift in the log-normal model is not equal to zero.

Using the normal model, the implied normal volatility term structure is shown in Figure 11.7, together with the forward. The normal volatilities are expressed in absolute terms. At the short end, in a low interest rate environment, they are in the same order of magnitude of the forward.

Caplet Volatility Stripping

Stripping caplet volatility surface from the market-quoted flat volatility surface involves standard bootstrapping techniques. For a given maturity T, the cap price can be written either with the flat volatility $\sigma(T)$:

$$Cap(T) = Notional \cdot \sum_{i=1}^{n} Caplet_i \left(F_i, \alpha_i, D_i, \sigma(T), K \right)$$

or caplet volatilities σ_i:

$$Cap(T) = Notional \cdot \sum_{i=1}^{n} Caplet_i \left(F_i, \alpha_i, D_i, \sigma_i, K \right)$$

For a given strike (K) expressed in actual interest rate, by arranging the flat volatilities (hence cap prices) in ascending order of maturity, the caplet volatilities can be bootstrapped incrementally by iterating the above two equations. Repeating the process for all strikes one by one, a caplet volatility surface can be constructed.

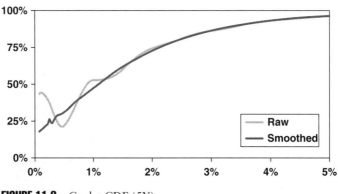

FIGURE 11.8   Caplet CDF (5Y)

During the caplet volatility stripping and subsequent re-pricing of vanillas and exotics, one has to pay attention to the interpolation and extrapolation schemes. In fact this applies to any local volatility surface stripping schemes. It is important to ensure that the caplet volatility surface is arbitrage-free in both T and K directions in the interpolation and extrapolation process. In T direction, typically piece-wise constant or linear interpolation in volatility or variance can be used in practice. In K direction, however, it can be more complex as volatility smile/skew needs to be handled properly to avoid arbitrage. Depending on the model used and/or the prevailing level of interest rate, the task of constructing an arbitrage-free caplet volatility surface can either be relatively simple or very complex.

In K direction, a non-arbitrage volatility curve will be corresponding to a monotonically increasing cumulative density function (CDF), which can be calculated from undiscounted digital prices. Figure 11.8 compares an example case where the Black caplet volatilities at year 5 are used to generate CDFs, by using the raw and smoothed volatilities. In the raw method, cubic spline is used for interpolation/extrapolation among the raw stripped caplet volatilities. The raw CDF is not behaving properly, in particular in the low strike region. The smoothed volatilities are obtained by fitting a functional form (e.g. SABR or Heston) to the raw data. Its CDF is much better, at the small expense of minor re-pricing error of market-quoted caps.

Similar comparison for the Black caplet at the 2-year point is shown in Figure 11.9. Clearly smoothing is essential if one is to use the stripped volatilities for re-pricing the vanilla books and/or pricing interest rate exotics. Additionally, the risk sensitivities are also dependent on the smoothness of the volatility curves.

Whilst some of the irregular ripples in the raw CDFs are due to numerical interpolation/extrapolation methods, the most fundamental reason lies in the model assumptions. With the Log-Normal assumption in the Black model, the rate cannot be zero or negative, hence the very low strike quotes are not really reliable to imply out Black volatilities. In contrast, if one uses the Normal (Bachelier) quotes to implied out the Normal volatilities, the stripped caplet volatilities along the K axis can generate much more plausible CDFs without any smooth scheme. This is demonstrated in Figure 11.10, in which the raw CDFs generated under the Black and the Normal

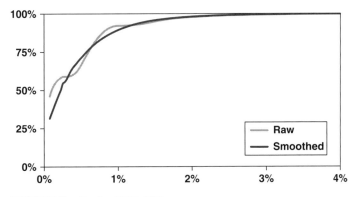

FIGURE 11.9 Caplet CDF (2Y)

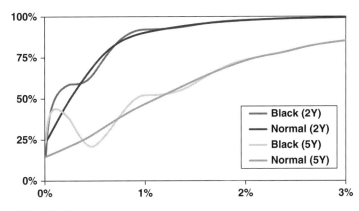

FIGURE 11.10 Caplet CDF (Black vs Normal)

model are compared. In the example, the caplet CDFs at 2 and 5 years are shown, the CDFs from the Normal model is monotonically increasing and arbitrage-free. In the very low strike region, both Normal and shifted Log-Normal model should perform much better than the Black model as their fundamental assumptions in that region is more sensible.

Tenor Volatility Transformation

The market-quoted cap/floor prices are associated with specified LIBOR tenors. The stripped caplet volatility surface from the market quotes is of course (LIBOR) tenor dependent. For example, if the market-quoted cap prices are based on 3-month LIBOR, then the stripped caplet volatility surface is for pricing relevant 3-month LIBOR instruments. It cannot be used directly for pricing, say, 6-month LIBOR instruments. A tenor volatility transformation or conversion is required if the caplet volatility surface is going to be used for different tenors. In the following, we shall explain the transformation methods that are model-independent.

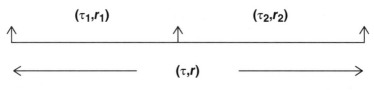

FIGURE 11.11 Tenor conversion diagram

Single Curve Environment   In the single yield curve environment, the tenor basis between LIBORs are zero. Using the schematic diagram in Figure 11.11, assuming the caplet volatilities for the shorter tenors (τ_1, τ_2) are known, we will convert them to the caplet volatility of a longer tenor (τ).

The corresponding forward rate (r) for the longer tenor (τ) in the compounding case is given by:

$$\tau r = \tau_1 r_1 \left(1 + \tau_2 r_2\right) + \tau_2 r_2$$
$$= \tau_1 r_1 + \tau_2 r_2 + \tau_1 \tau_2 r_1 r_2$$

which can be rewritten as:

$$r = a_1 r_1 + a_2 r_2 + a_3 r_3$$

where $a_1 = \dfrac{\tau_1}{\tau}$, $a_2 = \dfrac{\tau_2}{\tau}$, $a_3 = \dfrac{\tau_1 \tau_2}{\tau}$ and $r_3 = r_1 r_2$. Note that once the stochastic processes of r_1 and r_2 are given, the stochastic process of r_3 is also defined. For example, assuming r_1 and r_2 follow the Log-Normal process:

$$dr_1 = \left(\cdot\right)dt + r_1 \sigma_1 \sqrt{t}\,dw_1$$
$$dr_2 = \left(\cdot\right)dt + r_2 \sigma_2 \sqrt{t}\,dw_2$$
$$dw_1 dw_2 = \rho dt$$

where t is the time from today to the first caplet, the stochastic process for $r_3 = r_1 r_2$ is also Log-Normal, and given by:

$$dr_3 = \left(\cdot\right)dt + r_3 \sigma_3 \sqrt{t}\,dw_3$$

Since the longer tenor caplet (r) also starts at time t the variance integration will be from today to t. Hence:

$$\sigma_3^2 = \sigma_1^2 + \sigma_2^2 + 2\rho\sigma_1\sigma_2$$

It is clear that r is a basket of r_1, r_2, r_3. The volatility of a basket can be approximated in many different ways. One of the techniques is the moment matching, which matches the first and second moment. If the individual basket underlyings (r_1, r_2, r_3)

follow the Log-Normal processes, freezing and ignoring the drift, the basket volatility (σ_r) for r can be calculated from the following equation:

$$\sigma_r^2 t = ln\left[\frac{\sum_{i,j}^n a_i a_j r_i(0) r_j(0) exp\left(\rho_{i,j} \sigma_i \sigma_j t\right)}{\left[\sum_i^n a_i r_i(0)\right]^2} \right]$$

$$\rho_{i,j} = \rho \ \ if \ i \neq 3 \ j \neq 3$$

$$\rho_{i,3} = \frac{\sigma_i^2 + \sigma_1 \sigma_2 \rho}{\sigma_i \sigma_3} \ \ if \ i \neq 3 \ j = 3$$

$$\rho_{3,j} = \frac{\sigma_j^2 + \sigma_1 \sigma_2 \rho}{\sigma_j \sigma_3} \ \ if \ i = 3 \ j \neq 3$$

When interest rate is low the compounding term $r_3 = r_1 r_2$ can be ignored in practice. Figure 11.12 plots such an example for the 6-month caplet volatility given the 3-month caplet volatilities (σ_1, σ_2). The parameters used are $\sigma_1 = \sigma_2 = 60\%$, $\tau_1 = \tau_2 = 0.25$, $r_1(0) = r_2(0) = 0.5\%$ and $t = 2$. The 6-month caplet volatility approximated by the basket volatility is plotted against the correlation.

Market cap/floor tenor are typically 3 months or 6 months. In practice the required tenor volatility conversations are mostly between those tenors. Even if for other non-standard tenors, they are all within the range of 1 month – the shortest – to 12 months – the longest. The correlation between the two consecutive caplets is relatively high and stable. The basket approximation works well for the practical range and correlation levels. Also, for the 12-month caplet tenor, the equivalent swaption on the underlying 1-year swap may be of reference value for cross-checking.

If we use the Normal assumption for the interest rate, the compounding term $r_3 = r_1 r_2$ will almost certainly be negligible. This is because the Normal assumption is made usually when the interest rate is very low, in which case the compounding term

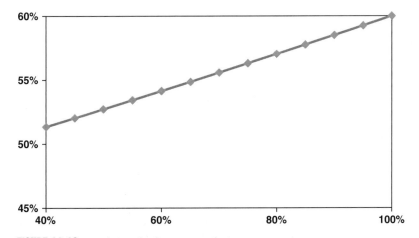

FIGURE 11.12 Basket volatility vs correlation

is very small. The forward rate (r) for the longer tenor (τ) is therefore given by the sum of two Normal variables:

$$r = a_1 r_1 + a_2 r_2$$

and the basket volatility (σ_r) for r can be obtained by the following equation:

$$\sigma_r^2 = a_1^2 \sigma_1^2 + a_2^2 \sigma_2^2 + 2\rho a_1 \sigma_1 a_2 \sigma_2$$

Basket techniques provide very simple ways to transform caplet tenor volatilities. There are other approximate approaches (e.g. Kienitz 2013) which are equally plausible. Note that the correlation parameters can be adjusted and practically most of the proposed approaches are equivalent if they are calibrated to each other.

We have so far discussed how to convert the volatilities of shorter tenor caplets (e.g. 3 month) to that of a longer tenor caplet (e.g. 6 month). What about the reverse, for example converting a 6-month caplet volatility into two 3-month caplets volatilities? The general setup is that, knowing the longer tenor caplet volatility (σ_r), we reach the solutions for the shorter tenor caplet volatilities $(\sigma_1, \cdots, \sigma_n)$ in the following basket volatility equation:

$$\sigma_r^2 t = ln\left[\frac{\sum_{i,j}^{n} a_i a_j r_i(0) r_j(0) exp\left(\rho_{i,j} \sigma_i \sigma_j t\right)}{\left[\sum_i^n a_i r_i(0)\right]^2} \right]$$

As always, the inverse problem is more difficult than the straight problem, and the answers are not unique. One must make assumptions to narrow down the possible solutions. It is also a good idea to reduce the dimensionality by keeping n as small as possible. Converting a 6-month tenor volatility into monthly tenor volatilities $(n = 6)$, one will have to solve for a 6-dimensional problem. In Table 11.2, using a 6-month caplet volatility $(\sigma_r$ is known), we discuss some of the practical solutions of converting it into two 3-month caplet volatilities $(n = 2$, solve for σ_1 and $\sigma_2)$.

TABLE 11.2 Solutions under different assumptions

Assumption	Solution
$\sigma_1 = \sigma_2$	This is the easiest. It works well when the volatility term structure is relatively flat.
$r_1(0)\sigma_1 = r_2(0)\sigma_2$	This is also easy. It assumes that the absolute (Normal) volatilities of two adjacent caplets are equal.
$\sigma_2 = f(\sigma_1)$	One can use a functional form to link up σ_1 and σ_2. It can be a linear relationship inferred from 6-month caplets.
$\sigma_t = b_t \cdot f(A, t)$	More generally, one can use a functional form $f(A, t)$, where A are constants, inferred from the known 6-month caplets, For example the hump functional form $\left[f(A,t) = (a_1 + a_2 t)exp(a_3 t) + a_4\right]$ can be a good candidate. The scaling parameter (b_t) associated with the 3-month caplet volatility (σ_t) can then be solved by using the basket volatility equation.

The tenor volatility transformation can be performed strike by strike using the same technique stated above. In general, the same volatility smile/skew shape will be preserved for the converted caplet volatility surface. Alternatively, one can explicitly use SABR functional form to preserve the smile/skew shape for different tenors. This can be done by superimposing the same smile/skew features (e.g. the smile/skew shape with respect to moneyness) in the SABR to the already-transformed ATM volatilities.

Multi-curve Environment In the multi-curve environment, one must take into account of the tenor basis (aka money market basis) between LIBORs. For simplicity, if we ignore the compounding term, using the same notations as above, the forward rate (r) for the longer tenor (τ) is given by:

$$
\begin{aligned}
r &= a_1(r_1 + b) + a_2 (r_2 + b) \\
&= a_1 r_1 + a_2 r_2 + (a_1 + a_2)b \\
&= r_s + (a_1 + a_2)b
\end{aligned}
$$

where b is the market-quoted tenor basis, for example between 3-month and 6-month LIBOR, and $r_s = a_1 r_1 + a_2 r_2$ is the equivalent single curve forward rate (without tenor basis) for the longer tenor (τ). The volatilities for r_s can be calculated using the basket technique outlined in the last section. We are therefore left with only needing to solve for the volatilities for r given those of r_s and b.

There are two possible approaches to transform shorter tenor caplet volatilities to longer tenor volatilities. Both approaches involve making certain assumptions on the tenor basis. The first is to assume that the tenor basis is deterministic. The second is to assume that the tenor basis is stochastic, and one has to estimate the volatility of the tenor basis and its correlations with LIBOR. In Table 11.3, we shall illustrate and compare the two approaches.

In Figure 11.13, assuming tenor basis is deterministic, we plot the tenor basis adjusted caplet volatilities versus tenor basis (b), using the same basket example in the single curve case with correlation fixed at 90%. As the tenor basis increases, the adjusted caplet volatility $\sigma(K)$ in the multi-curve case can be significantly different from that $\sigma_s(K)$ in the single curve case.

TABLE 11.3 Comparison of two approaches

	Tenor basis (b) is assumed to be deterministic	Tenor basis (b) is assumed to be stochastic (as it is in practice)
Equation	$r = r_s + (a_1 + a_2)b = r_s + d_b$	$r = r_s + (a_1 + a_2)b$
Stochastic Feature	$dr = d(r_s + d_b)$, a shifted Log-Normal (displaced diffusion) process can be used to obtain the implied volatility of $(r_s + d_b)$ or r.	Stochastic basis b can be viewed either as an additional component in the original basket (r_1, r_2, b), or as a component in the new basket of (r_s, b). The latter is obviously easier.

(continued)

TABLE 11.3 *Continued*

	Tenor basis (*b*) is assumed to be deterministic	Tenor basis (*b*) is assumed to be stochastic (as it is in practice)
Solution	Because: $$E^Q[(r_s - K)^+] = E^Q\left\{\left[(r_s + d_b) - (K + d_b)\right]^+\right\}$$ We have: $$BS\left(r_s, K, \sigma_s\left(K\right)\right) = BS\left(r_s + d_b, K + d_b, \sigma\left(K + d_b\right)\right)$$ d_b and $\sigma_s(K)$ of r_s, are known. The Black volatility $\sigma(K + d_b)$ of r can therefore be implied out. Note that its strike is shifted by d_b. The forward rate r is calculated from the longer tenor yield curve already including tenor basis.	One can therefore use the same basket approximation to obtain the basket volatility including tenor basis. The volatility of b and its correlations with LIBOR need to be estimated, primarily using historic data.
Intuition	Because b and d_b are positive, the resulting caplet volatility of r is lower than that of r_s.	Because b is typically negatively correlated to LIBOR, the resulting caplet volatility of L_{6M} is lower than that of L_{3M}, for example.
	Both approaches make the longer tenor caplet volatility lower.	

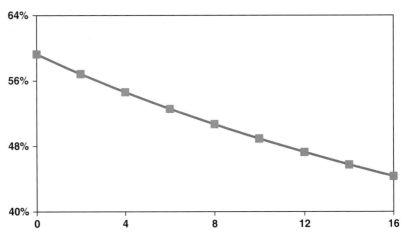

FIGURE 11.13 Tenor basis adjusted volatility

As can be seen above, there is a one-to-one relationship between $\sigma_s(K)$ and $\sigma(K)$. The caplet volatility in the single curve case can be converted to that in the multi-curve case with tenor basis adjustment, and vice versa. Hence if one needs to transform the longer tenor caplet volatility into shorter tenor ones in the multi-curve case, one can first of all convert it into the equivalent single curve volatility $(\sigma(K) \rightarrow \sigma_s(K))$. The techniques of transforming longer tenor to shorter tenor caplet volatilities described in the single curve section can then be applied to $\sigma_s(K)$.

Stripping and Transformation Examples

In the following, we shall examine some examples of caplet volatility stripping and tenor volatility transformation using a set of EUR cap market quotes. The quoted Black flat volatility surface and its equivalent shifted Log-Normal and Normal flat volatility surfaces are shown earlier in this chapter.

The quoting convention for the EUR caps is peculiar. Up to and including 2-years maturity, the cap underlying is 3M EURIBOR. From 3-years onwards, the underlying is 6M EURIBOR. Therefore during the caplet volatility stripping, if one needs to have the same tenor (either 3M or 6M) throughout, tenor volatility transformation is an important part of surface construction process.

Black Caplet Volatility Surfaces   The stripped and transformed caplet volatility surfaces for 3M and 6M tenor respectively are shown in the Figures 11.14 and 11.15.

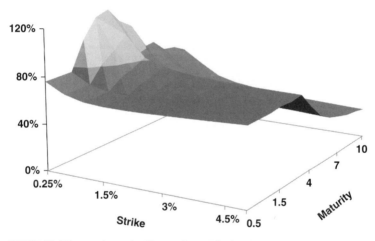

FIGURE 11.14   Caplet volatility surface (Black 3M)

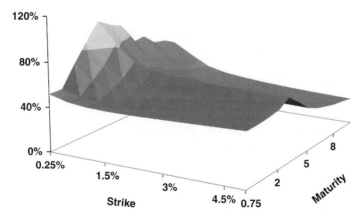

FIGURE 11.15   Caplet volatility surface (Black 6M)

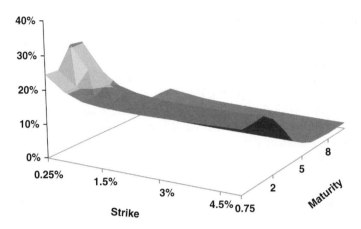

FIGURE 11.16   Caplet volatility difference (Black 3M-6M)

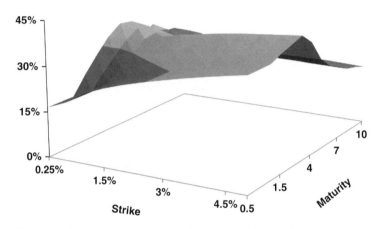

FIGURE 11.17   Caplet volatility surface (Shifted LN 3M)

The differences between the above two volatility surfaces are plotted in Figure 11.16. As expected, the 3M caplet volatilities are higher than those of 6M.

Shifted Log-normal Caplet Volatility Surface   The stripped and tenor transformed Log-Normal (LN) caplet volatility surfaces for 3M and 6M are shown in Figures 11.17 and 11.18.

The differences between them are plotted in Figure 11.19. The 3M shifted LN caplet volatilities are higher than those of 6M.

Normal Caplet Volatility Surface   The stripped and transformed 3M and 6M caplet Normal volatility surfaces are shown in Figures 11.20 and 11.21.

Figure 11.22 displays the differences between the 3M and 6M caplet Normal volatilities.

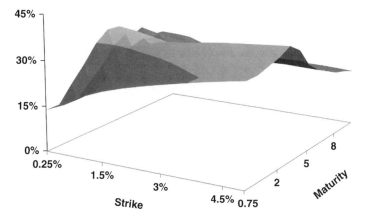

FIGURE 11.18   Caplet volatility surface (Shifted LN 6M)

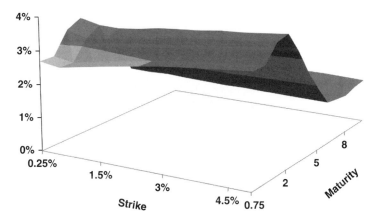

FIGURE 11.19   Caplet volatility difference (Shifted LN 3M-6M)

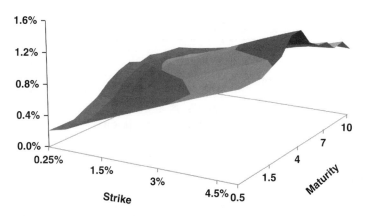

FIGURE 11.20   Caplet volatility surface (Normal 3M)

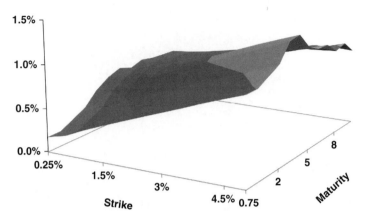

FIGURE 11.21 Caplet volatility surface (Normal 6M)

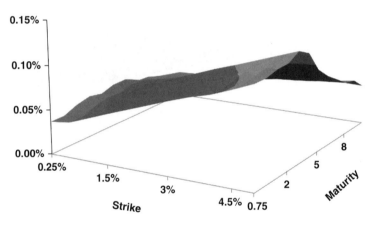

FIGURE 11.22 Caplet volatility difference (Normal 3M-6M)

EUROPEAN SWAPTION AND SABR

A swaption is an option on IRS. European swaptions for major currencies are quoted in the OTC markets. The market implied swaption volatilities are in turn used to price other vanilla as well as exotic instruments. SABR is an industry-standard model for swaption volatility smile and its dynamics. Note that due to credit elements, the traditional pricing link between a swaption and a bond option is no longer strong, and each has its own pricing setup.

Swaption Features

A payer swaption gives the holder the right (but not obligation) to exercise into a swap that pays the fixed (strike) and receives the floating. A receiver swaption gives the holder the right (but not obligation) to exercise into a swap that receives the fixed (strike) and pays the floating. The corresponding payoffs with a strike K are:

$$PaySwaption = Notional \cdot \max \left(S_{t,T}(0) - K, 0\right) \cdot A_{t,T}$$

$$RecSwaption = Notional \cdot \max \left(K - S_{t,T}(0), 0\right) \cdot A_{t,T}$$

$$K_{ATM} = S_{t,T}(0) = \frac{P(0,t) - P(0,T)}{\sum_{i=1}^{n} \tau_i P(0, T_i)}$$

where $S_{t,T}(0)$ is the forward swap rate at option maturity t, and the underlying swap tenor is $(T - t)$. $A_{t,T}$ is either the PVBP annuity or cash annuity, depending on whether the swaption is physical-settled or cash-settled. Settlement rules can indeed impact pricing. Table 11.4 summarizes the key swaption settlement rules and features.

TABLE 11.4   Swaption settlement rules and key features

Swaption Settlement	Rules and Key Features
Cash-Settled (Market convention for European currencies, including EUR and GBP)	■ On option expiry, the payoff is settled in cash. ■ The cash annuity is calculated using the IRR formula: $A_{t,T}(S) = \frac{1}{m}\sum_{i=1}^{n}(1 + S/m)^{-i} = \left[1 - (1 + S/m)^{-n}\right]/S$, where S is the settlement swap rate, m is the coupon frequency and n is the total number of coupons. ■ The cash value is not necessarily the accurate market value of the prevailing par swap with fixed rate equal to the strike, due to the fact that it is not the prevailing discount curve and year-fractions. ■ Whilst it is easy to calculate the settlement cash value, the actual swaption payoff is modified by the inclusion of S.
PVBP Cash-Settled (Market convention for USD)	■ On option expiry, the payoff is still settled in cash. ■ However, the cash annuity is calculated in the same way as phys-ical-settled, using the prevailing discount curve and relevant year-fractions. ■ The two counterparties will have to negotiate and agree their dis-count curves for the cash annuity. ■ The calculated cash value is in line with the market value of prevailing swap, equivalent to physical-settled value. However, cash-settled avoids the counterparty risks of the underlying swap.
Physical-Settled	■ On option expiry, if it is exercised, the two counterparties physi-cally transact a swap defined by the swaption. ■ For settlement purposes, one does not need to calculate annuity. ■ For pricing purposes, the PVBP annuity is calculated using the pre-vailing discount curve and relevant year-fractions: $A_{t,T}(0) = \sum_{i=1}^{n} \tau_i P(0, T_i).$ ■ The underlying swap will prolong the counterparty risks and credit lines.

Swaption Market Quotes

In the "old days" when there was only one yield curve (single-curve environment) and only one model (Black model), European swaption market quotes were either Black implied volatilities or spot premiums. One could easily convert one to another, and the two were regarded as equivalent.

In today's multi-curve and low interest rate environment, European swaptions can be priced with different curves and using different models. Therefore the swaption market quotes need to specify the curve for the premium quotes, and the model if the quotes are implied volatilities. Table 11.5–11.7 show three example sets of ATM swaption straddles premium quotes in bps: spot premiums with EONIA discounting for

TABLE 11.5 ATM swaption straddles – spot premium (EONIA)

Option Expiry	1Y	2Y	5Y	10Y	20Y	30Y
1M	4.0	9.0	52.0	185	387	544
3M	6.5	14.0	79.5	276	582	805
6M	10.0	23.0	113	369	753	1069
1Y	20.5	47.5	180	509	990	1398
2Y	45.5	100	297	723	1341	1879
5Y	116.5	231	581	1153	1956	2649
10Y	162.5	322	759	1430	2328	3153
20Y	169.0	338	783	1459	2322	3108
30Y	154.0	307	693	1274	2084	2853

Spot premium is the premium discounted to the spot date.

TABLE 11.6 ATM swaption straddles – forward premium (EONIA)

Option Expiry	1Y	2Y	5Y	10Y	20Y	30Y
1M	4.0	9.0	52.0	185	387	544
3M	6.5	14.0	79.5	276	582	804
6M	10.0	23.0	113	368	752	1068
1Y	20.5	47.5	180	508	988	1396
2Y	45.0	99.5	296	722	1338	1875
5Y	118.0	234	589	1169	1983	2685
10Y	179.5	356	839	1581	2574	3487
20Y	234.0	469	1086	2022	3220	4309
30Y	257	512	1155	2123	3472	4753

Forward premium is the un-discounted premium at the option expiry.

TABLE 11.7 ATM swaption straddles – spot premium (EURIBOR)

Option Expiry	1Y	2Y	5Y	10Y	20Y	30Y
1M	4.0	9.0	52.0	185	387	544
3M	7	14.0	80	276	582	804
6M	10.0	23.0	113	368	752	1068
1Y	20	47	180	508	988	1396
2Y	45	100	296	721	1337	1874
5Y	115	229	577	1144	1942	2629
10Y	159	317	748	1409	2294	3107
20Y	163	331	766	1426	2270	3039
30Y	148	300	675	1242	2031	2780

option and underlying swap (Table 11.5), forward premiums with EONIA discounting for underlying swap (Table 11.6), spot premiums with EURIBOR discounting for option and underlying swap (Table 11.7).

The market-quoted premiums can easily be converted into model-dependent implied volatilities. For major currencies, there are market quotes of Black volatilities (Black model). Implied volatilities of shifted Log-Normal (LN) model and/or Normal model are also quoted, mainly for handling low or negative interest rates.

Swaption Volatilities (Black, Shifted LN)

In the following, we shall analyse an example set of European swaption implied volatility quotes for euro. The features of ATM swaption volatility surface (maturity/tenor) and smile are shown for both Black and shifted LN model. In the shifted LN quotes, the shifts are 0.2% for the 1Y and 2Y tenor, 0.17% for the 3Y tenor, 0.13% for the 4Y tenor and 0.1% for all the other tenors.

Swaption ATM Volatility Surface   Figures 11.23 and 11.24 show the Black and shifted LN ATM volatility surface. In the Black case, the volatilities for the short tenors are much higher than those longer tenors. In the shifted LN case, the volatilities are lower than those of Black as expected. The short tenor volatilities are still in general higher than those of long tenors, although there can be some exceptions.

Swaption Volatility Smile   Extending the swaption ATM volatility surface along the strike dimension, the swaption volatility cube (maturity/tenor/strike) includes the market information of volatility smile. In the following, we take a few cross-sectional slices from the swaption volatility cube to dive into volatility smile.

Figure 11.25 compares the Black volatility smiles of different maturities (1y, 2y, 5y, 10y) on the same tenor (10y). The horizontal axis is strike expressed as the distance from the ATM strike. It can be seen that the smile curve flattens and smile decreases for longer maturities.

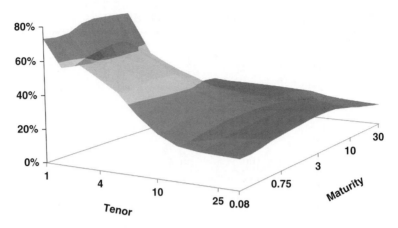

FIGURE 11.23 Swaption ATM volatility (Black)

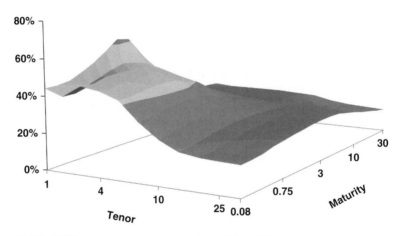

FIGURE 11.24 Swaption ATM volatility (shifted LN)

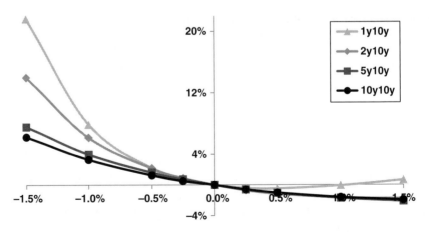

FIGURE 11.25 Swaption smile (Black)

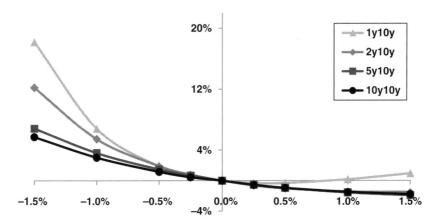

FIGURE 11.26   Swaption smile (Shifted LN)

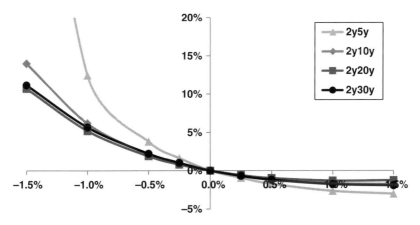

FIGURE 11.27   Swaption smile (Black)

The same conclusion can be drawn for the shifted LN volatility smile as shown in Figure 11.26: smile decreases for longer maturities. The curvature of the shifted LN smile curve is less than that of its relevant Black counterpart. In general, Black volatility smile is more pronounced than the shifted LN volatility smile.

Figure 11.27 exhibits the Black volatility smiles of the same maturity (2y) but of different tenors (5y, 10y, 20y, 30y). The smile (curvature) tends to decrease for longer tenors. The same can be observed for the shifted LN smile in Figure 11.28.

SABR Volatility Surface

SABR (Stochastic Alpha Beta Rho) model is a stochastic volatility model for the forward (swap) rate F_t, characterized by the following SDE:

$$dF_t = \sigma_t F_t^\beta dw_1$$
$$d\sigma_t = \nu \sigma_t dw_2$$
$$dw_1 dw_2 = \rho dt$$

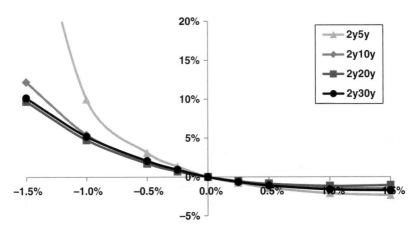

FIGURE 11.28 Swaption smile (Shifted LN)

where β, v and ρ are constant: $0 \leq \beta \leq 1$, $v \geq 0$ and $-1 < \rho < 1$. In the SABR name, stochastic Alpha means stochastic σ_t, as Beta and Rho are constant. The above SDE can be used to price European options and therefore derive the implied volatility of the Black model that reprices the same option. Numerically, one can solve the 2-D (F_t and σ_t) Kolmogorov PDE to obtain European option price. However, using asymptotic expansion approximation, Hagan et al (2002) derived the SABR implied volatility analytical formula, which is widely used in the industry either in its original or subsequently enhanced form. Denoting $F_0 = f$ and $\sigma_0 = \alpha$, the implied volatility at strike K expressed as Taylor expansion series in $v^2 T$ can be written as:

$$\sigma_{imp}(K, f, T) = \sigma_0(K, f)\big(1 + \sigma_1(K, f) \cdot T\big) + O((v^2 T)^2)$$

where:

$$\sigma_1(K, f) = \frac{(1 - \beta)^2 \alpha^2}{24(fK)^{1-\beta}} + \frac{\rho \beta v \alpha}{4(fK)^{(1-\beta)/2}} + \frac{2 - 3\rho^2}{24} v^2$$

For the term $\sigma_0(K, f)$, as pointed out by Obloj (2008), it can be better approximated by the enhanced method with slightly different outcomes, as compared in Table 11.8.

Figures 11.29 to 11.31 compare the original SABR to the enhanced SABR using an example set of swaption smile parameters at $T = 10$ years and $f = 3\%$. The differences around the ATM region are tiny and negligible. As we zoom into the low and high strike regions, the differences between the original and enhanced SABR become sizeable as shown in the figures. In fact, the enhanced SABR is less prone to the negative probability density problem, although it does not eliminate the problem completely.

With the enhanced SABR, the at-the-money volatility is obtained by setting $K = f$:

$$\sigma_{ATM} = \sigma_{imp}(f, f, T)$$
$$= \alpha f^{\beta-1}\big(1 + \sigma_1(f, f) \cdot T\big)$$
$$\sigma_1(f, f) = \frac{(1 - \beta)^2 \alpha^2}{24 f^{2(1-\beta)}} + \frac{\rho \beta v \alpha}{4 f^{(1-\beta)}} + \frac{2 - 3\rho^2}{24} v^2$$

TABLE 11.8   Original vs enhanced SABR

Original SABR [Hagan et al 2002]	Enhanced SABR [Berestycki 2004, Obloj 2008]
$$\sigma_0\left(K,f\right)=\frac{\left(f-K\right)\left(1-\beta\right)}{\left(fK\right)^{\beta/2}\left(f^{1-\beta}-K^{1-\beta}\right)}\cdot\frac{v\cdot\ln\left(f/K\right)}{x\left(z\right)}$$	$$\sigma_0\left(K,f\right)=\frac{v\cdot\ln\left(f/K\right)}{x\left(z\right)}$$
$$z=\frac{v\left(f-K\right)}{\alpha\left(fK\right)^{\beta/2}}$$	$$z=\frac{v\left(f^{1-\beta}-K^{1-\beta}\right)}{\alpha\left(1-\beta\right)}$$
$$x\left(z\right)=\ln\left(\frac{\sqrt{1-2\rho z+z^2}+z-\rho}{1-\rho}\right)$$	$$x\left(z\right)=\ln\left(\frac{\sqrt{1-2\rho z+z^2}+z-\rho}{1-\rho}\right)$$

After further expansion and simplification, the original SABR can be written as:

$$\sigma_0\left(K,f\right)=\frac{v\cdot\ln(f/K)}{\left\{1+\frac{(1-\beta)^2}{24}\ln^2(f/K)+\frac{(1-\beta)^4}{1920}\ln^4(f/K)+\cdots\right\}\cdot x(z)}$$

$$z=\frac{v}{\alpha}(fK)^{(1-\beta)/2}\cdot\ln\left(f/K\right)$$

The derivation is more rigorous in the context of calculating implied volatility given the local volatility. The formula is simpler. When $\beta\to1$, the term $\sigma_0(K,f)$ is continuous. It is more accurate when strike K is close to zero.

- The enhanced version modifies the $\sigma_0(K,f)$ term. It is just as simple (if not simpler) to implement.
- Although it is very close to the original version in most of the practical cases, the enhanced version does behave better in the low strike region. This can make a difference in the low interest rate environments.
- Overall, the enhanced version is preferred in practice.

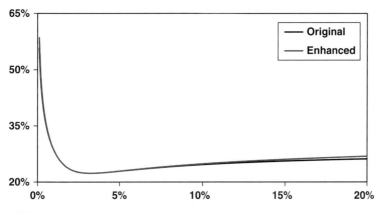

FIGURE 11.29   SABR (original vs enhanced)

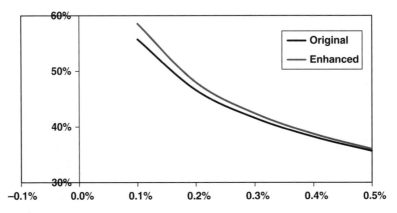

FIGURE 11.30   SABR at low strike

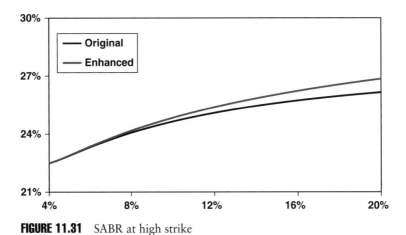

FIGURE 11.31   SABR at high strike

TABLE 11.9   The roles of SABR parameters

α	The main ATM volatility driver. It shifts the curve up and down;
β	The main driver of smile/skew dynamics. It affects the backbone and skew tilting. It may not be a good idea to use it "too much" for CMS calibration;
ρ	The correlation of forward and volatility, affecting skew tilting;
ν	Vol-on-vol, affecting the curvature, i.e. smile.

The four SABR parameters have distinctive roles in the shape and dynamics of the volatility smile. The details are listed in Table 11.9.

The SABR parameters can be calibrated to the market using numerical optimization routines at given time slices. One can adopt the global optimization approach and set up the minimization targets using logic procedure of:

- Estimating or in fact fixing β. For example, some practitioners fix β in the region between 0.35 and 0.6 for some major currencies.

- Calibrating ATM volatility and α.
- Calibrating ρ and ν.

As SABR is primarily used as the volatility functional form, its implied volatility analytical approximation is a superb fit-for-purpose volatility fitting tool in practice. When maturity T is larger, the approximation errors become larger compared to the numerical PDE solutions. If SABR is only used as volatility fitting tool, the approximation errors in themselves are not critical issues provided they do not cause negative probability densities in the wings. However, when β → 0 and/or vol-on-vol ν is large, an example scenario of the low interest rate environment, the negative probability densities in the wings do cause pricing problems. There have been continued efforts in searching for better analytical approximations that can minimize the negative density issues. Of course, one can also resort to the PDE solutions, in which case efficient PDE solvers (Hagan et al 2014, Park 2014) are critical.

In the low interest rate environment, shifted or displaced $(F_t + b)$ SABR (Hagan et al 2014) can be used to deal with negative interest rate scenarios in a non-arbitrage way. Typically, the shift b is user-defined for given expiry and tenor. The shifted-SABR parameters can then be calibrated to the market quotes in the same way as for standard SABR. Of course, the shifted-SABR parameters will be different from those of standard SABR if both are calibrated to the same swaption prices.

SABR Volatility Wings

European swaption is the primary market instrument the SABR volatility calibrates to. Additionally, it needs to be calibrated to CMS, which has quite different market drivers. The volatility wings at both high and low strike can impact calibration and derivatives pricing. The high strike wing tends to impact the CMS calibration more due to its level. The low strike wing tends to have arbitrage (negative probability density) issues, in particular when interest rate is low or even negative. A number of recent researches quoted earlier, either with better analytical approximation or with numerical PDE, have been aimed at reducing arbitrages on the wings and calibrating to the CMS market better as a result.

Nevertheless, getting the volatility wings right and calibrating to both vanilla option and CMS markets in practice is non-trivial. As observed during the recent financial crises, the CMS replication calibration is very hard when the market is in stress. Volatility wings may sound like a second order numerical effect, but they are definitely not a second order issue in this scenario. For CMS, the high strike wing impacts the numerical integration and results most, and it will need additional wing stitching to copy with the market realities and eventualities.

All four SABR parameters affect the middle part of the volatility curve in one way or another. Hence in the context of CMS calibration, if any of these parameters are changed, it will impact European swaption prices! This is certainly not desirable. As a matter of fact, the swaption market is quite separate from the CMS market, although both are dependent on volatility smile. In general, it is a much better practice to calibrate the central part of the volatility curve to the swaption market, and then modify wings subsequently for the CMS calibration. Treating volatility wings separately can avoid impacting on swaption prices and Greeks, and avoid impacting on smile dynamics embedded in β. We shall explain the additional wing stitching in chapter 13.

TABLE 11.10 Standard swap conventions of major currencies

	Fixed Leg		Floating Leg	
Currency	Frequency	Day Count	Frequency	Day Count
USD (NY)	6M	30/360	3M	ACT/360
USD (London)	1Y	ACT/360	3M	ACT/360
EUR (1Y)	1Y	30/360	3M	ACT/360
EUR (> 1Y)	1Y	30/360	6M	ACT/360
GBP (1Y)	1Y	ACT/365	3M	ACT/365
GBP (> 1Y)	6M	ACT/365	6M	ACT/365
CHF (1Y)	1Y	30/360	3M	ACT/360
CHF (> 1Y)	1Y	30/360	6M	ACT/360

Non-standard Swaption

In pricing non-standard swaption whereby the underlying swap is non-standard, or equivalently transforming the swaption volatility of standard swap to that of non-standard swap, one needs to take into account of both fixed and floating leg conventions. To illustrate this clearly, Table 11.10 summarizes the standard swap conventions of a few major currencies.

The non-standardness includes changes in frequency and day count convention in both fixed and floating legs. Frequency changes, however, are the major drivers of the swaption volatility transformation from standard to non-standard. The non-standard pricing and volatility transformation are made more complex by the advent of the multi-curve environment.

The principle in pricing non-standard swaption is to find its equivalent standard forward swap rate and strike. The equivalent standard strike can be used to sample the standard swaption volatility cube to get an equivalent standard volatility. The equivalent standard volatility may be subject to further adjustment, due to the frequency change in the fixed leg. The non-standard swaption can then be priced using an equivalent standard swaption pricing with the equivalent standard forward swap rate, strike and volatility as inputs. Let's us examine an example to illustrate the practical steps taken in pricing a non-standard swaption.

Assuming the standard swap has the fixed and floating leg frequency of $m_1 = 1Y$ and $m_2 = 6M$ respectively, and $F_{t,T}^m$ is the corresponding standard forward swap rate, we need to price a non-standard swaption with fixed and floating leg frequency of $n_1 = 6M$ and $n_2 = 3M$, and strike K_n. We can take the following steps:

1. The non-standard forward swap rate $F_{t,T}^n$ is calculated. Because the floating leg frequency is changed from $m_2 = 6M$ to $n_2 = 3M$, one needs to switch the index curve and use 3M (instead of 6M) LIBOR curve to calculate $F_{t,T}^n$. The OIS discount curve is the same and the non-standard fixed leg frequency ($n_1 = 6M$) needs to be taken into account;

2. One searches for an equivalent standard strike K_m. By the rationale of keeping the absolute moneyness the same: $F_{t,T}^m - K_m = F_{t,T}^n - K_n$, we have: $K_m = F_{t,T}^m - F_{t,T}^n + K_n$;

3. One can therefore sample the standard swaption volatility cube to obtain an equivalent standard volatility $\sigma_m = GetVol(tenor, maturiry, K_m)$;
4. The equivalent standard volatility (σ_m) needs to be further adjusted for the annuity $(A_{t,T})$ in the swaption payoff. The annuity is primarily dependent on the fixed leg frequency, and the compounding effect is the reason for further adjustment. For two different fixed leg frequencies f_n and f_m, day counts τ_n and τ_m, and rates r_n and r_m:

$$\left(1 + \frac{\tau_n r_n}{f_n}\right)^{f_n} = \left(1 + \frac{\tau_m r_m}{f_m}\right)^{f_m}$$

$$\left(1 + \frac{\tau_n K_n}{f_n}\right)^{f_n} = \left(1 + \frac{\tau_m K_m}{f_m}\right)^{f_m}$$

where $\tau = 365 / 365$ if the day count convention is ACT/360, otherwise $\tau = 1$. Under the Black Log-Normal assumption $(dr_n = r_n \sigma_n dw, dr_m = r_m \sigma_m dw)$, by applying Ito differentiation to the compounding equations, one obtains after some algebra:

$$\sigma_n = \sigma_m \frac{\tau_m(r_m - K_m)}{\tau_n(r_n - K_n)} \frac{\ln(r_n / K_n)}{\ln(r_m / K_m)} \left(1 + \frac{\tau_n(r_n + K_n)}{2f_n}\right)\left(1 + \frac{\tau_m(r_m + K_m)}{2f_m}\right)^{-1}$$

Note that σ_n can still be viewed within the standard volatility domain, as the equivalent standard volatility. It is adjusted for non-standard compounding in the annuity.

A more general CEV volatility conversion formula is of the form:

$$\sigma_n = \sigma_m \frac{\tau_m(r_m - K_m)}{\tau_n(r_n - K_n)} \frac{r_n^{1-\beta} - K_n^{1-\beta}}{r_m^{1-\beta} - K_m^{1-\beta}} \left(1 + \frac{\tau_n(r_n + K_n)}{2f_n}\right)\left(1 + \frac{\tau_m(r_m + K_m)}{2f_m}\right)^{-1}$$

Note that:

$$\lim_{\beta \to 1}\left(\frac{r_n^{1-\beta} - K_n^{1-\beta}}{r_m^{1-\beta} - K_m^{1-\beta}}\right) = \frac{\ln(r_n / K_n)}{\ln(r_m / K_m)}$$

The CEV formula converges to the Black version.

5. The non-standard (payer) swaption price can therefore be obtained as follows:

$$V(t, K_n) = D_t \cdot \max\left(S_{s,T}^n - K_n, 0\right) \cdot A_{t,T}^n$$

$$= D_t \cdot \max\left(S_{t,T}^m - K_m, 0\right) \cdot A_{t,T}^m$$

$$= Black(F_{t,T}^m, K_m, \sigma_n) \cdot A_{t,T}^m$$

6. If needed, the non-standard swaption volatility can be implied by using the Black implied volatility function:

$$\sigma_n(t, K^n) = BlackImpliedVol\,[V(t, K_n)]$$

TABLE 11.11   Fixed and floating leg frequency change in single and multi-curve environment

	Single Curve Environment	Multi-Curve Environment
Fixed Leg Frequency	Change in the fixed leg frequency has a major impact on the forward swap rate, strike and annuity compounding.	Change in the fixed leg frequency has a major impact on the forward swap rate, strike and annuity compounding.
Floating Leg Frequency	As there is no tenor basis, the change in the floating leg frequency does not impact on forward swap rate, strike or compounding.	Due to tenor basis, the change in the floating leg frequency means a change of index curve, e.g. from 6M to 3M LIBOR. The forward swap rate will be impacted as a result, in addition to the fixed leg frequency impact. The floating leg effects on volatility transformation can alternatively be captured by using shifted (displaced) diffusion with deterministic tenor basis as the shift.

The above steps allow one to transform standard swaption volatilities to non-standard swaption volatilities.

In both a single-curve and a multi-curve environment, it is necessary to go through the above steps to price non-standard swaptions and conduct volatility transformation. There are, however, some important differences between the two environments, which are highlighted in Table 11.11.

RISK SENSITIVITIES

The risk sensitivities of interest rate derivatives include standard Greeks, such as Delta, Gamma, Vega, etc. The most central one is the Delta w.r.t. the yield curve term structures, i.e. the time-bucketed Deltas. From pricing model and risk system perspective, Deltas w.r.t. the zero curve rates are convenient and efficient to compute. From hedging perspective, Deltas w.r.t. to the market instruments, e.g. FRA, Future, par swap rates are required.

In calculating Deltas w.r.t. the market instruments by brute force, every time a point is bumped, the entire zero curve has to be re-bootstrapped before position re-valuation. This method is highly inefficient. A much more efficient method is to use Jacobian transformation: the Deltas w.r.t. the zero curve rates $(z_1, z_2, \cdots, z_n)$ can be transformed to w.r.t. market instruments $(r_1, r_2, \cdots, r_m)$, without having to re-bootstrap. In the trading/risk systems where there are many curves and many time buckets, the efficiency enhancement will be substantial.

Jacobian Transformation

Denoting a derivative position as P, and we need to calculate its time-bucketed Deltas w.r.t. market instrument par yields $(r_1, r_2, \cdots, r_m)$, namely:

$$\left(\frac{\partial P}{\partial r_1}, \frac{\partial P}{\partial r_2}, \cdots, \frac{\partial P}{\partial r_m} \right)$$

Assuming P's time-bucketed Deltas w.r.t. the zero rates $(z_1, z_2, \cdots, z_n)$ have already been calculated as:

$$\left(\frac{\partial P}{\partial z_1}, \frac{\partial P}{\partial z_2}, \cdots, \frac{\partial P}{\partial z_n} \right)$$

By simple chain rule:

$$\left(\frac{\partial P}{\partial r_1}, \frac{\partial P}{\partial r_2}, \cdots, \frac{\partial P}{\partial r_m} \right) = \left(\frac{\partial P}{\partial z_1}, \frac{\partial P}{\partial z_2}, \cdots, \frac{\partial P}{\partial z_n} \right) \begin{pmatrix} \frac{\partial z_1}{\partial r_1} & \cdots & \frac{\partial z_1}{\partial r_m} \\ \vdots & \ddots & \vdots \\ \frac{\partial z_n}{\partial r_1} & \cdots & \frac{\partial z_n}{\partial r_m} \end{pmatrix}$$

The matrix $\begin{pmatrix} \frac{\partial z_1}{\partial r_1} & \cdots & \frac{\partial z_1}{\partial r_m} \\ \vdots & \ddots & \vdots \\ \frac{\partial z_n}{\partial r_1} & \cdots & \frac{\partial z_n}{\partial r_m} \end{pmatrix}$ is a Jacobian matrix. If it can be evaluated, the

Deltas w.r.t. the zero curve rates can be easily transformed to w.r.t. the market instrument par yields by the chain rule.

A Jacobian matrix consists of first order partial derivatives, and it has a very nice inverse property. Provided the Jacobian matrix is non-singular, the inverse of the Jacobian matrix is the Jacobian matrix of the inverse function, namely:

$$\begin{pmatrix} \frac{\partial z_1}{\partial r_1} & \cdots & \frac{\partial z_1}{\partial r_m} \\ \vdots & \ddots & \vdots \\ \frac{\partial z_n}{\partial r_1} & \cdots & \frac{\partial z_n}{\partial r_m} \end{pmatrix} = \begin{pmatrix} \frac{\partial r_1}{\partial z_1} & \cdots & \frac{\partial r_1}{\partial z_n} \\ \vdots & \ddots & \vdots \\ \frac{\partial r_m}{\partial z_1} & \cdots & \frac{\partial r_m}{\partial z_n} \end{pmatrix}^{-1}$$

The partial derivatives $\frac{\partial r_i}{\partial z_i}$ are simply the sensitivities of the par yields (e.g. par swap rate) to the zero rates. These are standard market instruments and their yield sensitivities to the zero rates can be readily calculated by trading and risk systems. Once the Jacobian matrix is calculated, the derivative position Delta sensitivities w.r.t. the par yields can then be obtained by matrix multiplications.

Note that quite often the PVs (rather than par yields) of the standard market instruments are calculated in the systems. For an instrument, if there is the relationship between its par yield (r) and PV (V) is monotonic then $\frac{dr}{dV} = \left(\frac{dV}{dr} \right)^{-1}$. This is indeed the case for most of the standard market instruments. Therefore the Jacobian yield derivatives in the matrix can be calculated as:

$$\frac{\partial r_i}{\partial z_i} = \frac{dr_i}{dV_i} \frac{\partial V_i}{\partial z_i} = \left(\frac{dV_i}{dr_i} \right)^{-1} \frac{\partial V_i}{\partial z_i}$$

where $\dfrac{dV_i}{dr_i}$ is the standard instrument's PV sensitivity to its par yield and $\dfrac{\partial V_i}{\partial z_i}$ is the standard instrument's PV sensitivity to the zero rate. Both of them can be calculated by systems.

In Figures 11.32 to 11.37, we compare the risk sensitivities w.r.t. the par rate using brute force Bump-and-Run (BnR) and the Jacobian technique. The risks w.r.t. the zero rate used in the Jacobian technique are plotted in the graphs for reference. All sensitivities are expressed as PV changes in bps for 1bp bump.

For a 30-year out-of-money payer swap, the time-bucketed Deltas obtained by Jacobian technique agree well with those obtained by BnR. This is true for both the OIS (discounting) and the LIBOR (forecasting) curve, as shown in Figures 11.32 and 11.33.

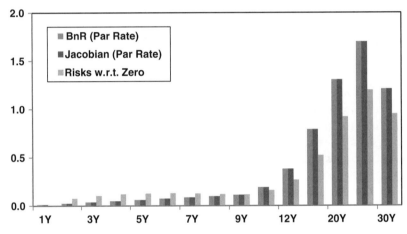

FIGURE 11.32   BnR risks vs Jacobian risks (OIS)

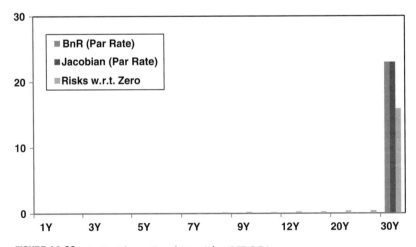

FIGURE 11.33   BnR risks vs Jacobian risks (LIBOR)

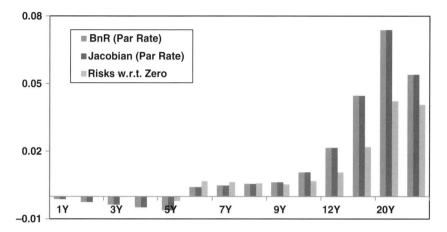

FIGURE 11.34 BnR risks vs Jacobian risks (OIS)

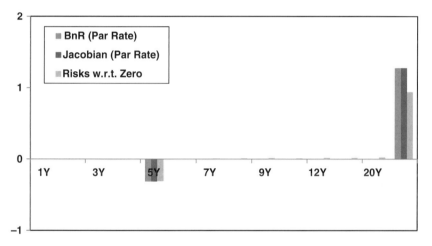

FIGURE 11.35 BnR risks vs Jacobian risks (LIBOR)

For a 5-year into 20-year European payer swaption, the time-bucketed Deltas obtained by Jacobian technique also agree well with those obtained by BnR. Figures 11.34 and 11.35 demonstrate this for both the OIS and the LIBOR curve.

For a 20-year cap, the time-bucketed Deltas obtained by Jacobian technique are in line with those obtained by BnR. Figures 11.36 and 11.37 demonstrate this for both the OIS and the LIBOR curve.

Although in the above examples the individual instruments are used, the conclusions also hold for a portfolio of trades. In summary, for calculating time-bucketed Deltas w.r.t. market instruments in the yield curves, Jacobian transformation technique is an extremely valuable tool for numerical efficiency. It is even more so in the multi-curve environment, where yield curve stripping is computationally more demanding. In fact, Jacobian technique is not only suitable for interest rate yield curve, but also

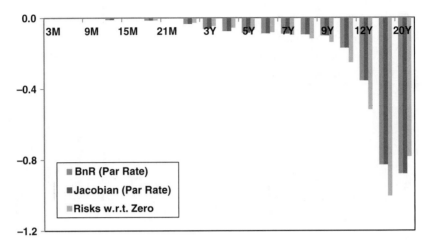

FIGURE 11.36   BnR risks vs Jacobian risks (OIS)

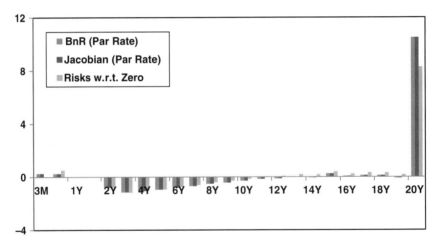

FIGURE 11.37   BnR risks vs Jacobian risks (LIBOR)

for other similar curve stripping situations, including CDS curve (credit Delta) and volatility surface (Vega).

Deltas Incorporating Smile Dynamics

As discussed in chapter 4, due to volatility and smile dynamics, the change in the underlying spot will result in a change of volatility, which in turn impacts the deltas. Different underlyings in different markets have their specific volatility and smile dynamics, which must be taken into account in calculating Greeks, in particular deltas.

For cap/floor, where the underlying is EURIBOR or LIBOR, practitioners tend to use sticky strike dynamics to calculate risk sensitivities, in particular deltas. With the

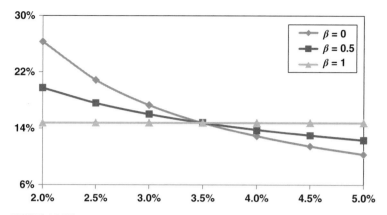

FIGURE 11.38 Swaption volatility backbones

sticky strike dynamics, when the forward EURIBOR or LIBOR is bumped, the corresponding ATM volatility changes as a result of ATM strike has changed. The volatilities at all other fixed strikes will stay the same.

For European swaption, some practitioners also use sticky strike dynamics for calculating risk sensitivities. However, as SABR model is widely used in the construction of swaption volatility cubes, many practitioners utilize the embedded volatility dynamics in the SABR model to calculate hedge parameters.

In SABR, once the model parameters are calibrated to the market, the ATM moves with the forward and the trace of ATM volatility in relation with the forward is known as backbone. Backbone effectively describes the embedded volatility dynamics and it is a function of β. In Figure 11.38, three example backbones for $\beta = 0$, $\beta = 0.5$ and $\beta = 1$ are plotted. In all three sets, the SABR model parameters are calibrated when forward $f_0 = 3.5\%$.

Depending on the chosen β, the embedded SABR dynamics can be used directly to generate bumped volatilities for all strikes. For a given bumped forward f_{new}, the corresponding bumped volatilities are $\sigma_{SABR}(f_{new}, K, \alpha, \beta, \rho, v)$. The bumped volatilities associated with the bumped forward f_{new} can then be used to re-value the book and obtain risk sensitivities.

Whilst SABR itself contains volatility and smile dynamics, some practitioners prefer to impose different empirical dynamics for hedging purposes. In this case, SABR is merely used as a volatility interpolation/extrapolation tool. One such example is to impose sticky delta dynamics: the ATM volatility is kept the same, and SABR model parameter α is re-calibrated to α_{new} using the bumped forward f_{new}. The bumped volatilities of other strikes can then be obtained according to $\sigma_{SABR}(f_{new}, K, \alpha_{new}, \beta, \rho, v)$, which in turn will be used to re-value the book and obtain hedging parameters.

Volatility dynamics in the context of hedging are based on statistical average behaviours. Markets do not always follow statistical average patterns. Nevertheless they serve as practical guidance. It is a bit of mystery, though, that practitioners believe their chosen volatility dynamics for hedging are correct, even though their hedging parameters can be quite different from each other under different chosen dynamics.

CHAPTER 12

Practical Interest Rate Derivative Models

The underlying of an interest rate derivative is that of the entire yield curve. The underlying stochastic processes are more complex as a result. Given the underlying complexity, it is not surprising that there exist many varieties of interest rate derivative models. In general, interest rate derivative models are less developed in handling volatility smile/skew for the same reason, compared to equity or FX derivative models.

KEY MODEL CATEGORIES

The Heath–Jarrow–Morton (HJM) modelling framework in its generic multi-factor form practically encompasses most of the interest rate derivative models. From this perspective, one can divide interest rate derivative models into low- and high-dimension categories, in addition to the short rate models.

Short Rate Models

In the short rate models, the short interest rate is the underlying and it is driven by specified stochastic processes. The underlying process is Markovian, allowing efficient numerical implementations. Table 12.1 summarizes key traditional 1-factor short rate models and their stochastic processes:

The Linear Gauss–Markov (LGM) model, a later variation, is theoretically equivalent to the HW short rate model. The LGM model, however, has a more efficient and reliable numerical implementation and calibration formulation, as we shall explain later in this chapter.

The short rate models can be formulated using 2-factors, to increase its capability in handling de-correlation along the T-axis. However, they do not have sufficient flexibility to handle volatility smile/skew along the K-axis. The same conclusions apply to the LGM model.

TABLE 12.1 Key 1-factor short rate models

Short Rate Models	Stochastic Process
Vasicek	$dr_t = (\theta - \kappa r_t)dt + \sigma dW$
Hull–White (HW)	$dr_t = (\theta_t - \kappa_t r_t)dt + \sigma_t dW$
Black–Derman–Toy (BDT)	$d\ln r_t = \left(\theta_t + \dfrac{\sigma_t'}{\sigma_t}\ln r_t\right)dt + \sigma_t dW$
Black–Karasinski (BK)	$d\ln r_t = (\theta_t - \kappa_t \ln r_t)dt + \sigma_t dW$
Cox–Ingersoll–Ross (CIR)	$dr_t = (\theta_t - \kappa_t r_t)dt + \sigma_t \sqrt{r_t}\,dW$
Constant Elasticity of Variance (CEV)	$dr_t = (\theta_t - \kappa_t r_t)dt + \sigma_t r_t^\beta dW$

Low-Dimensional HJM Models

The early attempts to reduce the dimensionality of HJM include the formulation of the single-factor Gaussian HJM model and the Cheyette model (Cheyette 1992). Those attempts were primarily aimed at making the forward rate stochastic process Markov, hence enhancing the efficiency of the numerical implementation. In the original HJM framework, the drift is a function of volatility and state-dependent, which makes the process non-Markov. Therefore a key technical ingredient of creating a Markovian representation in this context is to make appropriate assumptions on the volatility function. For example, by assuming the separability of the volatility, the forward rate processes can be made as functions of a Markov process. Whilst these models have succeeded in reducing dimensionality and handling various volatility term structure shapes, they are still not capable of capturing volatility smile/skew.

To be able to handle volatility smile/skew, more advanced models or extensions have since been developed within the scope of HJM but with low dimensionality. Some of the key models belong to this category are listed below:

- Quasi-Gaussian HJM model: Whereby the volatility has been made stochastic within the single factor Gaussian HJM framework.
- Cheyette model with stochastic volatility (Andreasen 2005): Stochastic volatility is introduced into the original Cheyette model.
- Cheyette model with local volatility (Chibane and Law 2013): A parameterized (quadratic) local volatility functional form is proposed for the original Cheyette model.
- Markov functional models (Hunt, Kennedy and Pelsser 2000): The zero bond values are explicitly made as functions of low-dimensional (1-factor or 2-factor) Markov process.

The low-dimensional HJM models can be implemented using efficient numerical techniques, such as PDEs or multi-nodal trees. From a practical application perspective, they can be a good compromise between choosing the short rate models and high-dimensional HJM models.

High-Dimensional HJM Models

The Libor Market Model (LMM), also known as the BGM/J model (Brace, Gatarek and Musiela 1997; Jamshidian 1997), has in fact reduced the original HJM dimensions dramatically, due to the LMM model's finite number of discrete forward rates (EURIBOR or LIBOR). Because the underlyings are market-observable and in fact tradable, LMM calibration is relatively straightforward. Nevertheless, LMM still in theory has far higher dimensions than the models in other categories, primarily due to LMM's non-Markov processes. As a result, LMM must be implemented using Monte Carlo, and this is an apparent disadvantage of the model. To price products with early and optimal exercise features, the least-square technique (Longstaff-Schwartz) needs to be used with the Monte Carlo simulations.

LMM in its original standard form cannot deal with volatility smile, which is widely observed in the cap/floor, swaption and CMS markets. Various stochastic volatility extensions have been proposed to enrich the LMM framework, to enable it to calibrate to volatility smile. The extended models have had decent degrees of success, although better model extensions and efficient calibration techniques are still in short supply.

The Swap Market Model (SMM) (Jamshidian 1997) is another model that belongs to the high-dimensional HJM category. Similar to LMM, it models the discrete market observable and tradable underlyings. Instead of Libors, SMM models a set of swap rates, either co-terminal or co-starting. The SMM setup is suitable only for pricing interest rate derivatives that are solely dependent on those swap rates. The drifts in the SMM are non-trivial to approximate well in practice. Because of the varying durations of the underlying swaps and the overlap nature of the swaps, the volatility and correlation structures are harder and more complex to determine or specify. Besides, many interest rate derivatives have some dependency on Libors. Therefore, overall LMM is much better and practical to work with than SMM.

In the following sections, we shall deep dive into four important interest rate derivative models, to gain good intuitions on their key features and characteristics. Each one of them can be representative of the respective model categories:

- LGM Model: To examine its mathematical formulation, numerical implementation and calibration process. The model limitations on de-correlation and volatility smile will also be explained.
- LMM: To look into the underlying mathematical formulation and practical implementation, as well as the smile model extension to calibrate and price in the volatility smile.
- Extended Cheyette Model: To explain its capabilities in calibrating and handling volatility smile, in addition to the underlying mathematics and numerical implementation.
- Interest rate local volatility model: To explore a brand new idea of modelling interest rate volatility smile.

LINEAR GAUSS–MARKOV MODEL

In the 1-factor Linear Gauss–Markov (LGM) model, a Gaussian process is assumed to be the driving factor. By skilfully selecting an appropriate numeraire (Hagan, Working Paper), it turns out that the short rate is a linear function of the Gaussian driver. The process by construction is Markovian. As can be seen later, the LGM short rate process is equivalent to that of HW model. Its numerical implementation and calibration can be more stable, as PDE can be used.

Formulation

For a tradable security $V_t(x)$ with a chosen numeraire $N_t(x)$, its deflated security value $V_t(x)/N_t(x)$ is a martingale. Namely:

$$\frac{V_t(x)}{N_t(x)} = E^Q\left\{\frac{V_T(X)}{N_T(X)} \mid X_t = x\right\}$$

$$= \int \frac{V_T(X)}{N_T(X)} p_{t,T}(x,X)dX$$

Given the 1-factor Gaussian driving factor:

$$dX_t = \alpha_t dW \qquad X_0 = 0 \qquad v_{t,T} = \int_t^T \alpha_\tau^2 d\tau$$

with its probability density function:

$$p_{t,T}(x,X) = \frac{1}{\sqrt{2\pi v_{t,T}}} exp\left[-\frac{(X-x)^2}{2v_{t,T}}\right]$$

the deflated security value can be written as:

$$\frac{V_t(x)}{N_t(x)} = \frac{1}{\sqrt{2\pi v_{t,T}}} \int \frac{V_T(X)}{N_T(X)} exp\left[-\frac{(X-x)^2}{2v_{t,T}}\right]dX$$

Denoting the deflated security value as $\hat{V}_t(\cdot) \equiv V_t(\cdot)/N_t(\cdot)$, the above can be simplified to:

$$\hat{V}_t(x) = \frac{1}{\sqrt{2\pi v_{t,T}}} \int \hat{V}_T(X) exp\left[-\frac{(X-x)^2}{2v_{t,T}}\right]dX$$

It is apparent that $\hat{V}_t(x)$ is the solution of the simple PDE:

$$\frac{\partial \hat{V}_t(x)}{\partial t} + \frac{1}{2}\alpha_t^2 \frac{\partial^2 \hat{V}_t(x)}{\partial x^2} = 0$$

The above formulation is the crux of the 1-factor LGM model. Its numerical implementation is simple and effective. All we need to do now is to define the deflated security value by choosing the numeraire $N_t(x)$.

A suitably chosen numeraire is crucial in the LGM model setup and subsequent numerical integrations. Hagan chose:

$$N_t(x) := \frac{1}{D(0,t)} exp\left(H_t x + \frac{1}{2}H_t^2 v_{0,t}\right)$$

where $D(0,t)$ is the discount factor, and:

$$H_t = \int_0^t exp\left(-\int_0^s \kappa_u du\right) ds$$

where k_u is a model parameter, often termed as mean reversion. Note that at $t = 0$, $N_0(0) = 1$. Using the above numeraire, noting that the real zero coupon bond price at maturity is 1, i.e. $P(X,T,T) = 1$, the deflated zero coupon bond price at t is given by:

$$\hat{P}(x,t,T) = \frac{1}{\sqrt{2\pi v_{t,T}}} \int \frac{1}{N_T(X)} exp\left[-\frac{(X-x)^2}{2v_{t,T}}\right] dX$$

$$= D_0(T) exp\left(-H_T x - \frac{1}{2}H_T^2 v_{0,t}\right)$$

where $D_0(T) = exp\left(-\int_0^T f_0(\tau)d\tau\right)$ is today's discount factor and $f_0(\tau)$ is today's forward curve.

Model Features

The above analytical solution of deflated zero coupon bond is a very valuable LGM model feature. It will facilitate faster numerical computations in pricing interest rate derivatives. From this analytical formula, one can also derive a number of interesting relationships and LGM model features, shown in Table 12.2.

The LGM model turns out to be equivalent to the Hull–White model $[dr_t = (\theta_t - \kappa_t r_t)dt + \sigma_t dW]$. The relationships between their model parameters are:

$$\kappa_t = -\frac{d^2 H_t}{dt^2}\Big/\frac{dH_t}{dt} \qquad \sigma_t = \frac{dH_t}{dt}\sqrt{\frac{dv_{0,t}}{dt}} = \frac{dH_t}{dt}\alpha_t$$

As noted above, the Hull–White model parameters are the differentiations of relevant LGM model parameters. Because the market vanilla instruments including European options depend on H_t and $v_{0,t}$, the LGM can be calibrated to the market without further differentiations. Numerical differentiation required in the Hull–White model calibration, for example to obtain the local volatility σ_t, can introduce noises. While the two models are equivalent mathematically, numerically LGM is much easier to calibrate to the market, and it is more stable in the subsequent pricing.

Calibration

The LGM model has two important invariances: shifting and scaling. In both cases, the transition probabilities $[p_{t,T}(x,X)dX]$ and zero coupon bond prices $[P(x,t,T)]$ remain unchanged after the model parameters transformation. Specifically, for a constant c:

▪ shifting transformation and invariance: $\begin{cases} H_t \to H_t + c \\ v_T \to v_T \end{cases}$ with $\begin{cases} x \to x + cv_T \\ X \to X + cv_T \end{cases}$

TABLE 12.2 LGM model features

Relationship	LGM Model Features
Relationship between numeraire and deflated instantaneous forward zero bond price is: $$\hat{P}(x,t,t) = \frac{1}{N_t(x)}$$ or: $$N_t(x) = \frac{1}{\hat{P}(x,t,t)}$$	The real instantaneous forward zero bond price $P(x,t,t)$ is 1. It is deflated by the numeraire, and the deflated counterpart is no longer equal to 1. So the chosen numeraire is a compounding factor under the "deflated" measure.
At $t = 0$, $x = 0$ and $N_0(0) = 1$, hence: $$P(0,0,T) = \hat{P}(0,0,T) = D_0(T)$$	The LGM model automatically fits and calibrates to today's discount curve $D_0(T)$.
By definition, a zero coupon bond is equal to: $$P(x,t,T) = exp\left(-\int_t^T f(x,t,\tau)d\tau\right)$$ where $f(x,t,\tau)$ is the instantaneous forward rate. $P(x,t,T)$ is also equal to: $$P(x,t,T) = \hat{P}(x,t,T)N_t(x)$$ $$= \frac{D_0(T)}{D_0(t)}exp\left[-(H_T - H_t)x - \frac{1}{2}(H_T^2 - H_t^2)v_{0,t}\right]$$	By differentiating the two equations of $P(x,t,T)$ w.r.t. T, one obtains: $$f(x,t,T) = f_0(T) + \frac{dH_T}{dT}x + H_T\frac{dH_T}{dT}v_{0,t}$$ Hence the short rate process $r_t = f(x,t,t)$ is: $$r_t = f_0(t) + \frac{dH_t}{dt}x + H_t\frac{dH_t}{dt}v_{0,t}$$ which is a linear function of Gaussian process in the form of $r_t = A_t x + B_t$

- scaling transformation and invariance: $\begin{cases} H_t \to cH_t \\ v_T \to v_T/c^2 \end{cases}$ with $\begin{cases} x \to x/c \\ X \to X/c \end{cases}$

The above invariances are important features that can be used during the calibration process. By making the appropriate transformations, the invariance features will facilitate the calibrations. The key vanilla instruments and their LGM analytical formulae are summarized here:

1. Swap

The receiver swap value is:

$$V_{rec}(x,t) = \sum_{i=1}^{n}\tau_i(K - s_i)P(x,t,t_i) + P(x,t,t_n) - P(x,t,t_0)$$

where τ_i is year-fraction and s_i is the floating leg spread transferred to the fixed leg, and

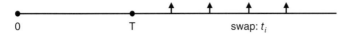

FIGURE 12.1 European swaption diagram

$$P(x,t,t_i) = \frac{D_0(t_i)}{D_0(t)} exp\left[-(H_{t_i} - H_t)x - \frac{1}{2}(H_{t_i}^2 - H_t^2)v_{0,t}\right]$$

The payer swap value is $V_{pay}(x,t) = -V_{rec}(x,t)$.

Their deflated values are $\dfrac{V_{rec}(x,t)}{N_t(x)}$ and $\dfrac{V_{pay}(x,t)}{N_t(x)}$ respectively.

2. European Swaption

As shown in Figure 12.1, for a receiver swaption with maturity T, its price is:

$$V_{rec}^{opt}(0,0) = \frac{1}{\sqrt{2\pi v_{0,T}}} \int exp\left(-\frac{X^2}{2v_{0,T}}\right) max\left[V_{rec}(X,T),0\right]dX$$

$$= D_n N\left(\frac{y^* + \left[H_{t_n} - H_{t_0}\right]v_{0,T}}{\sqrt{v_{0,T}}}\right) - D_0 N\left(\frac{y^*}{\sqrt{v_{0,T}}}\right) + \sum_{i=1}^{n}\tau_i(K-s_i)D_i N\left(\frac{y^* + \left[H_{t_i} - H_{t_0}\right]v_{0,T}}{\sqrt{v_{0,T}}}\right)$$

where y^* is the swap breakeven point for $V_{rec}\left(f(y^*),T\right) = 0$. It therefore solves for:

$$\sum_{i=1}^{n}\tau_i(K-s_i)D_i \ exp\left[-(H_{t_i} - H_{t_0})y^* - \frac{1}{2}(H_{t_i} - H_{t_0})^2 v_{0,T}\right]$$

$$+D_n \ exp\left[-(H_{t_n} - H_{t_0})y^* - \frac{1}{2}(H_{t_n} - H_{t_0})^2 v_{0,T}\right] = D_0$$

Because the above solver function is monotonic to y^*, the solution is unique and can be obtained by simple numerical root-finding routines.

Using call/put parity, the payer swaption price is given by:

$$V_{pay}^{opt}(0,0) = V_{rec}^{opt}(0,0) + D_0 - D_n - \sum_{i=1}^{n}\tau_i(K-s_i)D_i$$

3. Cap/Floor

A floorlet is simply a one-period receiver swaption. Its price is therefore the value of $V_{rec}^{opt}(0,0)$ with $n = 1$:

$$V_{fl}(0,0) = \left(1 + \tau_1(K-s_1)\right)D_1 N\left(\frac{y^* + \left[H_{t_n} - H_{t_0}\right]v_{0,T}}{\sqrt{v_{0,T}}}\right) - D_0 N\left(\frac{y^*}{\sqrt{v_{0,T}}}\right)$$

where y^* has an explicit solution given by:

$$y^* = \frac{ln\left[\dfrac{D_1\left(1+\tau_1\left(K-s_1\right)\right)}{D_0}\right] - \dfrac{1}{2}\left(H_{t_1}-H_{t_0}\right)^2 v_{0,T}}{H_{t_1}-H_{t_0}}$$

Using call/put parity, the caplet price is given by:

$$V_{cl}\left(0,0\right) = V_{fl}\left(0,0\right) + D_0 - D_1\left(1+\tau_1\left(K-s_1\right)\right)$$

During the calibration, given the market yield curve and vanilla instrument prices, the unknown LGM parameters (H_t and $v_{0,T}$ of the driving factor X_t) can be found using the above analytical formulae. Practitioners usually determine H_t by fixing the mean reversion parameter κ_t, and use the calibration process to search for $v_{0,T}$. For 1-factor LGM, the calibration is typically done at trade level for the specified option strike.

In the following, we shall examine an example of calibrating LGM to market swaption prices. Adopting co-terminal (30Y) calibration, the diagonal swaptions 1Y / 29Y, 2Y / 28Y, $\cdots$, 29Y / 1Y are used for calibration. Their market-quoted Black implied volatilities are shown in Figure 12.2.

The calibrated variance term structures ($v_{0,T}$ of X_t) for different mean reversion values (-1%, 0, 1%) are plotted in Figure 12.3.

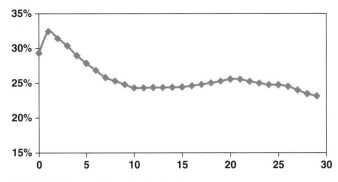

FIGURE 12.2 Black implied volatility

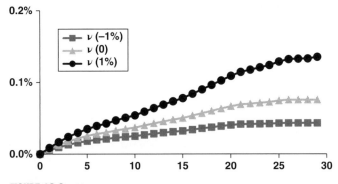

FIGURE 12.3 Variance term structure

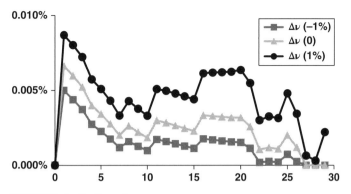

FIGURE 12.4 FwD variance term structure

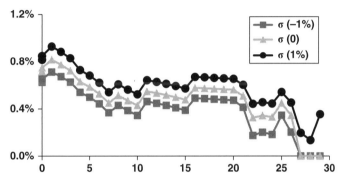

FIGURE 12.5 Local vol term structure

The forward variances $(\Delta v = v_{0,T_i} - v_{0,T_{i-1}})$ derived from the calibrated variance term structures for different mean reversion values (-1%, 0, 1%) are plotted in Figure 12.4. As expected, mean reversion does not have an impact to the forward variances. The higher the mean reversion is, the higher the calibrated forward variances are. This will in turn impact the pricing of path-dependent options, such as Bermudan swaptions.

For comparison purpose, the equivalent HW local volatility term structures calibrated to the same market data and instruments are shown in Figure 12.5. Calibrating HW local volatilities involves additional numerical differentiations compared to calibrating LGM variances. Hence, in general, LGM calibration is numerically easier and more stable.

If LGM is used for multi-factor hybrid modelling, e.g. in pricing interest rate and FX hybrids, the LGM local volatility (α_t) needs to be calibrated. In this case, one needs to conduct the same amount of numerical differentiations as in calibrating HW local volatility. Nevertheless, LGM still has the overall numerical advantages in that it can be formulated into relatively simple and standard PDE pricer.

The 1-factor LGM model exhibits similar de-correlation characteristics (or restriction) as other 1-factor short rate models. For two forward rates f_i and f_j with their instantaneous volatilities σ_i and σ_j, the terminal correlation between f_i and f_j is defined by:

$$\rho_{i,j}(T) = \frac{\int_0^T \sigma_i(t)\sigma_j(t)dt}{\sqrt{\int_0^T \sigma_i^2(t)dt \cdot \int_0^T \sigma_j^2(t)dt}}$$

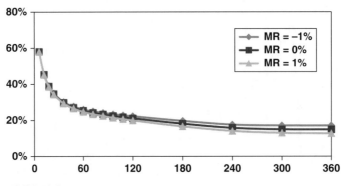

FIGURE 12.6   Correlation term structure

In Figure 12.6, we use the calibrated LGM variances to plot the calculated terminal correlation versus the gap between f_1 and f_2, for different mean reversion values (–1%, 0, 1%). The starting point for f_1 is fixed at 3 months, and the gap between f_1 and f_2 is labelled by the horizontal axis and in months.

As can be seen in Figure 12.6, mean reversion does not have much impact to the correlation and its decay shape. So for the 1-factor LGM model, once the model is calibrated, its implied correlation structure is almost "fixed" and restrictive. Because there is no de-correlation in the instantaneous volatilities, it can face problems in pricing certain types of derivative products that require richer correlation (de-correlation) dynamics.

PDE Pricing

One of the beauties of LGM is that the deflated security $\hat{V}_t(x) \equiv V_t(x) / N_t(x)$ satisfies the simple 1-D PDE:

$$\frac{\partial \hat{V}_t(x)}{\partial t} + \frac{1}{2}\alpha_t^2 \frac{\partial^2 \hat{V}_t(x)}{\partial x^2} = 0$$

Its boundary conditions are well defined as the payoff $V_T(X)$ and numeraire $N_T(X)$ at option expiry T are known. The local variances of x are already calibrated. Efficient numerical techniques, such as implicit or Crank-Nicolson can be readily used to roll back and solve the PDE.

The added benefit is that when pricing multi-factor hybrids, for example long-dated FX products, using LGM for interest rate allows one to easily set up standard 2-D or 3-D PDEs. Numerical techniques for solving standard PDEs are quite mature and readily available.

In the case of pricing path-dependent options, such as Bermudan swaption, the intrinsic node value of $\hat{V}_t(x)$ on the PDE grid is needed. With the calibrated parameters, the node intrinsic value can be easily obtained using the appropriate analytical formulae, for example that of swap or European swaption as listed in the calibration table. Note that the analytical formulae listed in the calibration uses the fact that $V_0(0) = \hat{V}_0(0)$. In fact, those formulae are directly applicable for $\hat{V}_t(x)$ given it is a martingale.

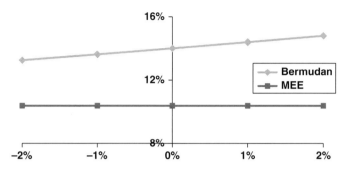

FIGURE 12.7 Swaption price vs mean reversion

Pricing a Bermudan involving rolling back PDE time slices and applying the optimum exercise condition on exercise dates: $\max\left(\hat{V}_{rollback}, \hat{V}_{intrinsic}\right)$. In Figure 12.7, the prices of an example 30-years Bermudan swaption are plotted against different mean reversion values. The embedded most expensive European (MEE) swaption prices, at 7-years into 23-years, are also plotted for reference.

As explained earlier, mean reversion impacts forward volatilities which the optimum exercise premium is sensitive to. For different mean reversion values, even though LGM is calibrated to the same European swaption prices, the Bermudan swaption prices will be different. Calibrating to the fixed European swaptions, larger mean reversion value will increase the price of a Bermudan swaption, as displayed in Figure 12.7.

Being a 1-factor model, LGM suffers the same problems of (lack of) de-correlation. It does not have much flexibility to handle volatility smile, although for some weak path-dependent products, one can choose to calibrate to the appropriate strikes.

LIBOR MARKET MODEL

In essence, LMM treats a collection of forward rates as a basket. The forward rates are clearly correlated, hence the specification of the correlation structure is important in the LMM framework. In the following, we shall illustrate the essential mathematical formulation of LMM, with a focus on the practical implementation of the model, as well as its extension to handle volatility smile.

Standard Formulation

As shown schematically in Figure 12.8, for $t < T_1$ and at times $T_1 < \cdots < T_i < \cdots < T_{n+1}$ the n corresponding forward rates are denoted as $f_1(t), \cdots, f_i(t), \cdots, f_n(t)$ and the $n+1$ corresponding zero coupon bonds are $P(t, T_1), \cdots, P(t, T_i), \cdots, P(t, T_{n+1})$.

By definition:

$$f_i(t)P(t, T_{i+1}) = \frac{P(t, T_i) - P(t, T_{i+1})}{\tau_i}$$

Because zero coupon bonds $(P(t, T_i), P(t, T_{i+1}))$ are tradable assets, $f_i(t)P(t, T_{i+1})$ must also be a tradable asset and its value with respect to the numeraire $P(t, T_{i+1})$ must

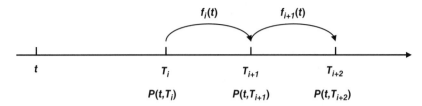

FIGURE 12.8 Diagram of forward rates and zero coupon bonds

be a martingale. Denoting Q_i as the measure associated with the numeraire $P(t, T_{i+1})$, under which the forward rate is a martingale (driftless). With the log-normal assumption, we have:

$$df_i(t) = \sigma_i(t)f_i(t)dW_i^{Q_i}$$

where $\sigma_i(t)$ is the instantaneous volatility, and $W_i^{Q_i}$ is the i-th element of n dimensional Brownian motion associated with the measure Q_i.

Whilst $f_i(t)$ is driftless under Q_i, the other forward rates $f_j(t)$ are not a martingale under Q_i. One can resort to the measure change technique to derive the drifts. The dynamics for all the forward rates under the measure Q_i are given by:

$$\frac{df_j(t)}{f_j(t)} = \mu_j^i(t)dt + \sigma_j(t)dW_j^{Q_i}$$

where:

$$
\begin{cases}
\mu_j^i(t) = \displaystyle\sum_{k=i+1}^{j} \frac{\tau_k f_k(t)\sigma_k\sigma_j\rho_{jk}}{1+\tau_k f_k(t)} & i < j \\[4mm]
\mu_j^i(t) = 0 & i = j \\[4mm]
\mu_j^i(t) = -\displaystyle\sum_{k=j+1}^{i} \frac{\tau_k f_k(t)\sigma_k\sigma_j\rho_{jk}}{1+\tau_k f_k(t)} & i > j
\end{cases}
$$

As can be seen from the above formulae, once the forward rate volatilities are specified, the forward rate drifts are determined as a result. This is also the outcome of HJM non-arbitrage framework which imposes a structure onto the drift of the forward rate process. Note that the drift term in the formulae can be rewritten as:

$$\frac{\tau_k f_k(t)\sigma_k\sigma_j\rho_{jk}}{1+\tau_k f_k(t)} = PV_{f_k(t)} \cdot \sigma_k\sigma_j\rho_{jk}$$

where $PV_{f_k(t)}$ is simply the present value of natural $f_k(t)$ payoff. The total drift for two forward measures is the sum of those terms of all forward rates in between. Clearly, the further apart the two forward measures are, the larger the total drift is.

The above formulation determine the following key LMM features:

- Because the drift terms are state-dependent, the forwards rate stochastic process is non-Markov.

- Therefore recombining tree or PDE cannot be used for LMM. At present, Monte Carlo simulation is the only feasible numerical technique for LMM implementation.
- For Monte Carlo simulation, a particular measure is chosen, and the drifts of the forward rates will be calculated thereof. The spot and terminal measure are the most commonly used in practice, although sometimes it is beneficial to choose a particular forward measure to make that particular forward rate martingale.
- Mathematically, the log-normal forward Libor assumption in the LMM does not lead to a log-normal process for the relevant forward swap rate. Therefore approximations are needed within the LMM to deal with swaptions or swaption features.

Numerical Implementation

For n forward rates, their joint dynamics under the measure Q_i can be written in the matrix form:

$$
\begin{pmatrix} df_1/f_1 \\ \vdots \\ df_n/f_n \end{pmatrix} = \begin{pmatrix} \mu_1 \\ \vdots \\ \mu_n \end{pmatrix} dt + \begin{pmatrix} \sigma_1 & \cdots & 0 \\ \vdots & \sigma_i & \vdots \\ 0 & \cdots & \sigma_n \end{pmatrix} \begin{pmatrix} dW_1 \\ \vdots \\ dW_n \end{pmatrix}
$$

For simplicity, the time and measure symbols have been omitted in the matrix form. The diagonal matrix $\{\sigma_i\}$ contains the instantaneous volatilities. The $\{dW_i\}$ column contains the correlated Brownian motions. The correlation matrix is implicitly included in the $\{dW_i\}$ column. The Black volatility of the i-th forward rate is related to its instantaneous volatility via:

$$
\sigma_B^2 = \frac{1}{T} \int_t^T \sigma_i^2 ds
$$

Theoretically up to n factors can be used to drive the above forward processes. In practice, however, it is desirable to use less factors for numerical efficiency. The reduced factors also make the application of Sobol numbers in the LMM Monte Carlo pricing more effective, with a much reduced problem in dimensionality.

Assuming we use m driving factors ($m \leq n$), the original matrix form describing the forward processes can be rewritten as:

$$
\begin{pmatrix} df_1/f_1 \\ \vdots \\ df_n/f_n \end{pmatrix} = \begin{pmatrix} \mu_1 \\ \vdots \\ \mu_n \end{pmatrix} dt + \begin{pmatrix} \sigma_{1,1} & \cdots & \sigma_{1,m} \\ \vdots & \sigma_{i,j} & \vdots \\ \sigma_{n,1} & \cdots & \sigma_{n,m} \end{pmatrix} \begin{pmatrix} dz_1 \\ \vdots \\ dz_m \end{pmatrix}
$$

where $\{\sigma_{i,j}\}$ is a $n \times m$ matrix, and the $\{dz_i\}$ column contains m independent Brownian motions. Each instantaneous volatility $\{\sigma_i\}$ in the original diagonal matrix has been decomposed into m Brownian motions:

$$
\sigma_i^2 = \sum_{j=1}^m \sigma_{i,j}^2
$$

and the i-th forward rate dynamics is:

$$\frac{df_i(t)}{f_i(t)} = \mu_i(t)dt + \sum_{j=1}^{m} \sigma_{i,j}\, dz$$

$$= \mu_i(t)dt + \sigma_i \sum_{j=1}^{m} \frac{\sigma_{i,j}}{\sigma_i}\, dz_j$$

The above decomposition allows the correlation structure to be included in the loading factors $\sigma_{i,j} / \sigma_i$. In other words, denoting $c_{ij} = \sigma_{i,j} / \sigma_i$ as the element in the $n \times m$ matrix C:

$$C \cdot C^T = \rho$$

where ρ is the full $n \times n$ instantaneous correlation structure of the n forward rates.

Practitioners usually use functional forms to exogenously specify instantaneous correlation structures in LMM. In Table 12.3, three functional forms are listed as examples.

Figure 12.9 compares the shape of the three correlation functional forms, with the same parameters $\rho_L = 30\%$ and $\beta = 0.5$. The horizontal axis is ΔT and in years. Whilst there are no fundamental reasons to prefer one to another, the concave shape at the short end ($\Delta T \to 0$) tends to calibrate to the market better.

TABLE 12.3 Possible correlation functional forms

Functional Form	Formula	Comments
Exponential	$\rho(\Delta T) = \rho_L + (1-\rho_L)e^{-\beta \cdot \Delta T}$	Convex function
Tanh	$\rho(\Delta T) = \rho_L + (1-\rho_L)\left[1 - Tanh(\beta \cdot \Delta T)\right]$	Convex function
Cosh	$\rho(\Delta T) = \rho_L + \dfrac{(1-\rho_L)}{Cosh(\beta \cdot \Delta T)}$	Short end concave, and long end convex

Where ρ_L and β are constants and they are positive numbers, and $\Delta T = |T_i - T_j|$.

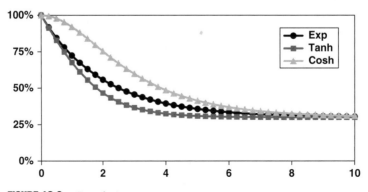

FIGURE 12.9 Correlation structures

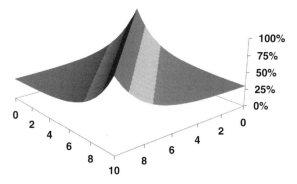

FIGURE 12.10 Correlation matrix (convex)

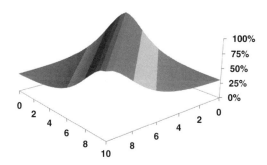

FIGURE 12.11 Correlation matrix (concave)

Figures 12.10 and 12.11 plot the correlation matrices of Exponential (convex) and Cosh (concave) functional form respectively. The x and y axes label T_i and T_j in years. The concave matrix or surface is numerically smooth across the line of $\Delta T = 0$, and its first order derivative is continuous.

LMM can accommodate much richer instantaneous correlation structures, as the forward rates on the entire forward curve is simulated. This is in contrast to the 1-factor models, such as LGM model, where the instantaneous volatilities are 100% correlated. Therefore LMM possesses the desired de-correlation effects, and is more suited to price and risk manage a wider range of path-dependent derivative products.

In Figure 12.12, the simulated forward curves are shown using an example EURI-BOR 6-month forward curve. The horizontal axis is expressed in months, and today's forward curve is labelled as T=0. As one simulates through time, at T=6m, the T=0 point is already fixed, hence only the remaining forward rates are being simulated. Moving past each time point, the relevant forward rate is fixed and drops out, and the rest of the forward rates are continuing the random walks specified by LMM.

Market Calibration

In LMM, each forward rate $f_i(t)$ has its associated instantaneous volatility σ_i. Each instantaneous volatility σ_i has a term structure spanning from t up to T_i, as illustrated in Figure 12.13.

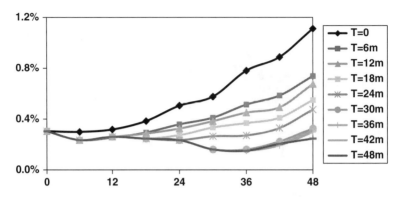

FIGURE 12.12 Simulated forward curves

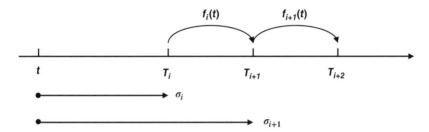

FIGURE 12.13 Forward rate volatility diagram

Calibrating to Cap/Floor It is relatively easy for LMM to be calibrated to the cap/floor prices, given its construction of modelling forward Libor rates directly. The market-quoted cap/floor implied volatility can be stripped into caplet/floorlet Black volatilities. A caplet/floorlet volatility $\sigma_B(T_i)$ is directly related to the forward rate's instantaneous volatility via:

$$\sigma_B^2(T_i) = \frac{1}{T}\int_t^T \sigma_i^2(s)\,ds$$

With a known $\sigma_B(T_i)$, the unknown $\sigma_i(s)$ term structure can be inversely calculated, in a variety of ways. The simplest is to assume $\sigma_i(s)$ is a piece-wise constant. So for n forward rates, there are n individual constant volatilities. The piece-wise constant approach allows easy calculations of bump-and-run Vega sensitivities.

Alternatively, one can assign a shared functional form to all instantaneous volatility term structures and solve for parameters. One such example is:

$$\sigma_i(s) = m_i\left[\left(a + b(T_i - s)\right)e^{-c(T_i - s)} + d\right]$$

where a, b, c, d are constants and they are the shared parameters for all forward rates, m_i is the parameter specifically associate with each i-th forward rate. During the calibration process, the common parameters a, b, c, d can be varied with the individual parameter m_i to achieve optimum time-homogenous fit. Whilst the functional form approach offers analytical and time-homogeneity convenience, it becomes very difficult when bump-and-run Vega sensitivities need to be calculated.

Calibrating to Swaption   Denoting a swap rate $S_{m,n}(t)$ spanning from m–th to n-th forward rates, it is defined by:

$$S_{m,n}(t) \cdot \sum_{i=m}^{n-1} P(t, T_{i+1}) \tau_i = P(t, T_m) - P(t, T_n)$$

The right-hand side of the above equation consists of zero bonds which are tradable assets. The left-hand side must also be a tradable asset, therefore its numeraire deflated value is a martingale (driftless):

$$dS_{m,n}(t) = \sigma_{m,n}(t) S_{m,n}(t) dW^{m,n}$$

where $dW^{m,n}$ is the Brownian motion under the annuity measure $Q^{m,n}$ associated with the numeraire $\sum_{i=m}^{n-1} P(t, T_{i+1}) \tau_i$. $\sigma_{m,n}(t)$ is the volatility of the swap rate.

Because a swap rate spans over a series of cascading forward rates, given instantaneous volatilities of the forward rates, the volatility of the swap rate is intuitively a basket average volatility. There is no exact analytical solution for the basket average volatility. There are, however, approximate formulae that are accurate and can be used to calibrate to the market European swaptions. By applying Ito's lemma on the swap rate, and after some algebra:

$$\sigma_{m,n}^2(t) = \frac{\sum_{i=m}^{n-1} \sum_{j=m}^{n-1} w_i(t) w_j(t) f_i(t) f_j(t) \sigma_i(t) \sigma_j(t) \rho_{ij}(t)}{S_{m,n}(t)^2}$$

$$\approx \frac{\sum_{i=m}^{n-1} \sum_{j=m}^{n-1} w_i(0) w_j(0) f_i(0) f_j(0) \sigma_i(t) \sigma_j(t) \rho_{ij}(t)}{S_{m,n}(0)^2}$$

where:

$$w_i(t) = \frac{P(t, T_{i+1}) \tau_i}{\sum_{i=m}^{n-1} P(t, T_{i+1}) \tau_i}$$

The weightings $w_i(t)$ can be further refined to take into account of the yield curve shape (Jäckel and Rebonato 2003). A shape correction term can be added to $w_i(t)$, to make the overall formulation more accurate.

The swaption Black volatility $\sigma_B(T_m)$ is simply given by:

$$\left(\sigma_B(T_m) \right)^2 = \frac{1}{T_m} \int_0^{T_m} \sigma_{m,n}^2(t) dt$$

To calibrate the forward rates volatilities to the swaption market, given the implied Black volatility $\sigma_B(T_m)$ is known, via the relationship between $\sigma_{m,n}(t)$ and $\sigma_i(t)$, one can set up numerical optimization schemes to solve for $\sigma_i(t)$. Note that in the standard LMM framework, the calibration is usually to the ATM swaption volatility matrix, using co-terminal and/or co-tenor swaptions depending on the products.

Whilst LMM is very realistic and flexible along the term structure axis, it cannot handle volatility smile properly. In the following, we shall examine how the standard LMM can be extended to include volatility smile.

Volatility Smile Extensions

Incorporating volatility smile in LMM is non-trivial. The avenues include using CEV or displaced diffusion process, and/or adding a stochastic volatility process into LMM. In the following, we shall examine how to incorporate displaced diffusion and Heston stochastic volatility process into LMM.

Displaced Diffusion and Stochastic Volatility (DDSV)   Displaced diffusion allows for better fitting to the skew, and stochastic volatility allows for better fitting to the smile. Together, they allow for much better calibration to the market volatility smile/skew. Additionally, in the low and negative interest rate environment, displaced diffusion has an inherent advantage of being able to accommodate negative rate.

Introducing displacement d_j into the forward rate SDEs, one arrives at the following displaced LMM process under the Q_i measure:

$$\frac{df_j(t)}{f_j(t)+d_j} = \mu_j^i(t)dt + \sigma_j(t)dW_j^{Q_i}$$

Adding a multiplicative stochastic volatility factor $V(t)$ (e.g. Wu and Zhang 2006) into the above displaced LMM process:

$$\begin{cases} \dfrac{df_j(t)}{f_j(t)+d_j} = V(t)\mu_j^i(t)dt + \sqrt{V(t)}\sigma_j(t)dW_j^{Q_i} \\ dV(t) = \kappa(t)\big(\theta(t)-V(t)\big)dt + \epsilon(t)\sqrt{V(t)}dZ \\ < dW_j^{Q_i} \cdot dZ >= \rho(t)dt \end{cases}$$

where $\kappa(t), \theta(t)$ and $\epsilon(t)$ are deterministic parameters, and forward rate drift is given by:

$$\begin{cases} \mu_j^i(t) = \displaystyle\sum_{k=i+1}^{j} \frac{\tau_k\big(f_k(t)+d_k\big)\sigma_k\sigma_j\rho_{jk}}{1+\tau_k f_k(t)} & i < j \\ \mu_j^i(t) = 0 & i = j \\ \mu_j^i(t) = -\displaystyle\sum_{k=j+1}^{i} \frac{\tau_k\big(f_k(t)+d_k\big)\sigma_k\sigma_j\rho_{jk}}{1+\tau_k f_k(t)} & i > j \end{cases}$$

The stochastic volatility process in the above setup is the well-known Heston type, which has the advantage of analytical tractability. With appropriate approximations in the underlying dynamics, the DDSV process can be mapped to standard Heston setup. The cap/caplet and swaption, which are key calibration instruments, can therefore be priced using standard Heston semi-analytical formulation.

DDSV-LMM Calibration DDSV-LMM has substantial degrees of freedom in the context of calibrating to market volatility smile/skew. There are three sets of parameters that need to be calibrated. In Table 12.4, their calibration instruments and key procedures are explained.

In the following, we shall compare a few examples of swaption smile calibration, using DD-LMM, SV-LMM, and DDSV-LMM. As can be visualized in Figures 12.14, 12.15 and 12.16, for maturity/tenor of 2Y5Y, 5Y10Y and 10Y20Y, DD-LMM calibration is the worst. SV-LMM is better but DDSV-LMM fits even better to the market.

In Figures 12.17 and 12.18, by removing the DD-LMM curve and zooming into the rest of 5Y10Y and 10Y20Y calibrations, it is shown that DDSV-LMM can fit the market swaption smile really well, much better than SV- alone.

The DDSV-LMM has enough degrees of freedom to calibrate to cap/floor and swaption market simultaneously if one chooses to. This may be desirable for pricing certain products that contact both cap/floor and swaption features. However,

TABLE 12.4 DDSV-LMM key calibration instruments and procedures

Parameter Sets	Calibration Procedures
Displacement d_j and stochastic volatility parameters $\kappa(t), \theta(t), \epsilon(t)$ and $\rho(t)$.	▪ This set is primarily used to calibrate smile/skew. The calibration instruments can be caps/floors or swaptions of all relevant strikes. ▪ CMS caps/floors can also be included in the calibration. ▪ Numerical optimization is typically used to back out parameters. ▪ This calibration does **not** need to be on-the-fly at trade level.
Forward rates correlation structure $\{\rho_{jk}\}$.	▪ The correlation structure can be exogenously specified by the practitioners using the functional forms as in the standard LMM. ▪ It can also be modified to calibrate to CMS spread options. Typically, more driving factors (e.g. 10) are required to have good fits, as CMS spread options contain rich correlation information. ▪ This calibration does **not** need to be on-the-fly at trade level.
Forward rates instantaneous volatilities $\sigma_j(t)$.	▪ Once the above two sets of parameters are calibrated, $\sigma_j(t)$ can be calibrated separately by bootstrapping the ATM caps/floors or swaptions as in the standard LMM. ▪ This set of parameters can be calibrated on-the-fly at trade level.

By calibrating to the relevant instruments, DDSV-LMM can be suitable for pricing a wide range of products with underlyings of Libor and/or CMS.

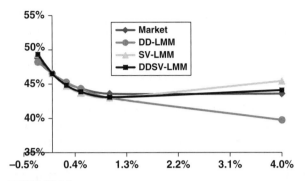

FIGURE 12.14 Smile calibration (2Y5Y)

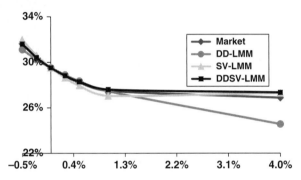

FIGURE 12.15 Smile calibration (5Y10Y)

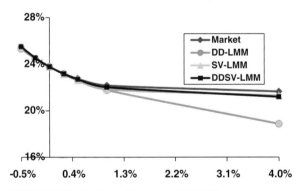

FIGURE 12.16 Smile calibration (10Y20Y)

numerical stability and hedging practicality are also two important factors to consider when deciding whether calibrating to both markets simultaneously has real pricing and hedging benefits.

EXTENDED CHEYETTE MODEL

We have so far examined two extreme model types, one is the simple 1-factor LGM model and the other is the complex high-dimensional LMM. Each model type has its pros and cons, limitations and suitability. Somewhere in the middle there is the

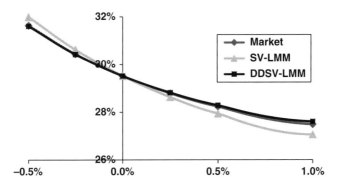

FIGURE 12.17   Smile calibration (5Y10Y)

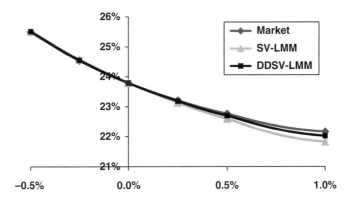

FIGURE 12.18   Smile calibration (10Y20Y)

Cheyette model (Cheyette 1992), which has lower dimension compared to LMM and more calibration flexibility compared to 1-factor LGM. While LMM can directly calibrate to the market instruments, its implementation is more cumbersome than the Cheyette model. With appropriate stochastic volatility or local volatility extension, the Cheyette model can handle and calibrate to market volatility smile efficiently.

Stochastic Process

Within the HJM framework, the forward rate $f(t, T)$ dynamics is specified by the following Normal process:

$$df(t, T) = \mu(t, T)dt + \sigma(t, T)dz$$

$$\mu(t, T) = \sigma(t, T)\int_t^T \sigma(t, s)ds$$

and the zero coupon bond $Z(t, T)$ is given by:

$$Z(t, T) = e^{-\int_t^T f(t, s)ds}$$

$\sigma(t,T)$ is forward rate volatility. The drift $\mu(t,T)$ determined by the martingale (no-arbitrage) condition is an integral of volatility. The explicit relationship between the drift and volatility of the forward rate is a cornerstone of HJM. Once the forward rate volatility structure is specified, a no-arbitrage term structure model is specified that fits the initial term structure automatically.

The HJM forward rate process is state-dependent, and HJM models are in general non-Markovian and have very high dimensions. This makes the numerical implementation difficult and inefficient: PDE-based techniques are not possible, and one has to use Monte Carlo in practice.

Volatility Separability

Cheyette model is essentially a Markov representation of HJM model, with much reduced dimensionality. This is achieved by assuming the volatility separability, i.e. the forward rate volatility can be written as the product of a time and rate (t,θ) dependent function and a maturity (T) dependent function:

$$\sigma(t,T) = \frac{\beta(t,\theta)}{\alpha(t)} \cdot \alpha(T) = \frac{\alpha(T)}{\alpha(t)}\beta(t,\theta)$$

The above can be generalized into the N-factor case whereby the forward rate volatility is the sum of N terms, and each term has the separability feature:

$$\sigma(t,T) = \sum_{i=1}^{N} \frac{\alpha_i(T)}{\alpha_i(t)}\beta_i(t,\theta)$$

One convenient assumption often made and used in practice is to set $\alpha_i(t) = \exp(-\kappa_i t)$, where κ_i is a constant. The forward rate volatility can then be rewritten as:

$$\sigma(t,t+\tau) = \sum_{i=1}^{N} exp[-\kappa_i \tau]\beta_i(t,\theta)$$

The exponential terms in the above equation depend on the tenor (τ) only. $\beta_i(t,\theta)$ terms generate time (t) and rate or state variable (θ) dependence. In Figure 12.19, three exponential terms together with their average are plotted against tenor (τ), each with different κ value as shown in the legend.

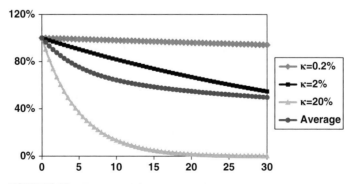

FIGURE 12.19 Exponential terms vs tenor

Clearly when N is large, it leads to richer dynamics and it can approximate better the continuous forward rate volatility postulated in the HJM framework. On the other hand, larger N makes the modelling more complex. Therefore in practice, a compromise has to be made. In the following, we use $N = 1$ to illustrate the underlying model details, which can be generalized into the multi-factor case using vector symbols.

Plugging the $N = 1$ volatility separability function into the HJM forward rate SDE, after some algebra, one obtains the following joint Markov representation:

$$f(t,T) = f(0,T) + \frac{\alpha(T)}{\alpha(t)}\left[x(t) + G(t,T)y(t)\right]$$

$$Z(t,T) = \frac{Z(0,T)}{Z(0,t)}exp\left[-G(t,T)x(t) - \frac{1}{2}G^2(t,T)y(t)\right]$$

where:

$$G(t,T) = \frac{A(T) - A(t)}{\alpha(t)} \quad A(t) = \int_0^t \alpha(s)ds$$

and the joint driving factors (state variables) $x(t)$ and $y(t)$ satisfy the following SDEs:

$$dx(t) = \left[-\frac{\alpha'(t)}{\alpha(t)}x(t) + y(t)\right]dt + \beta(t,\theta)dz$$

$$dy(t) = \left[\beta^2(t,\theta) - 2\frac{\alpha'(t)}{\alpha(t)}y(t)\right]dt$$

$$x(0) = 0$$

$$y(0) = 0$$

Note the special case of short rate $r(t) = f(t,t) = f(0,t) + x(t)$, hence $x(t) = r(t) - f(0,t)$ can be viewed as the centred version of short rate.

The volatility separability assumption has transformed the non-Markov HJM forward rate dynamics into a multi-factor Markov process. For $N = 1$, two state variables $\left[x(t), y(t)\right]$ drive the Markov process as shown above. For a given N, the total number of state variables is $N(N+3)/2$.

The above demonstrates that the Cheyette model has the features of a short rate model, and it also contains the relationships between short rate and different forward rates. Hence the Cheyette model has the advantage of being low-dimension and at the same time able to fit rates term structures similar to LMM.

Smile Model Formulation

In the Cheyette model the closed form solution of the zero coupon bond price holds even with local volatility or stochastic volatility. This is a very plausible model feature when it comes to practical numerical implementation. In the one-dimensional case, a PDE can also be set up for the driving factors.

Using $\alpha(t) = \exp(-\kappa t)$, where κ is a constant, going through standard non-arbitrage algebra, a contingent claim such as an European option (V) obeys the following PDE containing $x(t)$ and $y(t)$:

$$\frac{\partial V}{\partial t} + \left[y(t) - kx(t)\right]\frac{\partial V}{\partial x} + \frac{1}{2}\beta^2(t,\theta)\frac{\partial^2 V}{\partial x^2} + \left[\beta^2(t,\theta) - 2\kappa y(t)\right]\frac{\partial V}{\partial y}$$
$$= \left[x(t) + f(0,t)\right]V$$

This parabolic PDE can be solved by efficient numerical PDE solvers, such as that of the ADI scheme. The Cheyette model can potentially be very numerically efficient. Some path-dependent derivative features such as Bermudan early exercises can be readily incorporated and priced by the PDE solver as usual.

In order to capture and calibrate to the volatility smile, the Cheyette model has been extended to include either stochastic volatility (Andreasen 2005) or a quadratic local volatility functional form (Chibane and Law 2013). In the extended stochastic volatility Cheyette model, a selection of benchmark rolling forward rates (instantaneous forward rates) are linked to the volatility parameters in the Cheyette model. The selected forward rates hence become the driving factors, and the latent Cheyette model parameters are then calibrated to the volatility smile in a meaningful manner. The multi-factor stochastic volatility extension enables good volatility smile calibrations, and its numerical implementation is relatively efficient with appropriate and accurate approximations.

Local Volatility Functional Form   The local volatility functional form approach is simpler and by definition numerically more efficient. With a quadratic functional form (Chibane and Law 2013) for the local volatility $\beta(t, \theta)$, the volatility smile can be incorporated into the Cheyette model. For $\alpha(t) = \exp(-\kappa t)$ and $\beta(t, \theta)$ having a quadratic functional form, the Cheyette dynamics can be extended using the following SDEs:

$$dx(t) = \left[-\kappa x(t) + y(t)\right]dt + \beta(t,x(t))dz$$
$$dy(t) = \left[\beta^2(t,x(t)) - 2\kappa y(t)\right]dt$$
$$\beta(t,x(t)) = a(t)x^2(t) + b(t)x(t) + c(t)$$
$$x(0) = 0$$
$$y(0) = 0$$

where the deterministic parameters $a(t), b(t)$ and $c(t)$ need to be obtained via the smile calibration. The key is to link them to the observable market smile data, for example the swaption smile.

Denoting the forward swap rate as:

$$S(t) = S(t,x(t),y(t)) = \frac{Z(t,T_0) - Z(t,T_N)}{\sum_{i=1}^{N} Z(t,T_i)\tau_i}$$

and following Ito's lemma, the forward swap rate stochastic process under its annuity measure is given by:

$$dS(t) = \sigma(t,x(t),y(t))dz^A$$

$$\sigma\big(t,x(t),y(t)\big) = \frac{\partial S\big(t,x(t),y(t)\big)}{\partial x}\beta\big(t,x(t)\big)$$

$\sigma\big(t,x(t),y(t)\big)$ is therefore a function of $a(t)$, $b(t)$ and $c(t)$ contained in $\beta\big(t,x(t)\big)$.

The forward swap rate stochastic process under its annuity measure, on the other hand, is given by:

$$dS(t) = \sigma_S(t,S)dz^A$$

$$\sigma_S(t,S) = d(t)\Big[e(t)\big[S - S(0)\big]^2 + g(t)\big[S - S(0)\big] + S(0)\Big]$$

where $\sigma_S(t,S)$ is the local volatility of the forward swap rate, and is assumed to have a quadratic functional form, where $d(t)$, $e(t)$ and $g(t)$ are the deterministic parameters to be calibrated.

With the relationships established above, and the assumed quadratic functional forms for $\beta\big(t,x(t)\big)$ and $\sigma_S(t,S)$, the calibration process can be summarized in Table 12.5.

TABLE 12.5 Model calibration process

Steps	Descriptions
1. Calibrate the average quadratic parameters $\bar{d}(t), \bar{e}(t)$ and $\bar{g}(t)$ in $\bar{\sigma}_S(t,S)$;	With $dS(t) = \bar{\sigma}_S(t,S)dz^A$ and $\bar{\sigma}_S(t,S)$ specified by the quadratic functional form, there exist closed-form option pricing formulae, allowing the average quadratic parameters to be calibrated directly to the European swaption prices at given times.
2. The calibrated average quadratic parameters are: $$\bar{d}(t) = f\big(d(t)\big)$$ $$\bar{e}(t) = f\big(e(t),d(t)\big)$$ $$\bar{g}(t) = f\big(g(t),d(t)\big)$$	The average quadratic parameters are by definition the functions of time-dependent quadratic parameters $d(t)$, $e(t)$ and $g(t)$. Because of the linkage between $\{a(t), b(t), c(t)\}$ and $\{d(t), e(t), g(t)\}$, the equations on the left can be used to imply out $\{a(t), b(t), c(t)\}$.
3. Linkage between $\{a(t), b(t), c(t)\}$ and $\{d(t), e(t), g(t)\}$: $$\sigma\big(t, \bar{x}(t), \bar{y}(t)\big) = \sigma_S\big(t, S(0)\big)$$ $$\frac{\partial \sigma}{\partial x}\Big|_{\substack{x=\bar{x}(t) \\ y=\bar{y}(t)}} = \frac{\partial \sigma_S}{\partial x}\Big|_{S=S(0)}$$ $$\frac{\partial^2 \sigma}{\partial x^2}\Big|_{\substack{x=\bar{x}(t) \\ y=\bar{y}(t)}} = \frac{\partial^2 \sigma_S}{\partial x^2}\Big|_{S=S(0)}$$	As $\sigma\big(t, x(t), y(t)\big)$ is a function of $\{a(t), b(t), c(t)\}$ and $\sigma_S(t, S)$ a function of $\{d(t), e(t), g(t)\}$, the relationship between parameters $\{a(t), b(t), c(t)\}$ and $\{d(t), e(t), g(t)\}$ can be established by these three system equations: Solving these equation requires the calculation of the mean states $\bar{x}$ and $\bar{y}$; Approximations are made in the process of calculating $\bar{x}$ and $\bar{y}$, and subsequent numerical solver;
4. Calibrate the parameters $a(t)$, $b(t)$ and $c(t)$ in $\beta\big(t,x(t)\big)$.	By plugging $a(t)$, $b(t)$ and $c(t)$ into the equations explained in Step 2 and 3, these parameters can be solved numerically.

Once $\beta\big(t,x(t)\big)$ is calibrated including volatility smile, one can use PDE or Monte Carlo with state variable $x(t)$ and $y(t)$, to price relevant derivatives.

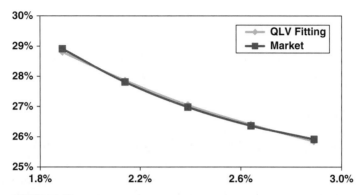

FIGURE 12.20   Implied Vol Calibration (5n15)

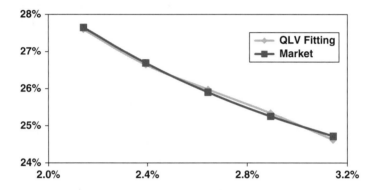

FIGURE 12.21   Implied Vol Calibration (15n5)

Smile Calibration Examples   Figures 12.20 and 12.21 show two swaption calibration examples, both calibrating to the market (Black) implied volatilities. Using the quadratic local volatility fitting procedure, the model generated implied volatilities are compared with the market. As shown in the figures, the calibration results are very good. Nevertheless they are not perfect, as parametric fitting has its limitations.

The smile calibration steps in the extended Cheyette model are fairly efficient compared to other interest rate smile models. While this represents a substantial progress, the smile calibration is still very convoluted with approximations in almost all steps.

- Is there a fundamentally simpler, more efficient and reliable way to model interest rate volatility smile?
- Is there a non-parametric local volatility model that can fit interest rate volatility smile?

LOCAL VOLATILITY MODEL

Up until now, given the available interest rate smile models, the volatility smile calibrations heavily rely on multi-dimensional numerical optimization. Unlike in equity and FX, there is no Dupire-type arbitrage-free local volatility model for interest rate smile. The basic smile modelling process is very different, as compared in Table 12.6.

TABLE 12.6   Comparison of smile modelling process

Local Volatility Model (in Equity/FX)	Interest Rate Smile Modelling
■ Strip Dupire local volatility directly from the market quotes (option prices or implied volatilities). ■ Price derivatives using the local volatilities.	■ Invent stochastic processes with multiple model parameters. ■ Derive European swaption price formula, which often does not have a closed-form solution. ■ Try to approximate the formula, in order to speed up calculations. ■ Apply multi-dimensional optimization scheme to numerically calibrate to the market quotes and iterate out the model parameters. ■ Price derivatives using the calibrated model parameters.
■ Local volatility can be non-parametric, and calibration via local volatility stripping is extremely efficient. More advanced smile models can be based on the local volatility model to leverage its numerical efficiency.	■ The calibration process is complex, convoluted and numerically inefficient. The outputs are less stable as a result.

So, why there is no Dupire equivalent local volatility model for interest rate smile? This is because the Dupire local volatility model requires the derivatives with respect to option maturity ($\partial C / \partial T$). In the equity market, the market option prices at different maturities are for the same underlying and therefore they are differentiable with respect to maturity. The underlying has a natural well-defined spot process.

This is not the case in the interest rate markets. For example, for a given forward swap rate only swaptions with expiry date equal to fixing date are traded. A swaption price at a given option maturity (t_1) is only for the forward swap fixing at t_1 with a fixed tenor. Another swaption price at different maturity (t_2) is for a different forward swap fixing at t_2 with a fixed tenor. These are seemingly two different underlyings driven by two separate forward processes, and there is no direct time evolution connecting these forward processes. Under this circumstance, the consensus was that it would be practically very hard to obtain meaningful $\partial C / \partial T$ from the market quotes.

However, can one invent a Dupire-type Local Volatility model for interest rate smile from a very different angle:

- allow a consistent process with that implied by the market swaption smile, hence
- able to calibrate to market-quoted swaptions directly and efficiently via local volatility stripping, hence
- price interest rate derivatives using local volatilities, to be consistent with market-quoted swaption (smile) prices?

Swap Local Volatility Stripping   Gatarek, Jablecki and Qu recently proposed a form of Dupire-type swap local volatility stripping. They worked on two key elements that are essential in a Dupire-type local volatility model:

- creating a modified swap spot dynamics (or diffusion process) that aims to reproduce implied swaption smile;

- formulating a swaption-based Dupire-type equation for the unique state-dependent diffusion coefficient.

In the following, we shall start the analysis with the log-normal case, and extend it later to the normal case.

Dynamics of Forward Swap Rate   For clarity, the time points $0 < u < t < T$ are schematically drawn in Figure 12.22:

A continuously compounded forward swap rate, seen at time u, starting (fixing) at time t and ending at time T is given by:

$$S_{tT}(u) = \frac{Z(u,t) - Z(u,T)}{\int_t^T Z(u,s)\,ds}$$

where $Z(\cdot)$ denotes the zero coupon bond and the swap tenor is $T - t$. Since this is a tradable forward swap rate, it must be a martingale under the forward annuity measure and satisfies the stochastic process:

$$dS_{tT}(u) = S_{tT}(u) \cdot \sigma_{tT}(u) \cdot dW_{tT}(u)$$

The market-quoted swaption prices can be used to obtain Black implied volatilities using this process. This process is on the forward and one cannot obtain the differentiation of price against the maturity. Therefore one cannot strip Dupire-type local volatilities using this process.

We need to create a spot process that allows us to differentiate against maturity, and subsequently strip local volatility. Let us introduce the concept of fixed-tenor **rolling swap**.

Dynamics of (Fixed-tenor) Rolling Swap   A fixed-tenor rolling swap has a fixed tenor (denoted as λ), and its fixing time t is rolling. The swap end point $t + \lambda$ rolls with t. For simplicity, fixed-tenor rolling swap rate is written as:

$$S_\lambda(t) = S_{t(t+\lambda)}(t)$$

The rolling process of the fixed-tenor (λ) swap is schematically shown in Figure 12.23, rolling from t_1 to t_2.

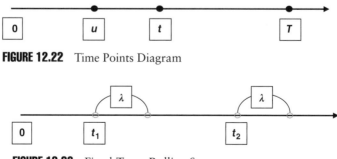

FIGURE 12.22   Time Points Diagram

FIGURE 12.23   Fixed-Tenor Rolling Swap

The fixed-tenor rolling swap is not a martingale. Its spot process can be derived by the following re-arrangement:

$$S_\lambda(t) - S_\lambda(u) = S_{t(t+\lambda)}(t) - S_{u(u+\lambda)}(u)$$

$$= \left(S_{t(t+\lambda)}(t) - S_{t(t+\lambda)}(u)\right) + \left(S_{t(t+\lambda)}(u) - S_{u(u+\lambda)}(u)\right)$$

Because $S_{t(t+\lambda)}(u)$ is a martingale (a market traded forward swap rate), we have:

$$S_{t(t+\lambda)}(t) - S_{t(t+\lambda)}(u) = S_\lambda(u)\sigma_{t(t+\lambda)}(u)\left(W_{t(t+\lambda)}(t) - W_{t(t+\lambda)}(u)\right)$$

and by expansion:

$$S_{t(t+\lambda)}(u) - S_{u(u+\lambda)}(u) = S_\lambda(u)\frac{\partial ln\left(S_{u(u+\lambda)}(t)\right)}{\partial u}(t-u) + o(t-u)$$

Taking the limit $u \to t$, one obtains an important SDE for the fixed-tenor rolling swap:

$$dS_\lambda(t) = S_\lambda(t)\sigma\left(S_\lambda(t), t\right)dW_{t(t+\lambda)} + S_\lambda(t)Q_{t(t+\lambda)}(t)dt \qquad Eq.(12.1)$$

where the drift:

$$Q_{t(t+\lambda)}(t) \approx \left.\frac{\partial ln S_{u(u+\lambda)}(t)}{\partial u}\right|_{u=t}$$

$$= \frac{Z(t, t+\lambda)f(t, t+\lambda) - r(t)}{1 - Z(t, t+\lambda)} - \frac{Z(t, t+\lambda) - 1}{\int_t^{t+\lambda} Z(t, s)ds}$$

$$= \left[S_\lambda(t) - r(t)\right] + \left[f(t, t+\lambda) - r(t)\right]\frac{Z(t, t+\lambda)}{1 - Z(t, t+\lambda)}$$

The instantaneous drift $Q_{t(t+\lambda)}(t)$ is approximated by a deterministic function which can be calculated from the "frozen" today's yield curve:

$$Q_{t(t+\lambda)}(t) \approx \left[S_{t(t+\lambda)}(0) - f(0,t)\right] + \left[f(0,t+\lambda) - f(0,t)\right]\frac{Z(0, t+\lambda)}{Z(0, t) - Z(0, t+\lambda)}$$

For convenience, in the following we shall denote the drift as $Q_\lambda(t) = Q_{t(t+\lambda)}(t)$.

Local Volatility Stripping of Co-tenor Swaption The European swaption (e.g. a payer swaption) for a given expiry (t) and tenor (λ) under the annuity measure can be written in terms of fixed-tenor rolling swap $S_\lambda(t)$:

$$\text{Swaption}(t, T, K) = E_{t(t+\lambda)}\left[S_\lambda(t) - K\right]^+ \cdot \int_t^{t+\lambda} Z(0, s)ds$$

where $E_{t(t+\lambda)}(\cdot)$ is the expectation under the swap measure associated specifically with annuity $\int_{t}^{t+\lambda} Z(t,s)ds$.

Denoting $C_{t(t+\lambda)}(u) = E_{t(t+\lambda)}\left[S_\lambda(u) - K\right]^+$ which is an undiscounted payoff, with the SDE Equation 12.1 for the fixed-tenor rolling swap $dS_\lambda(t)$, applying Fokker-Planck equation to its probability density function, a Dupire-type formula can be obtained:

$$\frac{K^2\sigma^2(K,t)}{2}\frac{\partial^2 C_{t(t+\lambda)}(t)}{\partial K^2} = \left.\frac{\partial C_{t(t+\lambda)}(u)}{\partial u}\right|_{u=t} + Q_\lambda(t)\left[K\frac{\partial C_{t(t+\lambda)}(t)}{\partial K} - C_{t(t+\lambda)}(t)\right]$$

Gatarek, Jablecki and Qu further approximated:

$$\left.\frac{\partial C_{t(t+\lambda)}(u)}{\partial u}\right|_{u=t} \approx \frac{\partial C_{t(t+\lambda)}(t)}{\partial t} - q(t,\lambda)C_{t(t+\lambda)}(t)$$

where $q(t,\lambda)$ is a deterministic function. $q(t,\lambda)$ is a complicated function and it can be calibrated numerically once $Q_\lambda(t)$ is calculated using the frozen today's yield curve.

The local volatility PDE (Dupire-type equation) for the fixed-tenor swaption can therefore be written as:

$$\frac{K^2\sigma^2(K,t)}{2}\frac{\partial^2 C_{t(t+\lambda)}(t)}{\partial K^2} = \frac{\partial C_{t(t+\lambda)}(t)}{\partial t} + Q_\lambda(t)K\frac{\partial C_{t(t+\lambda)}(t)}{\partial K} - \left[q(t,\lambda) + Q_\lambda(t)\right]C_{t(t+\lambda)}(t)$$

Comparing this local volatility PDE of undiscounted (rolling) swaption with that of undiscounted equity option, the swaption local volatility PDE has an additional term due to $q(t,\lambda)$. $q(t,\lambda)$ is a specific feature of the above approximation. From the PDE, the undiscounted market forward swap rate is solved by:

$$F_{t(t+\lambda)}(t) = S_\lambda(0)e^{\int_0^t q(s,\lambda)ds}e^{\int_0^t Q_\lambda(s)ds}$$

Therefore knowing $F_{t(t+\lambda)}(t)$ and $Q_\lambda(t)$ from today's yield curve, $q(t,\lambda)$ can be calculated.

By re-arranging the above PDE, the local volatility formula is:

$$\sigma(K,t) = \frac{1}{K}\sqrt{2\frac{\frac{\partial C_{t(t+\lambda)}(t)}{\partial t} + Q_\lambda(t)K\frac{\partial C_{t(t+\lambda)}(t)}{\partial K} - \left[q(t,\lambda) + Q_\lambda(t)\right]C_{t(t+\lambda)}(t)}{\frac{\partial^2 C_{t(t+\lambda)}(t)}{\partial K^2}}}$$

It can actually be stripped from the fixed-tenor swaption implied volatility (σ_I) directly:

$$\sigma(K,t) = \sqrt{\frac{2\dfrac{\partial \sigma_I}{\partial t} + \dfrac{\sigma_I}{t} + 2KQ_\lambda(t)\dfrac{\partial \sigma_I}{\partial K}}{\dfrac{1}{\sigma_I t}\left(1 + \dfrac{Ky}{\sigma_I}\dfrac{\partial \sigma_I}{\partial K}\right)^2 + K^2\dfrac{\partial^2 \sigma_I}{\partial K^2} - \dfrac{K^2\sigma_I t}{4}\left(\dfrac{\partial \sigma_I}{\partial K}\right)^2 + K\dfrac{\partial \sigma_I}{\partial K}}}$$

where $y = ln\left(F_\lambda(t)/K\right)$ and $F_\lambda(t)$ is the forward rolling swap rate.

Using the above stripping formula, one needs to pay attention to the following points:

- $dS_\lambda(t)$ is a process on the spot (rolling swap), and $dS_{tT}(u)$ is a process on the forward (swap rate). $F_\lambda(t)$ is the forward of $S_\lambda(t)$, and it is different from the market forward swap rate (denoted as F_t below).
- The implied volatility σ_I is that of the rolling swaption associated with the $dS_\lambda(t)$ process. The market-quoted implied swaption volatility (denoting it as σ_m) is associated the $dS_{tT}(u)$ process. We need to convert σ_m to σ_I. Denoting the market forward swap rate as F_t, the implied volatility conversion formula can be derived from the local volatility PDE as:

$$C_\lambda\left(F_t, \sigma_m, K, t\right) = e^{\int_0^t q(s,\lambda)ds} \, C_\lambda\left(S_\lambda(0)e^{\int_0^t Q_\lambda(s)ds}, \sigma_I, K, t\right)$$

where $C_\lambda(F,\sigma,K,t)$ is the undiscounted Black formula for the given forward (F), volatility (σ), strike (K), expiry (t) and tenor (λ). Once $Q_\lambda(t)$ and $q(t,\lambda)$ have been calibrated using today's yield curve as explained earlier, σ_I can be calculated from the market implied volatility σ_m. If and when $q(t,\lambda) = 0, \sigma_I = \sigma_m$, i.e. no volatility conversion is needed.

It is possible to simplify local volatility stripping:

- Instead of using the $Q_\lambda(t)$ formula, $Q_\lambda(t)$ can be numerically approximated by matching the market forward swap rates. For example, in the fixed-tenor lognormal case, using today's yield curve, $Q_\lambda(t) \approx ln\left[S_\lambda(t+\Delta t)/S_\lambda(t-\Delta t)\right]/(2\Delta t)$. This is equivalent to setting $q(t,\lambda) = 0$.
- Although $q(t,\lambda)$ is not in the local volatility stripping (from implied volatility) formula, it is in the implied volatility conversion formula and local volatility PDE. So when $q(t,\lambda) = 0$, it will simplify local volatility stripping and PDE calculations. In many practical cases, it is found that $q(t,\lambda)$ is indeed very small ($q(t,\lambda) \approx 0$).

The fixed-tenor (or co-tenor) swaption implied volatility (σ_m) can be easily extracted from the market-quoted swaption volatility cube. Figure 12.24 plots an example of co-tenor (log-normal Black) swaption implied volatility surface.

It is important to note that in the context of local volatility stripping, the cap/floor is effectively the fixed-tenor (co-tenor) swaption. Therefore the one can the fixed-tenor swaption formulation to strip the local volatility of caplet/floorlet.

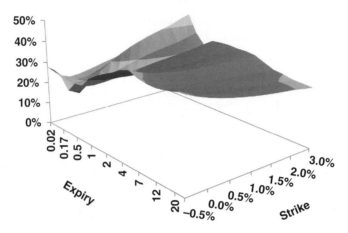

FIGURE 12.24   Co-Tenor Implied Vol Surface. The tenor is 1-year. Expiry is in years and strike is absolute.

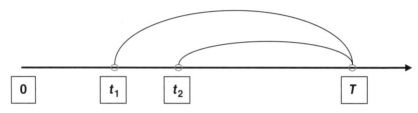

FIGURE 12.25   Fixed-Terminal Rolling Swap

Dynamics and Local Volatility Stripping of (Co-terminal) Swaption   Using exactly the same logic as for the fixed-tenor rolling swap, the dynamics of the fixed-terminal rolling swap can be formulated. The fixed-terminal rolling swap is defined as the swap with a fixed terminal T, and its starting point t is rolling, as schematically shown in Figure 12.25.

In order to strip local volatility for the co-terminal swaptions, one needs to derive a spot process for the fixed-terminal **rolling swap**. Following the same logic, the log-normal spot dynamics of the fixed-terminal rolling swap has a similar SDE as for the fixed-tenor rolling swap:

$$dS_{tT}(t) = S_{tT}(t)\sigma\big(S_{tT}(t),t\big)dW_{tT} + S_{tT}(t)Q_{tT}(t)dt$$

where T is the fixed terminal, and the drift is given by:

$$Q_{tT}(t) \approx \frac{\partial ln S_{uT}(t)}{\partial u}\bigg|_{u=t}$$

Given $S_{uT}(t) = \big[Z(t,u) - Z(t,T)\big] / \int_u^T Z(t,s)ds$, the drift equals to:

$$Q_{tT}(t) \approx \frac{1}{\int_t^T Z(t,s)ds} - \frac{r(t)}{1-Z(t,T)} = \frac{S_{tT}(t) - r(t)}{1-Z(t,T)}$$

Same as in the co-tenor case, $Q_{tT}(t)$ can be calculated from today's frozen yield curve analytically, or numerically by matching relevant forward swap rates.

The co-terminal swaption local volatility PDE and its local volatility stripping formula are identical to those for the fixed-tenor (co-tenor) swaptions. The only difference is in the formula of the drift ($Q_{tT}(t)$ instead of $Q_{\lambda}(t)$). Therefore by following the same procedure (calculating $Q_{tT}(t)$, $q(t)$, and converting σ_m to σ_l), one can strip the co-terminal local volatility in exactly the same way as tripping the co-tenor local volatility.

The co-terminal swaption implied volatility (σ_m) can be extracted from the market-quoted swaption volatility cube. Figure 12.26 shows an example of co-terminal (log-normal Black) swaption implied volatility surface.

Swap Local Volatility Stripping (Normal)   In order to deal with negative interest rates, swap rate dynamics can be assumed to follow the normal process. Using the same logic and reasoning as in the log-normal case, one can derive the dynamics for the fixed-tenor and fixed terminal rolling swap. The resultant stochastic processes and drifts are shown in Table 12.7 and Table 12.8.

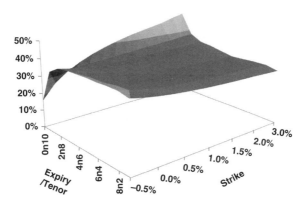

FIGURE 12.26   Co-Terminal Implied Vol Surface. The terminal is fixed at 10-years. Strike is absolute.

TABLE 12.7   Normal process for fixed-tenor rolling swap

	Fixed-Tenor (Co-Tenor)
SDE	$dS_{\lambda}(t) = \sigma(S_{\lambda}(t), t)\, dW_{t(t+\lambda)} + Q_{t(t+\lambda)}(t)\, dt$
Drift	$Q_{t(t+\lambda)}(t) \approx \left. \dfrac{\partial S_{u(u+\lambda)}(t)}{\partial u} \right|_{u=t}$
	$\approx S_{\lambda}(t)\left\{ \left[S_{\lambda}(t) - r(t)\right] + \left[f(t, t+\lambda) - r(t)\right] \dfrac{Z(t, t+\lambda)}{1 - Z(t, t+\lambda)} \right\}$

TABLE 12.8 Normal process for fixed-terminal rolling swap

	Fixed-Terminal (Co-Terminal)
SDE	$dS_{tT}(t) = \sigma\big(S_{tT}(t),t\big)dW_{tT} + Q_{tT}(t)dt$
Drift	$Q_{tT}(t) \approx \dfrac{\partial S_{uT}(t)}{\partial u}\bigg|_{u=t} \approx S_{tT}(t)\left[\dfrac{S_{tT}(t)-r(t)}{1-Z(t,T)}\right]$

To unify both fixed-tenor and fixed terminal cases, making the subscripts T and $t+\lambda$ interchangeable, the undiscounted call $\left(C_{tT}(t)=E_{tT}\Big[\big(S(t)-K\big)^+\Big]\right)$ satisfies the following local volatility PDE:

$$\frac{\sigma^2(K,t)}{2}\frac{\partial^2 C_{tT}(t)}{\partial K^2} = \frac{\partial C_{tT}(u)}{\partial u}\bigg|_{u=t} + Q(t)\frac{\partial C_{tT}(t)}{\partial K}$$

where $Q(t)$ is the instantaneous drift for either fixed-tenor or fixed-terminal rolling swap. Similar to the log-normal case:

$$\frac{\partial C_{tT}(u)}{\partial u}\bigg|_{u=t} \approx \frac{\partial C_{tT}(t)}{\partial t} - q(t)C_{tT}(t)$$

therefore:

$$\frac{\sigma^2(K,t)}{2}\frac{\partial^2 C_{tT}(t)}{\partial K^2} = \frac{\partial C_{tT}(t)}{\partial t} + Q(t)\frac{\partial C_{tT}(t)}{\partial K} - q(t)C_{tT}(t)$$

and:

$$\sigma(K,t) = \sqrt{2\frac{\dfrac{\partial C_{tT}(t)}{\partial t} + Q(t)\dfrac{\partial C_{tT}(t)}{\partial K} - q(t)C_{tT}(t)}{\dfrac{\partial^2 C_{tT}(t)}{\partial K^2}}}$$

As shown in §6.1, the normal local volatility can also be stripped directly from the normal implied volatility. With the Bachelier call, denoting the normal implied volatility as σ_N, the normal local volatility stripping formula is given by:

$$\sigma(K,t) = \sqrt{\frac{2\dfrac{\partial\sigma_N}{\partial t} + \dfrac{\sigma_N}{t} + 2Q(t)\dfrac{\partial\sigma_N}{\partial K}}{\dfrac{1}{\sigma_N t}\left(1+\dfrac{\big(F(t)-K\big)}{\sigma_N}\dfrac{\partial\sigma_N}{\partial K}\right)^2 + \dfrac{\partial^2\sigma_N}{\partial K^2}}}$$

where $F(t)$ is the forward of the rolling swap $S(t)$.

The remarks made on $F(t), Q(t), q(t)$ in the log-normal case are equally valid in the normal case. In particular:

- $Q(t)$ can either be calculated using the drift formula, or

- $Q(t)$ can be numerically approximated. For example, in the fixed-tenor normal case, using today's yield curve, $Q(t) = Q_\lambda(t) \approx \left[S_\lambda(t + \Delta t) - S_\lambda(t - \Delta t) \right] / (2\Delta t)$. This is equivalent to setting $q(t) = 0$.

Once $Q(t)$ and $q(t)$ have been calibrated using today's yield curve, an implied volatility conversion is needed to obtain σ_N from the market implied normal volatility σ_M. Denoting the market forward swap rate as F_t, the implied volatility conversion formula can be derived from the local volatility PDE as:

$$C_\lambda\left(F_t, \sigma_M, K, t\right) = e^{\int_0^t q(s)ds} C_\lambda\left(S_\lambda(0) + \int_0^t Q(s)ds, \sigma_N, K, t \right)$$

where $C_\lambda\left(F, \sigma, K, t\right)$ is the undiscounted Bachelier formula for the given forward (F), volatility (σ), strike (K), expiry (t) and tenor (λ). If and when $q(t) = 0$, $\sigma_N = \sigma_M$, i.e. no volatility conversion is needed.

To strip the local volatility for the cap/floor, one can use the fixed-tenor (co-tenor) swaption:

- The market-quoted cap/floor flat volatilities can be decomposed into caplet/floorlet volatilities by standard bootstrapping.
- For a given strike, each caplet (term) volatility is effectively the one-period fixed tenor swaption implied volatility.
- Therefore all the caplet implied volatilities, with a fixed tenor across different maturities and strikes, can be readily plugged into the above local volatility stripping procedure.

Feeding Local Volatility into Cheyette Model The stripped local volatilities can be conveniently applied and fed to the Cheyette model, to enable efficient interest rate derivatives pricing in the presence of smile. Recall the 1-factor Cheyette model driving factor SDEs:

$$dx(t) = \left[-\kappa x(t) + y(t) \right] dt + \beta\left(t, x(t)\right) dz$$

where $\beta\left(t, x(t)\right)$ is the local volatility of the driving factor $x(t)$. Since $S_\lambda(t) = S\left(x(t), t, \lambda\right)$, using the normal process for both $x(t)$ and $S_\lambda(t)$, we can link the local volatility of $x(t)$ with that of $S_\lambda(t)$ via:

$$\sigma(S, t) = \frac{\partial S\left(x(t), t, \lambda\right)}{\partial x(t)} \beta\left(t, x(t)\right)$$

where $\sigma(S, t)$ is the stripped normal local volatility of $S_\lambda(t)$. Therefore:

$$\beta\left(t, x(t)\right) = \left(\frac{\partial S\left(x(t), t, \lambda\right)}{\partial x(t)} \right)^{-1} \sigma(S, t)$$

and

$$dx(t) = \left[-\kappa x(t) + y(t) \right] dt + \left(\frac{\partial S\left(x(t), t, \lambda\right)}{\partial x(t)} \right)^{-1} \sigma(S, t) dz$$

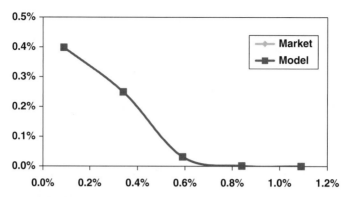

FIGURE 12.27 Swaption Price Calibration (1M×1Y)

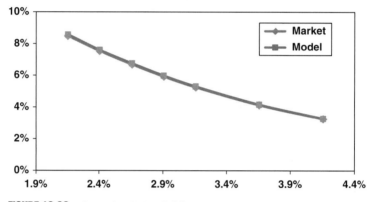

FIGURE 12.28 Swaption Price Calibration (10Y×10Y)

By feeding the Dupire-type local volatilities into the Cheyette model as such, the local volatilities of the driving factor can be calibrated efficiently to the market-implied volatility smile.

In the following, we examine a real market swaption price calibration with the normal model in which both $x(t)$ and $S_\lambda(t)$ follow the normal process. The model prices are obtained by feeding the stripped local volatilities into the Cheyette model and then reprice the European swaption via Cheyette 1D-PDE. During the local volatility stripping, the drift $Q(t)$ is calculated numerically by matching the market forward swap rates using today's yield curve, effectively setting $q(t) = 0$.

Figures 12.27 to 12.30 show two calibration examples at two different option maturities and tenors (labelled as Maturity × Tenor). In both figures, the market and model European swaption prices are plotted against the absolute strikes.

As shown above, the calibration and fitting is numerically stable. While the model prices match the market prices well at the short end, the calibration errors for long-dated swaptions are not negligible. The pricing errors for the $10Y \times 10Y$ European swaption examples are in the order of 10bps.

Note that if $S_\lambda(t)$ follows the log-normal process, the relationship between its local volatility $(\sigma_{LN}(S,t))$ and Cheyette normal local volatility is an approximation:

$$\beta\big(t,x(t)\big) \approx \left(\frac{\partial S\big(x(t),t,\lambda\big)}{\partial x(t)}\right)^{-1} S\big(x(t),t,\lambda\big)\sigma_{LN}\big(S,t\big)$$

In general, it is better to use the normal process for both $x(t)$ and $S_\lambda(t)$. The calibration to the market prices and subsequent local volatility stripping will be more accurate and consistent. During the calibration, if the Black implied volatilities are the market inputs, one should simply convert them into prices and then calibrate the (normal) model to the prices directly.

Libor Local Volatility Model

Stripping swap local volatility from swaption (explained in the last section) was a new idea and it introduced the concept of **rolling swap**. Based on the rolling swap concept a local volatility stripping formula was derived with some approximations, including in the drift $Q(t)$ and correction factor $q(t)$. The stripped local volatilities have to be fed into the Cheyette model for pricing.

In this section, we explore a brand new model on the rolling Libor. By working on the rolling Libor, we can derive a more rigorous spot process that permits the differentiation against option maturity, hence allows Dupire-type forward PDE for local volatility stripping. We can also build a backward pricing PDE to price exotics directly with local volatilities. The outcome is a self-consistent interest rate smile model that can:

- calibrate to the market volatility smile directly via local volatility stripping;
- price suitable path-dependent exotic interest rate derivatives with its own backward pricing PDE.

Dynamics of Fixed-tenor Rolling Libor   The fixed-tenor rolling Libor is defined as a fixed tenor (τ) Libor with its starting point t rolling, as schematically shown in Figure 12.29 ($0 \rightarrow t_1 \rightarrow t_2$):

One can directly assume a spot process for the rolling Libor. Let us start with the log-normal case. Denoting the time t rolling Libor as $L_{t(t+\tau)}(t)$ and zero bond as $Z(t,t+\tau)$, where τ is the fixed Libor tenor, the rolling Libor is assumed to follow the log-normal process:

$$\frac{dL_{t(t+\tau)}(t)}{L_{t(t+\tau)}(t)} = \mu_{t(t+\tau)}(t)dt + \sigma_{t(t+\tau)}(t)dW_{t(t+\tau)}(t) \qquad Eq.\,(12.2)$$

where $\mu_{t(t+\tau)}(t)$ is the drift, $\sigma_{t(t+\tau)}(t)$ is volatility, $W_{t(t+\tau)}(t)$ is the Brownian motion under the **spot measure** associated with the **local numeraire** $Z(t,t+\tau)$.

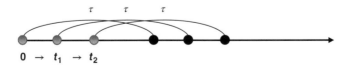

FIGURE 12.29   Schematic diagram of fixed-tenor rolling Libor

To define the local numeraire and search for the drift $\mu_{t(t+\tau)}(t)$ and diffusion $\sigma_{t(t+\tau)}(t)$ terms in the spot process (Equation 12.2), we can resort to the measure change technique. Denoting E^a as the expectation under the measure related to numeraire a, and E^b the expectation related to numeraire b, for a random variable X_t the Radon-Nikodym theorem states:

$$E^a[X_T] = E^b\left[\frac{a_T}{a_t}\frac{b_t}{b_T}X_T\right] \qquad t < T$$

This measure change technique will allow us to obtain the expectation under different measure with standard numeraire. For the spot process of the rolling Libor, however, instead of using a standard numeraire, we define a **local** numeraire $Z(t, t+\tau)$ such that a deterministic function of Libor $[f(L_{t,t+\tau}(t))]$ satisfies:

$$E^a\left\{f\left(L_{T,T+\tau}(T)\right) \mid t\right\} = E^{spot}\left\{\frac{a_T}{a_t}\frac{Z(t, t+\tau)}{Z(T, T+\tau)}f\left(L_{T,T+\tau}(T)\right) \mid t\right\}$$

where $E^a\{\cdot\}$ is an expectation under the measure associated with a standard numeraire (e.g. zero bond price or money market account). The use of **local** numeraire in $E^{spot}\{\cdot\}$ is permissible provided the drift $\mu_{t(t+\tau)}(t)$ and diffusion $\sigma_{t(t+\tau)}(t)$ are calibrated, for example to the market forward and option prices. Note that the **local** numeraire $Z(t, t+\tau)$ is only applicable to $f(L_{t,t+\tau}(t))$. In the rest of this section, we use the **local** numeraire for $f(L_{t,t+\tau}(t))$ in the measure change technique to obtain the expectation under the spot measure.

The rolling Libor $L_{t,t+\tau}(t)$ is not a martingale under the spot measure. In contrast, under the **forward measure** associated with the forward bond numeraire $Z(t, T+\tau)$, where $T > t$, the forward Libor is a martingale. Hence we have:

$$E^{fwd}\left\{L_{T(T+\tau)}(T) \mid t\right\} = L_{T(T+\tau)}(t)$$

By changing to the spot measure, we obtain:

$$E^{fwd}\left\{L_{T(T+\tau)}(T) \mid t\right\} = E^{spot}\left\{\frac{Z(T, T+\tau)}{Z(t, T+\tau)}\frac{Z(t, t+\tau)}{Z(T, T+\tau)}L_{T(T+\tau)}(T) \mid t\right\}$$

$$= \frac{Z(t, t+\tau)}{Z(t, T+\tau)}E^{spot}\left\{L_{T(T+\tau)}(T) \mid t\right\}$$

Therefore:

$$E^{spot}\left\{L_{T(T+\tau)}(T) \mid t\right\} = \frac{Z(t, T+\tau)}{Z(t, t+\tau)}L_{T(T+\tau)}(t)$$

By definition of Equation 12.2:

$$E^{spot}\left\{L_{T(T+\tau)}(T) \mid t\right\} = L_{t(t+\tau)}(t)e^{\int_t^T \mu_{s(s+\tau)}(s)ds}$$

therefore we obtain the formula for the drift:

$$\int_t^T \mu_{s(s+\tau)}(s)\,ds = \ln\left[\frac{Z(t,T+\tau)}{Z(t,t+\tau)}\frac{L_{T(T+\tau)}(t)}{L_{t(t+\tau)}(t)}\right] \qquad Eq.(12.3)$$

All quantities the drift formula can be calculated from today's yield curve. Hence the drift $\mu_{t(t+\tau)}(t)$ of the spot process of the rolling Libor can be accurately calculated or bootstrapped.

Local Volatility Stripping Formula Under the Spot Process   Akin to Equation 12.2, the spot process of the rolling Libor with local volatility $\sigma_{t(t+\tau)}(t,L)$ is given by:

$$\frac{dL_{t(t+\tau)}(t)}{L_{t(t+\tau)}(t)} = \mu_{t(t+\tau)}(t)\,dt + \sigma_{t(t+\tau)}(t,L)\,dW_{t(t+\tau)}(t)$$

Denoting $C = E^{spot}\left\{\left[L_{T(T+\tau)}(T) - K\right]^+\Big|t\right\}$ and applying Fokker–Planck equation to the probability density function, a Dupire-type local volatility forward PDE for **this spot process** can be derived:

$$\frac{K^2\sigma^2(T,K)}{2}\frac{\partial^2 C}{\partial K^2} = \frac{\partial C}{\partial T} + \mu(T)\left[K\frac{\partial C}{\partial K} - C\right]$$

For simplicity, the subscripts are omitted $[\mu(t) = \mu_{t(t+\tau)}(t)$ and $\sigma(L,t) = \sigma_{t(t+\tau)}(L,t)]$. The local volatility stripping formula is therefore:

$$\sigma(T,K) = \frac{1}{K}\sqrt{2\frac{\dfrac{\partial C}{\partial t} + \mu(T)\left[K\dfrac{\partial C}{\partial K} - C\right]}{\dfrac{\partial^2 C}{\partial K^2}}}$$

The (log-normal) local volatility can be stripped directly from the implied volatility of the spot process. With the Black call formula, denoting the Black implied volatility of spot rolling Libor as $\sigma_I = \sigma_I(T,K)$, the local volatility stripping formula is given by:

$$\sigma(T,K) = \sqrt{\frac{2\dfrac{\partial \sigma_I}{\partial T} + \dfrac{\sigma_I}{T} + 2K\mu(T)\dfrac{\partial \sigma_I}{\partial K}}{\dfrac{1}{\sigma_I T}\left(1 + \dfrac{Ky}{\sigma_I}\dfrac{\partial \sigma_I}{\partial K}\right)^2 + K^2\dfrac{\partial^2 \sigma_I}{\partial K^2} - \dfrac{K^2\sigma_I T}{4}\left(\dfrac{\partial \sigma_I}{\partial K}\right)^2 + K\dfrac{\partial \sigma_I}{\partial K}}} \qquad Eq.(12.4)$$

where $y = \ln(F(T)/K)$ and $F(T) = L_{0(0+\tau)}(0)e^{\int_0^T \mu_{s(s+\tau)}(s)\,ds}$ is the forward of the rolling Libor.

Note that the whole local volatility formulation is based on the spot process of the rolling Libor. The implied volatility (σ_I) of the rolling Libor is not the same as the market implied volatility, because the markets have been using the forward process to price vanilla options. To obtain the implied volatility of the rolling Libor from the market vanilla price or market implied volatility, we need to derive the vanilla pricing formulae using the spot rolling Libor process.

Vanilla Pricing Formulae Under the Spot Process   Vanilla options include cap/floor and European swaption. Cap or floor is the sum of caplets or floorlets respectively.

Caplet/Floorlet Pricing Formula   For a caplet with strike K starting at T and maturing at $T + \tau$, under the forward measure, the market caplet price is given by:

$$C(t;T,T+\tau,K) = \tau Z(t,T+\tau) E^{fwd}\left\{\left[L_{T(T+\tau)}(T) - K\right]^+ \Big| t\right\}$$

Using the measure change technique:

$$E^{fwd}\left\{\left[L_{T(T+\tau)}(T) - K\right]^+ \Big| t\right\} = E^{spot}\left\{\frac{Z(T,T+\tau)}{Z(t,T+\tau)} \frac{Z(t,t+\tau)}{Z(T,T+\tau)}\left[L_{T(T+\tau)}(T) - K\right]^+ \Big| t\right\}$$

$$= \frac{Z(t,t+\tau)}{Z(t,T+\tau)} E^{spot}\left\{\left[L_{T(T+\tau)}(T) - K\right]^+ \Big| t\right\}$$

Therefore:

$$C(t;T,T+\tau,K) = \tau Z(t,t+\tau) E^{spot}\left\{\left[L_{T(T+\tau)}(T) - K\right]^+ \Big| t\right\}$$

If rolling Libor $L_{t(t+\tau)}(t)$ follows the log-normal process Equation 12.2, a Black–Scholes pricing formula can be obtained:

$$C(t;T,T+\tau,K) = \tau Z(t,t+\tau)\left[F(T)N(d_1) - KN(d_2)\right] \qquad Eq.(12.5)$$

where $N(\cdot)$ is the Gaussian cumulative distribution function and

$$F(T) = L_{t(t+\tau)}(t) e^{\int_t^T \mu_{s(s+\tau)}(s)ds}$$

$$d_1 = \frac{\ln\left[F(T)/K\right]}{\sigma_I(T,K)\sqrt{T-t}} + \frac{1}{2}\sigma_I(T,K)\sqrt{T-t}$$

$$d_2 = d_1 - \sigma_I(T,K)\sqrt{T-t}$$

     The drift $\mu_{s(s+\tau)}(s)$ is given by Equation 12.3. $\sigma_I(T,K)$ is the implied volatility of $L_{t(t+\tau)}(t)$ specific to the caplet under the spot process. In other words, $\sigma_I(T,K)$ is the implied volatility of $L_{t(t+\tau)}(t)$ that should reprice the market caplet using Equation 12.5.
     The pricing formula for the floorlet is given by:

$$P(t;T,T+\tau,K) = \tau Z(t,t+\tau)\left[KN(-d_2) - F(T)N(-d_1)\right]$$

European Swaption Pricing Formula   Let us consider a European payer swaption with strike K and expiry T, on a underlying swap starting at T_0 and ending at T_n $(T \le T_0)$. For simplicity without losing generality, we assume the swap floating and fixed leg have the same frequency and payment schedule on $T_0, T_1, \ldots, T_n$. The underlying swap value at time T is given by:

$$U(T; T_0, T_n, K) = \sum_{i=1}^{n} \tau Z(T, T_{i-1} + \tau) \left[E^{fwd} \left\{ L_{T_{i-1}(T_{i-1} + \tau)}(T_{i-1}) \middle| T \right\} - K \right]$$

$$= \sum_{i=1}^{n} \tau Z(T, T + \tau) \left[E^{spot} \left\{ L_{T_{i-1}(T_{i-1} + \tau)}(T_{i-1}) \middle| T \right\} - K \frac{Z(T, T_{i-1} + \tau)}{Z(T, T + \tau)} \right]$$

$$= \sum_{i=1}^{n} \tau Z(T, T + \tau) \left[L_{T(T + \tau)}(T) e^{\int_{T}^{T_{i-1}} \mu_{s(s+\tau)}(s) ds} - K \frac{Z(T, T_{i-1} + \tau)}{Z(T, T + \tau)} \right]$$

$$= \tau Z(T, T + \tau) \left[L_{T(T + \tau)}(T) \sum_{i=1}^{n} e^{\int_{T}^{T_{i-1}} \mu_{s(s+\tau)}(s) ds} - K \sum_{i=1}^{n} \frac{Z(T, T_{i-1} + \tau)}{Z(T, T + \tau)} \right] \qquad Eq.(12.6)$$

In deriving Equation 12.6, we have used measure change technique to convert $E^{fwd}\{\cdot\}$ to $E^{spot}\{\cdot\}$.

Denoting:

$$\tilde{\mu} = \sum_{i=1}^{n} e^{\int_{T}^{T_{i-1}} \mu_{s(s+\tau)}(s) ds} \qquad \text{and} \qquad \tilde{K} = \frac{K \sum_{i=1}^{n} \frac{Z(T, T_{i-1} + \tau)}{Z(T, T + \tau)}}{\tilde{\mu}}$$

and in $\tilde{K}$ using the freezing technique to calculate the forward bond prices from today's yield curve, i.e. $Z(T, T + \tau) \approx Z(0; T, T + \tau)$ and $Z(T, T_{i-1} + \tau) \approx Z(0; T, T_{i-1} + \tau)$, Equation 12.6 becomes:

$$U(T; T_0, T_n, K) = \tau Z(T, T + \tau) \tilde{\mu} \left[L_{T(T + \tau)}(T) - \tilde{K} \right]$$

and the European payer swaption payoff at time T is therefore:

$$U(T; T_0, T_n, K)^+ = \tau Z(T, T + \tau) \tilde{\mu} [L_{T(T + \tau)}(T) - \tilde{K}]^+$$

Denoting $E^A(\cdot)$ as the expectation under the **annuity measure** associated with the annuity numeraire $A(t; T_0, T_n)$, using the measure change technique, the swaption price $V(t; T_0, T_n, K)$ at time t $(t < T)$ is:

$$V(t; T_0, T_n, K) = A(t; T_0, T_n) E^A \left\{ \frac{U(T; T_0, T_n, K)^+}{A(T; T_0, T_n)} \middle| t \right\}$$

$$= A(t; T_0, T_n) E^{spot} \left\{ \frac{A(T; T_0, T_n)}{A(t; T_0, T_n)} \frac{Z(t, t + \tau)}{Z(T, T + \tau)} \frac{U(T; T_0, T_n, K)^+}{A(T; T_0, T_n)} \middle| t \right\}$$

$$= \tau Z(t, t + \tau) \tilde{\mu} E^{spot} \left\{ [L_{T(T + \tau)}(T) - \tilde{K}]^+ \middle| t \right\}$$

Hence, with the log-normal spot process of $L_{T(T+\tau)}(t)$ defined by Equation 12.2, the swaption price formula is of the Black–Scholes form:

$$V(t;T_0,T_n,K) = \tau Z(t,t+\tau)\tilde{\mu}\left[F(T)N(d_1) - \tilde{K}N(d_2)\right] \qquad Eq.(12.7)$$

where

$$F(T) = L_{t(t+\tau)}(t)e^{\int_t^T \mu_{s(s+\tau)}(s)ds}$$

$$d_1 = \frac{\ln\left[F(T)/\tilde{K}\right]}{\sigma_I(T,K)\sqrt{T-t}} + \frac{1}{2}\sigma_I(T,K)\sqrt{T-t}$$

$$d_2 = d_1 - \sigma_I(T,K)\sqrt{T-t}$$

The drift $\mu_{s(s+\tau)}(s)$ is given by Equation 12.3. $\sigma_I(T,K)$ is the implied volatility of $L_{t(t+\tau)}(t)$ specific to the swaption expiry T and tenor $T_n - T_0$. It is the implied volatility of $L_{t(t+\tau)}(t)$ that should reprice the market European swaption using Equation 12.7.

Backward Pricing PDE Under the Spot Process   To complete the model, we derive an appropriate backward partial differential equation (PDE) for pricing contingent claims. In interest rates, if one tries to formulate a PDE on a contingent claim directly, one faces the complication of handling stochastic discount and annuity on PDE nodes. To bypass this problem, we instead derive a backward pricing PDE for the **deflated** value of the contingent claim. For a contingent claim $V\left[L_{T(T+\tau)}(T)\right]$, its zero bond numeraire **deflated** value is defined as:

$$\hat{V}\left[L_{T,T+\tau}(T)\right] = \frac{V\left[L_{T(T+\tau)}(T)\right]}{Z(T,T+\tau)}$$

As an example, for a contingent claim payoff $V\left[L_{T(T+\tau)}(T)\right] = Z(T,T+\tau)$ $\cdot\left[L_{T(T+\tau)}(T) - K\right]^+$, its zero bond numeraire **deflated** value is $\hat{V}\left[L_{T(T+\tau)}(T)\right]$ $= \left[L_{T(T+\tau)}(T) - K\right]^+$.

Denoting the expectation of deflated value under the spot measure as:

$$\hat{P} = \hat{P}\left(L_{t(t+\tau)}(t),t\right) = E^{spot}\left\{\hat{V}\left[L_{T(T+\tau)}(T)\right]\middle| t\right\}$$

when $L_{t(t+\tau)}(t)$ follows the log-normal local volatility process, applying Feynman-Kac theorem one arrives at the following Kolmogorov backward PDE:

$$\frac{\partial \hat{P}}{\partial t} + \mu(t)L\frac{\partial \hat{P}}{\partial L} + \frac{1}{2}\sigma^2(t,L)L^2\frac{\partial^2 \hat{P}}{\partial L^2} = 0 \qquad Eq.(12.8)$$

This backward pricing PDE provides an efficient way to price exotic interest rate derivatives in the presence of volatility smile. European swaptions can also be priced using the terminal payoffs given by Equation 12.6. The volatility smile is incorporated by the local volatility $\sigma(t,L)$ which can be stripped using Equation 12.4. This completes the model in the log-normal case.

Model Formulation in the Normal Case   To better handle low and negative interest rates, the rolling Libor dynamics can also be assumed to follow the normal process. The modelling logics are identical to the log-normal case. In the following, all relevant model formulae in the normal case are summarized:

- The normal process of the rolling Libor:

$$dL_{t(t+\tau)}(t) = \mu_{t(t+\tau)}(t)dt + \sigma_{t(t+\tau)}(t)dW_{t(t+\tau)}(t)$$

- The drift formula:

$$\int_t^T \mu_{s(s+\tau)}(s)ds = \frac{Z(t,T+\tau)}{Z(t,t+\tau)} L_{T(T+\tau)}(t) - L_{t(t+\tau)}(t)$$

- The local volatility stripping formulae:

$$\sigma(T,K) = \sqrt{2 \frac{\dfrac{\partial \hat{V}}{\partial T} + \mu(T)\dfrac{\partial \hat{V}}{\partial K}}{\dfrac{\partial^2 \hat{V}}{\partial K^2}}}$$

where $\hat{V} = E^{spot}\left\{ \left[L_{T,T+\tau}(T) - K \right]^+ \middle| t \right\}$.

$$\sigma(T,K) = \sqrt{\frac{2\dfrac{\partial \sigma_I}{\partial T} + \dfrac{\sigma_I}{T} + 2\mu(T)\dfrac{\partial \sigma_I}{\partial K}}{\dfrac{1}{\sigma_I T}\left(1 + \dfrac{(F(T)-K)}{\sigma_I}\dfrac{\partial \sigma_I}{\partial K}\right)^2 + \dfrac{\partial^2 \sigma_I}{\partial K^2}}} \qquad Eq.(12.9)$$

where $\sigma_I = \sigma_I(T,K)$ is the implied (normal) volatility of the rolling Libor.
- The caplet/floorlet pricing formula:

$$C(t;T,T+\tau,K) = \tau Z(t,t+\tau)\left[(F(T)-K)N(d) + \sigma_I(T,K)\sqrt{T-t}\,\phi(d)\right] \qquad Eq.(12.10)$$

where:

$$d = \frac{F(T)-K}{\sigma_I(T,K)\sqrt{T-t}} \qquad F(T) = L_{t(t+\tau)}(t) + \int_t^T \mu_{s(s+\tau)}(s)ds$$

$N(\cdot)$ is the Gaussian cumulative distribution function, $\phi(\cdot)$ is the Gaussian probability density function $\phi(x) = \dfrac{1}{\sqrt{2\pi}} exp(-x^2/2)$. $\sigma_I(T,K)$ is the implied (normal) volatility of $L_{t(t+\tau)}(t)$ specific to the caplet under the spot process.

- European swaption pricing formula:
  With the normal spot process of $L_{T(T+\tau)}(t)$, the European payer swaption price formula is of the Bachelier form:

$$V(t; T_0, T_n, K) = n\tau Z(t, t+\tau) \left[\left(F(T) - \tilde{K} \right) N(d) + \sigma_I(T, K) \sqrt{T-t} \; \phi(d) \right] \quad Eq.(12.11)$$

where

$$F(T) = L_{t(t+\tau)}(t) + \int_t^T \mu_{s(s+\tau)}(s) \, ds$$

$$\tilde{K} = \frac{K}{n} \sum_{i=1}^n \frac{Z(T, T_{i-1} + \tau)}{Z(T, T+\tau)} - \frac{1}{n} \sum_{i=1}^n \int_T^{T_{i-1}} \mu_{s(s+\tau)}(s) \, ds$$

$$d = \frac{F(T) - \tilde{K}}{\sigma_I(T, K) \sqrt{T-t}}$$

$\sigma_I(T, K)$ is the implied (normal) volatility of $L_{t(t+\tau)}(t)$ specific to the swaption expiry T and tenor $T_n - T_0$. In calculating $\tilde{K}$ we can use the freezing technique to obtain the forward bond prices from today's yield curve.

- Backward pricing PDE:
  For a contingent claim $V\left[L_{T,T+\tau}(T) \right]$, its zero bond numeraire deflated value is:

$$\hat{V}\left[L_{T,T+\tau}(T) \right] = \frac{V\left[L_{T,T+\tau}(T) \right]}{Z(T, T+\tau)}$$

Denoting the expectation of deflated value under the spot measure as:

$$\hat{P} = \hat{P}\left(L_{t,t+\tau}(t), t \right) = E^{spot} \left\{ \hat{V}\left[L_{T,T+\tau}(T) \right] \middle| t \right\}$$

$\hat{P}$ satisfies the following backward PDE:

$$\frac{\partial \hat{P}}{\partial t} + \mu(t) \frac{\partial \hat{P}}{\partial L} + \frac{1}{2} \sigma^2(t, L) \frac{\partial^2 \hat{P}}{\partial L^2} = 0 \qquad Eq.(12.12)$$

where $\sigma(t, L)$ is the (normal) local volatility of the rolling Libor.

From local volatility stripping (smile calibration) to backward PDE pricing, the formulations constitute the Libor Local Volatility model. We can now examine how the model can be used in practice.

Local Volatility Stripping and Smile Calibration Examples   First, we show examples of local volatility stripping from caplet and swaption in the normal case. The implied volatility of the rolling Libor can be obtained via the vanilla pricing formulae:

- For caplet: Using the market-quoted cap/floor prices, the caplet/floorlet prices can be obtained in the usual way. Equation 12.10 can then be used directly to calculate the implied volatility $\sigma_I(T,K)$ of the rolling Libor.
- For European swaption: Using the market-quoted European swaption prices, for a given swaption with known expiry, tenor, strike, Equation 12.11 can be used to calculate implied volatility $\sigma_I(T,K)$.
- If the market quotes are market implied volatilities (e.g. Black), they shall be converted into prices first. The implied volatility $\sigma_I(T,K)$ of the rolling Libor can then be backed out via Equation 12.10 or Equation 12.11.

Plugging the drift $\mu(T)$ and implied volatility $\sigma_I(T,K)$ into Equation 12.9, the local volatility of the rolling Libor can be stripped. The local volatility stripping is sensitive to the volatility interpolation and extrapolation scheme, so caution should apply to avoid numerical noises. To interpolate the implied volatilities between market quotes, a linear variance $\left[\sigma_I^2(T,K)\cdot T\right]$ scheme can be used. The examples below are for the 6-month rolling Libor.

Figure 12.30 shows an example of stripped local volatility from the caplet implied volatility at a time slice. Both local and implied volatility are normal. The implied volatility is for the $T = 3.5Y$ caplet, and the local volatility is at 3.5Y point.

Figure 12.31 shows an example of stripped local volatility from the swaption implied volatility at a time slice. Both local and implied volatility are normal. The implied volatility is for the $1Y \times 19Y$ swaption, and the local volatility is at the 1Y point.

Secondly, for the smile calibration, when the stripped local volatilities are plugged into the backward pricing PDE Equation 12.12, they should automatically reprice the market-quoted vanilla options, albeit with numerical errors.

To illustrate the market smile calibration for the co-terminal swaptions, Figures 12.32 and 12.33 compare the market prices with the model prices for different

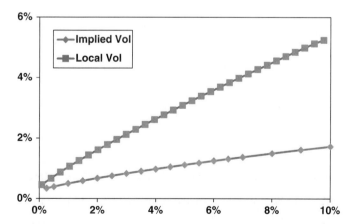

FIGURE 12.30 Local and implied volatility of the rolling Libor (caplet)
The horizontal axis is absolute strike (for implied vol) and spot (for local vol).

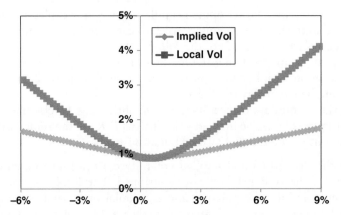

FIGURE 12.31 Local and implied volatility of the rolling Libor (swaption)
The horizontal axis is absolute strike (for implied vol) and spot (for local vol).

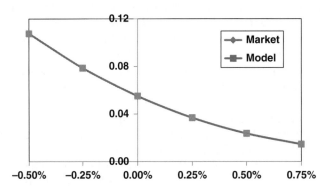

FIGURE 12.32 Market vs model swaption prices $(1Y \times 19Y)$

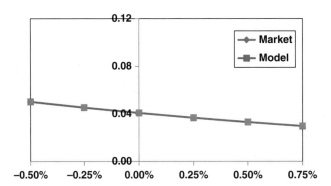

FIGURE 12.33 Market vs model swaption prices $(15Y \times 5Y)$
Strike is relative to ATM.

swaption expires/tenors. In both figures, the fixed co-terminal is 20 years. The model prices are obtained by plugging the relevant stripped local volatilities into the backward pricing PDE Equation 12.12 to reprice the European swaptions.

As can be seen in the figures, the model prices match the market prices very well and the numerical errors are small. The numerical errors (difference between market and model price) are in the order of 0.5bp for swaption $(1Y \times 19Y)$ and 0.04bp for swaption $(15Y \times 5Y)$. The market smile calibration via local volatility stripping is numerically accurate, stable and efficient.

Derivatives Pricing With Smile The stripped local volatilities can be plugged into the backward pricing PDE (Equation 12.8 for log-normal or Equation 12.12 for normal) to price a wide range of interest rate derivatives in the presence of volatility smile. Such a local volatility model is extremely efficient for pricing suited callable products, such as Bermudan swaption. One should remember, though, that the local volatility model is not suitable for pricing cliquet products such as "vol bond".

Bermudan Swaption A standard Bermudan swaption gives the holder an option to enter into a fixed-floating swap on any of the fixing dates. For a given Bermudan swaption tenor structure $\{T_0, T_1, \cdots, T_n\}$, the possible exercise dates are $\{T_1, T_2, \cdots, T_{n-1}\}$. On an exercise date T_i $(i = 1, 2, \cdots, n-1)$, the Bermudan value is the maximum of exercise value $V_e(T_i)$ and the holding value $V_h(T_i)$:

$$V(T_i) = max\left[V_e(T_i), V_h(T_i)\right]$$

- The exercise value is the intrinsic value. In the log-normal case, it is given by Equation 12.6 with the appropriate periods:

$$V_e(T_i) = \tau Z(T_i, T_i + \tau)\left[L_{T_i(T_i+\tau)}(T_i)\sum_{j=i}^{n-1} e^{\int_{T_i}^{T_j}\mu_{s(s+\tau)}(s)ds} - K\sum_{j=i}^{n-1}\frac{Z(T_i, T_j + \tau)}{Z(T_i, T_i + \tau)}\right]$$

In the normal case, it is given by:

$$V_e(T_i) = \tau Z(T_i, T_i + \tau)(n - i)\left[L_{T_i(T_i+\tau)}(T_i) + \frac{1}{n-i}\sum_{j=i}^{n-1}\int_{T_i}^{T_j}\mu_{s(s+\tau)}(s)ds - \frac{K}{n-i}\sum_{j=i}^{n-1}\frac{Z(T_i, T_j + \tau)}{Z(T_i, T_i + \tau)}\right]$$

- The holding value reflects the Bermudan value associated with the remaining exercise dates $\{T_{i+1}, T_{i+2}, \cdots, T_{n-1}\}$. It has an iterative relationship with the Bermudan values at different exercise dates. On the final exercise date T_{n-1}, the Bermudan value $V(T_{n-1}) = max\left[V_e(T_{n-1}), 0\right]$. At other exercise dates $\{T_1, T_2, \cdots, T_{n-2}\}$, the holding value follows a recursive relationship:

$$V_h(T_i) = E\left\{e^{-\int_{T_i}^{T_{i+1}} r(s)ds} V(T_{i+1})\middle| T_i\right\}$$

$$= E\left\{e^{-\int_{T_i}^{T_{i+1}} r(s)ds} max\left[V_e(T_{i+1}), V_h(T_{i+1})\right]\middle| T_i\right\} \qquad Eq.(12.13)$$

where $r(s)$ is the instantaneous interest rate.

- The Bermudan value at time T_0 is:

$$V(T_0) = E\left\{ e^{-\int_{T_0}^{T_1} r(s)ds} V(T_1)\bigg| T_0 \right\} \qquad\qquad Eq.(12.14)$$

Bermudan Pricing PDE Under the Spot Measure The expectations in Equation 12.13 and Equation 12.14 are under the bank account measure associated with the numeraire $B(t) = e^{\int_0^t r(s)ds}$. We need to convert them into the (spot rolling Libor) measure such that the backward pricing PDE (Equation 12.8 or Equation 12.12) can be utilized.

Denoting the numeraire deflated values $\hat{V}_e(T_{i+1})$ and $\hat{V}_b(T_{i+1})$ as:

$$\hat{V}_e(T_{i+1}) = \frac{V_e(T_{i+1})}{Z(T_{i+1}, T_{i+1} + \tau)} \qquad\qquad \hat{V}_b(T_{i+1}) = \frac{V_b(T_{i+1})}{Z(T_{i+1}, T_{i+1} + \tau)}$$

where $Z(T_{i+1}, T_{i+1} + \tau)$ is the zero bond. Using zero bond as numeraire and applying the measure change technique, Equation 12.13 can be rewritten as:

$$V_b(T_i) = E^{spot}\left\{ \frac{B(T_{i+1})}{B(T_i)} \frac{Z(T_i, T_i + \tau)}{Z(T_{i+1}, T_{i+1} + \tau)} e^{-\int_{T_i}^{T_{i+1}} r(s)ds} max\left[V_e(T_{i+1}), V_b(T_{i+1})\right]\bigg| T_i \right\}$$

$$= E^{spot}\left\{ Z(T_i, T_i + \tau) max\left[\frac{V_e(T_{i+1})}{Z(T_{i+1}, T_{i+1} + \tau)}, \frac{V_b(T_{i+1})}{Z(T_{i+1}, T_{i+1} + \tau)} \right]\bigg| T_i \right\}$$

$$= Z(T_i, T_i + \tau) E^{spot}\{max[\hat{V}_e(T_{i+1}), \hat{V}_b(T_{i+1})]| T_i \}$$

Hence:

$$\hat{V}_b(T_i) = \frac{V_b(T_i)}{Z(T_i, T_i + \tau)} = E^{spot}\left\{ max\left[\hat{V}_e(T_{i+1}), \hat{V}_b(T_{i+1}) \right]\bigg| T_i \right\}$$

The zero bond numeraire deflated quantity $\hat{V}_b(T_i)$ is a contingent claim that satisfies the backward pricing PDE (Equation 12.8 for log-normal or Equation 12.12 for normal). Therefore by working in the $\hat{V}(T_i)$ space instead of $V(T_i)$, we can use the backward pricing PDE to roll back $\hat{V}(T_i)$. At time T_0, the Bermudan swaption value is simply given by:

$$V_b(T_0) = Z(T_0, T_0 + \tau) E^{spot}\left\{ max\left[\hat{V}_e(T_1), \hat{V}_b(T_1) \right]\bigg| T_0 \right\}$$

For co-terminal calibration, the rolling Libor local volatilities between T_i and T_{i+1} in the PDE are related to the swaptions with expiry of T_{i+1} and tenor of $(T_n - T_{i+1})$.

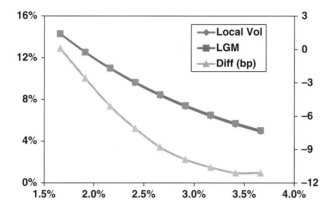

FIGURE 12.34 20Y Bermudan swaption prices using the Libor local volatility and LGM model
The horizontal axis is absolute strike. The left vertical axis labels the price, and right vertical axis labels the price difference in basis point.

Bermudan Pricing Example We use the normal case formulae to show the Bermudan pricing example. Because $\hat{V}_b(T_i)$ satisfies the backward pricing PDE Equation 12.12, the stripped (normal) local volatilities can be plugged into this PDE and one can roll back $\hat{V}(T_i)$ until T_0.

Figure 12.34 plots the 20-year Bermudan swaption prices at different strikes, all with annual exercise dates. The Bermudan prices calculated using the Libor local volatility model are compared with those using the Linear Gauss–Markov (LGM) model. The price differences (Local Vol – LGM) are also shown in the figure.

The Bermudan prices using the two models are comparable, although the smile calibrations are totally different. For Bermudan at different strikes, since the LGM model does not include smile, it has to calibrate to individual strikes separately, effectively using different internal model parameters for different strikes. The Libor local volatility model, however, calibrates to the entire smile in one-sweep and uses the same internal parameters (i.e. local volatilities) to price all strikes.

Further Model Development

Libor local volatility model is a self-contained interest rate local volatility model that is capable of capturing interest rate volatility smile. The model is based on the spot process of the rolling Libor and is arbitrage-free. The model can calibrate to either cap/floor or swaption market. It can easily accommodate OIS discounting. For example, the Libor process can be based on the projection (Libor) curve, and the discount (zero bond numeraire) can be based on the OIS curve.

This interest rate smile model is much simpler and flexible. It possesses the good features of Dupire local volatility model, including numerical simplicity and efficiency. The smile calibration is via local volatility stripping, accommodating non-parametric local volatility too. The stripped local volatilities can be plugged into backward pricing PDE to price a range of interest rate exotics, such as Bermudan swaption. The Libor local volatility model can generate consistent Greeks including smile/skew risk sensitivities.

Because of its efficiency in the smile calibration, the model can be used to price hybrids such as CVA, where the smile effects on a portfolio of instruments with different maturities and strikes are notoriously difficult to capture. By combining Libor local volatility dynamics with other factors (e.g. FX), the hybrid (e.g. CVA) model can price in interest rate smile efficiently.

The Libor local volatility model can potentially make interest rate smile modelling as efficient as equivalent smile modelling in equity or FX. Due to its simplicity and numerical efficiency, it is conceivable that the Libor local volatility model can play a very important role in interest rate smile modelling. The model can be extended to multi-factor:

- to accommodate more demanding yield curve dynamics as well as volatility smile;
- to allow simultaneous smile calibrate to both cap/floor and swaption markets.

The interest rate local volatility models are fundamentally different from the other types of interest rate smile models. This will open the door for researches and developments of a new category of simpler and more realistic interest rate smile models. Such local volatility models can potentially be extended to model options on other underlyings, for example CMS options or CDS index swaptions.

CHAPTER 13

CMS Replication and CMS Spread Options

Replication (pricing) is an interesting model paradigm that was originally associated with static hedge practices. In the presence of pronounced volatility smile/skew, replication, which is used to capture smile/skew information, is a very valuable tool. It is widely used in the interest rate derivatives pricing, in particular for (Constant Maturity Swap) CMS products. This chapter will focus on this subject to examine some of the practical issues, as well as practical solutions.

This chapter will also examine replication consistent copula pricing of CMS spread option products widely used in yield curve shape products. In the context of CMS spread options, CMS rates, though derived from the same yield curve and the same swaption volatilities, can be viewed as correlated individual components in a basket. The marginal distributions of CMS rates are important in volatility smile/skew calibration and analysing joint statistical characteristics. We shall demonstrate that a good model (a replication consistent market model) exhibits self-consistency to the vanilla markets, in terms of underlyings calibrations as well as their marginal distributions (volatility smile/skew). It will have a simple and transparent specification of co-dependence between rates, and simple and stable numerical implementation scheme.

CMS CONVEXITY

In a standard interest rate swap (IRS), one leg pays fix and the other pays floating (e.g. OIS, 3-month LIBOR/EURIBOR) rate. In a Constant Maturity Swap (CMS), one of the legs pays a floating rate indexed to a swap rate of a fixed maturity (e.g. 20-year swap rate). At the reset dates, the swap rates with a pre-determined maturity (e.g. 20 years) are taken for the calculation of cash flows (payable on the payment dates). Note that while a standard IRS contains the information or perception of rolling short end interest rate, a CMS contains much richer information over a longer period of the yield curve. Market practitioners have long used CMS to take views or hedge the overall yield curve movement, including future evolutions of the curve. CMS spread (e.g. 20-year swap minus 2-year swap) contains the information about the slope of the yield curve, which can be used to take position or hedge the relative movements in different parts of the yield curve.

To value a standard IRS, one can simply discount the expected cash flows. The present value of IRS is a linear combination of the floating rates (e.g. LIBOR/EURIBOR). The valuation of a CMS is much more complex. As can be seen later, the present value of a CMS is **not** a linear combination of the forward swap rates. This non-linearity in the CMS valuation is known as convexity. Convexity adjustment to CMS is non-trivial, as it is a function of rates, rates volatility and volatility smile. It becomes more complex in the context of CMS spread and option on CMS spread. In the following, we shall explain how the replication techniques can be used effectively to deal with CMS convexity and CMS derivatives pricing.

CMS REPLICATION

The concept of replication is not unfamiliar in the context of derivatives pricing. The very first principle of setting up the Black–Scholes equation is to replicate the option payoff with a portfolio of linear (hedging) instruments, and then dynamically rebalance the hedging. The dynamic hedging based on dynamic replication is one of the cornerstones of modern derivatives pricing theory. In a static replication, one assembles a set of vanilla instruments to form a static hedge to a typically non-linear payoff. Comparing to dynamic hedge, static hedge is more robust by construction. However, the product range suited for static hedge is rather limited.

In the presence of pronounced volatility smile/skew, static replication (referred to in the following as "replication") is a very valuable tool which allows one to capture and calibrate to the smile/skew. Let's review some of the key replication principles.

Replication Principles

For a non-linear monotonically increasing terminal payoff function $f(S)$, with $f(K_0) = 0$ as shown in Figure 13.1, one can replicate the function with the following approximation:

$$f(S) \approx \sum_i w(K_i) \cdot (S - K_i)^+$$

The weightings in the replication formula are:

$$w(K_0) = f'(K_0)$$
$$w(K_1) = f'(K_1) - f'(K_0) = f''(K_1) \cdot \Delta K$$

$$\dotsb$$

$$w(K_i) = f'(K_i) - f'(K_{i-1}) = f''(K_i) \cdot \Delta K$$

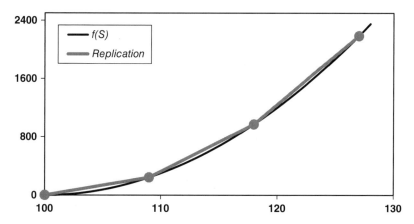

FIGURE 13.1   Monotonically increasing payoff

When $\Delta K \to 0$, we have the following golden replication formula 1:

$$f(S) = f'(K_0)(S - K_0)^+ + \int_{K_0}^{\infty} f''(K) \cdot (S - K)^+ dK$$

Essentially this particular non-linear terminal payoff can be replicated by a continuum of calls. As long as the payoff curve is monotonic, the formula holds for both convex and concave curves.

Similarly for a non-linear monotonically decreasing terminal payoff function $f(S)$, with $f(K_0) = 0$, as shown in Figure 13.2, it can be replicated by:

$$f(S) \approx \sum_{i} w(K_i) \cdot (K_i - S)^+$$

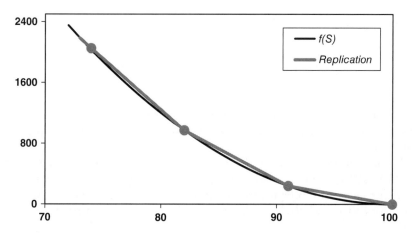

FIGURE 13.2   Monotonically decreasing payoff

The weightings are:

$$w(K_0) = -f'(K_0)$$
$$w(K_1) = -f'(K_1) + f'(K_0) = -f''(K_1) \cdot \Delta K$$

....

$$w(K_i) = -f'(K_i) + f'(K_{i-1}) = -f''(K_i) \cdot \Delta K$$

When $\Delta K \to 0$, we have the following replication golden formula 2:

$$f(S) = -f'(K_0)(K_0 - S)^+ + \int_0^{K_0} f''(K) \cdot (K - S)^+ dK$$

This particular non-linear terminal payoff can be replicated by a continuum of puts. As long as the payoff curve is monotonic, the formula holds for both convex and concave curves.

Armed with the above Golden Formulae, one can replicate (or convexity adjust) many exotic terminal payoffs in all asset classes. The key advantage in this type of replication is that one can capture volatility smile and skew in the process of integrating over the strike K. Let's examine a few examples, in which non-linear terminal payoffs are replicated.

Replication Examples

The first example is a general square terminal payoff: $f(S) = [(S - K_0)^+]^2$

By applying the golden formula 1 to it:

$$[(S - K_0)^+]^2 = 2\int_{K_0}^{\infty} (S - K)^+ dK$$

Taking expectation on both sides:

$$\left\langle [(S - K_0)^+]^2 \right\rangle^Q = 2\int_{K_0}^{\infty} \left\langle (S - K)^+ \right\rangle^Q dK$$

So the square terminal payoff is replicated by the integration of linear payoffs over the strike K. Note that the integration over K will effectively allow us to pick volatility smile and skew.

Let's take another replication example, which is widely used in FX derivatives, termed "FX self-Quanto". A FX self-Quanto call option $[(S_T - K_0)^+]$ states that its payoff currency is in foreign currency. Payoff in foreign currency is actually equivalent to a payoff converted into the home currency using the prevailing exchange rate S_T:

$$(S_T - K_0)^+ \cdot S_T$$

The above payoff can be rewritten as:

$$(S_T - K_0)^+ \cdot S_T = (S_T - K_0)^+ \cdot (S_T - K_0 + K_0)$$
$$= [(S_T - K_0)^+]^2 + (S_T - K_0)^+ \cdot K_0$$

Applying the golden formula:

$$\langle (S_T - K_0)^+ \cdot S_T \rangle = 2 \int_{K_0}^{\infty} \langle (S_T - K)^+ \rangle \cdot dK + \langle (S_T - K_0)^+ \rangle \cdot K_0$$

As can be seen, the integration over K indicates that FX self-Quanto pricing is sensitive to volatility smile.

A third replication example is the Equity Variance Swap. Its payoff can be expressed as a log contract:

$$\int_0^T \sigma_t^2 dt = 2 \cdot \int_0^T \frac{dS_t}{S_t} - 2 \cdot \ln\left(\frac{S_T}{S_0}\right)$$

$$\left\langle \frac{1}{T} \int_0^T \sigma_t^2 dt \right\rangle = \frac{2}{T} \left\langle \ln\left(\frac{F}{S_T}\right) \right\rangle$$

Applying the golden formulae on the log payoff:

$$PV = \frac{2}{T} \left[\int_0^F \frac{1}{K^2} \langle (K - S_T)^+ \rangle dK + \int_F^{\infty} \frac{1}{K^2} \langle (S_T - K)^+ \rangle dK \right]$$

Let's now examine an interest rate derivative replication example. Broadly speaking, an in-arrear cap/swap pays its coupon cash flow at the same time of the rate fixing. For a cap, the i-th caplet in-arrear payoff can be written as:

$$D(0, T_i) \cdot (F_{i,i+1} - K)^+ \cdot \tau_i$$
$$= D(0, T_{i+1}) \cdot \frac{1}{P(T_i, T_{i+1})} (F_{i,i+1} - K)^+ \cdot \tau_i$$
$$= D(0, T_{i+1}) \cdot \{\tau_i^2 \cdot [(F_{i,i+1} - K)^+]^2 + (\tau_i + \tau_i^2 \cdot K) \cdot (F_{i,i+1} - K)^+\}$$

So taking the expectation:

$$\left\langle D(0, T_i) \cdot (F_{i,i+1} - K)^+ \cdot \tau_i \right\rangle^{T_{i+1}} = P(0, T_{i+1}) \cdot \tau_i^2 \cdot \left\langle [(F_{i,i+1} - K)^+]^2 \right\rangle^{T_{i+1}} + \cdots$$

When $K = 0$, it is converging to an in-arrear swap (the floating leg).

Once again, we see the familiar squared payoff which can be replicated using the golden formula.

One of the most used applications of the replication technique is on the constant maturity swap (CMS). The CMS floating leg pays the cash flows indexed to the prevailing swap rate of fixed maturity. The i-th cash flow (x-year swap index) is given by:

$$S_{i,x}(t) = \frac{P(t, T_i) - P(t, T_{i+x})}{A_i(t)}$$

where the annuity is defined as:

$$A_i(t) = \sum_{j}^{x} \tau_j \cdot P(t, T_j)$$

Under $T_i + \delta$ measure, CMS rate is expressed as $\langle S_{i,x}(t) \rangle^{T_i + \delta}$. Using the Radon–Nikodym theorem, one can change T-measure to A-measure, so the CMS rate can be rewritten as:

$$\langle S_{i,x}(T_i) \rangle^{T_i + \delta} = \frac{A_i(0)}{P(0, T_i + \delta)} \cdot \left\langle S_{i,x}(T_i) \cdot \frac{P(T_i, T_i + \delta)}{A_i(T_i)} \right\rangle^{A_i}$$

$$= \frac{A_i(0)}{P(0, T_i + \delta)} \cdot \left\langle S_{i,x}^2(T_i) \cdot \frac{P(T_i, T_i + \delta)}{1 - P(T_i, T_i + x)} \right\rangle^{A_i}$$

The "squared" convex function can be approximated and differentiated with respect to $S_{i,x}$, and the golden formula can then be applied to replicate the CMS rate numerically.

In the presence of pronounced volatility smile/skew, stable replication is not straightforward. The above CMS replication technique does involve some approximations in the expansion of the convexity term. The expansion is on the single rate $S_{i,x}$. This implies that the CMS rate risk sensitivities are concentrated on that particular tenor at various time slices. Alternatively, one can use the approach suggested by Cedervall and Piterbarg, to value the convexity term using all tenors. This will effectively spread the risk sensitivities to all tenors. Clearly, in practice, the hedging will be affected if the risk sensitivities are spread differently. There is balance to be made between theoretical formulation and hedging practicality.

Let us now examine some real market CMS quotes, for the given yield curves. Figure 13.3 shows two yield curves (two EURO swap curves) with quite different term structures. The CMS quotes are obviously derived from the relevant yield curves and they are expressed as the basis points over 3-month EURIBOR.

The CMS quotes for the 10-year index derived from the two yield curves are plotted in Figure 13.4. The notion of EUCM10X in the graph means a swap of X years, one leg pays 3-month EURIBOR, the other leg pays 10-year swap rates. The shape of the yield curve is a key driver of the CMS quotes. In this particular case, given the CMS quotes from YC2 are higher than those of YC1, it states that, on average, the spread of forward 10-year swap rates against forward 3-month EURIBOR is higher in YC2 than YC1. This can be seen more clearly in the CMS quotes for the 30-year index shown in Figure 13.5. The average spreads of forward 30-year swap rates over forward 3-month EURIBOR are much higher in YC2 than YC1.

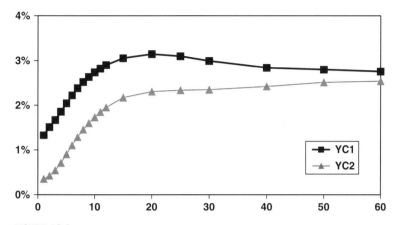

FIGURE 13.3 Swap curves (EUR)

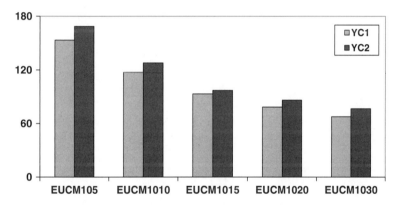

FIGURE 13.4 CMS – 10Y Index

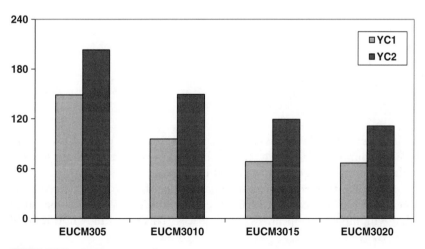

FIGURE 13.5 CMS – 30Y Index

The shape of the yield curve is not the only driving factor for CMS; the volatility as well as volatility smile all impact CMS rates due to the need of convexity adjustment by means of replication. The intuitions in CMS quotes relative to the shape of the yield curve can therefore be quite convoluted.

CMS CALIBRATION

The CMS replication technique provides a valuable tool to calibrate CMS to market volatility smile. In the interest rate derivatives world, SABR is widely used as a functional form for the swaption volatility surfaces. In the following, we shall discuss how to deal with some of the practical issues in calibrating CMS to the SABR volatility surfaces.

Calibration in SABR Framework

All replications in the presence of volatility smile share the same issue: volatility wings! CMS replication is no exception. As one needs to integrate along the relevant swaption volatility curve across all strikes, the volatility wings will impact the numerical integration and results. The enhanced SABR functional volatility curve (Berestycki 2004, Obloj 2008) has the following form, given the forward f and strike K at time T:

$$\sigma_{imp}(K,f,T) \approx \sigma_0(K,f)\big(1+\sigma_1(K,f)\cdot T\big)$$

where

$$\sigma_0(K,f) = \frac{v\cdot\ln\left(\dfrac{f}{K}\right)}{x(z)}$$

$$x(z) = \ln\left(\frac{\sqrt{1-2\rho z+z^2}+z-\rho}{1-\rho}\right)$$

$$z = \frac{v\big(f^{1-\beta}-K^{1-\beta}\big)}{\alpha(1-\beta)}$$

and

$$\sigma_1(K,f) = \frac{(1-\beta)^2\alpha^2}{24(fK)^{1-\beta}} + \frac{\rho\beta v\alpha}{4(fK)^{(1-\beta)/2}} + \frac{2-3\rho^2}{24}v^2$$

The at-the-money volatility is obtained by setting $K=f$, $\sigma_{ATM}(T) = \sigma_{imp}(f,f,T)$.

There are four SABR parameters, and all play key roles in the shape and dynamics of the volatility smile. The details are listed in Table 13.1.

All four SABR parameters affect the middle part of the volatility curve in one way or another. Hence in the context of CMS calibration, if any of these parameters are changed, it will impact European swaption prices! This is certainly not desirable. As a

TABLE 13.1 SABR parameters

α	The main ATM volatility driver;
β	The main driver of smile/skew dynamics. It may not be good idea to use it "too much" for CMS calibration;
ρ	The correlation of forward and volatility, affecting skew tilting;
v	vol-on-vol, affecting the smile.

matter of fact, the swaption market is quite separate from the CMS market, although both are dependent on volatility smile. In general, it is a much better practice to calibrate the central part of the volatility curve to the swaption market, and then modify wings subsequently for the CMS calibration. Treating volatility wings separately can avoid impacting on swaption prices and Greeks, and avoid impacting on smile dynamics embedded in β.

Stitching Volatility Wings

Getting the volatility wings right is important in the CMS replication calibration. Volatility wings may sound like a second order numerical effect, but are definitely not a second order issue practically speaking. In particular, when market volatilities shoot up, the untreated SABR wings can break the CMS calibration. To ensure additional degree of freedom to fit stressed market scenarios, one should stitch wings to the volatility smile. In stitching a volatility wing function [$f(K, A, B)$] to the original SABR volatility curve, one needs to ensure the wing function behaves well when K goes to infinity. For the high strike wing, we could use the following hyperbolic tangent functional form, which has the desired property:

$$V(K) = A \cdot \tanh(B \cdot K)$$

where A and B are constants, to be determined by matching the volatility as well as the slope (first derivative) of the SABR smile at a chosen high strike K.

Assuming SABR volatility at a high strike (K_h) is V, and the slope at that point is S:

$$V = V_{SABR}(K_h)$$

$$S = \frac{dV_{SABR}(K)}{dK}\bigg|_{K=K_h}$$

by matching the value as well as first derivative to those of the tail functional volatility, we have:

$$V = A \cdot \tanh(B \cdot K_h)$$

$$S = \frac{A \cdot B}{\cosh^2(B \cdot K_h)}$$

The solutions for A and B are:

$$A = \frac{V}{\tanh(B \cdot K_h)}$$

$$\frac{B}{\sinh(B \cdot K_h) \cdot \cosh(B \cdot K_h)} = \frac{S}{V}$$

B can be obtained by a simple numerical routine, and so can A. Once A and B are known, the wing can be stitched to SABR in a smooth way. A simple smooth stitching example is shown in Figure 13.6, with the following parameters:

$$K_h = 20\% \ V = 29.93\% \ S = 0.35 \text{ and } A = 0.32 \ B = 8.443$$

Note that the high strike K_h is a variable that can be used to match the CMS quotes. K_h provides a valuable additional degree of freedom for CMS calibration.

Let's examine some real-life CMS calibration examples. First, the SABR volatility surface is fully calibrated to the swaption market. As in general, the liquid swaption prices are in the central part of the SABR curve, the wings have no or little effect on the swaption market prices. We shall in the following compare calibrated CMS rates using SABR alone and those using SABR with a stitched wing.

Figure 13.7 shows the calibrated CMS rates against market quotes for the 10 year swap rate index. It is clear that SABR alone does not match the CMS market quotes well for a number of maturities (5Y, 10Y, 15Y and 20Y). However, if the volatility wings are stitched onto the SABR on the coupon fixing dates at the chosen K_h (in the example, $K_h = 2.3 \times f$), one obtains a much better calibration as shown in the figure.

In Figure 13.8, we compare the CMS Delta (bumping zero curve) for the calibrations with and without stitched wings. Different calibrations do result in different delta values. The same conclusion can be made for Vega.

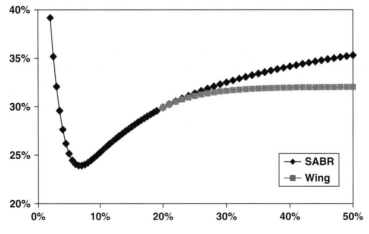

FIGURE 13.6   SABR vol smile

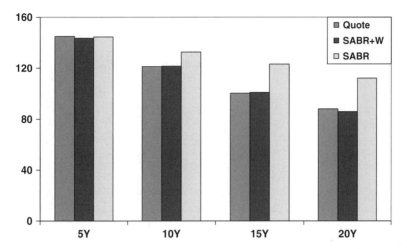

FIGURE 13.7 CMS calibration (10Y index)

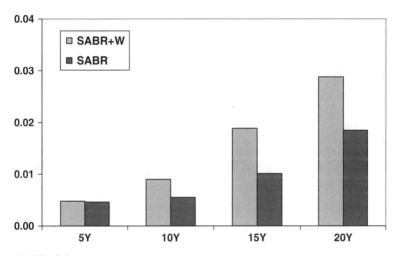

FIGURE 13.8 Delta (10Y index)

The Vega (bumping ATM volatility) comparison is shown in Figure 13.9.

A similar CMS calibration example is shown in Figure 13.10 for the 30-year swap rate index. The high strike $K_h = 1.9 \times f$ is chosen for the wing stitch. The calibration results are much enhanced as a result.

The Delta and Vega differences between the two different calibrations (SABR vs SABR + W) are evident as shown in Figures 13.11 and 13.12. Adequately stitched volatility wings not only help calibrating CMS to market properly, but also improve the hedging and risk managing of the CMS products.

Although wings are extremely important in the context of CMS replication and calibration, they have little impact on the overall probability density function (PDF).

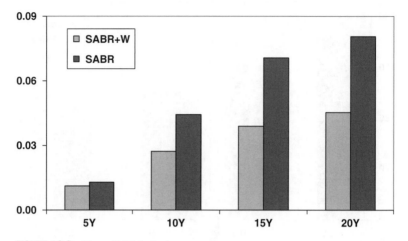

FIGURE 13.9 Vega (10Y index)

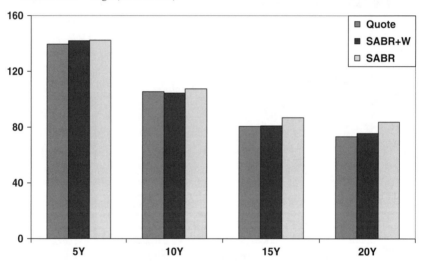

FIGURE 13.10 CMS calibration (30Y index)

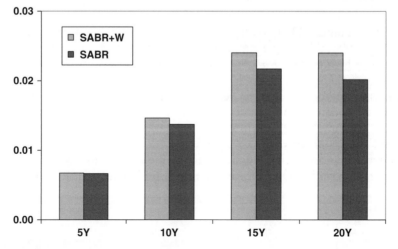

FIGURE 13.11 Delta (30Y index)

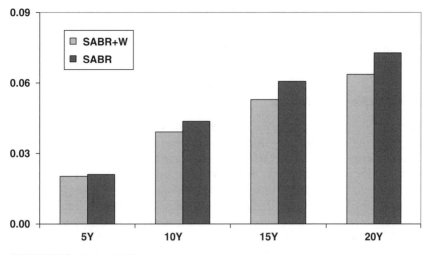

FIGURE 13.12   Vega (30Y index)

This can be clearly seen in Figure 13.13, where we compare the PDFs of SABR and SABR with wing. The difference is small and only on the wing, as one would expect. The conclusion is that the wing, if handled properly, won't affect standard option pricing whereby the dependency is on the PDF. But the wing will impact pricing of those dependent on replication, such as CMS, CMS cap and floor and CMS spread options. Note that we discussed the SABR right wing on the high strike end. We did not discuss the SABR left wing when strike is close to zero. The left wing is an entirely different yet much bigger topic as to how to handle negative interest rates in the context of option models. Again SABR original left wing cannot perform on its own as the PDF can go negative. These topics will be discussed elsewhere in the context of modelling interest rate derivatives when the rates are very low and negative.

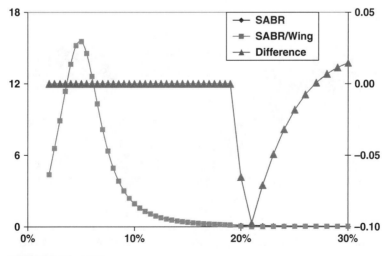

FIGURE 13.13   PDF

CMS SPREAD OPTION PRICING FRAMEWORK

In this section, we shall discuss the marginal distributions of CMS rates and the criteria for self-consistent pricing of CMS spread option.

Marginal Distributions of CMS Rates

Different CMS rates, though derived from the same yield curve and the same swaption volatility cube, in the context of CMS spread options can be treated as correlated individual components in a basket. CMS marginal distributions carry fundamental information of vanilla option markets, including volatility smile/skew. They can facilitate consistent analysis of the joint statistical characteristics of CMS rates. This will in turn allow us to achieve the self-consistency in CMS spread option pricing where the joint statistical characteristics in the presence of volatility smile/skew can be calibrated. In the following, some historical CMS statistical behaviours (PDFs) are examined, followed by the examination of implied PDFs, calculated by using different methodologies.

Figure 13.14 plots some historical CMS rates over many years. They all have a maturity of 10 years, and are linked to 2-year, 10-year and 30-year indices. It appears that the spreads were narrowing during the crises. The spreads between the 10-year and 30-year index have been narrower than those against the 2-year index.

The historical correlations from the above data (10Y maturity) are listed in Table 13.2. The correlations seem to follow the "distance rule", namely, the shorter the distance, the more correlated they are. The spread correlation (30s2s vs 10s2s) is also shown in this table (~ 63%), and it is less "predictable" in terms of intuition.

The historical correlations for the 30Y maturity are listed in Table 13.3. They follow very similar patterns as for the 10Y maturity.

The historical probability density function (PDF) for the 10Y CMS rates with 2Y, 10Y and 30Y indices are shown in Figure 13.15. The PDFs are calculated from the log-returns. The shapes of the distribution curves for all indices seem to suggest that

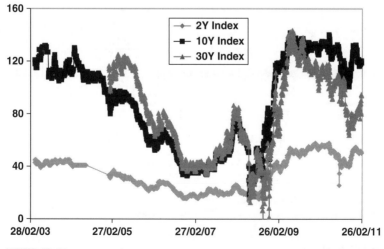

FIGURE 13.14   10Y CMS rates

TABLE 13.2   Historical correlations (10Y maturity)

Index	2Y	10Y	30Y	30s2s
2Y		~ 95%	~ 75%	
10Y			~ 85%	
30Y				
10s2s				~ 63%

TABLE 13.3   Historical correlations (30Y maturity)

Index	2Y	10Y	30Y	30s2s
2Y		~ 90%	~ 62%	
10Y			~ 82%	
30Y				
10s2s				~ 76%

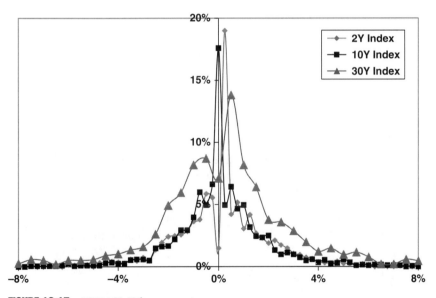

FIGURE 13.15   PDF (CMS log-return)

the log-normal fat tail assumption can be reasonable. It is tempting to simply assume that CMS underlyings follow log-normal processes, and various vanilla types of CMS options can be priced using the Black formula directly. Actually, there is much more to it, as we shall explain in the following sections.

Implied marginal distributions of CMS, in the form of its PDF or CDF, are calculated via a continuum of CMS digitals. There are two different methods of calculating CMS digitals. One is to use the full replication technique, by replicating the CMS cap/floor or digital pricing formulae directly. The other (temptation) is to use the Black formula, replicating CMS first, then re-basing swaption volatilities to CMS forward (re-based swaption volatilities can be obtained by re-calculating SABR alpha using the new CMS forward), then using Black cap/floor or digital formula.

Method 1 is clearly self-consistent, although numerically it is more expensive. The put-call parity will hold by construction. Method 2 is not self-consistent, as it will violate put-call Parity. For the full replication method 1:

- Following Radon–Nikodym, changing T-measure to A-measure, a cap can be written as:

$$\left\langle (S_{i,x}(T_i) - K)^+ \right\rangle^{T_i + \delta} = \frac{A_i(0)}{P(0, T_i + \delta)} \cdot \left\langle (S_{i,x}(T_i) - K)^+ \cdot \frac{P(T_i, T_i + \delta)}{A_i(T_i)} \right\rangle^{A_i}$$

$$= \frac{A_i(0)}{P(0, T_i + \delta)} \cdot \left\langle S_{i,x}(T_i) \cdot (S_{i,x}(T_i) - K)^+ \cdot \frac{P(T_i, T_i + \delta)}{1 - P(T_i, T_i + x)} \right\rangle^{A_i}$$

- A digital can be written as:

$$\left\langle 1_{|S_{i,x}(T_i) \geq K} \right\rangle^{T_i + \delta} = \frac{A_i(0)}{P(0, T_i + \delta)} \cdot \left\langle 1_{|S_{i,x}(T_i) \geq K} \cdot \frac{P(T_i, T_i + \delta)}{A_i(T_i)} \right\rangle^{A_i}$$

$$= \frac{A_i(0)}{P(0, T_i + \delta)} \cdot \left\langle S_{i,x}(T_i)_{|S_{i,x}(T_i) \geq K} \cdot \frac{P(T_i, T_i + \delta)}{1 - P(T_i, T_i + x)} \right\rangle^{A_i}$$

So the implied PDFs can be calculated from the above digital or cap spread. Figure 13.16 compares the PDFs obtained using method 1 and method 2 at 5-year time slice. The underlying is the 2-year CMS index. There is a visible difference between the two PDFs.

The same PDF comparison can be made at the 5-year time slice for the 10-year CMS index. The difference is much larger, as shown in Figure 13.17. This is understandable

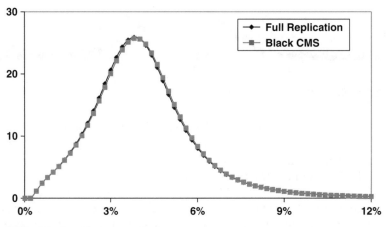

FIGURE 13.16 PDF (5Y on CMS2)

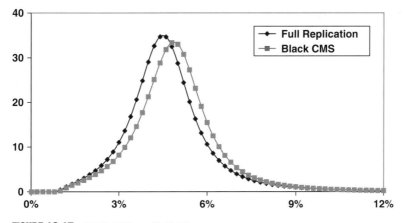

FIGURE 13.17   PDF (5Y on CMS10)

as the convexity adjustment via replication for a 10-year CMS index is proportionally larger than that for a 2-year CMS index.

The differences in PDFs will of course result in the differences in the relevant CMS implied volatilities. Implied volatilities are calculated by plugging into the prices into the Black formula. Figure 13.18 illustrates the departure of replication (CMS) implied from the equivalent swaption volatilities. It is a 5-year time slice on a 10-year CMS index. The correct CMS implied volatilities are quite different from swaption volatilities, which represent the convexity premium, including contributions from the smile.

In summary, a market implied CMS marginal CDF captures full volatility smile information. It ensures put-call parity by construction, which is embedded in the appropriate replication equations. Properly calibrated CMS marginals can be used in copula techniques to price CMS spread options. Market implied marginal CDF can provide self-consistency if blended properly with copula.

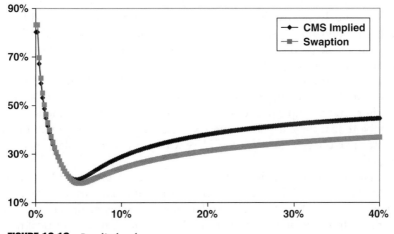

FIGURE 13.18   Implied vols

Criteria for Self-consistent Pricing of CMS Spread Option

Some of the typical CMS spread option payoffs are as follows:
- Standard spread option:

$$max\left(w_1S_1 - w_2S_2 - K,0\right)$$

- Curve sap (stochastic cap):

$$max\left[w_1\left(S_1 - S_2\right), w_2S_2 + c\right]$$

- Floored curve cap (stochastic cap and floor):

$$min\left[\max\left(w_1S_1 - w_2S_2 + c_1,K_1\right), \max\left(w_3S_2 + c_2,K_2\right)\right]$$

Where w_1 and w_2 are weightings, c_1 and c_2 are constant, S_1 and S_2 are the CMS underlyings.

There has been a variety of models used by banks for pricing CMS spread options, ranging from Black, to bi-variate, to multi-factor term structure models. A good model, however, should exhibit self-consistency to the vanilla markets, in terms of underlyings calibrations as well as their marginal distributions (volatility smile/skew). It should have simple and transparent specifications of co-dependence between CMS underlyings, and simple and stable numerical implementation schemes. There are many challenges in self-consistently pricing and risk managing CMS spread options. Some of the key challenges are how to calibrate to the CMS underlying market along both T and K axes; how to calibrate to CMS vanilla option (cap/floor) market that is consistent with the underlying replication; how to calibrate to the CMS spread option market where one might need to handle a correlation matrix, which is highly undesirable. Calibrating to three sets of CMS market simultaneously is never easy, never mind when the "wrong" model is used, one may have to handle "correlation skew". The calibration issues can be amplified in volatile markets. Therefore, self-consistency is extremely important, in particular in volatile markets.

In the following, we shall examine some real-life CMS spread option examples. Figures 13.19 and 13.20 are the market quotes of CMS spread cap and floor respectively. Both cap and floor price matrixes are for the CMS spread of 10-year index against 2-year index (CMS10-CMS02). The x-axis is the maturity in years, and the y-axis is the strike in basis points.

It is clear that if one uses the simple bi-variate model to fit those price matrixes, the obtained implied correlation matrixes will exhibit smile or skew. Figure 13.21 illustrates the short end example of the correlation matrix, which is a function of maturity and strike. Note that the correlation matrix is also a function of spread forward. Risk managing such an uneven correlation surface with so many dependencies is not a good idea in practice.

Note that the correlation also changes with time. In Figure 13.22, the implied correlations over a period of 225 days are plotted for different strikes. The change over time is significant, which makes the correlation risk management very difficult. Hence choosing the right model in the context of CMS spread options is critical not only for pricing but also for ongoing risk management activities.

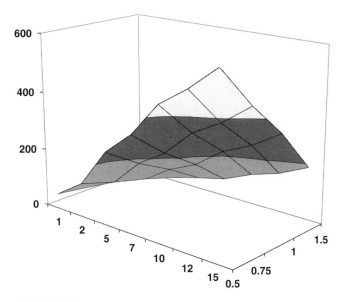

FIGURE 13.19   CMS spread option quotes (10s2s Cap)

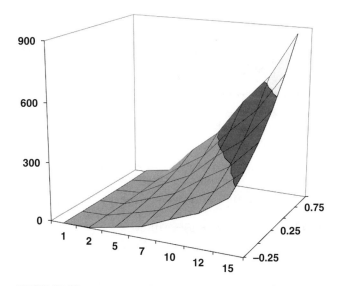

FIGURE 13.20   CMS spread option quotes (10s2s Floor)

So what are the self-consistency criteria in a good CMS spread option model? In a nutshell, in addition to standard yield curves, one should ensure consistency to the three CMS specific markets during the course of calibration: CMS replication underlyings, CMS vanilla options (cap/floor) and CMS spread options (correlation matrix). Calibrating to three markets simultaneously is hard enough, calibrating replication underlyings to the three markets in a self-consistent manner is even more challenging.

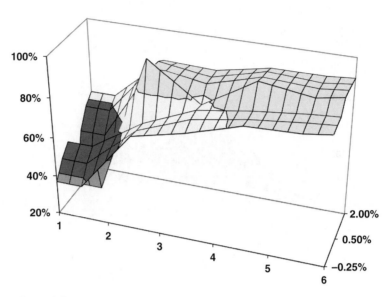

FIGURE 13.21   Implied correlation surface

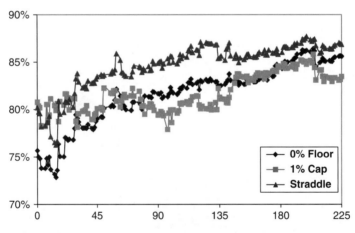

FIGURE 13.22   Implied correlation (10s2s)

COPULA PRICING WITH FULL MARKET MARGINAL DISTRIBUTIONS

Copula in its various forms has been widely used in pricing basket options. CMS spread options can also be priced using copula blended with full market calibrated marginal distributions. A good copula model should exhibit the following features:

■ self-consistency to the vanilla markets, in terms of underlying yield curve and CMS market calibrations;

■ fully consistent with the marginal distributions of the relevant CMS rates, which include swaption volatility smile/skew;

- simple and transparent specification of co-dependence or terminal correlation structure between the CMS underlyings (S_1, S_2), which allows sensible and meaningful calibration of the spread options (correlation market);
- simple and stable numerical implementation scheme.

In contrast to equity or FX underlying, the special feature of the CMS spread option is that the underlying prices (CMS rates) are also function of volatility smile, in addition to their random walks. Such a convoluted relationship make it crucial to blend copula (driving the random walks) with the replication (driving the underlying price), in order to maintain the self-consistency principle throughout the model. Copula can be a stable technique, and can do a good job in the overall consistent calibration to relevant markets.

According to Sklar's theorem, given marginals in uniforms, there exists a copula that binds the marginal uniforms to give the joint distribution of the multivariates:

$$F(S_1, S_2) = C(F_1(S_1), F_2(S_2))$$

Hence the joint PDF is given by:

$$f(S_1, S_2) = \frac{\partial^2 C(F_1(S_1), F_2(S_2))}{\partial S_1 \partial S_2}$$

$$= \frac{\partial^2 C(u_1, u_2)}{\partial u_1 \partial u_2} f_1(S_1) f_2(S_2)$$

Note that the joint PDF is completely specified once the copula or copula density is specified for the given underlying marginal distributions. The detailed formulation of Gaussian and t-copula can be found in the chapter of "Basket Products". These two types of copulas are widely used by practitioners because of their simplicity and tractability.

For the spread option, integrating spread option payoff with the joint PDF:

$$\max(S_1 - S_2 - K, 0)$$

$$= \int_{-\infty}^{\infty} \int_{-\infty}^{\infty} (S_1 - S_2 - K) \cdot 1_{S_1 - S_2 - K > 0} \cdot f(S_1, S_2) \cdot dS_1 dS_2$$

$$= P_1 - P_2$$

These two-dimensional integrations $(P_1$ and $P_2)$ can be can be reduced to one-dimensional integrations, which are of course far more efficient computationally:

$$P_1 = \int_{-\infty}^{\infty} \int_{-\infty}^{\infty} (S_1 - K) \cdot 1_{S_1 - S_2 - K > 0} \cdot f(S_1, S_2) \cdot dS_1 dS_2$$

$$= \int_{-\infty}^{\infty} (S_1 - K) \cdot \left(\int_{-\infty}^{\infty} 1_{S_1 - S_2 - K > 0} \cdot \frac{\partial^2 C(F_1(S_1), F_2(S_2))}{\partial S_1 \partial S_2} \cdot dS_2 \right) \cdot dS_1$$

$$= \int_{-\infty}^{\infty} (S_1 - K) \cdot \frac{\partial C(F_1(S_1), F_2(S_1 - K))}{\partial S_1} dS_1$$

$$P_2 = \int\limits_{-\infty}^{\infty}\int\limits_{-\infty}^{\infty} S_2 \cdot 1_{S_1-S_2-K>0} \cdot f(S_1,S_2) \cdot dS_1 dS_2$$

$$= \int\limits_{-\infty}^{\infty} S_2 \cdot \left(\int\limits_{-\infty}^{\infty} 1_{S_1-S_2-K>0} \cdot \frac{\partial^2 C(F_1(S_1), F_2(S_2))}{\partial S_1 \partial S_2} \cdot dS_1 \right) \cdot dS_2$$

$$= \int\limits_{-\infty}^{\infty} S_2 \cdot \left(f(S_2) - \frac{\partial C(F_1(S_2+K), F_2(S_2))}{\partial S_2} \right) dS_2$$

Power Copula

Both Gaussian and t-copula can be powered up as:

$$C_p(u,v,\rho,\theta_1,\theta_2) = u^{1-\theta_1} v^{1-\theta_2} C\left(u^{\theta_1}, v^{\theta_2}, \rho\right)$$

where θ_1 and θ_2 are constant. When $\theta_1 = \theta_2 = 1$, the power copula converges to the standard copula:

$$C_p(u,v,\rho,1,1) = C(u,v,\rho)$$

The power copula has two additional degrees of freedom (θ_1, θ_2), which allows more flexibility in the copula calibration process. In the power t-copula, at each time slice, four parameters $(\rho, d, \theta_1, \theta_2)$ can be used for calibration against the spread option quotes, while in standard t-copula one can only use (ρ, d) for calibration. The flexibility of the power t-copula comes at a cost, its partial derivatives require the calculation of bi-variate CDF. The standard t-copula counterparts do not require that, hence it is much more computationally efficient.

There are two typical ways to include the full market marginal distributions in the copula. One can either adopt large-step Monte Carlo or perform numerical integration over the given marginals. In the following, we shall examine the two methods for pricing spread options.

Large-step Monte Carlo Copula Implementation

In Figure 13.23, the marginal CDFs at 5-year time slice for the 2-year and 10-year CMS index are given.

In order to sample a marginal CDF, one can generate n independent random Gaussian numbers (g_j), and correlate the n Gaussian numbers as follows, for example via Cholesky decomposition:

$$G_i = \sum_j \rho_{ij} \cdot g_j$$

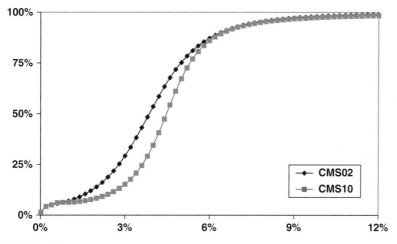

FIGURE 13.23 CDF (5Y on CMS02 and CMS10)

Those correlated Gaussian numbers can then be converted back to uniformly distributed numbers by inverse Wiener process:

$$U_i = W^{-1}(G_i)$$

Where $U_i[0,1]$ can be used to sample the CDF to obtain S_i. Clearly, once S_i are known, one can use them to calculate spread payoffs.

The above large-step Monte Carlo is equivalent to using Gaussian copula, but performed on the full market calibrated marginal distributions (CDFs). As those CDFs are in numerical forms, i.e. they are not expressed as functional forms, the above numerical sampling scheme (Monte Carlo) can in principle capture the full market CMS marginal distributions. In doing so, it is important to make some simple yet effective numerical corrections to minimize the Monte Carlo errors. One such correction is to modify S_i for all Monte Carlo runs, to ensure the correct forward for the simulated spread. The average spread forward prior to correction is calculated by:

$$F^i = S_1^i - S_2^i \qquad F^N = \sum_{i=1}^{N} \frac{F_i}{N}$$

Given we know exactly what the spread forward S_F should be (F), we can calculate a correction factor f, which can then be used to modify all simulated S_i:

$$f = \frac{F}{F^N} \qquad S_i' = f \cdot S$$

The spread option price using corrected S_i' will have much better convergence, considering there are several source of possible random errors, from volatility smile to replicated CDFs. Provided the fundamental setup is done properly and consistently, the large-step Monte Carlo copula is a versatile technique allowing one to easily price a variety of spread payoffs listed earlier. Of course, with any numerical technique, a numerical method has numerical advantages as well as problems. In the following, we examine some alternative semi-analytical implementation techniques, which can be implemented efficiently for a wide range of spread payoffs. In general, semi-analytical implementations have better computational efficiencies.

Semi-analytical Copula Implementation

In order to implement the copula pricing model semi-analytically, one needs to find a functional form or distribution that fits the market calibrated CMS marginal distribution. Given the fact that many practitioners in the industry use SABR to mark their swaption volatilities, Gaussian distribution is not the best choice, as fitting Gaussian to SABR is known to be very difficult. Student's t-distribution can be a good candidate for fitting to CMS CDF. Its skewed version has a number of degrees of freedom to tailor for fat tails often exhibited in SABR.

A standard Student's t-distribution expressed as PDF and CDF is as follows:

$$f_d(x) = \frac{\Gamma\left(\dfrac{d+1}{2}\right)}{\sqrt{d\pi} \cdot \Gamma\left(\dfrac{d}{2}\right)} \cdot \left(1 + \frac{x^2}{d}\right)^{-\frac{d+1}{2}}$$

$$F_d(x) = \frac{1}{2} + x\Gamma\left(\frac{d+1}{2}\right) \cdot \frac{{}_2F_1\left(\dfrac{1}{2}, \dfrac{d+1}{2}; \dfrac{3}{2}; -\dfrac{x^2}{d}\right)}{\sqrt{d\pi} \cdot \Gamma\left(\dfrac{d}{2}\right)}$$

Where $\Gamma(\cdot)$ is the Gamma function, ${}_2F_1(\cdot)$ is the hypergeometric function, and d is the degree of freedom. Examining the Standard t-distribution CDF, when $d \to \infty$ (i.e. when the degree of freedom goes to infinity), t-distribution converges to Gaussian. It is certainly much more flexible, being able to fit distributions with fat tails as well as normal distribution. Figure 13.24 illustrates this fact by comparing t-CDFs with different degrees of freedom ($d = 2$, $d = 20$) and a Gaussian.

Note that the standard t-distribution is symmetric around the mean, although it can handle fat tails. In order to fit asymmetric distributions often encountered in real life, one can extend the standard version to skewed t-distribution. Using a general method developed by Fernandez and Steel, a symmetric standard t-distribution can be transferred into a skewed t-distribution:

$$f_d(x, \varepsilon) = \begin{cases} \dfrac{2\varepsilon}{\sigma(1+\varepsilon^2)} \cdot f_d\left(\dfrac{\varepsilon(x-\mu)}{\sigma}\right), & x \le \mu \\[3mm] \dfrac{2\varepsilon}{\sigma(1+\varepsilon^2)} \cdot f_d\left(\dfrac{x-\mu}{\varepsilon\sigma}\right), & x > \mu \end{cases}$$

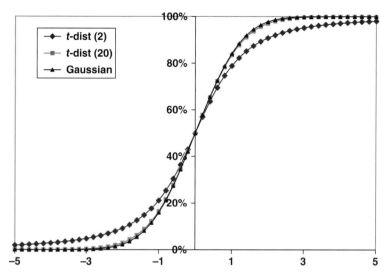

FIGURE 13.24 Student's *t*-CDF

Skewed *t*-distribution CDF is given by

$$F_d(x,\varepsilon) = \frac{2}{1+\varepsilon^2} \cdot F_d\left(\varepsilon \cdot y_1(x)\right) + \frac{2\varepsilon^2}{1+\varepsilon^2} \cdot \left[F_d\left(\frac{y_2(x)}{\varepsilon}\right) - \frac{1}{2} \right]$$

$$y_1(x) = \min\left(\frac{x-\mu}{\sigma}, 0\right) \qquad y_2(x) = \max\left(\frac{x-\mu}{\sigma}, 0\right)$$

The skewed *t*-distribution has four parameters $(d,\mu,\sigma,\varepsilon)$ determining the shape and size of PDF and CDF. They can be used to fit CMS marginal CDFs. The four parameters have intuitive meanings: d influence the heavy tails, $\propto$ is the location of the peak, σ is the scale factor and ε determines the skew. In Figures 13.25 and 13.26, the marginal CDFs at 5-year time slice are plotted against the fitted skewed *t*-distribution. For the 2Y CMS index (Figure 13.25), the fitted four parameters have the value of $d = 2.4236$, $\mu = 0.0377$, $\sigma = 0.0139$, $\varepsilon = 1.0452$.

For the 10-year CMS index (Figure 13.26), the fitted *t*-distribution parameters have the value of $d = 1.4562$, $\mu = 0.0454$, $\sigma = 0.0094$, $\varepsilon = 0.957$.

As can be seen from the above examples, skewed *t*-distribution can fit the CMS marginal CDF very well. It is very flexible to fit asymmetric shapes and fat tails. Very importantly, it is tractable and can be an ideal candidate as a functional form to represent CMS marginal CDF. Therefore, by combining fitted skewed *t*-distribution with copula one can blend the marginal distribution with copula effectively. The CMS spread option pricing model using this technique will have the advantages of combining self-consistent replication calibration with analytical tractability in the presence of volatility smile/skew.

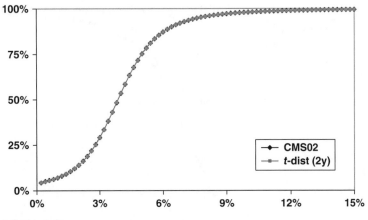

FIGURE 13.25   CDF (CMS02 vs *t*-dist)

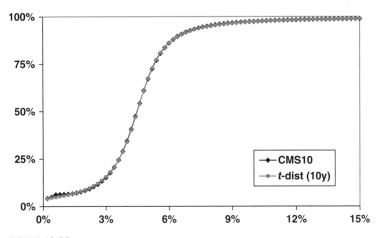

FIGURE 13.26   CDF (CMS10 vs *t*-dist)

Semi-analytical Copula Results Comparison

The results shown below are obtained by blending copula with full replication marginals. The underlying marginals are first of all calculated using full replication. These marginals are then fitted with skewed *t*-distributions. The fitted skewed *t*-distributions are effectively the analytical functional form of the marginals which can then be conveniently implemented with various copula models, including Gaussian, *t* and power-*t* copula.

Figure 13.27 compares the last caplet prices of 2-year caps at various strikes. The underlying is the 10-year vs 2-year CMS spread (10s2s). It is shown that all copulas achieving good results against the market quotes. Note that in all copula implementations we did not use different correlations for different strikes. Only one correlation at that time point is used: $\rho = 0.88$ for G-copula, $\rho = 0.865(d = 4.5)$ for *t*-copula and $\rho = 0.9(d = 4.5, \theta_1 = 0.96, \theta_2 = 0.96)$ for power *t*-copula.

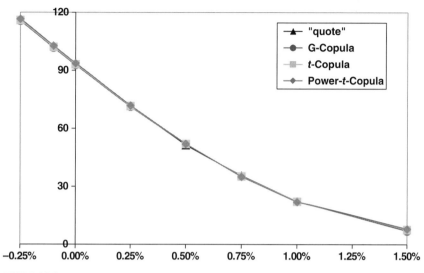

FIGURE 13.27   Calibration (2Y CMS caplet 10s2s)

The calibration errors are plotted in Figure 13.28. *t* and power-*t* copula is slightly better, with smaller errors. The good fitting of *t*-distribution to the marginals rather than the choice of copula seems to have the first order effect in terms of pricing and calibration accuracy.

The price comparisons for the 2-year caps at various strikes are shown in Figure 13.29. The cap price includes all relevant caplets. The underlying is the 10-year vs 2-year CMS spread (10s2s). Only one correlation at any particular time point is

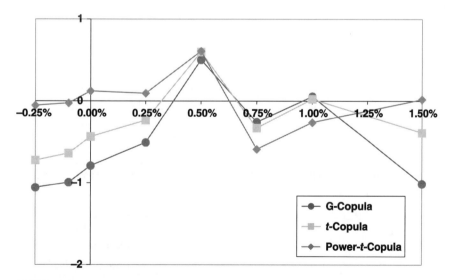

FIGURE 13.28   Calibration error (2Y CMS caplet 10s2s)

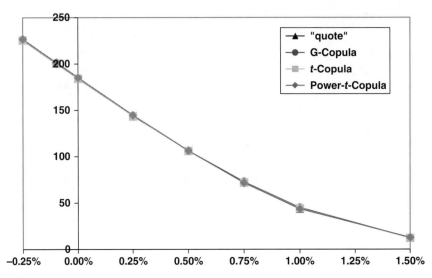

FIGURE 13.29   Calibration (2Y CMS cap 10s2s)

used. The two yearly correlations for G-copula are $\rho_1 = 0.72$, $\rho_2 = 0.83$, for t-copula $\rho_1 = 0.72$, $\rho_2 = 0.825$ and for power t-copula $\rho_1 = 0.77$, $\rho_2 = 0.91$.

The calibration errors of the above prices are plotted in Figure 13.30. The conclusion obtained for the caplets still holds for the cap.

Similar price comparisons for the last caplets of 5-year caps (CMS spread 10s2s) at various strikes are shown in Figure 13.31. The calibrated correlation is $\rho = 0.915$ for G-copula, $\rho = 0.88(d = 2.1)$ for t-copula and $\rho = 0.91(d = 2.1, \theta_1 = 0.99, \theta_2 = 0.98)$ for power t-copula.

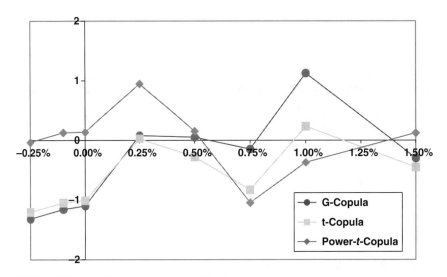

FIGURE 13.30   Calibration error (2Y CMS cap 10s2s)

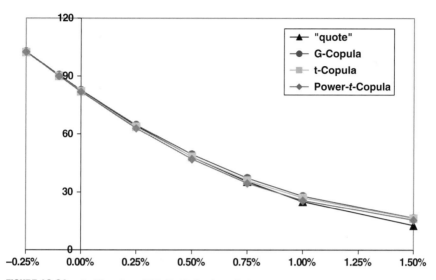

FIGURE 13.31 Calibration (5Y CMS Caplet 10s2s)

The calibration errors are plotted in Figure 13.32. Again, *t*- and power-*t* copula perform slightly better than the Gaussian copula, although in general they can all calibrate to the market quotes well.

The prices comparison for the 5-year caps (CMS spread 10s2s) at various strikes, and the corresponding calibration errors are shown in Figures 13.33 and 13.34 respectively. Very similar conclusions hold as for the 2-year caps: the copulas with adequately fitted marginals can calibrate to the market well.

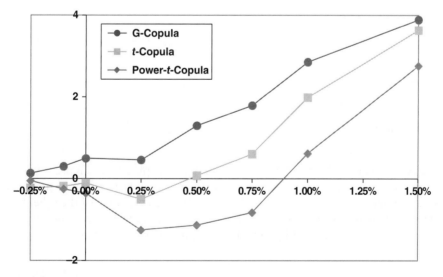

FIGURE 13.32 Calibration Error (5Y CMS caplet 10s2s)

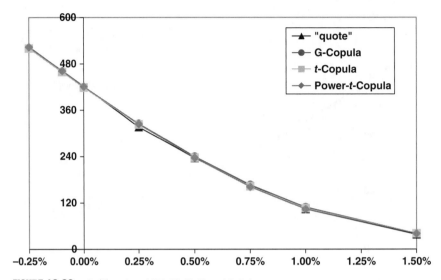

FIGURE 13.33 Calibration (5Y CMS Cap 10s2s)

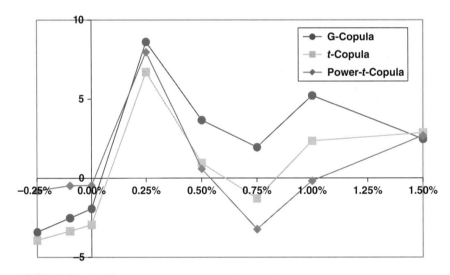

FIGURE 13.34 Calibration error (5Y CMS Cap 10s2s)

The yearly calibrated correlation term structure is plotted in Figure 13.35. Only one correlation at a given time slice is required in a copula to calibrate to the CMS markets. Comparing to the correlation matrices required for some of the other models, copula models with appropriately fitted marginals (e.g. skewed *t*-distribution) are far more superior in terms of simplifying and managing correlation structures.

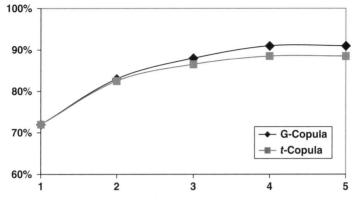

FIGURE 13.35 Correlation term structure

Concluding Remarks

CMS and its spread products belong to one of the most important yet difficult categories of interest rate derivatives. They are quite unique in that the replication of the underlying as well as the spread optionality is the function of the volatility smile. Copula blended with full replication marginal distributions can be a valuable technique to price and risk manage CMS spread products. Blending copula with marginal distributions can achieve good consistency with the underlying vanilla markets, including yield curve and swaption volatilities. It can maintain the full consistency with the CMS market and its associated smile/skew features. Besides, copula can specify explicit and simple co-dependence, and has the flexibility in calibrating to the "correlation market" in the spread option quotes. The resultant correlation term structure is much better and easier to risk manage than a correlation matrix, which is far more complex and volatile.

With the help of skewed *t*-distribution, one can simplify the blending of copula with the replication. Using a well fitted skewed *t*-distribution to represent replication marginal distributions, one is able to not only maintain the self-consistency but also adopt efficient numerical technique to implement the model. In practice, the technique is flexible in that the marginal distributions do not need to be SABR, as skewed *t*-distribution is capable of fitting to various marginal distributions.

As a general statement on using copula to price basket options, numerical integration in general works well for baskets with up to three underlyings. For baskets with more than three underlyings, large step Monte Carlo technique may be more efficient, and it can be made numerically equivalent to Gaussian copula on full marginal distributions. In the case of CMS spread options, fitting *t*-distributions to the full marginal distributions can greatly enhance the numerical efficiency. It is shown that both Gaussian copula and *t*-copula can do very well when blended with the well fitted *t*-distribution, in calibrating to the spread option prices. The most important thing is to use the full marginal calibrations, which seems to have the first order effect. One can then impose copula onto the full marginals numerically or semi-analytically. The choice of copula is also important: Gaussian copula is the simplest, t-copula is more flexible as it has heavy tails and non-zero tail dependence.

As a research interest, one may ask: why not use a fitted bi-variate t-distribution as the joint PDF directly in the pricing of CMS spread options? After all, once the joint PDF is found, pricing spread options should be straightforward. The numerical calibration of bi-variate t-distribution to the market could be quite expensive. However, it is worth researching the use of an EM (expectation-maximization) algorithm to speed up t-distribution calibration.

Finally, over the years, practitioners have been looking for a derivative model paradigm in which the exotics are derived purely from a map of vanilla prices without going through the underlying stochastic processes. In such a paradigm, everything is derived along the line of vanilla hedging. Does such a paradigm exist? It could exist for certain products when the copula techniques are applicable. Note that copula tends to use PDF and CDF directly. If the dynamics of PDF can be used to model smile/skew dynamics in a sensible way, then there is a natural link to such a model paradigm in which one does not need to go into stochastic processes.

CHAPTER 14

Interest Rate Derivative Products

Interest rate derivative products are designed to meet customers' hedging and/or investment needs. The customers include retail, institutional and corporate clients, asset and portfolio managers. Customers do have their own business rationales in transacting specific products. For example, pension funds and life insurers need to use interest rate swaps to hedge their liabilities. They tend to be the fixed rate receivers, and can be active users of swaption-based products. In the following, we shall examine some key categories of interest rate derivative products, understand their rationales, pricing and risk characteristics.

PRODUCT DESIGN AND PRODUCT RISKS

Interest rate derivative products can be issued in a variety of wrappers, such as certificates of deposit issued by banks and medium-term notes (MTN) issued by institutions and corporates. No matter what forms these products are in, they obey the general rules of derivative products design and pricing. Some of such golden rules are summarized in Table 14.1:

Yield Curve Movement

Interest rate derivative products are driven by the movement of the entire yield curve. In the following, a few real-life examples are shown to illustrate a combination of yield curve movements including parallel shift, shape change and curve inversion.

Figure 14.1 displays some example euro yield curves (EUR swap curves annual fixed rate vs 6M EURIBOR), showing the changing yield curves over time due to a combination of curve shifting, steepening or flattening.

Most of the time, the yield curve is upward sloping for a good reason: lenders or savers expect higher returns for locking up their money longer. However, there are times, for example due to expected economic downturns, when the yield curve is inverted (downward sloping). Figure 14.2 shows a real-life example of inverted yield curve (EUR), whereby the downward sloping is between 0 and 4 years.

TABLE 14.1 Products design golden rules

Golden Rule	Description
Zero Sum Game	While interest rate derivative products can change the payoff and risk profiles, the overall cost and benefit must observe the zero sum rule. For example, if investors receive above-market coupons under certain scenarios (benefit), they must also forgo coupons or receive much reduced coupons or even lose capital under the other scenarios (cost). There is no free lunch.
Favourable Pricing Environment (Payoff-Specific)	If investors' preference or view is contrary to the given market data including yield curve and implied volatilities, the pricing tends to work out better for both sell and buy sides. For example, in a range accrual, investors hope and expect the rate stay the same, implicitly hoping for a flat yield curve and low volatility. If the actual market yield curve is strongly sloping and volatilities are high, then the price of range accrual will be attractive for both seller and buyer.
Quanto	Quanto allows investors to benefit from some desirable features in foreign indices without taking exchange risks. For example, if USD LIBOR has higher volatility than its EUR counterpart, the USD range accrual products may offer much better terms. Euro investors could benefit from a Quanto range accrual, receiving payoffs in euro without entering a cross-currency swap. The product providers must price and take in Quanto risks.
Model Choice	For all PRACTICE PURPOSE, it is very difficult to find a ToE (theory of everything) or a MoE (model of everything). Therefore an appropriate model needs to be chosen for pricing a specific interest rate derivative product. In general, if a product is mainly sensitive to the parallel movement of the yield curve, the single factor models will be adequate for pricing it. Otherwise, multifactor models are required to capture the risks of shape variations in the yield curve.

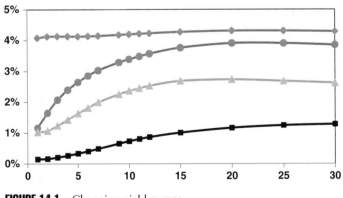

FIGURE 14.1 Changing yield curves

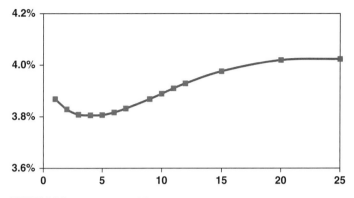

FIGURE 14.2 Inverted yield curve (0 to 4Y)

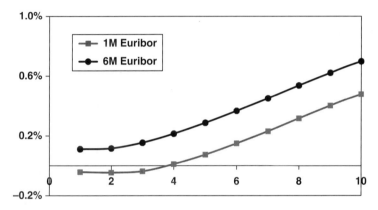

FIGURE 14.3 Negative interest rates

Historically, inverted yield curve scenarios occurred from time to time, but they rarely stayed inverted for long. While curve inversion is a risk, it is also an opportunity. For example, one can structure certain CMS spread products that will benefit when the inversion ends.

Last but not the least, yield curve can indeed become negative. In Figure 14.3, a snapshot of two EUR swap curves (fixed vs 1M EURIBOR and fixed vs 6M EURIBOR) are plotted. The negative rates in the 1M EURIBOR curve at the near end are in the order of −5bps for up to 3 years.

As expected, the EONIA curve snapped at the same time exhibits more negative rates at the near end. As displayed in Figure 14.4, EONIA is negative for up to 4 years, and the most negative point is about −10bps in this example.

In the above, we purposely used the term "near end" instead of "short end", as the negative rates extend to 3 or 4 years, which are not short. This has already forced an important model paradigm shift in that the negative interest rates must be priced into the interest rate derivative products.

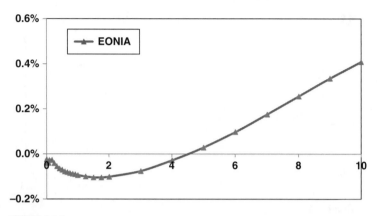

FIGURE 14.4 Negative interest rates

Vanilla Products and Risks

Vanilla products contain embedded vanilla options such as cap/floor, collar, digital on LIBOR/EURIBOR, European swaption, etc. For example, a 100% capital-protected product can have coupon incomes linked to the 6M EURIBOR, and the coupons can be floored (e.g. at 0%) and capped (e.g. at 4.00% pa). A fixed to floating note can mature in 4 years, paying a fixed rate of 4% in the first year, and 3-month LIBOR+1.5% floored at 0% for the remaining 3 years.

Numerous vanilla products can be created using combinations of vanilla payoffs. Customers' needs do vary with the market conditions. From a product design perspective, a high interest rate environment offers better scope and room for flexibility. In a low interest rate environment, the product scope is much more restricted.

While vanilla product features and risks are well understood by the (sell side) practitioners, these products can still cause serious damages if not designed and used properly. In the following, we explain how some of the very simple vanilla Interest Rate Hedging Products (IRHR) burnt UK small and medium-sized enterprise (SME) customers.

In 2013/14, at the request of the UK regulator FCA, some major UK banks reviewed and redressed the possible mis-selling of IRHR to businesses since 2001. The instruments concerned were interest rate swap, cap, collar and structured collar. Many of the businesses these IRHP were sold to were SMEs, classified as unsophisticated customers.

The instruments were sold as part of commercial loan packages, e.g. in fixed rate commercial loans and loans with collars. A fixed-rate loan consists of a floating rate loan and a swap to exchange floating with fixed-rate interest payment. When SMEs took out the fixed-rate loans, the interest rates were very high. They would face huge losses when the interest rates had since become very low.

The so-called "structured" collar embedded in some of the commercial loans sold to SMEs further amplified their losses. As shown in Figure 14.5, the upside of a "structured" collar is the same as the standard collar, but the downside is twice leveraged. When the market floating interest rate moved close to zero, the loan rate for those SMEs became doubly higher, leading to huge amplified losses.

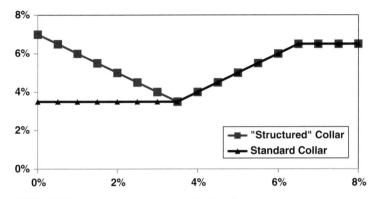

FIGURE 14.5   Loan rates with embedded collars

By early 2015, the affected banks had to set aside more than GBP 2 billion to compensate victims. So what had gone wrong with these seemingly very simple vanilla products?

Duty of Customer Care

In the above "structured" collar example, many loss scenarios were very evident and predictable. A simple analysis can reveal that the loss scenarios clearly violated the original purpose of the product, which was to "hedge" the commercial loan rates. For the customers who got the "structured" collar loans, they actually increased the risks rather than hedged or reduced the risks. So the product design was bad at the outset and they were not fit-for-purpose.

Vanilla products are very simple to the sell side practitioners, but they are **not** necessarily simple for unsophisticated customers. Have the banks really explained the risks clearly to unsophisticated customers, and do they really understand the risks and loss scenarios of the products? Sell side practitioners need to answer those questions rigorously. Duty of customer care plays a pivotal role when selling products to customers, in particular to unsophisticated customers.

Low Interest Rate and Multi-curve Impact

The low interest rate and multi-curve environment have certainly caused complications and made many interest rate derivative products more risky, even for seemingly simple products. Investors and practitioners need to be aware that the "less visible" risk factors can emerge to alter the risk characteristics of the products and/or hedging portfolios.

One example is that many standard or structured floating notes floor the coupon payments at zero. These type of notes therefore contain zero or negative strike floors. In the days when interest rates were high and markets were using the log-normal model for pricing, because the model inherently forbade negative interest rate, a zero or negative strike floor had no value. In the low or ultra-low interest rate environment when markets are using the normal or shifted log-normal model, a zero or negative strike floor can have material value. Hence such floating notes also have non-negligible floor risks.

Another real-life example is the hedging of zero-coupon interest rate swap (zIRS) which has been significantly affected by the multi-curve reality. Many pension funds traditionally use zIRSs to hedge their liabilities. In the fixed leg of a zIRS, the payment is only made at maturity. The risk exposure of this leg is therefore only to the one point on the discount curve, typically an OIS curve. Dealers who transact zIRSs with the pension funds have always hedged their zIRS positions with standard par swaps. A par swap has regular coupon payments before maturity, and it has risk exposures to both discount curve (OIS) and LIBOR curve (forecasting coupon cash flows). Hence:

- In a single curve environment where LOIS (basis between LIBOR and OIS) is negligible, a par swap can perfectly hedge the zIRS in terms of market risks, although the counterparty credit risk differs;
- In the multi-curve environment where LOIS is material, hedging zIRS with a par swap has a basis exposure to LOIS, in addition to time bucketed exposures of OIS and LIBOR curve;
- The basis risk can become one of the main risk factors in the volatile markets. As a result of more complicated risk exposures which make hedging more challenging and costly, the end user such as pension funds may have to burden the increased hedging costs.

Risks of Exotic Products

Exotic products contain more complex risks. How to capture and price in the key risks depends on the chosen model and how the model is calibrated to the vanilla markets. Naturally all exotic products have standard risk factors, such as Delta, Gamma, Vega etc. Additionally, practitioners need to pay attention to the fact that some interest rate derivative products have risk exposures to both cap/floor and swaption markets. While cap/floor market is closely related to the swaption market, they are two distinctive markets from hedging perspective. Table 14.2 lists some product categories with their characteristic risk exposures to the cap/floor and swaption markets.

In the rest of this chapter, we shall discuss some exotic products and deep dive into some of their specific product and risk features.

TABLE 14.2 Some exotic product categories

Product	Key Risk and Calibration
Non-callable LIBOR products; Pure cap/floor products (e.g. auto-caps).	Risk and calibration to the cap/floor market.
Bermudan swaption; Callable on CMS or CMS spread; Target redemption note on CMS spread.	Risk and calibration to the swaption market.
Callables on LIBOR-based payoffs such as: ■ Callable reverse floater ■ Callable range accrual ■ Knock-in or knock-out swap ■ Target redemption note	Reference index exposes to the cap/floor market and callability exposes to the swaption market. Hence need to calibrate to both cap/floor and swaption markets when practically feasible.

BERMUDAN SWAPTION

Bermudan swaptions are mainly used as hedging or positioning instruments by financial institutions. They are also embedded in some callable instruments, such as a callable swap which consists of a swap plus/minus a Bermudan swaption.

Product and Model Summary

In a bullet Bermudan swaption, the holder has the right to exercise into a swap on exercise dates. In essence, if there are N exercise dates, there will be N co-terminal swaptions (1 to N, 2 to $(N – 1)$, ..., N to 1) and one has to make an optimum decision as to which one to exercise. A schematic graph is drawn in Figure 14.6 to show the first two (1Y5Y and 2Y4Y) co-terminal swaptions in a 6Y Bermudan swaption in which there are five annual exercise dates.

Bullet Bermudan swaption is mainly sensitive to the parallel movement of the yield curve. Therefore the single factor models such as the LGM model can be adequate for pricing them in general. The calibration is co-terminal to be in line with the co-terminal European swaptions. The calibration strike can either be the contractual strike or the effective strike, which takes into account the optimal exercise boundary.

In an accreting Bermudan swaption, also known as a zero Bermudan swaption, on exercise dates the holder can exercise into an accreting swap with a pre-determined notional profile. An example accreting Bermudan swaption notional profile is shown in Figure 14.7, and the exercise dates are annual.

Accreting Bermudan swaption is often designed to hedge a zero-coupon bond. A callable zero bond is schematically shown in Figure 14.8:

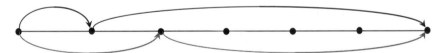

FIGURE 14.6   Diagram of co-terminal swaptions

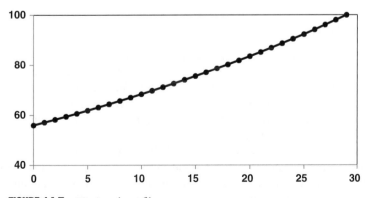

FIGURE 14.7   Notional profile

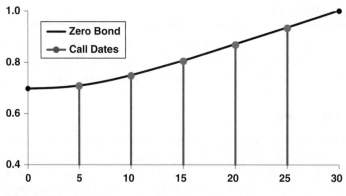

FIGURE 14.8 Callable zero bond

Accreting or amortizing Bermudan swaption payoff can be decomposed into a callable basket option. There are of course different ways of decomposing the payoff into a basket. The basket components can either share the initial starting point, which requires co-initial calibration, or share the end point, which needs co-terminal calibration.

Accreting or amortizing Bermudan swaption is sensitive correlation. Therefore how the basket is constructed can matter in practice. It is in general much better to have positive basket component weightings (a real basket option) than a mixture of positive and negative weightings (spread-type option). This is mainly because the correlation in a real basket option is technically and intuitively much easier to understand and manage than that in a spread-type option.

As for any basket options, correlation will impact prices as well as Greeks. Using a single factor model naively to price accreting or amortizing Bermudan swaptions implies that all basket components are driven by a single factor. This is equivalent to pricing a basket option with a correlation of 100%, leading to mispricing. For accreting or amortizing Bermudan swaptions, one therefore requires either a multi-factor model which naturally de-correlates the yield curve term structure, or a modified single-factor model in which the term correlations are factored into the basket decomposition and calibration process.

Economic Value Analysis

An important measure of a Bermudan swaption's economic value is the valuation difference between the Bermudan and the Most-Expensive European (MEE) swaption. In the bullet Bermudan swaption setup, there are finite number of co-terminal European swaptions. The most expensive one must be the lower boundary of the Bermudan swaption, as the holder of Bermudan has the right to exercise optimally (only once) among those European swaptions.

The gap between a Bermudan and its MEE reflects the true economic value of holding the Bermudan exercise right. The Bermudan-MEE gap need to be realized in terms of P&L during the life cycle of the Bermudan, assuming the hedging is correctly managed. It is important to emphasize that the MEE can be directly calibrated to the

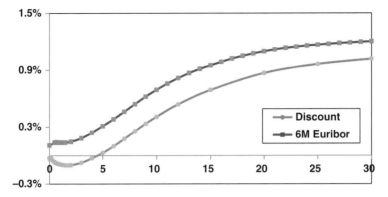

FIGURE 14.9   Yield curves

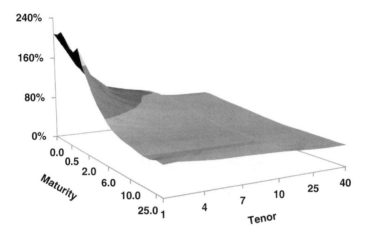

FIGURE 14.10   ATM swaption volatility surface

market European swaption quotes, and there is no or little model risk in MEE itself. Hence the Bermudan-MEE gap can also be used as a handle to assess the Bermudan model risks.

In the following, we use examples to visualize the behaviours of Bermudan and MEE. The examples Bermudans have a maturity of 30 years and they can exercise annually into a swap (annual fixed versus 6M EURIBOR). The yield curves and ATM swaption volatility surface used in the calculations are shown in Figures 14.9 and 14.10 respectively.

In Figures 14.11 and 14.12, the payer and receiver Bermudan and the corresponding MEE prices are plotted at various strikes. The Bermudan prices are always higher than the corresponding MEE prices.

In Figure 14.13, for payer and receiver, the Bermudan-MEE gap (price difference between Bermudan and MEE) versus strike is plotted. Because the gap represents the economic value of optimal (early) exercise, its peak indicates where the maximum exercise premium lies.

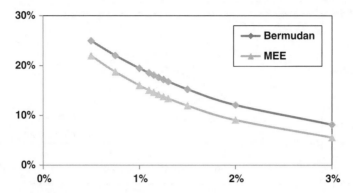

FIGURE 14.11 Payer Bermudan vs strike

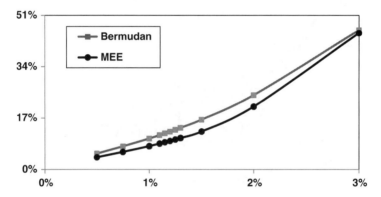

FIGURE 14.12 Receiver Bermudan vs strike

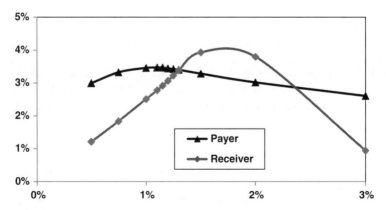

FIGURE 14.13 Bermudan-MEE gap vs strike

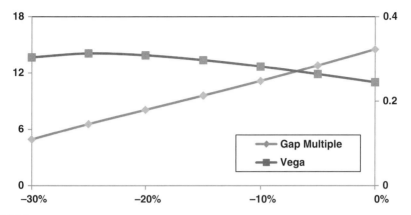

FIGURE 14.14   Gap multiple vs volatility shift. The left vertical axis labels the gap multiple and right vertical axis labels Vega. The horizontal axis is the parallel absolute shift of the ATM swaption volatility surface.

It is often convenient to measure the Bermudan-MEE gap in terms of ATM Vega (1% absolute volatility shift). The gap multiple (*gap/Vega*) is a relative measure stating how many volatility points are needed to pay for the optimal exercise premium.

In Figure 14.14, with a fixed strike of 1%, the gap multiples and Vegas are plotted against the absolute downward shifts of ATM volatility (the starting ATM volatilities are very high). The gap multiple increases or decreases linearly with the volatility, and Vega only changes moderately.

There are different ways of analysing Bermudans in practice. Bermudan-MEE gap analysis offers a reliable and intuitive handle to assess the economic value of optimal exercise, market and to some extend model risks. Therefore tracking historic Bermudan-MEE gap values will help to monitor and understand Bermudan risks. Any anomalies in the gap values can serve as early warnings to potential issues.

Volatility Exposures

Bermudan swaptions are typically hedged with European swaptions, and then supplemented by appropriate delta hedging instruments. Understanding volatility exposures is critical in managing Bermudan positions. Using the same 30-years Bermudan example, Figure 14.15 plots the ATM Vega at various strikes for the pay and receiver Bermudan swaption.

Figure 14.16 shows the ATM Vega map of a payer Bermudan with a strike of 1%. The Vega is for the maturity and tenor buckets. The bucketed volatility sensitivities are spread from 3-years to 25-years along the maturity and from 2-years to 25-years along the tenor axis.

The ATM Vega map of a receiver Bermudan of the same strike is shown in Figure 14.17. The bucketed sensitivities have similar maturity and tenor range, spreading from 3-years to 25-years along the maturity and from 2-years to 25-years along the tenor axis.

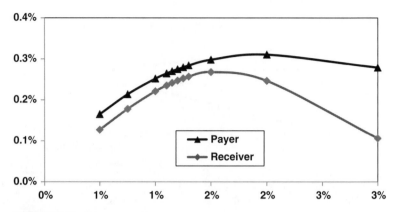

FIGURE 14.15   Vega vs strike

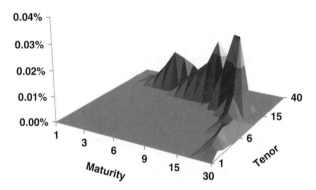

FIGURE 14.16   Vega buckets (payer)

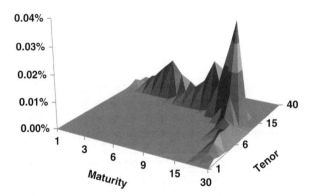

FIGURE 14.17   Vega buckets (receiver)

It is evident that to hedge a Bermudan swaption, a number of European swaptions are required in order to match the Vega buckets. Another dimension of the volatility sensitivities is, of course, the strike. The Vega map together with the volatility sensitivities along the strike (Vega cube) provide essential information for constructing European swaption hedges. The constructed European hedging portfolio should have a matching Vega cube to that of the Bermudan portfolio.

CALLABLE PRODUCTS

Callable products have higher headline coupons than their non-callable counterparts. Investors who bought callable products have effectively sold options to the issuers. Therefore the investment is exposed to more market volatility and early termination as a result. Some callable products offer initial lock-in period, for example a 20nc10 product has a 20-years maturity, and it cannot be called in the first 10 years (a lock-in period of 10 years). In the following, we shall examine a few (past or present) popular callable interest rate products.

Callable Step-up Fixed-Rate Notes

These types of note are sometimes also known as "redeemable" notes. Typically 100% capital is returned at maturity or when called. Figure 14.18 illustrates an example. It has a 10-year maturity, and fixed coupons are 1.5% for year 1 to 3, 2.3% for year 4 to 6 and 3.3% for year 7 to 10. The coupons are paid half-yearly, and the note is callable on every coupon date.

The callable step-up fixed-rate note contains an embedded Bermudan swaption with a step function strike. In practice, the issuer makes the call if it can issue a new debt at lower coupon rates, due to market interest rate and/or credit movements. As a reward for the callability, the headline fixed rates in this type of callable notes will appear to be higher than the like-for-like market interest rates. In low interest rate environments, the callable step-up fixed-rate notes can be viable products for yield enhancement. At the same time, they have relatively low risks from investors' perspective.

Callable Reverse Floaters

In the following, we shall explain the key features of callable reverse floaters. A variation of callable reverse floater known as callable snowball will also be examined.

Callable Reverse Floater Features   A reverse floater pays coupons that are inversely proportional to the reference floating rate. For example, for coupon period i the coupon can be $max[g_i \cdot (F_i - L_i), r_{min}]$, where g_i is a pre-determined gearing factor, F_i is the fixed rate, r_{min} is the minimum rate and L_i is the reference floating rate (e.g. LIBOR). In a

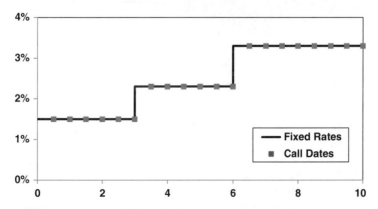

FIGURE 14.18   Callable step-up Fixed-Rate Note Coupons

callable reverse floater, the issuer has the right but not the obligation to terminate the note on any coupon date after the initial lockout period if defined.

While the callable reverse floater (CRF) payoff is rather straightforward, pricing it is not as straightforward. The coupons contain a floor or a series of floorlets, but the callable (Bermudan-style exercise) feature depends more on swaptions. From pricing model perspective, a multi-factor model is more appropriate as the product does have direct risk exposures to both cap/floor and swaption market. The model should ideally be calibrated to both cap/floor and swaption market to capture the joint risk exposures.

From the point of view of investor who bought a CRF note, the note is long caplet volatilities and short swaption volatilities beyond the lockout period. Using an example of 20nc10 (20-years expiry with 10-years non-call) CRF, Figures 14.19 and 14.20 exhibit the joint volatility sensitivities to the cap/floor and ATM swaptions respectively. The example CRF pays an annual coupon of $C_i = max(2\% - L_i, \ 0)$ which is long caplet volatilities as shown in Figure 14.19. In Figure 14.20, the note is shown to be short of swaption volatilities at expiries longer than 10-years.

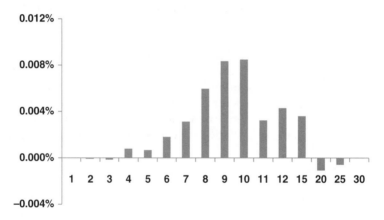

FIGURE 14.19   Caplet time bucketed volatility sensitivities
Horizontal axis is in years.

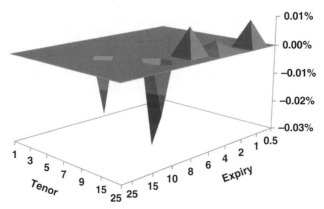

FIGURE 14.20   ATM swaption vol sensitivities
The Vega map shows the sensitivities around the 20-years
co-terminal region, including the interpolation effects.

The above joint-calibration approach is non-trivial to implement in practice. Some practitioners opt for simpler techniques to adjust the single-calibration models in order to capture some joint risk exposures. For example, if a callable model is calibrated to the swaptions only, one can adjust the price of a callable reverse floater (P_{crf}) as follows:

$$P_{crf} = P_{nc}^{cf} + \left(P_{call}^{sw} - P_{nc}^{sw}\right)$$

where P_{nc}^{cf} is the non-callable reverse floater price calibrated to cap/floor, P_{call}^{sw} is the callable and P_{nc}^{sw} the non-callable reverse floater price calibrated to the swaptions. $\Delta_{call} = P_{call}^{sw} - P_{nc}^{sw}$ represents the callability premium. P_{nc}^{cf} has the joint risk sensitivities to both cap/floor and swaption market. In the limiting case when the callability vanishes $(\Delta_{call} \to 0)$, the callable price converges to the non-callable price $(P_{crf} \to P_{nc}^{cf})$ with the correct cap/floor risk sensitivities.

Callable Snowball   A variation of callable reverse floater is the callable cumulative reverser floater, as known as callable snowball. As indicated by its name, a typical snowball coupon (C_i) pays:

$$C_i = min\left\{max\left[g_i \cdot (C_{i-1} + F_i - L_i), r_{min}\right], r_{max}\right\}$$

where C_{i-1} is the previous coupon cumulated into the current period, F_i is predetermined fixed rate, L_i is LIBOR, r_{min} and r_{max} are the minimum and maximum rate respectively.

Let us use the example in Figure 14.3 to understand the payoff features of snowball.

The value of F plays a crucial role. Figure 14.21 shows coupons at $i = 1,2...,10$ under different interest rate (L_i) scenarios when $F = 0$. In all cases, the coupons monotonically decrease over time until it is zero. This is easily explained, as when $F = 0$,

TABLE 14.3   Callable snowball example

Coupon Period	Coupon
$i = 1$	$C_1 = 6\%$
$i = 2,..., 10$	$C_i = max\left(C_{i-1} + F - L_i, 0\right)$

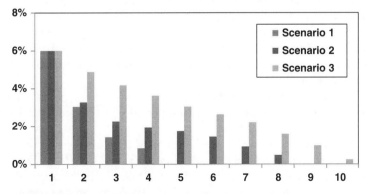

FIGURE 14.21   Snowball coupons $(F = 0)$

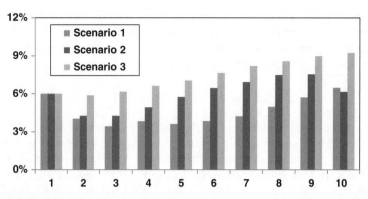

FIGURE 14.22 Snowball coupons ($F = 1\%$)

$C_i = C_{i-1} - L_i$ always decreases with L_i unless L_i is negative. This payoff has an attractive initial coupon, but coupons can deteriorate very quickly as time goes by.

For comparison purpose, the same interest rate scenarios are used to calculate coupons when $F = 1\%$, and the outcome is shown in Figure 14.22. The coupons are much healthier and the payoff features can be completely different from those of $F = 0$. From investors' perspective $F > 0$ is a much better product, although no doubt it will cost much more.

Callable Range Accrual Notes

In a typical range accrual note, one receives above-market rates (either fixed or floating) if a benchmark index (LIBOR, CMS or CMS spread) stays within a pre-determined range. To balance that, one receives sub-market rates if the benchmark index goes outside the range. In this non-callable range accrual note, investors short a series of digital caps and digital floors (short volatility) in return for higher headline coupons. The non-callable range accrual note can typically be priced by the vanilla cap/floor model, and by definition the calibration is to the cap/floor market.

A callable range accrual note (CRAN) can be called at the discretion of the issuer. The call dates typically coincide with the coupon dates. The callability will further enhance the yield as investors have sold a Bermudan style option to the issuer. Therefore in a CRAN there are cap/floor elements associated with coupons, as well as swaption elements associated with the callability. From a pricing perspective, a multi-factor model is more appropriate for pricing a CRAN as it has direct risk exposures to both cap/floor and swaption market. The model should ideally be calibrated to both cap/floor and swaptions, although there are cases where one can justify to calibrate to cap/floor only or swaptions only.

From an investor perspective, holding a CRAN is short caplet volatilities, and short swaption volatilities beyond the lockout period. In the example in Table 14.4, we examine an 20nc10 CRAN example.

Figures 14.23 and 14.24 exhibit the joint volatility sensitivities to the cap/floor and ATM swaptions respectively. In Figure 14.23, because this CRAN has embedded short digital positions it is shown to be short of caplet volatilities. Figure 14.24 shows the short swaption volatilities at expires beyond the 10-years non-call period.

FIGURE 14.4   Callable range accrual notes example

Coupon Period	Coupon
$i = 1,2...,20$	$C_i = \begin{cases} 2.5\% \text{ if } 0 \le L_i \le 4\% \\ \quad\ 0 \text{ else} \end{cases}$

The maturity is 20 years and non-call period is 10-years. After the non-call period, it is callable annually coinciding with the annual coupon dates.

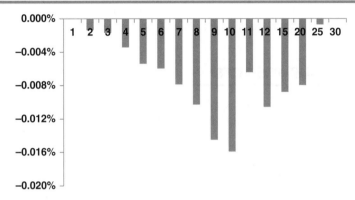

FIGURE 14.23   Caplet time bucketed volatility sensitivities
The horizontal axis is in years.

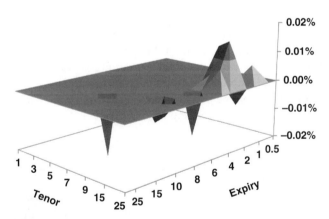

FIGURE 14.24   ATM swaption vol sensitivities
The Vega map shows the sensitivities around the 20-years co-terminal region, including the interpolation effects.

The multi-factor model with joint calibrating to both cap/floor and swaptions is non-trivial to implement in practice. Some practitioners opt for simpler techniques to adjust the single-calibration models in order to capture some joint risk exposures. For example, if a callable model is calibrated to the swaptions only, one can adjust the price of CRAN (P_{cran}) as follows:

$$P_{cran} = P_{nc}^{cf} + \left(P_{call}^{sw} - P_{nc}^{sw} \right)$$

where P_{nc}^{cf} is the non-callable range accrual price calibrated to cap/floor, P_{call}^{sw} is the callable and P_{nc}^{sw} the non-callable calibrated to the swaptions. $P_{call}^{sw} - P_{nc}^{sw}$ represents the callability premium. If the callability premium vanishes $(P_{call}^{sw} - P_{nc}^{sw}) \to 0$, the price of a CRAN automatically converges to that of the non-callable range accrual $P_{cran} \to P_{nc}^{cf}$.

Range accrual has its variations. For example, one variation is the zero coupon range accrual, which consists of a zero coupon bond plus a range accrual coupon payment stream. A maximum maturity is set in the zero coupon range accrual. The note can terminate early if the total return of the zero coupon bond and accrued coupons reaches the par. No matter of what variation it is, one needs to understand the embedded optionality and capture key risk exposures.

OTHER IMPORTANT PRODUCTS

In this section, we briefly explain a number of products including CMS products, target redemption note, volatility bond and credit-linked IRD note.

CMS Products

Many interest rate derivative products use CMS as the underlying index. CMS curves can be quite different from the yield curve from which they are derived from. Figure 14.25 shows such examples of the 2-year and 10-year CMS curves versus the original yield curve.

From investors' perspective, a CMS is a well-defined observable index when it comes to fixing. The CMS spread can be used to express a view on the changing shape of the yield curve, such as steepening. Many CMS products are designed to tailor investors' anticipation of CMS spread movement representing yield curve steepening or flattening or inverting. An example of a callable CMS steepener is shown in Table 14.5:

The dynamics of a CMS steepener is actually rather complex. Although investors' intuitions or views may be on the yield curve, CMS forward curve depends not only

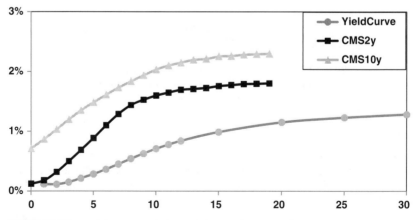

FIGURE 14.25   Yield curve and derived forward CMS curve

TABLE 14.5 Callable CMS steepener example

CMS Steepener Note	Coupons
Year 1 and Year 2	*LIBOR + spread*, the headline rate in this initial period is typically above-market, designed to be attractive.
Year 3 – Year 10	*min* {*max* [*m*(CMS10y – CMS2y), *floor*], *cap*}, *m* is the leverage factor, and the coupons can be *capped* and *floored*.

The note is callable by the issuer on the coupon dates from year 3 onwards.

Generally when the yield curve is flattening or inverting, CMS steepener note will be cheaper and offer better value to investors. However, the callable feature is against the investors as it will cut short the good payoffs soon after they occur.

TABLE 14.6 Quotes of CMS spread caps and floors

	floor	floor	floor	cap	cap	cap	cap	cap	
K →	−0.25%	−0.1%	0%	0.25%	0.5%	0.75%	1.0%	1.5%	ATM K
1y	0.1	0.2	0.2	44.7	26.9	11.8	3.6	0.3	0.83%
2y	0.5	0.8	1.2	114.2	73.7	39.3	17.3	2.7	0.88%
3y	1.4	2.1	2.8	189.8	127.1	73.5	36.8	7.5	0.91%
4y	3.1	4.5	5.7	266.0	181.9	110.0	59.0	14.2	0.92%
5y	6.3	8.7	10.9	338.4	234.3	145.3	81.3	21.9	0.91%
7y	23.8	30.1	35.5	462.1	323.8	207.1	122.5	39.9	0.85%
10y	96.5	113.4	127.0	623.6	446.3	299.7	193.1	83.6	0.71%
15y	316.1	351.7	380.3	915.1	690.4	510.5	380.9	243.0	0.56%
20y	545.5	602.3	647.6	1203.9	943.7	738.1	589.1	424.1	0.48%

on the shape of the yield curve, but also the swaption volatility and smile. Pricing CMS products requires the calibration of yield curves, swaptions and market-quoted spread options. Table 14.6 lists a set of example quotes of CMS spread caps and floors, where the price quotes are in basis points and caplet/floorlet frequency is quarterly. The underlying CMS spread is 10-years minus 2-years index (CMS10-CMS02). The spread cap/floor maturity is in years and the strike is absolute.

Calibrating to the standard spread options in the context of pricing non-callable non-standard CMS spread payoffs has been extensively discussed in the previous chapter. Economically, CMS spread options across different strikes can contain some dynamic information, such as:

- when yield curve is steepening (corresponding to increasing spread), it can lead to higher volatility potentially due to inflation expectation, etc.;
- when yield curve is inverting (corresponding to decreasing or negative spread), it can also lead to higher volatility, as typically this indicates recession scenarios and the real interest rate becomes negative.

TABLE 14.7   TARN with reverse floater example

TARN	Coupons
Year 1 and Year 2	A fixed rate F_0. The headline rate in this initial period is typically above-market, designed to be attractive.
Year 3 – Year 10	$min\{max[F - m \cdot L_i, 0], cap\}$, F is a constant, L_i is the reference index and m is the leverage factor. This coupon is a reverse floater payoff.

The note has a target/cap pre-determined at C.
Although the coupon in the initial period can be attractive, if the subsequent market-driven coupons become very low and unattractive, the investment will be stuck until maturity.

Target Redemption Note

In a typical target redemption note (TARN), the capital is protected and the sum of accumulated coupons has a cap, termed nicely as a target. The target/cap is a pre-determined constant. If the sum of accumulated coupons reaches the target/cap earlier than maturity, investors will receive a final payoff and the TARN terminates early. If the target/cap has not been reached during the lifetime of the note, investors will receive a final payoff at maturity so that the total coupons equal to the guaranteed target. The possibility of early termination is a distinctive feature of TARN.

The TARN coupons can be in a variety of payoffs, such as reverse floater, range accrual, etc. The reference index can be LIBOR, CMS or CMS spread. An example TARN with reverse floater coupons is illustrated in Table 14.7:

When the sum of accumulated coupons reaches the target/cap, the final coupon payoff can have different settlement types. Assuming one is in the last period in which the last possible coupon (denoted as X) will make the total sum exceeding the target/cap, the final coupon payoff can have the following settlement types:

1. **Receive the full coupon,** as shown in Figure 14.26, if X (the horizontal axis) is larger than the residual target (e.g. 3%). There is some digital risk for the note, but little for the final coupon payoff.
2. **Receive nothing,** as shown in Figure 14.27, if X (the horizontal axis) is larger than the residual target (e.g. 3%). There is a strong digital risk for the note and for the final coupon payoff.

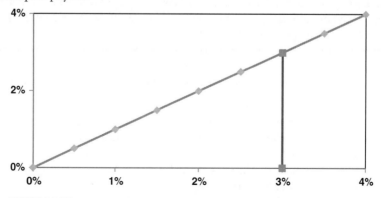

FIGURE 14.26   TARN final coupon payoff – full coupon

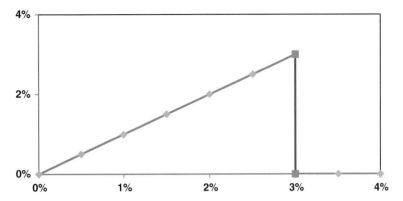

FIGURE 14.27   TARN final coupon payoff – no coupon

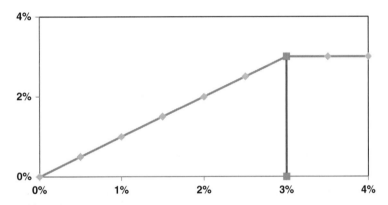

FIGURE 14.28   TARN final coupon payoff – partial coupon

3. **Receive up to the residual target,** as shown in Figure 14.28, if X (the horizontal axis) is larger than the residual target (e.g. 3%). There is a digital risk for the note and for the final coupon payoff.

Note:

- Digital risks in TARN need to be taken care of, e.g. adding softness by using call spread.
- TARN coupons can depend on other payoffs, such as reverse floater, range accrual, etc. The pricing and risks of TARN therefore should reflect the embedded option payoffs.

Intuitively the target redemption feature in TARN is analogous to a Asian barrier option where the running average is a state variable that can trigger a barrier event. In TARN, the running sum of accumulated coupons is the path-dependent state variable that can trigger a barrier knock-out. Depending on the actual coupon payoffs, the knock-out feature can be priced either by PDE or Monte Carlo technique.

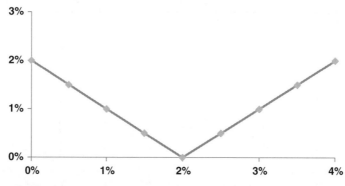

FIGURE 14.29   Vol bond coupon payoff

Volatility Bond

A volatility bond is also known as volatility note. Each of its coupons is linked to the absolute variation of a reference index over a given period. A volatility bond is essentially the sum of a series of forward start straddles:

$$V_{cpn} = \sum_{i=1}^{N} m \cdot |L_i - L_{i-1}| = \sum_{i=1}^{N} m \cdot (C_i + F_i)$$

where m is the leverage factor and L_{i-1} and L_i are the reference index at the beginning and end of each period respectively. The reference index can be LIBOR, CMS or CMS spread. C_i and F_i are the corresponding forward start caplets and floorlets.

A volatility bond coupon (straddle) payoff example is shown in Figure 14.29. Intuitively, given the embedded forward start straddles, when the implied volatility is lower and volatility surface is flatter (i.e. less smile/skew), the volatility bond is cheaper.

The volatility bond is designed to hedge the volatility exposures without taking directional risks. It can be a hedging instrument for institutions such as insurance companies, commercial banks and money managers, whose balance sheets are more exposed during the turbulent times. For example, for the holders of long-dated bonds:

- when interest rates become higher, the value of their fixed-rate bonds will fall;
- when interest rates become lower, their bond coupon income reinvests will suffer;
- the volatility bond can help to hedge both scenarios.

While the volatility bond can be an effectively hedging or positioning instrument for holders, it can be a nightmare for the sell side. As in every asset class, pricing and risk managing forward start options is never easy. Even though the de-correlation effects on forward-forward volatility could be priced in using a multi-factor term structure model, in practice the forward-forward volatility is very difficult to hedge, if at all possible. Hedging the associated strike risk, smile/skew risk and rolling risk can be expensive and ineffective. Therefore the volatility bond is in general considered to be a complex product even though its payoff sounds very simple.

Credit-Linked IRD Note

An interest rate derivative (IRD) note can also be linked to the creditworthiness of a third-party reference entity. In such a credit link IRD note, the coupon payoffs are still driven by interest rate (LIBOR or CMS) derivatives, but the capital and coupons can default due to the credit event of the third-party reference entity. If during the term of the note there is no credit event, the full capital will be redeemed at maturity. If a credit event of the reference entity occurs before maturity, the note will default and investors will only get back the recovery amount of the defaulted reference entity.

Because the capital and coupons of the note are not protected and investors have effectively sold the credit protection of the third-party reference entity to the issuer, the credit-linked note must offer investors better terms (such as higher coupons) in return. The issuer can in turn sell the reference entity credit default swap (CDS) protection on the market to receive CDS premium.

Strictly speaking, the credit-linked IRD note is a hybrid derivative product. Historically, CDS and swap rate tend to be negatively correlated. As an indicative example, using the weekly historical data between 2005 and 2015, the correlation between 5-year Citi Group CDS and 5-year USD swap rate was in the order of –45%.

Pricing and hedging credit and interest rate hybrid is a challenging task, not to mention hedging. Because the correlations between credit and interest rate mainly affect the coupons and the capital loss is primarily driven by the credit, credit-linked IRD notes can sometimes be priced and risk managed as the sum of two separate interest rate and credit derivative components. In general, however, one must assess and understand the hybrid risks, and make a sensible judgement and decision accordingly.

Four

Real Life Options and Derivatives

Real life options and derivatives (RLOD) tend to have complex behavioral and operational risks. But they do exist in real life, and many of them have a hybrid nature. The development and customisation of RLOD can be hampered by the fact that the risks are typically multi-factors and a variety of practicalities need to be managed. It is often easy to lose sight on what are the real risk factors in such a circumstance.

To deal with RLOD efficiently, it is vital to search for simpler and flexible techniques and models in the context of pricing, risk managing, reserving and capital calculations. In Part 4, we shall analyze a number of RLOD topics to understand and demystify them. By stripping away the surrounding details, we can drill down to the core part of risky elements embedded in these hybrids, and gain in depth understanding of their risk characteristics.

The RLOD topics discussed in Part 4 include:

- Long-dated FX;
- Portfolio CVA valuation techniques;
- Contingent convertibles (CoCo);
- Variable annuities;
- Interest rate optionality in fixed rate mortgages;
- Real estate derivatives;

In an increasingly tightened regulatory environment, banking and insurance industry have to deal with related RLOD topics. Some RLOD topics are directly related to the risk management and hedging of insurance solution products in the long term savings and reinsurance markets. Some RLOD topics are becoming day-to-day business ingredients in the context of building and optimising enterprise-wide risk and capital strategies.

CHAPTER 15

Long-dated FX Volatility and Hybrid Risks

Long-dated FX risks are present in many real-life situations, either in long-dated FX derivative products or in portfolio risk management such as CVA/FVA. Long-dated FX risks are mainly driven by three factors: FX spot and two yield curves of home and foreign currency. To capture and manage FX and interest rates hybrid risks which can be toxic, one needs to construct long-date FX volatility surfaces and implement appropriate hybrid pricing models.

FX VOLATILITY SURFACE

To price long-dated (e.g. up to 30 years) FX risks and manage them consistently with the short-dated hedging instruments, the entire FX volatility surface extending to the long end needs to be built. In reality, only a limited number of short-dated option or volatility quotes can be obtained directly from the market. Long-dated FX volatility surface can only be constructed by extrapolating to the long end both volatility term structure and volatility smile.

FX Volatility Market Quotes

The short end FX volatility market quotes have the following typical conventions:

- ATM volatility: quoted based on delta neutral, i.e. it is the volatility of a strike at which the call delta is the same as the put delta (with opposite sign of course).
- Smile: quoted against deltas, typically, 10% and 25% delta Risk Reversal (RR) and Butterfly (BF) are quoted.
- For a given delta (δ), $RR(\delta) = \sigma_{Call}(\delta) - \sigma_{Put}(\delta)$, $BF(\delta) = \left(\sigma_{Call}(\delta) + \sigma_{Put}(\delta)\right)/2$
- For G10 currencies, up to 2 years, quoted deltas are meant to be spot deltas (e.g. $\partial C / \partial S$). For longer than 2 years, quoted deltas are referencing forward deltas (e.g. $\partial C / \partial F$).

An example of EURUSD volatility surface quotes are shown in Table 15.1:

TABLE 15.1   Example EURUSD volatility surface quotes

Expiry	ATM	RR(10)	RR(25)	BF(10)	BF(25)
O/N	7.5%	–0.4%	–0.3%	0.3%	0.1%
1W	6.0%	–0.7%	–0.4%	0.3%	0.1%
2W	6.6%	–0.8%	–0.5%	0.3%	0.1%
3W	6.7%	–0.8%	–0.5%	0.3%	0.1%
1M	6.3%	–0.9%	–0.5%	0.4%	0.1%
2M	6.7%	–1.1%	–0.7%	0.5%	0.1%
3M	6.8%	–1.3%	–0.8%	0.7%	0.2%
6M	7.1%	–1.7%	–1.0%	0.8%	0.2%
1Y	7.6%	–2.0%	–1.1%	1.1%	0.3%
2Y	8.1%	–2.2%	–1.2%	1.0%	0.3%
3Y	8.4%	–2.3%	–1.2%	0.9%	0.3%
4Y	8.9%	–2.4%	–1.2%	0.8%	0.3%
5Y	9.3%	–2.4%	–1.2%	0.8%	0.3%

In the above quotes, the ATM volatilities have been subtracted from the *BF* quotes. These quotes can be easily rearranged into the following volatility surface as shown in Table 15.2 and plotted in Figure 15.1.

TABLE 15.2   Rearranged EURUSD volatility surface

Expiry	10P	25P	ATM	25C	10C
O/N	8.01%	7.74%	7.5%	7.49%	7.59%
1W	6.60%	6.30%	6.0%	5.90%	5.92%
2W	7.25%	6.92%	6.6%	6.47%	6.49%
3W	7.44%	7.05%	6.7%	6.58%	6.64%
1M	7.09%	6.67%	6.3%	6.17%	6.24%
2M	7.67%	7.12%	6.7%	6.47%	6.55%
3M	8.12%	7.38%	6.8%	6.63%	6.82%
6M	8.72%	7.81%	7.1%	6.86%	7.06%
1Y	9.66%	8.45%	7.6%	7.35%	7.67%
2Y	10.11%	8.91%	8.1%	7.76%	7.93%
3Y	10.50%	9.33%	8.4%	8.13%	8.22%
4Y	10.92%	9.79%	8.9%	8.59%	8.54%
5Y	11.27%	10.13%	9.3%	8.95%	8.85%

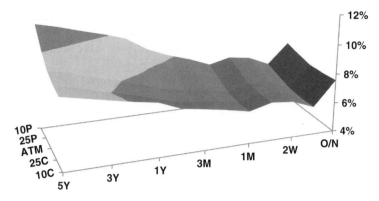

FIGURE 15.1   FX volatility surface

EXTRAPOLATING FX VOLATILITY TERM STRUCTURE TO LONG END

In the context of stochastic interest rates, it is important to make a distinction between spot FX volatility and forward FX volatility. The market-quoted FX volatilities are Black–Scholes volatilities, by definition they are the volatilities on FX forwards (forward volatilities) as they can reprice the options even if the interest rates are stochastic.

Extrapolating FX volatility term structure to the long end involves the following key steps:

- The spot volatilities need to be stripped out from the given market quotes which are forward volatilities.
- The spot volatility term structure needs to be extrapolated to the long end.
- The FX spot term structure can then be blended with volatility of the home and foreign currency interest rates to construct a long-dated FX forward volatility term structure.

Relationship Between Spot Volatility and Forward Volatility

By parity argument, the FX forward is expressed as:

$$F_{FX} = S \cdot \frac{Z_f}{Z_h}$$

where S is FX spot, Z_h and Z_f are the zero coupon bond of home and foreign currency respectively. For simplicity, the foreign zero coupon bond contains the cross-currency basis adjustment. The volatility of the long-dated FX forward is driven by the volatility of three factors: FX spot, home and foreign currency interest rates. The variance of FX forward is:

$$Var\left(dF_{FX}\right) = Var\left(dS\right) + Var\left(dZ_f\right) + Var\left(dZ_h\right)$$
$$+ 2\left[Cov\left(dS,\ dZ_f\right) - Cov\left(dS,\ dZ_h\right) - Cov\left(dZ_h,\ dZ_f\right)\right]$$

The variance and covariance of the three factor processes can be calculated analytically within the short rate model framework. Assuming FX spot (S), home currency short rate (r_h) and foreign currency short rate (r_f) have the following stochastic processes:

$$\frac{dS}{S} = (r_h - r_f)dt + \sigma dw_s$$

$$dr_h = (\mu_h - a_h r_h)dt + v_h dw_h$$

$$dr_h = (\mu_f - a_f r_f)dt + v_f dw_f$$

$$\langle dw_x dw_y \rangle = \rho_{(x,y)}dt$$

After some algebra, the volatility of the zero coupon bonds with a maturity of t in the home and foreign currencies can be derived as:

$$\sigma_h(t) = v_h \frac{1 - e^{-a_h t}}{a_h}$$

$$\sigma_f(t) = v_f \frac{1 - e^{-a_f t}}{a_f}$$

and the variance and covariance of FX spot and short rates as:

$$Var(dS) = \int_0^T \sigma^2(t)dt = \sigma_T^2 \cdot T$$

$$Var(dZ_h) = \int_0^T \sigma_h^2(t)dt = \frac{(4e^{-a_h T} - e^{-2a_h T} + 2a_h T - 3)v_h^2}{2a_h^3}$$

$$Var(dZ_f) = \int_0^T \sigma_f^2(t)dt = \frac{(4e^{-a_f T} - e^{-2a_f T} + 2a_f T - 3)v_f^2}{2a_f^3}$$

$$Cov(dS, dZ_h) = \int_0^T \rho_{(S,h)}\sigma(t)\sigma_h(t)dt = \rho_{(S,h)}\sigma_T v_h \frac{e^{-a_h T} + a_h T - 1}{a_h^2}$$

$$Cov(dS, dZ_f) = \int_0^T \rho_{(S,f)}\sigma(t)\sigma_f(t)dt = \rho_{(S,f)}\sigma_T v_f \frac{e^{-a_f T} + a_f T - 1}{a_f^2}$$

$$Cov(dZ_h, dZ_f) = \int_0^T \rho_{(h,f)}\sigma_h(t)\sigma_f(t)dt = \frac{v_h v_f}{a_h a_f}\left(\frac{1 - e^{-(a_h + a_f)T}}{a_h + a_f} + \frac{e^{-a_h T} -}{a_h} + \frac{e^{-a_f T} -}{a_f} + T\right)$$

The model and market parameters (a_h, v_h, a_f, v_f) can be calibrated to the market-quoted swaption volatility surface. Therefore using the forward variance equation:

- Knowing the variance and covariance of FX spot and short rates, the FX forward variance $Var(dF_{FX})$ can be obtained. FX forward volatility is $\sigma_F = \sqrt{Var(dF_{FX})/T}$.

- Knowing the FX forward variance $Var(dF_{FX})$, the forward variance equation becomes a quadratic equation for the FX spot volatility (σ_T). So σ_T can be obtained by solving a simple quadratic equation.

Spot Volatility Term Structure

After stripping out the short end spot volatilities from the quoted forward volatilities, one needs to build a spot volatility term structure, either by extrapolation or fitting a functional form. While flat extrapolation has its logic, a plausible functional form can provide better numerical stability and a reliable handle.

In the following, we derive a functional form assuming the instantaneous volatility-squared ($V_t = \sigma_t^2$) follows the Ornstein–Uhlenbeck (mean-reverting) process:

$$dV_t = \alpha\left(V_\infty - V_t\right)dt + \theta V_\infty dW_t$$

where α, V_∞, θ are constants and dW_t is the standard Wiener process. The integral solution of the above is:

$$V_t = V_\infty + \left(V_0 - V_\infty\right)e^{-\alpha t} + \theta V_\infty \int_0^t e^{-\alpha(t-s)}dW_s$$

The term volatility-squared at time T is:

$$\sigma_T^2 = \frac{1}{T}\int_0^T V_t dt$$

$$= \sigma_\infty^2 + \left(\sigma_0^2 - \sigma_\infty^2\right)\frac{1-e^{-\alpha T}}{\alpha T} + \theta \cdot \sigma_\infty^2 \cdot \int_0^T \frac{1-e^{-\alpha(T-t)}}{\alpha T}dW_t$$

The expected volatility-squared term structure therefore has the following functional form:

$$\sigma^2(T) = \left\langle\sigma_T^2\right\rangle = \sigma_\infty^2 + \left(\sigma_0^2 - \sigma_\infty^2\right)\frac{1-e^{-\alpha T}}{\alpha T}$$

and:

$$\sigma(\infty) = \sigma_\infty$$

$$\sigma(0) = \sigma_0$$

$$\frac{\partial\sigma(T)}{\partial T}\bigg|_{T\to\infty} = 0$$

By fitting to the short end market volatilities, the parameters (σ_∞, σ_0, α) can be obtained numerically using optimization techniques, such as Levenberg–Marquardt.

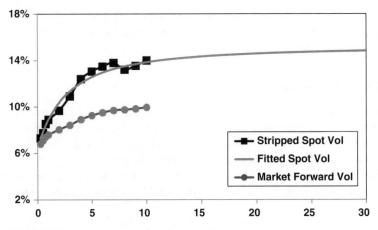

FIGURE 15.2 Stripped and fitted spot vol term structure

Since the intention is to use the functional form to extrapolate the long end volatilities, the parameters of the functional form should be fitted to medium-term (e.g. between 3 month or 5 years) data, rather than the very short end (0 to 3 months). The very short-dated FX volatilities are often driven by events.

Figure 15.2 shows an example of fitted spot volatility term structure. The short end spot volatilities are stripped from the short end market forward volatilities. The functional form is then fitted to the short end stripped spot volatilities resulting in a fitted long-dated spot volatility term structure.

Forward Volatility Term Structure

Once the spot volatility term structure is obtained, the forward volatility term structure can be constructed using the forward variance equation. Using the fitted spot volatility term structure in the example above, the constructed forward volatility term structure is shown in Figure 15.3.

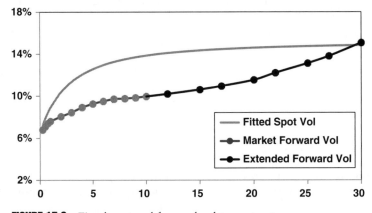

FIGURE 15.3 Fitted spot and forward vol term structure

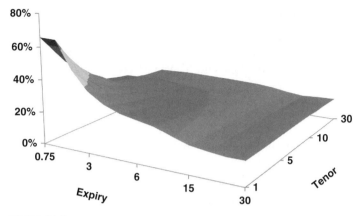

FIGURE 15.4   Swaption ATM vol surface (Home Ccy)

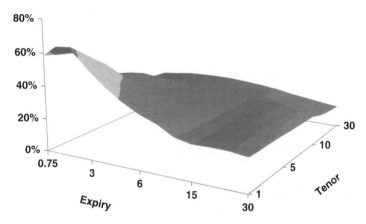

FIGURE 15.5   Swaption ATM vol surface (Foreign Ccy)

The home and foreign currency swaption ATM volatility surfaces used in the calculations are displayed in Figures 15.4 and 15.5.

The correlations used in the calculations are $\rho_{(s,h)} = -40\%$, $\rho_{(s,f)} = 45\%$ and $\rho_{(h,f)} = 20\%$. Note that the long end FX forward volatilities are heavily dependent on correlations. Although historic correlations can give sensible guidance, one will need to adjust them according to prevailing market conditions including central banks' monetary policies which impact $\rho_{(h,f)}$ most. The correlations need to be "calibrated" to the available market data or consensus one way or another.

EXTRAPOLATING FX VOLATILITY SMILE TO LONG END

In this section, the non-arbitrage smile boundaries will be examined, and extrapolation using smile boundaries will be discussed.

Non-arbitrage Smile Boundaries

As shown in chapter 4, when the Black–Scholes implied volatility is quoted against the strike, i.e. in the K space, the smile/skew boundary formulae can be used to extrapolate the short end smile/skew to the long end. The smile/skew at a given maturity T satisfies:

$$b_{skew} \leq \frac{\Delta \sigma}{\Delta K} \leq b_{smile}$$

where the non-arbitrage smile/skew boundaries are given by:

$$b_{smile} = -\frac{\partial C}{\partial K}\left(\frac{\partial C}{\partial \sigma}\right)^{-1} = \frac{N(d_2)}{KN'(d_2)\sqrt{T}} \qquad b_{skew} = -\frac{\partial P}{\partial K}\left(\frac{\partial P}{\partial \sigma}\right)^{-1} = \frac{[N(d_2)-1]}{KN'(d_2)\sqrt{T}}$$

Both b_{smile} and b_{skew} are functions of T and they can be used to extrapolate the short end smile to the long end in the K space.

In FX, however, the implied volatilities are quoted against deltas, mostly forward deltas. Therefore one needs to make the necessary conversion between the delta and K space. Denoting the option forward delta as δ, the non-arbitrage smile boundaries in the delta space are:

$$b_c^\delta = -\frac{\partial C}{\partial \delta}\left(\frac{\partial C}{\partial \sigma}\right)^{-1} \qquad b_p^\delta = -\frac{\partial P}{\partial \delta}\left(\frac{\partial P}{\partial \sigma}\right)^{-1}$$

For the call and put, Table 15.3 illustrates the steps taken to derive b_c^δ and b_p^δ:

Extrapolation Using Smile Boundaries

Figure 15.6 plots the delta space ATM smile boundaries (b_c^δ, b_p^δ) across different maturities, using $\sigma_{atm} = 10\%$, $r_h = 3\%$ and $r_f = 1\%$.

Unlike the typical decay patterns observed in the K space, the smile boundaries in the delta space are much flatter. This is illustrated in Figure 15.7, in which the equivalent boundary in the K and δ space are compared.

The reason for the above is that for a fixed delta difference (e.g. between 50C and 49C), the strike differences between them increase with the maturity, which offsets the K space decay and makes the delta space decay much flatter. Figure 15.8 plots an example of the strike differences per 1 delta change at different maturities, using $S = K = 1.141$, $\sigma_{atm} = 10\%$, $r_h = 3\%$ and $r_f = 1\%$.

To use the non-arbitrage boundaries to extrapolate the short end (e.g. 5-year) smile to the long end, the following steps can be taken:

1) At the extrapolation starting point, e.g. 5Y, calculate ATM smile boundaries $b_c^\delta(5Y)$ and $b_p^\delta(5Y)$.
2) For a given longer maturity T, calculate ATM smile boundary decay ratios, $R_c(T) = b_c^\delta(T)/b_c^\delta(5Y)$ and $R_p(T) = b_p^\delta(T)/b_p^\delta(5Y)$.

TABLE 15.3 Smile boundary derivation steps

Call	Put
$$\frac{\partial C}{\partial \delta} = \frac{\partial C}{\partial K} \cdot \frac{\partial K}{\partial \delta} = \frac{\partial C}{\partial K}\left(\frac{\partial \delta}{\partial K}\right)^{-1}$$	$$\frac{\partial P}{\partial \delta} = \frac{\partial P}{\partial K} \cdot \frac{\partial K}{\partial \delta} = \frac{\partial P}{\partial K}\left(\frac{\partial \delta}{\partial K}\right)^{-1}$$
therefore: $$b_c^\delta = b_{smile}\left(\frac{\partial \delta}{\partial K}\right)^{-1}$$	therefore: $$b_p^\delta = b_{skew}\left(\frac{\partial \delta}{\partial K}\right)^{-1}$$
For a call option, the FX forward delta is the ratio of the change in option PV to the change in forward PV, namely: $$\delta = \frac{\partial C}{\partial\left(Fe^{-r_b T}\right)} = \frac{\partial C}{\partial S} e^{r_f T} = N(d_1)$$ therefore: $$\frac{\partial \delta}{\partial K} = -N'(d_1)\frac{1}{K\sigma\sqrt{T}}$$	For a put option, the FX forward delta is the ratio of the change in option PV to the change in forward PV, namely: $$\delta = \frac{\partial P}{\partial\left(Fe^{-r_b T}\right)} = \frac{\partial P}{\partial S} e^{r_f T} = N(d_1) - 1$$ therefore: $$\frac{\partial \delta}{\partial K} = -N'(d_1)\frac{1}{K\sigma\sqrt{T}}$$
Hence: $$b_c^\delta = -\frac{\sigma N(d_2)}{N'(d_1)N'(d_2)}$$	Hence: $$b_p^\delta = \frac{\sigma\left[1 - N(d_2)\right]}{N'(d_1)N'(d_2)}$$

Note that $b_c^\delta < 0$ and $b_p^\delta > 0$, the smile in the delta space is therefore bound by:

$$b_{low} \le \frac{\Delta\sigma}{\Delta\delta} \le b_{up}$$

The smile boundaries in the delta space can be used to extrapolate the short end FX smile to the long end, ensuring it stays within the non-arbitrage band.

Compared to the boundaries in the K space, the delta space boundaries (b_c^δ, b_p^δ) no longer have the $1/\sqrt{T}$ decay factor.

3) Assuming the call and put delta space smile at the starting point (5Y) are $S_c(5Y)$ and $S_p(5Y)$ respectively, the call and put smile at T is extrapolated as $R_c(T) \cdot S_c(5Y)$ and $R_p(T) \cdot S_p(5Y)$ respectively.

Using the above methodology, a market-quoted FX volatility surface shown earlier in this chapter is extrapolated into a long-dated FX volatility surface, including extrapolated long end term structure and smile as shown in Figure 15.9.

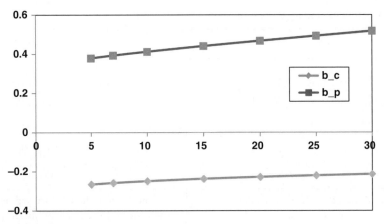

FIGURE 15.6 Smile/Skew δ space boundaries
Horizontal axis is the maturity in years.

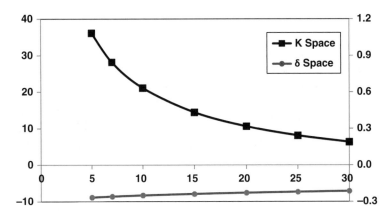

FIGURE 15.7 FX smile boundaries in K and δ space
K space boundary is labelled by left vertical axis and delta space by the right vertical axis. Horizontal axis is the maturity in years.

HYBRID OPTIONALITY

Modelling FX and interest rates hybrids is non-trivial in practice, considering both FX and interest rate options exhibit pronounced volatility smile/skew. These types of hybrids are in general quite complex and difficult to manage. Sometimes it is appropriate to simplify the overall modelling framework provided the principal hybrid risks can be captured. For example, sometimes one "ignores" the interest rate smile by incorporating standard short rate dynamics into FX smile models (e.g. FX stochastic local volatility model). In certain practical cases, both interest rate and FX smile are "ignored" in

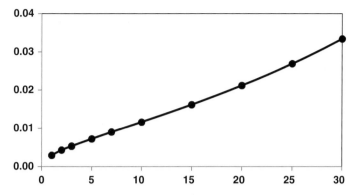

FIGURE 15.8 $\Delta K/\Delta\delta$ at different maturities
Horizontal axis is the maturity in years.

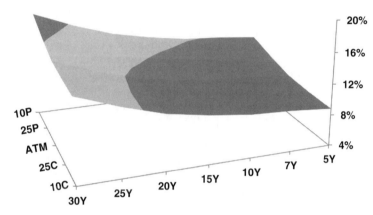

FIGURE 15.9 Long-dated FX volatility surface

order to relieve modelling and computational burden. The complex details on FX and interest rates hybrid models can be found in public domain literatures. In the following, we shall focus on understanding intuitively FX and interest rates hybrid risks.

PRDC Example

We shall use a Power Reverse Dual Currency (PRDC) swap as an example, to illustrate the embedded hybrid optionality and the associated risks. A PRDC trade typically involves three parties: investors, an issuer and a swap house (hedger). The cash flows are shown in Figure 15.10:

There are three key dates when important cash flows occur: the issue date, the coupon date and the maturity date **or** the date when the structure is called in the case of callable PRDC. Using USDJPY currency pair, detailed cash flows including coupons and notional exchanges are listed in Table 15.4.

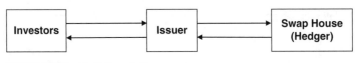

FIGURE 15.10 PRDC cash flows

TABLE 15.4 PRDC cash flows

	On Issue Date	On Coupon Dates	On Maturity Date OR Being Called
Investors	Pay JPY notional.	Receive FX-linked coupons (in JPY).	Receive JPY notional.
Issuer (The goal is to achieve favour-able sub-market USD funding)	Receive JPY notional. Pay JPY notional to the swap house. Receive USD notional from the swap house.	Receive FX-linked coupons (in JPY) from the swap house. Pay FX-linked coupons (in JPY) to investors. Pay USD sub-market coupons to the swap house.	Received JPY Notional. Pay JPY notional to investors. Pay USD notional to the swap house.
Swap House	Receive JPY notional. Pay USD notional.	Receive USD sub-market coupons. Pay FX-linked coupons (in JPY).	Received JPY notional. Pay JPY notional.

Note: A PRDC is usually structured as callable. The swap house that pays out the FX-linked coupons retains the right to call the entire structure on specified dates. The callable PRDC swap can be synthesized as a non-callable PRDC swap plus a Bermudan style swaption to enter an opposite swap.

From the point of view of the swap house, in addition to the initial and final notional exchanges, on the coupon dates, the following cash flows will occur:

- Receive leg: USD sub-market coupons $(L_i + s)$, L_i is LIBOR and s is spread.
- Pay leg: FX-linked coupon (in JPY) C_i. C_i can be a vanilla FX call option or collar, for example.
  The swap value (in JPY) of the above two legs is $V_0 = PV_{rec} = PV_{pay}$.

Optionality in Non-callable PRDC

Denoting N^{USD} as USD notional and N^{JPY} as JPY notional, for the non-callable swap:

$$PV_{rec} = \sum (L_i + s) \cdot D_t^{USD} \cdot FX_0 + N^{USD} \cdot D_T^{USD} \cdot FX_0 + N^{JPY}$$

$$PV_{pay} = N^{JPY} \cdot \sum C_i + N^{JPY} \cdot D_T^{JPY} + N^{USD} \cdot FX_0$$

Where D_t^{JPY} is the JPY discount factor and D_t^{USD} is the basis-adjusted USD discount factor. Given that:

$$\sum L_i \cdot D_t^{USD} \cdot FX_0 + N^{USD} \cdot D_T^{USD} \cdot FX_0 = N^{USD} \cdot FX_0$$

the swap value is:

$$V_0 = PV_{rec} - PV_{pay}$$

$$= \left[\sum s \cdot D_t^{USD} \cdot FX_0 + N^{JPY} \cdot \left(1 - D_T^{JPY}\right) \right] - N^{JPY} \cdot \sum C_i$$

The equation shows that the net PRDC swap position is a series of short FX call options, and the option maturities are on the coupon dates.

Optionality in Callable PRDC

For the callable PRDC swap, the swap value at time t is:

$$V_t = max\left(V_{rollback}, 0\right)$$

where $V_{rollback}$ is the swap value which includes embedded FX calls. Hence the swap value V_t will behave like a complex put-on-call compound option, with Bermudan exercise style.

When a PRDC swap is called, the intrinsic value resulted from the final notional exchange has the form:

$$V_{intrinsic} = N^{USD} \cdot FX_0 - N^{JPY}$$

Note that after the swap is called, the intrinsic value is a linear function of FX spot.

PRDC HYBRID RISKS

In this section, the risk sensitivities of non-callable and callable PRDC swap are analysed and compared. The example trade used for analysis is a USDJPY PRDC swap with a maturity of 30 years. There are the usual initial and final notional exchanges, and on coupon dates, the following cash flows occur:

- Receive leg: 3-month USD LIBOR.
- Pay leg: annual coupon in JPY linked to FX option: $max\left(X \cdot FX_t / FX_0 - Y, 0\right)$, where X and Y are pre-determined constants. In the callable PRDC case, the FX coupon payer has the option to call (off) the deal on the payer coupon dates.

FX Spot Sensitivity

The FX spot profiles for non-callable and callable PRDC are shown in Figure 15.11.

As shown in the figure, non-callable and callable PRDC exhibit very different characters:

- For a non-callable PRDC, as it is short a series of FX calls, when spot goes up, the price goes down.
- For a callable counterpart, at lower spot, the swap behaves like a put-on-call compound option. The profile there tends to be less varying. When spot goes up, at some point, the swap will be called and the option exercised into the intrinsic

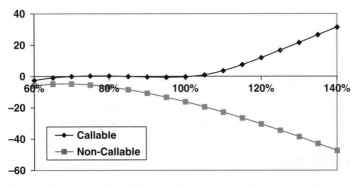

FIGURE 15.11 Price vs spot

value. From that point onwards, given the exercised intrinsic value is proportional to the FX spot as discussed earlier, the spot profile is a straight line upwards.

FX Volatility Sensitivity

The time-bucketed FX volatility sensitivities with 0.5% bump are shown in Figure 15.12:

- For the non-callable, the time-bucketed Vega profile is typical of a series of short FX call options. At the short end, the calls are very much in-the-money, the Vega is small. At the long end, given the FX forward is downwards trending (JPY rate is lower than USD rate), the calls are less in-the-money, hence larger Vega exposures are observed.
- For the callable, the Bermudan style compound option (put-on-call) is responsible for the wave-like Vega profile. There are two competing factors embedded in the callable PRDC swap. One is from the compounding puts, and the other is from the short call options. At the short end, the compounding puts on the long-dated calls are dominant, and they show positive Vega exposures. At the long end, the long-dated calls are more dominant, and they show negative Vega exposures.

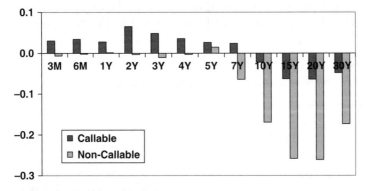

FIGURE 15.12 Time-bucketed FX Vega

The time-bucketed FX volatility sensitivities at the short end are very different from those at the long end. It is conceivable that the second order Greeks may not be negligible. The shapes of the sensitivity profiles can change depending on where the FX spot is. These make it difficult to use the short end FX volatility hedging the long end Vega exposures.

Interest Rates and Basis Sensitivity

The home currency (JPY) time-bucketed interest rate sensitivities with 10bps bump are plotted in Figure 15.13:

- For the non-callable, the sensitivities in the buckets before the maturity come from those of series FX calls. Given the corresponding forwards will increase for increased JPY rates, for short calls, negative sensitivities are expected. For the bucket including the maturity date, as V_0 is affected by D_T^{JPY}, a positive JPY exposure is expected.
- For the callable, the sensitivity profile should be similar to that of the non-callable, although the magnitudes differ. The callable behaves like a compound option, which tends to have lower magnitude in interest rate sensitivities.

The foreign currency (USD) time-bucketed interest rate sensitivities with 10bps bump are plotted in Figure 15.14:

- For the non-callable, all the bucket sensitivities including the one at maturity come from those of a series FX calls. Given the corresponding forwards will decrease for increased USD rates, for short calls, positive exposures are expected.
- For the callable, the sensitivity profile should be similar to that of the non-callable, although the magnitudes differ. The callable behaves like a compound option, which tends to have lower magnitude in interest rate sensitivities.

The time-bucketed basis sensitivities with 10bps bump are plotted in Figure 15.15:

- For the non-callable, as the basis curve mainly affects the FX forwards, the sensitivities are mainly due to short FX calls. Increased basis will increase the FX forwards, therefore negative basis exposures are observed.

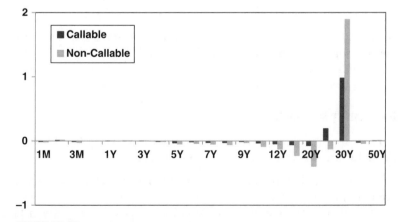

FIGURE 15.13 JPY interest rate sensitivities

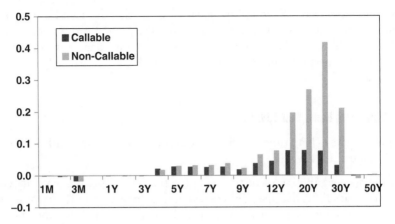

FIGURE 15.14   USD interest rate sensitivities

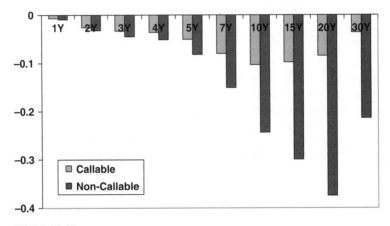

FIGURE 15.15   Basis sensitivity

- For the callable, the sensitivity profile should be similar to that of the non-callable, although the magnitudes differ. The callable behaves like a compound option, which tends to have lower magnitude in sensitivity.

Swaption Volatility Sensitivity

The ATM swaption volatility sensitivities with 10bps bump for the non-callable and callable PDRC are shown in Figures 15.16 and 15.17:

- For the non-callable, the swaption sensitivities are relatively small since the net positions are short FX calls.
- For the callable, the swaption sensitivities are positive and much larger. This is because the Bermudan-style callability is long swaption volatility.

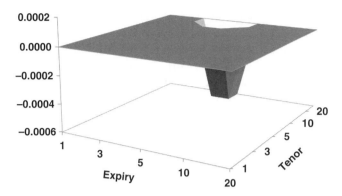

FIGURE 15.16   ATM swaption vol sensitivity (non-callable)

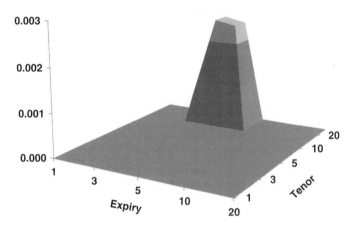

FIGURE 15.17   ATM swaption vol sensitivity (callable)

Correlation Sensitivity

The correlation sensitivity with 10bps bump for non-callable and callable PDRC is compared in Figure 15.18. The correlation is between JPY interest rate and FX rate

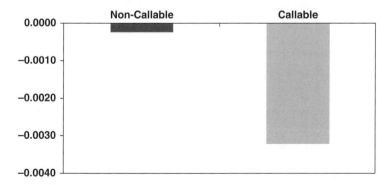

FIGURE 15.18   Correlation sensitivity

USDJPY. As can be seen in the graph, the correlation has a much bigger impact on the callable.

The hybrid risks in (callable) long-dated FX structures are difficult to manage in real life. Hedging long-dated FX Vega exposures can be very challenging, and hedging long-dated correlation exposures is close to impossible. Correlation had in the past caused big losses in banks' PRDC positions. It remains the biggest un-hedgeable risk factor in hybrid derivatives.

CHAPTER 16

Portfolio CVA: Efficient Numerical Techniques

Credit Value Adjustment (CVA) is a measure of credit risk exposures, and it has direct economic impacts on banks' profit and loss (P&L) under International Accounting Standard (IAS) 39, as accounting CVA contributes to P&L. CVA VaR and CVA Stressed VaR are also part of the RWA calculations, hence in turn impacting capital ratios under Basel III. CVA's flip side is Debit Value Adjustment (DVA) which includes own credit risks and issuer risks, etc.

CVA models are of hybrid nature. To a large extent CVA is akin to a credit contingent option on a portfolio of derivative instruments across asset classes. The computational overload is beyond many traditional derivatives business setups, and the associated risk measure and management systems are extremely demanding computationally.

Portfolio CVA valuation presents serious challenges to banks, as its implementation postulates a worst-case mixture: complex hybrid derivative modelling on large portfolios within enterprise-wide risk systems. This unique technical mixture makes it very difficult for banks to decide a practical and successful CVA implementation strategy. As far as CVA technologies are concerned, one should avoid the extreme of focusing too much on complex models. Equally one should avoid the other extreme of relying on traditional brute force risk systems. It is important to understand the specific features in CVA valuation and blend hybrid modelling effectively with the risk system implementation. An enhanced CVA numerical technique will not only represent an important quantitative advance, but also have a direct impact on banks' enterprise-wide CVA infrastructure design and its success.

In the following, we shall first give an overview of CVA modelling and valuation framework, followed by the outline of various numerical techniques for portfolio CVA valuation employed by the industry. We will then propose and discuss an efficient numerical technique, Grid Monte Carlo, which can be very effective in addressing the toxic mix of using Monte Carlo for large portfolios in risk systems.

CVA VALUATION IMPLEMENTATION FRAMEWORK

CVA bears all the hallmarks of hybrid derivatives. At the portfolio (a netting set) level, it is a credit contingent option on a basket of different instruments. The basket underlyings can be multi-asset and multi-currency, with a complex correlation structure. More often than not, the relevant positions are very long-dated, and the credit positions are subject to closing-out and funding assumptions. CVA is indeed a complex hybrid derivative problem. As most of the practitioners know, the hybrid models and their trading platforms are difficult to build, never mind hedging in practice. In the past, some practitioners may choose to avoid certain hybrid products or risks from product perspective for practical reasons. In the context of CVA, however, there is not much choice but to face up to CVA hybrid reality, given the counterparty risks of sizeable positions banks have. So, one will have to deal with all the difficult problems associated with long-dated hybrids, including modelling and numerical implementations, as well as other practical aspects, such as unobservable market data including correlations, jumps, long-dated volatilities, etc.

CVA and counterparty risks are very different from the traditional VaR type of risk factors in many aspects. Hence CVA framework design needs to recognize the facts, and avoid simplistic usage of the traditional risk system (e.g. VaR) framework. Simplistic usage of traditional systems with brute force for CVA valuation and risk sensitivities can be a very costly exercise, in dollars, operations, maintenance and computational burden. It is, however, possible to refine and modify the traditional risk systems to come up with a practical CVA valuation framework that is driven by efficient CVA numerical techniques, consisting of the following key elements:

- multi-factor RN (Risk-Neutral) scenario generation engines with appropriate calibrations;
- efficient numerical pricing functions and integrated EPE (Expected Positive Exposure) calculations that are consistent with the RN scenarios;
- advanced Greeks techniques (as opposed to brute force bumping).

NUMERICAL TECHNIQUES IN PORTFOLIO CVA VALUATION

There are two key numerical components in portfolio CVA valuation. The first is the multi-factor RN scenarios generation engine that includes calibrations. The second is the Monte Carlo pricer, for portfolios of a large number of instruments, at many forward points along the scenario paths. This is by definition a very computationally intensive process. Of course one can immediately think of using the latest computing architecture, e.g. Graphic Processing Units (GPU), but it is always better to first of all get the fundamental valuation design right. With optimized and efficient numerical techniques that are core to CVA valuation, the GPU can be leveraged more effectively and almost surely with much smaller costs.

The implementation of multi-factor RN scenario generation engine can be made modular and stand-alone. It should employ the same numerical routines and pricing models used in the front office, such as multi-dimensional Sobol, multi-currency swaption and FX option calibration tools, to name a few. Of course, one also needs to deal with correlation matrix calibration, long-dated market data, and general data cleaning issues, and so on. None of these tasks is trivial in practice, but there are standard methods and processes to follow.

The implementation of Monte Carlo pricer is very varied. Broadly speaking, there are two categories. One is the direct-call method. At each scenario point in time/state, the pricing model of the relevant derivative instrument is called directly in its entirety. For example, one can call a front office swaption model directly on the fly along a scenario path, passing in the prevailing forward market data. The direct call method obviously saves the need for re-implementing the instrument pricing models. However, it can be inconsistent with RN scenarios, e.g. in handling the forward volatilities. The main disadvantage though, is that it has much less room for computational efficiency gains. As the model pricer is effectively a black box, typically shared with the front office, one can only resort to techniques of reducing the number of calculations along and among the scenario paths, such as principal component analysis (PCA).

The other method of Monte Carlo pricing is the on-board scenario pricing, namely, at each scenario point in time/state, one specifically computes the conditional expectations for EPE, etc. The computation will naturally be consistent with RN scenarios. It can also be made fully consistent with the front office pricing models if the bank has a unified quantitative library written in object-oriented modules which can be shared. The on-board method has ample room for numerical optimization and computational efficiency gains. In the following, we shall focus on the on-board method, and discuss ways of achieving computational gains.

The CVA and EPE are defined as:

$$CVA = (1 - R) \int_0^T EPE_t \cdot dP_t$$

$$EPE_t = E^Q \left[DF_t \cdot max \left(V_t(\bar{x}) - C, 0 \right) \right]$$

where R is the recovery rate, DF_t the discount factor, C the collateral, and $V_t(\bar{x})$ is the conditional expectation of future portfolio value, for the given state variable $\bar{x}$. **The key question is how to compute the conditional expectation $V_t(\bar{x})$ efficiently.**

The conditional expectation for a portfolio of instrument is given by:

$$V_t(\bar{x}) = \sum_{i=1}^{N} v_t^i(\bar{x})$$

where $v_t^i(\bar{x})$ is the time t conditional expectation of i-th instrument in the portfolio. For a linear instrument, for example a swap value, $v_t^i(\bar{x})$ can be obtained efficiently including using analytical solutions on a path-by-path basis. For a simple nonlinear instrument, for example a European swaption, the conditional expectation can be also be valued either analytically on a path-by-path basis, or can be solved numerically using PDE. For a more exotic instrument, such as Bermudan swaption, one has to calculate the conditional expectation numerically. Given that all the valuations are done in a global Monte Carlo framework, the most obvious and least efficient way is to use brute force Monte Carlo. In such a scheme, at each scenario point, one does the Monte

Carlo pricing for the relevant derivative instrument, and this is repeated for all scenario points, over many scenarios. In this nested Monte Carlo approach, each inner scenario corresponding to many outer scenarios, which makes the nested Monte Carlo using brute force extremely computational intensive. As a very effective alternative, American Monte Carlo (AMC) (Longstaff and Schwartz) has been deployed to substantially reduce the computational burdens in CVA (Cesari et al). AMC uses least-square regression which has a capability of combining scenario generation and instrument pricing at the same time. Hence in AMC, one inner scenario corresponds to one outer scenario, and it is far superior to nested Monte Carlo for CVA valuations. However, given the huge scale in portfolio CVA valuation and Greeks calculation, a fundamentally better technique is called for to improve the overall situation substantially, in computational efficiency and accuracy.

GRID MONTE CARLO FOR CVA

Monte Carlo CVA pricing technique based on Grid (Qu and Zhu) can be very efficient and versatile. In essence, the Grid Monte Carlo (GMC) technique combines grids of forward values with the scenario paths. One first generates grids of forward values for all relevant instruments and states, then runs Monte Carlo scenario paths through them. Each scenario time point can be included in the grids. As illustrated in Figure 16.1, GMC consists of the following key steps:

1. generating raw Grids of forward values for the relevant instruments in the portfolio, e.g. using PDEs. This step is vital, and yet it can be done using relatively simple and standard derivative pricing models and techniques;
2. superimposing risk-neutral scenarios on to the Grids, effectively Monte Carlo within the Grids;
3. computing conditional expectations by sampling the Grids and interpolating.

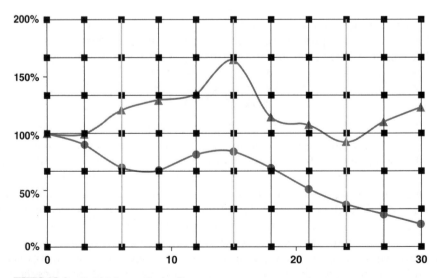

FIGURE 16.1 Grid Monte Carlo diagram

Each and every one of the three GMC steps can be computationally very efficient, given they are all standard and simple quantitative and numerical techniques. This fundamental simplicity explains why GMC implementation can be very efficient and accurate. In calculating conditional expectations from the raw grids, it is important to note that the conditional expectation values can be path-dependent. One needs to take into account various states determined by some specific instrument features, e.g. option exercise dates in cap/floor/swaption, as marked by every third vertical line in the graph. For a given portfolio (netting set), the Grids of the instruments in the portfolio can be constructed by the following rules:

- If a underlying instrument is linear without optionalities, e.g. standard swaps, the instrument grid values are simply the future values and can be obtained analytically.
- If a underlying instrument is a vanilla option with cash settlement on exercise, the instrument grid values are also simply the future values by PDE or analytically.
- If a underlying instrument is an option with physical or non-standard cash settlement, then there will be two time-dependent states due to option exercise feature.

Using a physically settled European swaption as example, the following illustrates how to take into account option exercise feature in computing conditional expectation. The conditional expectation $v_i(t)$ at time t is given by:

$$v_i(t) = E^Q\left[v_{swap}^+(T)\middle|t\right] \qquad\qquad t < T$$
$$v_i(t) = v_{swap}(t) \cdot 1_{\{v_{swap}(T)>0\}} \qquad\qquad t \geq T$$

where T is the swaption expiry. In the formulae, the conditional expectation is state- and time-dependent. It can be either a forward swaption or swap value after option expiry and exercise. Similarly for a Bermudan swaption, as a scenario passing through a given option exercise date, there are two possible states just after the exercise date: a swaption position if it is NOT exercised, or a swap position if it is exercised. Both states (exercise and not exercise) have their own grid, and both state (swaption and swap) grid need to be included in the portfolio grids for later conditional interpolation. To facilitate swaption exercise decision, one can first of all work out the optimal exercise boundary using PDE. For each (and entire) Monte Carlo scenario path, one can take the earliest point that is exercised, and assign all the subsequent points on the path with swap values. There will be two grids to choose from, either Bermudan grid or swap grid, depending on exercise status. The above can be clearly illustrated in Figure 16.2. Assuming the optimum exercise boundary is already calculated, at the large point on the central line (an exercise date), the exercise decision is known. Post the exercise at the slightly off-centre black point, and there are two possible states (Bermudan swaption or swap). Depending on the decision made at central point, the appropriate state grid at second point is sampled accordingly in the calculation of conditional expectation.

For other more complex instruments, the principle is the same: one needs to take into account various states due to exercise decisions or other features, and include those state grids at the portfolio level. Hence for a portfolio (netting set) of instruments, the collection of state grids consists of the grids for each instrument in the portfolio, plus additional exercise and/or feature grids. All grid values can be pre-calculated only once, and stored in memory. Multi-factor RN Monte Carlo scenarios can then be

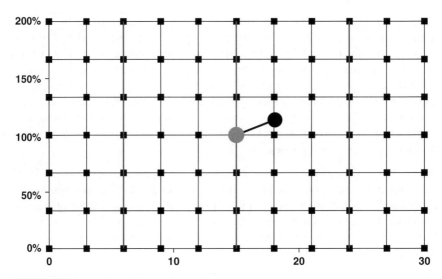

FIGURE 16.2 Exercise and post-exercise states

TABLE 16.1 Storage optimization

Storage	Description	Key Feature
State Variable Grid	The storage size is a function state variables, number of simulations, and number of time slices. For example, in a single currency case with 3000 simulations and 200 time slices, a state variable grid memory can be 5MB.	The size does **not** depend on number of instruments in the CVA portfolio. This can be reused for all instruments.
Instrument Price Grids	The storage size of an instrument price grid can simply be the size of a PDE, for example. In a 1-D PDE with 50 spot points and 200 time slices, the memory can be 80KB.	The overall size is the sum of all instruments concerned. However, one can aggregate each instrument one by one without having to store all instruments simultaneously.
Aggregation Grid	It has the same size of state variable grid. It can be overwritten during the aggregation process.	No dependency on number of instruments, and it is reuseable.

overlaid onto those state grids and the appropriate values for aggregation sampled out. Interpolation in GMC is numerically extremely efficient. At each scenario point, one can use simple interpolation scheme, e.g. linear in the state space $\bar{x}$, to calculate the future value. As most state variables in GMC are multi-dimension, linear interpolation in multi-dimension can further leverage the benefit in efficiency. EPE profile is simply the aggregation of the relevant future values.

Although GMC requires extensive use of computer memory for storing the grid values, the overall memory size can be made moderate using some efficient schemes. In practice, one can separately store the state variable grid, instrument price grid and aggregation grid, and reuse them as illustrated in Table 16.1.

As can be seen from the above table, if one aggregates EPE one by one sequentially, the number of instruments in the portfolio should not cause memory problems. The largest usage of memory is the state variable grid, which depends on number of currencies, spot points, simulations and time slices. Because it is re-usable for all instruments, it won't be a limitation either.

GMC IMPLEMENTATION EXAMPLE

Within the GMC CVA framework, a variety of appropriate derivatives pricing models can be used for grid generation. Let's examine some examples of using GMC technique to calculate EPE and ENE Profiles and CVAs. The example portfolio consists of one interest rate swap (IRS), one cross-currency swap (CCS) and one European swaption. We'll use a multi-currency Linear Gauss–Markov (LGM) modelling setup to price the instruments in the portfolio. For $M+1$ currencies, denoting the domestic currency as c_0 and foreign currencies $c_1, \cdots, c_M$, the associated FX pairs can be written as c_i / c_0, $i = 1, \cdots, M$, which is the number of c_0 per c_i. Let $x_i(t)$ be the state variable of the short rate process for currency c_i and $y_i(t)$ be the process for FX c_i / c_0, the multi-currency LGM model can be characterized as:

$$dx_0(t) = \alpha_0(t)dW_0(t)$$
$$dx_i(t) = -\rho_{i,y_i}\sigma_{y_i}(t)\alpha_i(t)dt + \alpha_i(t)dW_i(t) \qquad i = 1, 2, ..., M$$
$$dy_i(t) = y_i(t)\sigma_{y_i}(t)dW_{y_i}(t) \qquad i = 1, 2, ..., M$$

where ρ_{i,y_i} is the instantaneous correlation between $x_i(t)$ and $y_i(t)$, $\alpha_i(t) = \sigma_i(t)e^{\lambda_i t}$, $i = 0, 1, ..., M$ and λ_i is the mean reversion. In the single currency case (Hagan), a pricing measure associated with numeraire $N(t)$ is used to normalize zero coupon bonds. In the multi-currency setting, the domestic LGM pricing measure $N_0(t)$ is used to normalize all zero bonds in all currencies. The initial yield curves in all currencies are calibrated by construction. The model then evolves the normalized zero bonds together with associated numeraire-weighted FX rates $y_i(t)$ defined as:

$$y_i(t) = X^{i/0} \frac{N_i(t)}{N_0(t)} \qquad i = 1, ..., M$$

Where $N_i(t)$ is the numeraire for currency i and $X^{i/0}$ is the actual FX spot process.

Using standard LGM calculus, the currency i normalized zero coupon bonds under the domestic measure ($N_0(t)$) is given by:

$$\frac{dP_i(t, T)}{P_i(t, T)} = \rho_{i,y_i}\sigma_{y_i}(t)\alpha_i(t)H_i(T)dt - \alpha_i(t)H_i(T)dW_i(t)$$

where $H_i(T) = \int_0^T e^{-\lambda_i s}ds$. Note that FX forward is given by:

$$F^{i/0}(t, T) = y_i(t)\frac{P_i(t, T)}{P_0(t, T)}$$

The above global setting and measure governs the overall EPE aggregation as well as risk-neutral scenarios. For pricing instruments in a particular currency i, one can first use the measure $N_i(t)$ to calculate the grid values. For a tradable security $V(t,x_i)$, $V(t,x_i)/N_i(t)$ is a martingale:

$$\frac{V(t,x_i)}{N_i(t)} = E\left[\left.\frac{V(T,X_i)}{N_i(T)}\right|_{X_i(t)=x_i}\right]$$

Note that $N_i(0) = 1$. Denoting $\hat{V}(t,x_i) = V(t,x_i)/N_i(t)$, we have:

$$\hat{V}(t,x_i) = E\left[\left.\hat{V}(T,X_i)\right|_{X_i(t)=x_i}\right]$$

Its corresponding PDE is:

$$\frac{\partial \hat{V}}{\partial t} + \frac{1}{2}\alpha^2(t)\frac{\partial^2 \hat{V}}{\partial x_i^2} = 0$$

The grid values in the currency i measure can be used with the risk-neutral scenarios or states generated under the global measure, during the GMC interpretation and EPE aggregation process.

EPE and ENE Profiles

The above models are embedded within the GMC framework to value the example portfolio CVA. The individual instruments' stand-alone EPE and ENE profiles are shown in Figures 16.3 to 16.5.

The EPE and ENE Profile for the portfolio using GMC is shown in Figure 16.6, comparing to the simple sum of stand-alone profiles. The CVA of the netting set is 312bp, compared to the simple sum of 460bp.

Numerical Convergence

The numerical convergence and computational efficiency are shown in Figures 16.7. It can be seen that GMC converges very fast, showing robust numerical stability.

Computation Speed

One of the major advantages of GMC is its computation speed in calculating EPE profile. In the following, we compare the timing of GMC with that of AMC; both share the same pre-generated RN scenarios that are already calibrated to the markets, on a portfolio of Bermudan swaptions. In GMC, PDEs are used to create Grids for all trades, the EPE profile is then calculated by interpolation. In AMC, regression is used to compute the conditional expectation and hence EPE. Therefore the timing comparison boils down to the difference between (PDE + interpolation) and (regression + valuation) for achieving the same numerical accuracy. In general, PDE is much faster and more accurate than Monte Carlo path regression, and interpolation is much more efficient than

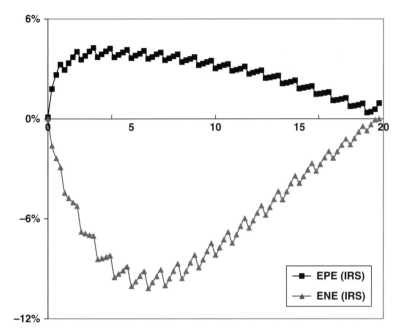

FIGURE 16.3   EPE and ENE profiles of an IRS, with CVA=85bp

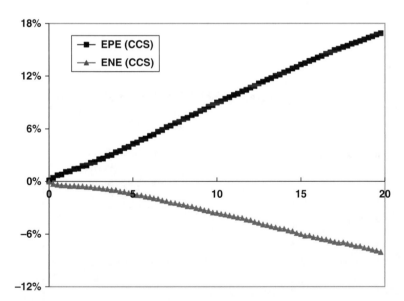

FIGURE 16.4   EPE and ENE profiles of a CCS, with CVA=159bp
In a CCS, the exposure at the long-end is mainly FX rate.

direct valuation. Both Figures 16.8 and 16.9 plot the timing against increasing number of Bermudan swaptions in the portfolio. Comparing the two figures (5Y Bermudan vs 20Y Bermudan), the GMC advantage over AMC for CVA becomes more significant for longer-dated trades and/or trades needing more time steps.

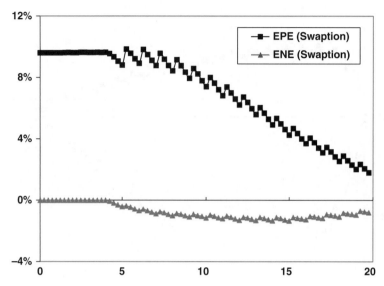

FIGURE 16.5 EPE and ENE Profiles of a European Swaption, with CVA=216bp
After the exercise date the flat lines become seesaws. This is in line with the fact that the profiles are the conditional exposures of the swap that exercised into.

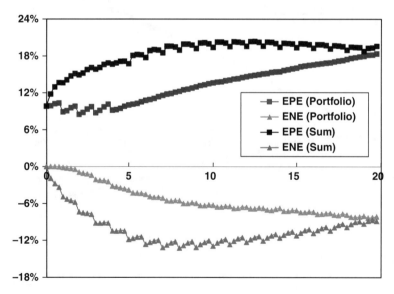

FIGURE 16.6 EPE and ENE profiles of the portfolio
Simple sums are plotted for comparison.

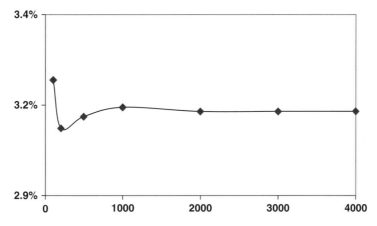

FIGURE 16.7 The numerical convergence of GMC on the example portfolio
CVA converges to the expected value of 312bp very quickly, exhibiting effective convenience and accuracy.

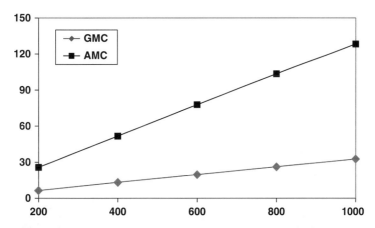

FIGURE 16.8 Timing comparison of GMC and AMC on portfolio CVA
Monte Carlo runs for both GMC and AMC is 3000. The portfolio consists of identical Bermudan swaptions, with a maturity of 5 years and annual exercise.

For GMC, excluding scenario generation and calibration, PDE timing and the incremental time increase due to interpolation are the key measures of its computational efficiency. In Figure 16.10, a 30-year cap is used as example. The first bar (0 scenario) is the PDE timing. The remaining three bars show the incremental time for scenario runs at 1000, 2000 and 3000 respectively, where the incremental time is due to interpolations in computing conditional expectations and EPE. As can be seen in the figure, the timing

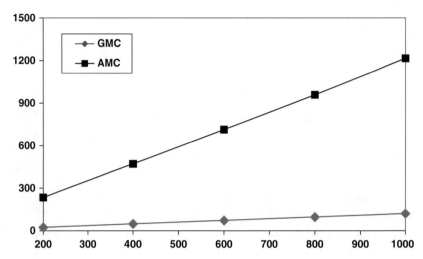

FIGURE 16.9 Timing comparison of GMC and AMC on portfolio CVA
Monte Carlo runs for both GMC and AMC is 3000. The portfolio consists of identical Bermudan swaptions, with a maturity of 20 years and annual exercise.

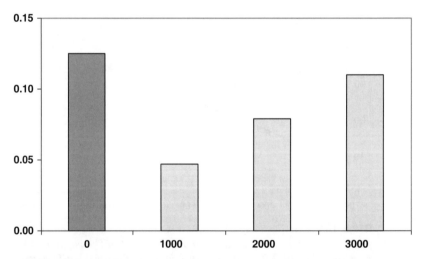

FIGURE 16.10 Timing of GMC on a 30-year EURIBOR (3-month) cap against the number of Monte Carlo scenarios
There are a total of 120 caplets, and the PDE used for generating grid has 1200 time slices.

due to interpolation is proportionally small or comparable to that of PDE. As we know, PDE is one of the fastest numerical techniques in quantitative finance. So it is not surprising that GMC can be extremely efficient in practice. For a large portfolio of instruments, a large portion of timing can come from PDEs due to increased number of Grids. The increase due to interpolation won't be too significant. So if one can find a way to reuse PDEs for a large portfolio, one can further enhance the computational efficiency.

GMC is applicable for a wide range of instruments across all major asset classes, including rates, FX and Equity. For example, interest rate swap, cross-currency swap, European swaption, cap/floor, callable swap, Bermudan swaptions, FX forward, etc. In practice, the instrument/trade PDE and their EPE profile calculations can be distributed among farms of many computers. The overall computing speed is largely dependent on the speeds of PDEs. In general a PDE is an order of magnitude more efficient than Monte Carlo for valuing most of the derivative instruments encountered in practice. In addition, GMC can price CVA on a portfolio of vanilla and exotic instruments in one sweep.

Risk Sensitivities

GMC also allows the implementation of path-wise Greeks using the adjoint technique, proposed originally by Giles and Glasserman. Adjoint method has been recently applied to CVA by Capriotti and M Peacock with remarkable results on Monte Carlo Greeks efficiency. Within the framework of GMC, the path-wise Greeks in the adjoint method can be not only readily implemented but also more efficient as the local Greeks on the Grid points are already calculated during the pricing. In addition, some of the local Greeks (e.g. $dv_i / d\bar{x}$) can be interpolated within the Grids which results in extra efficiency. Figures 16.11 and 16.12 show examples of time-bucketed interest rate Delta and Vega sensitivities respectively, for CVA on a 20-year swap, calculated within GMC framework. The adjoint Deltas and Vegas match those of brute force bump-and-run. The computational time of adjoint Deltas and Vegas is multi-magnitude faster that of brute force.

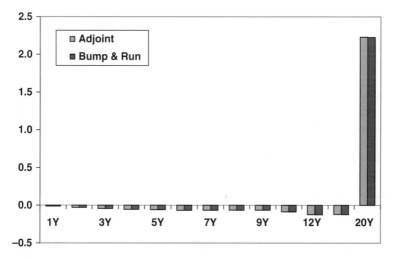

FIGURE 16.11 Comparison of time bucket zero rate Delta profiles of CVA on a 20Y swap using adjoint technique and brute force bump and run

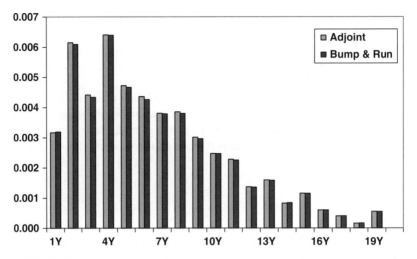

FIGURE 16.12   Comparison of time bucket Vega profiles of CVA on a 20Y swap using adjoint technique and brute force bump and run

GMC IN PRACTICE

CVA valuation on large portfolios is very challenging in practice, even after making some fundamental but reasonable assumptions (e.g. credit is not correlated to rates) to simplify the modelling. The fundamental computational problems remain and one needs to tackle those problems at the implementation level. For some linear instrument portfolios, e.g. swaps, one can of course use various techniques (e.g. cash flow aggregation) to speed up the calculations, but those techniques become complex and impossible once the portfolios contain non-linear instruments. Grid Monte Carlo (GMC) offers superior numerical capabilities in the context of valuing portfolio CVA of different types of derivative instruments, including the path-dependent ones. GMC is also scalable, from a single instrument to a large portfolio, without massive increase in computational overheads. Using GMC one can treat all instruments in the same fashion, and can include netting and projected collateral postings for the portfolio. The overall computational efficiency and accuracy in GMC is far more superior to its AMC counterpart. GMC's advantages become more apparent for larger portfolios, and/or for more exotic instruments even in smaller portfolios.

GMC Numerical Features

Some of the specific numerical features of GMC include:

- Grids can be fully calibrated to the market, hence the pricing can be consistent with the front office pricing model, overcoming the accuracy problems in AMC.
- Grids and the scenario generation model can share the same calibration routines; they are consistent with each other by construction.

- Conducting random walks within the grids is an extremely efficient process in calculating conditional expectations for EPE.
- Path-wise Greeks using adjoint technique can be readily implemented as the local Greeks on the Grid points are available.
- A wide range of derivative instruments can be covered, and their raw grids can be obtained using "standard" derivative pricing models.
- GMC overall has significant numerical advantages, in speed, convergence, stability and accuracy. It is applicable to RN CVA as well as credit counterparty risk systems where complexity and cost cause major problems.

Extending GMC for XVA

The implementation of XVA (CVA, DVA, FVA, AVA, KVA) calls for a holistic analysis of banks' computational infrastructure as well as their numerical techniques at the enterprise-wide portfolio level. The above GMC techniques can also be used to calculate other XVAs in addition to CVA. Let us use Funding Valuation Adjustment (FVA) to illustrate this.

FVA models the expected funding effects associated with uncollateralized derivatives trades. FVA measures the funding costs and benefits incurred when uncollateralized trades (e.g. with some corporates) are hedged with collateralized trades (e.g. OTC), or when the received collateral is not reusable. The asymmetry of the collateral agreements between the original and hedging trade causes the bias in the valuation of funding.

A funding cost example is when a client trade is in-the-money but the corporate counterparty is not posting collateral. The dealer, however, has to post collateral to the hedge counterparty. Similar asymmetry arises when a trade is collateralized but the asset cannot be rehypothecated.

A funding benefit example is when a client trade is out-of-the-money and the dealer does not post collateral to the corporate counterparty, yet the dealer receives collateral from the hedge counterparty. If the collateral is rehypothecable, the dealer can lend the collateral on, which should be recognized as a funding benefit.

For given EPE_t and ENE_t, defined as:

$$EPE_t = E_t^Q \left[DF_t \cdot max\left(V_t(\bar{x}) - C, 0\right)\right]$$

$$ENE_t = E_t^Q \left[DF_t \cdot min\left(V_t(\bar{x}) - C, 0\right)\right]$$

where R is the recovery rate, DFt the discount factor, C the collateral and $V_t(\bar{x})$ is the conditional expectation of future portfolio value for the given state variable $\bar{x}$, we can compare CVA and FVA:

$$CVA = (1 - R) \int_0^T EPE_t \cdot dP_t$$

$$FVA = (F - r) \int_0^T (EPE_t + ENE_t) \cdot dP_{\Delta t}$$

where dP_t is the default probability between t and $t + dt$, conditional on surviving to t. It can be either single or joint default/survival probability depending on whether the calculation is for unilateral or bilateral case. $dP_{\Delta t}$ is the survival probability between t and $t + dt$. It can be either single or joint survival probability, depending on whether the calculation is for a unilateral or bilateral case.

It is clear that FVA and CVA calculations share many common numerical features. One should leverage the CVA systems and infrastructures in the FVA calculations, or vice versa. One key practical decision in FVA calculations is which funding spread curve should be used. Incorporating FVA in the derivatives pricing has become a common place. The industry is moving towards recognizing FVA in earnings, which requires an adjustment at the portfolio level. Banks may take FVA charges directly, by incorporating them into the fair value adjustment.

CVA Hedging Consideration

Hedging CVA at portfolio level clearly requires numerically efficient and stable techniques that are capable of generating sensible and reliable Greeks. GMC can fulfil this important role. Additionally, practitioners need to consider a number of regulatory and accounting aspects.

The definitions of regulatory and accounting CVA are different. The CVA exposures in the regulatory capital requirements consist of two parts, one from the current exposures and the other from the expected future exposures (as in CVA VaR). Accounting rules, however, only recognize the current exposure. Therefore the hedges put for CVA VAR will be viewed as naked positions from an accounting perspective, leading to accounting P&L volatilities.

Because of the gap between regulatory and accounting definitions of CVA, a hedge deemed as effective by regulators may not be considered effective by accountants.

Practitioners are therefore working hard trying to ways and solutions to satisfy both sets of rules – an effective CVA VAR hedge at the same time avoiding P&L volatility.

The Basel III-compliant CVA hedging instruments include single-name CDSs, index CDSs and equivalent hedging instruments referencing the counterparty directly, which can be used to reduce CVA charges. Some single-name and index credit swaptions are also eligible for hedging CVA. Previously, the primary CVA hedge instruments used in practice are vanilla single-name CDSs.

Credit swaption can be a potential CVA hedging instrument. As it is an option, the maximum loss is the option premium, and its P&L is typically less volatile than CDSs. Credit swaptions hedge will be more efficient if the CVA VaR is very sensitive to stressed scenarios and volatile markets. It can potentially reduce the P&L volatility while still delivering a capital benefit at a reasonable cost.

Another possible way to reduce P&L volatility is to use a financial guarantee as the CVA hedge. Because a financial guarantee is not marked to market, one can theoretically hedge the regulatory CVA exposure without P&L volatility due to the hedge. However, because a financial guarantee is not marked to market, regulators have serious doubts about such hedging instruments.

CHAPTER 17

Contingent Convertibles (CoCo)

CoCos are contingent capital instruments that have an explicit trigger. When the trigger is breached, CoCo investors will lose capital. Comparing to the dated subordinated debt which absorbs losses in the event of default, CoCos will absorb losses whenever the predefined trigger is breached, regardless of default event. From issuer's perspective, the trigger event will write off part of the liabilities associated with the CoCos.

CoCos are the riskiest debt from European banks. The European policy makers created such securities in the wake of the financial crises to ensure the investors, rather than the governments and taxpayers, contribute to banks' rescues in future financial crises. With the implementation of Basel III, banks have stronger regulatory incentives to issue hybrid debt, which has characteristics of pure debt (e.g. bonds) and equity (e.g. stocks). CoCos are such debt instruments designed to meet strict capital rules.

COCO FEATURES

CoCo with appropriate features can be treated as AT1 and less risky Tier 2 in the capital structure, as schematically shown in Figure 17.1. It is an important component in the Basel III compliant capital structure.

As AT1, CoCos are perpetual but can be callable after an initial non-call period. Conversely, all AT1 under Basel III has explicit trigger (5.125%) that leads to loss absorption. Therefore AT1 instruments by definition are CoCos. As Tier 2, CoCos have fixed maturity and coupons must be paid to avoid default.

The regulatory requirements on capital and leverage ratio are the main drivers in the debt issuance markets, including CoCos. Since its inception, CoCos have become an important class of debt instruments, attracting not only hedge funds but also intuitional investors, as they can offer attractive compensations for the level of real risks. Key players in this field are joining efforts in compiling contingent capital indices to track their performances. From banks' perspective, if AT1s are treated as debt rather than equity, interest

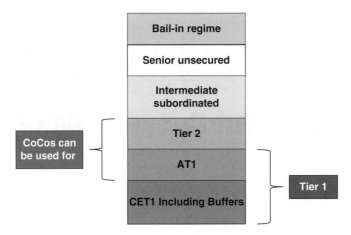

FIGURE 17.1   Basel III-compliant capital structure

payments are out of pretax earnings and therefore tax-deductible. This contributes to the fact that CoCos are cheaper to issue than stocks and preference shares.

COCO CATEGORIES

There are different types of CoCos. Upon the trigger event, i.e. when the relevant capital ratio falls below the trigger level, the payoff types include:

- Write-down: In a write-down CoCo, all or part of capital will be written down if the trigger is breached. This is a cleaner way from issuer's perspective to settle the CoCo trigger event, as the equity conversion often needs specific shareholder approval due to dilution concerns.
- Equity Conversion: Upon trigger event, the equity conversion CoCo will be forced to convert into equity. The conversion price is either fixed (e.g. 50% of share price at issuance) or the higher of the market price and floor price [$\max(S_T, floor)$]. The higher the conversion price, the more capital loss there will be for the CoCo investors upon the trigger event. Compared to the write-down version, an equity conversion CoCo is therefore equivalent to having a recovery value when the trigger event happens. One can evaluate how much cheaper the equity conversion feature is compared to the permanent write-down structure by using probability of default or barrier hitting probability.
- Write-down/Write-up: In this version, when the trigger is breached, the capital will be written down for the amount that needs to fill the capital shortfall. The loss will be on a pro rota basis with other loss-absorbing securities. If, however, the issuer manages to return to financial health, at issuer's discretion in accordance with certain rules, the issuer can write up the CoCo. While this "temporary" write-down arrangement may appear to have value, its value is actually rather limited. First, the distress can last a long time after writing-down. Secondly, the issuer can call the bond at the very low value after writing-down, effectively cancelling the chance of recovery or writing-up.

Examples of CoCo bond features are listed in Table 17.1:

TABLE 17.1 An real example of a CoCo bond

Term Sheet	Explanation	A Real Example
Issuer	A bank	UniCredit
Host Instrument	Tier 1 or LT2 or Senior	AT1, CRD IV compliant
Rating	Credit rating	BB-(Fitch)
Currency	Notional currency	EUR
Issue Size	Notional size	1 billion
Issue Date	Issue date	10 September 2014
Maturity	Perpetual (if Tier 1) or Dated (if LT2)	Perpetual
Next Call Date	First call date	At year 7, 10 September 2021
Coupon	Fixed coupon	6.75% until the first call date
Coupon Structure	Fixed coupon first, can then be floating which is reset periodically	Fixed-Floating reset every five years to 5-years Mid-Swap rate + 610bp
Coupon Cancellable?	Yes or No	Yes
Coupon Cancellation	Optional Cancellation at the sole discretion of the issuer. Mandatory Cancellation if insufficient distributable items, **or** distribution exceeding Maximum Distributable Amount, **or** upon trigger event.	Optional Cancellation at the sole discretion of the issuer. Mandatory Cancellation if insufficient distributable items b distribution exceeding Maximum Distributable Amount, **or** upon trigger event.
Principal Loss Absorption	Permanent principal write-down; or Write down/write up; or Full conversion into shares.	Write-down/write-up (temporary write-down)
Trigger for Principal Loss Absorption	Specified capital ratio and trigger level.	CET1 < 5.125%
Trigger Test Date	Periodically (e.g. last day of relevant fiscal quarter) or continuously.	Any time
Early Calls	For example, regulatory calls	Regulatory call
PoNV (Point of Non-Viability)	Statutory (risk factors disclosure) or Contractual	Statutory

As CoCos are designed to prop up capitals during the crises, typical CoCo trigger levels also reflect the minimum regulatory requirements of the capital structures. For example, the following trigger levels are found in the CoCo markets:

- 5.125% CET1: AT1 principle loss trigger. This is the minimum trigger level for a CoCo to qualify as AT1 capital under Basel III;
- 6% Tier 1: current solvency measure;
- 7% CET: minimum CET plus buffer.

COCO RISK FACTORS

As hybrid debt instruments, CoCos are exposed to interest rate risks. In addition, CoCos have their specific risks. Table 17.2 itemizes such risk factors and features embedded in CoCos.

TABLE 17.2 CoCo risk features

Risk Factors	Risk Features
Trigger Level and Distance to Trigger	■ CoCo triggers are typically accounting triggers, namely, they are the book value (as opposed to market value) of the relevant capital ratio. ■ The higher the trigger level is, the more risky the CoCo bond is. Fundamentally the distance to trigger from the current capital level is the key risk measure in a CoCo. ■ The frequency of publicly disclosing the book value is of relevance in the CoCo valuation. The relationship between the trigger level and company default can be quite complex. For example: ■ If the trigger level is high, a CoCo bond can be triggered before default happens. This is the case where a CoCo bond is more risky than its standard default bond counterpart. ■ On the other hand, for a low trigger CoCo bond, default can happen without the trigger or before the trigger level is breached. In such a scenario, a CoCo bond can be less risky than its default bond counterpart.
Point of Non-Viability (PoNV) Trigger	■ PoNV trigger is the discretionary trigger which can be activated by the regulators, based on their judgement of bank's solvency prospects.
Loss Absorption Mechanism	■ Write-down ■ Equity conversion: note that if the conversion price is set at the prevailing market price without floor, it will cause too much dilution, and theoretically the CoCo investors will not loss any capital at the time of mandatory conversion ■ Write-down/write-up
Coupon Cancellation (Automatic Restriction)	■ All CoCos have the possibility of early coupon cancellations. ■ CRD IV imposes the distribution restrictions known as Maximum Distribution Amount (MDA). This MDA risk in CoCos can be sizeable. ■ If CET1 breaches the capital conservation buffer, even if it still meets the minimum requirement of 4.5%, the (coupon) distributions will be automatically restricted. ■ In practice, due to banks' stricter internal rules and how the losses can occur during the crisis, it is reasonable to expect that the (coupon) distributions will be cancelled even before CET1 reaches the buffer line.

Risk Factors	Risk Features
Market Implied Cost of Equity	■ As AT1, CoCos' pricing must be cheaper than the relevant market implied cost of equity. Equity capital is permanent and loss-absorbing, and the return (e.g. dividends, earnings) can be reduced to zero. These risk features can be compared to CoCo risk features, to assess their relative costs.
Others	■ Credit spread on senior unsecured debt, a measure of default risk ■ Rating, as a reference ■ Coupon deferability ■ etc.

INDIRECT MODELLING APPROACHES

A CoCo pricing model needs to capture key risks and features embedded in CoCos, including capital loss trigger. The vast majority of real-life CoCos have an accounting trigger, as opposed to a market trigger. The accounting trigger event reflects the issuer's solvency position, so a CoCo has an embedded down-and-in put option on issuer's solvency positions. Because the option underlying the issuer's solvency position is not tradeable or hedgeable, deriving a CoCo pricing model is fraught with difficulties.

Credit or Equity Derivative Approach

In the credit derivative approach, the CoCo spread is modelled in a similar way to CDS. The default intensity or hazard rate λ_{CoCo} is the central parameter for quantifying the trigger event (CoCo "default"). As the CoCo trigger event must happen before the real default, the implied CoCo "default" must occur before the CDS default, we have $\lambda_{CoCo} \geq \lambda_{CDS}$. The mathematics is quite simple as it is practically the same as that of CDS. The fundamental problem with this approach, though, is that it only works if the CoCo trigger is a so-called market trigger, i.e. the trigger is CDS or stock price directly. It is not suitable for the vast majority of CoCos in the marketplace, which have the account triggers (e.g. CET1).

In the equity derivative approach, CoCo is synthesized and modelled by down-and-in forward for the equity conversion, plus a strip of down-and-out put options for the coupons. Stock price touching a barrier is used as the trigger. At the time of conversion, stock price is hence artificially set at the barrier. The mathematics is simple as the Black-Scholes closed-form solutions can be used to price the barrier options. The fatal problem of the equity derivative approach is the same as the credit derivative approach: it only works for market trigger CoCos, which rarely exist, and it does not work well for the accounting trigger CoCos, which account for the vast majority of issuances.

Let us also compare CoCos with traditional Convertible Bonds (CBs). They are in fact very different. Table 17.3 illustrates their key differences in behaviours and risk features.

TABLE 17.3 Comparison of CoCos and CBs

	CoCos	CBs
Underlying	Capital ratio, CET1 or CT1 or Tier 1 ratio.	Equity stock price.
Conversion	Automatically triggered conversion: investors are forced to write down capital or convert into equity with loss of capital, when the **down** market triggers the conversion.	Investors have options to convert into equity. Therefore the conversion only happens when investors can benefit in the **up** market.
Risk for Investors	Investors sold down-and-in put option on the underlying with the risk of losing capital.	Investors bought call option on the underlying with the limited risk of losing premium.
Coupons	Having higher fixed coupons than the prevailing market benchmark.	Having lower coupons than the prevailing market benchmark.

Based on the fact that CoCos have very different risk features compared to CBs, the equity stock-driven pricing models used for CBs are not adequate for CoCos.

Historic analyses and market experiences have demonstrated that the CoCo spreads are rather weakly correlated to CDS spread (only ~40%) or equity stock price (only ~ 25%). Fundamentally, the CoCo underlying (capital ratio) cannot be approximated reliably by either CDS or stock price. Models using CDS or stock price directly as proxy to the CoCo underlying will have difficulties in capturing the real risks, and the risk of wrong model assumptions is substantial. This calls for a model that is better connected to the underlying capital ratio which drives the CoCo dynamics.

Structural Asset Approach

The structural asset approach (Brigo et al 2013) aims to better capture CoCos underlying dynamics. It models the issuer's asset and links the asset parameters to CDS and equity price by model assumptions. The asset is also linked to the capital ratio by historic analysis. Detailed steps of the structural modelling are summarized here:

1. Model the issuer's asset V_t:
   - following Merton's approach, the issuer's asset is assumed to be Log-Normal: $dV_t / V_t = \mu_t dt + \sigma_t dZ$
2. Treat the issuer's debt as a barrier B_t:
   - it is assumed that when asset V_t touches the debt barrier B_t, it represents a default;
   - therefore the barrier touching probability is linked to the CDS implied default probability.
3. Link asset V_t and debt barrier B_t to market-observable CDS quotes:
   - For a given barrier level and CDS implied default probability, the model parameters such as volatility term structure σ_t can be calculated. One can make barrier B_t time-dependent, and use CDS term structure in the calculation.
   - However, at this stage, both barrier B_t and volatility term structure σ_t are unknown.

4. Link asset V_t and debt barrier B_t to equity price:
   - Equity price, on the other hand, can be modelled as a down-and-out European call.
   - This provides an additional constraint to enable the simultaneous calibration of B_t and σ_t.

   The above calibration steps are purely for the model parameters B_t and σ_t, with the help of standard CDS and barrier option analytical formulation. They are not related to the CoCo trigger event which is triggered by the capital ratio.

5. Relate asset V_t to capital ratio C_t
   - This step establishes a historic relationship between asset to equity (AE) ratio and C_t. The AE ratio is approximated by $X_t \approx V_t / (V_t - B_t)$;
   - Figure 17.2 shows a bank's example of historic relationship between CET1 ratio (vertical axis) and AE ratio (horizontal axis):
   - The scattered data in the above figure can be best fit using an exposure function $C_t = a \cdot exp(b \cdot X_t) + c$, where a, b, c are constants. An example best fit with $a = 6.5, b = -0.22$ and $c = 0.056$ is shown in Figure 17.3.
   - When the AE ratio becomes larger and the company is more leveraged, its capital ratio will become smaller.

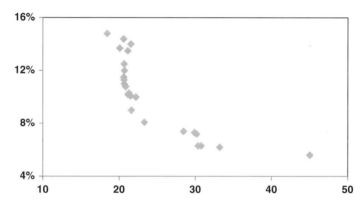

FIGURE 17.2   CET1 ration vs AE ratio

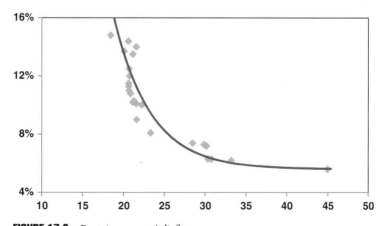

FIGURE 17.3   Best (exponential) fit

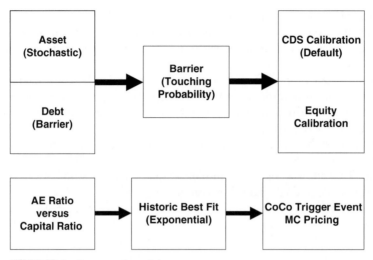

FIGURE 17.4 Structural model steps

6. Monte Carlo pricing
   - Through the random walks of V_t, one can derive the random walks of capital ratio C_t via the best fit functional form (e.g. exponential), such that the CoCo trigger event can be modelled and priced.
   - It is possible to calibrate to the market price of CoCo, and re-adjust certain model parameters, including those in the (exponential) functional form.

Schematically, the above steps can be illustrated in Figure 17.4:

The structural model provides some insight into the CoCo fundamentals, in terms of where the CoCo spread premium comes from or whether it is justified. However, the structural model is quite convoluted. There are explicit and implicit assumptions in the modelling steps. The CoCo's trigger underlying, the capital ratio is modelled indirectly requiring historic and empirical analysis. The overall modelling process is non-trivial from a risk measurement and management perspective. The natural question to ask is: "Why not model the CoCo trigger underlying (say CET1) directly?"

DIRECT MODELLING APPROACHES

In the indirect approaches, the capital ratio (e.g. CET1 ratio) is derived and modelled by going through a number of intermediate steps containing explicit and implicit assumptions. To remove those intermediate steps and substantially reduce the complexity, one can model the capital ratio (e.g. CET1) directly. The implicit assumptions made in the direct approach are not more than the assumptions made in the indirect approach.

Historic Time Series

To understand CoCo pricing features better and formulate the direct modelling approach accordingly, let us examine some example historic time series.

- CoCo price versus stock price: Figure 17.5 compares the CoCo price (labelled on the left vertical axis) with the issuer's stock price (labelled on the right vertical axis) over the same period. There is a clear strong longer-term correlation between the CoCo and stock prices, although the localized correlation over a shorter period can be weak.
- CoCo price versus CDS spread: Figure 17.6 plots the CoCo price and issuer's CDS spread (right vertical axis label) over the same period. There is a strong long-term correlation between the CoCo price and CDS. The localized correlation over short period can vary.

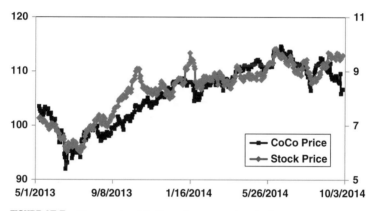

FIGURE 17.5 Time series (CoCo price vs stock price)

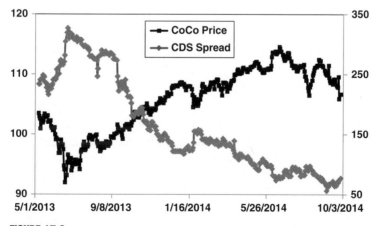

FIGURE 17.6 Time series (CoCo price vs CDS spread)

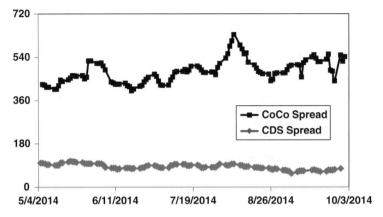

FIGURE 17.7   Time series (CoCo spread vs CDS spread)

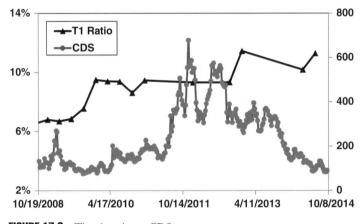

FIGURE 17.8   Tier 1 ratio vs CDS

By zooming in over a short period in Figure 17.7, the CoCo spread derived from the price is compared with CDS spread. Over this particular time period, they are very weakly correlated with each other.

- Tier 1 capital ratio versus CDS spread: in Figure 17.8, the published accounting Tier 1 capital ratio (left vertical axis label) is plotted with the CDS spread (right vertical axis label) over the same period. The accounting capital ratio is published only periodically, say quarterly or half-yearly. It has much lower volatility, in the order of 17% compared to the CDS historic volatility of 79% over the same sample period. Also, Tier 1 capital ratio is rather weakly correlated with the CDS spread.
- Tier 1 capital ratios: in Figure 17.9, the published accounting Tier 1 capital ratios for two European banks are plotted. They are quite correlated. The annualized volatilities of Tier 1 capital ratio for both banks are in the order of 17%.

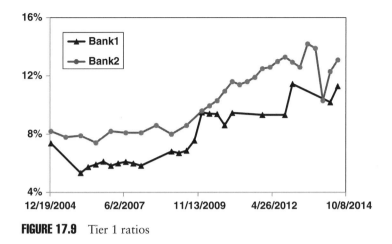

FIGURE 17.9   Tier 1 ratios

Model Criteria and Formulation

A sensible CoCo pricing model should reflect the market realities and include the key behaviour features, as exhibited in the above historic time series analysis. There is strong market evidence that CoCo spreads are correlated to the spreads of other subordinated debt, and higher trigger level weakens the correlation. The spread of a CoCo must be consistent with where it is in the issuer's capital structure. AT1 CoCo is the most risky, so its spread should be wider than other subordinated debt. For Tier 2 CoCos, rating agencies normally rate them between issuer's viability rating and default rating. Viability ratings measure the intrinsic creditworthiness, and default ratings measure the relative risk of non-payment on obligations. Theretofore the viability rating is lower (say, BB-) than the default rating (say A), and Tier 2 CoCos (classed as subordinated debt) can be rated 1 or 2 levels below the issuer's default rating.

Therefore in the direct modelling approach:

- The CoCo model shall reference directly the spread of relevant subordinated debt as the base spread. One can use the spread of CDS associated with the relevant subordinated debt as the base spread.
- The additional spread due to CoCo's accounting trigger event can be modelled directly by assuming capital ratio dynamics. The trigger event is viewed as the capital ratio touching a barrier.
- The barrier touching approach is directly related to the write down version of CoCo. One can actually treat the equity conversion CoCo as merely having an equivalent recovery upon the trigger event. Therefore the equity conversion CoCo can be modelled using the same barrier touching approach with a recovery rate.

Based on the above practical criteria, one can have the simple 1-factor CoCo models as listed in Table 17.4, assuming the CoCo trigger is the CET1 ratio.

For the default bond price, one needs to calibrate to the relevant subordinated CDS. For debts of different ratings or credit grades, their CDSs should in theory imply the same default probability, but with different recovery rates. One therefore needs

TABLE 17.4 1-factor CoCo models

Models	Formulations	Features
Diffusion ▪ CDS base spread is assumed deterministic. ▪ CET1 (c) follows a diffusion process (e.g. Log-Normal).	$$\frac{dc}{c} = \mu_c dt + \sigma_c dz$$ $$V_C = V_D \cdot 1_{\{\tau_c > T\}} + R_c \cdot 1_{\{\tau_c \leq T\}}$$	The CoCo price (V_C) consists of standard CDS default bond price including coupons (V_D), and an additional element due to CoCo trigger event (τ_c) and recovery (R_c). The model cannot price callable features in most of the CoCos.
Jump Diffusion ▪ CDS base spread is assumed deterministic. ▪ CET1 (c) follows a jump diffusion process.	$$\frac{dc}{c} = (\mu_c - \beta\lambda) dt + \sigma_c dz + dQ_t$$ $$V_C = V_D \cdot 1_{\{\tau_c > T\}} + R_c \cdot 1_{\{\tau_c \leq T\}}$$	One can use Poisson jumps $Q_t = \sum Y_i$, $\beta = E[Y_i]$ is the expected jump size and λ is the jump intensity. Jumps can make the trigger event modelling more flexible, as one has more degree of freedom to calibrate the underlying volatility. The model cannot price callable features.

to use the correct recovery rate to imply the correct default probability in the default bond pricing. For example, CDS recovery for some senior debt is quoted at 40%, and for some subordinated debt is at 20%.

For the accounting trigger event pricing, one can resort to barrier option pricing.

Model Analysis and Market Calibration

The above 1-factor models ignore the perpetual and callable features, as the call is really on the relevant credit spread. They can, however, price in the dominant feature of CoCo accounting trigger. The accounting trigger event pricing boils down to a pay-at-touch (barrier) rebate option. With the CET1 as the underlying directly, once it touches the trigger barrier, the pay-at-touch rebate on the default bond including coupons can be priced using standard barrier rebate analytical formula.

When Poisson jumps are introduced into the 1-factor diffusion model, the pricing principle is the same as pay-at-touch rebate, although Monte Carlo may be needed in implementation. In the following, some example pricing and calibration results for a real-life CoCo bond will be discussed.

The example CoCo bond has a perpetual maturity, although it is callable at year 7. The trigger is on CET1 and the trigger level is set at 5.125%, and the spot CET1 is 10%. The CoCo pays a coupon of 6.5%. The relevant subordinated debt CDS is 250bp with a recovery of 20%. With the 1-factor direct modelling approach, the price versus CET1 volatility is plotted in Figure 17.10, for no jump and two jump cases. In the pricing, the maturity is set to 7 years and the callable feature is ignored.

The black horizontal line in the graph is the market-quoted price to calibrate to:

▪ In the "no jump" case, implied volatility of CET1 is about 17.5% as marked by the red circle. It is broadly in line with the historic volatility of Tier 1 capital ratio, which is analysed earlier and in the order of 17%.

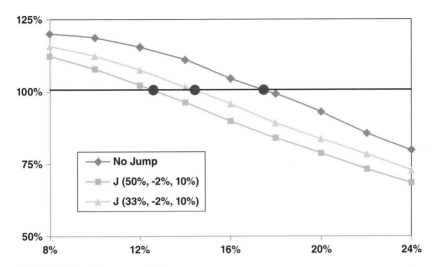

FIGURE 17.10 Price vs volatility

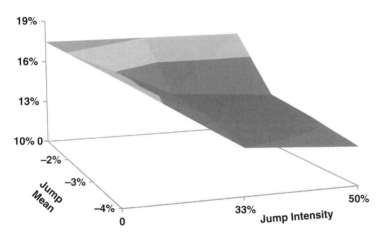

FIGURE 17.11 Implied volatility

- Setting jump intensity to 50%, jump mean to –2% and jump variance to 10%, implied volatility of CET1 reduces to 14.3%. When the jump intensity is reduced to 33% and jump mean and variance is kept unchanged, implied volatility of CET1 reduces to 12.5%. Clearly, jumps allow for lower diffusion volatility in order to calibrate to the same market price.

The implied volatilities for different jump intensities and jump means are plotted in the surface graph (Figure 17.11). More frequent jumps (larger jump intensity) and larger average jump sizes (more negative jump mean) will lead to lower implied volatility of CET1.

In Figure 17.12, the same "no jump" case is compared with two other jump cases. The two jump cases have the same jump intensity (33%) and jump mean (–2%), but different jump variance of 10% and 20%. Implied volatilities of CET1 in the two jump cases are 14.3% and 8.8% respectively.

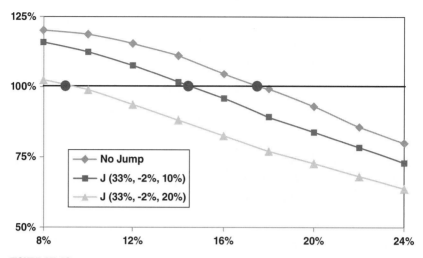

FIGURE 17.12 Price vs volatility

TABLE 17.5 A 2-factor CoCo model

Model	Formulations	Features
2-Factor Diffusion CDS (s) and CET1 (c) follow a joint diffusion process (e.g. joint Log-Normal).	$$\begin{cases} \dfrac{ds}{s} = \mu_s dt + \sigma_s dz_1 \\ \dfrac{dc}{c} = \mu_c dt + \sigma_c dz_2 \\ dz_1 \cdot dz_2 = \rho dt \end{cases}$$ $$V_C = V_D \cdot 1_{\{\tau_c > T\}} + R_c \cdot 1_{\{\tau_c \leq T\}}$$ $$V_C = max\left(V_{\text{intrinsic}}, V_C^t\right)$$	2-D PDE solver or Monte Carlo can be used for pricing. CET1 is for pricing trigger events, and CDS is for pricing call features. For the CDS part, one can also model the hazard rate instead.

Extending to 2-factor Model

In order to capture and price the call features in the CoCo, one needs to use a 2-factor model, as the call decision is mainly on the prevailing credit spread. For example, if a CoCo's floating part of the coupon at the call dates (e.g. every five years) is reset to the 5-year Mid-Swap rate plus 600bp, the issuer will call if its prevailing implied CoCo credit spread is materially less than 600bp. The reset spread (600bp) is effectively the CoCo credit spread option strike. Therefore in addition to CET1, the CoCo credit spread dynamics needs to be modelled. A relevant CDS can be a proxy for modelling the CoCo credit spread dynamics. Table 17.5 summarizes the key formations and features of such a model.

The price of the callable CoCo is impacted by two correlated contributors: the potential CET1 trigger event (knockout) before the call dates and the distributions of forward CDS spreads (affecting exercise decisions) at the call dates. This is qualitatively

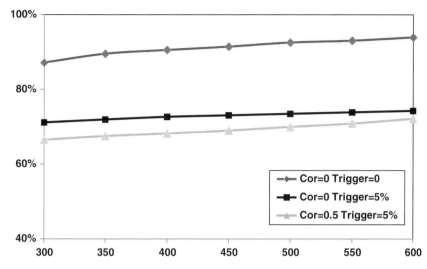

FIGURE 17.13 Exercise probability vs CDS strike

similar to the single-name default swaptions (e.g. White 2014) whereby the potential default before expiry and optionality at expiry contributing to the price.

Using the above 2-factor diffusion process, an example CoCo with callable feature is priced below. It has one call date at 7 years. If not called, the CoCo will continue for 5 more years and its coupon will be reset to the 5-year Mid-Swap rate plus "reset spread". Using CDS spread of 260bp and implied volatility of 80%, Figure 17.13 plots the call (or exercise) probabilities at year 7 against the reset spread (CDS strike) for three cases:

- Correlation between CDS and CET1 is 0, CET1 trigger level is 0.
- Correlation between CDS and CET1 is 0, CET1 trigger level is 5%.
- Correlation between CDS and CET1 is 0.5, CET1 trigger level is 5%.

Higher trigger level reduces the probability of call (exercise), as the higher trigger increases the chance of knockout before the call (exercise) date. Increased correlation between CDS and CET1 slightly reduces the probability of call, as larger correlation increases the chance of knock-out before the call date.

Concluding Remarks

In CoCo modelling, the advantages of modelling capital ratio (e.g. CET1 ratio) directly as underlying include:

- One can make simple and transparent assumptions on the underlying dynamics.
- The model parameters, such as implied volatility of CET1, can be calibrated to the market price directly.
- Consequently the implied volatility can be compared to the historic volatility if there is sufficient capital ratio time series data. The comparison will allow one to assess whether the CoCo price is broadly fair, or too expensive, or too cheap.

- One can price in the callable features in addition to accounting trigger event, by relatively simple model extension (to 2-factors).
- The risk sensitivities of a CoCo are directly related to CET1, and relevant subordinated debt spread (or CDS on such debt). One can use the model directly in the relevant risk assessment calculations, such as for VaR.

The main risky driving factor in a CoCo is the capital ratio, such as the CET1 ratio. While this is captured by the direct modelling approach, one cannot really hedge such risks at present. In certain scenarios, for example when the relevant capital ratio is very close to the trigger level, a CoCo bond can be more risky than the equity itself, even though CoCo in general has higher grade in the capital structure. This is not surprising, as a CoCo bond can also be viewed as a structured product, whereby certain specific product features can cause capital loss. Note that the capital ratio includes RWA, which is affected by many market and credit risk factors. In these contexts, CoCo is a highly complex product, and it may only suitable for sophisticated investors and customers.

CHAPTER 18

Variable Annuity Products

Annuity products are primarily for people who make financial arrangements for their retirement. They are important pension products, which are often associated with certain tax advantages, either in the form of contribution tax relief or benefit tax deferral, depending on jurisdictions. There are many different types of annuity product. The aim of this chapter is to drill down to those having embedded derivatives, and analyse their valuation and risks. Some of the key risks in the annuity products include equity and interest rate hybrid risks, and embedded mortality risks. We will analyse the pricing of these hybrid options and discuss their risk management issues. Given the long-dated nature of these products, several related key issues need to be addressed, including long-dated equity forward and long-dated volatility.

In a traditional annuity, referred to as **immediate annuity,** a customer makes a lump sum payment to an insurance company. Starting immediately, the insurance company pays the customer a series of income payments either for a fixed period or for life. The regular income payments can either be fixed using a fixed interest rate or variable by indexing to market indices, e.g. S&P500.

In a deferred annuity (Figure 18.1), a customer makes a lump sum payment or series of payments to an insurance company during the accumulation phase. The insurance company in return will pay regular incomes to the customer from a future date (start of annuitization phase). In the accumulation phase the customer invests his/her contributions and accumulates the fund. In the annuitization phase, the insurance company pays out using the fund accumulated.

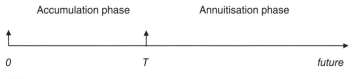

FIGURE 18.1 Deferred annuity

TABLE 18.1   Annuity types

Annuity Type	Accumulation phase	Annuitization phase	Regulatory treatment
Fixed Deferred Annuities	Fund return is no less than a specified minimum interest rate. Very similar to certain fixed income instruments and there is little volatility in the investment.	Becomes an immediate annuity.	Not securities, and not regulated by the SEC.
Fixed Indexed Annuities	Fund return tracks an index, e.g. S&P500. There may be various other features, such as guaranteed minimum fund value.	Becomes an immediate annuity.	May or may not be securities. Most not registered with SEC.
Variable Annuities	Choice of investments is varied, typically mutual funds. The underlying markets can be equity, bonds or other assets. This is the most volatile type as customers are exposed to the market volatility. There are various product features which include guarantees. These guarantees are effectively the embedded optionalities.	Flexible, with a variety of payout types which include guarantees (embedded optionalities). The payout can be drawdown and/ or annuitization regular incomes.	Securities and regulated by the SEC.

Again within the deferred annuity class, there are various types. Table 18.1 summarize three key types with their different features: fixed deferred, fixed indexed and Variable Annuity.

The US fixed indexed annuity market has been growing in recent years as it is widely considered to be able to deliver better value for money than the traditional annuities, in particular in the low interest rate environment. The indexed annuities can contain attractive features, such as protection against loss of capital and guarantee of minimum income for life. There are also increased uses of proprietary indices (smart beta or strategy indices) as opposed to the well-known equity indices (e.g. S&P500). The fact that indexed annuities are classified as pure insurance products and not securities means that they are outside the scope of the Securities and Exchange Commission (SEC) and the Financial Industry Regulatory Authority (Finra). This has lowered the business hurdle, as the product providers don't need a license to advise on securities.

Variable annuities have been very popular products in the USA and part of Asia. They have also attracted attention in Europe. Traditional annuities effectively force customers on a single day to lock into an annuity rate for the rest of their life, and also loss access to the capital. Variable annuities (VA), however, allow the payout benefits determined over a period of time. Besides, some VA products allow drawdown –access to the capital. As can be seen in the table above, variable annuities (VA) are in general more exposed to the market risks and volatilities, in both the accumulation and the annuitization phase. The returns on the investment and the payoff amount depend on investment performances as well as embedded guarantees. The guarantees offer protections against adverse market movements, and compensate interest rate and longevity risks for the customers.

VA has the capacity to include structured product features. One example of structured annuities is the indexed variable annuity product category, which includes many combination choices across time periods, underlying indices and downside barriers. Investors have choices of time periods (e.g. 1, 3, 5-years term), underlying indices (e.g. equity or commodity indices, or exchange-traded funds) and first loss downside buffers (e.g. 10%, 20%, 30%). Each investment option has a cap rate, which is the maximum upside appreciation of the index that may be applied at the end of the specific term. Tapered surrender charges (e.g. starting at 7%, reducing to 0% by year seven) apply in order to discourage early redemptions. These types of annuity product can be used in both accumulation and annuitization phase.

The real-life optionalities embedded in most of the VA products deserve serious attention of derivatives practitioners. The techniques of valuing the guarantees (optionalities) and managing VA risks are clearly complex. Guarantees in annuity products can became major liabilities; worse still, they can be open-ended, long-dated **liabilities**. Some of the life industry "traditional ways", which include setting aside capital reserves by actuarial estimation or by simulating tail exposures (VaR like methodologies), are unable to measure or capture true risks, which are often path-dependent. It is important to modernize those "traditional ways" in terms of managing such liabilities, in order to hedging and risk managing more appropriately. In the following, we discuss four typical types of VA features. The embedded optionalities and associated risks will be analysed.

KEY VA PRODUCT TYPES

In the USA, there are several typical types of variable annuity products.

GMAB (Guaranteed Minimum Accumulation Benefit)

The GMAB allows investors to protect their premiums paid into the fund during the accumulation phase. The premium may be rolled up at a guaranteed rate, or with a "ratchet" feature which allows investors to lock in the upside gain. At the end of the accumulation phase, the fund value is guaranteed to be above a minimum level, plus a participation of the market gain within a given limit. The above can be schematically expressed as a call spread:

$$V(T) = min\left[max\left(F(T), floor\right), cap\right]$$

Note that the *floor* and *cap* can be a function of time, taking into account the ratchet features. $V(T)$ will be used to purchase an annuity at the prevailing market rate.

GMDB (Guaranteed Minimum Death Benefit)

This is the benefit paid out typically during the accumulation phase, upon the death of the policy holder. The payout can be either the greater of total premium paid and prevailing fund value, or an amount calculated using a pre-determined fixed rate to roll up the premium. In some policies, the death benefit can apply in the annuitization phase. Clearly this particular benefit should be valued by explicitly in the mortality framework. Schematically, it can be expressed as:

$$V(T) = (1-p) \cdot F(T) + p \cdot min\big[max\big(F(T), floor\big), cap\big]$$

where p is the death probability.

GMIB (Guaranteed Minimum Income Benefit)

GMIB is a common and popular type of variable annuity feature that guarantees a minimum level of income benefit, regardless of the performance of the annuity. The guaranteed minimum level of income benefit can be either in the form of guaranteed minimum annuity rate or guaranteed minimum amount that pays out as an annuity. Denoting the prevailing accumulated fund value at annuitization as $F(T)$, which includes the charges, and a_T the prevailing market value of annuity with annual payment of 1, let us examine two cases in Table 18.2:

GMWB (Guaranteed Minimum Withdrawal Benefit)

GMWB, as its name indicates, gives annuitants the right to withdraw at a specified rate at specified intervals until their initial investment has been recouped. It offers protection against downside market risk when investment losses have been incurred, while keeping the benefit of upside gain. For example, a GMWB allows an annuitant to withdraw a maximum 8% of your total investment each year, regardless of market performance, until the annuitant has recovered 100% of original investment. If the

TABLE 18.2   GMIB case study

GMIB Type	Payoff	Comments
Guaranteed amount (paying out as annuity)	$V(T) = \max(F(T), F_T \cdot G \cdot a_T)$, where F_T is the guaranteed fund value, which may also include a lookback feature, i.e. $F_T = \max_t(F(t))$.	Either the prevailing fund value purchasing an annuity at the prevailing annuity rate, or the guaranteed fund value purchasing an annuity at the guaranteed annuity rate G.
Guaranteed annuity rate	$V(T) = \max\big(F(T), F_T\big) \cdot \max(r_T, G) \cdot a_T$, where r_T is the prevailing annuity rate, G is the guaranteed annuity rate.	The fund value $F(T)$ itself may be subject to a guarantee F_T. The terminal fund value will be used to purchase an annuity at a rate greater of r_T and G.

annuitant wishes to withdraw more than 8% at any withdraw points, there will be a penalty charge. In GMWB contracts, there may be other provisions that insurance companies wish to use to discourage withdraws. Such provisions include giving the policy holders incentives not to withdraw, such as extending withdrawals and increasing benefit amount. They can also include clauses to further penalize the policy holders when they withdraw, e.g. lowering the guaranteed minimum amount.

Stripping away various wrapping features, the core embedded optionality in GMWB comes from two key elements:

▪ The withdrawal guarantee: a guaranteed amount for withdrawal, and this explicit protection feature constitutes an option.
▪ The withdrawal process optimization: note that withdrawal is only allowed at pre-determined intervals (e.g. yearly), and each individual withdrawal amount is capped (e.g. 8% of guaranteed amount). If a withdrawal amount is more than the cap, then there will be a penalty charge. Hence, the withdraw amount (or withdrawal rate) itself is a factor to be optimized in order to **maximize** the overall economic value in GMWB.

The above two key optionality elements can be formulated as follows. Denoting A_t as the annuity investment account balance (asset) and G_t as the total guaranteed amount allowed being withdrawn, the log-normal asset underlying process can be expressed as:

$$dA_t = \mu \cdot A_t \cdot dt + \sigma \cdot A_t \cdot dz + dG_t$$

The withdrawal cash flow at time t can be written as:

$$CF(g_t) = \begin{cases} g_t & \text{if } 0 \le g_t \le g_{max} \\ g_{max} + (1-c)(g_t - g_{max}) & \text{if } g_t > g_{max} \end{cases}$$

Where g_{max} is the cap (maximum allowed withdrawal amount) at time t and c is the penalty charge if withdrawal is more than the cap. The present value of a GMWB is therefore of the following form:

$$V(A_t, G_t) = \max_{g_t} \left[E_t \left(DF_T \cdot \max(A_T, 0) + \sum_i DF_t^i \cdot CF(g_t) \right) \right]$$

Within the expectation brackets, the first term is simply the annuity investment account balance floored at 0, if there are withdrawals. The second term consists of cash flows coming from the withdrawals. After taking expectation, one needs to maximize the economic value by optimizing withdrawal amount g_t (or withdrawal rate). Intuitively this is similar to a Bermudan exercise feature in which one decides whether a faster withdrawal speed (which may result in penalty charge) is better than a slower withdrawal speed. The present value of the expected future cash flows at the decision (exercise) point will be maximized by varying the control variable g_t.

MAJOR RISK FACTORS IN VA PRODUCTS

VA products have many practical risk exposures, including fees, lock-in period, premium frequency, customer lapse behaviour (e.g. early withdrawal, surrender), mortality, etc. All of them can influence the pricing significantly.

Practical Risk Factors

For lapse and mortality risks, most of the industry hedging programmes assumes that the mortality and lapse profiles are static. In reality, they of course fluctuate! As for the mortality risks, there are no traded instruments in the markets can be used to hedge the longevity, hence mortality assumption can be a key driver for the VA products.

Policy holder behaviours measured at the overall level may be correlated to the market performance. For example, in GMAB, the charge of the guaranteed fund value is set as a percentage of the prevailing fund value. When the market performs badly, the charge in absolute term is small, while the guarantee itself is of better value. In this scenario, rational policy holders are less likely to lapse (early withdraw). In the opposite scenario, when market performs well, as it is deep in the money, the guarantee itself is of small value, but the policy holder pays a higher charge in absolute term. Hence rational decision is more likely to lapse the policy. Another example is in GMWB. When market performs badly and the fund value becomes very small, the optimal action is to exercise the withdrawal right and withdraw the allowed portion of fund as early as possible. When market performs well and the fund value is high, rational policy holders should choose to lapse the guarantee as it has little value, while the charge is higher in this scenario.

Out of all the practical risk factors, some can be "modelled" and assessed, and some can only be "guessed" and assessed. Although in the following we shall focus on market risk factors in the context of derivatives pricing, one should not forget that the practical risk factors cannot be ignored. For example, depending on the product features, one may need to formulate the lapse rate as a function of market level, instead of just a constant.

Market Risk Factors

There are two key types of market risk in VA products: one is equity/fund risks, which include FX and other factors affecting underlying fund performance. The other is interest rate risks coming from discounting but more importantly from explicit annuity guarantees. Of course in most of the VA products, both types of risk exist, although one may be more dominant than the other.

As GMDB is specifically the death benefit, we shall focus on GMAB, GMIB and GMWB to examine their riskiness in terms of underlying equity/fund exposures. By plotting the price changes against the equity/fund spot movement, one can broadly assess these products' risk exposures (Figure 18.2).

Figure 18.1 shows a plot for the comparable contracts of the three types: GMAB, GMIB and GMWB. GMAB tends to be flatter, indicating it is a less risky VA type, given the fact that its payoff resembles a call spread. GMWB, however, can enjoy the full market upside (less charge), but may suffer downside due to the fact that the guaranteed withdrawal needs to be in instalment over a long period time. Although

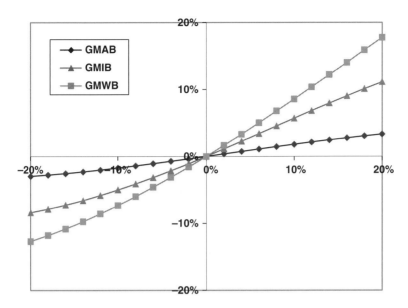

FIGURE 18.2 Price change vs spot move

the guaranteed withdrawal amount in GMWB can be the same amount of the original investment, the present value of the guarantee is much reduced. So comparably GMWB is most exposed to the underlying fund market risks. The optionalities embedded in GMAB and GMWB affect the accumulation phase most. The most predominant risk factor is the underlying fund fluctuations. For GMIB, it will also benefit from underlying market upside, but not as much as for GMWB. The downside risk in a GMIB due to adverse underlying market movement can be limited, as the explicit annuity guaranteed in the annuitization phase will kick in and act as a floor.

Stochastic interest rate will impact all three types of products, as all of them are long-dated products and stochastic discounting can affect prices. Stochastic interest rate also has a more direct impact on GMIB types as the guaranteed annuity is an option on interest rate. Hence pricing GMIB types of products requires hybrid derivative models, typically equity and interest rate hybrids.

Market Value of Annuity

The market value of annuity (MVA) a_T is defined as:

$$a_T = \sum_{i=1}^{n} (_x p_{t_i}) \cdot D_{t_i}$$

where $_x p_{t_i}$ is the survival probability from age x to age t_i and D_{t_i} is the discount factor. By definition, the prevailing annuity rate is:

$$r_T = \frac{1}{a_T}$$

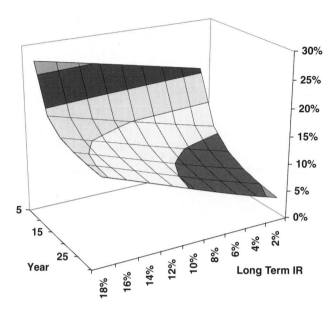

FIGURE 18.3   Annuity rate vs long-term IR and life expectancy

MVA (or the annuity rate) is an explicit function of mortality (life expectancy) and interest rate term structure. A schematic illustration of the relationship is shown in Figure 18.3, which indicates the risk exposures to those factors.

HYBRID PRICING MODELS FOR VA PRODUCTS

When it comes to derivatives pricing, assumptions are often made about the mortality element. One usually uses a deterministic survival probability curve, which is estimated conservatively, together with the assumption that the volatility of the survival probability is much lower than that of interest rates and equity markets.

General Multi-factor Model Framework

The stochastic process for the fund value F_t can be modelled as log-normal, and Hull–White model can be used for the interest rate r and average dividend yield q:

$$\frac{dF_t}{F_t} = (r - q) \cdot dt + \sigma_{F_t} \cdot dw_{F_t}$$

$$dr = (\mu_r - a_r \cdot r) \cdot dt + \nu_r \cdot dw_r$$

$$dq = (\mu_q - a_q \cdot q) \cdot dt + \nu_q \cdot dw_q$$

with correlations defined as:

$$\langle dw_{F_t} \cdot dw_r \rangle = \rho(F_t, r) \cdot dt$$

$$\langle dw_{F_t} \cdot dw_q \rangle = \rho(F_t, q) \cdot dt$$

$$\langle dw_r \cdot dw_q \rangle = \rho(r, q) \cdot dt$$

Note that in most VA products the guarantees are paid for not by an upfront option premium, but by annual charges based on a fixed percentage of the fund value. So the terminal fund value at time T includes the fees. Denoting the fixed percentage charge rate as c, the present value of GMWB payoff can be expressed:

$$V(A_0,G_0,c) = \max_{g_t} \left[E^Q \left(e^{-\int_0^T r(t)dt} \cdot \max(A_T,0) + \sum_i e^{-\int_0^{t_i} r(t)dt} \cdot CF(g_t) \right) \right]$$

and the present value of GMIB payoff can be expressed:

$$V(0,\ c) = E^Q \left[e^{-\int_0^T r(t)dt} \cdot V(T) \right]$$

Armed with the stochastic processes stated above, the GMWB and GMIB present values can be numerically evaluated by a PDE or Monte Carlo. The fair value of the charging rate c^f should solve for the following equations for GMWB and GMIB respectively:

$$V(A_0,G_0,c^f) = F(0)$$
$$V(0,\ c^f) = F(0)$$

Note that if the funds in VA products are the total return funds, i.e. no dividends, then one can reduce the three-factor model to two-factor only: F_t and r. This will substantially simplify the numerical implementation and increase the computational efficiency. If the funds consist of fixed income instruments (e.g. bonds), the above multi-factor model framework is flexible enough to model the underlying instruments consistently with the rates evolution in appropriate VA products. For example, one can use the same stochastic rate process for (bonds) fund diffusion, discounting and annuity guarantee.

Stochastic interest rate will of course impact the valuation of long-dated VA products. For GMWB, it is mainly affecting discounting. For GMIB, however, given the explicit annuity guarantees which are optionalities on rate, the stochastic interest rates effect will be dominant. Detailed analyses of GMIB optionalities will be presented in the section below.

Analysis of Hybrid Optionalities in GMIB

GMIB types of products have different variations in different countries. The similar European version of it is referred to as Guaranteed Annuity Option (GAO). There were high-profile losses suffered by insurance companies (e.g. Equitable Life) who failed to understand the embedded risks, never mind managing the risks. In this section, we shall specifically analyse the hybrid optionalities in GMIB or GAO. The values of GMIB are clearly affected by stochastic interest rate, underlying fund performance which determines the amounts to which the guaranteed applied, and the mortality assumption implicit in the guarantee impact the length of the policy. In the following, we will focus on equity and interest rate hybrid. Let us recall first the two types of GMIB payoffs: guaranteed amount and guaranteed annuity rate.

Guaranteed Amount This annuity payout is the greater of the prevailing fund value purchasing an annuity at the prevailing annuity rate, and the guaranteed fund value purchasing an annuity at the guaranteed annuity rate G:

$$V(T) = \max(F(T), F_T \cdot G \cdot a_T)$$

Rewriting it into the annuity form:

$$V(T) = \max(F(T) \cdot r_T \cdot a_T, F_T \cdot G \cdot a_T)$$
$$= F_T \cdot G \cdot a_T + a_T \cdot \max(F(T) \cdot r_T - F_T \cdot G, 0)$$

Note that the option payoff $\max(F(T) \cdot r_T - F_T \cdot G, 0)$ is intuitively similar to the well-known composite option. In a traditional compo option, the underlying stochastic process is driven by the product of the equity and foreign exchange rate, and Black–Scholes formula can be used with a modified volatility. If we assume geometric Brownian motion for both $F(T)$ and r_T, the above payoff has some similar pricing and risk features to a compo option.

Guaranteed Annuity Rate (GAR) The terminal fund value which is greater of the prevailing value $F(T)$ and the guarantee F_T, will be used to purchase an annuity at a rate greater of r_T and G:

$$V(T) = \max\big(F(T), F_T\big) \cdot \max(r_T, G) \cdot a_T$$

where r_T is the prevailing annuity rate, G is the guaranteed annuity rate and a_T is the prevailing market value of annuity with annual payment of 1. The key interest rate guarantee is the guaranteed annuity rate, specified at the outset of the contract, conservatively with respect to future mortality and interest rate assumptions.

Assuming the two underlyings ($F(T)$ and r_T) follow log-normal process, there exists an analytical solution (see Appendix A) for the above double-call payoff in $V(T)$. The analytical solution is of course an approximation, which assumes a fixed maturity, among other assumptions. However, it can be useful and convenient, in terms of understanding product pricing and risks qualitatively.

Replication Pricing and Hedging

The GMIB products can be priced within the general multi-factor model framework, and they can also be assessed using the analytical approximations explained above. Both are based on the foundation of continuous hedging. Hedging long-dated interest rate optionalities is never easy. Besides, continuous delta hedge will incur costs, which can be significant if the deal is very long dated. A semi-static hedging, in which the initial "static hedge" only needs to rebalance occasionally, will be highly desirable. Pricing models that are related to better hedging strategies (semi-static) are the topic of this section. For some simpler version of guaranteed annuity option (GAO), their payoffs suggest that a collection of bond option or swaption can be used as hedging

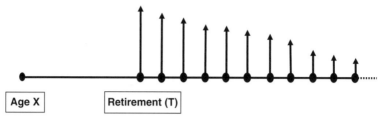

FIGURE 18.4 Diagram of payout cash flows

instruments. The bond options and swaptions can then be evaluated, either analytically or numerically, to price the annuity payoffs.

Let's examine an equity-linked GAO which guarantees a minimum annuity rate of G, with the optionality liability payoff at time T expressed as:

$$P_T = F_T \cdot \max(G - r_T, 0) \times a_T$$
$$= F_T \cdot \max\left(G \cdot a_T - 1, 0\right)$$
$$= F_T \cdot \max\left(G \cdot \sum_{i=1}^{n} ({}_x p_{t_i}) \cdot D_{t_i} - 1, 0\right)$$

For a given mortality table with deterministic survival probabilities, the payout cash flows can be illustrated in Figure 18.4:

When $G \geq r_T$, it is apparent that the guarantee is very similar to a receiver swaption on an amortizing annuity.

Decomposition Using Bond Options   Rewriting the GAO payoff into:

$$P_T = F_T \cdot \max\left(G \cdot \sum_{i=1}^{n} ({}_x p_{t_i}) \cdot D_{t_i} - 1, 0\right)$$
$$= F_T \cdot \max\left(G \cdot \sum_{i=1}^{n} ({}_x p_{t_i}) \cdot D_{t_i} - G \cdot \sum_{i=1}^{n} ({}_x p_{t_i}) \cdot D_{t_i}^*, 0\right)$$

where $D_{t_i}^*$ are chosen to satisfy the following equation:

$$G \cdot \sum_{i=1}^{n} ({}_x p_{t_i}) \cdot D_{t_i}^* = 1$$

Since the bond price is a monotonic function of the interest rate, the option on a sum of zero bond can be decomposed into a sum of options on zero bonds, with corresponding strikes of $D_{t_i}^*$:

$$P_T = F_T \cdot \sum_{i=1}^{n} G \cdot ({}_x p_{t_i}) \cdot \max\left(D_{t_i} - D_{t_i}^*, 0\right)$$

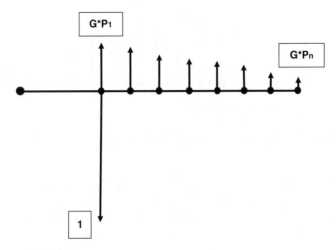

FIGURE 18.5   Diagram of payoff cash flows

So theoretically, one can replicate this type of GAO using a collection of bond options with appropriate weightings. Note that the fund value F_T is still stochastic, so it is not a complete static hedge unless the fund value is a fixed quantity or with little volatility.

In general, the bond options are less liquid instruments than swaptions. Let's try now a different decomposition.

Decomposition Using Swaptions: Given the GAO payoff, let us analyse its cash flows from the retirement time T:

$$G \cdot \sum_{i=1}^{n} (_x p_{t_i}) \cdot D_{t_i} - 1$$

A schematic diagram of the payoff cash flow is shown in Figure 18.5:

We intend to use a basket of swaps to match the above GAO payoff cash flows. Assuming the following basket of swaps (r_i) are used to replicate the GAO cash flows:

$$R_1 = w_1 \cdot (k_1 - r_1) \cdot D_1 = w_1 \cdot (k_1 \cdot D_1 + D_1 - 1)$$

$$R_2 = w_2 \cdot (k_2 - r_2) \cdot \sum_{i=1}^{2} D_i = w_2 \cdot (k_2 \cdot \sum_{i=1}^{2} D_i + D_2 - 1)$$

$$\ldots \ldots$$

$$R_n = w_n \cdot (k_n - r_n) \cdot \sum_{i=1}^{n} D_i = w_n \cdot (k_n \cdot \sum_{i=1}^{n} D_i + D_n - 1)$$

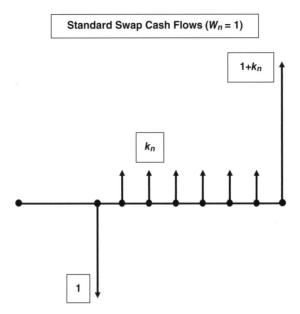

FIGURE 18.6 Standard swap cash flows ($w_n = 1$)

where R_i represents a swap with a particular maturity coinciding with a GAO cash flow date. The swap weightings w_i and fixed rates k_i are the parameters to be determined. A standard swap cash flow is illustrated in Figure 18.6:

By matching swaps' cash flows to those of GAO's on every cash flow date, we obtain the following simultaneous equations:

$$G \cdot P_n \cdot Y_n = w_n \cdot (k_n \cdot Y_n + 1)$$
$$G \cdot P_{n-1} \cdot Y_{n-1} = w_n \cdot k_n \cdot Y_n + w_{n-1} \cdot (k_{n-1} \cdot Y_{n-1} + 1)$$
$$\cdots\cdots$$

$$G \cdot P_i \cdot Y_i = \sum_{j=i+1}^{n} w_j \cdot k_j \cdot Y_j + w_i \cdot (k_i \cdot Y_i + 1)$$
$$\cdots\cdots$$

$$1 - G \cdot P_0 \cdot Y_0 = \sum_{i=1}^{n} w_i$$

where p_i is used for $_x p_{t_i}$, D_i for D_{t_i} and Y_i is the year fraction.

From the above simultaneous equations, one can solve for the swap weightings w_i and fixed rates k_i, by backward induction starting from the n-th date. Note that the very last equation has to be maintained during iterating k_i. Typically the first guess/ iteration is the at-the-money forward swap rates. Numerically the above simultaneous equations are easy to solve, as they are linear.

Once those swap parameters have been determined, the cash flows in the GAO payoff can be replaced by:

$$P_T = F_T \cdot \max\left(G \cdot \sum_{i=1}^{n} (x p_{t_i}) \cdot D_{t_i} - 1, 0 \right)$$

$$= F_T \cdot \max\left(\sum_{i=1}^{n} R_i, 0 \right)$$

The above shows that the GAO liabilities can be replicated by an option on a basket of swaps. The basket option approach allows for good intuition and sensible calibration decisions. If one wishes to further simplify the replications, note the following inequality:

$$F_T \cdot \max\left(\sum_{i=1}^{n} R_i, 0 \right) \le F_T \cdot \sum_{i=1}^{n} \max(R_i, 0)$$

As indicated by the inequality, the basket option on the swaps can be "over-hedged" by a basket of swaptions. The semi-static hedge provides a conservative pricing model.

Comparing the bond option and swaption hedging method, although the bond option method mathematically is more straightforward, the bond options tend to be less liquid than swaptions. In general, hedging with swaptions is more desirable.

Joint Equity and Swap Rate Process

In the last section only the annuity cash flows are replicated. In practice the replication is static only if the fund value is a fixed quantity or having very little volatility. In cases where the fund value is strongly stochastic, one can include the stochastic fund value by assuming a joint log-normal process for the fund value forward (F) and forward swap rate (r):

$$dF = F \cdot \sigma_F \sqrt{t} \cdot dz_1$$
$$dr = r \cdot \sigma_r \sqrt{t} \cdot dz_2$$
$$\langle dz_1 \cdot dz_2 \rangle = \rho \cdot dt$$

The payoff $F(T)[k - r(T)]^+$ is effectively a swaption with a stochastic notional. This can be intuitively understood as a Quanto under the swap measure! The Black's swaption model can be used with a Quanto adjustment to the forward swap rate. The present value of the GAO can be expressed as:

$$D_T \cdot E^Q \left\langle F(T) \cdot (k - r(T)^+) \right\rangle \cdot \sum D_i$$

$$= D_T \cdot E^Q \left\langle F_T \exp\left(Z_1 - \tfrac{1}{2}\sigma_F^2 \right) \cdot \left[k - r_T \exp\left(Z_2 - \tfrac{1}{2}\sigma_r^2 \right) \right]^+ \right\rangle \cdot \sum D_i$$

where D_T is the discount factor, F_T is the equity fund forward and r_T is the forward swap rate seen at time zero. Z_1 and Z_2 are jointly normal with zero mean. This is a familiar Quanto expression and hence the price becomes:

$$D_T \cdot F_T \cdot B\left(r_T \cdot e^{Z_1 \bullet Z_2}, k, \sigma_r \right) \cdot \sum D_i$$

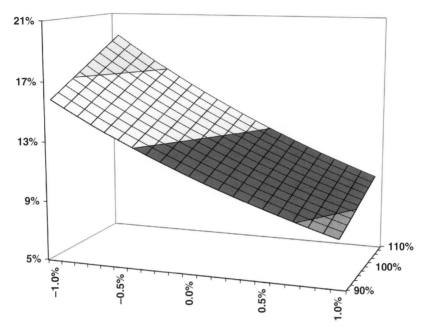

FIGURE 18.7 Price vs spot and rate

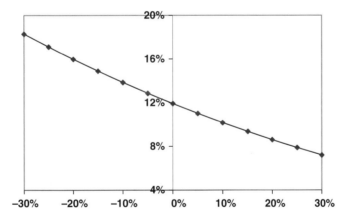

FIGURE 18.8 Price vs correlation

where $B(forward, strike, volatility)$ is the Black pricing formula for a put option. $Z_1 \bullet Z_2$ is the covariance, it is equal to $\rho \sigma_F \sigma_r$.

Figure 18.7 shows example prices versus the changes in equity fund spot and swap rate. It is a typical receiver swaption with varying notionals.

The price versus correlation is plotted in Figure 18.8. In the region where the fund value and swap rate are positively correlated, the price is less as the fund value and swap rate co-movements have opposite effect on the option price. In the region where the correlation is negative, fund value and swap rate have a positive effect on price, for example, when the fund value becomes larger and swap rate becomes less.

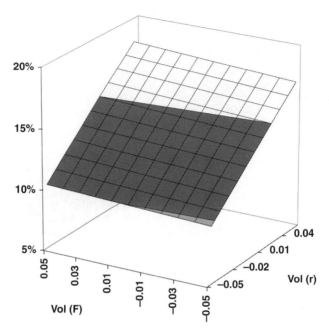

FIGURE 18.9   Price vs vol (F) and vol (r)

Figure 18.9 shows the price against the volatility of swap rate and fund value when the rate and fund correlation is set at –10%. The sensitivity to the swap rate volatility is much larger as the payoff is a direct option on rate. The sensitivity to the fund volatility is a result of the Quanto effect.

PRACTICALITIES OF HANDLING LONG-DATED VA PRODUCTS

In this section, we shall discuss some practical factors that affect VA products hedging decisions. These factors include transaction costs, long-dated forward and long-dated volatility.

Transaction Costs

For hedging long dated optionalities, transaction costs can be significant. Taking the above payoff as an example, the swaption with a variable notional requires the rebalancing of the swaption position when notional changes. There will be a transaction cost associated with the buying or selling swaptions where the bid-offer spread are substantial. For the swaption itself, one can use Leland's formula in which the transaction costs are included in the pricing by adjusting the swaption volatility. Transaction cost is proportional to the underlying volatility, as the more volatile the underlying is, the more frequent the rebalancing is. The transaction costs associated with the variable notional can be analysed and assessed in a similar way. The adjusted volatility needs to be plugged into both option formulation and the Quanto adjustment.

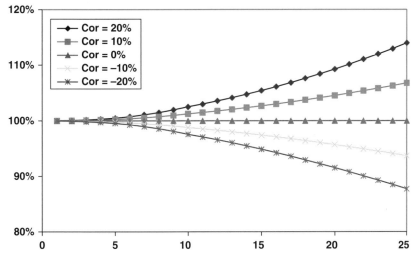

FIGURE 18.10   Convexity adjusted future

Note that the Quanto adjustment makes the option strike moving away from at-the-money. The adjustment itself changes with time as market parameters vary. Although the model suggests an optimum hedge using various strikes, the transaction costs make it impossible to sell the old position and repurchase at slightly different strikes. A more practical strategy is to adjust the hedge using swaps and ATM swaptions to offset first order risks, and carry out a relatively static hedge to offset any second order risks. In practice, transaction costs may determine hedging strategies that are more cost-effective.

Long-dated Fund (Equity) Forward

As can be seen above, most of the VA products involve buying or selling long-dated fund (equity) forward. To delta hedge the equity forward positions, typically exchange-traded equity index futures are used. Theoretically, **forward** is **not** equal to **future** if the interest rate is stochastic. For long-dated delta hedges, the difference between them could be so significant that an adjustment, termed below is essential. The convexity adjustment will affect pricing as well as hedging ratio.

Figure 18.10 shows the convexity adjustments versus the maturity, at various correlation levels for a typical set of equity index market data. As can be seen in the figure, the longer the term, the larger the convexity adjustment is. In general, the long-dated convexity adjustments become significant after 10 years.

The correlation effect on the convexity adjustment can be understood as follows:

- If one longs a future, with a **positive** correlation between the equity forward and interest rate (i.e. on average both go up or both go down together):
  - when market and rate go up, the margin account will be settled with a credit which in turn earns a higher interest;
  - when market and rate go down, the margin account will be settled with a debit which in turn incurs a lower funding cost;
  - this constitutes a systematic **advantage** for the person who longs the future, hence the future price must be higher than the forward;

- If one longs a future, with a **negative** correlation between the equity forward and interest rate (i.e. on average they move in opposite ways), the same logic as above indicates that there is a systematic **disadvantage** for the person who longs the future. Hence the future price must be lower than the forward.

Long-dated Fund (Equity) Volatility

The expected future fund value can be expressed as:

$$F_T = F_t \cdot \frac{\exp[r \cdot (T - t)]}{\exp[q \cdot (T - t)]}$$

Where F_t is the current fund value, r is the expected average fund growth rate and q is expected average dividend yield.

If both r and q are stochastic, the volatility of the expected future fund value is driven by three factors: volatility of F_t, r and q.

Denoting:

$$Z_r = \exp[-r \cdot (T - t)]$$
$$Z_q = \exp[-q \cdot (T - t)]$$

The variance of F_T is given by:

$$Var(dF_T) = Var(dF_t) + Var(dZ_r) + Var(dZ_q)$$
$$+ 2\left[Cov(dF_t, dZ_q) - Cov(dF_t, dZ_r) - Cov(dZ_r, dZ_q)\right]$$

where

$$Var(dF_t) = \int_0^T \sigma_{F_t}^2 \cdot dt$$

$$Var(dZ_r) = \int_0^T [\sigma_r(t)]^2 \cdot dt$$

$$Var(dZ_q) = \int_0^T [\sigma_q(t)]^2 \cdot dt$$

$$Cov(dF_t, dZ_r) = \int_0^T \rho(F_t, r) \cdot \sigma_{F_t} \cdot \sigma_r(t) \cdot dt$$

$$Cov(dF_t, dZ_q) = \int_0^T \rho(F_t, q) \cdot \sigma_{F_t} \cdot \sigma_q(t) \cdot dt$$

$$Cov(dZ_r, dZ_q) = \int_0^T \rho(r, q) \cdot \sigma_r(t) \cdot \sigma_q(t) \cdot dt$$

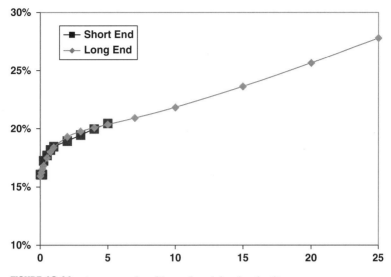

FIGURE 18.11   An example of long-dated fund volatility

Once the variance of F_T can be calculated, its volatility can simply be calculated backed out as:

$$\sigma_F = \frac{Var\left(dF_T\right)}{T}$$

If r and q follow the mean-reverting Ornstein–Uhlenbeck process, the volatility of r and q can be derived as:

$$\sigma_r\left(t\right) = v_r\,\frac{1 - e^{-a_r t}}{a_r}$$

$$\sigma_q\left(t\right) = v_q\,\frac{1 - e^{-a_q t}}{a_q}$$

Substituting these into the variance and covariance equations, the variance of F_T, i.e. $Var(dF_T)$ can be calculated.

The long-dated volatility can therefore be obtained from the variance. An example of long-dated fund volatility term structure derived from short end market quotes is shown in Figure 18.11.

IMPORTANCE OF UNDERSTANDING VA RISKS

Demographic changes, together with the changing company pension landscape, are driving the growth of VA products in various continents. As people live longer, there will be greater needs for a wider range of annuity products which allow the annuitants to participate market upside, in order to maintain the life styles. Equally, long-term protection against market downside, asset value volatility and longevity will also become more desirable. While VA products are flexible and can potentially meet those increasing needs, it is important that derivatives embedded in the VA products are fully understood and the risks are properly managed. In addition, the charges associated with the risks should be transparent to ensure the overall transparency of the VA products.

Managing and hedging long dated VA products is a very challenging task. It is vital for the product providers to fully understand the embedded derivatives in the VA products hence the associated risks in the balance sheet. The economic and regulatory capital costs for the risks in the books need to be calculated and understood properly. In addition, for the sake of transparency, the charges for various guarantees which are effectively the prices of embedded derivatives need to be valued accurately. Many lessons in the past told us that opaque in pricing may lead to mis-selling scandals.

While VA products represent attractive business opportunities, it is important to remember some key points:

- Pricing VA risks "correctly" is non-trivial, hedging them is even harder. Hedging costs could be substantial if the "wrong" pricing/hedging models are used.
- For long-dated liabilities, economic and market regimes change, hence one may need a variety of models suitable for dealing with different economical environments in order to manage the liabilities accordingly.
- Effectiveness of dynamic hedge needs to be examined, and whenever possible, semi-static hedge may be deployed. Semi-static hedging strategy can reduce model risks and hedging costs. It can be done by careful analysis of VA products cash flows. An example is to use a basket of swaptions to construct a semi-static hedge. It is likely that if semi-static hedging strategy is chosen, the construction tends to "over-hedge" the liabilities.
- VA products will be affected by the introduction of tougher financial regulations, including Solvency II Directive for the EU insurers. One must consider the impact of capital requirements under Solvency II, as well as the central clearing rules under EMIR.

In real life, VA policies are exposed to stochastic "everything", including financial markets, mortality/longevity, etc. In-depth understanding of VA risks will also help the products providers to use better structuring techniques to make the new products less risky. Avoiding unnecessary complex risks is the first line of defence. The seemingly "tail risks" in VA can be easily amplified due to correlation. One needs to pay particular attention to such "tail risks". For example, Figure 18.12 shows historic FTSE and GBP swap co-movements, which together drove up the historical GAO liabilities dramatically as shown in Figures 18.13 and 18.14. Strong stock market performance meant that the amounts to which the guaranteed applied increased significantly. Low interest rate leads to the fact that the prevailing annuity rates are lower than those guarantees, the insurer has to make up the difference and their liabilities become very serious.

This was the case in several high-profile losses suffered by insurance companies (e.g. Equitable Life), due to the mis-selling and mis-management of Guaranteed Annuity Options (GAOs). Most of the GAOs in the UK were issued in the 1970s and 1980s when long-term interest rates were high. At that time, the options were very far out

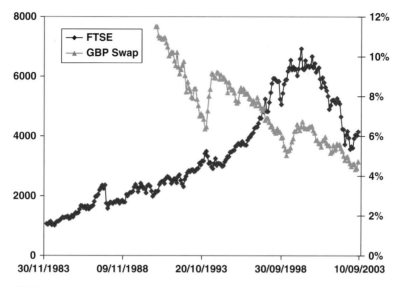

FIGURE 18.12   Historical FTSE and GBP long rate

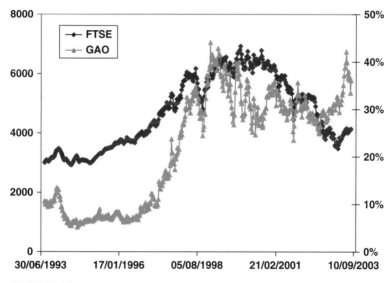

FIGURE 18.13   Historical FTSE and calculated GAO liability

of the money and insurance companies apparently assumed that interest rates would remain high and thus that the guarantees would never become active. Perhaps they did **not** even know such tail risks existed. In the early 1990s, when long-term interest rates began to fall, the guarantees became a major concern. Coupled with strong stock market performance which meant that the amounts to which the guaranteed applied increased significantly, the tail risks became major risks.

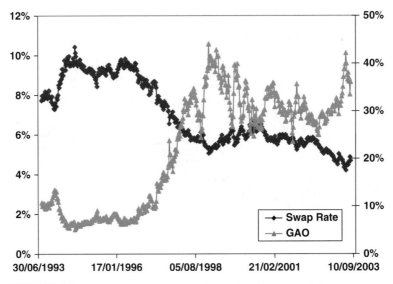

FIGURE 18.14   Historical swap rate and calculated GAO Liability

The correlation between equity (fund) and the long-term interest rate is a very important source of tail risks in VA. Over the past two decades, the long-term interest rate has been falling, coupled with the equity market volatility, the combined effect further highlighted the liability and solvency concerns, reserve issues, more importantly the hedges. There are other tail risks, including potential mis-selling compensation liabilities to the non-GAO policyholders. If they can prove they were mis-sold policies because they were not told about insurance companies' financial positions when they bought their non-GAO investments.

Interest Rate Optionality in Fixed-Rate Mortgage

In a fixed-rate mortgage portfolio, the rights of customers to prepay will impact the fair value as well as the risk characteristics of the mortgage portfolio. The embedded prepayment optionality is not a simple Bermudan swaption as it seems. The prepayment characteristics including speed and profile depend on many factors, which can be broadly divided into two distinguished yet entangled categories:

- Propensity factors: human- and circumstances-driven factors including customer behaviour, seasonality, burnout, house price and housing turnover, etc.
- Financial market factors: refinancing-driven market factor including (stochastic) interest rate movement, which is the main driver of the embedded interest rate optionality.

PREPAYMENT OPTIONALITY

Prepayment optionality is closely associated with the convexity effect. In this section, after explaining the convexity effect, we shall discuss the topic of quantifying prepayment option.

Convexity Effect

For a mortgage with a fixed rate of R_F from 0 to T_1 and floating rate L_i (LIBOR) from T_1 to T_2, ignoring prepayments and spreads for simplicity, its marking-to-market value is simply a fixed-floating amortizing bond:

$$
\begin{aligned}
M_{PV}^0 &= \sum_{i=0}^{T_1} \left(DF_i \cdot R_F \cdot \tau_i \cdot N_i \right) + \sum_{i=T_1}^{T_2} \left(DF_i \cdot L_i \cdot \tau_i \cdot N_i \right) \\
&= \sum_{i=0}^{T_1} \left[DF_i \cdot (R_F - L_i) \cdot \tau_i \cdot N_i \right] + \sum_{i=0}^{T_2} \left(DF_i \cdot L_i \cdot \tau_i \cdot N_i \right)
\end{aligned}
$$

$$= \sum_{i=0}^{T_1} \left[DF_i \cdot (R_F - L_i) \cdot \tau_i \cdot N_i \right] + N_0$$

where N_i is the outstanding notional, DF_i is the discount factor and τ_i is the year-fraction. The marking-to-market P&L is:

$$PnL^0 = \sum_{i=0}^{T_1} \left[DF_i \cdot (R_F - L_i) \cdot \tau_i \cdot N_i \right]$$

Including prepayments, the marking-to-market P&L can be expressed as the expectation of:

$$\langle PnL^1 \rangle = \left\langle \sum_{i=0}^{T_1} DF_i \cdot \left[(R_F - L_i) \cdot YF_i \cdot N_i^1 - N_i^p (R_F - L_i) \cdot FwdAnnuity \right] \right\rangle$$

where N_i^p is the prepaid notional and N_i^1 is remaining notional after prepayment at the i-th point.

The prepayment term N_i^p is critical in the analysis of convexity effect. It is dependent upon human propensity factors as well as financial market factors. Among the financial market factors, interest rate-driven refinancing is a key factor. Figure 19.1 shows historical GBP 2Y and 5Y swap rates over a period of 4 years in the 2000s, compared with the actual monthly prepayments of a fixed-rate GBP mortgage portfolio over the same period. The historical interest rates and prepayments were apparently anti-correlated: when interest rates became higher, there was less prepayment (N_i^p); when interest rates became lower, there was higher prepayment.

The above observed effect has a clear explanation: when market interest rates become higher, the fixed-rate mortgage holder is more likely to be content with the fixed-rate deal he/she had already, hence it is less likely to prepay. When the market

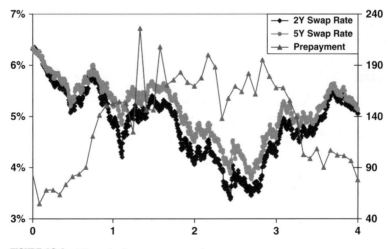

FIGURE 19.1   Historical swap rates and prepayments

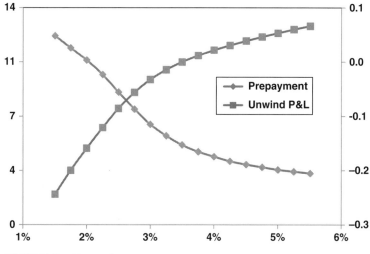

FIGURE 19.2 Convexity

interest rates become lower, there may be more competitive lower fixed-rate mortgages on offer, therefore there tend to be more prepayments as a result. This type of prepayment in the fixed-rate mortgage can cause headaches for banks on their linear swap hedging positions. If banks fully hedge the fixed-rate mortgage using swaps at the outset, they have to unwind the swap positions whenever there is a prepayment. For banks, because prepayments happen more at unfavourable swap rates than at favourable swap rates, the overall unwinding tends to result in losses. This is referred to as the convexity effect in the fixed-rate mortgage prepayment.

The convexity effect is schematically displayed in Figure 19.2. The prepayment profile is labelled by the left vertical axis, and corresponding unwinding P&L is labelled by the right vertical axis. The horizontal axis is the interest rate. Assuming the bank fully hedges the initial mortgage notional using a swap, when customers prepay the bank unwinds the prepaid amount of initial swap hedge, the convexity in P&L will manifest as:

- When the interest rate is **higher**, the bank's swap hedge is in the money, unwinding it will **make** money, but at a **lower** (prepaid) notional.
- When the interest rate is **lower**, the bank's swap hedge is out of the money, unwinding it will **lose** money, and at a **higher** (prepaid) notional.

The convexity effect causes losses during the unwinding because banks effectively hold short Gamma positions. The fixed-rate mortgage holders long the embedded interest rate options. A substantial portion of risks in a fixed-rate mortgage book are similar to those of an interest rate option book. It needs to be emphasized that the market mortgage rate consists of pure interest rate element and credit spread element. The same convexity effect is applicable to the combined market mortgage rate. Under a given economic and social environment, market mortgage rate is a key driver to the variation (uncertainty) of fixed-rate mortgage prepayments. It is true that human propensity factors convolute with the rate option risks. This does not necessarily mean that the rate option risks are not important. The rate option risks need to be captured and risk managed in the course of managing fixed-rate mortgage portfolios. The question is how to quantify such risks.

Quantifying Prepayment Option

In the following, we shall discuss an option-based prepayment technique (OBPT) which aims to capture key mortgage prepayment risk features by "calibrating" to both propensity (behaviour) "market" and financial (derivatives) markets. It inter-connects the two "markets" and models prepay decision-making process using the market yield curve information and the associated dynamics. The OBPT can be used to assess prepayment risks and earning exposures. It can also be used to calculate fair early redemption charges in the fixed-rate mortgages and derive efficient hedging strategies.

"Calibrating" to propensity (behaviour) "market" is very difficult in practice. It requires large amount of historical data, and different countries or regions have different behaviours. There are many different ways of prepayment modelling, and there is no universal technique that works for all. The OBPT focuses on a generic propensity distribution in terms of "virtual" transaction cost. Because the transaction cost is not directly tied in with the prepayment speed, it blends nicely with the option market and can include the prepayment burnout effects naturally. In the following, we use a real example of fixed-rate mortgage pool to illustrate key steps of deriving a propensity density function from the observable historical prepayment data.

Step 1: Single Monthly Mortality (SMM) Data   SMM is an actuarial name and it measures the monthly prepayment of a mortgage pool. After data cleaning, the SMM data (vertical axis) versus incentive (horizontal axis) is plotted in Figure 19.3. The incentive is defined as percentage of cash benefit at the time of prepayment. The cash benefit is simply how much money the borrowers saved by prepaying compared with the prevailing interest rate.

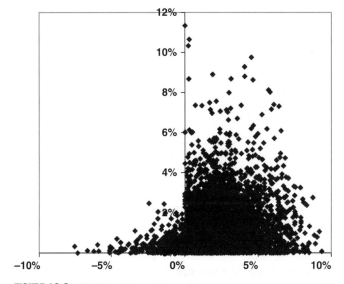

FIGURE 19.3   SMM vs incentive

Another related mortgage prepayment measure is the Conditional Prepayment Rate (CPR), which is effectively annualized SMM: $CPR = 1 - (1 - SMM_1)(1 - SMM_2) \cdots (1 - SMM_{12})$.

Step 2: Instantaneous Prepayment Distribution   The SMM can be viewed as the instantaneous prepayment data, and its relationship to the prevailing interest rate (via incentive) should be analysed. By taking the average within each of the pre-determined incentive buckets, one can obtain an instantaneous prepayment distribution as shown in Figure 19.4.

From the above instantaneous prepayment distribution, it is clear that most of the prepayments happened when there were positive market incentives. Due to various reasons such as moving house, there were still prepayments even if market incentives were negative.

Step 3: Cumulative Prepayment Distribution   The instantaneous prepayment distribution can be aggregated and converted into a cumulative distribution as shown in Figure 19.5. The cumulative distribution is numerically nicer to work with, as it is monotonic and smoother.

The above cumulative distribution has a clear intuition. If we pick a point on the curve, say (4%, 29%), it states that a total of 29% in the specified mortgage pool has a "virtual" transaction cost less than 4%. In other word, if the incentives are larger than 4%, those people will cash in or have already cashed in via prepayment. Also, the cumulative distribution is capped at 57%, meaning that a maximum of 57% will prepay if the incentive is large enough and remaining 43% will never prepay no matter what incentive is. The cap therefore includes the burn-out effects.

To facilitate subsequent numerical pricing, the kinks in the cumulative distribution curve shall be smoothed. One can also fit a functional form to it, and vary the shape of

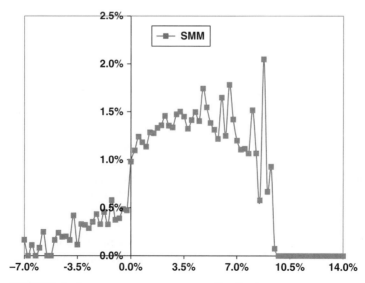

FIGURE 19.4   Instantaneous prepayment distribution

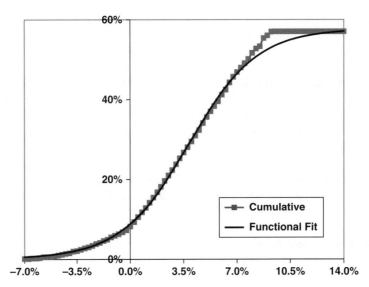

FIGURE 19.5 Cumulative prepayment distribution and a functional form (T, R, s, x) fit

propensity distribution curve as part of the propensity calibration process. An example functional form can be:

$$CumuDist = T + \frac{R}{1 + exp\left[-s\left(Incentive + x\right)\right]}$$

where T, R, s and x are constants which can be fitted to the given cumulative distribution data as shown in the graph above. The prepayment turnover effect is included in the parameter T which floors the distribution on the left-hand side.

Step 4: Monte Carlo Pricing Clearly, different historic prepayments data will result in different prepayment distributions and these distributions reflect the specific markets and propensities manifested as "virtual" transaction costs. The OBPT can then price in and capture the behaviour-related/induced option value and risks:

- Generate risk-neutral interest rate scenarios: this can be done using a standard Monte Carlo interest rate derivative pricing model (e.g. HW or BGM) and its calibration routine. The simulated interest rates (short rate or LIBOR) can then be converted into mortgage rates.
- Calculate incentives: given the known fixed-rate mortgage information and interest rate scenarios, the incentives along a path can be valued by the difference between prevailing mortgage rates and fixed contractual rate.
- Decide the prepayment: using the calculated incentives to sample the cumulative prepayment distribution curve to get the prepayment amount. Note that the prepayment is path-dependent, and one needs to take into account earlier prepayments along the scenario path.
- Once the prepayment profile is obtained, the prepayment valuations and risk sensitivities can be calculated.

■ The PV of the mortgage book including prepayment options can be calculated by valuing all cash flows along the scenario path for both scheduled payments and prepayment.

The OBPT combines stochastic interest rate with the historical (human propensity) prepayment distribution. It is flexible and able to take in different shapes of the distribution function. The OBPT will price in interest rate optionality, but not as much as for an outright Bermudan swaption. While theoretically the borrowers of fixed-rate mortgages hold Bermudan swaptions against the lending banks, the propensity factors dampen the optionalities. The prepayment optionality is therefore closer to the auto-callable than to the callable. Since OBPT takes into account the historical propensity, it is able to capture and value the embedded interest rate optionality more realistically.

PREPAYMENT RISK CHARACTERISTICS

In this section, the OBPT will be used to analyse a real-life example of fixed-rate mortgage portfolio. The portfolio has a range of fixed rates and fixed periods. The notional distribution against the fixed rate is plotted in Figure 19.6, with fixed rates ranging from 3.5% to 9%.

The portfolio's notional distribution versus the fixed period is plotted in Figure 19.7. The fixed periods have a range from 3-month to 5-years.

The distribution figures above will help us to understand peaks and troughs of the prepayment profiles and the associated risk profiles.

Prepayment Profile

Running the OBPT on large number of individual mortgages will incur massive computational burden. A pre-processing aggregation methodology should be adopted to

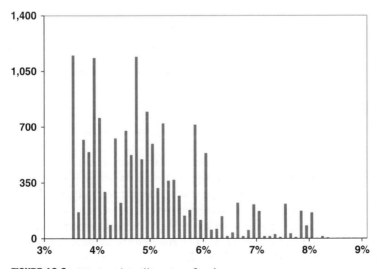

FIGURE 19.6 Notional (millions) vs fixed rate

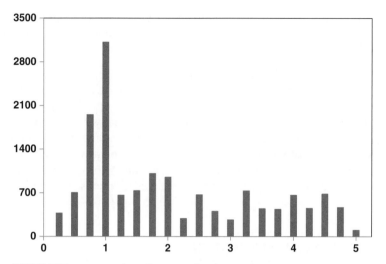

FIGURE 19.7 Notional (millions) vs fixed period (years)

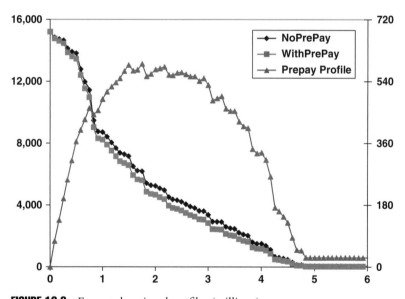

FIGURE 19.8 Expected notional profiles (millions)

shrink the portfolio, including aggregating similar fixed rates and fixed periods. For the example portfolio, the scheduled amortizing notional profile (no prepayment) and expected notional profile (including prepayment) are plotted in Figure 19.8. The differences between the two form the prepayment profile.

The expected notional profile (including prepayment) can be further calibrated to the current market data and information. The risk sensitivity analyses below are bench marked against the expected notional profile.

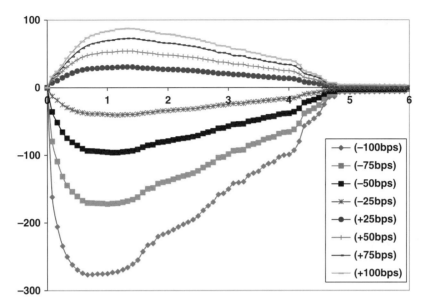

FIGURE 19.9 Interest rate sensitivity – parallel shifts (millions)

Interest Rate Risk Sensitivity

The expected notional profile is sensitive to the yield curve movement. Figure 19.9 shows such sensitivities to parallel shifts in the zero yield curve using the OBPT. The notional profile shifts indicate increased or reduced prepayment: negative shift in the notional profile corresponds to increased prepayment, positive shift in the notional profile corresponds to reduced prepayment. The notional profile shifts are labelled by the vertical axis in units of millions.

As can be seen in Figure 19.9, the sensitivity is non-linear. When the rate moves down, the prepayment increases at a faster pace, comparing to the reduced pace of prepayment when the rate moves up. This non-linearity in sensitivity is a classic sign of convexity and prepayment optionality, which can be further highlighted by the change in mortgage portfolio PV with the rate shift. In Figure 19.10, the mortgage PV change (labelled by middle vertical axis in millions) against the zero rate parallel shifts (labelled by horizontal axis in bps) is plotted. The right vertical axis labels the convexity which is the difference between the PV change curve and its tangential line at point (0, 0).

As can be seen in Figure 19.10, when the fair value of a fixed-rate mortgage portfolio includes the prepayment, its interest rate sensitivities are not linear. Linear swap hedges can only hedge the first order risks.

The expected notional profile changes to the time-bucketed +10bps shift to each of the zero rate pillars are plotted in Figure 19.11. These time-bucketed sensitivities show which time buckets have larger impacts on the notional profile, and subsequently on the mortgage portfolio PV. In this particular example, the 35-month interest rate has the biggest impact on the prepayment profile.

The expected notional profile changes to the interest rate curve tilting are plotted in Figure 19.12. The tilted curves are created by fixing the short end (1-day) rate, and moving the long end (50Y) rate by specified amounts shown in the graph. The

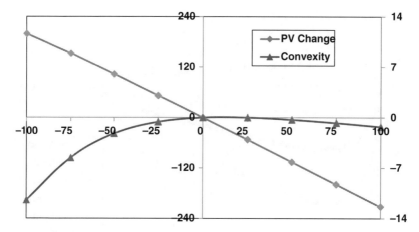

FIGURE 19.10   Mortgage PV change vs rate shift

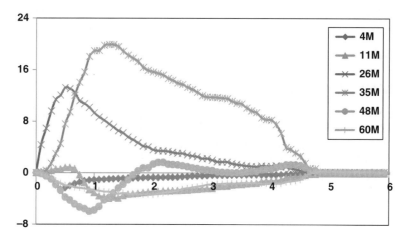

FIGURE 19.11   Time-bucketed sensitivity (millions)

increments (decrements) for the rates in between are linearly interpolated. The prepayment profile sensitivities to the tilting are also biased and they are not symmetric the up (+) and down (-) tilting.

Volatility Risk Sensitivity

The expected notional (and prepayment) profile is also sensitive to the volatility of the yield curve. Figure 19.13 shows the swaption sensitivities, by parallel shifting the ATM swaption volatility surface. The existence of volatility sensitivities indicates the non-linear risky behaviours, and such risky profiles can be used to determine appropriate option hedging ratios.

The mortgage portfolio PV sensitivities to the swaption ATM volatility surface are plotted in Figure 19.14. The vertical axis is in millions and horizontal axis is the absolute shift. The fixed-rate mortgage portfolio contains short Vega positions as expected.

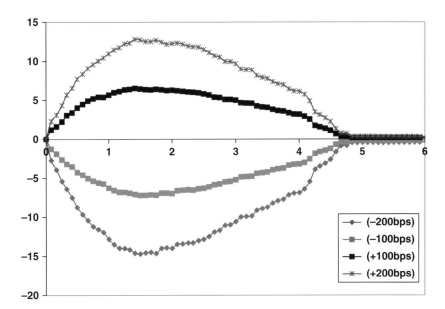

FIGURE 19.12   Interest rate sensitivity – tilts (millions)

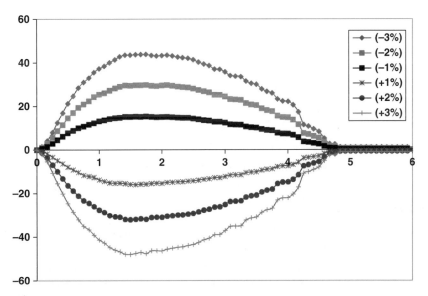

FIGURE 19.13   Volatility sensitivity – parallel shifts (millions)

The volatility expiry/tenor bucketed sensitivities shown in Figure 19.15 exhibit the mortgage portfolio Vega map along the expiry and tenor axis. They are the sensitivities to absolute 1% bump to each of the expiry/tenor pillars in the ATM swaption volatility surface. The highest Vega concentration for the example portfolio is in the region of 2Y-expiry and 1Y-tenor.

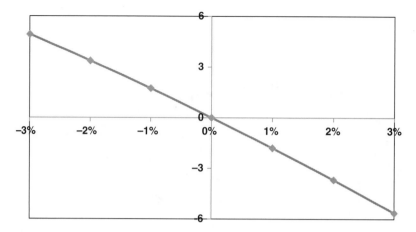

FIGURE 19.14   Mortgage PV change vs volatility shift

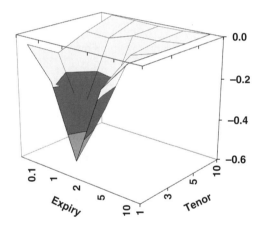

FIGURE 19.15   Mortgage PV bucketed Vega

Propensity Risk Sensitivity

The propensity sensitivities are obtained by shifting the propensity curve vertically and horizontally. Figure 19.16 shows the propensity curve used in the OBPT. It is a virtual transaction cost curve, whereby the horizontal axis is the transaction cost and vertical axis is the percentage of the aggregated mortgage prepayment associated with that transaction cost.

As shown in Figure 19.17, when the propensity curve is shifted upwards, the notional profile shifts down, indicating more prepayment. The higher the propensity curve, the higher the percentage of people who have lower virtual transaction cost, hence the higher prepayments are expected.

The notional profile sensitivities to the horizontal parallel shifts of the propensity curve are shown in Figure 19.18. Shifting propensity curve left (minus shifts) effectively reduces the virtual transaction costs, hence higher prepayments are observed.

The mortgage portfolio PV is also sensitive to the propensity curve. The sensitivities to the horizontal parallel shifts are shown in Figure 19.19. Shifting propensity curve

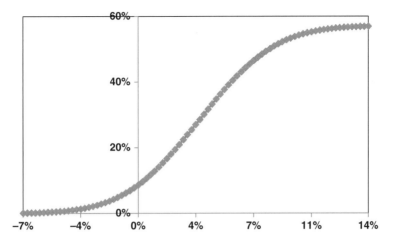

FIGURE 19.16   Propensity curve

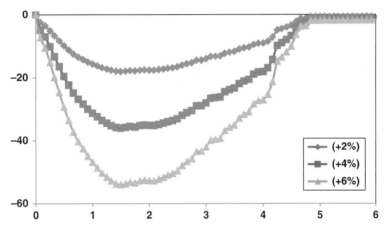

FIGURE 19.17   Propensity risks – vertical parallel shifts
Horizontal axis is in years, and vertical axis is in units of millions.

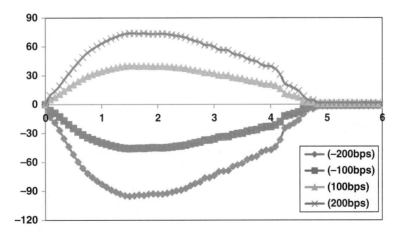

FIGURE 19.18   Propensity risks – horizontal parallel shifts
Horizontal axis is in years, and vertical axis is in units of millions.

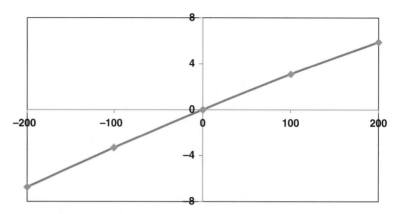

FIGURE 19.19 Mortgage PV sensitivity to propensity
Horizontal axis is in bps, and vertical axis is in units of millions.

left (minus shifts) effectively increases prepayments, hence more negative mortgage book values are observed due to larger short option positions.

The above prepayment risk analyses can help banks to understand better various risk factors in practice and formulate adequate risk management and hedging policies. Assessing the fair value of early redemption charge for a fixed-rate mortgage is an important hedging decision for the bank as well as for the customers.

EARLY REDEMPTION CHARGE

Early Redemption Charge (ERC) has two effects: it can deter prepayment as well as offset the prepayment resulted hedging costs. The fair value of ERC should therefore be based on the resultant prepayment and expected unwinding P&L of the initial swap hedges. The OBPT can easily include ERC as it simply adds to the virtual transaction costs during the simulation:

- For each interest rate scenario run, the prepayment at each step is calculated in the same way as in the previous sections including ERC deterrence.
- The resultant prepayment amount needs to be unwound from the original swap hedge. The ERC income together with the unwinding P&L is the total hedging P&L.

ERC can have either flat or stepped scheme and both of them can be included in the OBPT Monte Carlo.

Flat ERC Scheme

Flat ERC scheme is the most common charging structure and it levies a fixed penalty for those who prepay throughout the fixed period. Its deterrence to prepayment increases linearly with time as the early redemption benefit decreases with time. Using two fixed-rate mortgage examples, Figure 19.20 plots the total hedging P&L (ERC + unwinding P&L) versus ERC expressed in penalty days at the fixed rate. The example mortgages have fixed period of 5-years and 10-years, both have 25-years maturity.

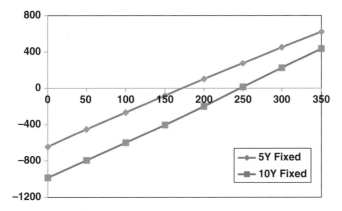

FIGURE 19.20   Hedging P&L vs ERC (days)

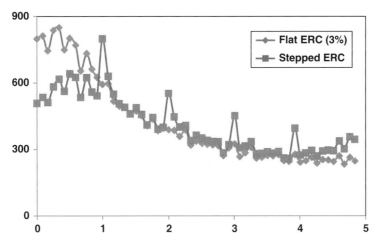

FIGURE 19.21   Prepayment profiles with different ERC schemes

The ERC has a flat rate expressed in penalty days. For the 5-years fixed period, at the 170-days point, the total hedging P&L is zero, indicating that the ERC fair value is 170-days penalty. For the 10-years fixed period, the ERC fair value is 250-days penalty in this particular example.

Step ERC Scheme

Step ERC scheme levies stepped penalties for those who prepay during the fixed period. For example, it can levy a higher penalty in the first year, and then step down every year during the fixed period. The step ERC scheme can alter prepayment profiles significantly, in particular over different time periods divided by the stepping points.

The OBPT can be applied for the step ERC scheme in the same way as for the flat ERC scheme. Figure 19.21 compares two example prepayment profiles: one uses a 3% flat rate ERC, and the other using an annual stepping down ERC scheme, starting at 5%. As shown in the figure, higher early ERC has depressed the prepayment in the early period.

Some banks tend to treat ERC as earnings, and their ERCs are often much higher than the fair values. From customers' perspective, ERC calculations should be made more transparent and fairer. Regulators in a number of jurisdictions have already demanded banks to justify their ERCs.

APPLYING OPTION-BASED PREPAYMENT TECHNIQUE

In this section, we shall clarify the scope and suitability of the OBPT, and also explain how to analyse the fixed-rate mortgage selling period optionality.

Scope and Suitability

The OBPT is **not** a mortgage prepayment model. A mortgage prepayment model is designed to forecast prepayments in the future considering all real-life factors. The OBPT is not about forecasting. It is about the optionality analysis given the historical data and/or certain market assumptions.

Optionality exists in many other mortgage investment products, including mortgage-backed securities (MBS). Assessing and quantifying optionalities in mortgage derivatives is a very challenging task, even more so for their risks and hedges. In practice, it involves a large quantity of historical and customer behaviour data, effective methodologies of mortgage data aggregation and smart numerical computation techniques. The human propensity characteristics are clearly country- and region-dependent, and there is no universal model or technique that works for all.

The OBPT, or the spirit of OBPT, can be used to assess and quantify prepayment-induced risk exposures and calculate the fair value of ERC. It allows banks to have a simpler handle on the risks involved and hence improve the decision making process in risk management and mortgage product development. The OBPT applications include:

- calculating fair value of the mortgage portfolio incorporating prepayment optionalities;
- assessing the potential hedging costs and Earning-at-Risk (EaR);
- formulating self-consistent hedging and risk management strategies for non-linear mortgage risks;
- calculating and justifying ERCs.

Selling Period Optionality

Another smaller but noticeable optionality in the fixed-rate mortgage lies in its selling period. The total notional size is variable, and it can be a function of market interest rate:

- If market interest rate goes up during the selling period, more people will take up the (lower) fixed rate offered and bigger notional is expected.
- If market interest rate falls, smaller notional is expected as the (higher) fixed rate offered is no longer attractive.
- There is an observable correlation between the market interest rate and notional to be sold.

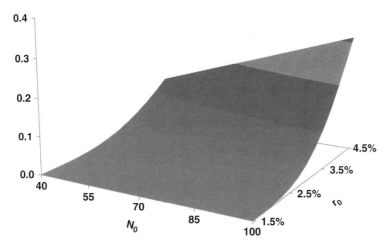

FIGURE 19.22 Variable size option during selling period

As the mortgage rate is already fixed, the customers effectively long an interest rate option. Mathematically, the fixed-rate mortgage variable size optionality during the selling period can be expressed:

$$N_t \left(r_t - K \right)^+ \cdot A_t^T$$

where the selling period is between 0 and t, K is the fixed-rate mortgage offered, r_t is the relevant interest rate at time t and N_t is the total notional sold by time t, A_t^T is the annuity over the mortgage fixed period spanning from t to T.

Assuming both N_t and r_t follow log-normal process, the variable size option can be calculated analytically (see Appendix A). Figure 19.22 schematically shows the option values for different rates and notionals at time 0, using an example of 3-month selling period ($t = 0.25$), $K = 3\%$, rate volatility of 50%, notional volatility of 10%, correlation between them is 50% and a 5-years fixed period.

Real Estate Derivatives

Real estate derivatives are embedded in a number of real-life financial products, such as equity release schemes and lifetime roll-up mortgages. These real estate-linked schemes are important sources of real estate exposures which allow financial institutions to warehouse risks and structure real estate derivative products for retails.

There are also commercial real estate indices that one can use to take exposures and hedge valuations of commercial properties.

EQUITY RELEASE SCHEME AND RELATED DERIVATIVES

The equity release schemes are financial tools used to release values locked in residential properties. Essentially a customer sells a stake in their property in return for a lump sum and lease for life. Within such schemes, people who are cash-poor but (property) capital-rich can release a portion of their property value without having to sell the property. Typically, the scheme holder is paid a lump sum for a portion of his property, retains the right to live in the property for the rest of his/her life. Upon death and/or when the property is sold, the scheme provider receives the portion of the property value he effectively bought and realizes any appreciation or depreciation in the property portfolio value.

A typical reversion scheme allows the property owner to sell a portion of the property and retain the right to live in it for the rest of his/her life. Upon death or when the property is sold early (reversion crystallization time), the reversion scheme provider who has purchased a portion of the property will receive the portion of the prevailing property value and realize any appreciation or depreciation. In almost all cases, it makes sense that the reversion is less than 100% and the occupier maintains a stake in the equity release property.

For example, a single male aged 80 takes 80% of the property reversion on a house currently valued at £200,000. To enter an equity release scheme, assuming the reversion discount rate is 65%, the customer will be paid a lump sum of £104,000 (80% * £200,000 * 65%). The reversion discount takes into account property forwards, mortality rate, interest rate and rent. Upon the death of the property owner, assume the property is sold for £250,000. Given 80% of the property is in the reversion scheme, the scheme provider will receive £200,000 lump sum, and 20% (£50,000) will go to scheme holder's family.

Equity release schemes offered in the traditional forms are designed mainly to meet social needs, such as for the elderly. They can also be in the newer form in which the lump sum released is used for other purposes, such as investment in other properties. This can be a suitable form of funding for purchasing a second home or investment property, in particular when the equity release property is in a much more expensive area than that of the second home or investment property. Effectively this is a form of equity release mortgage in which the released lump sum is interest-free but at the expense of parting with a portion of equity.

The embedded real estate derivatives in such schemes are a function of the property owners' life expectancy (longevity), long-term interest rates and the expected property forward value. In order to hedge the risks of property portfolio risks, the scheme providers can use property derivative products to offset the property risks embedded in their portfolios. The pricing models for the property derivative products have to broadly capture the characteristics of life expectancy, long-term interest rate and the property forward curve.

The equity release scheme provider can either retain all the risks in their book, or enter an equity reversion swap agreement, with a bank for example, to pass on the real estate exposures.

MORTALITY IN DERIVATIVES PRICING

Mortality risks are embedded in many long dated real estate derivatives products. The methodology of pricing in mortality risks is mainly based on mortality tables widely used in the insurance industry. The mortality rates raw data consist of various statistical functions of the age and gender, population groups, etc. The most fundamental mortality tables are the base tables which contain the relevant annualized mortality rates derived from realized statistics as well as forecasts into years ahead. For the sake of pricing real estate derivative products, let us examine two examples of the mortality base tables: male base and female base table.

Male Mortality Base Table

In the example male mortality base table (Table 20.1), the first column lists age (x), and the first row the forward years. The percentage numbers in the table are the death rate q(x),[1] which is a function of age (x) and forward year. q(x) is the forecasted probability that a person aged x dies within the next year (x+1) in the given year. For example, the table forecasts that a male aged 75 has a death rate of 1.801% in 2018, and 1.687% in 2023. The forecasted mortality rates take into account medical and technological advances and indicate that in the future we shall all live longer (with a

---

[1] It is also worth noting that another measure the insurance industry uses is called the force of mortality u(x), which is the conditional probability that a life of attains the age x and dies within the next year (x+1). In this book, we only use q(x), which is sufficient as u(x) can be derived from q(x).

TABLE 20.1 An example of male mortality base table

x	31/12/2015	31/12/2016	31/12/2017	31/12/2018	31/12/2019	31/12/2020	31/12/2021	31/12/2022	31/12/2023
70	1.119%	1.099%	1.079%	1.060%	1.042%	1.024%	1.007%	0.991%	0.975%
71	1.237%	1.216%	1.195%	1.175%	1.156%	1.137%	1.119%	1.102%	1.085%
72	1.368%	1.345%	1.324%	1.303%	1.282%	1.263%	1.244%	1.225%	1.207%
73	1.518%	1.495%	1.471%	1.449%	1.428%	1.407%	1.387%	1.367%	1.348%
74	1.687%	1.662%	1.638%	1.614%	1.591%	1.569%	1.548%	1.527%	1.507%
75	1.879%	1.852%	1.826%	1.801%	1.777%	1.753%	1.731%	1.709%	1.687%
76	2.101%	2.073%	2.046%	2.019%	1.993%	1.968%	1.944%	1.920%	1.898%
77	2.356%	2.325%	2.296%	2.268%	2.240%	2.214%	2.188%	2.163%	2.138%
78	2.646%	2.614%	2.583%	2.553%	2.523%	2.495%	2.467%	2.440%	2.414%
79	2.986%	2.951%	2.918%	2.885%	2.854%	2.823%	2.793%	2.764%	2.736%
80	3.383%	3.339%	3.303%	3.268%	3.234%	3.201%	3.169%	3.138%	3.108%
81	3.849%	3.792%	3.747%	3.709%	3.673%	3.637%	3.603%	3.570%	3.537%
82	4.396%	4.325%	4.267%	4.227%	4.187%	4.149%	4.112%	4.076%	4.041%
83	5.039%	4.950%	4.877%	4.825%	4.783%	4.742%	4.701%	4.662%	4.625%
84	5.791%	5.679%	5.589%	5.522%	5.469%	5.424%	5.381%	5.338%	5.297%
85	6.665%	6.526%	6.414%	6.330%	6.263%	6.215%	6.168%	6.122%	6.078%

small probability to die). Note that when one calculates a male's expected life, the q(x) trail goes diagonal. For example, for a male aged 75 in 2018, he will be 76 in 2019 and 77 in 2020. Hence the q(x) trail goes along the diagonal marked blue in the table. The corresponding mortality rates are 1.801%, 1.993% and 2.214%.

The above male mortality base table is plotted in the surface graph Figure 20.1. As in an implied volatility surface, **mortality surface is also skewed**. The shape of the surface is clear and intuitive: for a person whose age is older in the same year, the mortality rate is higher. For a person of the same age, the mortality rate in the far end (future years) is less than in the short end (closer to now).

Female Mortality Base Table

An example of a female mortality base table is displayed in Table 20.2. Taking an example, the table forecasts a female aged 75 has a death rate of 1.487% in 2018, and 1.393% in 2023. Comparing this to the equivalent male mortality rates, a female's q(x) is smaller and of course she is less likely to die. Note that when one calculates a female's life expectancy, the q(x) trail goes diagonal. For example, for a female aged 75 in 2018, she will be 76 in 2019 and 77 in 2020. Hence the q(x) trail goes along the diagonal shaded in the table. The corresponding mortality rates are 1.487%, 1.722%, 1.992%.

The female mortality base table is plotted in the surface graph in Figure 20.2. Again it is a skewed surface, for the same reason as for the male mortality surface.

Survival Probability

The above mortality tables and their features are an important base for pricing real estate derivatives. In fact, mortality in many ways is very much similar to credit derivatives. A company's default event in the credit derivatives is conceptually similar to a person's death, although a person's death is certain eventually. The concept of a company's

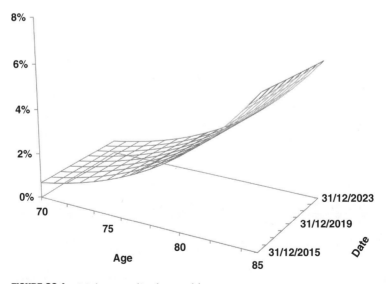

FIGURE 20.1 Male mortality base table

TABLE 20.2 An example of female mortality base table

x	31/12/2015	31/12/2016	31/12/2017	31/12/2018	31/12/2019	31/12/2020	31/12/2021	31/12/2022	31/12/2023
70	0.678%	0.666%	0.654%	0.643%	0.632%	0.621%	0.611%	0.601%	0.591%
71	0.804%	0.790%	0.777%	0.764%	0.751%	0.739%	0.727%	0.716%	0.705%
72	0.951%	0.935%	0.920%	0.906%	0.891%	0.878%	0.865%	0.852%	0.839%
73	1.122%	1.105%	1.088%	1.071%	1.055%	1.040%	1.025%	1.010%	0.997%
74	1.321%	1.301%	1.282%	1.264%	1.246%	1.228%	1.212%	1.195%	1.180%
75	1.550%	1.528%	1.507%	1.487%	1.467%	1.447%	1.428%	1.410%	1.393%
76	1.815%	1.791%	1.767%	1.744%	1.722%	1.700%	1.679%	1.659%	1.639%
77	2.119%	2.092%	2.066%	2.040%	2.016%	1.992%	1.968%	1.946%	1.924%
78	2.468%	2.438%	2.408%	2.380%	2.353%	2.326%	2.300%	2.275%	2.251%
79	2.865%	2.832%	2.799%	2.768%	2.738%	2.709%	2.680%	2.652%	2.626%
80	3.316%	3.280%	3.244%	3.210%	3.177%	3.145%	3.113%	3.083%	3.053%
81	3.827%	3.787%	3.749%	3.711%	3.675%	3.639%	3.605%	3.571%	3.539%
82	4.403%	4.360%	4.318%	4.277%	4.237%	4.199%	4.161%	4.125%	4.089%
83	5.051%	5.004%	4.958%	4.914%	4.871%	4.829%	4.788%	4.748%	4.710%
84	5.776%	5.725%	5.676%	5.628%	5.581%	5.536%	5.491%	5.448%	5.407%
85	6.584%	6.530%	6.476%	6.425%	6.374%	6.325%	6.278%	6.231%	6.186%

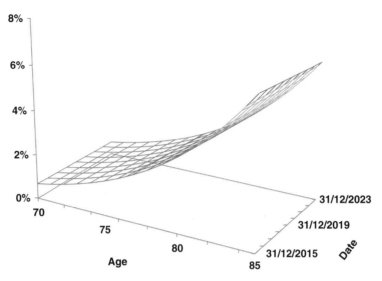

FIGURE 20.2 Female mortality base table

survival is identical to that of a person's survival. Therefore, the mortality calculation methodology is very much similar to that used in credit default swap (CDS). Default (death) and survival probability can be calculated and used to price various instruments. By converting the annualized death rates in the mortality table into exponential rates, one can derive something equivalent to the hazard rate h (as in pricing CDS).

Single Holder Denoting the mortality hazard rate as h, which is very similar to the instantaneous default density in the credit derivatives world, and a person's survival probability to time T as $Q(T)$, the survival probability to $T + dt$ is by definition:

$$Q(T + dt) = Q(T)(1 - h \cdot dt)$$

Solving this differential equation, one obtains:

$$Q(T) = e^{-\int_0^T h \cdot dt}$$

The probability of a person surviving to time T **and** then dying in a subsequent interval dt is:

$$Q_D(T) = Q(T) - Q(T + dt)$$

Joint Holders The joint mortality rates need to be derived and they can then be used in the same pricing model as for the single holder.

Given individual survival probabilities $Q_1(T)$ and $Q_2(T)$, the probability of any one or both surviving is:

$$Q_J(T) = 1 - \left[1 - Q_1(T)\right]\left[1 - Q_2(T)\right]$$

The probability of one or both surviving to time T **and** then both dying in subsequent interval dt is:

$$Q_{DJ}(T) = Q_J(T) - Q_J(T + dt)$$

The joint mortality rates can be simply backed out from the above calculated probabilities.

REVERSION DERIVATIVES PRODUCTS

Reversion derivatives products are types of transactions designed to transfer or protect risks embedded in real-life property-linked schemes, such as equity release schemes. They are meant to hedge property and mortality exposures. The real tradable underlying for the real estate derivatives is the property itself. Trading properties takes a long time and settlement and liquidity are major issues. One alternative is to structure the derivative transaction on published property indices. In UK the residential property derivatives can be written on the HPI (House Price Index). For example, Halifax publishes periodically the UK HPI as well as the geographical regional HPIs. The geographical regional HPIs can be mixed with appropriate weightings to represent a specific property portfolio with a specific geographic exposures. The derivative products based on such HPIs can be used for hedging and risk managing those specific property portfolios.

Assuming HPI at the time 0 is $S(0)$, and at reversion crystallization time T is $S(T)$, the following reversion derivatives products referencing HPI can be created:

- Reversion Swap: $S(T) - K$
- Reversion Call: $\max(S(T) - K, 0)$
- Reversion Put: $\max(K - S(T), 0)$

Where the contractual strike K is defined as:

$$K = LTV \cdot (1 + R)^T$$

where R is a pre-determined contractual annualized rate, which can be related to the expected property growth rate, and LTV is either the portion of the property under reversion or loan to value in the case of life mortgage.

The values of the above reversion products are functions of the property owners' life expectancy, long-term interest rates and expected property forward values. Pricing models need to capture the characteristics of these facts, and broadly reflect the key features of mortality statistics.

For Single Holder

$$REVERSION\_Swap = \sum_i Q_D(t_i) \cdot DF_i \cdot (S_i - K_i)$$

$$REVERSION\_Call = \sum_i Q_D(t_i) \cdot DF_i \cdot HPI\_Call\_Option(t_i, \sigma_i, K_i, F_i)$$

$$REVERSION\_Put = \sum_i Q_D(t_i) \cdot DF_i \cdot HPI\_Put\_Option(t_i, \sigma_i, K_i, F_i)$$

Note that the strikes $K_i = RolledUp(t_i)$ which include LTV.

For Joint Holders

The joint mortality rates as derived in the last section will be used in the following formulae:

$$REVERSION\_Swap = \sum_i Q_{DJ}(t_i) \cdot DF_i \cdot (S_i - K_i)$$

$$REVERSION\_Call = \sum_i Q_{DJ}(t_i) \cdot DF_i \cdot HPI\_Call\_Option(t_i, \sigma_i, K_i, F_i)$$

$$REVERSION\_Put = \sum_i Q_{DJ}(t_i) \cdot DF_i \cdot HPI\_Put\_Option(t_i, \sigma_i, K_i, F_i)$$

Note that the strikes $K_i = RolledUp(t_i)$ which include LTV.

Model Formulation

Although in general the pricing models for real estate derivative products can be complicated, in real life it is better to focus on simpler models that capture key risks. Besides mortality discussion, another key question is how to model the property underlying. There are two frameworks: one is to model the property index itself, the other is to model the property forward rate. The advantage of the formal is that the index can never go negative. Hence it is plausible to assume the HPI spot (S) follows a geometric Brownian process:

$$\frac{dS}{S} = \mu dt + \sigma dz$$

where μ is the drift and σ is the volatility. In estimating the drift μ one should be aware that it is not the usual risk-neutral drift. The risk-free rate, HPI growth and rental market information can be used to estimate the drift. This log-normal assumption of a property index makes the model tractable, even if one has to combine the mortality calculations.

The second framework is to model the HPI instantaneous forward rate (r) using the mean reversion process:

$$dr = (\mu - ar)dt + \sigma dz$$

The underlying (S) can then be integrated as:

$$S_{t+dt} = S_t e^{r \cdot dt}$$

which is equivalent to:

$$\frac{dS}{S} = e^{r \cdot dt} - 1$$

Reversion Products Analyses

In the following, we shall use the lognormal index modelling framework to price the reversion products. Four cases with different mortality features are selected. Using the given mortality base tables and the mortality calculation methodology, the expected life of the four cases are listed in Table 20.3:

The market parameters used are: interest rate is 3%, HPI forward is flat at 0% and HPI volatility is 15%. The strikes for the reversion products are listed in Table 20.4. Note that by choosing the strike of reversion swap at 0, the reversion price is effectively the present value (PV) a policy holder receives as a lump sum up front.

Figure 20.3 compares the reversion prices versus property forward for a single male at age 70 and 85. It is interesting to note the cross point when the property forward rate is larger than the interest rate (for discounting). Note that the expected life difference (18 years vs 7 years) is an important factor in the calculation: when the property growth is less than the interest rate, the person who has a shorter expected life benefits more, hence we see higher reversion price for the male aged 85. When the property growth is higher than the interest rate, the person who is expected to live longer will benefit more from the property growth. Therefore the reversion price for the male aged 70 is higher in the region that forward is higher than interest rate.

The same explanation is for the joint policy holder as shown in Figure 20.4.

Figure 20.5 shows the call and put prices against the property forward. Again the cross point indicates the interplay among the three factors: expected life, interest rate and property growth.

TABLE 20.3   Examples of expected life

Policy holder	Expected Life
Male aged 70	18 years
Male aged 85	7 years
Joint (male 70 female 70)	23 years
Joint (male 85 female 85)	10 years

TABLE 20.4   Reversion products and strikes

Product	Strike
Reversion Swap	0
Reversion Call	$K = 40\% \left(1 + 5\%\right)^{T}$
Reversion Put	$K = 40\% \left(1 + 5\%\right)^{T}$

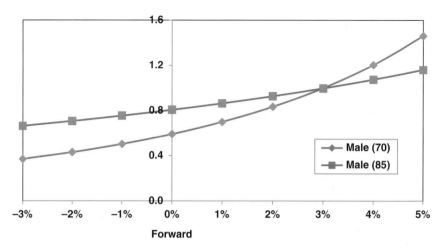

FIGURE 20.3   Reversion price vs forward

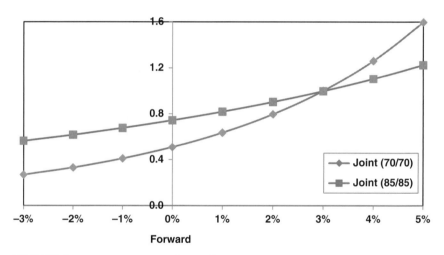

FIGURE 20.4   Reversion price vs forward

For the put prices as shown in Figure 20.6, clearly the protection against down side is dominated by the expected life, namely, the male at age 70 benefits more from the downside protection than the male aged 85.

Figures 20.7 and 20.8 show the call and put prices respectively for the joint policy/ protection holders. The same logic applies here in terms of understanding the shape of the price ladder curve.

Figure 20.9 illustrates the time-bucketed interest rate risk sensitivities for a reversion price for a male aged 70, with a bump size of 10 basis points. As stated previously, the expected life is around 18 years. This is why we see the sensitivity is largely around that region. Clearly as the interest rate goes up and discount factor is smaller, the reversion price comes down as expected.

In addition to the usual market risk factors such as forward and interest rate, the reversion prices are sensitive to mortality rates. The mortality risks can be shown in Figures 20.10 and 20.11 by plotting prices against the mortality rate shift in the

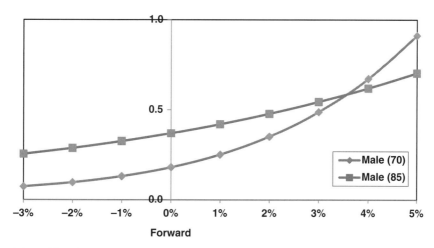

FIGURE 20.5   Call price vs forward

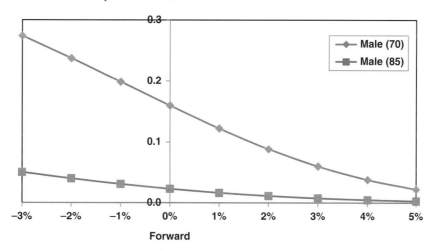

FIGURE 20.6   Put price vs forward

mortality table. Figure 20.10 shows the change in expected life: as the mortality rate decreases, the expected life is longer, and vice versa. Figure 20.11 shows the corresponding reversion price versus the mortality rate shift.

Reversion swap is clearly insensitive to volatility of HPI, and reversion call and put are clearly long volatility. Note that there is no real OTC market for HPI volatility. The mortality risks embedded within HPI reversion trades can potentially be warehoused for other mortality products if and when they occur (say, in the insurance business).

REAL ESTATE PORTFOLIO DERIVATIVES

The reversion derivatives products stated in the last section are simplified and standardized. In practice, the originators of the equity release schemes often seek to hedge their portfolios in a customized manner. This means that one has to structure and price different, often path-dependent, payoffs.

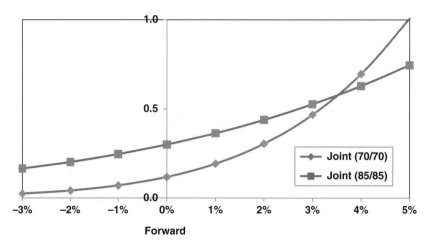

FIGURE 20.7 Call price vs forward

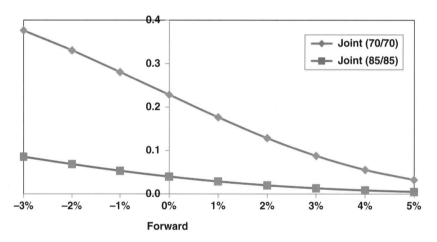

FIGURE 20.8 Put price vs forward

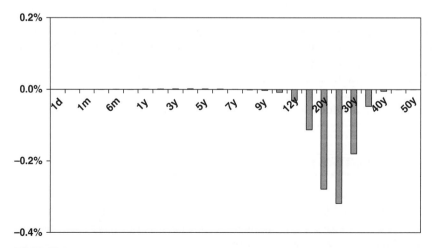

FIGURE 20.9 Time-bucketed interest rate sensitivity

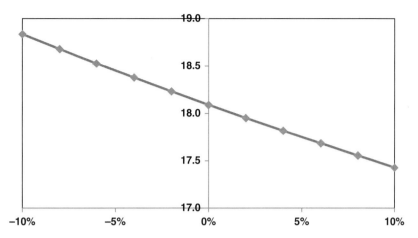

FIGURE 20.10   Expected life vs mortality shift

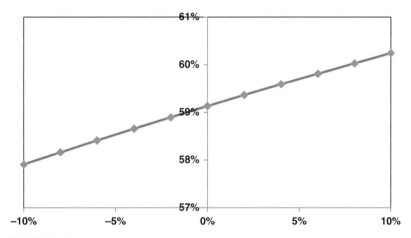

FIGURE 20.11   Reversion price vs mortality shift

Equity Release Portfolio

Let's examine such an example which is designed to hedge a property portfolio in an equity release scheme. The structure has a fixed maturity and a payoff depending on regular (e.g. monthly) fixing of HPI. The Net Exposure Amount (NEA) is defined as the sum of the payoffs at those monthly time slices:

$$NEA = \sum_{i=1}^{n} N_i \cdot \left[(S_i - K_i^u) + \max(K_i^d - S_i, 0) \right]$$

Where K_i^u and K_i^d are upper and down side strike, defined as:

$$K_i^u = \left(1 + \frac{r_u}{4} \right)^{\frac{i}{3}}, \quad K_i^d = \max \left[\left(1 - \frac{r_d}{4} \right)^{\frac{i}{3}}, floor \right]$$

Both upper and down side strikes are reset monthly. r_u and r_d are the annualized rates with quarterly compounding, and *floor* is the minimum down side strike level. N_i is the time-dependent notional, which we shall discuss later.

The payoff at each time slice $(S_i - K_i^u) + max(K_i^d - S_i, 0)$, designed to protect the down side risks, is plotted in Figure 20.12:

Note that *NEA* is the sum of those individual payoffs:

$$NEA = \sum_i NEA_i$$

The individual NEA_i are typically rolled up to the maturity at LIBOR. If *NEA<0*, the overall negative value of the equity release originators will be compensated with $abs(NEA)$, subject to a *cap*. So the product payout formula is:

$$payout = min(cap, abs(min(NEA, 0)))$$

Both upper and down side strikes are time-dependent. Together with the floor, they form a strike cone. Figure 20.13 shows an example strike cone ($r_u = r_d = 3\%$, *floor* = 80%)

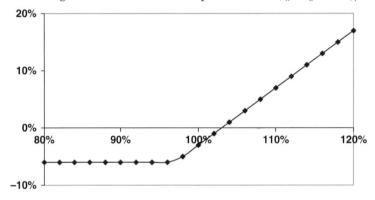

FIGURE 20.12 Payoff at a time slice

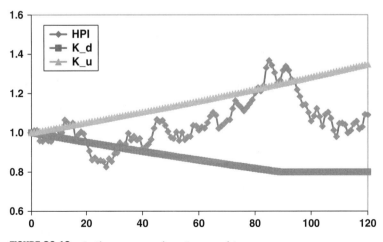

FIGURE 20.13 Strikes cone vs date (in month)

together with a simulated HPI spot path. Clearly this is a path-dependent option whose absolute strikes and payoff are functions of time.

Note that in the payoff formula the notionals (N_i) of HPI structure are also a function of time. In an equity release scheme, the scheme provider's payoff largely depends on the mortality rate and the notionals are effectively the estimate of how much property is going to be released from the property owners at a given time. Figure 20.14 shows an example notional curve versus dates (in month). As can be seen in the figure, initially the notionals are zeros as it is assumed that the properties will be released immediately. The curve then trends gradually upwards, indicating an increased amount of equity release. It peaks at a certain point, where the maximum expected mortality rate and hence the maximum amount of equity release lie. The notional curve is effectively the mirror curve of the expected mortality rate. The value of the derivative structure is dependent on the shape of the curve.

Risk Analysis

Using the above example notional profile, in the following risk analysis, the forward, volatility, 2D rate and forward risks will be examined. In the conventional option pricing models, the risk-free rate drives the forward and the forward growth rate is dependent on the risk-free rate. In the HPI option model, the risk-free interest rate is **not** used to drive the forward and the forward growth rate is treated as a separate input variable.

Figure 20.15 shows the price versus the HPI forward growth rate at different cap values. The risk-free rate is kept unchanged at 3%. Given the put spread nature designed to protect downside risks, the combined price is short forward. Clearly the structure is designed to hedge the downside risks and the option holder is protected when the property market goes down, with the maximum payoff capped by the cap value.

Figure 20.16 shows the volatility sensitivity of the price, with the forward fixed at 1%. The cap in the payoff formulae is removed, and all prices are calculated without a cap. The curve plots the price against a wide range of volatility given the general low

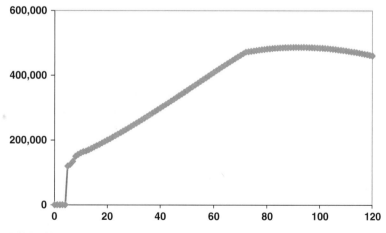

FIGURE 20.14 Notional vs date (in month)

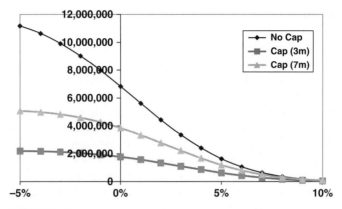

FIGURE 20.15   Price vs forward rate

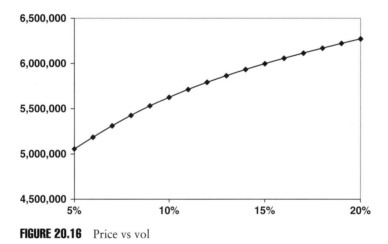

FIGURE 20.16   Price vs vol

volatility nature of the real estate market. The historic UK HPI volatility is typically within the range of 4% to 10%. The combined position is long volatility.

Rate and Forward Risks

As mentioned earlier, the risk-free rate and HPI forward are treated separately in the model as the HPI pricing is **not** considered as non-arbitrage. In reality, there is a real chance that the risk-free rate and HPI forward move in different directions. The combined HPI position will have risk exposures to the joint movement, either correlated or un-correlated. Figure 20.17 illustrates such risks by plotting the 2D sensitivity, with one axis being the risk-free rate and the other HPI forward. In the calculations, the volatility is fixed at 10%. The cap in the payoff formulae is removed, and all prices are calculated without a cap.

As can be seen in Figure 20.17, when the forward is −10% (property market crashes) and the interest rate is low (0%), the protection is of the most value. This type of scenarios are not viewed as extreme any more, it indeed happened in the late

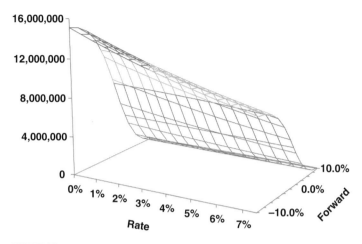

FIGURE 20.17   2D risks (rate and forward)

1980s and early 1990s, and during the sub-prime crisis. The other end of scenarios are when the forward is very high (a booming property market) and the interest rate is high, the protection then has very little value. The 2D risk map provides the joint risk scenarios (either correlated or un-correlated) between the risk-free rate and HPI forward. Although the risk-free rate and HPI forward are modelled as independent variables, their joint risks can be very important in considering hedging strategies.

PROPERTY-LINKED ROLL-UP MORTGAGE

A property-linked roll-up mortgage is essentially a fixed rate (roll-up rate) loan for life. The borrower does not need to repay until death. The loan is repaid as a lump sum, and it is **capped** by the borrower's prevailing property value. Mathematically, the repayment (upon death) at time T can be expressed as:

$$\begin{aligned} Mortgage\_Leg(T) &= \min\left[LoanRolledUp(T), HPI(T)\right] \\ &= LoanRolledUp(T) - \max\left[LoanRolledUp(T) - HPI(T), 0\right] \\ &= LoanRolledUp(T) - HPI\_Put\_Option \end{aligned}$$

The mortgage lender has effectively sold a mortality adjusted HPI Put option to the borrower.

The other leg of the swap – the LIBOR leg has the coupon at time t:

$$Libor\_Leg(t) = N_0 \cdot Libor(t) + C \cdot LoanRolledUp(t)$$

where N_0 is the original loan amount and C is the pre-determined spread.

Note that the both HPI and LIBOR legs are functions of **mortality**. Both legs will be terminated upon death, and they need to be modelled in **complete sync** as far as the mortality rates are concerned, to avoid potential numerical instability.

Taking into the mortality, the probability of a person surviving to T **and** dying in subsequent dt is:

$$Q_D(T) = Q(T) - Q(T + dt)$$

For Single Holder

$$Mortgage\_Leg = \sum_i Q_D(t_i) \cdot DF_i \cdot \left[LoanRolledUp(t_i) - HPI\_Option(t_i, \sigma_i, K_i, F_i) \right]$$

$$Libor\_Leg = \sum_i Q_D(t_i) \cdot DF_i \cdot \left[Accural_i + Spread \cdot LoanRolledUp(t_i) \right], \quad t_i\, between\, cpn\, dates$$

$$Libor\_Leg = \sum_i Q(t_i) \cdot DF_i \cdot \left[CF_i + Spread \cdot LoanRolledUp(t_i) \right], \quad t_i\, on\, cpn\, dates$$

Note that the strikes used in *HPI_Option* are $K_i = LoanRolledUp(t_i)$, and they include LTV.

For Joint Holder

The joint mortality rates need to be derived and they can then be used in the same pricing model as for the single holder.

$$Mortgage\_Leg = \sum_i Q_{DJ}(t_i) \cdot DF_i \cdot \left[LoanRolledUp(t_i) - HPI\_Option(t_i, \sigma_i, K_i, F_i) \right]$$

$$Libor\_Leg = \sum_i Q_{DJ}(t_i) \cdot DF_i \cdot \left[Accural_i + Spread \cdot LoanRolledUp(t_i) \right], \quad t_i\, between\, cpn\, dates$$

$$Libor\_Leg = \sum_i Q(t_i) \cdot DF_i \cdot \left[CF_i + Spread \cdot LoanRolledUp(t_i) \right], \quad t_i\, on\, cpn\, dates$$

Note that the strikes used in *HPI_Option* are $K_i = LoanRolledUp(t_i)$, and they include LTV.

Case Study and Analysis

Let's examine some examples, in which the roll-up mortgages are offered to four borrowing groups: a single female aged 70, a single female aged 85, a joint male and female both aged 70, and a joint male and female both aged 85. Using the example mortality base table given in the previous section, the expected life for the four cases are calculated and plotted in Figure 20.18.

Accordingly, the roll-up loan values (excluding put options) are calculated and shown in Figure 20.19. The calculation is done for LTV=20% and LTV=40%. The figures are quite intuitive and the roll-up loan values are in line with the expected life and LTV. Clearly the four cases, and indeed the differences of the four cases, illustrate the mortality risks in the roll-up mortgage products.

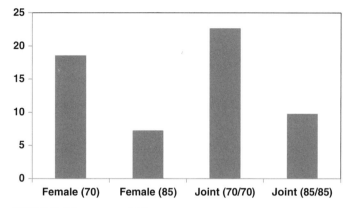

FIGURE 20.18 Expected life

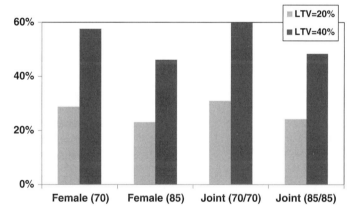

FIGURE 20.19 Roll-up loan PV

Next, let's examine the put option values. It is evident that the put option is sensitive to the property forward value. Figure 20.20 shows the option prices versus property forward rate when the LTV=20%. The values of (property) put option increase as the property forward rate decrease.

The corresponding mortgage PV (roll-up loan + put option) when LTV=20% is shown in Figure 20.21. The mortgage PV decreases when the property forward rate decrease, as the put option acting as a cap to the loan starts to restrict the size of the loan repayment. It is also interesting to note the cross points of the curves around region where the forward rate is –1%.

When the property forward is higher than the cross point (in this particular case, –1%), the longer the expected life, the higher the mortgage values are. When the property forward is lower than the cross point (in this particular case, –1%), the longer the expected life, the less the mortgage values are. This is because when the property forward is decreasing, and the put options playing more important capping roles, those who have longer expected life (e.g. joint 70/70) are affected more in terms of their mortgage values. In contrast, as the property forward is increasing, the put options have less restrictive roles to play, those who have longer expected life (e.g. joint 70/70) are associated with higher mortgage values.

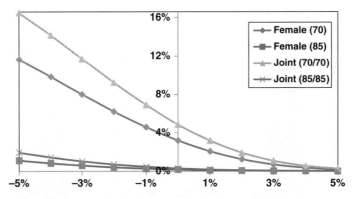

FIGURE 20.20   Put option price (LTV=20%)

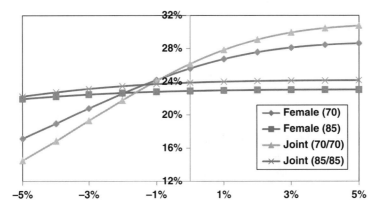

FIGURE 20.21   Mortgage PV (LTV=20%)

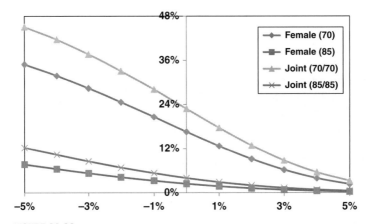

FIGURE 20.22   Put option price (LTV=40%)

Similarly, the put option values versus forward are plotted in Figure 20.22 when LTV=40%. The shape of the curves are as intuitive as in the case of LTV=20%.

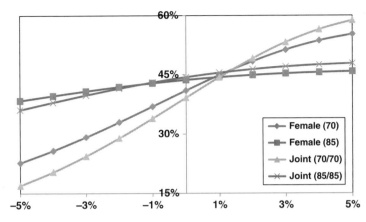

FIGURE 20.23 Mortgage PV (LTV=40%)

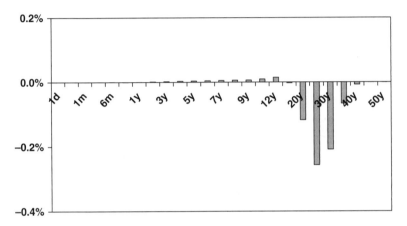

FIGURE 20.24 Interest rate sensitivity (joint 70/70, LTV=20%)

However, if we examine the mortgage PV (roll-up loan + put option) when LTV=40% as shown in Figure 20.23, the mortgage PV decreases at a much faster speed when the property forward rate decreases. Clearly the put option starts to cap the size of the loan repayment much earlier given a much higher LTV. Also note that the cross point where the expected life plays a balancing role is different from that when LTV=20%. The cross point for LTV=40% is at 1% versus –1% for LTV=20%, due to the fact that the put options kick in earlier in the case of higher LTV.

Risk Sensitivities

The time bucket interest rate sensitivities of the mortgage value are shown in Figure 20.24. The interest rate bump size is 10 basis points, and it is for a joint policy holder (male/female) both aged 70, with a LTV of 20%. The most sensitive region is of course around their expected life, which is around 23 years. The (fixed-rate) mortgage is of less value when the interest rate is higher.

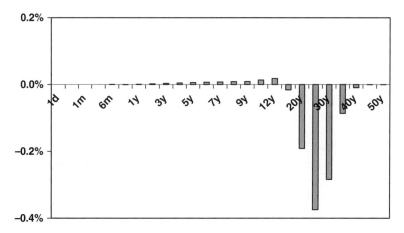

FIGURE 20.25   Interest rate sensitivity (joint 70/70, LTV=40%)

The time bucket interest rate sensitivities for the same joint policy holder (male/female, 70/70), but with a LTV of 40% is shown in Figure 20.25. Again the most sensitive region is around the expect life (about 23 years), but the sensitivities have much larger magnitudes.

HPI RETAIL PRODUCTS

On the back of the reversion products, banks can issue retail products linked to real estate index. There are a variety of HPI options issued by financial institutions. For example, vanilla options, Asian and auto-callable.

- HPI European Option:

$$Call = \max(S_T - K, 0)$$
$$Put = \max(K - S_T, 0)$$

where S_T is the HPI spot at maturity T, and K is the option strike.
- HPI Asian Option:

$$Call = \max(S_A - K, 0)$$
$$Put = \max(K - S_A, 0)$$

where S_A is the arithmetic average of HPI spot during the specified average period, and K is the option strike.
- Callable:
    The payoff is as follows:

$$Payoff = N + G \cdot Option$$

where N is the notional (say 100%), G is the gearing and the *Option* can be either a call or put. The whole payoff is subject to "being kicked out" at pre-determined dates, if certain trigger levels are breached.

Embedded Risks

Although the HPI option payoffs listed above are simple by standard derivative pricing theory, in reality it is not easy to manage those products, remembering that the property underlying is not a liquid tradable asset. The biggest risk factor is the HPI forward.

Additionally, several practical issues need to be considered, including how the long-term drift of the property underlying is estimated and how the stochastic interest rate is taken into account. As the property index underlying is typically calculated and fixed periodically, the discrete nature of the underlying also needs to be considered. In addition, the correlation between the interest rate and the property index may also contribute towards the pricing of property derivative products. One also needs to consider the following risks specifically:

- Gap Risk: This is the risk involved in hedging an amortizing risk with a bullet retail product. The negative gap over the first a few years would be offset to some extent by a positive gap over the next years.
- Maturity Risk: There is a mismatch between the average reversions life and the proposed retail product maturity, which is shorter.
- Basis Risk: The regionally re-weighted HPI is a measure of the reversion portfolio. Halifax publishes 12 regional indexes; the weighted average of these indexes based on the regional breakdown of the portfolio of reversions is the re-weighted HPI. Should a product be based on the national HPI (as opposed to the regionally re-weighted HPI), one will be exposed to basis risk. The basis risk is portfolio-specific, and the difference between a regionally re-weighted HPI representing the reversion portfolio and the national HPI can be substantial.

HPI Risk Scenarios

HPI risk scenarios are valuable in analysing the embedded structural risks. Forward growth is a key risk factor to be simulated. For example, one can parameterize and create the following scenarios:

- initial growth: Bull, Mean, Bear;
- long-term growth: Bear, Flat, Trend and Bull;
- mean-reversion: Weak, Strong.

The initial growth parameter will provide a view of short-term HPI. The bullish view will see HPI growing rapidly, the mean will assume an initial zero growth and the bearish view will assume a marked falling in the short term. In a similar manner the long-term growth parameter will give a view of the market far into the future. The mean-reversion parameter will describe how fast and how strong the paths revert to the long-term growth behaviour. Thus for example a path that is Short Bear Long Strong Bear will have the HPI index falling in the short term and continuing to fall in the long term, with little variation of the index from the falling trend.

The cyclic nature of the HPI needs to be captured in scenarios. For example, the cyclic paths can be parameterized by four stages of observed historical cyclic behaviour. The order, duration and magnitude of these stages vary between scenarios creating a comprehensive set of possible historic-based HPI trends. The four cyclic stages are described below:

- growth – stage during which there is bullish HPI growth;
- decline – stage of falling HPI where there is distinct bearish HPI growth;
- stagnation – stage of faltering/zero HPI growth;
- recovery – stage where HPI sees steady growth.

Each cyclic path can be split into several periods of which the 4 stages described above fill the periods in a rolling manner. An example path over 20 years may be split into the following 6 periods {4, 2, 1, 4, 5, 4} with the starting stage being bearish growth.

PRODUCT OF TWO CALLS

Dealing with real-life options, one sometimes come across the following payoff (P) involving two stochastic underlyings (S_1 and S_2) and two strikes (K_1 and K_2):

$$P = \max(S_1, K_1) \cdot \max(S_2, K_2)$$

The above payoff can find applications in:

- Annuity products as in chapter 18, whereby the equity underlying in the investment portfolio during the accumulation period is correlated with the swap rate driving the annuity.
- Assessing fixed-rate mortgage variable size risk as in chapter 19, whereby during the selling period the market interest rate and total notional sold is correlated: if the market rate goes up, more people will take up the fixed-rate mortgage offer and a bigger notional is expected; if the market rate falls, a smaller notional is expected.

DECOMPOSITION

$$
\begin{aligned}
P &= \max(S_1, K_1) \cdot \max(S_2, K_2) \\
&= \left[K_1 + \max(S_1 - K_1, 0) \right]\left[K_2 + \max(S_2 - K_2, 0) \right] \\
&= K_1 K_2 + K_1 max(S_2 - K_2, 0) + K_2 max(S_1 - K_1, 0) + max(S_1 - K_1, 0) \cdot max(S_2 - K_2, 0)
\end{aligned}
$$

The first term is a constant, and the second and third terms are standard European calls. The fourth term is a product of two calls. Denoting $G = max(S_1 - K_1, 0) \cdot max(S_2 - K_2, 0)$:

$$G = \int\limits_{K_1}^{\infty} \int\limits_{K_2}^{\infty} (S_1 - K_2)(S_1 - K_2)\varphi(S_1, S_2, \rho)\, dS_1\, dS_2$$

where $\varphi(S_1, S_2, \rho)$ is the joint probability distribution with correlation ρ. Assuming both S_1 and S_2 follow the log-normal process, and by making the following changes of variables:

$$V = \sigma\sqrt{t} \quad u = \mu \cdot t$$

$$X = \frac{ln\left(S_t / S_0\right) - u + V^2/2}{V}$$

$$S_t = S_0 \exp\left(X \cdot V + u - V^2/2\right)$$

G can be written as:

$$G = \int_{K_1}^{\infty} \int_{K_2}^{\infty} \left(S_1 - K_1\right) \cdot \left(S_2 - K_2\right) \cdot \varphi(S_1, S_2, \rho) \cdot dS_1 \cdot dS_2$$

$$= \int_{X_{1K}}^{\infty} \int_{X_{2K}}^{\infty} \left(S_1^0 \cdot \exp\left(X_1 \cdot V_1 + u_1 - \frac{V_1^2}{2}\right) - K_1\right) \cdot \left(S_2^0 \cdot \exp\left(X_2 \cdot V_2 + u_2 - \frac{V_2^2}{2}\right) - K_2\right) \cdot \varphi(X_1, X_2, \rho) \cdot dX_1 \cdot dX_2$$

$$= S_1^0 \cdot S_2^0 \cdot \exp\left(u_1 - \frac{V_1^2}{2} + u_2 - \frac{V_2^2}{2}\right) \cdot \int_{X_{1K}}^{\infty} \int_{X_{2K}}^{\infty} \exp\left(X_1 \cdot V_1\right) \cdot \exp\left(X_2 \cdot V_2\right) \cdot \varphi(X_1, X_2, \rho) \cdot dX_1 \cdot dX_2$$

$$- S_1^0 \cdot K_2 \cdot \exp\left(u_1 - \frac{V_1^2}{2}\right) \cdot \int_{X_{1K}}^{\infty} \int_{X_{2K}}^{\infty} \exp\left(X_1 \cdot V_1\right) \cdot \varphi(X_1, X_2, \rho) \cdot dX_1 \cdot dX_2$$

$$- S_2^0 \cdot K_1 \cdot \exp\left(u_2 - \frac{V_2^2}{2}\right) \cdot \int_{X_{1K}}^{\infty} \int_{X_{2K}}^{\infty} \exp\left(X_2 \cdot V_2\right) \cdot \varphi(X_1, X_2, \rho) \cdot dX_1 \cdot dX_2$$

$$+ K_1 \cdot K_2 \cdot \int_{X_{1K}}^{\infty} \int_{X_{2K}}^{\infty} \varphi(X_1, X_2, \rho) \cdot dX_1 \cdot dX_2$$

where:

$$X_{1K} = \frac{ln\left(K_1 / S_1^0\right) - u_1 + V_1^2/2}{V_1}$$

$$X_{2K} = \frac{ln\left(K_2 / S_2^0\right) - u_2 + V_2^2/2}{V_2}\Big|$$

THREE KEY INTEGRALS

By examining the components in G, we need to calculate the following three types of integrals:

$$I_1 = \int\limits_{X_{1K}}^{\infty} \int\limits_{X_{2K}}^{\infty} \varphi(X_1, X_2, \rho) dX_1 dX_2$$

$$I_2 = \int\limits_{X_{1K}}^{\infty} \int\limits_{X_{2K}}^{\infty} \exp(A \cdot X_2) \cdot \varphi(X_1, X_2, \rho) dX_1 dX_2$$

$$I_3 = \int\limits_{X_{1K}}^{\infty} \int\limits_{X_{2K}}^{\infty} \exp(V_1 \cdot X_1) \cdot \exp(V_2 \cdot X_2) \cdot \varphi(X_1, X_2, \rho) dX_1 dX_2$$

Integral 1

$$I_1 = \int\limits_{X_{1K}}^{\infty} \left[\int\limits_{X_{2K}}^{\infty} \varphi(X_1, X_2, \rho) dX_2 \right] dX_1$$

$$= \int\limits_{X_{1K}}^{\infty} \varphi(X_1) \cdot N\left(\frac{\rho}{\sqrt{1-\rho^2}} X_1 - \frac{X_{2K}}{\sqrt{1-\rho^2}} \right) dX_1$$

where $N(\cdot)$ is the cumulative normal density function. Note that:

$$\int\limits_{X_K}^{\infty} \varphi(X) \cdot N(\alpha \cdot X + \beta) \cdot dX = N\left(\frac{\beta}{\sqrt{1+\alpha^2}} \right) - N_2\left(X_K, \frac{\beta}{\sqrt{1+\alpha^2}}, \frac{-\alpha}{\sqrt{1+\alpha^2}} \right)$$

where $N_2(\cdot)$ is the joint cumulative normal density function, we obtain:

$$I_1 = N(-X_{2K}) - N_2(X_{1K}, -X_{2K}, -\rho)$$

Integral 2

$$I_2 = \int\limits_{X_{1K}}^{\infty} \left[\int\limits_{X_{2K}}^{\infty} \exp(A \cdot X_2) \cdot \varphi(X_1, X_2, \rho) dX_2 \right] dX_1$$

$$= \exp\left(\frac{A^2(1-\rho^2)}{2} \right) \int\limits_{X_{1K}}^{\infty} \exp(\rho A X_1) \cdot \varphi(X_1) \cdot N\left(\frac{\rho}{\sqrt{1-\rho^2}} X_1 - \frac{X_{2K} - A(1-\rho^2)}{\sqrt{1-\rho^2}} \right) dX_1$$

Note that:

$$\int_{X_K}^{\infty} \exp(\delta \cdot X) \cdot \varphi(X) \cdot N(\alpha \cdot X + \beta) \cdot dX$$

$$= \exp\left(\frac{\delta^2}{2}\right) \cdot \left[N\left(\frac{\alpha \cdot \delta + \beta}{\sqrt{1+\alpha^2}}\right) - N_2\left(X_K - \delta, \frac{\alpha \cdot \delta + \beta}{\sqrt{1+\alpha^2}}, \frac{-\alpha}{\sqrt{1+\alpha^2}}\right) \right]$$

therefore:

$$I_2 = \exp\left(\frac{A^2}{2}\right)\left[N\left(A - X_{2K}\right) - N_2(X_{1K} - \rho A, A - X_{2K}, -\rho)\right]$$

Integral 3

$$I_3 = \int_{X_{1K}}^{\infty}\left[\int_{X_{2K}}^{\infty} \exp(V_2 \cdot X_2) \cdot \varphi(X_1, X_2, \rho) dX_2 \right] \exp(V_1 \cdot X_1) dX_1$$

$$= \exp\left(\frac{V_2^2(1-\rho^2)}{2}\right) \int_{X_{1K}}^{\infty} \exp\left[(\rho V_2 + V_1)X_1\right] \cdot \varphi(X_1) \cdot N\left(\frac{\rho}{\sqrt{1-\rho^2}} X_1 - \frac{X_{2K} - V_2(1-\rho^2)}{\sqrt{1-\rho^2}}\right) dX_1$$

Note that:

$$\int_{X_K}^{\infty} \exp(\delta \cdot X) \cdot \varphi(X) \cdot N(\alpha \cdot X + \beta) \cdot dX$$

$$= \exp\left(\frac{\delta^2}{2}\right) \cdot \left[N\left(\frac{\alpha \cdot \delta + \beta}{\sqrt{1+\alpha^2}}\right) - N_2\left(X_K - \delta, \frac{\alpha \cdot \delta + \beta}{\sqrt{1+\alpha^2}}, \frac{-\alpha}{\sqrt{1+\alpha^2}}\right) \right]$$

therefore:

$$I_3 = \exp\left(\frac{V_1^2 + V_2^2 + 2\rho V_1 V_2}{2}\right)\left[N\left(\rho V_1 + V_2 - X_{2K}\right) - N_2(X_{1K} - \rho V_2 - V_1, \rho V_1 + V_2 - X_{2K}, -\rho)\right]$$

ANALYTICAL FORMULA

Once we have the answers for the three key integrals, the closed-form solution for G can be found by plugging in the appropriate parameters:

$$G = max\left(S_1 - K_1, 0\right) \cdot max\left(S_2 - K_2, 0\right)$$
$$= G_1 + G_2 + G_3 + G_4$$

where:

$$G_1 = S_1^0 S_2^0 \exp\left(u_1 + u_2 + \rho V_1 V_2\right)\left[N\left(\rho V_1 + V_2 - X_{2K}\right) - N_2(X_{1K} - \rho V_2 - V_1, \rho V_1 + V_2 - X_{2K}, -\rho)\right]$$

$$G_2 = -S_1^0 K_2 \exp(u_1)\left[N\left(V_1 - X_{1K}\right) - N_2(X_{2K} - \rho V_1, V_1 - X_{1K}, -\rho)\right]$$

$$G_3 = -S_2^0 K_1 \exp(u_2)\left[N\left(V_2 - X_{2K}\right) - N_2(X_{1K} - \rho V_2, V_2 - X_{2K}, -\rho)\right]$$

$$G_4 = K_1 K_2 \left[N\left(-X_{2K}\right) - N_2(X_{1K}, -X_{2K}, -\rho)\right]$$

If one needs to value $S_1 \cdot \max(S_2 - K_2, 0)$, the above formulae can be substantially simplified by setting $K_1 = 0$.

Bibliography

Acerbi, C., Szekely, B., "Back-testing expected shortfall", *Risk* (Dec. 2014) pp. 76–81.

Ahn, D.M., Dittmar, R.F., Gallant, A.R., "Quadratic term structure models: Theory and evidence", *Review of Financial Studies*, vol. 15 (2002) pp. 243–288.

Andersen, L.B.G., Andreasen, J., "Jumping Smiles", *Risk* (Nov. 1999) pp. 65–68.

Andersen, L., Broadie, M., "Primal-dual simulation algorithm for pricing multi-dimensional American options", *Management Science*, vol. 50(9) (2004) pp. 1222–1234.

Andersen, L.B.G., Brotherton-Ratcliffe, R., "The equity option volatility smile: an implicit finite-difference approach", *The Journal of Computational Finance* (Winter 1997/98) pp. 5–37.

Andersen, L., Piterbarg, V., *Interest Rate Modeling*, Atlantic Financial Press (Feb. 2010).

Andreasen, J., "The pricing of discretely sampled Asian and lookback options: A change of numeraire approach", *Journal of Computational Finance*, vol. 2 (1998) pp. 5–30.

Andreasen, J., "Back to the future", *Risk* (Sept. 2005) pp. 104–109.

Andreasen, J., Huge, B., "Random grids", *Risk* (July 2011) pp. 66–71.

Antonov, A., Spector, M., "Advanced analytics for the SABR model", (March 2012), http://papers.ssrn.com/sol3/papers.cfm?abstract_id=2026350

Barone-Adesi, G., Whaley, R.E., "Efficient analytic approximation of American option values", *Journal of Finance*, vol. 42(2) (1987) pp. 301–320.

Basel Committee on Banking Supervision, "Basel III: A global regulatory framework for more resilient banks and banking systems", (Dec. 2010, rev June 2011), http://www.bis.org/publ/bcbs189.pdf

Basel Committee on Banking Supervision, "Basel III: The Liquidity Coverage Ratio and liquidity risk monitoring tools", (Jan. 2013), http://www.bis.org/publ/bcbs238.pdf

Basel Committee on Banking Supervision, "Fundamental review of the trading book: A revised market risk framework", (Oct. 2013), http://www.bis.org/publ/bcbs265.pdf

Basel Committee on Banking Supervision, "Fundamental review of the trading book: outstanding issues", (Dec. 2014), http://www.bis.org/bcbs/publ/d305.pdf

Bensaid, B., Lesne, J.P., Pages, H., Scheinkman, J., "Derivative asset pricing with transaction costs", *Mathematical Finance*, vol. 2 (April 1992) pp. 63–86.

Berestycki, H., Busca, J., Florent, I., "Computing the implied volatility in stochastic volatility models", *Communications on Pure and Applied Mathematics*, vol. 57 (Oct. 2004) pp. 1352–1373.

Bianchetti, M., "Two curves, one price", *Risk* (Aug. 2010) pp. 74–80.

Black, F., Karasinski, P., "Bond and option pricing when short rates are lognormal", *Financial Analysts Journal* (July 1991) pp. 52–59.

Black, F., Scholes, M., "The pricing of option and corporate liabilities", *Journal of Political Economy*, vol. 81 (1973) pp. 637–659.

Black, F., Derman, E., Toy, W., "A one-factor model of interest rates and its application to Treasury bond options", *Financial Analysts Journal* (Jan. 1990) pp. 33–39.

Boyle, P.P., "A lattice framework for option pricing with two state variables", *Journal of Financial and Quantitative Analysis*, vol. 23 (March 1988) pp. 1–12.

Boyle, P.P., "New life forms on the option landscape", *Journal of Financial Engineering*, vol. 2(3) (1993) pp. 217–252.

Boyle, P., Broadie, M., Glasserman, P., "Monte Carlo methods for security pricing", *Journal of Economic Dynamics and Control*, vol. 21 (June 1997) pp. 1267–1321.

Boyle, P.P., Tian, Y., "An implicit finite difference approximation to the pricing of barrier options", *Applied Mathematical Finance*, vol. 5 (1998) pp. 17–43.

Brace, A., Gatarek, D., Musiela, M., "The market model of interest rate dynamics", *Mathematical Finance*, vol. 7 (1997) pp. 127–155.

Brace, A., Musiela, M., "A multifactor Gauss Markov implementation of Heath, Jarrow, and Morton", *Mathematical Finance*, vol. 4 (1994) pp. 259–283.

Brace, A., Gatarek, D., Musiela, M., "The market model of interest rate dynamics", *Mathematical Finance*, vol. 7 (1997) pp. 127–147.

Brigo, D., Garcia, J., Pede, N., "CoCo Bonds Valuation with Equity- and Credit-Calibrated First Passage Structural Models", (Feb. 2013), http://arxiv.org/pdf/1302.6629v1.pdf

Brigo, D., Liinev, J., "On the distributional distance between the lognormal LIBOR and swap market models", *Quantitative Finance*, vol. 5(5) (2005) pp. 433–442.

Broadie, M., Detemple, J., "American capped call options on dividend-paying assets", *Review of Financial Studies*, vol. 8 (1995) pp. 161–191.

Broadie, M., Detemple, J., "American option valuation: New bounds, approximations, and a comparison of existing methods", *Review of Financial Studies*, vol. 9 (1996) pp. 1211–1250.

Broadie, M., Glasserman, P., "Pricing American-style securities using simulation", *Journal of Economic Dynamics and Control*, vol. 21 (1997) pp. 1323–1352.

Broadie, M., Glasserman, P., Kou, S., "A continuity correction for discrete barrier option", *Mathematical Finance*, vol. 7 (1997) pp. 325–349.

Broadie, M., Glasserman, P., Kou, S.G., "Connecting discrete and continuous path dependent options", *Finance and Stochastics*, vol. 3 (1999) pp. 55–82.

Brogden, A., "The taming of the skew", *Risk*, (Nov. 2000) pp. 112–115.

Brogden, A., Qu, D., "Hedging dynamic volatility in equity markets using an L-factor dynamic volatility surface model", *Global Derivatives* 2000, April 2000.

Capriotti L, J Lee and M Peacock, "Real-time counterparty credit risk management in Monte Carlo", *Risk* (June 2011) pp. 86–90.

Carr, P., Jarrow, R., Myneni, R., "Alternative characterizations of American put options", *Mathematical Finance*, vol. 2 (1992) pp. 87–106.

Cedervall, S., Piterbarg, V., "CMS: covering all bases", *Risk* (March 2012) pp. 64–69.

Cheuk, T.H.F., Vorst, T.C.F., "Currency lookback options and observation frequency: A binomial approach", *Journal of International Money and Finance*, vol. 16(2) (1997) pp. 173–187.

Cheyette, O., "Markov representation of the Heath-Jarrow-Morton model", (May 1992), Barra Inc.

Chiarella, C., Kwon, O.K., "Finite dimensional affine realizations of HJM models in terms of forward rates and yields", *Review of Derivatives Research*, vol. 6 (2003) pp. 129–155.

Chibane, M., Law, D., "A quadratic volatility Cheyette model", *Risk* (July 2013) pp. 60–63.

Chung, S.L., Shackleton, M., Wojakowski, R., "Efficient quadratic approximation of floating strike Asian option values", *Finance*, vol. 24 (2003) pp. 49–62.

Clément, E., Lamberton, D., Protter, P., "An analysis of a least squares regression algorithm for American option pricing", *Finance and Stochastic*, vol. 6 (2002) pp. 449–471.

Conze, A., Viswanathan, "Path dependent options: The case of lookback options", *Journal of Finance*, vol. 46(5) (1991) pp. 1893–1907.

Cox, D.R., Miller, H.D., *The Theory of Stochastic Processes*, Chapman and Hall, London (1995).

Cox, J.C., Ingersoll, J.E. Jr., Ross, S.A., "An analysis of variable rate loan contracts", *Journal of Finance*, vol. 35 (1980) pp. 389–403.

Cox, J.C., Ingersoll, J.E. Jr., Ross, S.A., "A theory of the term structure of interest rates", *Econometrica*, vol. 53 (March 1985) pp. 385–407.

Crepey, S., Douady, R., "Lois: credit and liquidity", *Risk* (June 2013) pp. 78–82.

Curran, M., "Valuing Asian and portfolio options by conditioning on the geometric mean price", *Management Science*, vol. 40(12) (1994) pp. 1705–1711.

Dai, M., Kwok, Y.K., "Knock-in American options", *Journal of Futures Markets*, vol. 24(2) (2004) pp. 179–192.

Dai, M., Kwok, Y.K., "American options with lookback payoff", *SIAM Journal of Applied Mathematics*, vol. 66(1) (2005a) pp. 206–227.

Dai, M., Kwok, Y.K., "Optimal policies of call with notice period requirement for American warrants and convertible bonds", *Asia Pacific Financial Markets*, vol. 12(4) (2005b) pp. 353–373.

Dai, M., Kwok, Y.K., "Options with combined reset rights on strike and maturity", *Journal of Economic Dynamics and Control*, vol. 29 (2005c) pp. 1495–1515.

Dai, M., Kwok, Y.K., "Characterization of optimal stopping regions of American Asian and lookback options", *Mathematical Finance*, vol. 16(1) (2006) pp. 63–82.

Dai, M., Kwok, Y.K., "Optimal multiple stopping models of reload options and shout options", to appear in *Journal of Economic Dynamics and Control* (2008).

Dai, M., Kwok, Y.K., Wu, L., "Options with multiple reset rights", *International Journal of Theoretical and Applied Finance*, vol. 6(6) (2003) pp. 637–653.

Dai, Q., Singleton, K.J., "Specification analysis of affine term structure models", *Journal of Finance*, vol. 55 (2000) pp. 1943–1978.

Dai, M., Wong, H.Y., Kwok, Y.K., "Quanto lookback options", *Mathematical Finance*, vol. 14(3) (2004) pp. 445–467.

Daniluk, A., Gatarek, D., "A fully lognormal LIBOR market model", *Risk* (Sept. 2005) pp. 115–118.

Davis, M.H.A., Panas, V.G., Zariphopoulou, T., "European option pricing with transaction costs", *SIAM Journal of Control*, vol. 31 (1993) pp. 470–493.

Dempster, M.A.H., Hutton, J.P., "Pricing American stock options by linear programming", *Mathematical Finance*, vol. 9 (1999) pp. 229–254.

Derman, E., "Regimes of volatility", *Risk* (April 1999), 55–59.

Derman, E., Kani, I., "Riding on a smile", *Risk* (Feb. 1994) pp. 32–39.

Derman, E., Kani, I., "Stochastic implied tress: Arbitrage pricing with stochastic term and strike structure of volatility", *International Journal of Theoretical and Applied Finance*, vol. 1 (1998) pp. 61–110.

Duffie, D., Huang, C.F., "Implementing Arrow–Debreu equilibria by continuous trading of a few long-lived securities", *Econometrica*, vol. 53(6) (1985) pp. 1337–1356.

Duffie, D., Kan, R., "A yield-factor model of interest rates", *Mathematical Finance*, vol. 6(4) (1996) pp. 379–406.

Dupire, B., "Pricing with a smile", *Risk*, vol. 7(1) (Jan. 1994) pp. 18–20.

El-Karoui, N., Geman, H., "A probabilistic approach to the valuation of floating rate notes with an application to interest rate swaps", *Advances in Options and Futures Research*, vol. 1 (1994) pp. 41–64.

Erras, E., Mauri, G., Mercurio, F., "Capturing the skew in interest rate derivatives: a shifted lognormal LIBOR model with uncertain parameters", (November 2004), http://www.fabiomercurio.it/sllmup.pdf

Evans, J.D., Kuske, R., Keller, J.B., "American options on assets with dividends near expiry", *Mathematical Finance*, vol. 12(3) (2002) pp. 219–237.

Fernandez, C., Steel, M.F.J., "On Bayesian Modeling of Fat Tails and Skewness", *Journal of the American Statistical Association*, vol. 93, no. 441 (March, 1998) pp. 359- 371.

Figlewski, S., Gao, B., "The adaptive mesh model: A new approach to efficient option pricing", *Journal of Financial Economics*, vol. 53 (1999) pp. 313–351.

Fong, H.G., Vasicek, O.A., "Fixed-income volatility management", *Journal of Portfolio Management* (Summer 1991) pp. 41–46.

Forsyth, P.A., Vetzal, K.R., Zvan, R., "Convergence of lattice and PDE methods for valuing path dependent options using interpolation", *Review of Derivatives Research*, vol. 5 (2002) pp. 273–314.

Fouque, J.P., Papanicolaou, G., Sircar, K.R., *Derivatives in Financial Markets with Stochastic Volatility*, Cambridge University Press, Cambridge, U.K. (2000).

Galluccio, S., Ly, J.M., "Theory and calibration of swap market models", *Mathematical Finance*, vol. 17 (Jan. 2007) pp. 111–141.

Garman, M., "Recollection in tranquillity", in *From Black–Scholes to Black Holes: New Frontiers in Options*, Risk Magazine, Ltd, London (1992) pp. 171–175.

Gatarek, D., Bachert, P., Maksymiuk, R., *The LIBOR Market Model in Practice*, John Wiley & Sons Ltd, 2007.

Gatarek, D., Jablecki, J., Qu, D., "Non-Parametric Local Volatility Model", ICBI Conference – Global Derivatives Trading & Risk Management, Amsterdam, May 2015.

Gatheral, J., *The Volatility Surface: A Practitioner's Guide*, John Wiley & Sons Ltd, 2006.

Geman, H., El Karoui, N., Rochet, J.C., "Changes of numeraire, changes of probability measure and option pricing", *Journal of Applied Probability*, vol. 32 (1995) pp. 443–458.

Gentle, D., "Basket Weaving", *Risk*, Vol.6(6) (1993) p. 51.

Geske, R., "The valuation of compound options", *Journal of Financial Economics*, vol. 7 (1979) pp. 375–380.

Geske, R., Johnson, H.E., "The American put option valued analytically", *Journal of Finance*, vol. 39 (1984) pp. 1511–1524.

Giese, A., "Quanto adjustments in the presence of stochastic volatility", *Risk* (May 2012) pp. 67–71.

Giles M and P Glasserman, "Smoking adjoints: fast Monte Carlo Greeks", *Risk* (January 2006) pp. 92–96.

Glasserman, P., *Monte Carlo methods in financial engineering*, Springer, New York (2004).

Glasserman, P., Yu, B., "Number of paths versus number of basis functions in American option pricing", *Annals of Applied Probability*, vol. 14(4) (2004) pp. 2090–2119.

Grannan, E.R., Swindle, G.H., "Minimizing transaction costs of option hedging strategies", *Mathematical Finance*, vol. 6 (Oct. 1996) pp. 341–364.

Grzelak, L. A., Oosterlee, C. W., "An equity–interest rate hybrid model with stochastic volatility and the interest rate smile", *The Journal of Computational Finance*, vol. 15(4) (Summer 2012), pp.1-33.

Guyon, J., Henry-Labordere, P., "From spot volatilities to implied volatilities", *Risk*, (June 2011) pp. 79–84.

Gyongy, I., "Mimicking the one-dimensional marginal distributions of processes having an Ito differential", *Probability Theory and Related Fields*, vol. 71 pp. 501–516.

Hagan, P., "Evaluating and Hedging Exotic Swap Instruments via LGM", (Working Paper), http://www.scribd.com/doc/198899911/Evaluating-and-Hedging-Exotic-Swap-Instruments-via-LGM

Hagan P., "Methodology for Callable Swaps and Bermudan 'Exercise Into' Swaptions", www.scribd.com/doc/6911871/.

Hagan, P., Kumar, D., Lesniewski, A.S., Woodward, D.E., "Managing Smile Risk", *Wilmott Magazine* (Sept. 2002) pp. 84–108.

Hagan, P., Kumar, D., Lesniewski, A.S., Woodward, D.E., "Arbitrage-Free SABR", *Wilmott* (January 2014) pp. 60–75.

Harrison, J.M., Kreps, D.M., "Martingales and arbitrage in multiperiod securities markets", *Journal of Economic Theory*, vol. 20 (1979) pp. 381–408.

Harrison, J.M., Pliska, S.R., "A stochastic calculus model of continuous trading: Complete markets", *Stochastic Processes and Their Applications*, vol. 15 (1983) pp. 313–316.

Heath, D., Jarrow, R., Morton, A., "Bond pricing and the term structure of interest rates: A new methodology for contingent claims valuation", *Econometrica*, vol. 60 (Jan. 1992) pp. 77–105.

Henderson, V., Wojakowski, R., "On the equivalence of floating and fixed-strike Asian options", *Journal of Applied Probability*, vol. 39 (2002) pp. 391–394.

Henrard, M., "Explicit bond option and swaption formula in Heath–Jarrow–Morton one factor model", *International Journal of Theoretical and Applied Finance*, vol. 6(1) (2003) pp. 57–72.

Henrard, M., "LIBOR market model and Gaussian HJM explicit approaches to option on composition", *Working paper* (2005).

Henrard, M., "Swaptions in Libor market model with local volatility", (June 2010), http://papers.ssrn.com/sol3/papers.cfm?abstract_id=1098420

Henry-Labordere, P., "Calibration of local stochastic volatility models to market smiles", *Risk* (Sept. 2009) pp. 112–117.

Heston, S.L., "A closed-form solution for options with stochastic volatility with applications to bond and currency options", *Review of Financial Studies*, vol. 6 (1993) pp. 327–343.

Heston, S., "Discrete-time versions of continuous-time interest rate models", *Journal of Fixed Income* (Sept. 1995) pp. 86–88.

Heston, S., Zhou, G., "On the rate of convergence of discrete-time contingent claims", *Mathematical Finance*, vol. 10(1) (2000) pp. 53–75.

Heynen, R., Kat, H., "Partial barrier options", *Journal of Financial Engineering*, vol. 3(3/4) (1994a) pp. 253–274.

Heynen, R., Kat, H., "Selective memory", *Risk*, vol. 7 (Nov. 1994b) pp. 73–76.

Heynen, R.C., Kat, H.M., "Lookback options with discrete and partial monitoring of the underlying price", *Applied Mathematical Finance*, vol. 2 (1995) pp. 273–284.

Heynen, R.C., Kat, H.M., "Discrete partial barrier options with a moving barrier", *Journal of Financial Engineering*, vol. 5 (1996) pp. 199–209.

Ho, T.S.Y., Lee, S.B., "Term structure movements and pricing interest rate contingent claims", *Journal of Finance*, vol. 41 (Dec. 1986) pp. 1011–1029.

Hodges, S.D., Neuberger, A.J., "Optimal replication of contingent claims under transaction costs", *Review of Futures Markets*, vol. 8 (1989) pp. 222–239.

Hull, J.C., White, A., "The pricing of options on assets with stochastic volatilities", *Journal of Finance*, vol. 42 (June 1987) pp. 281–300.

Hull, J., White, A., "Pricing interest-rate-derivative securities", *Review of Financial Studies*, vol. 3(4) (1990) pp. 573–592.

Hull, J., White, A., "Bond option pricing based on a model for the evolution of bond prices", *Advances in Futures and Options Research*, vol. 6 (1993a) pp. 1–13.

Hull, J., White, A., "Efficient procedures for valuing European and American path-dependent options", *Journal of Derivatives* (Fall 1993b) pp. 21–31.

Hull, J., White, A., "Numerical procedures for implementing term structure models I: Singlefactor models", *Journal of Derivatives* (Fall 1994) pp. 7–16.

Hull, J., White, A., "Forward rate volatilities, swap rate volatilities, and the implementation of the LIBOR market model", *Journal of Fixed Income*, vol. 10(3) (2000) pp. 46–62.

Hunt, P.J., Kennedy, J.E., Pelsser, A., "Markov-functional interest rate models", *Finance and Stochastics* vol.4 (Aug. 2000) pp. 391–408.

Huynh, C.B., "Back to Baskets", *Risk*, vol. 7(5) (1994) p. 59.

Inui, K., Kijima, M., "A Markovian framework in multi-factor Heath–Jarrow–Morton models", *Journal of Financial and Quantitative Analysis*, vol. 33(3) (1998) pp. 423–440.

Jäckel, P., Rebonato, R., "The link between caplet and swaption volatilities in a Brace-Gatarek-Musiela/Jamshidian framework: approximate solution and empirical evidence", *Journal of Computational Finance*, vol. 6(4) (2003) pp. 41–59.

Jamshidian, F., "An exact bond option formula", *Journal of Finance*, vol. 44 (Mar. 1989) pp. 205–209.

Jamshidian, F., "An analysis of American options", *Review of Futures Markets*, vol. 11(1) (1992) pp. 72–82.

Jamshidian, F., "Hedging quantos, differential swaps and ratios", *Applied Mathematical Finance*, vol. 1 (1994) pp. 1–20.

Jamshidian, F., "A simple class of square-root interest-rate models", *Applied Mathematical Finance*, vol. 2 (1995) pp. 61–72.

Jamshidian, F., "Bond, futures and option evaluation in the quadratic interest rate model", *Applied Mathematical Finance*, vol. 3 (1996) pp. 93–115.

Jamshidian, F., "LIBOR and swap market models and measures", *Finance and Stochastics*, vol. 1 (1997) pp. 293–330.

Jamshidian, F., "Volatility Estimation, Modelling & Risk Management", *Global Derivatives*, 2000, Paris, April, 2000.

Jamshidian, F., Zhu, Y., "Scenario Simulation: Theory and Methodology", *Finance Stochastics* 1 (1997) pp. 43–67.

Jarrow, R., Rudd, A., "Approximate option valuation for arbitrary stochastic processes", *Journal of Financial Economics*, vol. 10 (1982) pp. 347–369.

Jarrow, R.A., Rudd, A., *Option Pricing*, Richard D. Irwin, Homewood (1983).

Jex, M., Henderson, R., Wang, D., "Pricing exotics under the smile", *Risk* (Nov. 1999) pp. 72–75.

Ju, N., "Pricing an American option by approximating its early exercise boundary as a multipiece exponential function", *Review of Financial Studies*, vol. 11(3) (1998).

Ju, N., "Pricing Asian and Basket Options Via Taylor Expansion", *Journal of Computational Finance*, 5(3) (2002) pp. 79–103.

Karatzas, I., "On the pricing of American options", *Applied Mathematics and Optimization*, vol. 60 (1988) pp. 37–60.

Karatzas, I., Shreve, S.E., *Brownian motion and stochastic calculus*, second edition, Springer, New York (1991).

Kat, H., Verdonk, L., "Tree surgery", *Risk*, vol. 8 (Feb. 1995) pp. 53–56.

Kemna, A.G.Z., Vorst, T.C.F., "A pricing method for options based on average asset values", *Journal of Banking and Finance*, vol. 14 (1990) pp. 113–129.

Kienitz, J., "Transforming Volatility – Multi Curve Cap and Swaption Volatilities", (March 2013), http://papers.ssrn.com/sol3/papers.cfm?abstract_id=2204702

Kijima, M., Nagayama, I., "Efficient numerical procedures for the Hull–White extended Vasicek model", *Journal of Financial Engineering*, vol. 3(3/4) (1994) pp. 275–292.

Kolkiewicz, A.W., "Pricing and hedging more general double-barrier options", *Journal of Computational Finance*, vol. 5(3) (2002) pp. 1–26.

Kunitomo, N., Ikeda, M., "Pricing options with curved boundaries", *Mathematical Finance*, vol. 2 (Oct. 1992) pp. 275–298.

Kwok, Y.K., Lau, K.W., "Pricing algorithms for options with exotic path dependence", *Journal of Derivatives*, (Fall 2001a) pp. 28–38.

Kwok, Y.K., Lau, K.W., "Accuracy and reliability considerations of option pricing algorithms", *Journal of Futures Markets*, vol. 21 (2001b) pp. 875–903.

Kwok, Y.K., Wu, L., "Effects of callable feature on early exercise policy", *Review of Derivatives Research*, vol. 4 (2000) pp. 189–211.

Kwok, Y.K., Wu, L., Yu, H., "Pricing multi-asset options with an external barrier", *International Journal of Theoretical and Applied Finance*, vol. 1(4) (1998) pp. 523–541.

Kwok, Y.K., Wong, H.Y., Lau, K.W., "Pricing algorithms of multivariate path dependent options", *Journal of Complexity*, vol. 17 (2001) pp. 773–794.

Leland, H.E., "Option pricing and replication with transaction costs", *Journal of Finance*, vol. 40 (Dec. 1985) pp. 1283–1301.

Lee, P., Wang, L., Karim, A., "Index volatility surface via moment-matching techniques", *Risk*, Dec. 2003 pp. 83–89.

Levy, E., "Pricing European average rate currency options", *Journal of International Money and Finance*, vol. 11 (1992) pp. 474–491.

Levy, E., Mantion, F., "Discrete by nature", *Risk*, vol. 10 (Jan. 1997) pp. 74–75.

Li, A., "The pricing of double barrier options and their variations", *Advances in Futures and Options Research*, vol. 10 (1999) pp. 17–41.

Lo, C.F., Yuen, P.H., Hui, C.H., "Pricing barrier options with square root process", *International Journal of Theoretical and Applied Finance*, vol. 4(5) (2002) pp. 805–818.

Longstaff, F.A., Schwartz, E.S., "Interest rate volatility and the term structure: A two-factor general equilibrium model", *Journal of Finance*, vol. 47 (Sept. 1992) pp. 1259–1282.

Longstaff, F.A., Schwartz, E.S., "A simple approach to valuing risky fixed and floating rate debt", *Journal of Finance*, vol. 50 (July 1995) pp. 789–819.

Longstaff, F.A., Schwartz, E.S., "Valuing American Options by Simulation: A simple Least-Squares Approach", *The Review of Financial Studies*, vol. 14 (2001) pp. 113–147.

Luo, L.S.J., "Various types of double-barrier options", *Journal of Computational Finance*, vol. 4(3) (2001) pp. 125–138.

MacMillan, L.W., "Analytic approximation for the American put option", *Advances in Futures and Options Research*, vol. 1 (Part A 1986) pp. 119–139.

Maghsoodi, Y., "Solution of the extended CIR term structure and bond option valuation", *Mathematical Finance*, vol. 6(1) (1996) pp. 89–109.

Margrabe, W., "The value of an option to exchange one asset for another", *Journal of Finance*, vol. 33 (March 1978) pp. 177–186.

Merton, R.C., "Theory of rational option pricing", *Bell Journal of Economics and Management Sciences*, vol. 4 (Spring 1973) p. 141–183.

Merton, R.C., "On the pricing of corporate debt: The risk structure of interest rates", *Journal of Finance*, vol. 29 (1974) pp. 449–470.

Merton, R.C., "Option pricing when the underlying stock returns are discontinuous", *Journal of Financial Economics*, vol. 3 (March 1976) pp. 125–144.

Meyer, G.H., "Numerical investigation of early exercise in American puts with discrete dividends", *Journal of Computational Finance*, vol. 5(2) (2001) pp. 37–53.

Milevsky, M.A., Posner, S.E., "Asian options, the sum of lognormals, and the reciprocal Gamma distribution", *Journal of Financial and Quantitative Analysis*, vol. 33 (1998) pp. 409–422.

Milevsky, M.A., Posner, S.E., "A Closed-Form Approximation for Valuing Basket Options", *The Journal of Derivatives*, Summer 1998, p. 54.

Miltersen, K.R., Sandmann, K., Sondermann, D., "Closed form solutions for term structure derivatives with Log-Normal interest rates", *Journal of Finance*, vol. 52(1) (1997) pp. 409–430.

Munk, C., "Stochastic duration and fast coupon bond option pricing in multi-factor models", *Review of Derivatives Research*, vol. 3 (1999) pp. 157–181.

Neuberger, A., "Option replication with transaction costs – an exact solution for the pure jump process", *Advances in Futures and Options Research*, vol. 7 (1994) pp. 1–20.

Nielsen, J.A., Sandmann, K., "The pricing of Asian options under stochastic interest rates", *Applied Mathematical Finance*, vol. 3 (1996) pp. 209–236.

Nielsen, J.A., Sandmann, K., "Pricing of Asian exchange rate options under stochastic interest rates as a sum of options", *Finance and Stochastics*, vol. 6 (2002) pp. 355–370.

Nielsen, J.A., Sandmann, K., "Pricing bounds on Asian options", *Journal of Financial and Quantitative Analysis*, vol. 38(2) (2003) pp. 449–473.

Nunes, J.P.D., "Multifactor valuation of floating range note", *Mathematical Finance*, vol. 14(1) (2004) pp. 79–97.

Obloj, J., "Fine-Tune Your Smile: Correction to Hagan et al", *Wilmott* (May 2008).

Park, H., "SABR symmetry", *Risk* (Jan. 2014) pp. 106–111.

Paskov, S., Traub, J.F., "Faster valuation of financial derivatives", *Journal of Portfolio Management* (Fall 1995) pp. 113–120.

Pelsser, A., "Pricing double barrier options using Laplace transforms", *Finance and Stochastics*, vol. 4 (2000) pp. 95–104.

Piterbarg, V., "A stochastic volatility forward Libor model with a term structure of volatility smiles", (October 2003), http://www.javaquant.net/papers/piterbarg_2003_stochastic.pdf

Pliska, S.R., *Introduction to mathematical finance*, Blackwell Publishers, Oxford, U.K. (199).

Qu, D., "Discrete Dividends In Equity Derivatives", *Derivatives Week*, (August 2000).

Qu, D., "Hedging Volatility Dynamics In Equity Derivatives", *Derivatives Week*, (October 2000).

Qu, D., "Managing Barrier Risks Using Exponential Soft Barriers", *Derivatives Week*, (15 January 2001).

Qu, D., "Basket Implied Volatility Surfaced", *Derivatives Week*, (4 June 2001).

Qu, D., "Risk Managing Long-Dated FX Derivatives", *Derivatives Week*, (7 October 2002).

Qu, D., "Pricing Basket Options With Skew", *Wilmott* (July 2005) pp. 58–64.

Qu, D., Zhu, D., "Efficient CVA Valuation Techniques", ICBI Conference – Global Derivatives Trading & Risk Management, Amsterdam, April 2013.

Qu, D., Zhu, D., "Grid Monte Carlo in Portfolio CVA Valuation", *Wilmott* vol. 2014(70) (March 2014) pp. 64–70.

Ren, Y., Madan, D., Qian, M.Q., "Calibrating and pricing with embedded local volatility models", *Risk* (Sept. 2007) pp. 138–143.

Ritchken, P., Sankarasubramanian, L., "Volatility structures of forward rates and the dynamics of the term structure", *Mathematical Finance*, vol. 5(1) (1995) pp. 55–72.

Roberts, G.O., Shortland, C.F., "Pricing barrier options with time-dependent coefficients", *Mathematical Finance*, vol. 7 (Jan. 1997) pp. 83–93.

Rogers, L., Shi, Z., "The value of an Asian option", *Journal of Applied Probability*, vol. 32(4) (1995) pp. 1077–1088.

Rossi, A., "The Britten–Jones and Neuberger smile-consistent with stochastic volatility option pricing model: A further analysis", *International Journal of Theoretical and Applied Finance*, vol. 5(1) (2002) pp. 1–31.

Rubinstein, M., "Options for the undecided", in *From Black–Scholes to Black–Holes: New Frontiers in Options*, Risk Magazine Ltd, London (1992) pp. 187–189.

Schaefer, S.M., Schwartz, E.S., "A two-factor model of the term structure: An approximate analytical solution", *Journal of Financial and Quantitative Analysis*, vol. 19 (Dec. 1984) pp. 413–424.

Schrager, D.F., Pelsser, A.A., "Pricing swaptions and coupon bond options in affine term structure models", *Mathematical Finance*, vol. 16 (2006) pp. 673–694.

Selby, M.J.P., Strickland, C., "Computing the Fong and Vasicek pure discount bond price formula", *Journal of Fixed Income* (Sept. 1995) pp. 78–84.

Sepp, A., "Analytical pricing of double-barrier options under a double-exponential jump diffusion process: Applications of Laplace transform", *International Journal of Theoretical and Applied Finance*, vol. 7(2) (2004) pp. 151–175.

Sidenius, J., "Double barrier options: Valuation by path counting", *Journal of Computational Finance*, vol. 1 (1998) pp. 63–79.

Singleton, K.J., Umantsev, L., "Pricing coupon-bond options and swaptions in affine term structure models", *Mathematical Finance*, vol. 12(4) (2002) pp. 427–446.

Stein, E., Stein, J., "Stock price distributions with stochastic volatility: an analytic approach", *Review of Financial Studies*, vol. 4 (1991) pp. 727–752.

Steinrucke, L., Zagst, R., Swishchuk, A., "The Markov-switching jump diffusion LIBOR market model", *Quantitative Finance*, vol. 15(3) (2015), pp.455-476.

Tataru, G., Fisher, T., "Stochastic local volatility", *Bloomberg Technical Paper*, Feb. 2010.

Tavella, D., Randall, C., *Pricing Financial Instruments: The Finite Difference Method*, John Wiley & Sons, New York (2000).

Ticot, Y., Charvet, X., "LPI swaps with a smile", *Risk*, vol. 26 (May 2013) pp. 66–71.

Tsao, C.Y., Chang, C.C., Lin, C.G., "Analytic approximation formulae for pricing forwardstarting Asian options", *Journal of Futures Markets*, vol. 23(5) (2003) pp. 487–516.

Tsitsiklis, L., Van Roy, B., "Regression methods for pricing complex American style options", *IEEE Transactions on Neural Networks*, vol. 12 (2001) pp. 694–703.

Turnbull, S. & Wakeman, L., "A quick algorithm for pricing European average options", *Journal of Financial and Quantitative Analysis* (1991), No. 26, p. 377–389.

Vasicek, O., "An equilibrium characterization of the term structure", *Journal of Financial Economics*, vol. 5 (1977) pp. 177–188.

Wei, J.Z., "Valuing differential swaps", *Journal of Derivatives*, (Spring 1994) pp. 64–76.

Wei, J.Z., "A simple approach to bond option pricing", *Journal of Futures Markets*, vol. 17(2) (1997) pp. 131–160.

Whaley, R., "On the valuation of American call options on stocks with known dividends", *Journal of Financial Economics*, vol. 9 (1981) pp. 207–211.

Whalley, E., Wilmott, P., "Counting the costs", *Risk*, vol. 6 (Oct. 1993) pp. 59–66.

Wilmott, P., *Paul Wilmott on Quantitative Finance*, John Wiley & Sons Ltd, Chichester (2006).

Wilmott, P., *Paul Wilmott Introduces Quantitative Finance*, John Wiley & Sons Ltd, (2007).

Wong, H.Y., Kwok, Y.K., "Sub-replication and replenishing premium: Efficient pricing of multi-state lookbacks", *Review of Derivatives Research*, vol. 6 (2003) pp. 83–106.

Wu, L., Zhang, F., "Libor Market Model With Stochastic Volatility", *Journal of Industrial and Management Optimization*, vol. 2(2) (May 2006) pp. 199–227.

Xu, C., Kwok, Y.K., "Integral price formulas for lookback options", *Journal of Applied Mathematics*, vol. 2005(2) (2005) pp. 117–125.

Zhang, P.G., "Flexible Asian options", *Journal of Financial Engineering*, vol. 3(1) (1994) pp. 65–83.

Zhu, Y.L., Sun, Y., "The singularity-separating method for two-factor convertible bonds", *Journal of Computational Finance*, vol. 3 (1999) pp. 91–110.

Zou, J., Derman, E., "Strike-Adjusted Spread: A New Metric For Estimating The Value Of Equity Options", Goldman Sachs Quantitative Strategies Research Notes, July 1999.

Zvan, R., Forsyth, P.A., Vetzal, K.R., "Robust numerical methods for PDE model of Asian options", *Journal of Computational Finance*, vol. 1 (Winter 1998) pp. 39–78.

Zvan, R., Vetzal, K.R., Forsyth, P.A., "PDE methods for pricing barrier options", *Journal of Economic Dynamics and Control*, vol. 24 (2000) pp. 1563–1590.

Index